Lecture Notes in Computer Sci

T0238386

Commenced Publication in 1973
Founding and Former Series Editors:
Gerhard Goos, Juris Hartmanis, and Jan van Leeuwen

Teddy Furon   François Cayre
Gwenaël Doërr   Patrick Bas (Eds.)

Information Hiding

9th International Workshop, IH 2007
Saint Malo, France, June 11-13, 2007
Revised Selected Papers

 Springer

Volume Editors

Teddy Furon
INRIA Rennes - Bretagne Atlantique Research Centre
Campus universitaire de Beaulieu, 35042 Rennes cedex, France
E-mail: teddy.furon@irisa.fr

François Cayre
Gipsa-lab Grenoble, CNRS
961, rue de la Houille Blanche, 38402 St. Martin d'Hères Cedex, France
E-mail: cayre@inpg.fr

Gwenaël Doërr
University College London
Adastral Park, Ross Building 2, Martlesham IP5 3RE, UK
E-mail: g.doerr@adastral.ucl.ac.uk

Patrick Bas
Gipsa-lab Grenoble, CNRS
961 rue de la Houille Blanche, 38402 Saint Martin d'Hères cedex, France
E-mail: Patrick.Bas@inpg.fr

Library of Congress Control Number: 2007941939

CR Subject Classification (1998): E.3, K.6.5, K.4.1, K.5.1, D.4.6, E.4, C.2, H.4.3, H.3, H.5.1

LNCS Sublibrary: SL 4 – Security and Cryptology

ISSN	0302-9743
ISBN-10	3-540-77369-X Springer Berlin Heidelberg New York
ISBN-13	978-3-540-77369-6 Springer Berlin Heidelberg New York

Springer is a part of Springer Science+Business Media

springer.com

© Springer-Verlag Berlin Heidelberg 2007
Printed in Germany

Typesetting: Camera-ready by author, data conversion by Scientific Publishing Services, Chennai, India
Printed on acid-free paper   SPIN: 12207015   06/3180   5 4 3 2 1 0

Preface

We are glad to present in this volume the proceedings of the ninth edition of Information Hiding (IH 2007). The conference was held in Saint Malo, the Corsairs town, France, during June 11–13, 2007. It was organized by a team of four French pirates supported by the valuable help of the conference organization cell of INRIA Rennes.

Continuing the tradition of the previous editions, we tried to provide a balanced program covering the different aspects of information hiding. This being said, the selection of the program was a very challenging task. This year, 105 papers from 25 countries were submitted. This was the highest number of submissions in IH history. We would like to take the opportunity to thank all the authors who submitted a paper to IH 2007 and thus contributed to consolidate the reputation of this conference. Each paper was refereed by at least three reviewers. Since this event was run with a single track, it implied that only 25 papers were accepted for presentation. This unusually low acceptance rate will further promote Information Hiding as the top forum of our community. Although watermarking and steganography still receive most of the interest, new topics emerged during the conference such as the use of Tardos codes for fingerprinting and digital forensics.

We would like to thank all the members of the Program Committee and all the external reviewers for the enormous effort that they put into the reviewing process. We thank again Edith Blin Guyot for handling all local organizational issues. Finally, we are most grateful to our different sponsors with a special mention of the European Office Aerospace R&D (USA) for its early support and of the Fondation Michel Métivier for funding three travel scholarships and a best paper prize for young authors.

We hope that you will enjoy reading these proceedings and find inspiration for your future research.

June 2007

Teddy Furon
François Cayre
Gwenaël Doërr
Patrick Bas

Organization

General Chairs

Teddy Furon   INRIA Rennes, France
Gwenaël Doërr   University College London, UK

Program Chairs

Patrick Bas   LIS/INPG, France
François Cayre   LIS/CNRS, France

Program Committee

Ross J. Anderson	University of Cambridge, UK
Mauro Barni	Università di Siena, Italy
Patrick Bas	LIS/INPG, France
Jack Brassil	HP Labs, USA
Jan Camenisch	IBM Zurich Research Laboratory, Switzerland
François Cayre	LIS/CNRS, France
Ee-Chien Chang	National University of Singapore, Singapore
Christian Collberg	University of Arizona, USA
Ingemar J. Cox	University College London, UK
Gwenaël Doërr	University College London, UK
Jessica Fridrich	SUNY Binghampton, USA
Teddy Furon	INRIA Rennes, France
Neil F. Johnson	Booz Allen Hamilton, USA
Stefan Katzenbeisser	Philips Research, Netherlands
Darko Kirovski	Microsoft Research, USA
John McHugh	Dalhousie University, Canada
Ira S. Moskowitz	Naval Research Laboratory, USA
Andreas Pfitzmann	Dresden University of Technology, Germany
Phil Sallee	Booz Allen Hamilton, USA

Local Organization

Edith Blin Guyot   INRIA Rennes, France

Logo Design

Violaine Tygréat   INRIA Rennes, France
Cédric Gerot   LIS/INPG, France

External Reviewers

Gabriela Barrantes
Rainer Böhme
Roberto Caldelli
Edward Carter
Mo Chen
Mehmet, Celik,
Pedro Comesaña
Scott Craver
Alessia De Rosa
Mirek Dobsicek

Hany Farid
Elke Franz
Thomas Gloe
Miroslav Goljan
Shan He
Andrew Ker
Negar Kiyavash
Norka Lucena
Jan Lukáš
Ginger Myles

Alessandro Piva
Mila Dalla Preda
Bart Preneel
Hans Georg Schaathun
Dagmar Schönfeld
Clark Thomborson
Andreas Westfeld
Antje Winkler
Brecht Wyseur

Sponsoring Institutions

Conseil Général d'Ille et Vilaine, France
Direction Générale des Armées, France
European Office Aerospace R&D, USA
Fondation Michel Métivier, France
INRIA Rennes, France
Lecture Notes in Computer Science (LNCS)
Pôle de Compétitivité "Image et Réseaux", France
Région Bretagne, France
Thomson, France
Université de Rennes, France

Table of Contents

Watermarking Security

Steganalysis

Watermarking and Re-synchronization

Fingerprinting

Forensics

Steganalysis

MPSteg-color: A New Steganographic Technique for Color Images

Giacomo Cancelli and Mauro Barni

Università degli Studi di Siena
Dipartimento di Ingegneria dell'Informazione, Italy
{cancelli,barni}@dii.unisi.it

Abstract. A new steganographic algorithm for color images (MPSteg-color) is presented based on Matching Pursuit (MP) decomposition of the host image. With respect to previous works operating in the MP domain, the availability of three color bands is exploited to avoid the instability of the decomposition path and to randomize it for enhanced security. A selection and an update rule working entirely in the integer domain have been developed to improve the capacity of the stego channel and limit the computational complexity of the embedder. The system performance are boosted by applying the Matrix Embedding (ME) principle possibly coupled with a Wet Paper Coding approach to avoid ambiguities in stego-channel selection. The experimental comparison of the new scheme with a state-of-the-art algorithm applying the ME principle directly in the pixel domain reveals that, despite the lower PSNR achieved by MPSteg-color, a classical steganalyzer finds it more difficult to detect the MP-stego messages.

1 Introduction

The adoption of a steganographic technique operating in the Matching Pursuit (MP) domain has been recently proposed [1] as a possible way to improve the undetectability of a stego-message against conventional blind steganalyzers based on high order statistics (see for instance [2,3]). The rational behind the MP approach is that blind steganalyzers do not consider the semantic content of the host images, hence embedding the stego-message at a higher semantic level is arguably a good solution to improve its undetectability.

As reported in [1], however, trying to put the above idea at work is a difficult task due to some inherent drawbacks of the MP approach including computational complexity, and instability of the decomposition. The latter problem, in particular, represents a serious obstacle to the development of an efficient steganographic algorithm working in the MP domain.

To explain the reason for these difficulties, let us recall that MP works by decomposing the host image by means of a highly redundant basis. Due to the redundant nature of the basis the decomposition is not unique, hence the MP algorithm works by selecting an element of the basis at a time in a greedy fashion with no guarantee of global optimality (only a locally optimum decomposition is found). Consider now a typical steganographic scenario in which the embedder first decomposes the image by using the MP algorithm, then modifies the decomposition coefficients to insert the stego-message

T. Furon et al. (Eds.): IH 2007, LNCS 4567, pp. 1–15, 2007.

and at the end it goes back to the pixel domain. When the decoder applies again the MP algorithm it will select a different set of elements (in a different order) from the redundant basis hence making it impossible for the decoder to correctly extract the hidden message. Worse than that, even by assuming that the subset of elements of the basis (and their order) is fixed, changing one coefficient of the decomposition usually leads to a variation of all the coefficients of the decomposition when the MP is applied again to the modified image (this phenomenon is due to the non-orthogonality of the elements of the redundant basis).

In this paper we propose a new steganographic system (MPSteg-color) that, by exploiting the availability of three color bands, and by adopting a selection and an update rules working entirely in the integer domain, permits to avoid the instability problems outlined above, thus augmenting the capacity of the stego channel and limiting the computational complexity of the embedder. The system performance are boosted by applying on top of the basic embedding scheme the Matrix Embedding (ME) principle possibly coupled with a Wet Paper Coding approach to avoid ambiguities in the stego-channel selection.

The effectiveness of MPSteg-color has been tested by evaluating the detectability of the stego-message. Specifically, the images produced by MPSteg-color has been analyzed by means of a state-of-the-art steganalyzer [3] and the results compared to those obtained when the steganalyzer is applied to the output of a conventional ME-based scheme operating in the pixel domain. Despite the lower PSNR of the images produced by MPSteg-color, the steganalyzer finds it more difficult to detect the stego-message produced by MPSteg-color, thus providing a first, preliminary, confirm of the original intuition that embedding the stego-message at a higher semantic level improves the undetectability of the system.

2   Introduction to MP Image Decomposition

The main idea behind the use of redundant basis with a very high number of elements is that for any given signal it is likely that a few elements of the basis may be found and that these are enough to represent the signal properly. Of course, since the number of signals in the basis greatly exceeds the size of the space the host signal belongs to, the elements of the basis will no longer be orthogonal as in standard signal decomposition. In this class of problems, the elements of the redundant basis are called atoms, whereas the redundant basis is called the dictionary, and is indicated as $\mathcal{D}$:

$$\mathcal{D} = \{g_n\}_{n:1..N},\tag{1}$$

where g_n is the n-th atom. Let $\mathcal{I}$ be a generic image, we can describe it as the sum of a subset of elements of $\mathcal{D}$:

$$\mathcal{I} = \sum_{k=1}^{N} c_k g_k,\tag{2}$$

where c_k is the specific weight of the k-th atom, and where as many c_k as possible are zero. There are no particular requirements concerning the dictionary: in fact, the main advantage of this approach is the complete freedom in designing $\mathcal{D}$ which can then be efficiently tailored to closely match signal structures. Due to the non-orthogonality of the atoms, the decomposition in equation (2) is not unique, hence one could ask which is the best possible way of decomposing $\mathcal{I}$. Whereas many meanings can be given to the term *best decomposition*, in many cases, for instance in compression applications, it is only necessary that a suitable approximation of the image $\mathcal{I}$ is obtained. In this case it is useful to define the residual signal $\mathcal{R}^n$ as the difference between the original image $\mathcal{I}$ and the approximation obtained by considering only n atoms of the dictionary:

$$\mathcal{I}_n = \sum_{k=1}^{n} c_k g_{\gamma_k}, \tag{3}$$

$$\mathcal{R}^n = \mathcal{I} - \mathcal{I}_n. \tag{4}$$

where γ_k ties the atom identifier to the k-th position of the decomposition sum.

Given the above definitions, the best approximation problem can be restated as follows:

$$\text{minimize } n \text{ subject to } \|\mathcal{R}^n\|^2 \leq \varepsilon, \tag{5}$$

where ε is a predefined approximation error. Unfortunately, the above minimization is a NP-hard problem, due to the non-orthogonality of the dictionary [4]. Matching Pursuit is a greedy method that permits to decrease the above NP problem to a polynomial complexity [4].

MP works by choosing, at the k−th step, the atom $g_{\gamma_k} \in \mathcal{D}$ which minimizes the MSE between the reconstructed image and the original image, i.e. the atom that minimizes $\|\mathcal{R}^n\|^2$. While MP finds the best solution at the each step, it generally does not find the global optimum. In the following we will find convenient to rephrase MP as a two-step algorithm. The first step is defined through a selection function that, given the residual $\mathcal{R}^{n-1}$ at the n-th iteration, selects the appropriate element of $\mathcal{D}$ and its weight:

$$[c_n, g_{\gamma_n}] = \mathcal{S}(\mathcal{R}^{n-1}, \mathcal{D}) \tag{6}$$

where $\mathcal{S}(\cdot)$ is a particular selection operator, and then updates the residual

$$\mathcal{R}^n = \mathcal{U}(\mathcal{R}^{n-1}, c_n, g_{\gamma_n}), \tag{7}$$

Note that at each step the initial image $\mathcal{I}$ can be written as:

$$\mathcal{I} = \sum_{k=1}^{n} c_k \cdot g_{\gamma_k} + \mathcal{R}^n. \tag{8}$$

To complete the definition of the MP framework, other specifications must be given like the description of the dictionary and the selection rule.

2.1 Dictionary

There are several ways of building the dictionary. Discrete- or real-valued atoms can be used and atoms can be generated manually or by means of a generating function.

Fig. 1. A subset of the atoms the dictionary consists of

In classical MP techniques applied to still images [5], the dictionary is built by starting from a set of generating functions that generate real-valued atoms. A problem with real-valued atoms is that when the modified coefficients are used to reconstruct the image in the pixel domain, non-integer values may be produced, thus resulting in a quantization error when the grey levels are expressed in the standard 8-bit format allowing only integer values in the [0,255] range. This is a problem in steganographic applications where the hidden message is so weak that the quantization error may prevent its correct decoding. For this reason we decided to work with integer-valued atoms having integer-valued coefficients.

The most important property of the dictionary is that it should be able to describe each type of image with a linear combination of few atoms. To simplify the construction of the dictionary and to keep the computational burden of the MP decomposition low, we decided to work on a block basis, thus applying the MP algorithm to 4×4 blocks. At this level, each block may be seen as the composition of some fundamental geometric structures like flat regions, lines, edges and corners.

Bearing the above ideas in mind and by remembering that our aim is to embed the message at a semantic level, we designed the dictionary by considering elements which describe uniform areas, contours, lines, edge C-junctions, H-junctions, L-junctions, T-junctions and X-junctions. Each atom is formed by pixels whose value is either 0 or 1. In Fig. 1 the basic (non-shifted) atoms forming the dictionary are shown.

The complete dictionary is built by considering all the possible 16 shifts of the atoms reported in the figure.

2.2 MP Selection Rule

In order to derive the requirements that the selection rule must satisfy, let us observe that the stego message will be embedded in the MP domain (i.e. by modifying the coefficients c_k in equation (3)), but after embedding the modified image must be brought back in the pixel domain. If we want to avoid the introduction of quantization errors it is necessary that the reconstructed image belongs to the *Image class*, where the *Image class* is defined by the following property:

Property 1. *Let $\mathcal{I}$ be a generic gray image[1] in the pixel domain and let $n \times m$ be its size. Let $\mathcal{I}(x, y)$ be the value of the image $\mathcal{I}$ at x-row and y-column. We say that $\mathcal{I}$ belongs to the* Image class *if:*

$$\forall x \in 1..n, \forall y \in 1..m \qquad 0 \leq \mathcal{I}(x, y) \leq 255 \qquad and \qquad \mathcal{I}(x, y) \in \mathbb{Z}$$

the value of 255 is used by considering 8 bit color depth for each color band. The necessity of ensuring that each step the approximated image and the residual belong to thew *Image class* suggested us to consider only integer-valued atoms, and to allow only integer atom coefficients. In this way, we ensure that the reconstructed image takes only integer values. As to the constraint that the pixel values must be included in the [0,255] range, this property is ensured by the particular choice of the selection and update rule (see next section). As a side effect of the choice of working only with integer values, a considerable reduction of the computation time is also obtained.

The second requirement the MP decomposition must satisfy regards the necessity of avoiding (or at least limiting) the instability of the MP decomposition. As we outlined in the introduction, MP instability has two different facets. The former source of instability is due to the fact that the insertion of the message may change the order in which the atoms are chosen by the MP algorithm. As a matter of fact, if this is the case, the decoder will fail to read the hidden message correctly [2].

The second source of MP instability derives from the non-orthogonality of the dictionary: if we modify one single c_{k*} coefficient, reconstruct the modified image and apply the MP algorithm again, even if we do not change the order in which the atoms are selected, it may well be the case that all the coefficients will assume different values. Even worse, there is not guarantee that the coefficient of the k^*-th atom will be equal to the value we set it to [3].

A final, obvious, requirement stems from the very goal of all our work, that is to embed the stego-message at as high as possible a semantic level, hence the selection rule must be defined in such a way that at each step the most relevant atom is selected to describe the residual image.

By summarizing, we are looking for a selection rule that:

- contrasts atom instability;
- works in integer arithmetic without exiting the *Image class*;
- selects atoms based on their structural significance.

In the next section we describe the MPSteg-color algorithm, by paying great attention to describe the MP selection rule and prove that the first two requirements are indeed satisfied (the extent to which the third requirement is satisfied will be judged globally by evaluating the performance of the whole stego-system).

---

[1] It is possible to extend this definition to RGB images by considering each color band as a gray image.

[2] Note that in image compression, where the image is reconstructed from a list of weighed atoms, the fact that a successive decomposition generates a different list of atoms is not a problem.

[3] It is easy to show that this is the case, for example, if the selection and update rules are based on the classical projection operator.

3   MPSteg-color

Since we have to deal with color images, we will use the following notation:

$$
\mathcal{I} = \begin{pmatrix} \mathcal{I}_r \\ \mathcal{I}_g \\ \mathcal{I}_b \end{pmatrix}
$$

where $\mathcal{I}_r$, $\mathcal{I}_g$ and $\mathcal{I}_b$ are the three RGB bands of a traditional color image.

As we said, MPSteg-color works on a non-overlapping, 4×4 block-wise partition of the original image, however for simplicity we continue to refer to image decomposition instead of block decomposition. The use of blocks, in fact, is only an implementation detail, not a conceptual strategy.

The main idea behind MPSteg-color is to use the correlation of the three color bands to stabilize the decomposition path. Specifically we propose to calculate the decomposition path on a color band and to use it to decompose the other two bands. Due to the high correlation between color bands, we argue that the structural elements found in a band will also be present in the other two. Suppose, for instance, that the decomposition path is computed on the $\mathcal{I}_r$ band, we can decompose the original image as follows

$$
\mathcal{I} = \begin{pmatrix} \sum_{k=1}^{n} c_{r,k} \cdot g_{\gamma_{r,k}} + \mathcal{R}_r^n \\ \sum_{k=1}^{n} c_{g,k} \cdot g_{\gamma_{r,k}} + \mathcal{R}_g^n \\ \sum_{k=1}^{n} c_{b,k} \cdot g_{\gamma_{r,k}} + \mathcal{R}_b^n \end{pmatrix} \tag{9}
$$

where $g_{\gamma_{r,k}}$ are the atoms selected on the red band, $c_{r,k}, c_{g,k}$ and $c_{b,k}$ are the atom weights of each band and $\mathcal{R}_r^n, \mathcal{R}_g^n$ and $\mathcal{R}_b^n$ are the partial residuals. By using (9) we do not obtain the optimum decomposition of $\mathcal{I}$, but this kind of decomposition has a good property: if the red band does not change, the $\mathcal{S}(\mathcal{I}_r)$ function chooses the same decomposition path even if the other two bands have been heavily changed. Therefore, we can embed the message within two bands without modifying the decomposition path since it is calculated on the remaining band. Having avoided that the insertion of the stego-message produces a different decomposition path, we must define the selection and update rules in such a way that any modification of a coefficient does not influence the other weights. We achieved such a results by defining the selection rule as follows. At each step k let:

$$
\mathcal{S}(\mathcal{R}^{k-1}, \mathcal{D}) = [c_k^*, g_{\gamma_k^*}] \tag{10}
$$

with

$$
g_{\gamma_k^*} = \arg \min_{g_{\gamma_k} \in \mathcal{D}} \sum_{i,j} |\mathcal{R}^k(i,j)| \qquad \text{with} \qquad \mathcal{R}^k = \mathcal{R}^{k-1} - c_k^* g_{\gamma_k}, \tag{11}
$$

and in which c_k^* is computed as follows:

$$
c_k^* = \max\{c \geq 0 : \mathcal{R}^{k-1} - c g_{\gamma_k} \geq 0 \quad \text{for every pixel}\} \tag{12}
$$

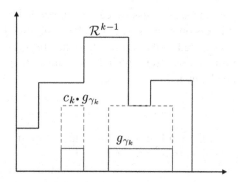

Fig. 2. The Selection Rule

the behavior of the selection rule is illustrated in Fig.2, where the choice of c_k is shown in the one-dimensional case. By starting from the residual R^{k-1} (the highest signal) and the selected atom g_{γ_k} (the lowest signal), the weight c_k is calculated as the maximum integer number for which $c_k g_{\gamma_k}$ is lower or equal to R^{k-1} (the dashed signal in the figure). Note that given that the atoms take only 0 or 1 values, at teach step the inclusion of a new term in the MP decomposition permits to set to zero at least one pixel of the residual. Note also that the partial residual $\mathcal{R}^k$ continues to stay in the *Image class*.

We must now determine whether the selection rule described above is able to contrast the instability of the MP decomposition. This is indeed the case, if we assume that the decomposition path is fixed and that only non-zero coefficients are modified, as it is shown in the following theorem.

Theorem 1. *Let $\mathcal{I} = \mathcal{R}^0$ be an image and let $g_\gamma = (g_{\gamma_1}, \ldots, g_{\gamma_n})$ be a decomposition path. We suppose that the atoms are binary valued, i.e. they take only values 0 or 1. Let assume that the MP decomposition coefficients are computed iteratively by means of the following operations:*

$$c_k = \max\{c \geq 0 : \mathcal{R}^{k-1} - cg_{\gamma_k} \geq 0 \quad \text{for every pixel}\} \tag{13}$$
$$\mathcal{R}^k = \mathcal{R}^{k-1} - c_k g_{\gamma_k}, \tag{14}$$

and let $\mathbf{c} = (c_1, c_2 \ldots c_n)$ be the coefficient vector built after n iterations. Let c_k be an element of $\mathbf{c}$ with $c_k \neq 0$, and let $\mathbf{c}'$ be a modified version of $\mathbf{c}$ where c_k has been replaced by c'_k. If we apply the MP decomposition to the modified image

$$\mathcal{I}' = \sum_{i=1, i\neq k}^{n} c_i \cdot g_{\gamma_i} + c'_k g_{\gamma_k} + \mathcal{R}^n \tag{15}$$

by using the decomposition path g_γ, we re-obtain exactly the same vector $\mathbf{c}'$ and the same residual $\mathcal{R}^n$.

The proof of Theorem 1 is shown in the Appendix A.

The above theorem can be applied recursively to deal with the case in which more than one coefficient in $\mathbf{c}$ is changed.

Theorem 1 tells us that the stego message can be embedded by changing any non-zero coefficient of the MP decomposition vector c. By assuming, for instance, that the decomposition path is computed in the red band, then, MPSteg-color can embed the stego-message by operating on the vector with the decomposition weights of the green and blue bands. Specifically, by letting

$$c_{gb} = (c_{g,1}, c_{b,1}, \ldots, c_{g,n}, c_{b,n}) \tag{16}$$

be the host feature vector, the marked vector is obtained by quantizing each feature according to a 3-level quantizer (more on this below).

By indicating with $c_{gb}^w = (c_{g,1}^w, c_{b,1}^w, \ldots, c_{g,n}^w, c^w b, n)$ the marked coefficient vector, we then have:

$$\mathcal{I}^w = \begin{pmatrix} \sum_{k=1}^{n} c_{r,k} \cdot g_{\gamma_{r,k}} + \mathcal{R}_r^n \\ \sum_{k=1}^{n} c_{g,k}^w \cdot g_{\gamma_{r,k}} + \mathcal{R}_g^n \\ \sum_{k=1}^{n} c_{b,k}^w \cdot g_{\gamma_{r,k}} + \mathcal{R}_b^n \end{pmatrix} \tag{17}$$

As a last step we must define the embedding rule used to embed the message into c. Given that the coefficients of c are positive integers, we can apply any method that is usually applied to embed a message in the pixel domain. However we must consider that the embedder can not touch zero coefficients (due to the hypothesis of theorem 1), but in principle it could set to zero some non-zero coefficients. If this is the case a de-synchronization is introduced between the embedder and the decoder since the decoder will not know which coefficients have been used to convey the stego-message. In the steganographic literature this is a well know problem (the channel selection problem), for which a few solutions exist.

3.1 ± 1 (Ternary) Matrix Embedding

The simplest (non-optimal solution) to cope with the channel selection problem consists in preventing the embedder to set any coefficient to zero. In other words, whenever the embedding rule would result in a zero coefficient a sub-optimal embedding strategy is adopted and a different value is chosen (see below further details). Having said this, a very efficient way to minimize the embedding distortion for low payloads and when a sufficiently large number of host coefficients is available is the ± 1 (or ternary) Matrix Embedding (ME) algorithm described by Fridrich et al. [3]. The ME algorithm derives from the simpler ± 1 scheme that, by working with a ternary alphabet, is able to embed a ternary symbol by adding or subtracting at most 1 to the host coefficients. It can be shown that by using the ternary alphabet the payload increases by a $\log_2 3$ with respect to the binary case.

For low payloads the ± 1 algorithm can be greatly improved by using the ME extension [3]. In its simplest form, the ME approach uses a Hamming code to embed a message. By using a specific parity check matrix, it is possible to embed more symbols in a predefined set of features by changing at most one coefficient. In general, it is possible to prove that for a ternary alphabet $\dfrac{3^i - 1}{2}$ coefficients must be available to embed i ternary symbols by changing only one element [3].

In the MPSteg-color scenario the ME algorithm can be applied to the non-null coefficients of $c_{g,b}$. However, the embedder must pay attention to increase all coefficient set to zero by the ME algorithm to a value of 3 to preserve the cardinality of the non-null set. Note that this results in a larger distortion.

3.2   Wet Paper Coding and Matrix Embedding

A very elegant and optimal solution to the channel selection problem can be obtained by applying the Wet Paper Coding paradigm, which in turn can be coupled with the Matrix Embedding algorithm (WPC-ME) as described by Fridrich et al. [6].

In brief, all the available features of a signal, in our case all the elements of c_{gb}, are used to embed the secret message. The embedder selects the changeable elements in $c_{g,b}$ and the WPC-ME algorithm tries to embed the message through syndrome coding, without touching non-changeable coefficients (in our case the null coefficients). If WPC-ME finds a solution, it is at the minimum distance from the starting c_{gb} in terms of Hamming distance. With WPC-ME, all coefficients are used to recover the secret message even if the cardinality of the null-coefficient set is changed during the embedding phase. Fridrich et al. [6] describe a binary version of the WPC-ME algorithm, however, at least in principle, it is possible to extend WPC-ME to a ternary alphabet but the resulting algorithm is very expensive in terms of execution time because it uses a complete NP search to find the optimum solution that achieves the right syndrome. For this reason we did not implement the WPC-ME version of MPSteg-color leaving it for future work. We rather evaluated the potential performance of a binary version of MPSteg-color with WPC-ME by extrapolating some of the results presented in *Embedding Efficiency* section of [6]. In practice, the number of changes that must be introduced for a given payload has been derived from the analysis by Fridrich et al. then such changes have been randomly introduced in the MP decomposition of the host image and the steganalyzer was run on these images.

The overall schemes of the MPSteg-color embedder and decoder are reported in Fig. 3

3.3   A Few Implementation Details

Some minor modifications to the general scheme described so far have been incorporated in the final version of MPSteg-color to improve its performance from a couple of critical points.

As a first thing, let us recall that the redundant bases and the MP algorithm have been introduced for image representation and, more specifically, in order to represent an image with a small number of atoms. The first atoms selected by MP are thus able

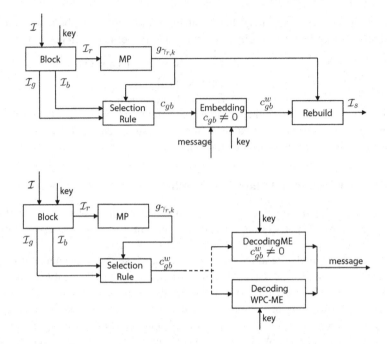

Fig. 3. MPSteg-color embedding (up) and decoding (bottom) schemes

to describe most of the image compared to the remaining residual. For each block we observed that a great deal of the block's energy is extracted by the first atom. For this reason, when the selected embedding scheme modifies the first atom, this modification is more perceptible to the human eye, hence to improve undetectability, MPSteg-color does not mark the first atom.

A second significant problem is the security of the algorithm. To increase it, a secret key is introduced. This key is a seed for a random number generator that decides on a block by block basis which color band will be used to calculate the decomposition path. The MP decomposition is applied at the chosen band, while the secret message is embedded within the other bands.

4   Experimental Results

We executed several tests on a set of, non-compressed, 600 256×256 color images taken with a Canon EOS 20D. A subset of 400 images are used as the training set and 200 images for testing. Images were acquired and stored in raw format. From the original 600 images, a database of 1200 images, half of which marked has been produced. The MP algorithm was applied to blocks of 4×4 pixels. The dictionary contains 32 centered atoms of 4x4 pixels, plus all possible shifts. Thus the MP algorithm worked with 512 atoms. The maximum decomposition depth was set to 16.

Table 1. Results the steganalyzer. The Spc column reports the symbol per change inserted by the ME methods.

Payload$_{bpp}$	±1 ME			MPSteg & ±1 ME			MPSteg & WPC-ME	
	Spc	PSNR	Accuracy	Spc	PSNR	Accuracy	PSNR	Accuracy
0.5	2	57.9122	0.8561	1	48.7702	0.8078	50.2423	0.6936
0.25	3	61.0855	0.6037	2	53.4482	0.5400	53.5247	0.5294
0.1154	4	65.5842	0.2938	3	58.5014	0.3012	57.9467	0.2777
0.05	5	70.1466	0.1562	4	63.2808	0.1489	63.4285	0.1154

To test the new steganographic technique, the steganalyzer developed by Goljan et al. [3] was extended and used. From the initial gray scale steganalyzer we implemented a color version by joining the 3 band feature vectors in a unique feature vector with triple components (81 components). To detect stego-images a Fisher's linear discriminant was used.

This steganalysis tool was used to compare MPSteg with the ±1 ME algorithm [7] . Section 3.2 showed how ±1 works. Considering that each pixel is an RGB pixel, 256 × 256 × 3 usable host coefficients were available for ±1 ME. Note that the number of coefficients MPSteg-color can rely on is much lower due to the necessity to skip one band, to leave null coefficients unchanged and to the low number of atoms necessary to describe each block.

In this scenario we calculated the average payload and the accuracy obtained by the steganalyzer when it is applied to both ±1 ME and MPSteg-color in the ME and WPC-ME versions. Table 1 shows the results of the steganalyzer applied to four different payloads. The results are those obtained on the training set, however the results we obtained on the test set are similar to those given in the table.

In the first column the payload in terms of bit per pixel per band is given and, for ME techniques the Spc column contains the Symbol per change characterizing the various algorithms. We remember that if we want embed i symbols with one change, we must have $\dfrac{3^i - 1}{2}$ non-null coefficients, i.e. we must have 121 weights. The average PSNR was obtained by taking the average on the linear quantities and then passing to the logarithmic scale. In the accuracy column the ability of the steganalyzer to detect the presence of the stego-message is indicated.

As it can be seen from Table 1 (PSNR column), the ±1 ME algorithm is less intrusive than MPSteg algorithm because the embedding procedure of the first technique changes only one pixel value rather than the value of a set of pixels as MPSteg-color does. Moreover, the compared technique works on a much bigger set of coefficients which are the pixels of the color image. Our technique instead works on the weights of the atoms of only two subbands, thus resulting in a lower payload. Indeed, in the table the systems are compared by keeping the same payload, however higher payload would be possible for the ±1 ME scheme, whereas for MPSteg-color a payload higher than 1bpp per band is not achievable.

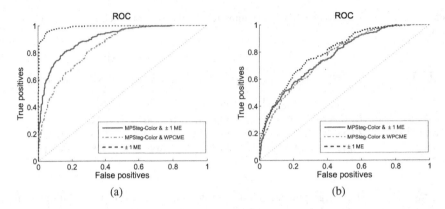

Fig. 4. ROCs on 400 training set images for two embedding capacities: (a) 1 bpp and (b) 0.25 bpp. Three steganographic methods are analyzed: solid = MPSteg-color ME, dot-dashed = MPSteg-color WPCME, dot = ± 1 ME (non-adaptive embedding). The dashed diagonal line represents the lower bound of the steganalyzer.

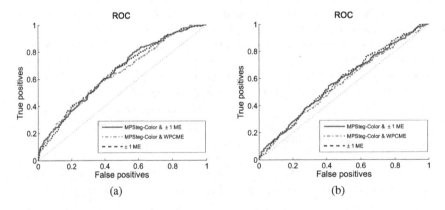

Fig. 5. ROCs on 400 training set images for two embedding capacities: (a) 0.1154 bpp and (b) 0.05. Three steganographic methods are analyzed: solid = MPSteg-color ME, dot-dashed = MPSteg-color WPCME, dot = ± 1 ME (non-adaptive embedding). The dashed diagonal line represents the lower bound of the steganalyzer.

We recall that ± 1 ME and MPSteg-color with ME work with a ternary alphabet, while the results of the WPC-ME version of MPSteg-color have been estimate by considering a binary alphabet, $15 \times 2 \times 4096$ coefficients and by assuming that only non-null coefficients are modified. The ultimate performance of WPC-ME MPSteg-color, then, are superior to those reported in the table (though they may not be easy to achieve).

In Fig. 4 and Fig. 5 the ROC curves are shown for four different payloads. How it is possible to see, ROCs are similar in Fig. 5(a) and Fig. 5(b) for low payloads while, in Fig. 4(a) and Fig. 4(b), ROCs are more separated and MPSteg curves are under the ± 1 ME.

The results that we obtained suggest that, despite the lower PSNR, the message embedded by MPSteg-color is the less detectable, with a significant difference for larger payloads (for the lower payloads all the schemes are sufficiently secure).

5   Discussion and Conclusions

In this paper an high redundant basis data hiding technique is developed for color images. The embedding method based on the MP algorithm bypasses the instability of the decomposition path by using two independent and high correlated sets: a color band is used exclusively to obtain the decomposition path used to decompose the other two. In this manner, by changing non-null weights we can embed the message within two bands without modifying the decomposition band. Under specific hypothesis, Theorem 1 guarantees that by using the proposed selection rule we can correctly extract the secret message. Moreover, by using an integer arithmetic we can increase the performance of MPSteg-color by simplifying the MP decomposition operations. In addition, the stability of our approach allows to use several kinds of embedding methods like ± 1 ME and WPC-ME and binary and ternary alphabets.

Results that obtained by means of a sophisticated blind steganalyzer shows that despite the ± 1 ME technique introduces less artifacts in comparison to our technique (in terms of PSNR), the security of the proposed approach is superior. Moreover, the results empirically show that, we can increase the undetectability of the stego-message by embedding the message at a higher semantic level.

The undetectability of MPSteg-color encourages new research in MP-domain steganography. Specifically, a number of improvements of the basic algorithm described here can be conceived. First of all, an additional level of security can be introduced. So far, in fact, a fixed dictionary is used, hence making it easier to conceive a steganalyzer specifically designed to detect the MP-stego-message. Possible solutions consist in making the dictionary dependent on a secret key, or in randomizing the image partition into sub-blocks. Moreover it should be observed that in MPSteg-color the length of the host feature vector is rather low with respect to the number of pixels. By using a ternary alphabet we can contrast the decrease of the payload, or by using the same payload, we can increase the security. Thus, we should investigate new embedding schemes which gets close to the theoretical rate-distortion bound. New techniques introduced in [8] show how advanced codes called LDGM can decrease the gap to the rate-distortion curve by using high dimensional codebooks.

Acknowledgments

This work was partially supported by the European Commission through the IST Programme under projects ECRYPT (Contract number IST-2002-507932) and SPEED (Contract number 034238). The information in this paper is provided as is, and no guarantee or warranty is given or implied that the information is fit for any particular purpose. The user thereof uses the information at its sole risk and liability.

We also would like to thank Miroslav Goljan and Jessica Fridrich for providing us the steganalyzer software.

References

1. Cancelli, G., Barni, M., Menegaz, G.: Mpsteg: hiding a message in the matching pursuit domain. In: Proc. SPIE, Security, Steganography, and Watermarking of Multimedia Contents VIII, San Jose, California USA. vol. 6072 (2006)
2. Holotyak, T., Fridrich, J., Voloshynovskiy, S.: Blind statistical steganalysis of additive steganography using wavelet higher order statistics. In: Proc. of the 9th IFIP TC-6 TC-11 Conference on Communications and Multimedia Security, Salzburg, Austria, September 19-21 (2005)
3. Fridrich, J., Goljan, M., Holotyak, T.: New blind steganalysis and its implications. In: Proc. SPIE, Security, Steganography, and Watermarking of Multimedia Contents VIII, San Jose, California USA. vol. 6072 (2006)
4. Mallat, S., Zhang, Z.: Matching pursuit with time-frequency dictionaries. IEEE Trans. on Signal Processing 41 (1993)
5. Vandergheynst, P., Frossard, P.: Image coding using redundant dictionaries. Marcel Dekker Publishing (2005)
6. Fridrich, J., Goljan, M., Soukal, D.: Wet paper codes with improved embedding efficiency. IEEE Transactions on Information Forensics and Security 1(1), 102–110 (2006)
7. Fridrich, J., Goljan, M., Lisonek, P., Soukal, D.: Writing on wet paper. IEEE Transactions on Information Security and Forensics 53, 3923–3935 (2005)
8. Fridrich, J., Filler, T.: Practical methods for minimizing embedding impact in steganography. In: Proc. SPIE, Security, Steganography, and Watermarking of Multimedia Contents IX, San Jose, California USA. vol. 6505 (2007)

Appendix A

Theorem 1. *Let $\mathcal{I} = \mathcal{R}^0$ be an image and let $g_\gamma = (g_{\gamma_1}, \ldots, g_{\gamma_n})$ be a decomposition path. We suppose that the atoms are binary valued, i.e. they take only values 0 or 1. Let assume that the MP decomposition coefficients are computed iteratively by means of the following operations:*

$$c_k = \max\{c \geq 0 : \mathcal{R}^{k-1} - cg_{\gamma_k} \geq 0 \quad \text{for every pixel}\} \tag{18}$$
$$\mathcal{R}^k = \mathcal{R}^{k-1} - c_k g_{\gamma_k}, \tag{19}$$

and let $c = (c_1, c_2 \ldots c_n)$ be the coefficient vector built after n iterations. Let c_k be an element of c with $c_k \neq 0$, and let c' be a modified version of c where c_k has been replaced by c'_k. If we apply the MP decomposition to the modified image

$$\mathcal{I}' = \sum_{i=1, i \neq k}^{n} c_i \cdot g_{\gamma_i} + c'_k g_{\gamma_k} + \mathcal{R}^n \tag{20}$$

by using the decomposition path g_γ, we re-obtain exactly the same vector c' and the same residual $\mathcal{R}^n$.

Proof. To prove the theorem we introduce some notations. We indicate by $S(g_{\gamma_k})$ the support of the atom $(\gamma_k)^4$. This notation, and the fact that $g_{\gamma_k}(x, y) \in \{0, 1\} \; \forall(x, y)$,

---

[4] The support of an atom is defined as the set of coordinates (x, y) for which $g_{\gamma_k}(x, y) \neq 0$.

permits us to rewrite the rule for the computation of c_k as follows:

$$c_k = \min_{(x,y) \in S(g_{\gamma_k})} \mathcal{R}^{k-1}(x,y). \tag{21}$$

We indicate by j_k the coordinates for which the above minimum is reached, i.e.:

$$j_k = \arg \min_{(x,y) \in S(g_{\gamma_k})} \mathcal{R}^{k-1}(x,y). \tag{22}$$

Note that after the update we will always have $\mathcal{R}^k(j_k) = 0$. We also find it useful to define the set $\mathcal{J}_k = \bigcup_{i=1}^{k} j_i$. Let now c_k be a non-zero element of c. We surely have $S(g_{\gamma_k}) \cap \mathcal{J}_{k-1} = \emptyset$ since otherwise we would have $c_k = 0$. Let us demonstrate first that by applying the MP to $\mathcal{I}'$ the coefficients of the atoms g_{γ_h} with $h < k$ do not change. To do so let us focus on a generic atom g_{γ_h}, two cases are possible: $S(g_{\gamma_k}) \cap S(g_{\gamma_h}) = \emptyset$ or $S(g_{\gamma_k}) \cap S(g_{\gamma_h}) \neq \emptyset$. In the first case it is evident that the weight c_h will not change, since a modification of the weight assigned to $S(g_{\gamma_k})$ can not have any impact on (21) since the minimization is performed on $S(g_{\gamma_h})$. When the intersection between $S(g_{\gamma_h})$ and $S(g_{\gamma_k})$ is non-empty, two cases are again possible, $c'_k > c_k$ and $c'_k < c_k$. In the former case some of the values in $\mathcal{R}^{h-1}$ are increased, however $\mathcal{R}^{h-1}(j_h)$ does not change since $S(g_{\gamma_k}) \cap \mathcal{J}_{k-1} = \emptyset$, hence leaving the computation of the weight c_h unchanged. If $c'_k < c_k$, some values in $\mathcal{R}^{h-1}$ are decreased while leaving $\mathcal{R}^{h-1}(j_h)$ unchanged. However $\forall (x,y) \in S(g_{\gamma_k}) \cap S(g_{\gamma_h})$ we have $\mathcal{R}^{k-1}(x,y) \leq \mathcal{R}^h(x,y)$ since due to the particular update rule we adopted, at each iteration the values in the residual can not increase. For this reason at the h-th selection step, the modification of the k-th coefficient can not decrease the residual by more than $\mathcal{R}^{h-1} - c_h$ (remember that $c_h = \mathcal{R}^{h-1}(j_h)$). In other words, $\mathcal{R}^{h-1}(x,y)$ computed on the modified image $\mathcal{I}'$ will satisfy the relation $\mathcal{R}^{h-1}(x,y) \geq \mathcal{R}^{h-1}(j_h)$ hence ensuring that $c'_h = c_h$.

We must now demonstrate that the components $h \geq k$ of the vector c do not change as well. Let us start with the case $h = k$. When the MP is applied to the image $\mathcal{I}'$ we have

$$c''_k = \min_{(x,y) \in S(g_{\gamma_k})} \left[\mathcal{R}^{k-1}(x,y) + (c'_k - c_k)g_{\gamma_k}(x,y) \right]. \tag{23}$$

From equation (23) it is evident that

$$c''_k = c'_k = \min_{(x,y) \in S(g_{\gamma_k})} \mathcal{R}^{k-1}(x,y), \tag{24}$$

since the term $(c'_k - c_k)g_{\gamma_k}$ introduces a constant bias on all the points of $S(g_{\gamma_k})$.

As to the case $h > k$ it is trivial to show that $c'_h = c_h$ given that the residual after the k-th step will be the same for $\mathcal{I}$ and $\mathcal{I}'$. $\qquad \square$

YASS: Yet Another Steganographic Scheme That Resists Blind Steganalysis

Kaushal Solanki[2], Anindya Sarkar[1], and B.S. Manjunath[1]

[1] Department of Electrical and Computer Engineering,[*]
University of California,
Santa Barbara, CA 93106
[2] Mayachitra Inc.,
5266 Hollister Avenue,
Santa Barbara, CA 93111
solanki@mayachitra.com,anindya@ece.ucsb.edu,manj@ece.ucsb.edu

Abstract. A new, simple, approach for *active* steganography is proposed in this paper that can successfully resist recent blind steganalysis methods, in addition to surviving distortion constrained attacks. We present *Yet Another Steganographic Scheme* (YASS), a method based on embedding data in randomized locations so as to disable the self-calibration process (such as, by cropping a few pixel rows and/or columns to estimate the cover image features) popularly used by blind steganalysis schemes. The errors induced in the embedded data due to the fact that the stego signal must be *advertised* in a specific format such as JPEG, are dealt with by the use of erasure and error correcting codes. For the presented JPEG steganograhic scheme, it is shown that the detection rates of recent blind steganalysis schemes are close to random guessing, thus confirming the practical applicability of the proposed technique. We also note that the presented steganography framework, of hiding in randomized locations and using a coding framework to deal with errors, is quite simple yet very generalizable.

Keywords: data hiding, error correcting codes, steganalysis, steganography, supervised learning.

1 Introduction

Secure communication of a secret message has always been important to people, and it is not surprising that *steganography*, the art of communicating without revealing its existence, as well as *cryptography*, the art of concealing the meaning of a message, have a rich history. In this paper, we consider the problem of secure steganography via hiding information in digital images. In steganography, a *message* signal is embedded into a *host* or *cover* signal to get a *composite* or *stego* signal in such a way that the presence of hidden information cannot be

---

[*] This research is supported in part by a grant from ONR # N00014-05-1-0816. Corresponding author: K. Solanki (solanki@mayachitra.com)

T. Furon et al. (Eds.): IH 2007, LNCS 4567, pp. 16–31, 2007.

detected by either *statistical* or *perceptual* analysis of the stego signal. In case of *active* steganography, there is an additional requirement that the hidden data must be recoverable even after benign or malicious processing of the stego signal by an adversary.

JPEG is arguably the most popular format for storing, presenting, and exchanging images. It is not surprising that steganography in the JPEG format, and its converse problem of steganalysis of JPEG images to find ones with hidden data, have received considerable attention from researchers over the past decade. There are many approaches and software available for JPEG steganography, which include OutGuess [1], StegHide [2], model-based steganography [3], perturbed quantization [4], F5 [5], and statistical restoration [6,7].

Approaches for JPEG steganography have focused on hiding data in the least significant bit (LSB) of the quantized discrete cosine transform (DCT) coefficients. In order to avoid inducing significant perceptual distortion in the image, most methods avoid hiding in DCT coefficients whose value is 0. To detect the presence of data embedded in this manner, steganalysis algorithms exploit the fact that the DCT coefficient histogram gets modified when hiding random information bits. Hence recently proposed steganographic approaches attempt to match, as closely as possible, the original DCT histogram or its model. Westfield's F5 algorithm [5] increases, decreases, or keeps unchanged, the coefficient value based on the data bit to be hidden, so as to better match the host statistics. Provos's OutGuess [1] was the first attempt at explicitly matching the DCT histogram. Sallee proposed a model based approach for steganography [3] wherein the DCT coefficients were modified to hide data such that they follow an underlying model. Fridrich et al's perturbed quantization [4] attempts to resemble the statistics of a double-compressed image. Statistical restoration method proposed by Solanki et al [6,7] can match the DCT histograms exactly, thus providing provable security so long as only the marginal statistics are used by the steganalyst.

Many steganalysis schemes (see [8,9,10]) have been able to successfully detect the above steganographic techniques that match marginal statistics or models. They exploit the fact that higher order statistics get modified by data hiding using these stego methods. It is known that, the higher order statistics, in general, are difficult to match, model, or restore. Recently, blind steganalysis algorithms [9,10,11,12,13,14,15,16] have been proposed that employ supervised learning to distinguish between the plain cover and stego images, and also identify the particular hiding algorithm used for steganography. These techniques bank on the fact that there are some image *features* that are modified during the embedding process which can be used as an input to the learning machine. For the success of this approach, it is crucial that these features are very sensitive to the embedding changes, but insensitive to the image content. This requires a good model for natural images against which the suspected stego images can be evaluated.

In spite of the absence of good universal models, recent steganalysis algorithms have been very successful by using a *self-calibration* method to approximate the statistics of the original cover (see, for example, Pevny and Fridrich [9,10], and

Dabeer et al [17]). The calibration method typically used for JPEG steganography is quite simple; a few pixel rows and/or columns are cropped from the image so as to desynchronize it from the original JPEG grid and the resulting image is compressed again, which forms a good approximation of the cover image. The results reported in [10], the most recent multi-class JPEG steganalysis method that employs such self-calibration, are close to perfect: the steganalyst can determine one out of 6 stego algorithms employed for hiding with a detection accuracy of more than 95% in most cases, even at low embedding rates.

We present *yet another steganographic scheme* (YASS), a method for secure, active, steganography that can successfully resist the aforementioned blind steganalysis schemes. The technique is based on a simple idea of embedding data in random locations within an image, which makes it difficult for the steganalyst to get a good estimate of the cover image features via the self-calibration process. This approach works by desynchronizing the steganalyst, which is similar in spirit to what *stirmark* does for watermarks. Although data is hidden in randomly chosen blocks in the image, the image must be advertised in JPEG format. This leads to errors in the recovered data bits, which are dealt with by using erasure and error correcting codes in a manner similar to [18].

We evaluate the method against several recent blind steganalysis schemes, which include Farid's 72-dimensional wavelet-based features [19], Pevny and Fridrich's 23-dimensional DCT-based features [9] and 274-dimensional merged Markov and DCT features [10], a feature vector comprising of histogram of DCT coefficients, Xuan et al's statistical moments based spatial domain steganalysis features [13], and Chen et al's 324-dimensional JPEG steganalysis feature [20]. We find that the presented method, YASS, is completely undetectable for most of the embedding configurations, while the competing algorithms, OutGuess and StegHide, are detectable at the same hiding rates. We also note here that, because we use error correction coding framework, our method provides robustness against distortion constrained attacks thus enabling active steganography.

The rest of the paper is organized as follows. In Section 2, we motivate the use of the proposed randomized hiding for steganography. Next, in Section 3, we introduce and describe our JPEG steganographic technique: YASS. Experimental setup and results are presented in Section 4, followed by the concluding remarks in Section 5.

2   Resisting Blind Steganalysis

The notion of ϵ-security proposed by Cachin [21] states that a steganographic scheme is ϵ-secure if the Kullback-Leibler divergence between the cover and the stego signal distributions is less than a small number ϵ. This definition inherently assumes that cover signals can be described by "natural" distributions, which are known to the steganalyst. Statistical steganalysis schemes work by evaluating a suspected stego signal against an assumed or computed cover distribution or *model*. Most recent steganalysis schemes fall in this category [22,10,9].

Blind statistical steganalysis schemes use a supervised learning technique on *features* derived from plain cover as well as stego signals. This class of methods has been very successful in detecting steganographic methods available today. For example, detection results presented in [10] and also our own experiments indicate that popular JPEG steganographic schemes such as OutGuess [1], StegHide [2], model-based steganography [3], and 1D statistical restoration schemes [6,7] can be successfully detected. Following are the key ingredients that contribute to the success of these blind steganalysis schemes.

1. **Self-calibration mechanism:** Calibration process is used by the blind steganalysis schemes to estimate the statistics of the cover image from the stego image. For JPEG steganography, this is typically achieved by decompressing the stego image to the spatial domain followed by cropping the image by a few pixels on each side and compressing the image again using the same compression parameters.
2. **Features capturing cover memory:** Most steganographic schemes hide data on a per-symbol basis, and typically do not explicitly compensate or preserve statistical dependencies. Hence, features that capture higher dimensional dependencies in the cover symbols are crucial in detecting the embedding changes. Cover memory has been shown to be very important to steganalysis [22], and is incorporated into the feature vector in several ways, e.g. [23,15].
3. **Powerful machine learning:** Use of powerful machine learning techniques and training with several thousand images ensures that even the slightest statistical variation in the features is *learned* by the machine.

The calibration process is perhaps the most important of the above that allows the steganalyst to get an accurate underlying model of the cover image despite not having access to it. With this approach, statistical steganalysis is successful eventhough good *universal* statistical models for images are not available. In the following section, we discuss a simple approach that can potentially defeat these steganalysis schemes.

2.1   The Proposed Approach for Steganography

In order to enable secure communication in the presence of blind steganalysis, the steganographer must embed information into host signals in such a way that no image features are significantly perturbed during the embedding process. However, we must not forget that the steganalyst must depend on the stego image to derive the approximate cover image statistics via some sort of self-calibration process. The steganographer can, instead of (or along with) trying to preserve the feature vectors, embed data in such a way that it distorts the steganalyst's estimate of the cover image statistics. This can practically be achieved using the following approaches.

1. **Hiding with high embedding strength:** By embedding data with high strength, the cover image is distorted so much that the cover image statistics

can no longer be derived reliably from the available stego image. This is indeed found to be true and reported in recent work by Kharrazi et al [24].
2. **Randomized hiding:** By randomizing the embedding approach, the algorithm to estimate the cover statistics can be effectively disabled. Things that can be randomized include the spatial location of hiding, the transform coefficient to hide, the choice of transform domain, or even the embedding method. In this manner, the steganalyst cannot make any consistent assumptions about the hiding process even if the embedding algorithm is known to everyone as per the Kerckhoff's principle.

There are some obvious disadvantages of using the first approach of hiding with high strength. First, the likelihood of perceptual distortion is high. Second, the data can possibly be detected by a steganalyst evaluating the stego image against a *universal* image model even if it is not that precise.

The second approach of hiding in a randomized manner is quite appealing, and we explore its simplest realization in this paper: embedding data in randomized locations within an image. One issue with hiding data in random locations is the possibility of encountering errors in the hidden bits due to the fact that the stego image must be *shipped* or *advertised* in a standard format such as JPEG. This is dealt with by the use of erasures and error correction coding framework previously employed in [18]. In the next section, we describe yet another steganographic scheme (YASS), a JPEG stegosystem based on the aforementioned framework.

3 YASS for JPEG Steganography

We now present a JPEG steganography scheme, YASS, that embeds data in 8×8 blocks whose locations are chosen randomly so that they do not coincide with the 8×8 grid used during JPEG compression. Let the host image be denoted by a $M \times N$ matrix of pixel values. For simplicity, we assume that the image is grayscale (single channel); if it is not, we extract its luminance. Below we describe the main steps involved in this randomized block hiding method.

1. Divide the image into blocks of size $B \times B$, where B, which we call *big block size*, is always greater than 8, the size of a JPEG block. Thus we have $M_B \times N_B$ big blocks in the image where $M_B = \lfloor \frac{M}{B} \rfloor$ and $N_B = \lfloor \frac{N}{B} \rfloor$.
2. For each block (i, j) ($0 \leq i < M_B, 0 \leq j < N_B$), we pseudorandomly select a 8×8 sub-block in which to hide data. The key for the random number generator is shared between the encoder and the decoder. The pseudorandom number generator determines the location of the smaller 8×8 block within the big block. This process is illustrated in Figure 1(a) where four example blocks are shown, whose top leftmost corner (s_x, s_y) is randomly chosen from the set $\{0, 1, ..., B - 8\}$. Figure 1(b) shows the blocks as seen by the steganalyst who gets *out-of-sync* from the embedding blocks, and cannot resynchronize even if the embedding mechanism is known.

3. For every 8×8 block thus chosen, we compute its 2D DCT and divide it by a JPEG quantization matrix at a *design* quality factor QF_h. Data is hidden in a predetermined band of low frequency AC coefficients using quantization index modulation. For maintaining perceptual transparency, we do not hide in coefficients that quantize to zero by the JPEG quantizer (following the selective embedding in coefficients scheme proposed in [18]).

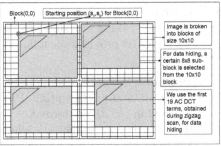
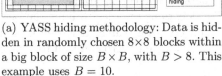
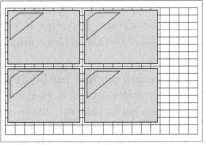

(a) YASS hiding methodology: Data is hidden in randomly chosen 8×8 blocks within a big block of size $B \times B$, with $B > 8$. This example uses $B = 10$.

(b) The block structure as seen by a steganalyst, who gets *out-of-sync* with the blocks used during embedding, and cannot synchronize even if the hiding method and its parameters are known.

Fig. 1. The embedding method and its detection

Note that using this approach, we can effectively de-synchronize the steganalyst so that the features computed by him would not directly capture the modifications done to the image for data hiding (see Figure 1). It should be noted that with this embedding procedure, we are reducing the embedding rate in two ways. First, some *real estate* of the image is wasted by choosing bigger blocks from which an 8×8 block is chosen to hide data. Note that the above framework can be further generalized to enable lesser *wastage*, by using larger big blocks and putting more 8×8 blocks into them. For example, we can use big blocks of size 33×33 and embed in sixteen 8×8 blocks within. We report results for such implementations as well (Section 4). The second cause of decrease in rate is that since the embedding grid does not coincide with the JPEG grid, there are errors in the received data which must be corrected by adding redundancy. This process is briefly described in the following section.

3.1 Coding Framework

In order to deal with the errors caused in the image due to JPEG compression, we use a coding framework using repeat-accumulate (RA) codes [25], similar to that proposed in [18]. This framework also allows us to hide in an adaptive fashion, avoiding coefficients that quantize to zero so as to control the perceptual distortion to the image.

For every block, we consider an embedding band comprising of first n low frequency coefficients which forms the *candidate embedding band*. Data bits are hidden in a coefficient lying in the band if it does not quantize to zero using the JPEG quantizer at QF_h. Before the hiding process, the bit stream to be hidden is coded, using a low rate code, assuming that all host coefficients that lie in the candidate embedding band will actually be employed for hiding. A code symbol is *erased at the encoder* if the local adaptive criterion (of being quantized to zero) for the coefficient is not met. A rate $1/q$ RA encoder is employed, which involves q-fold repetition, pseudorandom interleaving and accumulation of the resultant bit-stream. Decoding is performed iteratively using the sum-product algorithm [26]. The use of this coding framework for YASS provides the following advantages.

1. **Protection against initial JPEG compression:** Use of the coding framework provides error-free recovery of the hidden data after the initial JPEG compression so that the image can be advertised in the JPEG format.
2. **Flexibility in choosing hiding locations:** The coding framework allows us to dynamically select the embedding locations in order to limit the perceptual distortion caused to the host image during hiding. It is well known that embedding in DCT coefficients that quantize to zero can lead to visible artifacts in the stego image.
3. **Enabling active steganography:** The use of error correcting codes also provides protection against several distortion constrained attacks that an active warden might perform. The attacks that can be survived include a second JPEG compression, additive noise, limited amount of filtering, and so on. This provides a significant advantage over most other stego methods available in the literature.

4   Experiments and Results

We conduct a comprehensive set of experiments and present the results demonstrating the applicability of the presented approach. First, the results for the embedding capacity are presented for some standard images (Section 4.1). Next, in Section 4.2, we present the detection results of our scheme using recent blind steganalysis methods for a couple of datasets (comprising of several thousand natural images). We also compare the detection results of our method with those of OutGuess and StegHide in Section 4.3, and show that our methods clearly outperform these approaches. As a control experiment, in Section 4.4, we compare our hiding method with a *naive* standard hiding approach, in which data is hidden in randomly chosen low-frequency DCT coefficients using standard JPEG grid, while keeping the same embedding rate.

4.1   Embedding Rates

In Table 1, we list the number of bits that can be hidden in several standard images using YASS with different embedding parameters. QF_h denotes the design quality factor used during hiding, and QF_a denotes the output or advertised image quality factor. Note that for the presented scheme, these two can be different and their values do affect the steganalysis performance (see Section 4.2). The same notations are used in other tables presented in this paper. Also note that the number of bits reported in this section are before coding and can be recovered without any errors, even in the presence of distortion constrained attacks. For all the results presented in this paper, we use 19 low-frequency DCT coefficients as the candidate embedding band.

Table 1. Number of information bits that can be hidden in some standard images of size 512×512. The big-block size $B = 9$.

$QF_h \rightarrow QF_a$	baboon	peppers	airplane	lena	couple	crowd
$50 \rightarrow 50$	1453	1295	2128	1702	1655	2979
$50 \rightarrow 75$	14896	6620	7448	7448	9930	11916
$75 \rightarrow 75$	1453	1805	2590	2128	2128	3972
$60 \rightarrow 75$	11916	6620	7448	6620	8512	9930

From this table, we see that the number of bits that can be embedded increases when $QF_a > QF_h$, however this also leads to slightly more successful steganalysis performance (to be shown in Tables 4 and 6), which gives us a trade-off between the embedding rate and the detection performance. When QF_a equals QF_h, there are more physical errors in the channel leading to a reduced embedding rate.

In Table 2, we study the effect of using different big-block sizes B on the embedding capacity. Here we also report the bits per non-zero coefficients (*bpnc*). It is seen from this table that using lower B provides higher embedding capacity, which is because we end-up using more *real estate* of the host image for hiding. We can ensure even higher percentage of image utilization by using larger big-blocks and putting greater number of 8×8 blocks within. For example, we can put four 8×8 blocks in a 17×17 block, thus making an effective big-block size of $B_{eff} = \frac{17}{2} = 8.5$. We experiment with block-size $B = (n \times 8 + 1)$ and use n^2 8×8 blocks for hiding, and report the results in Table 3. The embedding rate improves as we use more image area for hiding, but the detection results get worse (from the steganographer's viewpoint, see Tables 4 and 6). Also, using a lower B_{eff} does not always guarantee a higher embedding capacity because of the fact that more errors may be induced due to JPEG compression, which forces us to use a larger redundancy factor, q, of the RA code.

4.2   Detection Results

The steganographic security of our scheme is evaluated against the following blind steganalysis schemes. The names in **bold** are the ones used to denote the steganalysis schemes in the tables presented in this paper.

1. **Farid:** 72-dimensional feature vector based on moments in the wavelet domain [19].

Table 2. Hiding rates for the 512×512 Lena image for different big-block sizes B. *bpnc* denotes bits per non-zero coefficients and *databits* denotes the number of hidden information bits.

$QF_h \to QF_a$	B	9	B	10	B	12	B	14
50 → 50	databits	1702	databits	1497	databits	882	databits	464
	bpnc	0.072	bpnc	0.064	bpnc	0.038	bpnc	0.020
50 → 75	databits	7448	databits	5491	databits	4189	databits	2736
	bpnc	0.213	bpnc	0.159	bpnc	0.118	bpnc	0.077
75 → 75	databits	2128	databits	2059	databits	1457	databits	794
	bpnc	0.059	bpnc	0.057	bpnc	0.040	bpnc	0.022
60 → 75	databits	6620	databits	5491	databits	3724	databits	2462
	bpnc	0.187	bpnc	0.158	bpnc	0.105	bpnc	0.069

Table 3. Hiding rates for the 512×512 Lena image for larger big-block sizes $B = 9$, 25, 49, 65 and 81, which can incorporate several 8×8 blocks

$QF_h \to QF_a$	B	9	B	25	B	49	B	65	B	81
50 → 75	databits	7448	databits	7834	databits	8064	databits	7963	databits	8064
	bpnc	0.213	bpnc	0.224	bpnc	0.235	bpnc	0.228	bpnc	0.229
75 → 75	databits	2128	databits	2350	databits	2341	databits	1837	databits	1577
	bpnc	0.059	bpnc	0.065	bpnc	0.065	bpnc	0.051	bpnc	0.044
60 → 75	databits	6620	databits	7050	databits	8064	databits	7166	databits	7258
	bpnc	0.187	bpnc	0.200	bpnc	0.231	bpnc	0.203	bpnc	0.205

2. **PF-23:** Pevny and Fridrich's 23-dimensional DCT feature vector [9].
3. **PF-274:** Pevny and Fridrich's 274-dimensional feature vector that merges Markov and DCT features [10].
4. **DCT hist.:** Histogram of DCT coefficients from a low-frequency band [7].
5. **Xuan-39:** Spatial domain steganalysis proposed by Xuan et al [13] (a 39-dimensional feature vector).
6. **Chen-324:** JPEG steganalysis based on statistical moments of wavelet characteristic functions proposed by Chen et al [20].

Since we decompress the images at the time of hiding, it can be argued that spatial domain steganalysis schemes may be able to detect the presence of embedded data. Hence we include a recent spatial domain steganalysis scheme in our tests.

We conduct our experiments on two datasets: the first having 4500 images in compressed (JPEG) format and the other having 2000 images in uncompressed TIFF format. For each dataset, we use half the data for training and the other half for testing. The training and testing sets have an equal number of cover and stego images. The idea behind using datasets in different formats is to study the effect of using already compressed images verses uncompressed images for our method since it hides in a desynchronized 8×8 grid. As we see later, there is not much difference in the observed detection rates for the two datasets. As in all published blind steganalysis approaches, we train a support vector machine (SVM) on a set of known stego and cover images and use the threshold thus obtained, to distinguish between the cover and stego images at the time of testing.

The SVM classifier has to distinguish between two class of images: cover (class '0') and stego (class '1'). Let X_0 and X_1 denote the events that the actual image being observed belongs to classes '0' and '1', respectively. On the detection side, let Y_0 and Y_1 denote the events that the observed image is classified as belonging to classes '0' and '1', respectively. We use the probability of detection, P_{detect} as our evaluation criteria, which is defined as follows.

$$P_{detect} = 1 - P_{error}$$
$$P_{error} = P(X_0)P(Y_1|X_0) + P(X_1)P(Y_0|X_1)$$
$$= \frac{1}{2}P_{FA} + \frac{1}{2}P_{miss}, \text{ for } P(X_0) = P(X_1) = \frac{1}{2}$$

where $P_{FA} = P(Y_1|X_0)$ and $P_{miss} = P(Y_0|X_1)$ denote the probability of false alarm and missed detection respectively. Note that the above equation assumes an equal number of cover and stego images in the dataset. For the steganalysis results, we report P_{detect} upto 2 significant digits after the decimal point. An uninformed detector can classify all the test images as stego (or cover) and get an accuracy of 0.5. Thus, P_{detect} being close to 0.5 implies nearly undetectable hiding, and as the detectability improves, P_{detect} should increase towards 1.

In Tables 4 and 5, we present the detection accuracy obtained on the JPEG and TIFF image dataset respectively. Note that even for the TIFF dataset, the output is always a JPEG image at an advertised quality factor. For this dataset, the plain cover images are JPEG compressed at QF_a during the training as well as testing. It can be seen from the tables that our scheme is undetectable using any of the steganalysis features. The only time the detection is not completely random is when the design quality factor is lower than the advertised one ($QF_h = 50$ and $QF_a = 75$). We also present, in Table 6, the steganalysis results when larger big-block sizes are used, so as to incorporate more 8×8 blocks within. P_{detect} remains close to 0.5 in most cases, but for PF-274, it increases as B increases (in Table 6), since more area of the image is used for hiding when employing larger big-blocks. Note that since we are using a set of images and the embedding rate varies for individual images, we cannot provide *bpnc* values in these tables.

4.3   Comparison with Competing Methods

In Table 7, we present a comparison of our steganographic scheme, YASS, to OutGuess[1] and StegHide[2]. To enable fair comparison, we must use the same hiding rate for all the schemes. This is complicated by the fact that YASS uses an error correcting code whose redundancy factor, q, determines the actual number of information bits hidden in the image. Experiments indicate that, for images in our dataset, the redundancy factor required to ensure zero BER was in the range 10-40, which depends on the particular image and the level of JPEG compression

Table 4. JPEG dataset: Steganalysis results for randomized block based hiding, when big-block size B is varied. It can be seen that the detection is random for most of the configurations.

QF_h (used for hiding)	QF_a (advertised QF)	Steganalysis Method	Detection accuracy: P_{detect}			
			$B=9$	$B=10$	$B=12$	$B=14$
50	50	Farid	0.52	0.51	0.52	0.51
50	75	Farid	0.55	0.55	0.54	0.51
75	75	Farid	0.52	0.51	0.52	0.51
50	50	PF-23	0.56	0.55	0.54	0.54
50	75	PF-23	0.59	0.59	0.56	0.60
75	75	PF-23	0.53	0.57	0.53	0.52
50	50	PF-274	0.58	0.56	0.53	0.55
50	75	PF-274	0.77	0.79	0.74	0.65
75	75	PF-274	0.59	0.60	0.62	0.54
50	50	DCT-hist	0.53	0.53	0.51	0.53
50	75	DCT-hist	0.64	0.64	0.60	0.54
75	75	DCT-hist	0.55	0.54	0.55	0.53
50	50	Xuan-39	0.54	0.56	0.54	0.51
50	75	Xuan-39	0.63	0.64	0.57	0.53
75	75	Xuan-39	0.52	0.54	0.53	0.52
50	50	Chen-324	0.57	0.51	0.55	0.54
50	75	Chen-324	0.75	0.65	0.60	0.55
75	75	Chen-324	0.54	0.55	0.53	0.53

involved. Hence we present results where the amount of data embedded using OutGuess and StegHide corresponds to the hiding rate obtained using $q = 10$ and $q = 40$. It can be seen from the table that both OutGuess and StegHide are almost completely detectable (especially when using PF-23, PF-274, and DCT-hist features), but YASS is not detectable at equivalent hiding rates.

We also experimented with the F5 steganographic scheme [5], which uses *matrix embedding* (see for example [27]), and found that this scheme is also undetectable at equivalent embedding rates using PF-274 and PF-23 features. Matrix embedding allows hiding at *embedding efficiencies* (defined as number of bits hidden for every change made to the host symbols), potentially much higher than the trivial efficiency of 2 bits per change (bpc). Thus for passive steganography, schemes that employ matrix embedding (such as F5) can enable undetectable hiding at embedding rates equivalent to YASS. However, an added advantage of YASS is that it can provide protection against active adversaries by its use of error correcting codes.

4.4   Comparison with Standard Hiding at Same Rate

In the previous sections, it is seen that our proposed steganographic approach performs quite well against blind steganalysis schemes that we have tested against. We must, however, note that the improved steganographic security comes at the

Table 5. TIFF dataset: Steganalysis results for randomized block based hiding, when the big-block size B is varied. It can be seen that the detection is random for most of the configurations.

QF_h (used for hiding)	QF_a (advertised QF)	Steganalysis Method	Detection accuracy: P_{detect}			
			$B=9$	$B=10$	$B=12$	$B=14$
50	50	Farid	0.51	0.51	0.51	0.51
50	75	Farid	0.53	0.51	0.52	0.51
75	75	Farid	0.50	0.51	0.51	0.51
50	50	PF-23	0.53	0.55	0.53	0.53
50	75	PF-23	0.59	0.66	0.53	0.53
75	75	PF-23	0.54	0.51	0.53	0.53
50	50	PF-274	0.52	0.56	0.55	0.51
50	75	PF-274	0.72	0.81	0.65	0.60
75	75	PF-274	0.56	0.56	0.52	0.53
50	50	DCT-hist	0.51	0.53	0.52	0.48
50	75	DCT-hist	0.60	0.59	0.56	0.56
75	75	DCT-hist	0.52	0.52	0.51	0.52
50	50	Xuan-39	0.52	0.51	0.52	0.48
50	75	Xuan-39	0.57	0.60	0.53	0.48
75	75	Xuan-39	0.47	0.51	0.49	0.47
50	50	Chen-324	0.55	0.55	0.53	0.53
50	75	Chen-324	0.65	0.64	0.56	0.54
75	75	Chen-324	0.55	0.51	0.51	0.50

cost of reduced embedding rate. To further investigate whether the good performance of YASS is simply because of reduced rate or not, we present another *simpler* extension of the idea of embedding in random locations: we now embed data in randomly chosen low-frequency AC DCT coefficients computed using the original JPEG grid. This approach would incur minimal distortion to the original cover during the hiding process, and hence would be an ideal *control* experiment for testing our scheme. The results are reported in Table 8, where we compare the YASS embedding scheme with this randomized frequency (RF) scheme for three hiding rates: 2 out of 64 (one 8×8 block), 1 out of 64, and 1 out of 128 coefficients. It can be seen that the naive RF scheme performs quite well, however, the performance of YASS is consistently better.

We end this section by noting that the reported results (for RF) are for embedding at trivial embedding efficiency of 2 bpc. As stated earlier, the detectability can be reduced by causing fewer changes to the DCT coefficients by using matrix embedding. One of the key factors that determines detectability is the change rate. This change rate can be thought of as the encoders' "budget", which can be "used" either way: to provide robustness by using redundancy and giving up some embedding efficiency, or to improve the embedding efficiency via matrix embedding but causing an increase in the fragility of the system. YASS goes the

Table 6. Using larger big-block size B: Steganalysis results for randomized block based hiding on the TIFF image dataset, for block-size $B = 9$, 25 and 49. For 9×9, 25×25 and 49×49 blocks, we use 1, 9 and 36 8×8 sub-blocks respectively for hiding

QF_h (used for hiding)	QF_a (advertised QF)	Steganalysis Method	Detection accuracy: P_{detect}		
			$B=9$	$B=25$	$B=49$
50	50	Farid	0.51	0.50	0.50
50	75	Farid	0.53	0.51	0.52
75	75	Farid	0.50	0.49	0.51
50	50	PF-23	0.53	0.53	0.57
50	75	PF-23	0.59	0.58	0.67
75	75	PF-23	0.54	0.53	0.53
50	50	PF-274	0.52	0.57	0.59
50	75	PF-274	0.72	0.73	0.78
75	75	PF-274	0.56	0.58	0.68
50	50	DCT-hist	0.51	0.50	0.51
50	75	DCT-hist	0.60	0.56	0.50
75	75	DCT-hist	0.52	0.51	0.50
50	50	Xuan-39	0.52	0.52	0.52
50	75	Xuan-39	0.57	0.53	0.50
75	75	Xuan-39	0.47	0.52	0.51
50	50	Chen-324	0.55	0.53	0.52
50	75	Chen-324	0.65	0.58	0.57
75	75	Chen-324	0.55	0.52	0.51

Table 7. Steganalysis results for comparing the randomized block based scheme (YASS) with OutGuess and Steghide schemes, used at rates of $\frac{1}{10}$ and $\frac{1}{40}$, for the TIFF image dataset. For OutGuess and Steghide, the images are JPEG compressed using a quality factor of QF_a before being presented to the steganographic scheme. Note that the QF_h parameter is applicable only for the YASS scheme.

QF_h	QF_a	Steganalysis Method	Detection accuracy: P_{detect}				
			YASS	OutGuess-$\frac{1}{10}$	Steghide-$\frac{1}{10}$	OutGuess-$\frac{1}{40}$	Steghide-$\frac{1}{40}$
50	50	Farid	0.51	0.74	0.50	0.77	0.52
50	75	Farid	0.53	0.59	0.50	0.50	0.55
75	75	Farid	0.50	0.59	0.50	0.50	0.55
50	50	PF-23	0.53	0.98	0.78	0.97	0.80
50	75	PF-23	0.59	1.00	0.99	0.99	0.99
75	75	PF-23	0.54	1.00	0.99	0.99	0.99
50	50	PF-274	0.52	1.00	0.98	1.00	0.96
50	75	PF-274	0.72	1.00	1.00	1.00	1.00
75	75	PF-274	0.56	1.00	1.00	1.00	1.00
50	50	DCT-hist	0.51	0.95	0.59	0.94	0.60
50	75	DCT-hist	0.60	1.00	0.91	1.00	0.93
75	75	DCT-hist	0.52	1.00	0.91	1.00	0.93

first way: it can provide robustness against an active adversary by using error correcting codes but the embedding efficiency is quite low. However, we emphasize that for passive warden steganography, an equivalent level of undetectability can be achieved at the same embedding rates using matrix embedding.

Table 8. Comparison of steganalysis results for randomized block (RB) hiding (i.e., YASS) with $B = 9$, and randomized frequency (RF) based hiding

QF_h (used for hiding)	QF_a (advertised QF)	Steganalysis Method	Detection accuracy: P_{detect}			
			RB (YASS)	RF 1/128	RF 1/64	RF 2/64
50	50	Farid	0.51	0.66	0.65	0.67
75	75	Farid	0.50	0.52	0.58	0.67
50	50	PF-23	0.53	0.69	0.83	0.92
75	75	PF-23	0.54	0.58	0.72	0.83
50	50	PF-274	0.52	0.71	0.79	0.90
75	75	PF-274	0.56	0.62	0.75	0.82
50	50	DCT-hist	0.51	0.55	0.68	0.86
75	75	DCT-hist	0.52	0.54	0.59	0.80

5   Conclusions

In this paper, we have demonstrated a simple yet very effective steganographic approach that provides security against recent blind steganalysis schemes. The method embeds data in randomly chosen host blocks, thus relying on confusing the steganalyst's estimate of the cover statistics, rather than preserving the host image features. We note that the improved security comes at the cost of embedding capacity, and in the future, we will investigate schemes that can significantly increase the hiding capacity while maintaining the steganographic security. We will also explore other mechanisms for randomizing the embedding process, such as using randomly chosen transform domains.

References

1. Provos, N.: Defending against statistical steganalysis. In: 10th USENIX Security Symposium, Washington DC, USA (2001)
2. Hetzl, S., Mutzel, P.: A graph theoretic approach to steganography. In: 9th IFIP TC-6 TC-11 International Conference, Communications and Multimedia Security, Salzburg, Austria, vol. 3677, pp. 119–128 (2005)
3. Sallee, P.: Model-based steganography. In: Kalker, T., Cox, I., Ro, Y.M. (eds.) IWDW 2003. LNCS, vol. 2939, pp. 154–167. Springer, Heidelberg (2004)
4. Fridrich, J., Goljan, M., Lisoněk, P., Soukal, D.: Writing on wet paper. In: ACM Workshop on Multimedia and security, Magdeburg, Germany (2004)
5. Westfeld, A.: High capacity despite better steganalysis (F5 - a steganographic algorithm). In: Moskowitz, I.S. (ed.) Information Hiding. LNCS, vol. 2137, pp. 289–302. Springer, Heidelberg (2001)

6. Solanki, K., Sullivan, K., Madhow, U., Manjunath, B.S., Chandrasekaran, S.: Statistical restoration for robust and secure steganography. In: Proc. ICIP, Genova, Italy, pp. II 1118–1121 (2005)
7. Solanki, K., Sullivan, K., Madhow, U., Manjunath, B.S., Chandrasekaran, S.: Probably secure steganography: Achieving zero K-L divergence using statistical restoration. In: Proc. ICIP, Atlanta, GA, USA, pp. 125–128 (2006)
8. Wang, Y., Moulin, P.: Steganalysis of block-DCT image steganography. In: IEEE workshop on Statistical Signal Processing, IEEE Computer Society Press, Los Alamitos (2003)
9. Pevny, T., Fridrich, J.: Multi-class blind steganalysis for JPEG images. In: Proc. of SPIE, San Jose, CA (2006)
10. Pevny, T., Fridrich, J.: Merging Markov and DCT features for multi-class JPEG steganalysis. In: Proc. of SPIE, San Jose, CA (2007)
11. Avcibas, I., Sankur, B., Memon, N.: Image steganalysis with binary similarity measures. In: Proc. ICIP, pp. 645–648 (2002)
12. Lyu, S., Farid, H.: Detecting hidden messages using higher-order statistics and support vector machines. In: Ershov, A.P., Nepomniaschy, V.A. (eds.) International Symposium on Theoretical Programming. LNCS, vol. 5, Springer, Heidelberg (1974)
13. Xuan, G., Shi, Y.Q., Gao, J., Zou, D., Yang, C., Yang, C., Zhang, Z., Chai, P., Chen, C., Chen, W.: Steganalysis based on multiple features formed by statistical moments of wavelet characteristic functions. In: Schlender, B., Frielinghaus, W. (eds.) GI - 3. Fachtagung über Programmiersprachen. LNCS, vol. 7th International Workshop on Information Hiding, Springer, Heidelberg (1974)
14. Harmsen, J.J., Pearlman, W.A.: Steganalysis of additive noise modelable information hiding. In: Proc. of SPIE, pp. 131–142 (2003)
15. Shi, Y.Q., Chen, C., Chen, W.: A Markov process based approach to effective attacking JPEG steganography. In: Leilich, H.-O. (ed.) GI-NTG Fachtagung Struktur und Betrieb von Rechensystemen. LNCS, Springer, Heidelberg (1974)
16. Wang, Y., Moulin, P.: Optimized feature extraction for learning-based image steganalysis. IEEE Transactions on Information Forensics and Security 2(1), 31–45 (2007)
17. Dabeer, O., Sullivan, K., Madhow, U., Chandrasekaran, S., Manjunath, B.: Detection of hiding in the least significant bit. IEEE Transactions on Signal Processing, Supplement on Secure Media I 52, 3046–3058 (2004)
18. Solanki, K., Jacobsen, N., Madhow, U., Manjunath, B.S., Chandrasekaran, S.: Robust image-adaptive data hiding based on erasure and error correction. IEEE Trans. on Image Processing 13, 1627–1639 (2004)
19. Farid, H.: Code for generating wavelet-based feature vectors for steganalysis, http://www.cs.dartmouth.edu/farid/research/steg.m
20. Chen, C., Shi, Y.Q., Chen, W., Xuan, G.: Statistical moments based universal steganalysis using JPEG-2D array and 2-D characteristic function. In: Proc. ICIP, Atlanta, GA, USA, pp. 105–108 (2006)
21. Cachin, C.: An information theoretic model for steganography. In: 2nd Int'l Workshop on Info. Hiding. LNCS, vol. 1525, pp. 306–318 (1998)
22. Sullivan, K., Madhow, U., Chandrasekaran, S., Manjunath, B.: Steganalysis for Markov cover data with applications to images. IEEE Transactions on Information Forensics and Security 1, 275–287 (2006)
23. Fu, D., Shi, Y.Q., Zou, D., Xuan, G.: JPEG steganalysis using empirical transition matrix in block dct domain. In: International Workshop on Multimedia Signal Processing, Victoria, BC, Canada (2006)

24. Kharrazi, M., Sencar, H.T., Memon, N.: Cover selection for steganographic embedding. In: Proc. ICIP, pp. 117–120 (2006)
25. Divsalar, D., Jin, H., McEliece, R.J.: Coding theorems for turbo-like codes. In: 36th Allerton Conf. on Communications, Control, and Computing, pp. 201–210 (1998)
26. Kschischang, F.R., Frey, B.J., Loeliger, H.A.: Factor graphs and the sum-product algorithm. IEEE Trans. on Info. Theory 47, 498–519 (2001)
27. Fridrich, J., Soukal, D.: Matrix embedding for large payloads. In: Proc. of SPIE, pp. 727–738 (2006)

Steganographic Communication
with Quantum Information

Keye Martin

Center for High Assurance Computer Systems, Code 5540
Naval Research Laboratory
Washington, DC 20375
kmartin@itd.nrl.navy.mil

Abstract. We introduce a scheme for steganographic communication based on a channel hidden within the quantum key distribution protocol of Bennett and Brassard. An outside observer cannot establish evidence that this communication is taking place for the simple reason that no correlations between public data and hidden information exist. Assuming an attacker guesses hidden communication is underway, we obtain a precise quantitative bound on the amount of hidden information they can acquire, and find that it is very small, less than 10^{-7} bits per channel use in typical experimental settings. We also calculate the capacity of the steganographic channel, including an analysis based on data available from experimental realizations of quantum protocols.

1   Introduction

The representation of classical information by quantum states is ideally suited for secure communication. One reason is that quantum states cannot be copied in general, so anyone trying to listen in has to try and gain information from the original source. However, attempts to gain information from the original source often lead to a detectable disturbance in the signal. An important illustration of the value of these fundamental principles is *quantum key distribution* (QKD), a protocol which provides a secure method for establishing a secret key between two participants. This key can then be used by the participants to encrypt information, providing them with the ability to communicate securely. QKD has already been experimentally realized many times and is even commercially available. Currently, it is the most developed of all the proposed quantum technologies.

In this paper, we explain how fundamental quantum components like QKD can be manipulated in ways that until now do not appear to have been anticipated. Using any one of a number of techniques, ranging from simple covert tricks to more intricate aspects of quantum information, a quantum protocol can be used to obtain a new protocol which is physically indistinguishable from the original, but which also contains a channel whose existence is undetectable by any currently known technology. Such 'hidden channels' have the potential to provide secure transmission of quantum information via teleportation, new and

T. Furon et al. (Eds.): IH 2007, LNCS 4567, pp. 32–49, 2007.

powerful schemes for authenticating communication and perhaps even the ability to provide *secure communication without encryption*: the protection offered to keys by quantum mechanics may be extendable to the information transmitted during communication itself, making key-based encryption unnecessary.

2   QKD

In this section, we will review the basic protocol for quantum key distribution. We intend for this paper to be readable by someone with no prior knowledge of quantum mechanics. For this reason, we discuss only the minimal background needed to understand quantum key distribution. The few ideas we make use of are very simple.

Like all systems, a quantum system has *state*. The state of a quantum system is represented by a unit vector in a vector space that has a lot more structure than most, known as a Hilbert space. The state of a quantum system is also called a *ket*. Here are two examples of kets: $|0\rangle$ and $|1\rangle$. It is useful to think about these two particular kets as being quantum realizations of the classical bits 0 and 1. Each refers to a legitimate state of a quantum system. A photon is an example of a quantum system and its polarization (state) is something we need kets to describe.

One of the neat things about a quantum system is that it can also be in any state 'in between' $|0\rangle$ and $|1\rangle$, such as

$$|+\rangle = \frac{1}{\sqrt{2}}(|0\rangle + |1\rangle) \quad \text{or} \quad |-\rangle = \frac{1}{\sqrt{2}}(|0\rangle - |1\rangle)$$

which we also think of as representing the classical bits 1 and 0 respectively. Any ket $|\psi\rangle$ that can be written

$$|\psi\rangle = a|0\rangle + b|1\rangle, \text{ for } |a|^2 + |b|^2 = 1$$

is called a *qubit*. There are only four qubits that we care about in this paper: $|0\rangle$, $|1\rangle$, $|+\rangle$ and $|-\rangle$.

Like all systems, one would like to extract information from a quantum system. One way to extract information from a quantum system is to perform a measurement on it. Before an observer can perform a measurement on a quantum system, they must say what they want to measure. One way an observer can specify what they want to measure is by specifying a *basis* and then "performing a measurement in the specified basis." Two examples of bases are $X = \{|+\rangle, |-\rangle\}$ and $Z = \{|0\rangle, |1\rangle\}$. They are the only bases we care about in this paper[1]. What happens when we measure a quantum system?

If the state of a quantum system is described by the qubit $|\psi\rangle = a|0\rangle + b|1\rangle$, then a measurement in the Z basis will yield the result $|0\rangle$ with probability $|a|^2$

---

[1] Many bases are possible, and each offers a *different* way of representing the classical bits 0 and 1. The ability to alternate between such representations helps prevent eavesdropping in QKD.

and the result $|1\rangle$ with probability $|b|^2$. Notice that these are the only possibile outcomes of this measurement because qubits satisfy $|a|^2 + |b|^2 = 1$, a property they have because they are unit vectors. In this paper, we only care about measuring the following four states in the Z basis: $|0\rangle$, $|1\rangle$, $|+\rangle$ and $|-\rangle$. If we measure a system with state $|0\rangle$ in the Z basis, we get $|0\rangle$ with probability 1; the same is true of the state $|1\rangle$. If we measure either $|+\rangle$ or $|-\rangle$ in the Z basis, we obtain $|0\rangle$ with probability 1/2 and $|1\rangle$ with probability 1/2.

It is also possible to measure a system in the X basis. If a system is in the state $|+\rangle$ and we measure it in the X basis, we get $|+\rangle$ with probability 1, similarly for $|-\rangle$. But what happens when we measure a system with state $|0\rangle$ or $|1\rangle$ in the X basis? Well, first we have to express these states as sums of states in the X basis:

$$|0\rangle = \frac{1}{\sqrt{2}}(|+\rangle + |-\rangle)$$

$$|1\rangle = \frac{1}{\sqrt{2}}(|+\rangle - |-\rangle)$$

Now we can see that if we measure $|0\rangle$ in the X basis, we get $|+\rangle$ with probability 1/2 and $|-\rangle$ with probability 1/2, similarly for $|1\rangle$. We are now ready to recall one of the standard accounts of QKD, the BB84 protocol [8]:

(1) Alice chooses a random string k of about $4n$ bits containing the eventual key
(2) Alice randomly codes each bit of k in either the $X = \{|+\rangle, |-\rangle\}$ or $Z = \{|0\rangle, |1\rangle\}$ bases
(3) Alice sends each resulting qubit to Bob
(4) Bob receives the $4n$ qubits, randomly measuring each in either the X or the Z basis
(5) Alice announces in which basis she originally coded each bit of k
(6) Bob tells Alice which bits he received correctly; they now share about $2n$ bits
(7) Alice selects a subset of n bits from the group she formed in step (6) that will be used to check on Eve's interference, and tells Bob which bits she selected.
(8) Alice and Bob compare their values of the n check bits; if more than an acceptable number disagree, they abort the protocol (eavesdropping)
(9) Alice and Bob perform information reconciliation and privacy amplification to select a smaller m-bit key from the remaining n bits

Definition 1. The bits in step (6) are called the *sifted bits.*

If Alice has coded a classical bit in either of the X or Z bases, and later Bob measures in the same basis, he will receive the bit sent by Alice with probability 1. Such a bit will be one of the sifted bits. But now suppose that an eavesdropper wishes to know the bit Alice is sending Bob. Well the eavesdropper, named Eve, has to guess which basis Alice coded the bit in, and then measure it herself. When Eve guesses, she introduces an error into the sifted bits with probability 1/4 – but an error that Alice and Bob will know about, and this is the reason they are able to detect the presence of an eavesdropper.

It is fundamental in QKD that Alice and Bob insist on an error rate within the sifted bits that is less than $1/4$ to defend themselves from precisely this type of attack, or else the security of QKD cannot be guaranteed [2]. For instance, assuming errors only due to Eve, if Eve has measured all the qubits sent from Alice to Bob, then Eve knows which of the sifted bits Bob and Alice share, and which of the sifted bits they may not share[2]. This is something that Bob himself does not even know. With an error rate beyond $1/4$, Bob cannot have more information than Eve about any key generated – remember that after the sifted bits are identified, Eve can listen in on the rest of the protocol, since it takes place over a public channel.

3   QKD is Not Communication

There are a lot of places in the literature that QKD is loosely termed "communication." But strictly speaking, it really is not communication. We understand communication as the transfer of information from a sender to a receiver, with the implicit understanding that the information received is independent of any action taken by the receiver. This independence between sender and receiver is what makes communication a worthwhile endeavor: it grants the sender the freedom to "say whatever they want." For instance, if every time you talked to your friend on a noiseless telephone he received only a subset of roughly half the words you spoke, and if this subset were randomly determined by the number of times a hummingbird in the room flapped its wings between words, you would not feel as though communication were taking place. And that is what is going on with QKD.

Ideally, Alice hopes that the entire bit string k will be received correctly by Bob. But even if we ignore effects due to environmental noise and eavesdropping, Bob still only receives about half the bits in k, and this half is randomly determined by his ability to guess the basis in which Alice prepared the qubit. The key that Alice and Bob eventually share is thus determined by an *interaction* between the two parties. So initially, Alice is not sending Bob information, she is sending him data. To send information to Bob would imply that up front she decides on a message to send to Bob and that he receives it with high probability, independent of his own actions. That is, an instance of communication is taking place when Alice has some measure of *control* over the data Bob receives. To quote from a standard reference [8] on quantum information,

> "Quantum cryptography is sometimes thought of not as secret key exchange or transfer, but rather as secret key *generation*, since fundamentally neither Alice nor Bob can pre-determine the key they will ultimately end up with upon completion of the protocol."
> – Nielsen and Chuang, page 591.

Assuming we have generated a key k of many bits using QKD, why can't Alice and Bob just use this key to communicate by having Alice announce "yes/no" for each bit of k over the public classical channel? Answer: Eve might be able to

---

[2] Eve knows when she guessed the right basis and when she did not.

flip classical bits with probability $1/2$ and neither Bob nor Alice would have any idea that Eve interfered. Nevertheless, the QKD protocol can be easily modified to allow Alice and Bob to communicate.

4   A Hidden Channel Within a Quantum Protocol

To illustrate, we will use one of the 'simple covert tricks' mentioned earlier. Assume Alice would like to send Bob a single bit of information. All we have to do is make a simple change to step (7) in QKD:

(7) Alice randomly selects a bit from the group of $2n$ whose value is the information she wants to transmit. Then she randomly selects $n - 1$ check bits from the remaining $2n - 1$. The nth check bit is chosen from the remaining $n + 1$ as being the bit to the immediate left of the information[3].

Bob now has the information Alice sent: he knows its relation to the last check bit, because the two parties have agreed on this scheme in advance. They have agreed that Alice will covertly send Bob a 'pointer' to the information. Here is an example:

Example 1. Alice and Bob share the $2n$ bits

$$0\ 0\ 1\ 0\ 1\ 0\ 1\ 1\ 0\ 0\ 1\ 0\ 1\ 0\ 1\ 1\ 1\ 0\ 1\ 0\ 1\ 1\ 0\ 1\ 1\ 0\ 0$$

Alice selects the information bit

$$0\ 0\ 1\ 0\ 1\ 0\ 1\ 1\ 0\ 0\ 1\ 0\ 1\ 0\ 1\ 1\ \overline{1}\ 0\ 1\ 0\ 1\ 1\ 0\ 1\ 1\ 0\ 0$$

Now she selects $n - 1$ check bits at random

$$\mathbf{0}\ 0\ 1\ 0\ 1\ 0\ \mathbf{1}\ \mathbf{1}\ 1\ 0\ 0\ \mathbf{1}\ 0\ \mathbf{1}\ 0\ \mathbf{1}\ \mathbf{1}\ \overline{1}\ \mathbf{0}\ 1\ 0\ 1\ \mathbf{1}\ \mathbf{0}\ \mathbf{1}\ 1\ \mathbf{0}\ \mathbf{0}$$

This leaves Alice and Bob with $n + 1$ remaining bits

$$0 * 1\ 0 * 0\ 1 * 1 * 0 * 0 * 0 * * \overline{1} * 1\ 0 * 1 * 1\ 1 * *$$

Alice now selects the last check bit as being the pointer to the information i.e. the bit to the immediate left of the information bit:

$$0 * 1\ 0 * 0\ 1 * 1 * 0 * 0 * \overset{\rightarrow}{\mathbf{0}} * * \overline{1} * 1\ 0 * 1 * 1\ 1 * *$$

Is Bob *guaranteed* to receive the information sent by Alice? No. But he is not guaranteed to receive all the bits perfectly in the case of QKD either. There are many reasons why. Suppose an eavesdropper *just happens* to measure only the qubit that holds the information in the wrong basis, then there is a 50 percent

---

[3] The case when the $2n$ bits are all zero or all one are handled with a simple convention. For instance, the nth check bit could be chosen as the first of the remaining bits to mean '0', while choosing it as the last of the remaining bits would signify '1'.

chance that Bob has the wrong bit, even though he believes he has the right bit. Or suppose that background light acts as noise which causes the information bit to flip. In either case, Bob would have no idea, and neither would Alice. But chances are good that such errors, whether caused by the environment or an eavesdropper, would also manifest themselves in the check bits as well, which would then enable them to estimate the likelihood that their attempt to communicate will succeed. Alice and Bob always have the option of aborting the protocol if their chances of success are not deemed high enough. The capacity of this channel is of course important to consider – and later we will – but there is a more fundamental issue that needs to be addressed first: just how hidden is this communication?

Rather surprisingly, we now describe a procedure which *may* allow an attacker, named Eve, to not only uncover the existence of the hidden communication taking place in the protocol above, but also to gain a nonzero amount of information about the hidden message being passed from Alice to Bob. Eve will assume that Alice and Bob are communicating in the manner above. Specifically, Eve will assume that if the location of the last check bit announced by Alice is i, then the bit at location $f_1(i) = (i \mod n + 1) + 1$ is a covert information bit Alice wishes to communicate to Bob, and seek to establish evidence in support of this.

Eve reasons that if Alice and Bob are not using the last check bit as a pointer to the information bit, then the distribution of 0's and 1's found in position $f_1(i)$ over several trial runs of QKD should be $(1/2, 1/2)$. The reason is that Alice initially generates a random bit string. If Eve finds that the actual distribution over m trials of QKD is different from $(1/2, 1/2)$, she may have evidence that things are not on the up and up. This is not an easy task for Eve to accomplish.

First, Eve has to *know* the value of the bit Alice holds at location $f_1(i)$. The only way for Eve to know this bit is to measure it. If she measures too many of the qubits sent from Alice to Bob, she will be detected by Alice and Bob. Thus, Eve can only measure *some* of the qubits. However, she still needs a way to detect the existence of all the qubits she doesnt measure – but without introducing errors – or else she will not know the correct location of the information bit. It is possible for Eve to actually achieve this. In addition, there is more good news for Eve: in a given trial run of QKD, she can know with absolute certainty whether or not she knows the value of the bit Alice holds at location $f_1(i)$, the bit she assumes Alice is trying to send to Bob. The bad news is that it may take Eve a long time to acquire enough data for m trial runs.

In a particular trial run of QKD, Eve should use the following procedure:

(i) Eve performs a quantum nondemolition measurement [6] on *every* qubit passed from Alice to Bob. This allows Eve to detect the existence of a qubit but leaves its polarization invariant: she is able to count qubits and record their respective positions without introducing errors detectable by Alice and Bob[4].

---

[4] Many current realizations of QKD require Bob to detect a photon within a certain window of time. Eve's desire to count photons but not measure them may require her to 'slow down' the photons, causing them to arrive outside of the alloted time frame, meaning that even this interference would be detectable.

(ii) Every time Eve detects and counts a qubit, she makes the decision to either measure its polarization or not to. If she measures a qubit, she records the value obtained; if not, she guesses a value. When Eve measures a qubit, there is a 1/4 probability that she introduces an error into the sifted bits[5]. Thus, in measuring a proportion p of the qubits sent by Alice, Eve introduces a percentage of errors equal to $p/4$.

(iii) When Alice is finished sending qubits to Bob, and announces the last check bit as being located in position i, Eve checks to see if she knows the value Alice holds at $f_1(i)$ [6]. If she does, she records the bit; if not, she ignores it.

The most important detail for Eve to sort out now is how to keep the error rate down. We know that $p/4 < 1/4$ which means that she should not measure all qubits. But even if she does not measure all of them, Eve may still introduce enough errors to be detected. The way for Eve to estimate p is to realize that she is looking at a sample of $2n$ sifted bits in which the probability of an error in a given bit is $p/4$. Using the normal approximation to the binomial, Eve should choose p so that the interval

$$\left[\frac{p}{4} - \frac{3\sqrt{2n(p/4)(1-p/4)}}{2n}, \frac{p}{4} + \frac{3\sqrt{2n(p/4)(1-p/4)}}{2n} \right]$$

does not contain $1/4$ i.e. so that the probability of introducing an error rate near $1/4$ is very small (outside of three deviations). This first requires Eve to obtain the value of n, which she can do by simply observing a particular run of QKD and counting the number of check bits announced by Alice. After Eve knows n, choosing a value of p that satisfies

$$0 < p < \frac{2n+18}{2n+9} - 3 \cdot \frac{\sqrt{6n+36}}{2n+9}$$

allows her to measure a proportion p of the qubits while having better than a ninety nine percent chance of escaping detection by Alice and Bob: for $n = 100$, she can measure about 68 percent of the qubits, while for $n = 325$, she can measure 81 percent[7]. In a given trial, Eve will know the value of the bit Alice holds in the $f_1(i)$ location with probability $p \cdot (1/2)$, so on average it will take her about $2/p$ trials of QKD before she obtains her first known bit. So much for a given trial.

If Eve observes m trial runs of QKD in which she knows the value Alice holds at the $f_1(i)$ location, and records the result each time, she obtains a distribution $p_0 = (\text{\# of 0's})/m$, $p_1 = (\text{\# of 1's})/m$. If $0's$ and $1's$ are truly equally likely, then this distribution should be in the range

$$p_0, p_1 \in \left[\frac{1}{2} - \frac{3}{2\sqrt{m}}, \frac{1}{2} + \frac{3}{2\sqrt{m}} \right]$$

---

[5] Eve chooses the wrong basis with probability 1/2 and then Bob's measurement in the correct basis causes a bit flip with probability 1/2.

[6] Eve knows this because she knows which qubits she measured, and of those, she knows which qubits she measured in the same basis that Alice used.

[7] The value $n = 325$ is from an experiment we will see later on.

after m trials i.e. it should be within three deviations of $(1/2, 1/2)$. If it is not, Eve has evidence of an unusual relationship between the last check bit and the bit to its immediate right, and in future runs of QKD she can try to use this knowledge to help her steal covert information.

So how good are Eve's chances at actually uncovering the existence of the hidden communication? Intuitively, we think not very good, since Alice has every reason in the world to send 0's and 1's with equal probability: if the hidden channel is binary symmetric, this is how Alice achieves capacity; if it is not (a condition which can only potentially be caused by the environment, since Eve cannot distinguish between 0's and 1's before measurement), Alice knows that sending bits according to $(1/2, 1/2)$ gets her to within ninety four percent of capacity[7]. Another problem with this strategy by Eve: who says Alice will follow a distribution at all?

So suppose for a moment that Eve forgets all about distributions, and instead just decides to try and match the bits in a fixed location to a coding of, say, the English alphabet. The problem for her then is that she won't know the value of the bit in a fixed location every time QKD is run, but at best, every *other* time, since on average it takes Eve $2/p$ trials of QKD before obtaining a bit. Thus, at least half the bits in the code words she observes will be bits that Eve herself has guessed.

Nevertheless, if Alice consistently follows a distribution different from $(1/2, 1/2)$, Eve may have reason to believe that covert communication is taking place, and that fact alone is cause enough for concern that we now take a closer look at just *why* Eve's attack may be successful once in a blue moon.

5   The Detection of Hidden Communication

The reason the attack in the last section is even conceivable is that the displacement between the last check bit and the information bit is always the same. That is, before Alice announces the last check bit, she has a binary string

$$a_1, \ldots, a_{n+1}$$

When she announces the last check bit a_i, the information bit is always located at position

$$f_1(i) = (i \mod n + 1) + 1.$$

That is, the displacement between the last check bit and the information bit is 1. Alice and Bob could just as well have used a displacement of d

$$f_d(i) = (i \mod n + 1) + d$$

for any $1 \leq d \leq n$, and the results of the last section would carry over equally well. The reason is that whenever a fixed displacement is used, there always exists a *correlation* between the position of the last check bit and the position of the information bit.

To establish this formally, and to calculate the strength of this correlation, we realize that from the point of view of Eve, there is an implicit 'channel' at work: in this channel, the input is the location $i \in \{1, \ldots, n+1\}$ of the last check bit chosen by Alice, and the output is the location $j \in \{1, \ldots, n+1\}$ of the information bit calculated by Bob. If Alice and Bob use a displacement of $k \in \{1, \ldots, n\}$ with probability d_k, and Alice chooses the location of the last check bit according to $(x_1, \ldots, x_{n+1})$, then the distribution $y = (y_1, \ldots, y_{n+1})$ on the location of the information bit calculated by Bob is given by

$$y = (x_1, \ldots, x_{n+1}) \cdot \begin{pmatrix} P(1|1) = 0 & P(2|1) = d_1 & \cdots & P(n+1|1) = d_n \\ P(1|2) = d_n & P(2|2) = 0 & \cdots & P(n+1|2) = d_{n-1} \\ \vdots & \vdots & & \vdots \\ P(1|n+1) = d_1 & P(2|n+1) = d_2 & \cdots & P(n+1|n+1) = 0 \end{pmatrix}$$

The mutual information between x and y, which measures the correlation between the location of the last check bit and that of the information bit, is given by

$$H(y) - \sum_{i=1}^{n+1} x_i H(d_1, \ldots, d_n) = H(y) - H(d_1, \ldots, d_n)$$

where H is the base two Shannon entropy. In particular,

- If Alice and Bob use a fixed displacement, then the mutual information between the location of the last check bit and the information bit is $H(x)$: the correlation depends only on how Alice selects last check bits.
- If Alice and Bob alternate randomly between all possible displacements, so that each is equally likely $((\forall k)\, d_k = 1/n)$, then the mutual information is zero.

So the mathematics tells us that if Alice and Bob can come up with a way of forcing $d_k = 1/n$ for all possible displacements k that the mutual information is zero: the correlation no longer exists. Because the correlation does not exist, there should be no test Eve can perform to uncover the existence of the hidden communication between Alice and Bob. But does it actually work? How does it affect Eve's ability to exploit the attack given in the last section?

Suppose Alice and Bob use a displacement of k with probability d_k, that Alice sends hidden bits according to $(x, 1-x)$, and that Eve expects as usual to see bits distributed as $(1/2, 1/2)$. The proportion of 0's that Eve will find in the location displaced k units from the last check bit in several trial runs of QKD is[8]

$$d_k x + (1 - d_k)(1/2) = d_k(x - 1/2) + 1/2$$

Assuming that Alice follows a distribution different from $(1/2, 1/2)$, so that $x \neq 1/2$, Eve will observe a proportion of 0's different from $1/2$. But if $d_k = 1/n$ for all k, then the proportion of 0's observed by Eve is the *same* for all displacements

---

[8] Either Alice uses the displaced location to place a 0 with probability x or she does not use the location, in which case there is a $1/2$ probability that the bit in the location is a zero.

k i.e. even though Eve will observe a proportion different from $1/2$, she can no longer detect that one particular displacement is being favored by Alice over any other. In addition, assuming $x \neq 1/2$, this is the *only* way that Eve cannot detect a favored displacement:

$$(\forall j, k)\, d_j(x - 1/2) + 1/2 = d_k(x - 1/2) + 1/2 \implies (\forall j, k)\, d_j = d_k \implies (\forall k)\, d_k = 1/n$$

For instance, if Alice and Bob use a constant displacement [9], we can see that the proportion of 0's in the favored location will be x, while in all others it will be $1/2$.

Then it is clear that if Alice and Bob would like to keep their communication hidden, they need to find a way to force $d_k = 1/n$. They can do this by *randomizing* the choice of displacement each time a single bit is sent. At first this sounds difficult, until we remember that their channel is hidden within a quantum protocol whose sole reason for existing is the production of secret keys!

6   A Steganographic Channel Within a Quantum Protocol

First, before any communication ever takes place, Alice and Bob agree on an initial displacement. They could choose $d = 1$ for instance; even if Eve knows, this only gives her a chance of stealing the first bit. Then, the next time they wish to communicate over the hidden channel, they use the key generated in the previous run of QKD to randomly choose a new displacement, which is used to covertly transmit the next bit. They can use any scheme they like. For instance, if the key k is a binary string of length n, then it represents a number that in general can be much larger than n, so they could use $d = (k \mod n) + 1$. Here is the scheme in detail:

(1) Alice chooses a random string k of about $4n$ bits containing the eventual key
(2) Alice randomly codes each bit of k in either the $X = \{|+\rangle, |-\rangle\}$ or $Z = \{|0\rangle, |1\rangle\}$ bases
(3) Alice sends each resulting qubit to Bob
(4) Bob receives the $4n$ qubits, randomly measuring each in either the X or the Z basis
(5) Alice announces in which basis she originally coded each bit of k
(6) Bob tells Alice which bits he received correctly; they keep $2n$ of these bits. (With high probability, they will have at least this many; if not, they abort the protocol)

(*) Alice and Bob calculate the displacement d using n and the key they share from the previous run of QKD[10] ; initially they can take $k = n$.

---

[9] An interesting question about the use of a constant displacement is just how small Alice can make the correlation between the last check bit and information bit.
[10] Alice and Bob do not have to use QKD to generate keys, just any scheme they both have access to that an outside party cannot possibly have.

(7) Alice randomly selects a bit from the group of $2n$ whose value is the information she wants to transmit. Then she randomly selects $n - 1$ check bits from the remaining $2n - 1$. The nth check bit is chosen from the remaining $n + 1$ so that its displacement from the information bit is d.

(8) Alice and Bob compare their values of the n check bits; if more than an acceptable number disagree, they abort the protocol (eavesdropping)

(9) Alice and Bob perform information reconciliation and privacy amplification to select a smaller m-bit key from the remaining n bits

We have three questions about this scheme:

(a) Is there a way for Eve to detect the existence of this communication?
(b) If Eve either knows or assumes the communication is taking place between Alice and Bob, how much can she learn about what they are saying?
(c) How much information does Bob receive from Alice i.e. what is the capacity of the hidden channel between the two of them?

The answer to (a) depends only on the secrecy of quantum key distribution: if it generates truly random keys only possessed by Alice and Bob, then $d_k = 1/n$ for all k, which means no correlation exists between the last check bit and the information bit, and thus there is no way to detect the existence of the hidden channel. On these grounds, the answer to (a) is No. Answering (b) is more subtle.

Because of (a), the most Eve can do now is *assume* that Alice and Bob are communicating. We seek a quantitative upper bound on exactly what Eve can learn. When Eve measures a qubit sent from Alice in a randomly chosen basis, she has a 3/4 probability of obtaining the value of the bit[11] held by Alice. Thus, if Eve measures some fraction p of the qubits sent from Alice, the proportion of measured bits she shares with Alice is $(3/4)p$. For all qubits that Eve does not measure, she tries to guess the value of the bit.

Thus, if Eve measures a proportion p of the qubits sent from Alice, the probability that Eve has the value of a bit held by Alice is

$$a = \left(\frac{3}{4}\right)p + (1 - p)\frac{1}{2} = \frac{1}{2} + \frac{p}{4}$$

So it is in Eve's best interest to measure as many qubits as possible. However, in measuring a proportion p of qubits, she introduces a corresponding proportion $p/4$ of errors into the sifted bits. Thus, to obtain an upper bound on the amount of information Eve can obtain, we must allow her to cause as many errors as possible. This means in particular that in trying to obtain an upper bound on Eve's information we must assume the environment causes no errors. Now consider the implicit channel from Alice to Eve. When Alice sends a hidden bit to Bob, there are only two ways that Eve can know this bit:

– Either Eve guesses the correct location of the hidden bit and has the same value for that bit as Alice, or

---

[11] Either Eve guesses the right basis, in which case she gets the bit, or guesses the wrong basis, in which case her measurement yields the bit with probability 1/2.

- Eve guesses the wrong location of the hidden bit, but has the same value in the incorrect location as Alice does in the correct location.

The first event happens with probability $(1/n)a$. To calculate the probability of the second event, assuming Eve guesses the wrong location, call it k, she will still have the information bit if either (1) Eve has the same value in location k as Alice (prob. a) and Alice has the same value in location k as in the location of the information bit (prob. $1/2$), or (2) Eve does not have the same value in location k as Alice (prob. $1 - a$) and Alice does not have the same value in location k as in the location of the information bit (prob. $1/2$). Thus, the probability that Eve knows the value of the hidden bit sent from Alice to Bob is

$$\left(\frac{1}{n}\right)a + \left(1 - \frac{1}{n}\right)\left(a\frac{1}{2} + (1 - a)\frac{1}{2}\right) = \left(a - \frac{1}{2}\right)\frac{1}{n} + \frac{1}{2}$$

which can also be expressed in terms of the proportion p of qubits measured by Eve:

$$\frac{p}{4n} + \frac{1}{2}$$

The channel from Alice to Eve is thus a binary symmetric channel with capacity

$$C(n, p) = 1 - H\left(\frac{p}{4n} + \frac{1}{2}\right)$$

where H is the base two Shannon entropy. The capacity of the Alice-Eve channel is an upper bound on the amount of information Eve can acquire about a message passed from Alice to Bob over the steganographic channel. This capacity in turn is bounded as follows:

Theorem 1. *The information Eve can acquire about the message from Alice to Bob satisfies*

$$C(n, p) \leq \frac{1}{\ln(2)} \cdot \frac{p^2}{4n^2 - 2np}.$$

Proof. First, consider any binary symmetric channel, with capacity

$$C(x) = 1 - H(x)$$

where $x \in (1/2, 1)$. By the mean value theorem,

$$C(x) = H(1/2) - H(x) = \left(\frac{1}{2} - x\right) \cdot H'(c)$$

for some $c \in (1/2, x)$. Since $c < x$,

$$H'(c) = \frac{1}{\ln(2)} \cdot \ln\left(\frac{1}{c} - 1\right) > H'(x)$$

and since $x > 1/2$, we can bound the capacity as

$$C(x) \leq \left(\frac{1}{2} - x \right) H'(x)$$

$$= \left(x - \frac{1}{2} \right) \ln \left(\frac{x}{1-x} \right) \frac{1}{\ln(2)}$$

$$\leq \left(x - \frac{1}{2} \right) \left(\frac{x}{1-x} - 1 \right) \frac{1}{\ln(2)} \qquad \text{(using } \ln(x) \leq x - 1\text{)}$$

$$= \frac{1}{\ln(2)} \cdot \frac{(2x-1)^2}{2(1-x)}$$

Now consider the capacity $C(n, p)$ of the Alice-Eve channel. Assume $p > 0$, since otherwise the claim is trivial. Setting $x = p/4n + 1/2 \in (1/2, 1)$ and using our observation above,

$$C(n, p) \leq \frac{1}{\ln(2)} \cdot \frac{p^2}{4n^2 - 2np}$$

which finishes the proof.   □

Corollary 1. *The amount of information Eve can acquire never exceeds*

$$\frac{1}{\ln(2)} \cdot \frac{1}{4n^2 - 2n}$$

Proof. This is immediate since $p \leq 1$.   □

Finally, we answer (c). Because Bob knows the location of the information bit, the capacity of the hidden channel from Alice to Bob is determined by the error rate in the sifted bits.

Theorem 2. *If the error rate $\alpha \in [0, 1/4)$ is due solely to interference caused by Eve, then the capacity of the Alice-Bob steganographic channel is $1 - H(\alpha)$. In particular, the capacity of the Alice-Bob channel is never smaller than $1 - H(1/4) \approx 0.1887$.*

Proof. The important point is that the probability of a 0 flipping to a 1 is the same as the probability that a 1 flips to a 0. The reason this is true when Eve causes all errors is that she cannot tell which classical bit a qubit represents before she performs a measurement and that Alice sends bits with equal frequency.
                                                                                □

What is very important in the result above is that Alice and Bob can force the error rate to be smaller than 1/4 by simply aborting the protocol when it is too high i.e. they can increase the capacity of the steganographic channel at will[12]. As the capacity of their channel approaches its maximum value of one, the amount of information Eve acquires tends to zero: as the steganographic

---

[12] But it will cost them something: *time.*

capacity increases to one, the error rate decreases to zero, which means Eve can measure fewer and fewer qubits ($p \to 0$), so by Theorem 1, Eve's information tends to zero. Even if Alice and Bob do not insist on a small error rate, they do no worse than 0.18, while Eve's information in realistic settings will always be small. An example will help make this drastic difference clear.

Example 2. Take $n = 100$. Then no matter what Eve does, the information she acquires is less than $3.62 \cdot 10^{-5}$ bits per channel use.

Actual error rates will be a combination of errors caused by an eavesdropper and errors caused by the environment: $\alpha = \epsilon + p/4$. Notice though that a positive value of ϵ does nothing to help Eve acquire hidden information, since the proportion p of qubits she can measure decreases as the error rate due to the environment increases: $p < 1 - 4\epsilon$. In this more general case, it is also intuitively clear that $1 - H(\alpha)$ is still a lower bound on the capacity of the Alice-Bob channel.

In fact, if we can obtain a decent model of the error rate imposed by the environment, Alice and Bob can then reject any error rate that on average is not likely to be caused by the environment alone. This will result not only in a more secure version of QKD, but also in a higher steganographic capacity. To develop a feel for the kinds of error rates due to the environment, we now calculate the capacity of our steganographic channel in an experimental realization of freespace QKD.

7   Experimental Capacity

Most experimental realizations of QKD thus far have either been based on sending photons through fiber optic cables (coding bits with phase) or sending photons through open air (coding bits with polarization) i.e. *freespace quantum key distribution*. It is the latter that we find especially fascinating. In several trial runs of freespace QKD [9], total error rates ranged from a low of $\alpha = 0.006$ to a high of $\alpha = 0.089$, with the great majority being $\alpha = 0.04$ or less. The number of sifted bits reported in the experiment is 651, meaning that $n = 325$.

Error Rate	Capacity (Alice→Bob)	Eve's Information ($C(n,p)$)
0.089	0.566	$4.3 \cdot 10^{-7}$
0.081	0.594	$3.5 \cdot 10^{-7}$
0.072	0.626	$2.8 \cdot 10^{-7}$
0.064	0.656	$2.2 \cdot 10^{-7}$
0.058	0.680	$1.8 \cdot 10^{-7}$
0.047	0.726	$1.2 \cdot 10^{-7}$
0.039	0.762	$8.3 \cdot 10^{-8}$
0.031	0.800	$5.2 \cdot 10^{-8}$
0.022	0.847	$2.6 \cdot 10^{-8}$
0.014	0.893	$1.0 \cdot 10^{-8}$
0.006	0.947	$1.9 \cdot 10^{-9}$

Here is a table showing the total error rate, a lower bound on the capacity of the steganographic channel from Alice to Bob and an upper bound (Theorem 1) on the amount of information Eve would be able to acquire about the hidden message in bits per channel use.

The reason we used Theorem 1 to calculate upper bounds on Eve's information is that the numbers very quickly become difficult to manage. For instance, to find the actual value $C(n, p)$ of Eve's information when $\alpha = 0.089$, which turns out to be $2.16 \cdot 10^{-7}$, one needs to calculate $1 - H(0.500273846)$. As the error rate gets smaller, the calculations become more and more tedious. In the ideal case of no errors $\alpha = 0$, Alice and Bob achieve a maximum capacity of 1, while Eve acquires the minimum amount of information 0.

Conservatively then[13], a decent upper bound on the error rate introduced by the environment ϵ in the freespace QKD experiment is around $\epsilon \leq 1/10 = 0.10$. If we then decide that only environmental errors are allowed, this constrains $\alpha \leq 1/10$, which in turn means that an eavesdropper can only measure a proportion p of qubits that satisfies $p \leq 2/5$ i.e. Eve can measure no more than 40% percent of the qubits.

8   Applications

We consider a few uses for quantum steganographic channels.

8.1   Authentication

A party contacts Alice over an open channel claiming that he is Bob, that he has lost the key they once shared, and that he needs Alice to send him the latest instructions for his mission. Bob is known to be separated from Alice by an ocean. Understandably so, Alice tells the party that the two of them should establish a secret key using QKD and that then she will happily send "Bob" his instructions.

However, what Bob knows, but the contacting party may not know, is that after Alice selects check bits, she will deliberately announce fradulent values, causing them to repeatedly abort and rerun the QKD protocol in the name of "environmental noise." Each time QKD is run though, Alice is transmitting a hidden bit to the party[14], until she has transmitted a string of a previously agreed upon length. If the party is really Bob, he will know this, receive the complete string from Alice, and then announce to her over the public channel "Maybe we would be more successful trying to establish a key if I initiated the QKD session," at which point he uses the same trick to send back the string to Alice. If the party is not Bob, he will have no knowledge of of the hidden channel, and after Alice is finished transmitting the string, he will not offer to

---

[13] Assuming that there was no eavesdropper during this experiment!.

[14] Since they are not generating keys in this setup, the hidden channel is implemented using a constant displacement scheme, which works fine as long as Alice sends bits with equal probability.

try and initiate the session himself. At that point, Alice says "Sorry, seems like we have a bad connection right now, try again later."

Provided the length of the string sent by Alice is long enough, she will have proof that the contacting party knows about the existence of the hidden channel and how it works. From there, she can make him jump through further hoops if she likes, until she is convinced that the contacting party is really Bob.

8.2 Teleportation of Quantum States

Teleportation allows Alice to send Bob a *qubit* as follows:

– At the start, Alice and Bob share an entangled pair of qubits.
– Later, Alice would like to send a qubit $|\psi\rangle = a|0\rangle + b|1\rangle$ to Bob; Alice has no knowledge of a and b, neither does Bob.
– Alice interacts $|\psi\rangle$ with her half of the entangled pair, and then measures the two qubits she now has, obtaining one of four possible results: $m = 00$, $m = 01$, $m = 10$ or $m = 11$.
– The state of Bob's qubit is now determined by the result of the measurement Alice performed in the previous step; specifically, Bob's state is

$$\begin{cases} a|0\rangle + b|1\rangle \text{ if } m = 00 \\ a|1\rangle + b|0\rangle \text{ if } m = 01 \\ a|0\rangle - b|1\rangle \text{ if } m = 10 \\ a|1\rangle - b|0\rangle \text{ if } m = 11 \end{cases}$$

Thus, if there is a *secure way* for Alice to send Bob the result m of her measurement, Bob can then determine the appropriate quantum operations that will transform his qubit into the original qubit $|\psi\rangle$ that Alice wanted to send. Since the result of Alice's measurement is simply a two bit binary string, the steganographic channel given here can be used to do exactly that. This improves the security of teleportation since it can now be implemented with a classical channel that cannot be eavesdropped on or interfered with. For instance, if an attacker eavesdrops on the classical channel, they may gain valuable information about the teleportation session; but if the channel hidden in QKD is used to transmit the two classical bits, we know that there is very little chance of an eavesdropper learning anything. In addition, using the hidden channel to transmit the two bits helps to cover up the fact that teleportation is taking place – the parties appear to be generating an innocent key, as opposed to what they are really doing, which is teleporting qubits.

8.3 Secure Communication Without Encryption

If Alice and Bob use a single displacement, then the hidden channel provides legitimate secure communication without encryption. The question is: how secure? This depends on how small Alice can force the mutual information between locations of the last check bit and information bit to be, but mostly it seems to depend on whether Alice follows a $(1/2, 1/2)$ distribution in transmitting hidden bits – something Information Theory encourages her to do.

If Alice and Bob don't use a single displacement, then it is debatable as to whether or not they are really using encryption. The function of the key is to destroy the correlation between the location of the last check bit and information bit – assuming Alice does not follow a $(1/2, 1/2)$ distribution. The key is used to prevent an outside observer from having reason to believe that steganographic communication is underway. The hidden information itself though is not encrypted, it is protected from eavesdropping by quantum mechanics, by the fact that if an eavesdropper wants to know the value of a bit, they have to measure a qubit, thus introducing errors into the sifted bits that are detectable by Alice and Bob.

A good question would be: if Alice and Bob use the hidden channel to communicate, this requires them to repeatedly run QKD, which might tip off an outside observer about the existence of the hidden communication. However, if Alice and Bob want to send small but important messages, as in the case of teleportation already discussed, a possible justification for the repeated use of QKD would be the use of the one time pad algorithm in cryptography.

9   The Flip Side

Suppose *you* think parties are covertly communicating. What can you do to stop them? Measure as many qubits as possible. Doing this, you can shrink the capacity to about 0.18 – assuming they let you!

10   Closing

One of the interesting aspects of the steganographic channel described herein is that Alice and Bob can abort the protocol whenever the error rate is too high i.e. whenever they detect "too much noise in the line" they can try again. This is a positive aspect of the channel because it allows them to reduce the likelihood of eavesdropping while simultaneously increasing the channel capacity per channel use. But what it ignores is the expense of aborting a trial run of QKD.

A good approximation on the amount of time a trial of freespace QKD takes is about a second. That means that every time Alice and Bob abort QKD it costs them *a second of time*. This cost has to be incorporated into our analysis in future work. Specifically, our steganographic channel is implicitly a timing channel, precisely because it makes decisions based on error rates. As such, we would like to see its capacity when measured in bits per unit time[10].

The steganographic form of communication we have considered here is one aspect of a larger subject that could be called "quantum security." From the author's point of view, quantum security centers on three interrelated concerns: the threats to security posed by quantum technology on systems, the new capabilities it offers for ensuring the security of systems and the determination of the extent to which either of these is realizable.

Acknowledgements

The idea of a hidden channel within QKD stems from an interesting two day brainstorming session between the author and James Troupe of NSWC. The author thanks both he and Ira Moskowitz of NRL for discussions of genuine value. The author also wishes to express his gratitude to the anonymous referees whose insights improved the presentation in this paper. Finally, the author thanks Teddy Furon, but we cannot say why.

References

1. Bennett, C.H., Brassard, G.: Quantum cryptography: public key distribution and coin tossing. In: Proceedings of IEEE International Conference on Computers, Systems and Signal Processing, pp. 175–179. IEEE Computer Society Press, Los Alamitos (1984)
2. Brassard, G., Lütkenhaus, N., Mor, T., Sanders, B.: Limitations on practical quantum cryptography. Physical Review Letters 86(6) (2000)
3. Calsamiglia, J., Barnett, S., Lütkenhaus, N., Suominen, K.: Removal of a single photon by adaptive absorption. Physical Review A 64 (2000)
4. Gea-Banacloche, J.: Hiding messages in quantum data. Journal of Mathematical Physics 43(9), 4531–4536 (2002)
5. Hughes, R.J., et al.: Practical free-space quantum cryptography. In: Williams, C.P. (ed.) QCQC 1998. LNCS, vol. 1509, pp. 200–213. Springer, Heidelberg (1999)
6. Kok, P., Lee, H., Dowling, J.: Single-photon quantum-nondemolition detectors constructed with linear optics and projective measurements. Physical Review A 66, 063814 (2002)
7. Majani, E.E., Rumsey, H.: Two results on binary-input discrete memoryless channels. In: Proceedings of the IEEE International Symposium on Information Theory, pp. 104–104. IEEE Computer Society Press, Los Alamitos (1991)
8. Nielsen, M., Chuang, I.: Quantum computation and quantum information. Cambridge University Press, Cambridge (2000)
9. Nordholt, J.E., Hughes, R.J.: A new face for cryptography. Los Alamos Science 27, 68–86 (2002)
10. Martin, K., Moskowitz, I.S.: Noisy timing channels with binary inputs and outputs. In: Moskowitz, I.S. (ed.) Information Hiding. LNCS, vol. 2137, Springer, Heidelberg (2001)
11. Shannon, C.E.: A mathematical theory of communication. Bell Systems Technical Journal 27, 379–423, 623–656 (1948)

Three-Dimensional Meshes Watermarking: Review and Attack-Centric Investigation

Kai Wang[1], Guillaume Lavoué[1], Florence Denis[2], and Atilla Baskurt[1]

[1] LIRIS, UMR 5205 CNRS, INSA-Lyon, F-69621 Villeurbanne, France
[2] LIRIS, UMR 5205 CNRS, Université Lyon 1, F-69622 Villeurbanne, France
{kwang,glavoue,fdenis,abaskurt}@liris.cnrs.fr

Abstract. The recent decade has seen the emergence of 3D meshes in industrial, medical and entertainment applications. Therefore, their intellectual property protection problem has attracted more and more attention in both the research and industrial realms. This paper gives a synthetic review of 3D mesh watermarking techniques, which are deemed to be a potential effective solution to the above problem. We begin with a discussion on the particular difficulties encountered while applying watermarking on 3D meshes. Then some typical algorithms are presented and analyzed, classifying them in two categories: spatial and spectral. Considering the important impact of the different attacks on the design of 3D mesh watermarking algorithms, we also provide an attack-centric viewpoint of this state of the art. Finally, some special issues and possible future working directions are discussed.

Keywords: 3D mesh, digital watermarking, copyright protection, authentication, attack, robustness.

1 Introduction

Recently, 3D meshes have been widely used in virtual reality, medical imaging, video games and computer aided design. A 3D mesh is a collection of polygonal facets targeting to constitute an appropriate approximation of a real 3D object. It possesses three different combinatorial elements: *vertices*, *edges* and *facets*. From another viewpoint, a mesh can also be completely described by two kinds of information. The *geometry* information gives the positions (coordinates) of all its vertices, while the *connectivity* information provides the adjacency relations between the different combinatorial elements. Figure 1 shows an example of 3D mesh. As illustrated by the close-up, the *degree* of a facet is the number of its component edges, and the *valence* of a vertex is defined as the number of its incident edges. Although there are many other 3D representations, such as cloud of points, parametrized surface, implicit surface and voxels, 3D mesh has been the *de facto* standard of numerical representation of 3D objects thanks to its simplicity and usability. Furthermore, it is quite easy to convert other representations to 3D mesh, which is considered as a low-level but effective model.

Digital watermarking has been considered as a potential efficient solution for copyright protection of various multimedia contents. This technique carefully

T. Furon et al. (Eds.): IH 2007, LNCS 4567, pp. 50–64, 2007.

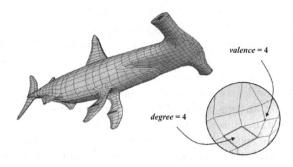

Fig. 1. Example of 3D mesh and a close-up illustrating the *valence* of a *vertex* and the *degree* of a *facet*

hides some secret information in the cover content. Compared with traditional cryptography, digital watermarking technique is able to protect digital works after the transmission phase and the legal access. There exist different classifications of watermarking techniques. We distinguish *non-blind* and *blind* watermarking schemes depending on whether the original digital work is needed at extraction, or not. Usually, one hopes to construct a *robust* watermark, which is able to go through common malicious attacks, for copyright protection purpose. But sometimes, the watermark is intentionally designed to be *fragile* for authentication applications. Finally, researchers have the habit to group practical watermarking algorithms in two categories, to say *spatial* or *spectral*, according to the insertion domain.

This paper reviews the nearly 10-year history of the research on 3D meshes watermarking techniques since the publication of the first relevant algorithms in 1997 [24]. The remainder of this paper is organized as follows. Section 2 discusses the special difficulties encountered when watermarking 3D meshes, and provides an overview of the most important techniques proposed in the literature. Attacks on watermarked meshes play an important role in the elaboration of suitable watermarking algorithms. They are much more intractable than their counterparts on images. So section 3 is dedicated to analyzing various possible attacks and discussing the corresponding solutions to resist them. Some open questions and possible research directions are given in the last section.

2   3D Meshes Watermarking Techniques

2.1   Difficulties and Classification

There still exist few watermarking methods for 3D meshes, in contrast with the relative maturity of the theory and practices of image, audio and video watermarking. This situation is mainly caused by the difficulties encountered while handling the arbitrary topology and irregular sampling of 3D meshes, and the complexity of possible attacks on watermarked meshes.

We can consider an image as a matrix, and each pixel as an element of this matrix. This means that all these pixels have an intrinsic order in the image, for example the order established by row or column scanning. On the contrary, there is no simple robust intrinsic ordering for mesh elements, which often constitute the watermarking primitives. Some intuitive orders, such as the order of the vertices and facets in the mesh file, and the order of vertices obtained by ranking their projections on an axis of the objective coordinate system, are easy to be altered. In addition, because of their irregular sampling, we are still short of an efficient and effective spectral analysis tool for 3D meshes. This situation, as you can see in the following sections, makes it difficult to put the well-known "secure spread spectrum" watermarking schemes into practices.

Besides the above point, robust watermarks have also to face to various intractable attacks. The reordering of vertices and facets do not have any impact on the shape of the mesh, while it can seriously desynchronize watermarks which rely on this straightforward ordering. The similarity transformations, including translation, rotation and uniform scaling, are supposed to be common operations through which a robust watermark should survive. Even worse, the original watermark primitives can disappear after a mesh simplification or remeshing. Such tools are available in many softwares, and they can totally destroy the connectivity information of the watermarked mesh while well conserving its shape. Usually, we distinguish geometric attacks, which only modify the positions of the vertices, and connectivity attacks, which also change the connectivity aspect. Section 3 provides a detailed investigation on these attacks and discusses the existing solutions to make the watermarks robust to them.

Watermarking 3D meshes in computer aided design applications introduces other difficulties brought by the design constraints. For example, the symmetry of the object has to be conserved and the geometric modifications have to be within a tolerance for future assembly. Under this situation, the watermarked mesh will no longer be evaluated only by the human visual system that is quite subjective, but also by some strict objective metrics.

Existing techniques concerning 3D meshes can be classified in two main categories, depending on whether the watermark is embedded in the spatial domain (by modifying the geometry or the connectivity) or in the spectral domain (by modifying some kind of spectral-like coefficients).

2.2 Spatial Techniques

As mentioned above, the spatial description of a 3D mesh includes geometry aspect and connectivity aspect. Most existing algorithms take the former as primitives, which shows superiority in both robustness and imperceptibility compared to the latter. This section focuses more on watermarking primitives than on robustness, which will be explored in detail in the next section.

Spatial Techniques Modifying the Geometry
Note that regardless of what the practical primitive is, all the techniques in this subsection are implemented by modifying the coordinates of involved vertices.

The algorithms that modify the vertices positions directly and individually are often fragile techniques. Yeo and Yeung [32] proposed such an algorithm that serves for mesh authentication. The basic idea is to search for a new position for each vertex where two predefined hash functions have an identical value, so as to make all vertices valid for authentication. At the extraction phase, they simply examine the validity of each vertex, and locate the possible attacks on the invalid vertices. In fact, this algorithm depends on a pre-established vertex order to avoid causality problem. Lin et al. [21] solved this defect and also proposed a more analytic and controllable modification scheme with a better attack localization capability. Cayre and Macq [8] proposed a high-capacity blind data-hiding algorithm for 3D triangular meshes. By choosing the projection of a vertex on its opposite edge in a triangle as the primitive (see Figure 2), the theoretical capacity can attain 1 bit per vertex. The synchronizing mechanism relies on the choice of the first triangle by a certain geometrical criterion, and a further spreading scheme that is piloted by a secret key. Combining the above embedding scheme with an indexing mechanism [24], which explicitly indicates the indexes of the embedded bits in the whole watermark sequence, Cayre et al. [10] devised an effective fragile watermark. Bors [7] also reported a blind algorithm. The primitive is the relative position of a vertex to its 1-ring neighbours. A two-state space division is established, and the vertex is assumed to be moved into the correct subspace according to the next watermark bit.

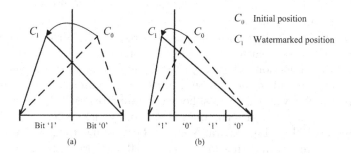

Fig. 2. Watermarking primitive in the algorithm of Cayre and Macq [8], the projection is moved to the nearest correct interval: (a) opposite edge is divided in two intervals; (b) opposite edge is divided in four intervals. The inserted bits are both '1'.

Some other algorithms choose positions of groups of vertices as watermarking primitives in order to strengthen the robustness. Yu et al. [34] gave a non-blind robust algorithm. Vertices are divided into several groups and in each of them is inserted one bit by modifying the lengths from its member vertices to the gravity centre of the mesh. The modulation scheme is a simple additive method with an adaptive intensity obtained by a local geometrical analysis of the mesh. The extraction is also quite simple, since it is sufficient to regroup the vertices and inverse the additive insertion model. However, to ensure a good robustness, a pre-processing step of registration and resampling is necessary, which needs the non-watermarked cover mesh and inevitably makes the algorithm non-blind. In Benedens's "Vertex Flood Algorithm (VFA)" [4], after grouping vertices according to their distances to the centre of a designated triangle, the range of the group interval is then divided into $m = 2^n$ subintervals, and all the group vertices distances to the chosen triangle centre are altered so that the new distances all fall into a certain subinterval that stands for the next n watermark bits.

Facets have several interesting measures for watermarking. Ohbuchi et al. [24] chose the ratio between the height of a triangle and its opposite edge length as primitive to construct a watermarking technique that is intrinsically invariant to similarity transformations (Triangle Similarity Quadruple (TSQ) algorithm). Benedens [4] reported a blind algorithm in which the triangular facet height is quantized. By quantizing the distance of a facet to the mesh centre, Wu and Chueng [30] gave a fragile but high-capacity scheme. In another Benedens's method [3], the Extended Gaussian Image (EGI) of a mesh is established by clustering facets according to their normal directions, then in each "bin" of the EGI, the average normal direction of the group of facets is modified to carry one watermark bit. Since these average normal directions approximately describe the mesh shape, this scheme is demonstrated to be relatively robust to simplification and remeshing. Instead of EGI, Lee et al. [19] adopted Complex EGI for watermarking. One inconvenience of this class of algorithms is that the modification of the positions of the involved vertices is indirect and sometimes quite complicated, especially in the last two algorithms.

Watermark embedding can be done in the spherical coordinate system, especially in the distance component $r_i = \sqrt{x_i^2 + y_i^2 + z_i^2}$. We can benefit to elaborate some similarity-transformation-invariant algorithms if the distance component is relative to the mesh centre. Since the component r_i represents the shape of the mesh, its modification is supposed to be more robust than a single x_i, y_i, or z_i component modification. These are two main reasons for why numerous researchers chose to watermark in spherical coordinate system [11,22,35].

There exist other spatial techniques that modify the geometry. Ohbuchi et al. [24] presented the "Tetrahedral Volume Ratio Embedding" algorithm that is invariant to affine transformation. Li et al. [20] converted the initial mesh in spherical parameterization domain and watermarked its 2D spherical harmonic transformation coefficients. In fact, parameterization transforms a 3D mesh into a bidimensional description, thus probably permits making use of the existing 2D image watermarking algorithms. At last, Bennour et al. [6] propose to insert watermarks in the 2D contours of 3D objects.

To summarize, the main drawback of the techniques that modify the geometry is the relatively weak robustness to both geometric and connectivity attacks. For blind schemes, the synchronization issue is really a difficult problem. However, these methods can have the advantages of high capacity and localization ability of malicious attacks.

Spatial Techniques Modifying the Connectivity
Actually, there are very few 3D meshes watermarking techniques based on connectivity modification. On the one hand, this kind of watermark is obviously

fragile to connectivity attacks, and on the other hand, the introduced modification can be very easy to detect. Ohbuchi et al. [24] presented two such algorithms. In the first one, the local triangulation density is changed to insert a visible watermark. The second algorithm first cuts one band of triangular facets off the mesh, and then glues it to the mesh with just one edge. This facet band can be a meaningful pattern or be simply determined by a secret key. Both methods are visible and fragile, but the local distribution of the embedded watermark stops them from being a useful fragile watermark for integrity authentication.

2.3 Spectral Techniques

Most of the successful image watermarking algorithms are based on spectral analysis. A better imperceptibility can be gained thanks to a dilution effect of the inserted watermark bits in all the spatial/temporal and spectral parts of the carrier. A better robustness can also be achieved if the watermark is inserted in the low and median frequency parts. Unfortunately, for 3D meshes, we haven't yet an efficient and robust spectral analysis tool. Moreover, the lack of a natural parameterization makes spectral analysis even more difficult. As it can be seen in the following subsections, almost all the existing tools have their limitations. Besides the algorithms that embed watermarks in the spectrum obtained by a direct frequency analysis, we also present here the class of algorithms that are based on multiresolution analysis. The basic idea behind both of them is the same: modification of some spectral-like coefficients.

Spectral Techniques Based on Direct Frequency Analysis

Researchers have tried different types of basis functions for this direct frequency analysis. For Laplacian basis functions, a matrix of dimension $N \times N$ (N being the number of vertices) is constructed based on mesh connectivity. Then $3 * N$ spectral coefficients are calculated as the projections of the three coordinates vectors of all the vertices on the N ordered and normalized eigenvectors of this Laplacian matrix. Based on this analysis, Ohbuchi et al. [26] proposed a non-blind method (additive modulation of the low and median frequency coefficients) while Cayre et al. [9] gave a semi-blind one (quantization of the low and median frequency coefficients). There exist two serious problems with the Laplacian frequency analysis. The computation time increases rapidly with mesh complexity due to the diagonalization of the $N \times N$ Laplacian matrix. Moreover, the analysis procedure depends on the mesh connectivity information. The first problem forced the authors to cut the original mesh into several patches possessing fewer vertices. To overcome the fragility to connectivity change, the authors proposed a pre-processing step of resampling at the extraction to recover exactly the same connectivity as the cover mesh.

Wu and Kobbelt [31] reported an algorithm that is based on radial basis functions. The construction of these basis functions is relative to the geometric information. This kind of analysis seems effective because it can give a good approximation of the original mesh with just a very limited number of basis functions. So calculation time can be greatly saved. In spite of this improvement, the algorithm remains sensible to various attacks, that's why the authors still proposed to do registration and resampling before the real extraction. With the similar objective to solve the computation performance issue, Murotani and Sugihara [23] proposed to watermark the mesh singular spectral coefficients. In this method, the matrix to be diagonalized has a much lower dimension.

Although current 3D mesh spectral analysis tools are not efficient enough, they provide the opportunity to directly transplant the existing mature spectral watermarking techniques of digital images.

Spectral Techniques Based on Multiresolution Analysis

Multiresolution analysis is a useful tool to reach an acceptable trade-off between the mesh complexity and the capacity of the available resources. Such an analysis produces a coarse mesh which represents the basic shape (low frequencies) and a set of details information at different resolution levels (median and high frequencies). These methods also permit realizing a synthesis process during which multiple representations with different complexities can be created.

The most interesting point of multiresolution analysis for watermarking is its flexibility. There are different available locations authorizing to meet different application demands. For example, insertion in the coarsest mesh ensures a good robustness, while embedding in the details parts provides an excellent capacity. The insertion in low resolution can be both more robust and more imperceptible thanks to a dilution effect. The insertion in high resolution level may permit constructing some effective fragile watermarks with a precise localization ability of the attacks.

Wavelets are a common tool for such a multiresolution analysis. Figure 3 shows the wavelet decomposition of a dense rabbit mesh, the watermark can be inserted either in the coarsest mesh, or in the wavelet coefficients at different levels. In fact, these wavelet coefficients are 3D vectors associated with each edge of the corresponding coarser mesh. Note that this kind of wavelet analysis is applicable only on semi-regular triangular meshes. Based on this wavelet analysis, Kanai et al. [15] proposed a non-blind algorithm that modifies the ratio between a wavelet coefficient norm and the length of its support edge, which is invariant to similarity transformations. Uccheddu et al. [28] described a blind one-bit watermarking algorithm with the hypothesis of the statistical independence between the wavelet coefficients norms and the inserted watermark bit string.

Thanks to a remeshing step, the above analysis could be extended to irregular meshes. With this idea, Cho et al. [12] built a fragile watermark to accomplish authentication task in the wavelet domain. This remeshing step can also be done in spherical parameterized space. Jin et al. [14] used such a technique to insert a watermark into both the coarsest representation and the spherical wavelet coefficients of an irregular mesh. Using a direct irregular mesh wavelet analysis tool without any assistant remeshing step, Kim et al. [16] elaborated a blind algorithm. Other multiresolution analysis tools, such as the edge-collapse iterations technique [27] and the Burt-Adelson pyramid decomposition [33], are employed to develop robust 3D mesh watermarking algorithms.

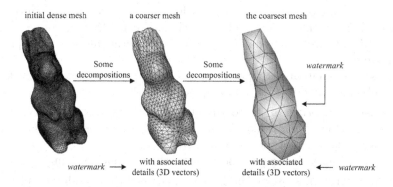

initial dense mesh   a coarser mesh   the coarsest mesh

Some decompositions   Some decompositions   watermark

watermark ⟶   with associated details (3D vectors)   with associated details (3D vectors)   ⟵ watermark

Fig. 3. 3D mesh watermarking techniques based on wavelet analysis

Nonetheless, as the current direct spectral analysis tools, the available multiresolution analysis schemes have either connectivity restrictions or robustness deficiencies (especially to connectivity attacks). And for majority of these techniques, registration and resampling are recommended to ensure a sufficient robustness. But this inevitably makes the algorithms non-blind.

3 Attack-Centric Investigation

As mentioned in subsection 2.1, attacks constitute an indispensable factor when designing 3D meshes watermarking algorithms. In this section, we carefully discuss three types of attacks and introduce the existing solutions in the literature.

3.1 Robustness to Geometric Attacks

This kind of attacks only modifies the geometric part of the watermarked mesh. Regardless of what the nature of the geometric change is, the attack is reflected by a modification of vertices positions.

Similarity Transformations. Similarity transformation is considered to be a common operation rather than an attack, against which even a fragile watermark should be able to stand. It includes translation, rotation, uniform scaling, and the combination of the above three operations. Generally speaking, there are three different strategies to build a watermark that is immune to this attack.

The first solution is to use some primitives that are invariant to similarity transformations. Ohbuchi et al. [24] gave a list of such primitives. The most utilized is the ratio between two measures of a triangle (height or edge length). The primitives in some blind spatial techniques are also invariant to similarity transformations, like the primitives in the methods of Cayre and Macq [8], Bors [7], and Cho et al. [11]. Practically, these primitives are all some relative measures between several absolute and individual ones. Fortunately, not only the watermarking primitives are kept unchanged, but also most synchronization schemes are insensible to this kind of attack. Moreover, if we expect a robustness even to affine transformations, the Nielson-Foley norm can be a good primitive candidate [5,29].

The second solution is to watermark in an invariant space. One such space can be obtained by doing the following steps [22,35].

1. Translate the origin of the coordinate system to the mesh gravity centre.
2. Calculate the principal axes of the mesh and rotate the object so that they coincide with axes of the coordinate system.
3. Do a uniform scaling so that the whole mesh is bounded in a unit sphere/cube.

Then the watermark is inserted in this new space. But the causality problem arises because the variables used in the above steps, such as the gravity centre and the principle axes orientations are probably changed after watermark insertion. So there will possibly exist some extent of errors when reconstructing this space at the extraction. If a precise extraction is demanded, then we have to memorize some feature values of the insertion space in order to help the reconstruction, but this will make the technique at least semi-blind.

The third solution is to carry out registration of the input mesh at extraction with the original non-watermarked one. Low-precision registration methods use singular spectral coefficients [23], eigenvectors of the vertices correlation matrices [25], inertial moments [26], and characteristic points [31] of the two meshes. High-precision methods often need user interactions to determine a good initial condition and the registration is realized by iteratively minimizing a sum of local errors [26,33]. This solution will obviously make the algorithms non-blind, but provides a better robustness.

Signal Processing Attacks. A mesh can be considered as a signal in a three-dimensional space. There are counterparts of the traditional one-dimensional signal processing techniques for 3D meshes, such as random additional noise, smoothing, enhancement, and lossless compression (usually realized by quantization). Figure 4.b and 4.c illustrate two examples. Although these operations can be very harmful to inserted watermarks, they are really common manipulations in animation and special effects applications.

Random noise, smoothing, and enhancement can be modeled in the spectral domain by a modification of the high-frequency part. Quantization can be thought as a certain form of noise, but its effect is somewhat complicated. Generally speaking, the spectral watermarking techniques that modify the low and median frequency parts are more robust to these attacks, as demonstrated by Praun et al. [27]. Their method is among the most robust in the literature. Note that for the additive watermarking scheme, insertion in the low frequency part is both more robust and more imperceptible. Different modulation schemes have been developed. Ohbuchi et al. [25] proposed to repeat the watermark insertion in the first half of the spectrum with a constant intensity. Wu and Kobbelt [31] watermarked only the very low frequency coefficients and proposed an adaptive insertion intensity that is proportional to the absolute value of the coefficient.

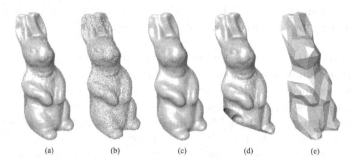

Fig. 4. Original mesh and four examples of attacked meshes: (a) original rabbit mesh; (b) random additive noise; (c) smoothing; (d) cropping; (e) simplification

Lavoué et al. [18] gave another modulation scheme, in which the intensity is linear for the low and median frequency coefficients and constant for the high frequency part.

Spatial techniques are less robust to signal processing attacks. One good measure is to search for an adaptive spatial insertion intensity founded on local geometric analysis. This analysis can be based on the average length of the incident edges of a vertex [2], the geometric distortion introduced by a vertex split operation [27], the minimal incident edge length of a vertex [33], or the possible normal direction variance of the incident facets of a vertex after insertion [34]. The basic idea is to increase the watermarking intensity while keeping the visual quality. At last, redundant insertion [25] and use of error correction code [18] can sometimes significantly reinforce the robustness to these attacks.

Local Deformation Attacks. A local deformation is sometimes imperceptible if we haven't the original mesh for comparison, but it can seriously disturb the watermark, especially the synchronization process. One natural solution is to divide the mesh into several patches and repeat the watermark insertion in each patch. The mesh division can be based on curvature or semantic analysis. This solution can be considered as a local embedding scheme described by Ohbuchi et al. [24]. As mentioned previously, division in patches may also decrease the insertion time for some spectral techniques. Another solution is to adopt an indexed watermarking method, like the TSQ algorithm described in [24] and the fragile watermarking scheme described by Cayre et al. [10].

3.2 Robustness to Connectivity Attacks

This class of attacks includes cropping, remeshing, subdivision and simplification. In general, they are quite difficult to handle.

Cropping is a special attack (see Figure 4.d for an example), and some researchers prefer to regard it as a geometric attack because its consequence is quite similar to the one caused by local deformation. Watermark repetition in different patches and the indexed method seem the most efficient ways to resist cropping.

As far as the other attacks (Figure 4.e illustrates an example of simplification), the algorithms which take the average normal direction of a group of facets [3,19], or the distances of a group of vertices to the mesh centre [11] as primitives, seem less sensible. Their primitives are approximately conserved after connectivity modification. Other spatial techniques are less robust by reasons of both the geometric change of the primitives and the desynchronization problem. The basis function construction and the frequency coefficients calculation in direct spectral analysis are either dependent on vertices order or on mesh connectivity. The existing multiresolution analysis tools often have connectivity restrictions, and the remeshing step is not robust enough to connectivity change. So, to attain a sufficient robustness for these methods, the authors usually recommend performing a pre-processing step of connectivity restoration before extraction. This restoration procedure can be considered as a resampling of the extraction input mesh (objective mesh) so as to obtain the same connectivity configuration as the cover mesh [26,33,34] or the non-attacked stego-mesh [31] (reference mesh). The task is to find, for each vertex in the reference mesh, a corresponding point on the surface of the objective mesh. This correspondence can be established by the nearest neighbour criterion [31], ray intersection [26,34], or iterations targeting to minimize a particular cost function [33].

Two other possibilities to handle connectivity attacks are to find a robust transformation or parameterization domain that is independent of connectivity, and to watermark in some robust mesh shape descriptors.

3.3 Robustness to Other Attacks

This group contains mainly three attacks: file attack, format attack, and representation attack. The file attack simply consists of reordering the vertices and/or the facets in the mesh description file. The mesh file format conversion attack may alter the underlying mesh data structure, so the intrinsic processing order of the vertices and facets can also be changed. To be invariant to these two attacks, it just needs to turn the synchronization scheme independent of these intrinsic orders. The representation conversion may be the most destructive attack to 3D mesh watermarks, because after such an attack, the mesh itself will no longer exist (for example, an approximation of a mesh with a NURBS model). Until now, not any researcher has mentioned robustness to this attack. In our opinion, the two ideas given at the end of the last subsection can also be potential solutions to this serious attack.

4 Discussions and Perspectives

Table 1 presents a comparison of some typical algorithms of each class. The values in the column "Inserted bits" are the ones reported in the original papers. Most robustness performances are evaluated by a sign ranging from '−−', which means the least robust, to '++', which stands for the most robust. In our opinions, there exist many valuable research topics in 3D meshes watermarking:

Classic Problem: Trade-off Between Capacity, Robustness, and Imperceptibility. These measures are often contradictory. For example, an important watermarking intensity gives a better robustness, but normally degrades the visual quality of the watermarked mesh and risks to make the watermark perceptible. The redundant insertion could considerably strengthen the robustness, but meanwhile unavoidably decreases the capacity. Local adaptive geometric analysis seems favorable to find optimal watermarking parameters in order to achieve a well compromise between these indicators.

Algorithms Evaluation. So far, the research community has been lacking of a widely used performance evaluation system of the existing algorithms. We need a standard attack benchmark and distortion measurement. The distortion introduced by watermarking can be either evaluated by objective geometric distortion measure, or by subjective perceptual distortion measure [13,17].

Construction of Blind and Robust Algorithms. The elaboration of such an algorithm attracts the attention of many researchers considering its satisfactory flexibility and reliability. In our opinion, this requires at least to overcome two difficulties. The first one is to build a robust and secure synchronization mechanism, especially for spatial techniques. Using certain robust aspect of the mesh to locate and index the watermarking primitives seems a good idea. At the same time, the separation of synchronization primitives from watermarking primitives can prevent the causality problem. The second difficulty is to avoid the registration and resampling pre-processing steps, which target to ensure the robustness. As mentioned before, global and robust shape descriptors or transformations, like geometric moments, spherical harmonic transformation, can be a good start point. Another possibility is to introduce a remeshing step at both insertion and extraction sides. First of all, the cover mesh (possibly irregular) is remeshed to generate a corresponding semi-regular mesh with a similar geometrical shape. Then watermarks are inserted in this semi-regular mesh. For extraction, we suppose that a mesh with the same semi-regular connectivity can be reconstructed. Here, the connectivity issue is supposed to be solved, and the watermarks in the semi-regular mesh are assumed to be blind and geometrically robust. The key point lies in elaborating a remeshing scheme which is insensitive to connectivity change. Alface and Macq [1] have made some efforts in this direction. They devised a remeshing scheme based on mesh feature points, which are umbilical points obtained by curvature analysis, but the robustness of their method seems not strong enough.

Other Perspectives. Other research topics include informed 3D mesh watermarking techniques, hierarchical watermarks, 3D mesh digital fingerprints, and the interplay between compression and watermarking, or between subdivision and watermarking.

Table 1. Comparison of different 3D mesh watermarking techniques

Categories	Algorithms	Clearly contro-llable intensity	Inserted bits	Blind	Local adaptability
Spatial techniques on vertices	Yeo and Yeung [32]	No	1 bit/vertex	Yes	No
	Lin et al. [21]	Yes	1 bit/vertex	Yes	No
	Cayre and Macq [8]	Yes	1 bit/vertex	Yes	No
	Yu et al. [34]	Yes	≈50 bits	No	Yes
	VFA [4]	Yes	≈900 bits	Yes	No
	Bors [7]	No	0.2 bits/vertex	Yes	Yes
	Cho et al. [11]	Yes	≈50 bits	Yes	No
Spatial techniques on facets	TSQ [24]	No	1.2 bits/facet	Yes	No
	Benedens [3]	Yes	≈30 bits	Semi	No
	Lee at al. [19]	Yes	≈50 bits	Semi	Yes
Other spatial techniques	Li et al. [20]	No	24 bits	No	No
	Bennour et al. [6]	Yes	≈500 bits	No	No
Direct spectral techniques	Ohbuchi et al. [26]	Yes	32 bits	No	No
	Cayre et al. [9]	Yes	64 bits	Semi	No
	Wu and Kobbelt [31]	Yes	24 bits	No	No
	Alface and Macq [1]	Yes	64 bits	Yes	No
Multiresolution spectral techniques	Kanai et al. [15]	Yes	≈620 bytes	No	No
	Uccheddu et al. [28]	Yes	Not clear	Yes	No
	Praun et al. [27]	Yes	50 bits	No	Yes
	Yin et al. [33]	Yes	250 bits	No	Yes

Continuation of Table 1. Robustness to different attacks

Algorithms	Similarity transform.	Signal proce-ssing attacks	Local deform. and cropping	Connectivity attacks	Elements reordering
Yeo and Yeung [32]	− −	− −	Localization*	− −	Fragile
Lin et al. [21]	− −	−	Localization*	− −	Invariant
Cayre and Macq [8]	++	−	−	− −	Invariant
Yu et al. [34]	Registration	+	−	Resampling	Invariant
VFA [4]	+	−	−	−	Invariant
Bors [7]	++	−	+	− −	Invariant
Cho et al. [11]	++	+	−	+	Invariant
TSQ [24]	++	−	+	− −	Invariant
Benedens [3]	Registration	+	−	+	Invariant
Lee et al. [19]	Registration	+	−	+	Invariant
Li et al. [20]	+	+	+	Resampling	Invariant
Bennour et al. [6]	Registration	+	+	−	Invariant
Ohbuchi et al. [26]	Registration	++	++	Resampling	Resampling
Cayre et al. [9]	+	+	+	− −	Fragile
Wu and Kobbelt [31]	Registration	++	++	Resampling	Resampling
Alface and Macq [1]	+	+	++	+	Fragile
Kanai et al. [15]	+	−	−	− −	Invariant
Uccheddu et al. [28]	−	+	−	−	Invariant
Praun et al. [27]	Registration	++	++	Resampling	Resampling
Yin et al. [33]	Registration	+	−	Resampling	Resampling

* "Localization" means the ability of localizing attacks for the fragile algorithms.

Acknowledgments. The research work of the first author is funded by China Scholarship Council of Chinese government.

References

1. Alface, P.R., Macq, B.: Feature-Based Watermarking of 3D Objects Towards Robustness against Remeshing and De-synchronization. In: Proceedings of the SPIE-IS and T Electronic Imaging, vol. 5681, pp. 400–408 (2005)
2. Ashourian, M., Enteshary, R.: A New Masking Method for Spatial Domain Watermarking of Three-Dimensional Triangle Meshes. In: Proceedings of the IEEE Region 10 Annual International Conference, vol. 1, pp. 428–431 (2003)
3. Benedens, O.: Geometry-Based Watermarking of 3D Models. IEEE Computer Graphics and Applications 19(1), 46–55 (1999)
4. Benedens, O.: Two High Capacity Methods for Embedding Public Watermarks into 3D Polygonal Models. In: Proceedings of the Multimedia and Security Workshop at ACM Multimedia, pp. 95–99 (1999)
5. Benedens, O., Busch, C.: Towards Blind Detection of Robust Watermarks in Polygonal Models. Computer Graphics Forum 19(3), 199–208 (2000)
6. Bennour, J., Garcia, E., Dugelay, J.L.: Watermark Recovery from 2D Views of a 3D Object Using Texture or Silhouette Information. Journal of Electronic Imaging (July-August, 2007)
7. Bors, A.G.: Watermarking Mesh-Based Representations of 3-D Objects Using Local Moments. IEEE Transactions on Image Processing 15(3), 687–701 (2006)
8. Cayre, F., Macq, B.: Data Hiding on 3-D Triangle Meshes. IEEE Transactions on Signal Processing 51(4), 939–949 (2003)
9. Cayre, F., Alface, P.R., Schmitt, F., Macq, B., Maitre, H.: Application of Spectral Decomposition to Compression and Watermarking of 3D Triangle Mesh Geometry. Signal Processing 18(4), 309–319 (2003)
10. Cayre, F., Devillers, O., Schmitt, F., Maitre, H.: Watermarking 3D Triangle Meshes for Authentication and Integrity, Research Report of INRIA, p. 29 (2004)
11. Cho, J.W., Kim, M.S., Prost, R., Chung, H.Y., Jung, H.Y.: Robust Watermarking on Polygonal Meshes Using Distribution of Vertex Norms. In: Proceedings of the International Workshop on Digital Watermarking, pp. 283–293 (2005)
12. Cho, W.H., Lee, M.E., Lim, H., Park, S.Y.: Watermarking Technique for Authentication of 3-D Polygonal Meshes. In: Proceedings of the International Workshop on Digital Watermarking, pp. 259–270 (2005)
13. Gelasca, E.D., Ebrahimi, T., Corsini, M., Barni, M.: Objective Evaluation of the Perceptual Quality of 3D Watermarking. In: Proceedings of the International Conference on Image Processing, vol. 1, pp. 241–244 (2005)
14. Jin, J.Q., Dai, M.Y., Bao, H.J., Peng, Q.S.: Watermarking on 3D Mesh Based on Spherical Wavelet Transform. Journal of Zhejiang University: Science 5(3), 251–258 (2004)
15. Kanai, S., Date, H., Kishinami, T.: Digital Watermarking for 3D Polygons Using Multiresolution Wavelet Decomposition. In: Proceedings of the International Workshop on Geometric Modeling: Fundamentals and Applications, pp. 296–307 (1998)
16. Kim, M.S., Valette, S., Jung, H.Y., Prost, R.: Watermarking of 3D Irregular Meshes Based on Wavelet Multiresolution Analysis. In: Proceedings of the International Workshop on Digital Watermarking, pp. 313–324 (2005)

17. Lavoué, G., Gelasca, E.D., Dupont, F., Baskurt, A., Ebrahimi, T.: Perceptually Driven 3D Distance Metrics with Application to Watermarking. In: Proceedings of the SPIE Applications of Digital Image Processing, p. 63120 (2006)
18. Lavoué, G., Denis, F., Dupont, F.: Subdivision Surface Watermarking. Computers and Graphics 31(3), 480–492 (2007)
19. Lee, J.W., Lee, S.H., Kwon, K.R., Lee, K.I.: Complex EGI Based 3D-Mesh Watermarking. IEICE Transactions on Fundamentals of Electronics, Communications and Computer Sciences 88(6), 1512–1519 (2005)
20. Li, L., Zhang, D., Pan, Z., Shi, J., Zhou, K., Ye, K.: Watermarking 3D Mesh by Spherical Parameterization. Computers and Graphics 28(6), 981–989 (2004)
21. Lin, H.S., Liao, H.M., Lu, C., Lin, J.: Fragile Watermarking for Authenticating 3-D Polygonal Meshes. IEEE Transactions on Multimedia 7(6), 997–1006 (2005)
22. Maret, Y., Ebrahimi, T.: Data Hiding on 3D Polygonal Meshes. In: Proceedings of the Multimedia and Security Workshop, pp. 68–74 (2004)
23. Murotani, K., Sugihara, K.: Watermarking 3D Polygonal Meshes Using the Singular Spectrum Analysis. In: Proceedings of the IMA International Conference on the Mathematics of Surfaces, pp. 85–98 (2003)
24. Ohbuchi, R., Masuda, H., Aono, M.: Watermarking Three-Dimensional Polygonal Models. In: Proceedings of the ACM International Multimedia Conference and Exhibition, pp. 261–272 (1997)
25. Ohbuchi, R., Takahashi, S., Miyazawa, T., Mukaiyama, A.: Watermarking 3D Polygonal Meshes in the Mesh Spectral Domain. In: Proceedings of the Graphics Interface, pp. 9–17 (2001)
26. Ohbuchi, R., Mukaiyama, A., Takahashi, S.: A Frequency-Domain Approach to Watermarking 3D Shapes. Computer Graphics Forum 21(3), 373–382 (2002)
27. Praun, E., Hoppe, H., Finkelstein, A.: Robust Mesh Watermarking. In: Proceedings of the ACM SIGGRAPH Conference on Computer Graphics, pp. 49–56 (1999)
28. Uccheddu, F., Corsini, M., Barni, M.: Wavelet-Based Blind Watermarking of 3D Models. In: Proceedings of the Multimedia and Security Workshop, pp. 143–154 (2004)
29. Wagner, M.G.: Robust Watermarking of Polygonal Meshes. In: Proceedings of the Geometric Modeling and Processing, pp. 201–208 (2000)
30. Wu, H.T., Chueng, Y.M.: A Fragile Watermarking Scheme for 3D Meshes. In: Proceedings of the Multimedia and Security Workshop, pp. 117–124 (2005)
31. Wu, J., Kobbelt, L.: Efficient Spectral Watermarking of Large Meshes with Orthogonal Basis Functions. Visual Computer 21(8-10), 848–857 (2005)
32. Yeo, B., Yeung, M.M.: Watermarking 3D Objects for Verification. IEEE Computer Graphics and Applications 19(1), 36–45 (1999)
33. Yin, K., Pan, Z., Shi, J., Zhang, D.: Robust Mesh Watermarking Based on Multiresolution Processing. Computers and Graphics 25(3), 409–420 (2001)
34. Yu, Z., Ip, H.H.S., Kwok, L.F.: A Robust Watermarking Scheme for 3D Triangular Mesh Models. Pattern Recognition 36(11), 2603–2614 (2003)
35. Zafeiriou, S., Tefas, A., Pitas, I.: A Blind Robust Watermarking Scheme for Copyright Protection of 3D Mesh Models. In: Proceedings of the International Conference on Image Processing, vol. 3, pp. 1569–1572 (2004)

Robust and High Capacity Image Watermarking Based on Jointly Coding and Embedding Optimization

Chuntao Wang[1], Jiangqun Ni[1,2,*], Jiwu Huang[1,2], Rongyue Zhang[1], and Meiying Huang[1]

[1] Department of Electronics and Communication Engineering,
Sun Yat-Sen University, Guangzhou, 510275, P. R. China
[2] Guangdong Key Laboratory of Information Security Technology,
Guangzhou, 510275, P.R. China
Ph: 86-20-84036167
issjqni@mail.sysu.edu.cn

Abstract. A new informed image watermarking algorithm is presented in this paper, which can achieve the information rate of 1/64 bits/pixel with high robustness. Firstly, the LOT (Locally Optimum Test) detector based on HMM in wavelet domain is developed to tackle the issue that the exact strength for informed embedding is unknown to the receiver. Then based on the LOT detector, the dirty-paper code for informed coding is constructed and the metric for the robustness is defined accordingly. Unlike the previous approaches of informed watermarking which take the informed coding and embedding process separately, the proposed algorithm implements a jointly coding and embedding optimization for high capacity and robust watermarking. The Genetic Algorithm (GA) is employed to optimize the robustness and distortion constraints simultaneously. Extensive simulations are carried out which demonstrates that the proposed algorithm achieves significant improvements in performance against JPEG, gain attack, low-pass filtering and so on.

1 Introduction

The digital watermarking can be treated as the process of communication with side information [1], where the original cover work is regarded as the side information known to the encoder. This investigation results in the concepts of informed watermarking which is used to design the robust watermarking algorithm with high capacity, and becomes the domain of intensive research [2-7]. The conventional informed watermarking [2-3] includes two separate stages, i.e., informed coding and informed embedding. The use of dirty–paper code [8] is the most common approach to informed coding, where the set of codewords is divided into different cosets, each of which contains multiple codewords representing the same single message. With the dirty-paper code, the to-be-embedded message is represented by the codeword from the associated coset, which fits the best the cover work in which the message will be embedded. While the informed embedding process tails each watermark code according to the cover work, attempting to put the watermarked cover work in the

---

* Corresponding author.

T. Furon et al. (Eds.): IH 2007, LNCS 4567, pp. 65–79, 2007.

detectable area of the code with respect to the detector under the robustness and fidelity constrains. Usually, a correlation-based detector is employed to incorporate the informed watermarking process [2-3].

Instead of the correlation-based one, a HMM based detector is developed in our previous works [9] with significant performance improvements. The HMM based watermarking scheme in [9] uses the HVS (Human Visual System) masking values as the embedding strength, which are kept almost unchanged even after most common signal processing attacks and ideal for blind watermarking application. However, for blind detection in the framework of informed watermarking, the exact strengths for informed embedding are unavailable to the receiver; consequently the performance of HMM based detector is expected to degrade considerably. To tackle this issue, a new HMM-based LOT detector is developed by applying the theory of the hypothesis testing in [10], which is then utilized to design the dirty-paper code and to define the robustness metric for the proposed informed watermarking algorithm.

High-capacity watermarking application requires the introduction of perceptual shaping based on perceptual model. Watson in [15] describes a perceptual model which has been proven to be far more efficient than the objective metric MSE (Mean Square Error) at estimating the perceptual effects of watermarks added to images. Considering the proposed the algorithm works on the framework of wavelet based HMM model, a perceptual distance in wavelet domain is constructed by following the spirit of Watson distance in DCT domain [15], which is then used to measure the fidelity of the watermarked image.

With the nonlinear HMM-based LOT detector, the informed watermarking can no longer be treated as two separate processes of coding and embedding. For a given message, the code determined from informed coding process is not necessary the optimal one for informed embedding process, and vice versa. Therefore, an algorithm of jointly coding and embedding optimization is proposed. Specifically, each codeword in the coset associated to the to-be-embedded watermark message is proceeded with informed embedding, among which the codeword with the best robustness and invisibility trade-off is taken as the optimum one for watermark embedding. By incorporating the HMM-based LOT detector and GA-based jointly coding and embedding optimization, the proposed informed watermarking algorithm can achieve information rate as 1/64 bits/pixel with high robustness against JPEG, Gaussian noise, gain attack and etc.

The remainder of this paper is organized as follows. The LOT detector is developed and analyzed in section 2. In section 3, the HVS distance in wavelet domain is constructed. The informed watermarking optimized with GA-based joint coding and embedding and the design of dirty-paper code are given in section 4 and 5, respectively. Simulation results are given in section 6. And finally the conclusion remarks are drawn in section 7.

2   HMM Based LOT Detector and Performance Evaluation

The HMM-based LOT detector is developed in this section to tackle the issue that the exact embedding strength is unknown to the receiver for the strategy of informed embedding, which is then used to define the robustness measure in subsequent section.

Let $\mathbf{w} = \left(w_{j,l}^1, w_{j,l}^2, w_{j,l}^3 \right)^T$ denote a *vector node* that consists of the wavelet coefficients at level j and location l in orientation d ($d=1, 2, 3$ for H, V and D, respectively). If only the coarsest 2-level wavelet pyramids are considered, then totally 5 vector nodes $\mathbf{w}_k (k = 0,1,...,4)$ are defined, which forms a 15-node vector tree as shown in Fig.1, where the 3 nodes with the same label constitute a vector node. To characterize the statistical dependency of wavelet coefficients, a vector DWT-HMM [9] with a set of parameters Θ is developed

$$\Theta = \{\mathbf{p}_1, \mathbf{A}_2,..., \mathbf{A}_J; \mathbf{C}_j^{(m)}, (j = 1,..., J, m = 1,2)\}. \tag{1}$$

The specification of Θ can be found in [9] and is trained with EM algorithm [11][9]. With the vector DWT-HMM, the pdf of the vector node $\mathbf{w}_k (k = 0,1,...,4)$ can be expressed as:

$$f(\mathbf{w}_k) = p_j^{(1)} g(\mathbf{w}_k; \mathbf{C}_j^{(1)}) + p_j^{(2)} g(\mathbf{w}_k; \mathbf{C}_j^{(2)}), \quad \begin{cases} j = J, & k = 0 \\ j = J-1, & \text{otherwise} \end{cases} \tag{2}$$

where $p_j^{(1)} + p_j^{(2)} = 1$ and $g(\mathbf{w}; \mathbf{C}) = (1/\sqrt{(2\pi)^n |\det(\mathbf{C})|}) \exp(-\mathbf{w}^T \mathbf{C}^{-1} \mathbf{w}/2)$. Hence, the pdf of a vector tree $\mathbf{T}$ can be constructed as

$$f(\mathbf{T} | \Theta) = \prod_{k=0}^4 f(\mathbf{w}_k). \tag{3}$$

If a 15-element codeword $\mathbf{CW}$ is embedded into the vector tree $\mathbf{T}$ and the watermarked vector tree is $\mathbf{T}_w$, then the pdf of $\mathbf{T}_w$ is

$$f(\mathbf{T}_w | \mathbf{CW}, \Theta) = f(\mathbf{T}_w - \mathbf{B} \cdot \mathbf{CW} | \Theta) \tag{4}$$

where $\mathbf{B}$ stands for the 15-element embedding strength.

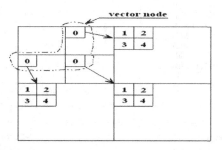

Fig. 1. Vector DWT-HMM model (2 levels)

Therefore, the log-form HMM-based detector as described in [9] can be constructed as follows:

$$L(\mathbf{T}, \mathbf{CW}) = \ln \frac{f(\mathbf{T}_w | \mathbf{CW}, \Theta)}{f(\mathbf{T} | \Theta)} = \ln \frac{f(\mathbf{T}_w - \mathbf{B} \cdot \mathbf{CW} | \Theta)}{f(\mathbf{T} | \Theta)} = \sum_{k=0}^4 \ln \frac{f(\mathbf{w}_k - \mathbf{B}(k) \cdot \mathbf{CW}(k))}{f(\mathbf{w}_k)}, \tag{5}$$

where $\mathbf{B}(k)$ and $\mathbf{CW}(k)$ are the 3-element embedding strength and sub-code corresponding to the vector node $\mathbf{w}_k$ ($k = 0,1,...,4$), respectively. If (5) is larger than zero, then $\mathbf{CW}$ exists. In the case of multiple codewords available, the codeword with the maximum $L(\mathbf{T},\mathbf{CW})$ value is taken as the detected one.

Unlike the previous approach in [9] where the vector $\mathbf{B}$ used in HMM detector is the HVS (Human Visual System) masking value and known to the detector, the exact embedding strength for the proposed informed watermarking algorithm is unavailable to the detector, and consequently the performance of the detector (5) is degraded considerably. To tackle this issue, the HMM based LOT detector is developed by applying the theory of locally optimum hypothesis testing in [10], i.e.:

$$L(\mathbf{T},\mathbf{CW})_{LOT} = \sum_{k=0}^{4} V_{LOT}(\mathbf{CW},k),$$ (6)

where $V_{LOT}(k)$ is defined as:

$$V_{LOT}(\mathbf{CW},k) = -\frac{f'(\mathbf{w}_k)}{f(\mathbf{w}_k)}\cdot\mathbf{CW}(k) = g_{LO}(\mathbf{w}_k)\cdot\mathbf{CW}(k), k = 0,1,...,4,$$ (7)

where $f'(\mathbf{w}_k)$ is the partial derivative of $f(\mathbf{w}_k)$, i.e.,:

$$f'(\mathbf{w}_k) = p_j^{(I)} g(\mathbf{w}_k;\mathbf{C}_j^{(I)})\cdot(-\mathbf{w}_k^{T}[\mathbf{C}_j^{(I)}]^{-I}) + p_j^{(2)} g(\mathbf{w}_k;\mathbf{C}_j^{(2)})\cdot(-\mathbf{w}_k^{T}[\mathbf{C}_j^{(2)}]^{-I}).$$ (8)

With the HMM based LOT detector in (6), the embedding strength $\mathbf{B}$ is no longer necessary for the detection of codeword $\mathbf{CW}$ in vector tree $\mathbf{T}_w$.

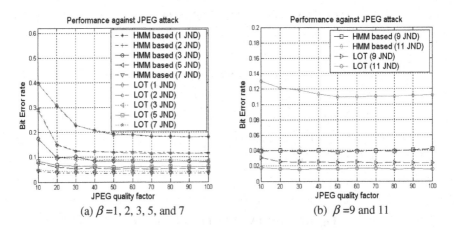

(a) β =1, 2, 3, 5, and 7   (b) β =9 and 11

Fig. 2. Performance comparison between the HMM-based detector and the LOT one

To evaluate the performance of the proposed LOT detector, an un-coded 5120-bit random sequence is embedded into the *512*512*8b* test image "Lena" with the algorithm in [9], and then detected with both the HMM-based detector in [9] and the

LOT detector defined in (6). In our simulation, the global adjustment factor β for embedding strength [9] are set to 1, 2, 3, 5, 7, 9 and 11, respectively. And the results are given in Fig.2, which demonstrate that: (1) the performance of LOT detector is almost the same as that of HMM based detector in [9] when the embedding strength is small (β =1, 2 and 3); (2) the performance of LOT is little worse when β ranges from 5 to 7; and (3) the LOT detector works better when β is greater than 9. The situation in case (3) is attributed to the fact that the estimated HVS values according to the watermarked image, which are used as the embedding strength, are deviated from the true one greatly.

We would like to further investigate the nonlinear characteristics of the LOT detector described in (6). Noticing that the 5 vector nodes in (6) are statistically same, only one vector node is analyzed and the result is then extended to the case with multiple vector nodes. Without loss of generality, the 1st (k=0) vector node $\mathbf{w}_0 = \begin{bmatrix} \mathbf{w}_0(1) & \mathbf{w}_0(2) & \mathbf{w}_0(3) \end{bmatrix}^{T}$ is taken for analysis. Let $\mathbf{w}_0(1)$ to be kept as constant, while both $\mathbf{w}_0(2)$ and $\mathbf{w}_0(3)$ to be independent variables ranging from $-\delta$ to δ. The distribution of $V_{LOT}(\mathbf{CW},0)$ in (7) against $\mathbf{w}_0(2)$ and $\mathbf{w}_0(3)$ is shown in Fig.3, where $\mathbf{w}_0(1) = -1$, $\delta = 500$, $\mathbf{CW}(0)$ is randomly set as [-1.512, 1.681, -1.074], and the parameter set Θ is trained with the $256*256*8b$ test image "Lena". The distribution would vary when $\mathbf{w}_0(1)$ and $\mathbf{CW}(0)$ are set to other values, but its outline is kept invariant. According to Fig.3, the characteristics of the LOT detector can be summarized as follows:

1. The distribution of LOT detector is symmetric around the original point;
2. There exist two peaks near the original point, which are similar to the 3-D Gaussian distribution;
3. For the same variation of independent variables, the LOT value near the peak areas varies more greatly than that in other areas, as illustrated in Fig.3 (b).

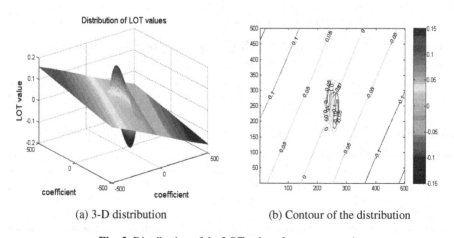

(a) 3-D distribution   (b) Contour of the distribution

Fig. 3. Distribution of the LOT values for a vector node

If $\mathbf{w}_0(1)$ is set as independent variable, the LOT distribution has the similar shape and would be illustrated in 4-D space. This can be extended to the case when all 5 vector nodes are considered, where the LOT distribution would be described in 16-D space.

3 HVS Distance in Wavelet Domain

As described in section 1, the perceptual distance in wavelet domain is more preferable as the distortion measure for the proposed informed watermarking algorithm. To our best knowledge, however, no such metric can be found in previous literatures. By following the spirit of Watson's perceptual model in DCT domain [13], the perceptual distance in wavelet domain is constructed.

Instead of the JND (Just Noticeable Difference) in [9], the IJND (Integrated JND) developed in [14] is adopted, which is developed as follows:

$$
\begin{aligned}
IJND(j,o,x,y) = frequence\_m(j,o)*luminance\_m(j,x,y) \\
*texture\_m(j,x,y)^{0.015}*entropy\_m(j,x,y),
\end{aligned} \tag{9}
$$

where j, o, x, y stands for the level of the wavelet pyramid, the orientation of wavelet subband, the coordination in x- and y-axis, respectively. The $frequence\_m(j,o)$, $luminance\_m(j,x,y)$, and $texture\_m(j,x,y)$ in (9) are the frequency masking, luminance masking, and texture masking, respectively, which are given in [9]; the $entropy\_m(j,x,y)$ is the entropy masking defined in [14]. The detailed specifications of these parameters can be found in [9] and [14].

To have a good granularity, the perceptual distances for a vector tree and an image are developed separately. Let $\mathbf{T}$ and $\mathbf{T}_w$ to be the original vector tree and the watermarked one, respectively, the difference between each element of the vector tree is defined as follows:

$$
\mathbf{e}(i) = \mathbf{T}_w(i) - \mathbf{T}(i), \ i = 1, 2, \dots, 15. \tag{10}
$$

It is then scaled by its corresponding IJND value calculated with (9) to generate the perceptual distance for each element, i.e.,

$$
\mathbf{d}(i) = \frac{\mathbf{e}(i)}{\mathbf{IJND}(i)}, \ i = 1, 2, \dots, 15. \tag{11}
$$

Next, the $\mathbf{d}(i)$ ($i = 1, 2, \dots, 15$) are pooled into one single metric to form the perceptual distance for the 15-node vector tree, i.e.,

$$
D_{DWT} = \left(\sum_{i=1}^{15} \mathbf{d}(i)^p \right)^{1/p} \tag{12}
$$

where $p = 4$ according to Watson's work [13]. Similarly, pooling together $\mathbf{d}(t,i)$ for all vector trees constitutes the perceptual distance in wavelet domain for an image:

$$D_{DWT} = \left(\sum_t \sum_{i=1}^{15} \mathbf{d}(t,i)^p \right)^{1/p}, \tag{13}$$

where $\mathbf{d}(t,i)$ denotes the $\mathbf{d}(i)$ $(i = 1, 2, ..., 15)$ of the tth vector tree.

4 Informed Watermarking Algorithm

In this section, based on the definition of robustness and distortion metrics, the informed watermarking algorithm with joint coding and embedding is described. More over, the GA based optimization algorithm under robustness and distortion constraints is also given.

Robustness and Distortion Measure

Under the framework of HMM-based watermarking [9], the vector trees are used as the carrier for watermark, and each of them has 15 nodes as shown in Fig.1. For informed coding, if one vector tree is assumed to be embedded with one bit, then two cosets with size N, namely C_0 and C_1, are required to correspond to the bit 0 and bit 1, respectively. Without loss of generality, assume that the bit 0 is embedded into the vector tree $\mathbf{T}$, and the codeword $\mathbf{CW}_i^0$ in C_0 is determined by the algorithm to represent the bit 0. Therefore, the objective of the informed watermarking is to adjust $\mathbf{T}$ in the way of $\mathbf{T}_w = \mathbf{T} + \mathbf{B} * \mathbf{CW}_i^0$ so as to put $\mathbf{T}_w$ into the *detectable area* of $\mathbf{CW}_i^0$ with respect to the LOT detector $L(\mathbf{T}, \mathbf{CW})_{LOT}$. In the case of attacks, the received vector tree is $\mathbf{T}_w'$, and the probability of correct detection is determined as follows:

$$\Pr\left\{ L(\mathbf{T}_w', \mathbf{CW}_i^0)_{LOT} > L(\mathbf{T}_w', \mathbf{CW}_j^1)_{LOT} \right\}$$
$$= \Pr\left\{ \sum_{k=0}^{4} \left(g_{LO}(\mathbf{w}_k') \cdot \mathbf{CW}_i^0(k) \right) > \sum_{k=0}^{4} \left(g_{LO}(\mathbf{w}_k') \cdot \mathbf{CW}_j^1(k) \right) \right\} \tag{14}$$
$$= \Pr\left\{ \sum_{k=0}^{4} \left(g_{LO}(\mathbf{w}_k') \cdot \left(\mathbf{CW}_i^0(k) - \mathbf{CW}_j^1(k) \right) \right) > 0 \right\}, \mathbf{CW}_j^1 \in C_1, j = 1, 2, ..., N.$$

For simplification, we define

$$\Delta R = \max_{1 \le j \le N} \sum_{k=0}^{4} \left(g_{LO}(\mathbf{w}_k') \cdot \left(\mathbf{CW}_i^0(k) - \mathbf{CW}_j^0(k) \right) \right). \tag{15}$$

Obviously, the larger the ΔR is, the higher the correct detection probability would be, and thus the stronger robustness could be achieved. Therefore, the formulation (15) can be served as the robustness measure.

As described in previous sections, the perceptual distance in wavelet domain is introduced to measure the perceptual distortion between the original cover work and the watermarked one. The proposed informed watermarking algorithm works with vector tree as the basic processing unit, therefore the formulation (12) can be incorporated as the perceptual distortion metric for each vector tree:

$$\Delta D = \left(\sum_{i=1}^{15} \mathbf{d}(i)^p \right)^{1/p} \quad \text{where } p = 4 \tag{16}$$

Informed Watermarking with Jointly Coding and Embedding Optimization

The image is firstly decomposed into the 3-level wavelet pyramid, and then the coarsest two levels (scale=2 and 3) are used to construct the vector trees (see Fig.1) which are used as the carriers of watermark message. For each vector tree, 1 bit message is informedly coded and embedded, which leads to an information rate as 1/64 bits/pixel. For informed coding, two cosets with size N, namely C_0 and C_1, are constructed with the method described in section 5; for informed embedding, the GA with powerfully global searching capability [12] is employed so as to obtain the optimal embedding strength under the robustness and distortion constraints. As the nonlinear feature of HMM-based LOT detector, a strategy of joint coding and embedding optimization is required to further trade off the robustness and invisibility constrains simultaneously. More specifically, the informed watermarking is implemented as follows:

1. Determine the coset C_i ($i = 0,1$) according to the to-be-embedded bit b ($b = 0,1$);
2. Select a codeword $\mathbf{CW}_n^i$ ($n = 1,2,\dots,N$) from C_i orderly;
3. For a given vector tree $\mathbf{T}$, deploy the GA to seek an optimal 15-node embedding strength $\mathbf{B}$ under constrain of the robustness and distortion, which put the vector tree to the detectable area of $\mathbf{CW}_n^i$. The implementation of GA will be given in the next sub-section;
4. With the generated $\mathbf{B}$ for $\mathbf{CW}_n^i$, the robustness to distortion ratio $RDR = \Delta R / \Delta D$ is computed;
5. Go to step 2 until all codewords in C_i are proceeded. The codeword, namely, $\mathbf{CW}_{opt}^i$, with maximum RDR value is determined as the optimal one in C_i for the given vector tree;
6. Embed the optimal codeword with the optimal strength $\mathbf{B}_{opt}$, i.e., $\mathbf{T}_w = \mathbf{T} + \mathbf{B}_{opt} * \mathbf{CW}_{opt}^i$.

After all vector trees are embedded with the above method, the inverse wavelet transformation is applied to obtain the watermarked image.

Robustness and Distortion Trade-off Optimized with GA

For a given codeword $\mathbf{CW}$ and a vector tree $\mathbf{T}$, the informed embedding process adjusts $\mathbf{T}_w$ to the detectable area of $\mathbf{CW}$ with respect to the LOT detector, which aims to obtain the maximum robustness with minimum distortion. This issue can be formulated as the multi-objective optimization problem, i.e.,

$$\max \{ z_1 = f_R(\mathbf{T}, \mathbf{B}, \mathbf{CW}), z_2 = -f_D(\mathbf{T}, \mathbf{B}, \mathbf{CW}) \}$$
$$s.t. \ z_1 \geq R_0 \text{ and } z_2 \leq D_0, \tag{9}$$

where $f_R(\cdot)$ and $f_D(\cdot)$ are the measure of robustness and distortion as defined in (15) and (16), respectively. The D_0 and R_0 in (17) are the upper-bound in D_{DWT} for distortion and the lower-bound for robustness, respectively.

The multi-objective optimization formulation in (17) can be further simplified as (18), i.e.,

$$\begin{aligned}
\max \quad & RDR = f_R(\mathbf{T},\mathbf{B},\mathbf{CW}) \,/\, f_D(\mathbf{T},\mathbf{B},\mathbf{CW}) \\
s.\ t. \quad & z_1 = f_R(\mathbf{T},\mathbf{B},\mathbf{CW}) \geq R_0 \ and\ z_2 = f_D(\mathbf{T},\mathbf{B},\mathbf{CW}) \leq D_0\,.
\end{aligned} \tag{10}$$

where $RDR = \Delta R / \Delta D$ is the robustness to distortion ratio. The GA with powerful capability of global searching [12] is then employed to solve the above optimization problem, which would generate an optimal embedding strength $\mathbf{B}$ for each vector tree $\mathbf{T}$ and the selected codeword $\mathbf{CW}$ under the above constraints.

For robust watermarking application, the mark embedded in each vector tree should be survived under the circumstances of deep attacks, especially in JPEG attack. In the interest of resisting JPEG attack, the process of JPEG attack simulation is incorporated with the GA to determine the embedding strength for each vector tree. According to [15], the quantization step Δ of different subbands at the same scale is the same for wavelet based image coding. Therefore, the quantization errors of those subbands at different QF of JPEG compression are also the same, which motivates the

process of JPEG simulation. Let vector $\bar{B} = \begin{bmatrix} \bar{b}_1 & \cdots & \bar{b}_{15} \end{bmatrix}^\tau$ represents the upper

bound for embedding strength in a GA process for a vector tree, the greater the bound $\bar{B}$ is, and the more robust the watermarking would be. And we take $\bar{b}_i = \alpha \cdot JND_i$, $\alpha \in [0.1, 3]$ in our simulation. For target JPEG QF, say JPEG 30, assume the variation of wavelet coefficient at scale 3 and 2 to be Δ_p and Δ_c, respectively. The simulation attack works as follows:

1. Let $t = 0$ and $\alpha_t = 0.1$. For a given vector tree $\mathbf{T}$, applying GA to generate the optimal embedding strength $\mathbf{B}_t$. Let r_p and r_c stand for the alterations of wavelet coefficients introduced by JPEG compression, and are set with $-\Delta_p$ and $-\Delta_c$, respectively.

2. Let $\mathbf{s} = \begin{bmatrix} s_i = \pm 1 \end{bmatrix}_{i=1\cdots3}$ be the 3-D random sign vector, which is used to increase the diversity of the attack simulation. The simulated coefficients for vector tree $\mathbf{T}_w$ under attack, i.e., $\mathbf{w}'_0 = \mathbf{w}_0 + r_p \cdot \mathbf{s}$ and $\mathbf{w}'_k = \mathbf{w}_k + r_c \cdot \mathbf{s}$, $(k = 1, \cdots, 4)$, which are then used to compute ΔR with (15).

3. If $\Delta R > 0$, then it passes the attack test in step 2. Set $r_p = r_p + step_p$ and $r_c = r_c + step_c$, where $step_c = step_p \cdot \Delta_c / \Delta_p$. And go to step 2 for further test until $r_p = \Delta_p$ and $r_c = \Delta_c$. Otherwise, set $\alpha_t = \alpha_t + step_\alpha$, $t = t+1$ and go to step 1 for next iteration until $\alpha_t = 3$.

As long as the above process is successfully completed, with high probability, $\mathbf{T}_w$ would survive all JPEG attacks by target JPEG QF. The computation complexity for the attack simulation is only $O(n)$, $n = 2r_p/step_p$. Also the feasibility and efficiency of the test are demonstrated in the experiments given in section 6.

Watermark Detection

For each constructed vector tree (refer to Fig.1), the LOT value is calculated for every codeword in C_0 and C_1, among which the one with max LOT value is taken as the detected codeword. And the corresponding coset index (0 or 1) is treated as the extracted message bit

5 Dirty-Paper Code Design

The 15-nodes vector in Fig.1 is used as the carrier for watermark message, and the codeword thus has 15 elements too. With m bits messages to be embedded into every tree, $M = 2^m$ cosets need to be constructed for dirty-paper coding, each of which has multiple codewords so that one can choose a best one according to the given carrier to obtain the optimal trade-off between the robustness and imperceptibility. To achieve this target, the codewords should be diverse enough so as to easily adapt to different carriers; on the other hand, the minimum distance among the different coset should be also kept as large as possible when considering the definition of LOT detector in (6) and (7) and in the interest of robust detection.

    As mentioned in previous section, the 15-element codeword can be divided into 5 independent sub-codewords $\mathbf{CW}(k)$ $(k = 0,1,\cdots,4)$ that corresponds to the vector node $\mathbf{w}_k$ $(k = 0,1,...,4)$, and thus the codeword can be independently designed based on $\mathbf{CW}(k)$. For the two-level vector tree shown in Fig.1, a hierarchical construction of the dirty-paper code is developed based on both the robustness analysis in [9] and the principles of dirty-paper coding. Codes from different coset are designed to have a relative large distance between the 3 code elements corresponding to the parent node $\mathbf{CW}(0)$, since the parent nodes in a vector tree would have more contribution to robust detection than their four children [9]. In addition, also based on the result in [9] and the principle of dirty-paper coding, a diversity configuration for the code elements corresponding to the children nodes would help to trade off the robustness and invisibility. Therefore, for the code elements corresponding to each four children with the same parent, two of them are set to be positive and others are negative as illustrated in Fig.1. The above two rules are employed in the process of dirty-paper code design.

    The proposed algorithm embeds 1 bit message to every 15-node vector tree. Therefore, two cosets C_0 and C_1 corresponding to message 0 and 1 are to be designed. Let N denotes the code number in each coset, and the dirty-paper code is constructed as follows:

1. For coset C_0, the sub-codeword $\mathbf{CW}(0)$ corresponding to parent nodes is set to be $\{-a - r_1 \quad -a - r_2 \quad a + r_3\}$; while for coset C_1 , the sub-code $\mathbf{CW}(0)$ is set to be $\{a + r_4 \quad a + r_5 \quad -a - r_6\}$, where a is positive integer and set as 1 in our design, and $r_i (i = 1\cdots 6)$ is random number in the range $(0,1)$;

2. The sub-codeword $\{CW(i)\}_{i=1\cdots4}$ correspond to the 4 children nodes at 3 orientations of the vector tree, as shown in Fig.1. The design rule of sub-code $\{CW(i)\}_{i=1\cdots4}$ for both coset C_0 and C_1 is same, i.e., two of them are set to be positive ($CW(1)$ and $CW(2)$) and others are negative ($CW(3)$ and $CW(4)$). For coset C_0, (1) $CW(1)$ and $CW(2)$ are set to be $\{a+r_7 \quad a+r_8 \quad a+r_9\}$ and $\{a+r_{10} \quad a+r_{11} \quad a+r_{12}\}$, respectively; and (2) $CW(3)$ and $CW(4)$ are set to be $\{-a-r_{13} \quad -a-r_{14} \quad -a-r_{15}\}$ and $\{-a-r_{16} \quad -a-r_{17} \quad -a-r_{18}\}$, respectively, where a is positive integer and set as 1 in our design, and $r_i(i=7\cdots18)$ is random number in the range $(0,1)$. The same design rule can be applied to $\{CW(i)\}_{i=1\cdots4}$ for coset C_1.

6   Experimental Results and Analysis

In our simulation, we test six *256*256*8b* gray level images with different texture, namely, Baboon, Boat, Einstein, F16, Harbor, and Lena. The images are decomposed with biorthogonal 9/7 wavelet into 3-level pyramid, among which the coarsest 2-level (scale=2 and 3) are used to construct vector trees. A 1024-bit random sequence is embedded with the related parameters set N=32 (coset size), $\Delta_p = 20$ and $\Delta_c = 60$. Fig. 4 shows the watermarked images.

Fig. 4. Watermarked image: (a) Baboon (PSNR=36.77dB, $D_{DWT} = 33.14$); (b) Boat (PSNR= 35.40dB, D_{DWT} =30.64); (c) Einstein (PSNR=37.19dB, D_{DWT} =27.44); (d) F16 (PSNR=36.10dB, D_{DWT} =25.40); (e) Harbor (PSNR= 36.50dB, D_{DWT} =29.36) (e) Lena (PSNR= 35.28dB, D_{DWT} =33.74)

We then investigate how the number of the codewords in a coset affects the performance of the proposed informed watermarking algorithm. In the simulation, we set the coset size N to be $1, 8, 16, 32$, and 64, and adjust D_{DWT} to be nearly same while keeping the other parameters invariant. Fig.5 gives the performance of the algorithm against JPEG attack for the images Boat and Lena, which show that the performance improves consistently as the number of code in the coset increases. It's observed that the performance in the case of multiple codewords has significant gain over that of only one codeword, which evidently demonstrates the benefits of dirty-paper coding. The simulation results also reveal the fact that the performance improvement is limited when $N > 16$, which suggests that the configuration of 32 codewords in a coset may be a reasonable trade-off between the performance and computation complexity. The similar results are observed for other test images.

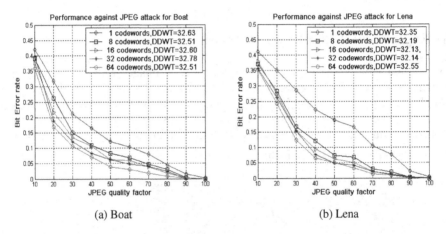

(a) Boat   (b) Lena

Fig. 5. Performance comparison in the case of $N=1, 8, 16, 32$, and 64

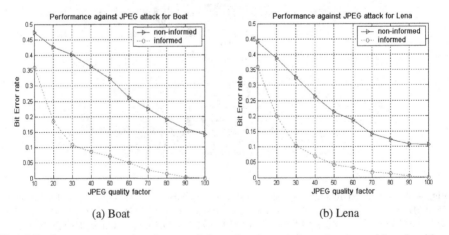

(a) Boat   (b) Lena

Fig. 6. Performance comparison between informed and non-informed watermarking algorithm against JPEG compression for test images Boat and Lena

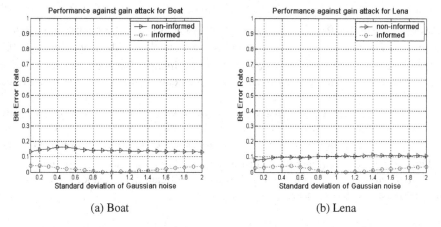

(a) Boat   (b) Lena

Fig. 7. Performance comparison between informed and non-informed watermarking algorithm against gain attacks for test images Boat and Lena

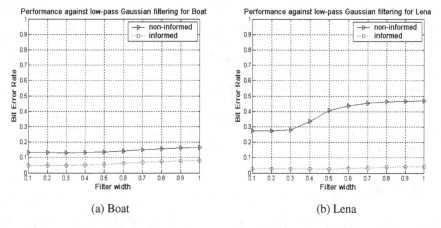

(a) Boat   (b) Lena

Fig. 8. Performance comparison between informed and non-informed watermarking algorithm against low-pass Gaussian filtering for test image Boat and Lena

To evaluate the feasibility of the proposed watermarking algorithm, we compare the performance of the proposed algorithm with the one in [9], which is also HMM based and among the state-of-the-art robust watermarking algorithm. For convenience, they are named as informed and non-informed watermarking algorithm, respectively. Out of impartiality, the same watermark message of 1024 bits is embedded into the images with each tree inserted with 1 bit, and the same D_{DWT} is set. The watermarked images in Fig.4 are attacked with JPEG compression by StirMark 4.0 [16-17]. Fig.6 gives the performance comparison between informed and non-informed watermarking algorithm against JPEG compression for test images Boat and Lena, where the significant performance gains are also observed.

The value-metric or gain attack means altering the amplitude of the cover, i.e., $I'(x, y) = \beta * I(x, y), \beta \in R^+$, which is a main weakness of lattice-based dirty paper coding [2]. The images Boat and Lena in Fig.4 are attacked with β varying from 0.1 to 2 and the results of watermark detection for test image Boat and Lena are given in Fig.7, where considerable performance improvements with the proposed informed watermarking algorithm are achieved.

Low-pass filtering attack is also tested with the informed watermarking algorithm and the non-informed one for test images in Fig.4 and the low-pass Gaussian filter of width σ_g varying from 0.1 to 1 is used. Performance comparison between informed and non-informed watermarking algorithm against low-pass Gaussian filtering for test image Boat and Lena are given in Fig.8, where significant performance gains with the informed one are also observed.

7   Conclusion

In this paper, we present a new informed image watermarking algorithm, which can achieve the information rate of 1/64 bits/pixel with high robustness. The HMM based LOT detector is developed to tackle the issue that the exact embedding strength is unavailable to the receiver when informed embedding strategy is employed. The LOT detector is then used to design the rules for dirty-paper code construction. The perceptual distance in wavelet domain is constructed to measure the fidelity of the watermarked image. The genetic algorithm is employed for joint coding and embedding optimization to trade-off the robustness and distortion constraints simultaneously. Extensive simulation results demonstrate that the proposed algorithm can achieve high watermarking capacity with high robustness against JPEG, Gaussian noise, gain attack and etc.

Acknowledgment

The authors appreciate the supports received from NSFC (60325208, 90604008, 60633030), 973 Program (2006CB303104), and NSF of Guangdong (04205407).

Reference

1. Cox, I.J., Miller, M.L., McKellips, A.L.: Watermarking as communications with side information. Proc. IEEE 87(7), 1127–1141 (1999)
2. Miller, M.L., Doerr, G.J., Cox, I.J.: Applying informed coding and embedding to design a robust, high capacity, watermark. IEEE Trans. Image Process 13(6), 792–807 (2004)
3. Abrardo, A., Barni, M.: Informed watermarking by means of orthogonal and quasi-orthogonal dirty paper coding. IEEE Trans. on Signal Processing 53(2), 824–833 (2005)
4. Moulin, P., O'Sullivan, J.A.: Information-theoretic analysis of information hiding. In: Proc. IEEE Int. Symp. Inf. Theory, Sorrento, Italy, p. 19 (June 2000)
5. Moulin, P.: The role of information theory in watermarking and its application to image watermarking. Signal Process 81(6), 1121–1139 (2001)

6. Cohen, A.S., Lapidoth, A.: The Gaussian watermarking game. IEEE Trans. Inf. Theory 48(6), 1639–1667 (2002)
7. Yu, W., Sutivong, A., Julian, D., Cover, T.M., Chiang, M.: Writing on colored paper. In: Proc. ISIT, June 24-29, 2001, Washington, DC (2001)
8. Costa, M.H.M.: Writing on dirty paper. IEEE Trans. Inf. Theory IT 29(3), 439–441 (1983)
9. Ni, J., Zhang, R., Huang, J., Wang, C.: HMM-based in wavelet domain robust multibit image watermarking algorithm. In: Barni, M., Cox, I., Kalker, T., Kim, H.J. (eds.) IWDW 2005. LNCS, vol. 3710, pp. 110–123. Springer, Heidelberg (2005)
10. Poor, H.V.: An introduction to signal detection and estimation. Springer, Heidelberg (1994)
11. Crouse, M.S., Nowak, R.D., Baraniuk, R.G.: Wavelet-Based Statistical Signal Processing Using Hidden Markov Models. IEEE Trans. on Signal Processing 46(4) (April 1998)
12. Mitsuo, G., Cheng, R.W.: Genetic algorithms and Engineering design. John Wiley & Sons Inc, New York (1997)
13. Watson, B.: DCT quantization matrices optimized for individual images. Human Vision, Visual Processing, and Digital Display IV SPIE-1913, 202–216 (1993)
14. Ni, J., Wang, C., Huang, J.: Performance enhancement for DWT-HMM image watermarking with content-adaptive approach. In: Proc. of ICIP 2006, pp. 1377–1380 (2006)
15. Chen, J., et al.: Scalar quantization noise analysis and optimal bit allocation for wavelet pyramid image coding. IEICE Trans. Fundamental E76-A, 1502–1504 (1993)
16. Petitcolas, F.A.P.: Watermarking schemes evaluation. IEEE Trans. on Signal Processing 17(5), 58–64 (2000)
17. StirMark. http://www.cl.cam.ac.uk/ fapp2/watermarking/stirmark/

A Graph Game Model for Software Tamper Protection

Nenad Dedić[*], Mariusz Jakubowski[**], and Ramarathnam Venkatesan[***]

Abstract. We present a probabilistic program-transformation algorithm to render a given program tamper-resistant. In addition, we suggest a model to estimate the required effort for an attack. We make some engineering assumptions about local indistinguishability on the transformed program and model an attacker's steps as making a walk on the program flow graph. The goal of the attacker is to learn what has been inserted by the transformation, in which case he wins. Our heuristic estimate counts the number of steps of his walk on the graph. Our model is somewhat simplified, but we believe both the constructions and models can be made more realistic in the future.

1 Introduction

In this paper, we consider the problem of protecting a complex program against tampering. The results of [3,11] mean that we cannot hope to solve this in general, namely in a model involving worst-case programs and polynomial-time adversaries. Hence it is natural to ask for practical solutions in some natural model with limited attacks. Here the hard problem is in building an appropriate model. A careful look at well known attacks (see overview in Section 3) and effects of program-transformation tools on local program properties (e.g., how homogeneous the code looks over 50 lines of assembly code) allows us to propose a security model of various protection schemes, based on some assumptions.

Our overall approach is as follows. First, we take a given program P and convert this into another program P', where we inject new code that modifies the control and data flow graphs by adding nodes and edges. The goal of the attacker is to find the new additions, and we would grant the attacker victory if he does this reliably. Thus, we specify a formal model by defining a game where the attacker's moves correspond to various attempts to break the protection, and the attacker's victory corresponds to a break. In the present state of software protection, models based on complexity theory offer mainly negative results [3,11], with a handful of positive results that essentially formalize hash-based comparisons [12,18]. Motivated by an assortment of heuristic techniques for tamper protection, we give a simplified model, which captures realistic scenarios and allows quantitative analysis of tamper-resistance. Our model makes

---

[*] Computer Science Department, Boston University. nenad@cs.bu.edu. Part of this work was done during internships at Microsoft Research (Redmond, WA).

[**] Microsoft Research (Redmond, WA). mariuszj@microsoft.com

[***] Microsoft Research (Redmond, WA and Bangalore, India). venkie@microsoft.com

T. Furon et al. (Eds.): IH 2007, LNCS 4567, pp. 80–95, 2007.

engineering assumptions about local indistinguishability of small code fragments and provides a lower bound on the attack effort required.

An adversary who tries to reverse-engineer and eventually "crack" the program is typically equipped with some software tools that allow him to analyze the static structure of the program, and execute it in some controlled way. It seems very difficult to design a scheme that transforms *any* program into a semantically equivalent one, but which is protected against malicious changes.

2   Our Approach

The rest of this article is structured as follows, with a main goal of motivating the model and an algorithm for protection.

1. An overview of known tamper-protection techniques and attacks.
2. A randomized algorithm for tamper-proofing complex programs.
3. A graph-game-based model of an attacker's interaction with programs.
4. Lower bounds on an attacker's resources to break the protected program.

Our approach involves inserting k *local tamper-detection checks* in the program. Each check is responsible for detecting tampering in a small portion of the program, consisting of s program fragments. At least f checks are required to fail before a tamper response is triggered, thus we have a *threshold tamper response*. Next we make use of *homogenizing transformations*. They a given program into a semantically equivalent one, but such that local observations (those confined to instruction sequences of length at most b) can be assumed to reveal no useful patterns.

Neither of the above methods offers sufficient security if used alone. The task of our algorithm is to inject the local checks in a randomized way, create the threshold tamper response and perform program homogenization.

We then show a model which we believe captures most of practical attacks against our method. This model does not necessarily cover tamper-protection schemes based on different ideas. Finally, relying on certain conjectures, we show some lower bounds on attacks. Some aspects and components of our algorithm have been implemented and studied in practice for the viability of our models and assumptions. This article presents a first effort in formalizing them. We believe that our methods can be further refined, and heuristic estimates on attack complexity can be made more realistic.

3   Some Typical Protection Schemes and Attacks

Our model is aimed at capturing most practical attacks. Its viewpoint involves forcing an attacker into learning and playing a graph game, whose winning strategy has a lower bound in the number of game steps under suitable assumptions. These come down to some engineering assumptions about certain code transformations, which we believe can be made to hold with further research. To justify this model and provide context, we survey prevalent tamper-protection techniques and attacks. We start from the easiest, which offer least security, and proceed to more sophisticated ones. We denote the program to be protected by P and the attacker by A.

3.1   Single-Point License Check

P is protected by adding a subroutine L which verifies some condition, such as a correct digital signature validating its authenticity or a license. L is called from other parts of P, and normal operation is resumed only if L returns "true".

   Attack. Using simple control flow analysis, A can identify L. A then patches L to return only "true".

3.2   Distributed License Check

To thwart the previous attack, L is broken into pieces or copied with some variations, additionally obfuscated, which are spread throughout P.

   Attack. A can make a preliminary guess for the location of one copy of L. A's goal now is to find the locations where variations of L or its components may be scattered. Robust binary matching tools such as [17] can be used to identify other copies of L. Other attacks use flow graph analysis. That is, A computes the flow graph of G. The guessed copy of L induces a subgraph H. A copy of L elsewhere in the program induces a subgraph similar to H, and it can be found via subgraph embedding. Another flow graph based attack uses the fact that typically, the code corresponding to L is a component which is weakly connected to the rest of G. After identification, A can patch the calls to L. These attacks are considerably advanced in comparison in terms of the tools needed to implement them in practice.

3.3   Code Checksums and Integrity-Verification Kernels

Tampering can be detected during runtime by loading code segments, and computing checksums. P runs only if they agree with precomputed values [2].

   Attack. The task of loading a code segment for reading is an unusual occurrence in typical programs, and can be trapped. Using some hardware support, more generic attacks on code-checksum schemes are described in [15]. Unusual execution patterns (read accesses to code segment, paging faults) can be exploited.

3.4   Oblivious Hashing

Consider a program fragment F that uses some set of variables X. For an assignment x to variables X, *execution trace* $e(x)$ is the sequence of all values of X during execution of $F(x)$. Oblivious hashing [4] is a method whereby for a subset of variables $Z \subseteq X$, $F(x)$ produces a hash $h_Z(e(x))$. For suitably chosen random inputs r, tampering with values of Z during execution of $F(r)$ will produce e' for which $h_Z(e') \neq h_Z(e(r))$ with high probability. OH can be used to detect code tampering. It is resistant to the attacks of [15] because the code segment is never read or used as data, and calls used to compute OH cannot be easily separated from regular calls.

Attack. If correct values of $h(e)$ are precomputed and stored for test inputs, then A may discover these values, since they may look special or random (see Subsections 3.8, 3.9). If one uses $h(t)$ indirectly (to encrypt some important variables) or computes $h(t)$ during runtime using a duplicate code segment, then without sufficient precaution, A can attack via program analysis. Methods for addressing these attacks are discussed in this paper.

3.5 Anti-disassembly and Diversity

Here an attacker converts a released executable into assembly so that it can be understood, using a disassembler which itself may have built-in graph-analysis tools [7]. A defense would be to cause incorrect disassembly by exploiting different instruction lengths to cause ambiguity involving data and code. At best one can cause a handful of attempts to disassemble, but it is unlikely using only these that one can force a significant number of runs of the disassembler. More flexibility is offered by virtualization and individualization [1], where the idea is to force A into learning a new virtual machine (VM) for attacking each copy. An instance I of the program P is implemented as a (V_I, P_I), where V_I is a virtual machine and P_I is code which implements P under VM V_I. To execute the instance I, one has to run $V_I(P_I)$. Disassembling is difficult because A does not have the specification of V_I. Furthermore, even if A disassembles (V_I, P_I), this is of little help in disassembling (V_J, P_J) for $I \neq J$, because of instance randomization.

Attack. The scheme is open to attacks which do not rely on detailed understanding of P_I. In a *copy attack*, A tampers with P_I and then learns which code is responsible for the resulting crash: It saves program state s before some suspect branch, and tries multiple execution paths from s. If most of these paths end up crashing in the same place, then it must be some previous branch that is causing the crash. A can now make a new guess and repeat the attack.

3.6 Defense Against Copy Attacks

A defense against the above attack involves *distributed tamper-detection checks* and *threshold tamper-protection scheme*. Distributed tamper-detection check is embedded in s program fragments $F_1, \ldots, F_s$, and it has a chance p of failing if each of $F_1, \ldots, F_s$ is tampered with. To disable a check, the attacker must identify all s code fragments $F_1, \ldots, F_s$. Threshold tamper-protection scheme embeds k checks in the program, and it causes the program to crash (or initiates some other security response, such as performance degradation or disabling features) only after at least f checks fail.

These two techniques make it difficult for the attacker to locate the protection scheme without detailed examination of the code and careful debugging. Additional ideas can be used to increase the security, for example delaying the crash even after f checks have failed.

Attack. A can reduce size of the search space by using control- and data-flow analysis.

3.7   Program-Analysis Tools

Against static control-flow analysis, the idea is to make the control-flow graph look like a complete graph. Computed jumps and opaque predicates can be used for this. A computed jump explicitly calculates the jump-target address, and this calculation can be obfuscated. Similarly, an opaque predicate [6] calculates the value of a predicate in an obfuscated way. Sufficiently strong obfuscation can reduce the usefulness of control-flow analysis.

Against data-flow analysis, the idea is to make the dependency graph of k variables look like a complete graph on k nodes. A should gain no useful information about dependencies of those variables. Lightweight encryption (LWE) can be used for this.

3.8   Unusual-Code-Detection Attacks

Certain transformations used in program protection can introduce unusual code patterns. For example XOR and other arithmetic instructions are less often used, but a protection mechanism or (light-weight) encryption may use them often, where they can be spotted by localized frequency counts of such opcodes. Semantics-preserving peephole transformations or adding chaff code can be used to make code appear more uniform. Iteration and randomization can be used to diffuse well.

3.9   Randomness Detection Attacks

Some protection mechanisms may embed encrypted code segments, which may make them vulnerable to attacks of [13]. This attack was designed to find high-entropy sections, such as cryptographic keys that may contain 1024 bits. To prevent code attacks, near-clear encryption of code may be used (by transforming a code fragment into another one that still looks like valid code). Protection of data segments against such attacks involves keeping all data in an encrypted-randomized form.

3.10   Secure-Hardware Oblivious Execution of Arbitrary Programs

In the scheme of [10], P is converted into P' whose data access pattern is completely random. In each step, a fresh random address is accessed, and a random value is written to it. The scheme offers very good security guarantees, but is impractical. For a program of size n, it suffers a $\log^2(n)$ overhead in running time, and because of random data access, locality of reference is lost.

By relaxing the notion of obliviousness [16] to an attacker's inability to narrow down the location of a variable observed in memory location at time $t = 0$ after $t = T$, one may restore locality of reference for some data-structure operations. This oblivious data structure also requires hardware, but may be simulated by software in practice. While this opens new attacks, defenses may use all the methods discussed in this paper, enabling a modular approach to designing protection systems.

4   The Protection Algorithm

At a high level, our protection scheme works as follows. Let P be the program which we wish to protect. Suppose that there is some programmer-specified *critical code* L. L returns a boolean output, indicating some condition required for proper program execution (such as validity of a license). However, L need not implement any otherwise useful functionality of P. Our goal is to link L and P so that P executes properly only if L returns "true" despite tampering attacks. The protection algorithm proceeds in phases:

Critical code replication and embedding. L is replicated into l copies $L_1, \ldots, L_l$. Each copy L_i is embedded into P, so that if L_i returns "false", then P is corrupted or terminated. This phase could require significant manual intervention: Specifying suitable points where L_i can be embedded could require programmers' insight into code.

Graph transformation. P is transformed suitably, so that we can assume that its flow graph can be adequately modeled as a random regular graph, and program executions look like random walks.

Check insertion. k checks $C_1, \ldots, C_k$ are randomly inserted into P. Each C_i locally checks for untampered execution.

Creating dependencies. P is transformed so that it crashes when a subset of f checks fails.

4.1   Primitives

We base our scheme on the existence of certain primitives. No single primitive suffices to achieve security against tampering. They must be used in conjunction to ensure adequate protection, and a meaningful model in which a security analysis is possible. Ideas that demonstrate plausibility of those primitives will be briefly mentioned, but a detailed discourse is beyond the scope of this paper. We believe that it is possible, with sufficient research effort, to implement them with satisfactory security.

Flow graph transformation. Our protection algorithm requires some way to change P into a functionally equivalent Q whose flow graph G has the following property. An execution of P cannot avoid any substantial (i.e., constant) fraction of nodes of G for too long (except with small probability). The precise formalization and quantification of these statements depend on the system parameters and desired security level, and some analysis will be given later in the text.

Roughly, we will assume that G can be modeled by an expander graph, and that P's execution resembles a random walk on G as much as possible (even when tampered by the attacker). We assume that there is a function $(V, E) =$ GraphTransform(P, n) that returns a program Q whose flow graph is a good expander graph of n nodes with the above properties.

This transformation can be approximately achieved by combining various obfuscating transformations, such as code replication, diversification and overlapping [1]; opaque constructs [6]; and data and control-flow randomization [5].

We will assume that the program is partitionied, where the partion is given by sets of flow graph nodes $F_1, \ldots, F_n$. By picking n properly and assuming the sizes of F_i's are approximately the same, we will assume that the flow graph induced by this partition is an expander graph.

Checks. A check C is specified by s code fragments $F_1, \ldots, F_s$. If some F_i is tampered, then with probability $\mathsf{p_{detect}}$ it will be *triggered*. If all of $F_1, \ldots, F_s$ are triggered, then the check C *fails*. We assume that the attacker cannot prevent the check failing, unless he identifies all $C_1, \ldots, C_s$. Let $C =$ InsertCheck$(F_1, \ldots, F_s)$ denote the function that produces a check C given code fragments $F_1, \ldots, F_s$. A brief outline of a possible check implementation follows.

Tampered code can be triggered using integrity verification kernels (IVK). If IVKs are implemented using oblivious hashing, then runtime tampering is detected and registered as an incorrectly computed hash value. For example, to insert a triggering mechanism in F_i, one embeds oblivious-hash computation in F_i, resulting in a hash value h_i. Some correct values h_i^* can be precomputed (or h_i can be compared against the hash of a copy of F_i elsewhere in the program). Suppose correct h_i^* are precomputed. To ensure that C fails only after all of $F_1, \ldots, F_s$ are triggered, some other code could compute the product $(h_1 - h_1^*) \cdot \cdots (h_s - h_s^*)$. This product can be nonzero only if all the hash values are incorrect. Product computation should, of course, be obfuscated. Appropriate action can be taken, depending on whether the product is zero. [4,2]

Check detection-response. We assume that check failures can be detected, and a response can be effected after some programmer-specified subset of checks has failed. More precisely, suppose k checks $C_1, \ldots, C_k$ are installed. The programmer will specify the *response structure* – a set R whose elements are subsets of checks (so R contains elements x, where each $x \subseteq \{C_1, \ldots, C_k\}$). The response will be triggered only upon failure of a subset of checks $y \subseteq \{C_1, \ldots, C_k\}$, such that $x \subseteq y$ for some $x \in R$.

For a detailed account on a possible check response implementation refer to [14]. We note here that their implementation provides for tampering response after a specified number f of checks fail. Let us denote the corresponding response structure by $R_f(C_1, \ldots, C_k)$. Then $x \in R_f(C_1, \ldots, C_k) \iff x \subseteq \{C_1, \ldots, C_k\} \wedge |x| = f)$. A practical advantage of their approach is is that the response is well separated both temporally and spatially from the checks that cause it.

We will denote with InsertResponse$(P, (C_1, \ldots, C_k), f)$ the function which transforms the program P into P' with the response structure $R_f(C_1, \ldots, C_k)$.

Critical code embedding. We assume that, given some program fragment F, it is possible to embed the critical code L into F as follows. The resulting code F' will execute L. If L returns "true", then F' behaves functionally identically to F. Otherwise F' executes some other programmer-specified action. This embedding could be as simple as: *if $L = true$ then run F else quit*. In practice, however, it is desirable to use obfuscation and individualized instances of L, to make it more difficult to circumvent L. We will denote with CodeEntangle(L, F) the function which returns F' as described above.

4.2   Protection Algorithm

```
Harden(P, L, l, n, k, s, f):
    Flow graph transformation:
        let G = (V, E) ← GraphTransform(P, n)
    Critical code embedding and replication:
        select at random a subset U ⊆ V with |U| = l
        for each v ∈ U do
            v ← CodeEntangle(L, v)
    Check embedding:
        for i = 1 to k do
            select at random v_1, ..., v_s ∈ V
            C_i = InsertCheck(v_1, ..., v_s)
    Creating tampering response:
        InsertResponse(G, (C_1, ..., C_k), f)
```

4.3   Design Goals of Tamper Protection

Before elaborating our model and analysis, we identify desirable properties of a tamper-protection scheme. We believe that our scheme, when instantiated with secure primitives, satisfies those properties. Our model and analysis serve to validate these intuitions.

Tampering response. An obvious goal is to cause improper program operation if tampering is detected. For brevity we will call this a *crash*, but we note that it need not be an actual program crash – it could be slow or unreliable operation, disabling some features, or generally any graceful degradation of program operation.

Thwarting local attacks. The attacker A should gain no information based only on local modifications and observations. For example, changing a single register could result in a crash soon after the change, and A could easily understand how the crash is caused. If tamper-protection is causing it, this provides vital clues to bypassing the protection.

Require multiple failed checks. A secure protection scheme triggers a response only after some minimal number f of checks fails. This makes the task of locating individual checks more difficult.

Hard global analysis. The protection scheme should be embedded as a random structure R in the flow graph G, and discovering R should be necessary for bypassing the protection. A should be able to obtain information about R only through observing walks on G and crashes. Observing the exact memory contents should give no significant advantage to A.

4.4   On Different Security Models

We wish to obtain lower bounds on the complexity of successful attacker A, and quantify them in terms of running time, memory or some other complexity measure. Broadly speaking, there are three approaches:

- *Information-theory*-based approach does not bound the resources of an adversary, but limits the number of probes or input-output queries to a function that is presumed to be a random function.

  Our model is akin to this. If our assumptions hold in practice, then what we derive is a probability bound that an adversary who makes so many probes running the program can learn all the edges he needs to break the system.

- *Complexity-theory* approach considers resource-bounded adversaries, and bases the security of a system on a problem that is intractable. As in cryptography, the instances are picked under some probability distribution.

  The fundamental difficulty in using this approach here is that the program P given to us may be developed by a vast community of programmers, and can only be altered minimally before running into objectionable performance. In particular, the instances do not admit a probabilistic generation model; if we are to base it on graph-theoretic models, no graph problem is known that can be attractive for cryptography, either.

- *Customized constructions* for secure hash and stream ciphers base their security on the best attacks known to the community (DES/AES/SHA-1).

5   Our Model

The model is motivated by practical considerations, namely the available implementations of primitives and currently known attacks and some foreseeable extensions. Denote the protected version of the program by Q, its flow graph by G, the critical code by L, and the attacker by A.

On the one hand, we have A equipped with various tools, including debuggers, data- and control-flow analyzers, graph tools, etc. A is capable of inspecting the code statically and observing its behaviour dynamically. A is also capable of *static tampering* (i.e., changing the code) or *dynamic tampering* (i.e., changing the state of a running program). All of these can be done manually or automated – e.g., using sophisticated programmable debuggers and program-analysis algorithms. A's goal is to ensure that Q runs correctly, even if the critical code L fails.

On the other hand we have the program Q, with critical code L replicated at many locations in Q, and various code-obfuscation transformations applied. If these transformations are secure, then local observations of Q should yield little useful information. Code-obfuscation techniques can make understanding small windows of code difficult. Data-flow obfuscation makes understanding the state of the running program difficult. Flow graph transformations ensure that the flow graph mimics a random graph, with good connectivity between nodes. Fake calls and random calls to replicated code make the execution appear like a random walk on the flow graph. Checks detect tampering, but based on local observations, it is difficult to tell apart checking code from regular code, and check variables from normal ones. Check response is triggered only after sufficiently many checks fail, making the task of pinpointing any check more difficult.

Above we stated some observations and desiderata regarding the protected program and the attacks. We distill them into the following idealized assumptions:

1. Execution of the program induces a random walk on the flow graph at the appropriate level of granularity of clustering the flow graph.
2. Observations restricted to small areas make local variables and code appear to have random values.
3. Tampering local variables or code causes corresponding inserted checks to fail.
4. A sufficient number of failed checks causes the program to crash.
5. In order to prevent the execution of a check, all the locations of variables and code from which the check is initiated need to be identified (e.g., a jump occurs from these locations into the checking code, possibly via computed jumps).

These are indeed simplified idealizations, but we believe that as the implementations of primitives become more secure, or suitable secure hardware is used, the assumptions become closer to reality. Under these assumptions, an attack on a program can be modeled as a game played on the flow graph G of Q.

Informally the game looks as follows. It is played on the flow graph $G = (V, E)$ of Q. A subset U of nodes contains instances of critical code. There are checks $C_1, \ldots, C_k \subseteq V$ in it, each of them consisting of s nodes. Certain subsets of checks are designated as dangerous (the activation structure R contains those dangerous subsets of checks). The attacker A runs Q, and the execution corresponds to a walk on G consisting of independent random steps. In each step A can either tamper with the current node, or leave it alone. A wins the game if he can run the program for at least N steps (N is the parameter), with the following restrictions: (1) Every node that contains the critical code must be tampered; and (2) the program must not crash.

Checks prevent A from winning this game trivially in the following way. Tampering is detected with probability p_{detect}. A check fails if all its nodes detect tampering. The program crashes when the set of failed checks contains some dangerous set of checks; A should then restart the program; else he cannot win. Finally, the attacker can also try to remove a check: He makes a guess

$C = \{v_1, \ldots, v_s\}$, and if $C = C_i$ for some i, then the check C_i becomes effectively disabled – it will no longer fail even if its nodes detect tampering.

Game 1.
BreakingGame($G = (V, E)$, v_0, U, $(C_1, \ldots, C_k)$, R, p, N):

Definitions and terminology. $v_0 \in V$ is called the *entry point*. $U \subseteq V$ is called the *critical code*. $C_i \subseteq V$ ($|C_i| = s$) are called *checks*. R is called the *response structure* and it is a set whose elements are subsets of V (i.e., $x \in R \implies x \subseteq V$). $p \in [0, 1]$ and $N \in \mathbb{N}$ are called the *tamper detection probability*, and the *required running time*, respectively.

Game state. The game state is of the form (Act, T, curr, time, steps, crash), and its components are called *activated check set, tampered node set, current node, running time, step counter* and *crash flag*, respectively.

Game description.

    Initial game state. Initial game state is set as follows: Act $= \{C_1, \ldots, C_k\}$, $T = \emptyset$, curr $= v_0$, time $= 0$ and steps $= 0$.

    Game moves. The game proceeds in *steps*, until the player wins or quits. In each step, the player chooses one of the following moves:

        RUN. If curr $\in U$ and curr $\notin T$ then crash $\leftarrow 1$. time $\leftarrow$ time $+ 1$. curr is replaced by its random neighbour in G.

        TAMPER. With probability p, curr is added to the set of tampered nodes T. time $\leftarrow$ time $+ 1$. curr is replaced by its random neighbour in G.

        GUESS($v_1, \ldots, v_s$). If $\{v_1, \ldots, v_s\} = C_i$ for some i, then C_i is removed from the activated check set Act.

        RESET. The game state is reset as follows: $T = \emptyset$, curr $= v_0$, time $= 0$ and crash $= 0$.

        QUIT. The game ends. The attacker loses.

    Before the next step, the game state is updated as follows. steps $\leftarrow$ steps $+ 1$. If there is a set of checks $C_{i_1}, \ldots, C_{i_m}$ such that $C_{i_1}, \ldots, C_{i_m} \subseteq T$ and $\{C_{i_1}, \ldots, C_{i_m}\} \cap$ Act $\in R$, then crash $\leftarrow 1$. If time $> N$ and crash $= 0$ then the attacker wins the game. Otherwise he gets to play the next step.

Note that the sequence of nodes visited between two consecutive RESET moves is a walk on G. Thus, we call the walk that occurs between $(i - 1)$-st and i-th reset moves *i-th walk of the game*.

6   Security Analysis

We now consider some statistical attacks on this scheme. To get a more transparent analysis, we will use specific settings of scheme parameters. The analyses indicate that, for these settings, attacks take time exponential in check size s.

Throughout this section we use the following notation. If $W = (v_1, \ldots, v_t)$ is a walk on some graph, we write W^s to denote $\{v_1, \ldots, v_t\}^s$. When no confusion is possible, we write W to denote $\{v_1, \ldots, v_t\}$.

6.1   Case Study: Dense Critical Code, Perfect Checks

1. $U = V$: all nodes of G contain the critical code L,
2. $p = 1$: tampering is detected with certainty,
3. $k = cn$ for some $c > 0$: there are cn checks in the program,
4. threshold $f = cn/2$: half the checks must fail to trigger the response,
5. $N = n^{1+d}$: a succesful attack must run for at least n^{1+d} steps.

Let I_n denote the set of all $((V, E), v_0, V, (C_1, \ldots, C_{cn}), R, 1, n^{1+d})$ where the following hold. (V, E) is an expander graph with $\lambda_2 \leq 1/2$ and $|V| = n$. Every $C_i \subset V$ contains exactly s nodes. $R = \{C_1, \ldots, C_{cn}\}^{cn/2}$, i.e., R contains all $cn/2$-element subsets of $\{C_1, \ldots, C_{cn}\}$. v_0 is arbitrary.

Then by construction, the uniform distribution on I_n is exactly the distribution of BreakingGame instances which correspond to the output of the protection algorithm Harden. We consider two simple attacker's strategies and analyze the expected effort, over random choice of game instance from I_n, and random walks that take place in the game.

Voting attack. This attack is based on the following idea. Let $X = (v_1, \ldots, v_s) \in V^s$ be some choice of s nodes. Suppose A runs the program and tampers it until it crashes, and let $Z = \{v_1, \ldots, v_t\}$ be the corresponding set of tampered nodes. Define $p(X) = \Pr[X \in Z^s]$, the probability that all nodes of X are tampered. We assume, favouring the attacker, that for most check assignments this probability will be concentrated in checks, i.e., there is some δ so that for any check C_i and any non-check $X = (v_1, \ldots, v_s)$, $p(C_i) - p(X) > \delta > 0$. This in particular means that checks are more likely to show up in Z than any other choice of s nodes. A could use this margin to isolate the checks, in the following simple attack.

initialize an s-dimensional $n \times n \times \cdots \times n$ array B to zeros
    (*B will store votes for each* $(v_1, \ldots, v_s) \in V^s$)
for $i = 1$ to $1/\delta^2$ do
    run A and tamper with it arbitrarily; let W be the set of tampered nodes
    for each $(v_1, \ldots, v_s) \in W$ do
        set $B[v_1, \ldots, v_s] \leftarrow B[v_1, \ldots, v_s] + 1$ (*add one vote for* $(v_1, \ldots, v_s)$)
find the n entries of B with most votes and output their addresses

The complexity of this attack is at least $\Omega(n^s)$. Indeed, barring exponentially unlikely events, each round produces a walk of length at least $n - 2n/s$ (else by Theorem 1 below, too few checks fail for the program to crash). A must now update $(n - 2n/s)^s \approx n^s/e^2$ entries in the array, so this is the least time he needs to spend. Note that this does not even depend on the margin δ. It could be quite big and the above attack would still be too expensive.

Intersection attack. The goal of this attack is to find any single check. A plays m rounds and obtains the walks $W_1, \ldots, W_m$. A hopes that there is at least one check C that fails in each walk $W_1, \ldots, W_m$, and tries to find that check. C obviously shows up in every W_i; i.e., $C \in B := (W_1 \cap \cdots \cap W_m)^s$. A's search space is thus reduced to B, and he can inspect every candidate from B until he finds C. This strategy, however, takes $n^{\Omega(s)}$ work on average, as indicated below.

By Theorem 1, $1 - 1/(2s) > |W_i|/n > 1 - 2/s$ (with prob. $1 - e^{-O(n)}$). For this simplified analysis, assume that W_i consist of independently drawn samples from V. The expected size of $\cap_{i=1}^m W_i$ is lower bounded by $(1 - 2/s)^m$. Therefore $\mathsf{E}B > n^s(1 - 2/s)^m s \approx n^s e^{-2m}$. Furhtermore $\Pr[C \in W_i]$ by $(|W_i|/n)^s$, so $\Pr[C \in \cap_{i=1}^m W_i] \leq (|W_i|/n)^{sm} \leq (1 - 1/(2s))^{sm} \approx e^{-m/2}$. Therefore, to get success probability ϵ, the attacker must set $m < 2 \log \epsilon$. But then his work (i.e., the size of B) is at least $n^s e^{-2m} > n^s \epsilon^4$.

6.2   Other Parameter Settings and Models

A more practical setting is the one where $U \subset V$ and $0 < p < 1$; i.e., critical code is distributed only through a fraction of the program code, and checks have a chance to miss tampering. In this case, the algorithm Harden should be modified to insert checks only in U. Using some random walk lemmas (see for example [9]) and techniques similar to those of the previous section, one can prove similar lower bounds. We do not provide details in this article.

In a more realistic model, the attack game can be changed to allow A to choose some steps in the walk, instead of just passively observing them. One could for example let A choose every other step adversarially. If A's strategy is non-adaptive (i.e., each adversarial step depends only on the current node), then the results of [8] can be used to analyze attack complexity, and derive bounds similar to those of the previous section. We do not provide any details in this article.

7   Conclusion and Future Work

This article presented a new graph-based framework for modeling and implementing specific tamper-resistance algorithms. Our scheme may yield practical program-transformation tools to harden software against malicious patching and interference. A crucial improvement over today's "ad hoc" protection methods is an attack-resistance model, which can help estimate how long particular protected applications will remain unbroken in practice. This is important in various business scenarios (e.g., DRM and software licensing), where measurable attack resistance can prevent unexpected breaches and enforce a consistent revenue stream.

Future work will involve making our models and assumptions more realistic, as well as performing more implementation and experimental verification. Upcoming efforts will study the exact theoretical resistance offered by our algorithms, and also develop new algorithms along similar lines. We note that theoretical impossibility results on obfuscation [3,11] do not pose roadblocks to development of such algorithms, because the attack resistance we require need not be exponential or even superpolynomial. As long as our techniques can predict such resistance (or lack thereof) accurately for typical programs, our approach should be useful in practice.

A Graph Lemmas

Lemma 1. *Consider a walk W which tampers $t = n - n/2s$ distinct nodes. Then:*

1. *Expected number of failed checks is $cn/\sqrt{e} + \epsilon(s)$ for some $\epsilon(s) \in o(s)$.*
2. *For $1 - e^{-O(n)}$ fraction of check assignments, the number of failed checks is at least $0.5cn$.*

Proof. Let $T \subseteq V$ be the set of tampered nodes. Denote $\mu = |T|/|V| = t/n$. Let p be the probability that a randomly chosen check $C = (v_1, \ldots, v_s)$ is contained in T. For sufficiently large s, we have $p = \mu^s = (1 - 1/2s)^s \approx 1/\sqrt{e}$.

1. There are cn checks, so the expected number of checks contained in T is cnp and this converges to $cn/\sqrt{e} > 0.6cn$ as $n \to \infty$.
2. Applying a Chernoff bound, one gets that the number of failed checks is exponentially unlikely to fall below $0.5cn$.

Lemma 2. *Consider a walk W which tampers at most $t = n - 2n/s$ distinct nodes. For $1 - e^{-O(n)}$ fraction of check assignments, the number of failed checks is at most $cn/4$.*

Proof. Let T, μ and p be as in the proof of Lemma 1. Then $p = \mu^s = (1-2/s)^s = ((1-2/s)^{(s/2)})^2$. For sufficiently large s we have $p \approx 1/e^2$. The expected number of failed checks is thus cn/e^2, and using a Chernoff bound one gets that at most $cn/4$ checks fail, except with probability $1 - e^{-O(n)}$.

It is easy to do a "quantifier switch" to make the probabilities of Lemmas 1,2 over random walks, using the following simple lemma.

Lemma 3 (Pigeonhole principle variant). *Let $I(a, b)$ $(a \in A, b \in B)$ be a 0-1 matrix. Let $p_b = \Pr_{a \in A}[I(a, b) = 1]$ and let $p = \Pr_{(a,b) \in A \times B}[I(a, b) = 1]$. If $p \leq \epsilon$ then*

$$\Pr_{b \in B}[p_b \geq \sqrt{\epsilon}] \leq \sqrt{\epsilon}.$$

Using Lemma 3, Lemmas 1,2 and taking into account that $U = V$, it is easy to show:

Theorem 1. *For $1 - e^{-O(n)}$ fraction of check assignments the following hold:*

1. *$1 - e^{-O(n)}$ fraction of walks shorter than $n - 2n/s$ do not crash.*
2. *for any constant $d > 0$, $1 - e^{-O(n)}$ fraction of walks longer than n^{1+d} crash.*

Proof. The first claim follows directly from Lemma 2. For the second claim, note that a random walk of length n^{1+d} covers G with probability $1 - e^{-O(n)}$. Therefore the subset U of nodes containing the critical code is covered. To avoid crashing due to untampered execution of critical code, the attacker must tamper with every node on the walk. So more than $n - n/2s$ nodes are tampered, and by Lemma 1 the walk with probability $1 - e^{-O(n)}$.

References

1. Anckaert, B., Jakubowski, M., Venkatesan, R.: Proteus: Virtualization for diversified tamper-resistance. In: Kurosawa, K., Safavi-Naini, R., Yung, M. (eds.) Proceedings of the Sixth ACM Workshop on Digital Rights Management, pp. 47–57. ACM Press, New York (2006)
2. Aucsmith, D.: Tamper resistant software: An implementation. In: Proceedings of the First International Workshop on Information Hiding, London, UK, pp. 317–333. Springer, Heidelberg (1996)
3. Barak, B., Goldreich, O., Impagliazzo, R., Rudich, S., Sahai, A., Vadhan, S., Yang, K.: On the (im)possibility of obfuscating programs. In: Kilian, J. (ed.) CRYPTO 2001. LNCS, vol. 2139, pp. 1–18. Springer, Heidelberg (2001), http://www.wisdom.weizmann.ac.il/boaz/Papers/obfuscate.ps
4. Chen, Y., Venkatesan, R., Cary, M., Pang, R., Sinha, S., Jakubowski, M.H.: Oblivious hashing: A stealthy software integrity verification primitive. In: Petitcolas, F.A.P. (ed.) IH 2002. LNCS, vol. 2578, pp. 400–414. Springer, Heidelberg (2003)
5. Collberg, C., Thomborson, C., Low, D.: Breaking abstractions and unstructuring data structures. In: International Conference on Computer Languages, pp. 28–38 (1998)
6. Collberg, C., Thomborson, C., Low, D.: Manufacturing cheap, resilient, and stealthy opaque constructs. In: POPL 1998, pp. 184–196 (1998)
7. DataRescue. IDA Pro
8. Ganapathy, M.K.: Robust mixing. In: Díaz, J., Jansen, K., Rolim, J.D.P., Zwick, U. (eds.) APPROX 2006 and RANDOM 2006. LNCS, vol. 4110, pp. 351–362. Springer, Heidelberg (2006)
9. Gillman, D.: A chernoff bound for random walks on expander graphs. In: IEEE Symposium on Foundations of Computer Science, pp. 680–691. IEEE Computer Society Press, Los Alamitos (1993)
10. Goldreich, O., Ostrovsky, R.: Software protection and simulation on oblivious RAMs. Journal of the ACM 43(3), 431–473 (1996)
11. Goldwasser, S., Kalai, Y.T.: On the impossibility of obfuscation with auxiliary input. In: FOCS 2005: Proceedings of the 46th Annual IEEE Symposium on Foundations of Computer Science, pp. 553–562. IEEE Computer Society Press, Los Alamitos (2005)
12. Lynn, B., Prabhakaran, M., Sahai, A.: Positive results and techniques for obfuscation. In: Cachin, C., Camenisch, J.L. (eds.) EUROCRYPT 2004. LNCS, vol. 3027, Springer, Heidelberg (2004)
13. Shamir, A., van Someren, N.: Playing hide and seek with stored keys. In: Franklin, M.K. (ed.) FC 1999. LNCS, vol. 1648, pp. 118–124. Springer, Heidelberg (1999)
14. Tan, G., Chen, Y., Jakubowski, M.H.: Delayed and controlled failures in tamper-resistant systems. In: Proceedings of 8th Information Hiding Workshop (2006)

15. van Oorschot, P.C., Somayaji, A., Wurster, G.: Hardware-assisted circumvention of self-hashing software tamper resistance. IEEE Trans. Dependable Secur. Comput. 2(2), 82–92 (2005)
16. Varadarajan, A., Venkatesan, R.: Limited obliviousness for data structures and efficient execution of programs. Unpublished manuscript
17. Wang, Z., Pierce, K., McFarling, S.: Bmat - a binary matching tool for stale profile propagation. J. Instruction-Level Parallelism 2 (2000)
18. Wee, H.: On obfuscating point functions. In: STOC 2005: Proceedings of the thirty-seventh annual ACM symposium on Theory of computing, pp. 523–532. ACM Press, New York,USA (2005)

Software Integrity Checking Expressions (ICEs) for Robust Tamper Detection

Mariusz Jakubowski[1,*] Prasad Naldurg[2], Vijay Patankar[2], and Ramarathnam Venkatesan[3]

[1] Microsoft Research Redmond
[2] Microsoft Research India
[3] Microsoft Research Redmond and Microsoft Research India
{mariuszj,prasadn,vij,venkie}@microsoft.com

Abstract. We introduce software integrity checking expressions (Soft-ICEs), which are program predicates that can be used in software tamper detection. We present two candidates, probabilistic verification conditions (PVCs) and Fourier-learning approximations (FLAs), which can be computed for certain classes of programs,. We show that these predicates hold for any valid execution of the program, and fail with some probability for any invalid execution (e.g., when the output value of one of the variables is tampered). PVCs work with straight-line integer programs that have operations $\{ *, +, - \}$. We also sketch how we can extend this class to include branches and loops. FLAs can work over programs with arbitrary operations, but have some limitations in terms of efficiency, code size, and ability to handle various classes of functions. We describe a few applications of this technique, such as program integrity checking, program or client identification, and tamper detection. As a generalization of oblivious hashing (OH), our approach resolves several troublesome issues that complicate practical application of OH towards tamper-resistance.

1 Introduction

We describe a general framework for generating and validating useful verification conditions of programs to protect against integrity attacks. We present two methods, one to generate probabilistic verification conditions (PVCs) and the other to compute Fourier-learning approximations (FLAs), which can both be viewed as instances of a general class of software integrity checking expressions (SoftICEs). These can be applied to a variety of problems, including software-client identification and tamper detection.

Our PVC technique relies on the transformation of straight line program fragments (without control-branching or loops) into a set of polynomial equations. With each set of equations, we compute a reduced basis that eliminates redundant variables and equations that do not contribute to the output. This basis

---

* Corresponding author.

T. Furon et al. (Eds.): IH 2007, LNCS 4567, pp. 96–111, 2007.

depends on program code, and is consistent with the input-output semantics of a given program fragment. We show how we can use this basis as an integrity checking expression (ICE) with provable security properties.

Similarly, in our FLA method, we view a code fragment as a function operating on variables read inside the fragment; the output is all variables potentially overwritten within the fragment. This scheme treats such a function as a series of component functions that map the input variables onto single bits. A Fourier-based machine-learning technique converts such functions into tables of Fourier coefficients, and an inverse transform can use this table to approximate the original function. Together with the coefficients, the inverse transform serves as an ICE to verify each individual bit of the target function.

Traditionally, verification conditions (VCs) are used formally (or axiomatically) to validate properties of programs without actually executing all possible paths in the program. In particular, these conditions characterize a computable semantic interpretation, which is a mathematical or logical description of the possible behaviors of a given program [1]. In this context, for example in [2,3], one typically has a specification of the property of interest, and the generation of VCs is driven by this property. These techniques typically work on a formal model that is an over-approximation or abstraction of program behavior. One of the challenges in abstraction is this loss of precision, and leads to false-errors. On the other hand, we are interested in capturing verification conditions that are precise, and characterize input-output behavior accurately.

In addition to this, we differ from traditional VC generation in many aspects: We are agnostic to particular property specifications and therefore completely automatic. Recently, a technique called random interpretation has been proposed [6], which combines abstract interpretation with random testing to assert probabilistic property-driven conditions for linear programs. Our framework describes how to generate generic semantic fingerprints of programs, independent of property specifications or particular verification frameworks (e.g., abstract interpretation). Furthermore, most existing techniques for generating verification conditions work only for linear constraints. Our methods are more general and work with nonlinear integer programs as well.

Our work on PVCs is also related to previous work on fast probabilistic verification of polynomial identities [4], but our polynomials are derived from actual programs.

We envision the application of these conditions in two scenarios: (a) In a setting when the program is *oblivious* to the checks being performed, and (b) in a non-oblivious setting, where an adversary can try to learn the checks, which reduces to finding the random primes that are chosen for these reductions and creation of VCs. Our analysis is universal in the sense that we do not assume anything about the inputs.

The techniques proposed in this paper have a number of interesting applications:

- One application of our technique is *program identification* and individualization. Consider a web portal W that distributes client software that is individualized with respect to some client identity information. Now, imagine some other portal W' that wants to use the database and services of W to re-package and sell the same software to its clients. If W wants to keep track of its original code, it can embed our ICEs in it.

- Another application is *software protection*. We believe that our probabilistic conditions can be used as primitives to build provably secure software protection mechanisms. Desirable properties of software protection include obfuscation and tamper-resistance. Security is determined by the minimum effort required to bypass such measures, and provable security means that we can accurately estimate this effort, even if it is mere hours or days.

The problem of tamper detection in an oblivious setting has been explored in [10]. This work proposes a technique called *oblivious hashing (OH)*, which computes hash values based on assignments and branches executed by a program. OH requires program inputs that exercise all code paths of interest; hashes may then be pre-computed by executing the program on these inputs. Alternately, OH may rely on code replicas to compute and compare redundant hashes. In contrast, we require no specific inputs, hash pre-computation, or code replicas, thus resolving a number of issues that have created roadblocks against practical adoption of OH.

A number of recent results [7,8,9] have explored the nature and scope of program obfuscation. These results have identified different classes of programs that can (or cannot) be obfuscated, for a general definition of obfuscation as being equivalent to black-box access to a program. So far these results have only shown very small classes of programs that can be provably obfuscated. The properties defined here are not quantitative and we believe we can extend the scope of these results to apply to a broader class of problems with probabilistic guarantees.

In a non-oblivious setting, the notion of proof-carrying code was developed in [5], where an untrusted program carries a proof for a property defined by the verifier. The verifier generates VCs automatically, using the same algorithm as the program developer, and checks the proof. If the proof cannot be verified, the program is considered unauthentic. In contrast, our probabilistic predicates assert invariants about input-output behavior, and we believe that they can be used to detect tampering and aid in obfuscation.

The rest of the paper is organized as follows: We present our program model in Section 2. Section 3 presents the main theorem, about the precision of these predicates, as well as their failure-independence when we trade precision for efficiency. Section 4 presents examples, including extensions to include branches and loops, and comparisons with traditional VC-generation techniques. Section 5 concludes with a discussion on future work.

2   Program Model and Basics

In this section, we describe our program model, along with our assumptions, and present mathematical preliminaries, including definitions and notations, that are needed to explain our PVC technique. We explain our FLA technique, and its associated model in Section 5.

We study this problem in the context of integer programs. Here we allow only integer values to variables in all (possibly infinite) reachable program-states, consistent with our program semantics. In particular, we restrict our variables to take values in the ring of rational integers (denoted by $\mathbb{Z}$). Here, we would like to point out that our method can be easily adapted to deal with programs with rational number inputs, i.e. inputs from $\mathbb{Q}$. This is achieved by considering a rational number input as a quotient of two integers. Thus, each variable (with rational number input) in an assignment is replaced by two distinct variables (quotient of two variables) that accept integer inputs. One can then *homogenise* the resulting assignment and produce an assignement with integer inputs. Repeated application of this process will covert a given program with rational number inputs into an equivalent program with integer inputs. Thus, without loss of generality, we may restrict our study to programs with integer inputs.

In our PVC technique we exploit the fundamental correspondence between ideals of polynomial rings and subsets of affine spaces, called affine varieties, to generate our probabilistic conditions.

Our goal is to capture a precise algebraic description of the relationship between input and output variables for a generic program. To this end, with each program P we associate an ideal or equivalently a system of polynomial equations $f_i(x_1, \cdots, x_n) = 0$. We then compute a basis of such an ideal by eliminating variables and redundant equations. This basis has the same set of zeros as the original program. In Section 3, we show how we can construct a probabilistic predicate from this basis and describe a testing framework to detect tampering.

2.1 Background and Notation

To make this paper self-contained, we present definitions of rings, polynomial rings, ideals and their bases. Our domain of program variables will be $\mathbb{Z}$, the ring of rational integers.

A *ring* R is a set equipped with two operations, that of multiplication and addition $\{+, .\}$, together with respective *identity* elements denoted by 1 and 0. A ring is *commutative* if the operation of multiplication is commutative. Henceforth we will only deal with commutative rings.

An *ideal* of a ring R is an additive subgroup of R. In other words, an ideal I of a commutative ring R is a nonempty subset R such that $(I, +)$ is a subgroup of $(R, +)$ and that for all $r \in R$ and $x \in I$, $r \cdot x \in I$. An ideal *generated* by a given subset S of R is by definition the smallest ideal of R containing S. This ideal is denoted by $\langle S \rangle$ and called as the ideal of R generated by S.

Let $\{x_1, x_2, \cdots, x_n\}$ be n indeterminate *algebraically* independent variables over a commutative ring R, where n is a positive integer. Let $R[x_1, x_2, \cdots, x_n]$ be the ring of polynomials over R. We will denote this for short by $R[\bar{x}]$. Note that, as said earlier, it is a ring under the operations of multiplication and addition of polynomials. We say that a commutative ring R is a field if every non-zero element is invertible or has an inverse. A field will be usually denoted by K or

k. Thus, let k be a field, and let $k[\bar{x}]$ denote the polynomial ring over k. If an ideal I of R is such that there exists a finite subset $X \subseteq R$(necessarily a subset of I) generating it, then the ideal I is said to be finitely generated. It is a basic theorem that every ideal of $\mathbb{Z}[x_1, x_2, \cdots, x_n]$, the polynomial ring of integers, is finitely generated.

We now focus on *Gröbner bases*, a particular type of generating subset of an ideal in a polynomial ring. It is defined with respect to a particular monomial ordering, say $\preceq$. By a monomial orderning, we mean a way of comparing two different monomials in n variables over R. It is a theorem that every ideal posseses a unique Gröbner basis depending only on the monomial ordering $\preceq$. Thus for a fixed monomial ordering $\preceq$, we will denote the Gröbner basis of an ideal I by G. Thus, we can write $G := \{g_1, \cdots, g_m\}$, for some polynomials g_i, and $< G >= I$.

Gröbner bases possess a number of useful properties. The original ideal and its Gröbner basis have the same zeros. The computation of a Gröbner basis may require time (in the worst case) that is exponential or even doubly-exponential (for different orderings) in the number of solutions of the underlying polynomial system (or ideals). However, we have observed that they are efficiently computable in practice, in a few seconds, for typical code fragments of interest, and most computer algebra packages such as Mathematica and MAGMA provide this support. We propose to validate their usefulness for checking program fragments related to license-checking and digital rights protection. Computation of our ICEs is off-line, in the sense that it can be viewed as a precomputation and this stage does not affect the runtime performance of our original applications.

Reduced Gröbner bases can be shown to be unique for any given ideal and monomial ordering. Thus, one can determine if two ideals are equal by looking at their reduced Gröbner bases.

Next, we show how one may use these properties to generate behavioral fingerprints of program executions.

2.2   Computing Bases

We explain our technique for straight-line programs in this subsection. We focus on program fragments that form a part of what is called a basic-block, without any additional control flow instructions. Subsquently, we present some engineering techniques with weaker guarantees that can handle control flow branching and looping. However, this section is of independent value as we can apply our general technique to only program fragments that are sensitive, trading coverage for performance.

Let P be a straight-line integer program fragment. Let $x_1, \cdots, x_r$ be all the input variables, and let $x_{r+1}, \cdots, x_n$ be all the output variables of P. We define the set of program states $V(P)$, as the set (possibly infinite) of all possible valuations to the variables $x_1, \cdots, x_n$ of P, consistent with the update semantics of variables in the program.

We assume that the *operations* of P are defined over the the integers $\mathbb{Z}$ and are restricted to addition, subtraction, and multiplication by integers and combinations of quantities obtained by these.

As mentioned earlier, with homogenisation and other algebraic simplifications, our method can be easily adapted for programs that include the division operation. We can convert a given assignment that contains quotients of polynomials into new assigment (or assignments) without quotients (or division operation), by introducing auxiliary variables when necessary.

Therefore, we view a straight-line program (without any branches and conditions) as a set of polynomial equations in some finite variables with integer coefficients. In order to view assignments as equations, we use a standard transformation technique called *Static Single Assignment (SSA)*, which converts an ordered sequence of program statements into a set of polynomials by introducing temporary variables. In SSA, if a program variable x is updated, each new assignment of x is replaced with a new variable in all expressions between the current assignment and the next. One thus gets a set of polynomial equations associated with a given program. Let $I(P)$ be the ideal generated by these polynomials. This ideal will be called as the *Program Ideal* of the given program P. Now, if we fix a monomial ordering of the variables that are involved in the definitions of $I(P)$, we can construct a Gröbner basis for $I(P)$. Let us denote it by $G(P)$. This gives us the following: The set of states that evaluate to zero for a Gröbner basis is identical to the set of states that evaluate to zero for the original polynomials. In this sense, as a VC, the Gröbner basis as an abstraction of the program behavior is **precise**.

This can be utilised as follows: Suppose $x_i = \lambda_i$ for $i = 1$ to n is a specific executable-instance of a program P. Then, $g_j(\bar{\lambda}) = 0$ for $j = 1$ to m, here $\bar{\lambda} := (\lambda_1, \cdots, \lambda_n)$. Thus, if we take up all the polynomials of G, and evaluate $\bar{\lambda}$ at these, then we can verify *authenticity* of program P with respect to its input-output behaviour by checking whether an execution-instance of P is satisfied by all the polynomials of G. However, this would constitute a lot of checking.

Rather than check for authenticity, it is easier to check for tampering. If a program is modified or tampered and its input-output behavior has changed, the bases produced by the original program and the modified program will be different. For a given set of inputs, if the program is not tampered, the Gröbner bases associated with this will evaluate to zero. However, if they evaluate to non-zero, then the two programs are not the same. If we can find an input-output for which the Gröbner Basis is non-zero for a tampered program, we can assert (by black-box testing) that the program has been tampered. Finding this particular input instance that will cause the basis to evaluate to non-zero is also difficult. However, with the reduction presented in the next section, we show how we can rely on a number-theoretic argument to quantify the security of our scheme for a general adversary without having to rely on particular input instances.

In the next section, we present our main theorem regarding probabilistic generation and validation of predicates using our basic idea.

3   Probabilistic Verification Conditions

In this section, we derive a probabilistic validation property that is independent of specific program inputs and outputs. We use a simple number-theoretic method of reduction modulo primes.

We now study how the Gröbner Basis polynomials behave when we apply reduction modulo primes. This is useful for a variety of reasons. If we can quantify how often the reduced polynomials produce the same set of zeros in comparison with the original polynomials, we can devise a probabilistic testing framework that complicates the task of a tampering adversary.

We employ the Schwartz-Zippel lemma [4] used in standard testing of polynomial identities to obtain this quantification, which is typically used to determine if a given multivariate polynomial is equal to zero.

Theorem 1 (Schwartz-Zippel). *Let* $P \in F[x_1, x_2, \cdots, x_n]$ *be a (non-zero) polynomial of total-degree* $d > 0$ *over a field* F. *Let* S *be a finite subset of* F. *Let* $r_1, r_2, r_3, \cdots, r_n$ *be selected randomly from* S. *Then*

$$Pr[P(r_1, r_2, \cdots, r_n) = 0] \leq \frac{d}{|S|}.$$

This is basically a generalised version of the fact that a one variable polynomial of degree d has at most d roots over a field F.

We will use a variation of the above lemma, which we state below. This variation follows from the earlier lemma by noting that a random choice of $r \in \mathbb{Z}$ amounts to a random choice of $r \mod p$ in $\mathbb{Z}/p\mathbb{Z}$ for a randomly chosen prime p and that $|S| = |\mathbb{Z}/p\mathbb{Z}| = p$.

Theorem 2 (Schwartz-Zippel-Variant). *Let* $P \in Z[x_1, x_2, \cdots, x_n]$ *be a (non-zero) polynomial of total-degree* $d > 0$ *defined over the integers* $\mathbb{Z}$. *Let* P *be the set of all primes numbers. Let* $r_1, r_2, r_3, \cdots, r_n$ *be selected randomly from* $\mathbb{Z}$. *Then*

$$Pr[P(r_1, r_2, \cdots, r_n) = 0 \mod p] \leq \frac{d}{p}.$$

Thus, the Schwartz-Zippel lemma bounds the probability that a non-zero polynomial will have roots at randomly selected test points. If we choose a prime $p > d$, given a polynomial from a Gröbner basis that is computed for a straight-line program as described earlier, the probability that this polynomial will be zero when evaluated at a random input-output (of the given program) is bounded above $\frac{d}{p}$.

This quantification provides us a basis for defining a probabilistic testing methodology as follows:

If we are given black-box access to tampered code, the probability of the code producing a *zero* (an input-output instance at which the polynomial evaluates to zero) will be bounded by $\frac{d}{p}$. But p is chosen at random and can be arbitrarily large. Thus, in order to pass tampered code as authentic, an adversary will have to guess a random prime from a possibly infinite set of choices, and this is a well-known hard problem.

Furthermore, granted that the adversary knows the prime, the adversary also needs to maximize the probability that a non-authentic input-output instance is passed on as authentic. Equivalently, the adversary needs to make sure that a random and tampered input-output instance be a zero of all the polynomials (of a Gröbner bases) modulo p. Given p and a finite set of polynomial equations, this can be achieved with some work, provided the polynomial equations are *simple*. Instead if randomized techniques are employed, and if the prime p is much larger than the total-degree of all the polynomial equations, then the difficulty of finding a zero has already been quantified by the Schwartz-Zippel lemma.

On the other hand, the verifier can test the program for random input-outputs, and modulo a randomly chosen large prime p. If the program is not tampered, all the input-outputs will be the zeros for the polynomials modulo any prime p. The more tests the verifier does, the lesser the error probability. But, by the arguments above, the probability that a tampered input-output instance passes as a zero of a polynomial modulo a random large prime p is bounded above by $\frac{d}{p}$. The probability of passing a specific non-authentic instance as authentic can be minimized by choosing many randomly chosen primes p_i and repeating the verification on the same given specific instance as needed.

4   Examples of PVCs

In this section, we present five examples to demonstrate how our technique can be used in practice. The first example shows how we can generate conditions for linear programs. We also show how our probabilistic conditions compare with traditional verification conditions. The second example has non-linear constraints. The third example presents is more exploratory and presents some preliminary ideas on branches and loops. In the fourth example, we show how we can compute these bases for small, overlapping, randomly selected code fragments to scale our solution to large programs. Finally we show how we can reduce the complexity of checking by using our results from our previous section.

4.1   Linear Programs

In the following example, the input and output variables in this progr are $\{x, y, z\}$.

$$x = x + y + z;$$
$$y = y + 5;$$
$$z = x + 1;$$
$$x = x + 1;$$

In order to treat these assignment as equations, we transform the program using SSA into the following:

$$x_1 = x_0 + y_0;$$
$$x_2 = x_1 + z_0;$$
$$y_1 = y_0 + 5;$$
$$z_1 = x_2 + 1;$$
$$x_3 = x_2 + 1;$$

In the example above:

$$I = \langle x_1 - x_0 - y_0, x_2 - x_1 - z_0,$$
$$y_1 - y_0 - 5, z_1 - x_2 - 1, x_3 - x_2 - 1 \rangle$$

The Gröbner basis of this ideal with respect to a fixed monomial order $\{x_0 < x_1 < x_2 < x_3 < y_0 < y_1 < z_1\}$ is given by:

$$G = \{5 + y_0 - y_1, x_3 - z_1, 1 + x_2 - z_1,$$
$$1 + x_1 + z_0 - z_1, -4 + x_0 + y_1 + z_0 - z_1\}$$

When the order is changed we get a different basis. For the ordering $z_0 < y_0 < y_1 < x_0 < x_1, x_2 < x_3$ the basis is $\{x_3 - z_1, 1 + x_2 - z_1, -5 + x_0 - x_1 + y_1, x_0 - x_1 + y_0, 1 + x_1 + z_0 - z_1\}$ For both these cases, the basis polynomials evaluate to zero for any valuations to input variable x_0, y_0, and z_0. However if the program output is changed (simulated by changing some intermediate outputs, these polynomials do not evaluate to zero.

Comparison with Traditional VC Generation. For comparison, we compute invariants using a standard strongest-precondition algorithm. Suppose we start with an assumption $x > 0, y > 0, z > 0$. The VC obtained in this case is $z_1 \geq 4 \wedge x_3 \geq 4 \wedge y_1 \geq 6$. Note that if we use these assertions in a black-box or oblivious setting, we can argue trivially that they are less resilient to program modification than the ones generated by our technique.

If we start with true as the initial assertion, i.e., $\top$, we get:

$$VC = \langle (z_1 = x_0 + y_0 + z_0 + 1) \wedge$$
$$(x_3 = x_0 + y_0 + z_0 + 1) \wedge$$
$$(y_1 = y_0 + 5) \rangle$$

While the strongest-postcondition algorithm now produces an equivalent set of conditions (and depended on what we gave to it initially), our technique can produce probabilistic conditions, and can be applied to nonlinear programs as well.

4.2   An Automated Nonlinear Example

Below we give an example of Gröbner-basis computation on typical code in an automated fashion. For this, we have implemented an SSA-remapping tool that converts C++ code into polynomials suitable for our basis computation. Consider the following code snippet:

$$x = b^2 + 2a - 17c;$$
$$y = x + 3ab;$$
$$z = 19b - 18yx^2;$$
$$y = x + 2y - z;$$

After processing the above input code, our tool generates the following polynomials:

```
t154 - (b0 * b0),        y0 - t161,
t155 - (2 * a0),         t162 - (19 * b0),
t156 - (t154 + t155),    t163 - (18 * y0),
t157 - (17 * c0),        t164 - (t163 * x0),
t158 - (t156 - t157),    t165 - (t164 * x0),
x0 - t158,               t166 - (t162 - t165),
t159 - (3 * a0),         z0 - t166,
t160 - (t159 * b0),      t167 - (2 * y0),
t161 - (x0 + t160),      t168 - (x0 + t167),
t169 - (t168 - z0),      y1 - t169
```

In the above, variables with names prefixed by 't' (e.g., t154) are new temporaries introduced by our SSA-remapping tool. Original variables (e.g., y) are extended with numerical suffixes to create SSA-remapped versions (e.g., y0,y1). Only the variable y requires more than one version, since only y is assigned more than once.

With variables t154 through t169 eliminated, a Gröbner basis for the above polynomials is the following:

$$x_0 + 2y_0 - y_1 - z_0,$$
$$2a_0 + b_0^2 - 17c_0 + 2y_0 - y_1 - z_0,$$
$$3a_0b_0 - 3y_0 + y_1 + z_0,$$
$$6a_0^2 - 51a_0c_0 + 6a_0y_0 + 3b_0y_0 - 3a_0y_1 -$$
$$b_0y_1 - 3a_0z_0 - b_0z_0,$$
$$-19b_0 + 72y_0^3 - 72y_0^2y_1 + 18y_0y_1^2 + z_0 -$$
$$72y_0^2z_0 + 36y_0y_1z_0 + 18y_0z_0^2$$

The above basis polynomials evaluate to zero on any set of proper assignments to the variables $a_0, b_0, c_0, x_0, y_0, z_0$, and y_1. For example, if $a_0 = 3$ and $b_0 = 14$

and $c_0 = 15$, we have $x_0 = -53$, $y_0 = 73$, $z_0 = -3690760$, $y_1 = 3690853$, and each basis polynomial evaluates to zero on these assignments. If an attack or a program error tampers with these values, this will most likely no longer hold. For example, if the the value of y_0 is changed from 73 to 72, the five basis polynomials evaluate to $\{-2, -2, 3, -60, -320130\}$.

Note that the variable y_0 corresponds to the value of y prior to its second assignment in the original C++ snippet; y_1 is the final value of y computed by the C++ code.

4.3   Conditionals and Loops

To generate VCs for conditional statements, we compute VC sets independently for each branch path; we then perform a cross product of these VC sets. Since all polynomials in at least one VC set must evaluate to zero, each polynomial in the cross product must also vanish. As an example, consider the following C++ snippet:

```
if (...)                    else
{                           {
    x = b*b - 17*a*b;           x = b*b - 2*a + 17*c;
    x = x - 3*x*c;              y = x + 2*a*b;
}                           }
```

Polynomials corresponding to the two branch paths are as follows:

$$x_0 - b^2 + 17ab,$$
$$x_1 - x_0 + 3x_0 c$$

$$x_0 - b^2 + 2a - 17c,$$
$$y - x_0 - 2ab$$

The respective Gröbner bases are:

$$-x_0 + 3cx_0 + x_1,$$
$$17ab - b^2 + x_0$$

$$-2a + b^2 + 17c - x_0,$$
$$2ab + x_0 - y,$$
$$4a^2 - 34ac + 2ax_0 + bx_0 - by$$

The cross product of these bases consists of 6 polynomials, each of which must evaluate to zero on any proper variable assignment:

$$(-x_0 + 3cx_0 + x_1)(-2a + b^2 + 17c - x_0),$$
$$(-x_0 + 3cx_0 + x_1)(2ab + x_0 - y),$$
$$(-x_0 + 3cx_0 + x_1)(4a^2 - 34ac + 2ax_0 + bx_0 - by),$$
$$(17ab - b^2 + x_0)(-2a + b^2 + 17c - x_0),$$
$$(17ab - b^2 + x_0)(2ab + x_0 - y),$$
$$(17ab - b^2 + x_0)(4a^2 - 34ac + 2ax_0 + bx_0 - by)$$

Note that this method produces VCs that ascertain the proper execution of each branch path; however, these VCs do not verify that the proper path was chosen according to the condition evaluated at runtime. To fix this, the condition itself may be treated as a polynomial for VC generation. Future work will include details of how this may be accomplished.

To handle a loop, we may compute a Gröbner basis for just the loop body. While this will not yield VCs that verify the actual loop iteration, we may additionally include loop variables and conditions in the set of input polynomials. Alternately, we may unroll loops, producing new instances of loop variables for each iteration. A more detailed description of these methods will appear in future work.

4.4 Overlapping

For larger code sections, computing Gröbner bases may be expensive. Even with modular reduction, the results may contain an unwieldy number of complex polynomials. Moreover, depending on the order of monomial elimination, the time and resources to compute a basis for large code sections may vary dramatically. In practice, well optimized software implementations are able to compute Gröbner bases for up to a few tens of variables.

To address this problem, we compute Gröbner bases for small, randomly overlapping fragments of input code; we then use a combination of the resulting VCs. This reduces the number and complexity of basis polynomials while retaining soundness and security. In addition, the overlapping creates links among the small code fragments, resulting in VCs that provide a probabilistic degree of precision.

As an example, consider the following C++ code segment:

```
x = b*b + 2*a - 17*c;
y = x + 3*a*b;
z = 19*b - 18*y*x*x;
y = x + 2*y - z;
```

We may split this into the overlapping fragments below, computing separate Gröbner bases for each:

```
x = b*b + 2*a - 17*c;
y = x + 3*a*b;
z = 19*b - 18*y*x*x;

y = x + 3*a*b;
z = 19*b - 18*y*x*x;
y = x + 2*y - z;
```

In general, the combined Gröbner bases from all fragments should be less complex and more usable than the single basis computed from the entire code segment. In future work, we will analyze the benefits and limitations of overlapping for purposes such as program analysis and tamper-resistance.

4.5 Reducing Complexity

We show a crucial number-theoretic trick with known bounds to reduce complexity and simplify analysis. We also emphasize the probabilistic nature of our conditions and highlight that we can analyze program behavior without making any assumptions on input-output models.

Consider a transformed program consisting of the following polynomials:

$$Q = \{x_1 - 2a + b + c,$$
$$x_2 - 17a + b - 7c - 10,$$
$$x_3 - 5b + a + 2,$$
$$x_4 + 18a - 7b + c - 14\}$$

The Gröbner Basis with $\{a, b, c\}$ eliminated is $-3154 + 497x_1 + 92x_2 - 88x_3 + 147x_4$. This evaluates to zero for any assignments to input variables. We now study how the polynomials reduce modulo a prime.

$$p = 2 : \{x1 + x_4\}$$
$$p = 3 : \{2 + 2x1 + 2x2 + 2x3\}$$
$$p = 7 : \{3 + x2 + 3x3\}$$
$$p = 11 : \{3 + 2x1 + 4x2 + 4x4\}$$
$$p = 17 : \{8 + 4x1 + 7x2 + 14x3 + 11x4\}$$
$$p = 23 : \{20 + 14x1 + 4x3 + 9x4\}$$
$$p = 101 : \{78 + 93x1 + 92x2 + 13x3 + 46x4\}$$

When we modify the outputs slightly, the bases now only evaluate to zero every $(1/p)$ times on an average, as expected. For example, with $p = 2$:

$$\{0\}\{1\}\{0\}\{1\}\{0\}\{1\}\{0\}\{1\}\{0\}\{1\}$$
$$\{0\}\{1\}\{0\}\{1\}\{0\}\{1\}\{0\}\{1\}\{0\}\{1\}$$
$$\{0\}\{1\}\{0\}\{1\}\{0\}\cdots$$

With $p = 11$:

$$\{0\}\{2\}\{4\}\{6\}\{8\}\{10\}\{1\}\{3\}\{5\}\{7\}$$
$$\{9\}\{0\}\{2\}\{4\}\{6\}\{8\}\{10\}\{1\}\{3\}\{5\}$$
$$\{7\}\{9\}\{0\}\{2\}\{4\}\cdots$$

With $p = 101$:

$$\{13\}\{40\}\{67\}\{94\}\{20\}\{47\}\{74\}\{0\}\{27\}$$
$$\{54\}\{81\}\{7\}\{34\}\{61\}\{88\}\{14\}\{41\}\{68\}$$
$$\{95\}\{21\}\{48\}\{75\}\{1\}\{28\}\{55\}\cdots$$

Subsequently, we hope to relax our restriction that the operations in our program be algebraic.

5   ICEs Via Fourier Learning

In this section, we show how to use a technique from machine learning to generate ICEs for arbitrary code, including mathematical operations and control-flow constructs. Our main idea is to treat a program fragment F as a function $f : \{0,1\}^n \to \{0,1\}^m$, and learn each such function via a standard training algorithm, as described shortly. The input to f is all variables read in F; the output of f is all variables potentially overwritten by F. For simplicity, assume that F modifies only a single bit and rewrite f as $f : \{0,1\}^n \to \{+1,-1\}$. For program fragments that change m bits, our scheme may consider m separate functions, one for each bit.

A Fourier-based learning procedure [13] essentially performs an approximate Fourier transform of a Boolean function $f : \{0,1\}^n \to \{+1,-1\}$. A basis for such functions is the family of functions $\chi_\alpha : \{0,1\}^n \to \{+1,-1\}$ defined as

$$\chi_\alpha(x) = (-1)^{\sum_{i=1}^n x_i \alpha_i}, \tag{1}$$

where α is an n-bit parameter, while x_i and α_i represent individual bits of x and α, respectively, for $i = 1..n$. Informally, each basis function $\chi_\alpha(x)$ computes the parity of a subset of x's bits, with the subset specified by the bit vector α. It can be shown that this function family is an orthonormal basis, so that a standard Fourier transform can map f onto 2^n Fourier coefficients c_α. These coefficients can be used to compute f:

$$f(x) = \sum_{\alpha \in \{0,1\}^n} c_\alpha \chi_\alpha(x) \tag{2}$$

With this basis, a full Fourier transform requires exponential time to compute an exponential number of coefficients. However, a typical function f can often be approximated by a small subset thereof. Efficient learning algorithms exist for functions that can be well approximated by a small number of coefficients or by a selection of "low-frequency" coefficients c_α, where α has low Hamming weight. These algorithms use sets of "training" inputs and outputs to estimate values of coefficients, essentially approximating a Fourier transform.

Within this framework, an ICE for a program fragment F is a table of learned Fourier coefficients c_α for an associated bit function f, along with the expression specified by eq. 2. The coefficients and eq. 2 can be used to approximate $f(x)$ on any input x. As with any ICE, this result should match the actual value of $f(x)$ computed at runtime; otherwise F has been tampered.

As an example, we applied a "low-frequency" learning algorithm [13] to the following C fragment, which accepts the 12-bit integer variable x as input and returns a single-bit output:

```
uint y;
if ((x & 1) == 0)          if ((x & 4) == 0)
    y = x >> 3;                y = y * 11 + 1;
else                       else
    y = x >> ((int)x & 7);     y = 3 * y - 45;

if ((x & 2) == 0)          return (0 == (y & 4)) ? 1 : -1;
    y = 19 * y + x;
else
    y = y - 3 * x;
```

To illustrate some specific figures, our learning procedure used 55690 random input-output pairs to approximate 1585 low-frequency Fourier coefficients c_α (with α having Hamming weight of 5 or less). This was sufficient to learn the above function well; e.g., for several random inputs x, the following lists the correct and approximated outputs:

```
x=372:   y=-1    y_approx=-1.54975758664033
x=648:   y=1     y_approx=0.855773029269167
x=3321:  y=1     y_approx=1.09868917220327
x=1880:  y=-1    y_approx=-0.807793140599749
```

This approach also provides other benefits for software protection, mainly due to obfuscation via homogenization. Programs turn into tables of Fourier coefficients, while execution becomes evaluation of inverse Fourier transforms (eq. 2). Thus, both representation and operation of transformed programs are highly uniform, which complicates analysis and reverse engineering. This is similar to representing functions as lookup tables, but Fourier-based learning works even when the size of such tables would be impractical. An adversary may be forced to treat Fourier-converted programs as black-box functions, since it is unclear how to recover original code from corresponding tables of coefficients. Future work will analyze the exact difficulty of this problem.

6   Future Work

This work should be considered as a preliminary investigation in our quest for robust, automatic, provably secure semantic fingerprints of programs. In future work, we will address computation of VCs for loops (with algebraic loop-variable updates) and conditionals. Moving beyond algebraic restrictions to accommodate bitwise and other operations, we may encode these computations as boolean formulas and arithmetize them suitably to treat them as algebraic polynomials (e.g., [11]). While this may increase the number of variables dramatically, we will use overlapping and other engineering techniques to manage this complexity for target applications.

References

1. Cousot, P., Cousot, R.: Abstract interpretation: A unified lattice model for static analysis of programs by construction or approximation of fix points. In: 4th Annual ACM Symposium on Principles of Programming Languages, pp. 234–252 (1977)
2. Ball, T., Majumdar, R., Millstein, T., Rajamani, S.K.: Automatic Predicate Abstraction of C Programs. PLDI 2001, SIGPLAN Notices 36(5), 203–213 (2001)
3. Henzinger, T.A., Jhala, R., Majumdar, R., Sutre, G.: Software Verification with Blast. In: Ball, T., Rajamani, S.K. (eds.) Model Checking Software. LNCS, vol. 2648, pp. 235–239. Springer, Heidelberg (2003)
4. Schwartz, J.T.: Fast probabilistic algorithms for verification of polynomial identities. JACM 27(4), 701–717 (1980)
5. Necula, G.C.: Proof Carrying Code. In: 24th Annual ACM Symposium on Principles of Programming Languages, ACM Press, New York (1997)
6. Gulwani, S., Necula, G.C.: Discovering affine equalities using random interpretation. In: 30th Annual ACM Symposium on Principles of Programming Languages, pp. 74–84 (January 2003)
7. Barak, B., Goldreich, O., Impagliazzo, R., Rudich, S., Sahai, A., Vadhan, S., Yang, K.: On the (Im)possibility of Obfuscating Programs. In: Kilian, J. (ed.) CRYPTO 2001. LNCS, vol. 2139, Springer, Heidelberg (2001)
8. Kalai, Y.T., Goldwasser, S.: On the Impossibility of Obfuscation with Auxiliary Inputs. In: Proc. 46th IEEE Symposium on Foundations of Computer Science (FOCS 2005) (2005)
9. Lynn, B., Prabhakaran, M., Sahai, A.: Positive Results and Techniques for Obfuscation. In: Cachin, C., Camenisch, J.L. (eds.) EUROCRYPT 2004. LNCS, vol. 3027, Springer, Heidelberg (2004)
10. Chen, Y., Venkatesan, R., Cary, M., Pang, R., Sinha, S., Jakubowski, M.: Oblivious hashing: a stealthy software integrity verification primitive. In: Proceedings of the 5th International Workshop on Information Hiding, pp. 400–414 (2002)
11. Shamir, A.: IP = PSPACE. Journal of the ACM 39(4), 869–877 (1992)
12. Jacobson, N.: Basic Algebra I. W H Freeman and Co., New York (1985)
13. Mansour, Y.: Learning boolean functions via the Fourier transform. In: Roychowdhury, V., Siu, K.-Y., Orlitsky, A. (eds.) Theoretical Advances in Neural Computation and Learning, Kluwer Academic Publishers, Dordrecht (1994)

Space-Efficient Kleptography
Without Random Oracles

Adam L. Young[1] and Moti M. Yung[2]

[1] Cryptovirology Labs
aly@cryptovirology.com
[2] RSA Labs and Columbia University
moti@cs.columbia.edu

Abstract. In the past, hiding asymmetric backdoors inside cryptosystems required a random oracle assumption (idealization) as "randomizers" of the hidden channels. The basic question left open is whether cryptography itself based on traditional hardness assumption(s) alone enables "internal randomized channels" that enable the embedding of an asymmetric backdoor inside another cryptosystem while retaining the security of the cryptosystem and the backdoor (two security proofs in one system). This question translates into the existence of kleptographic channels without the idealization of random oracle functions. We therefore address the basic problem of controlling the probability distribution over information (i.e., the kleptogram) that is hidden within the output of a cryptographic system. We settle this question by presenting an elliptic curve asymmetric backdoor construction that solves this problem. As an example, we apply the construction to produce a provably secure asymmetric backdoor in SSL. The construction is general and applies to many other kleptographic settings as well.

Keywords: Key exchange, elliptic curve, twisted elliptic curves, kleptography.

1 Introduction

Kleptography and the theory of subliminal channels has been actively investigated by many researchers over the years [3,21,29,22,28,8]. Building asymmetric backdoors into cryptographic algorithms (and protocols) is a challenging task, since devising a provably secure information hiding attack within a host cryptographic algorithm while maintaining the provably secure nature of the host is tricky. The field is challenged by a unique constraint that is not present in many other areas of modern cryptologic designs: i.e., the limited bandwidth of existing subliminal channels [26,9,27,4] in cryptographic algorithms. When we deal with kleptography, these small channels have to embed asymmetric encryption channels on the one hand (for security and speed of the attack) and look random (for undetectability of the attack).

In this paper we succeed in utilizing extremely small channels by introducing a new "Information Hiding Primitive" that achieves provably secure information

T. Furon et al. (Eds.): IH 2007, LNCS 4567, pp. 112–129, 2007.
© Springer-Verlag Berlin Heidelberg 2007

leakage in very low bandwidth subliminal channels, which we call a *space-efficient pseudorandom key exchange*. The primitive allows the cryptographic device in question to broadcast a very small key exchange message through the subliminal channel and employ the corresponding Diffie-Hellman [10] shared secret to produce coin flips that appear to be uniformly distributed (in a provable sense). This primitive has general applicability in Information Hiding, but we will skip many applications and will only show how to employ it to securely and subliminally compromise an SSL client. The attack has the advantage that it can be carried out when an SSL session is established, and it is not required to be carried out at the time that key pairs are generated (so the attack succeeds even when SSL key pairs are generated honestly in tamper-proof devices). Our attacks are purely algebraic (no hash functions, no random oracle model).

Our new problem of key exchange ties in closely with recent work on secure key exchange, steganography, and kleptography. An issue that has drawn attention is the fact that existing key exchange protocols generate symmetric keys using a biased distribution by taking bits directly from a Diffie-Hellman (DH) shared secret. It has been shown how to use the *leftover hash lemma* [17] to derive symmetric keys properly from DH secrets [12], i.e., so that the symmetric key bits are drawn independently using the uniform distribution. It was shown in [6] how to derive a shared secret that is a uniformly random bit string using an algebraic approach based on twisted elliptic curves. Related work includes [13] that shows a secure hashed DH transform over a non-DDH group G (a group in which DDH does not hold). Here Gennaro et al show that for the hashed DH transform to be secure it suffices that G contain a sufficiently large DDH subgroup.

Public key steganography has recently been placed on formal grounds [16,2]. Möller employed binary twists to produce a space-efficient public key stegosystem [24]. The construction has the property that the ciphertexts appear as uniformly random bit strings. The construction is hybrid and involves a key encapsulation mechanism, one-time MAC, and a stream cipher and relies on an oracle Diffie-Hellman assumption.

Finally, a recent kleptographic attack on RSA key generation utilizes twists [31]. The construction relies on ECDDH and employs twisted binary curves. The key exchange value, that appears as a random bit string, is encoded in the upper order bits of the RSA modulus that is being generated. The shared secret is supplied to a random oracle to produce a random bit string that is used as the uppermost bits of the RSA prime p. Coppersmith's factoring algorithm is used for recovery [7] (following [8]). This scheme has the property that Alice's key exchange message and the shared secret appear as random bit strings.

Thus, one can see that our new "space-efficient pseudorandom key exchange" advances the work in these areas by achieving space-efficiency without relying on non-traditional hardness problems. Our contributions are the following:

1. We formally define the space-efficient pseudorandom key exchange problem.
2. We give a construction for the exchange, based on a twisted pair of curves over GF(p), and we prove the security under ECDDH in the standard (random oracle devoid) model.

3. We apply the key exchange to construct the first kleptographic (asymmetric backdoor) attack on SSL that has a proof of security in the standard model.

2   Background, Definitions, and Primitives

An asymmetric backdoor in SSL was presented in [14] that follows the kleptography paradigm [29,30]. We remark that this SSL attack is a solid step in the direction of building an asymmetric backdoor in SSL. However, the construction has the following shortcomings. The constructions are heuristic in nature and there are no proofs in the paper. Also, an elliptic curve key exchange is employed but is not described in sufficient detail. For example, the set of all compressed points on a typical cryptographically secure elliptic curve do not form a set of bit strings having a cardinality that is a power of 2 (not even close). For example, the $(m + 1)$-bit compressed points on a binary curve over $GF(2^m)$ correspond to about half of $\{0,1\}^{m+1}$, thus allowing trivial identification of the backdoor in black-box SSL/TLS implementations (in kleptography, the implementation and hence the curves are given to the distinguisher).

Recent work on the problem includes [15] that presents sketches of attacks that rely on hashing (no formal security arguments are made). The authors mention the use of elliptic curve crypto for the backdoor but share the same oversight as [14] in regards to trivial distinguishability of compressed points. The paper also explores various means of information leakage in SSH as well as defensive measures.

A construction for a steganographic key exchange was presented in [2] which does not rely on random oracles but requires the use of a universal hash function. Although we do not apply our result to steganography in this paper, it is worth pointing out that kleptography and public key steganography are related areas of research and our results do not require a universal hash function.

We now cover some notation and conventions. Uppercase is used to denote a point on an elliptic curve and lowercase is used to denote a scalar multiplier. So, xG denotes scalar multiplication. Recall that $0G = O$ (point at infinity), $1G = G$, $2G = G + G$, and so on. Unless otherwise stated, an element that is selected randomly is selected using the uniform distribution.

Every finite commutative group A satisfies a unique isomorphism of the form $A \cong (\mathbb{Z}/n_1\mathbb{Z}) \times ... \times (\mathbb{Z}/n_r\mathbb{Z})$ where n_{i+1} divides n_i for $1 \leq i < r$ and $n_r > 1$. The integer r is called the *rank* of the group A, and the r-tuple $(n_1, ..., n_r)$ is called the *group structure*.

Definition 1. *Let A be a commutative group, and let $(n_1, ..., n_r)$ represent the structure of the group. A **generating tuple** for the group A is an ordered tuple $(G_1, ..., G_r) \in A^r$ for which every element $X \in A$ can be written uniquely as $X = a_1G_1 + ... + a_rG_r$ where $0 \leq a_i < n_i$.*

2.1   Review of Twists and Kaliski's PRBG

Twists using the general class of elliptic curves over $GF(p)$ were studied and applied by Kaliski [18,19,20]. Denote by $E_{a,b}(\mathbb{F}_p)$ the elliptic curve $y^2 = x^3 + ax + b$

over the finite field $\mathbb{F}_p$. Let $\#E_{a,b}(\mathbb{F}_p)$ denote the number of points on the curve $E_{a,b}(\mathbb{F}_p)$. We sometimes use $E_{a,b}$ as shorthand for $E_{a,b}(\mathbb{F}_p)$. Let k be the length in bits of the prime p. Below we give Lemma 6.5 and Definition 6.1 from [19].

Lemma 1. *Let $\beta \neq 0$ be a quadratic nonresidue in the field $\mathbb{F}_p$ and let $E_{a,b}(\mathbb{F}_p)$ be an elliptic curve. Then for every value x, letting $y = \sqrt{x^3 + ax + b}$:*

1. *If y is a quadratic residue, then the points $(x, \pm y)$ are on the curve $E_{a,b}(\mathbb{F}_p)$.*
2. *If y is a quadratic nonresidue, then the points[1] $(\beta x, \pm\sqrt{\beta^3}y)$ are on the curve $E_{a\beta^2, b\beta^3}(\mathbb{F}_p)$.*
3. *If $y = 0$, then the point $(x, 0)$ is on the curve $E_{a,b}(\mathbb{F}_p)$ and the point $(\beta x, 0)$ is on the curve $E_{a\beta^2, b\beta^3}(\mathbb{F}_p)$.*

A corollary to this lemma is that the number of points *on* the two curves *is* $2p + 2$, two points for each value of x and two identity elements.

Definition 2. *Let $E_{a,b}(\mathbb{F}_p)$ be an elliptic curve of parameter k and let β be a quadratic nonresidue modulo p. A twisted pair $T_{a,b,\beta}(\mathbb{F}_p)$ of parameter k is the union [sic][2] of the elliptic curves $E_{a,b}(\mathbb{F}_p)$ and $E_{a\beta^2, b\beta^3}(\mathbb{F}_p)$.*

A twisted pair may be a multiset, since the curves $E_{a,b}(\mathbb{F}_p)$ and $E_{a\beta^2, b\beta^3}(\mathbb{F}_p)$ may intersect.

2.2 Embedding for the General Class Using Twists

Kaliski uses the symbol $'$ (prime) to differentiate points originating from the two curves. In other words, he uses P to denote a point from $E_{a,b}$ and P' to denote a point from $E_{a',b'} = E_{a\beta^2, b\beta^3}$. The presence or absence of the $'$ in the input to Kaliski's generator is really a parameter by itself. To clarify things we add a Boolean input to the PRBG to indicate which curve P was selected from instead of appending $'$ to P. We let $c = 0$ denote that P is a point chosen from $E_{a,b}$ and we let $c = 1$ denote that P is a point chosen from $E_{a',b'}$.

We now review Lemma 6.6 from [19]. Define $sgn : \mathbb{F}_p \to \{0,1\}$ to be 0 if $(p-1)/2 \geq y > 0$ and 1 otherwise. Function $X_T[T_{a,b,\beta}(\mathbb{F}_p)](P, i)$ is,

$$X_T[T_{a,b,\beta}(\mathbb{F}_p)](P, i) = \begin{cases} 2x + \text{sgn}(y) & \text{if } P = (x, y),\ y \neq 0,\ i = 0 \\ 2x/\beta + \text{sgn}(y) & \text{if } P = (x, y),\ y \neq 0,\ i = 1 \\ 2x & \text{if } P = (x, 0),\ i = 0 \\ 2x/\beta + 1 & \text{if } P = (x, 0),\ i = 1 \\ 2p & \text{if } P = O,\ i = 0 \\ 2p + 1 & \text{if } P = O,\ i = 1 \end{cases}$$

---

[1] We reviewed this definition in Appendix A of [32]. It had a typo in which the square-root symbol erroneously stretched over y. We fix that here.

[2] It is perhaps more accurate to say "collection" instead of "union" since Kaliski's small example in Table 6.1 has $(0,0)$ appearing twice in $T_{5,0,3}(\mathbb{F}_7)$. He confirms this by noting the possibility that the twisted pair may be a multiset.

Lemma 2. *Let $T_{a,b,\beta}(\mathbb{F}_p)$ be a twisted pair. The function $X_T[T_{a,b,\beta}(\mathbb{F}_p)](P,i)$ is a polynomial time computable, probabilistic polynomial time invertible mapping between the set of points on the twisted pair $T_{a,b,\beta}(\mathbb{F}_p)$ and the set $\{0, ..., 2p+1\}$.*

The proof of this lemma defines the inverse function, broken down for the case that the input is even or odd. The probabilistic polynomial time algorithm to compute square roots is used [25,1] that can be assumed to return the principal square root (the one whose sign is 0). Define $w = x^3 + ax + b$ for $x \neq p$.

$$X_{T,even}^{-1}[T_{a,b,\beta}(\mathbb{F}_p)](2x) = \begin{cases} ((x, \sqrt{w}), 0) & \text{if } w \text{ is a quadratic residue} \\ ((\beta x, \sqrt{\beta^3 w}), 1) & \text{if } w \text{ is a quadratic nonresidue} \\ ((x, 0), 0) & \text{if } w = 0 \\ (O, 0) & \text{if } x = p \end{cases}$$

$$X_{T,odd}^{-1}[T_{a,b,\beta}(\mathbb{F}_p)](2x+1) = \begin{cases} ((x, -\sqrt{w}), 0) & \text{if } w \text{ is a quadratic residue} \\ ((\beta x, -\sqrt{\beta^3 w}), 1) & \text{if } w \text{ is a quadratic nonresidue} \\ ((x, 0), 1) & \text{if } w = 0 \\ (O, 1) & \text{if } x = p \end{cases}$$

For simplicity we sometimes refer to $E_{a,b}$ as curve 0 and $E_{a',b'}$ as curve 1. Below we introduce functions that allow us to do embeddings using fixed-length bit strings. The input P to function Encode is a point originating on curve $c \in \{0,1\}$.

Encode($T_{a,b,\beta}(\mathbb{F}_p), P, c$):
1. let t_s be the binary string representing $t = X_T[T_{a,b,\beta}(\mathbb{F}_p)](P,c)$
2. if $|t_s| > k+1$ then output 0^k and halt
3. output $P_s = 0^{k+1-|t_s|} \| t_s$

For the primes we use, Step 2 will never output 0^k. Decode outputs (P,c) where P is a point residing on curve $c \in \{0,1\}$.

Decode($T_{a,b,\beta}(\mathbb{F}_p), P_s$):
1. let $ysgn$ be the least significant bit of P_s
2. let α be the integer corresponding to P_s
3. if ($ysgn = 0$) then output $(P,c) = X_{T,even}^{-1}[T_{a,b,\beta}(\mathbb{F}_p)](\alpha)$ and halt
4. output $(P,c) = X_{T,odd}^{-1}[T_{a,b,\beta}(\mathbb{F}_p)](\alpha)$

The following fact derives from Lemma 2.

Fact 1: Let $T_{a,b,\beta}(\mathbb{F}_p)$ be a twisted pair. Encode is a polynomial time computable, probabilistic polynomial time invertible mapping between the set of points on the twisted pair $T_{a,b,\beta}(\mathbb{F}_p)$ and all $(k+1)$-bit strings corresponding to the integers in the set $\{0, ..., 2p+1\}$ padded with leading zeros as necessary. The inverse function of Encode is Decode.

The following is Definition 6.4 from [19].

Definition 3. *A **twisted instance** of parameter k consists of a twisted pair $T_{a,b,\beta}(\mathbb{F}_p)$ of parameter k, generating pairs (G_1, G_2) and (G'_1, G'_2) for, respectively, the curves $E_{a,b}(\mathbb{F}_p)$ and $E_{a\beta^2, b\beta^3}(\mathbb{F}_p)$ contained in the twisted pair, a point P in the twisted pair, and $c \in \{0,1\}$ that denotes the curve that P was chosen from. Notation: $\langle T_{a,b,\beta}(\mathbb{F}_p), (G_1, G_2), (G'_1, G'_2), P, c \rangle$.*

2.3 Kaliski's PRBG for the General Class

We now review Definition 6.5 and Theorem 6.15 from [19]. We changed the definition to incorporate bit c_i. The function η_1 is the most significant bit function. $\eta_1(c, n)$ is 1 if $c \mod n \geq n/2$ and $\eta_1(c, n)$ is -1 if $c \mod n < n/2$.

Definition 4. *Let n and (n_1, n_2) denote the size and structure of the group $E_{a,b}(\mathbb{F}_p)$ and let n' and (n'_1, n'_2) denote the size and structure of $E_{a\beta^2, b\beta^3}(\mathbb{F}_p)$. The **general elliptic pseudorandom bit generator** inputs $O(k^8)$ bits, outputs $O(k^9)$ bits, operates on twisted instances and, for each parameter k computes a sequence $v(x_{j-1})...v(x_0)$ where x_0 is a twisted instance of parameter k selected uniformly at random and $x_{i+1} = f(x_i)$. The function f is defined as,*

$$f(\langle T_{a,b,\beta}(\mathbb{F}_p), (G_1, G_2), (G'_1, G'_2), P_i, c_i \rangle) = \langle T_{a,b,\beta}(\mathbb{F}_p), (G_1, G_2), (G'_1, G'_2), P_{i+1}, c_{i+1} \rangle$$

where (P_{i+1}, c_{i+1}) is computed as,

$$(P_{i+1}, c_{i+1}) = \begin{cases} ((x \mod n_1)G_1 + \lfloor x/n_1 \rfloor G_2, 0) & \text{if } 0 \leq x < n \\ (((x-n) \mod n'_1)G'_1 + \lfloor (x-n)/n'_1 \rfloor G'_2, 1) & \text{if } n \leq x < 2p+2 \end{cases}$$

and the integer x is computed as, $x = X_T[T_{a,b,\beta}(\mathbb{F}_p)](P_i, c_i)$ where $c_i \in \{0,1\}$ is the curve that P_i was selected from. The function v is defined as,

$$v(\langle T_{a,b,\beta}(\mathbb{F}_p), (G_1, G_2), (G'_1, G'_2), P_i, c_i \rangle) = \begin{cases} \eta_1(x, n_1) & \text{if } 0 \leq x < n \\ \eta_1(x-n, n'_1) & \text{if } n \leq x < 2p+2. \end{cases}$$

Theorem 1. *If the general elliptic logarithm problem is intractable then the general elliptic pseudorandom bit generator is cryptographically strong.*

2.4 Review of ECDDH and ECDDH Randomization

A group family $\mathcal{G}$ is a set of finite cyclic groups $\mathcal{G} = \{E_{a,b}(\mathbb{F}_p)\}$ where each group has prime order. Let IG_0 be an instance generator for $\mathcal{G}$ that on input k (in unary) generates the pair $(E_{a,b}(\mathbb{F}_p), G)$ where $E_{a,b}(\mathbb{F}_p)$ is from $\mathcal{G}$, G is a generator of $E_{a,b}(\mathbb{F}_p)$, and $r = \#E_{a,b}(\mathbb{F}_p)$.

Definition 5. *An ECDDH algorithm A_0 for $\mathcal{G}$ satisfies, for some fixed $\alpha > 0$ and sufficiently large k:*

$$|\Pr[A_0(E_{a,b}(\mathbb{F}_p), G, aG, bG, abG) = 1] - \Pr[A_0(E_{a,b}(\mathbb{F}_p), G, aG, bG, cG) = 1]| > \tfrac{1}{k^\alpha}$$

The probability is over the random choice of $(E_{a,b}(\mathbb{F}_p), G)$ according to the distribution induced by $\mathrm{IG}_0(k)$, the random choice of integers a, b, c satisfying $0 \le a, b, c \le r - 1$, and the bits used by A_0.

The ECDDH assumption is that no such polytime A_0 exists for $\mathcal{G}$. The following is the ECDDH randomization method from [5] adapted for the case of elliptic curves. Let $(E_{a,b}(\mathbb{F}_p), G, X, Y, Z)$ be an ECDDH problem instance. Algorithm f chooses scalars u_1, u_2, v randomly satisfying $0 \le u_1, u_2, v \le r - 1$.

$$f(E_{a,b}(\mathbb{F}_p), G, X, Y, Z) = (vX + u_1 G, Y + u_2 G, vZ + u_1 Y + vu_2 X + u_1 u_2 G)$$

If the input triple is a DH triple then the output is a random DH triple. If the input triple is not a DH triple then the output is a random 3-tuple.

3   The Twisted DDH Problem

In this section we introduce a new problem TDDH and show how it relates to ECDDH. Let TW_k denote the set of all twists of parameter k in which both groups (curves) in each twist have prime order. Let IG_1 be an instance generator for TW_k that on input k (in unary) generates the instance given by $\tau = (T_{a,b,\beta}(\mathbb{F}_p), G_1, G_1')$ where $T_{a,b,\beta}(\mathbb{F}_p)$ is in TW_k, G_1 is a generator of $E_{a,b}(\mathbb{F}_p)$ and G_1' is a generator of $E_{a',b'}(\mathbb{F}_p)$.

Definition 6. *A TDDH algorithm A_1 for TW_k satisfies, for some fixed $\alpha > 0$ and sufficiently large k:*

$$|\Pr[A_1(\tau, (aG_1, bG_1, abG_1), (a'G_1', b'G_1', a'b'G_1')) = 1] -$$
$$\Pr[A_1(\tau, (aG_1, bG_1, cG_1), (a'G_1', b'G_1', c'G_1')) = 1]| > \frac{1}{k^\alpha}$$

The probability is over the random choice of τ according to the distribution induced by $\mathrm{IG}_1(k)$, the random choice[3] of $a, b, c \in \{0, 1, ..., r - 1\}$, the random choice of $a', b', c' \in \{0, 1, 2, ..., r' - 1\}$, and the bits used by A_1.

The TDDH assumption is that no such polytime A_1 exists for TW_k. We refer to this as the *twisted DDH* assumption.

A distinguishing characteristic between the two curves in the twists that we use is as follows. In one curve the Weierstrass coefficient b is a quadratic residue whereas in the other curve it is a non-residue. For this reason we treat ECDDH differently for each of the two curves. Theorem 2 is straightforward to show. Being able to compute ECDDH for just one of the two curves in the twist breaks TDDH.

Theorem 2. *The TDDH problem polytime reduces to the ECDDH problem over $(E_{a,b}(\mathbb{F}_p), G_1)$ or ECDDH over $(E_{a',b'}(\mathbb{F}_p), G_1')$*

The other direction is Theorem 3.

---

[3] These a and b are not to be confused with the Weierstrass coefficients.

Theorem 3. *ECDDH over $(E_{a,b}(\mathbb{F}_p), G_1)$ or ECDDH over $(E_{a',b'}(\mathbb{F}_p), G_1')$ polytime reduces to TDDH.*

Proof. Let $t = (E_{a,b}, G_1, X, Y, Z)$ and $t' = (E_{a',b'}, G_1', X', Y', Z')$ be ECDDH problem instances. Suppose there exists a distinguisher D that solves TDDH.

$M_0(E_{a,b}, G_1, X, Y, Z)$:
1. compute $u = f(E_{a,b}, G_1, X, Y, Z)$
2. generate a random 3-tuple u' over $(E_{a',b'}, G_1')$
3. output (τ, u, u')

$M_1(E_{a',b'}, G_1', X', Y', Z')$:
1. compute $u' = f(E_{a',b'}, G_1', X', Y', Z')$
2. generate a random DH triple u over $(E_{a,b}, G_1)$
3. output (τ, u, u')

Clearly M_0 and M_1 run in time polynomial in k. Let $S_{0,DH}$ be the set of all DH triples over $(E_{a,b}, G_1)$ and let $S_{1,DH}$ be the set of all DH triples over $(E_{a',b'}, G_1')$. Let $S_{0,T}$ be the set of all 3-tuples over $(E_{a,b}, G_1)$ and let $S_{1,T}$ be the set of all 3-tuples over $(E_{a',b'}, G_1')$.

Without loss of generality we may suppose that the TDDH distinguisher D outputs 1 with advantage δ_1 in k when both 3-tuples are DH triples and 0 with advantage δ_0 in k when both 3-tuples are random 3-tuples, where δ_1 and δ_0 are non-negligible. Observe that a slightly less powerful distinguisher can be used to construct D, e.g., one in which δ_1 is non-negligible but δ_0 is negligible.

Consider the case that $v_0 \in_R S_{0,DH}$ and $v_1 \in_R S_{1,T}$. There are 3 cases:

Case 1: Consider the case that $D(\tau, v_0, v_1)$ outputs 0 with probability $1/2 \pm \gamma(k)$ where γ is negligible. Let $d = D(M_0(E_{a,b}, G_1, X, Y, Z))$. Algorithm M_0 generates u' to be a random 3-tuple over $(E_{a',b'}, G_1')$. Suppose that (X, Y, Z) is a DH triple. Then by the correctness of algorithm f, u is a random DH triple. So, in this case $d = 0$ with probability $1/2 \pm \gamma(k)$ (negligible advantage). Suppose that (X, Y, Z) is not a DH triple. Then by the correctness of f, u is a random 3-tuple. So, $d = 0$ with probability $1/2 + \delta_0(k)$ (non-negligible advantage). There is a polynomial time observable difference in behavior here. Therefore, $D(M_0(E_{a,b}, G_1, X, Y, Z))$ solves ECDDH over $(E_{a,b}, G_1)$.

Case 2: Consider the case that $D(\tau, v_0, v_1)$ outputs 0 with probability $1/2 - \delta_2(k)$ and 1 with probability $1/2 + \delta_2(k)$ where δ_2 is non-negligible. Let $d = D(M_0(E_{a,b}, G_1, X, Y, Z))$. Algorithm M_0 generates u' to be a random 3-tuple over $(E_{a',b'}, G_1')$. Suppose that (X, Y, Z) is a DH triple. Then by the correctness of algorithm f, u is a random DH triple. So, in this case $d = 1$ with probability $1/2 + \delta_2(k)$. Suppose that (X, Y, Z) is not a DH triple. Then by the correctness of f, u is a random 3-tuple. So, $d = 0$ with probability $1/2 + \delta_0(k)$. Therefore, $D(M_0(E_{a,b}, G_1, X, Y, Z))$ solves ECDDH over $(E_{a,b}, G_1)$.

Case 3: Consider the case that $D(\tau, v_0, v_1)$ outputs 0 with probability $1/2 + \delta_3(k)$ and 1 with probability $1/2 - \delta_3(k)$ where δ_3 is non-negligible. Let $d = D(M_1(E_{a',b'}, G_1', X', Y', Z'))$. Algorithm M_1 generates u to be a random DH triple over $(E_{a,b}, G_1)$. Suppose that (X', Y', Z') is a DH triple. Then by the correctness of algorithm f, u' is a random DH triple. So, in this case $d = 1$ with probability $1/2 + \delta_1(k)$. Suppose that (X', Y', Z') is not a DH triple. Then by the correctness of f, u' is a random 3-tuple. So, $d = 0$ with probability $1/2 + \delta_3(k)$. Therefore, $D(M_1(E_{a',b'}, G_1', X', Y', Z'))$ solves ECDDH over $(E_{a',b'}, G_1')$. $\diamond$

We have therefore shown that Theorem 4 holds (equivalence).

Theorem 4. *TDDH is polytime equivalent to ECDDH over $(E_{a,b}(\mathbb{F}_p), G_1)$ or ECDDH over $(E_{a',b'}(\mathbb{F}_p), G_1')$*

4   The Space-Efficient Pseudorandom Key Exchange

We define the space-efficient pseudorandom key exchange problem below. It is an error prone exchange. Bob fails to compute the shared secret with probability $1 - p_1$. The primitive is nonetheless useful.

Definition 7. *Let $\tau = (T_{a,b,\beta}(\mathbb{F}_p), G_1, G_1')$ be agreed upon system parameters where $|p| = k$ is the security parameter, let $t_{\tau,\Pi}$ denote the set of all possible transcripts (Y, Y', m_A, m_k) resulting from protocol Π and the distribution over them resulting from Π, let $t_{\tau,U}$ denote $E_{a,b}(\mathbb{F}_p) \times E_{a',b'}(\mathbb{F}_p) \times \{0,1\}^{k+1} \times \{0,1\}^\ell$ and the uniform distribution over it, and let Alice and Bob be efficient algorithms. If in a two round protocol Π between Alice and Bob,*

1. *Bob sends two exchange messages (Y, Y') to Alice where Y is chosen randomly from $E_{a,b}(\mathbb{F}_p)$ and Y' is chosen randomly from $E_{a',b'}(\mathbb{F}_p)$, and*
2. *Alice receives (Y, Y'), generates a $(k+1)$-bit message m_A and an ℓ-bit shared secret m_k, and sends m_A to Bob, and*
3. *Bob succeeds in computing m_k with probability p_1, and*
4. *(confidentiality) the fastest algorithm that computes m_k with non-negligible probability in k on input the 4-tuple (τ, Y, Y', m_A) runs in time exponential in k, and*
5. *(indistinguishability) the fastest algorithm that distinguishes ensemble $t_{\tau,\Pi}$ from ensemble $t_{\tau,U}$ with an advantage that is non-negligible (in k) runs in time exponential in k,*

*then Π is a **space-efficient pseudorandom key exchange** having success probability p_1.*

5   The Key Exchange Construction

For the key exchange we require that the prime $p = 2^k - \delta$ be used where δ satisfies $1 \leq \delta < \sqrt{2^k}$. The value δ may be randomly chosen until p of this form is found. The curves $E_{a,b}(\mathbb{F}_p)$ and $E_{a',b'}(\mathbb{F}_p)$ have prime order and must provide a suitable setting for ECDDH. For shorthand we define $r = \#E_{a,b}(\mathbb{F}_p)$ and $r' = \#E_{a',b'}(\mathbb{F}_p)$ which are both prime. From Subsection 2.1 it follows that

$r + r' = 2p + 2$. We remark that these special curves may have other applications since they provide a secure setting for ECDDH while at the same time form a twisted pair of curves. Example for $k = 223$:

$\mathtt{p} = \mathtt{7FFFFFFFFFFFFFFFFFFFFFFFFFFFFFEB827AAD8FF16901B27758B57A11F}$

$\mathtt{a} = \mathtt{66B8D3AFB14D309911554443EAF593E6CDC0431376AD682FE0EDF029}$

$\mathtt{b} = \mathtt{3AC5CF725D8207054CC3BEC8D0CEEB2D569B03D467F21133DA080DE0}$

$\beta = \mathtt{5D0E74ABC6D516767E80F78C50A4D8BF8C0854D247BFFBFAA4837582}$

Alice and Bob agree on a twisted pair $T_{a,b,\beta}(\mathbb{F}_p)$ of this form. They then choose a generator G_1 of $E_{a,b}(\mathbb{F}_p)$ and a generator G_1' of $E_{a',b'}(\mathbb{F}_p)$.

The fact that we use generators rather than generating pairs means that we employ a slightly simplified version of Kaliski's PRBG. We replace the generating pairs (e.g., in Definition 4) with generators in Kaliski's work. So, for example, in the definition of (P_{i+1}, c_{i+1}) we may replace G_2 with the point at infinity and G_2' with the point at infinity.

Technically, Kaliski's generator outputs a value drawn pseudorandomly from $\{1, -1\}^j$. We define algorithm $\mathtt{ECPRBG}(T_{a,b,\beta}(\mathbb{F}_p), G_1, G_1', P, c, j)$ that passes the instance $\langle T_{a,b,\beta}(\mathbb{F}_p), G_1, G_1', P, c \rangle$ to Kaliski's PRBG (modified to use generators). However, instead of outputting the result of Kaliski's pseudorandom generator, namely, $v(x_{j-1})...v(x_0)$, it outputs $(\mathrm{msb}(v(x_{j-1}))...\mathrm{msb}(v(x_0)), P_j, c_j)$. We define the predicate $\mathrm{msb}(x) = (1 + x)/2$. The value $c_j = 0$ if P_j was chosen from $E_{a,b}$ and $c_j = 1$ otherwise.

Protocol Π utilizes the randomized algorithm $\mathtt{SelCurv}(1^k)$ that outputs 0 with probability $r/(2p + 2)$ and 1 with probability $r'/(2p + 2)$.

Step 1: Bob chooses x randomly such that $0 \leq x \leq r - 1$ and chooses x' randomly such that $0 \leq x' \leq r' - 1$. He sends $(Y, Y') = (xG_1, x'G_1')$ to Alice.

Step 2: Alice sends m_A to Bob where $(m_A, m_k) = \mathtt{GenPairA}(Y, Y')$.

$\mathtt{GenPairA}(Y, Y')$:
1. compute $u = \mathtt{SelCurv}(1^k)$ and $v = \mathtt{SelCurv}(1^k)$
2. if $(u = 0)$ then
3.   choose $w \in_R \{0, 1, ..., r - 1\}$ and set $m_A = \mathtt{Encode}(T_{a,b,\beta}(\mathbb{F}_p), wG_1, u)$
4. else
5.   choose $w \in_R \{0, 1, ..., r' - 1\}$ and set $m_A = \mathtt{Encode}(T_{a,b,\beta}(\mathbb{F}_p), wG_1', u)$
6. if $(u \neq v)$ then
7.   if $(v = 0)$ then choose $z \in_R \{0, 1, ..., r - 1\}$ and compute $P = zG_1$
8.   if $(v = 1)$ then choose $z \in_R \{0, 1, ..., r' - 1\}$ and compute $P = zG_1'$
9. else
10.   if $(v = 0)$ then compute $P = wY$ else compute $P = wY'$
11. compute $(m_k, P_\ell, c_\ell) = \mathtt{ECPRBG}(T_{a,b,\beta}(\mathbb{F}_p), G_1, G_1', P, v, \ell)$
12. output (m_A, m_k)

Step 3: Bob computes $m_k = \mathtt{RecSecret}(m_A, x, x')$.

$\mathtt{RecSecret}(m_A, x, x')$:
1. compute $(U, u) = \mathtt{Decode}(T_{a,b,\beta}(\mathbb{F}_p), m_A)$

2. if $(u = 0)$ then compute $P = xU$ else compute $P = x'U$
3. output m_k where $(m_k, P_\ell, c_\ell) = \texttt{ECPRBG}(T_{a,b,\beta}(\mathbb{F}_p), G_1, G'_1, P, u, \ell)$

6   Security

The proof of Lemma 3 uses an algorithm Adv with an unspecified running time (leaves open the possibility of being polytime, superpolytime, etc.).

Lemma 3. *TDDH polytime reduces to the problem of computing m_k with non-negligible probability in k on input τ, Y, Y', m_A from protocol Π.*

Proof. Suppose there exists an algorithm Adv that computes m_k with non-negligible probability in k on input τ, Y, Y', m_A. Consider the following algorithm M that takes as input the TDDH problem instance (τ, t_0, t_1) where $t_0 = (X, Y, Z)$ and $t_1 = (X', Y', Z')$.

$\text{M}(\tau, t_0, t_1)$:
1. compute $(X_r, Y_r, Z_r) = f(E_{a,b}(\mathbb{F}_p), G_1, X, Y, Z)$
2. compute $(X'_r, Y'_r, Z'_r) = f(E_{a',b'}(\mathbb{F}_p), G'_1, X', Y', Z')$
3. compute $u = \texttt{SelCurv}(1^k)$ and $v = \texttt{SelCurv}(1^k)$
4. if $(u = 0)$ then set $m_A = \texttt{Encode}(T_{a,b,\beta}(\mathbb{F}_p), X_r, u)$
5. if $(u = 1)$ then set $m_A = \texttt{Encode}(T_{a,b,\beta}(\mathbb{F}_p), X'_r, u)$
6. if $(u \neq v)$ then
7.   if $(v = 0)$ then choose $z \in_R \{0, 1, ..., r - 1\}$ and compute $P = zG_1$
8.   if $(v = 1)$ then choose $z \in_R \{0, 1, ..., r' - 1\}$ and compute $P = zG'_1$
9. else
10.   if $(v = 0)$ then set $P = Z_r$ else set $P = Z'_r$
11. compute $(m_k, P_\ell, c_\ell) = \texttt{ECPRBG}(T_{a,b,\beta}(\mathbb{F}_p), G_1, G'_1, P, v, \ell)$
12. compute $\sigma = \texttt{Adv}(\tau, Y_r, Y'_r, m_A)$
13. if $(\sigma = m_k)$ then output 1 else output 0

Ignoring the running time of Adv, clearly M runs in time polynomial in k.

    Suppose t_0 and t_1 are DH triples. Then from the correctness of algorithm f, both (X_r, Y_r, Z_r) and (X'_r, Y'_r, Z'_r) are random DH triples. It follows that the tuple (Y_r, Y'_r, m_A, m_k) is drawn from the same set and probability distribution as Π. So, $(\sigma = m_k)$ with non-negligible probability. Therefore, M outputs 1 with non-negligible probability.

    Suppose t_0 and t_1 are not DH triples. Then from the correctness of f, both (X_r, Y_r, Z_r) and (X'_r, Y'_r, Z'_r) are random 3-tuples. So, Adv can do no better than guess m_k (e.g., by guessing point P from the twist that is input to ECPRBG). It follows that $(\sigma = m_k)$ with negligible probability. Therefore, M outputs 1 with negligible probability. ◇

    Lemma 3 and Theorem 4 give the following theorem that shows that Property 4 of Definition 7 holds.

Theorem 5. *If ECDDH requires exponential time (in k) on both curves in $T_{a,b,\beta}(\mathbb{F}_p)$ then computing m_k with non-negligible probability (in k) on input the tuple (τ, Y, Y', m_A) from protocol Π is hard.*

Let Π_2 be Π except that GenPairA2 is used instead of GenPairA. Note that Y and Y' are not used by GenPairA2.

GenPairA2(Y, Y'):
1. compute $u = \texttt{SelCurv}(1^k)$ and $v = \texttt{SelCurv}(1^k)$
2. if $(u = 0)$ then
3.   choose $w \in_R \{0, 1, ..., r - 1\}$ and set $m_A = \texttt{Encode}(T_{a,b,\beta}(\mathbb{F}_p), wG_1, u)$
4. else
5.   choose $w \in_R \{0, 1, ..., r' - 1\}$ and set $m_A = \texttt{Encode}(T_{a,b,\beta}(\mathbb{F}_p), wG_1', u)$
6. if $(v = 0)$ then choose $z \in_R \{0, 1, ..., r - 1\}$ and compute $P = zG_1$
7. if $(v = 1)$ then choose $z \in_R \{0, 1, ..., r' - 1\}$ and compute $P = zG_1'$
8. compute $(m_k, P_\ell, c_\ell) = \texttt{ECPRBG}(T_{a,b,\beta}(\mathbb{F}_p), G_1, G_1', P, v, \ell)$
9. output (m_A, m_k)

Lemma 4. *TDDH polytime reduces to the problem of distinguishing $t_{\tau,\Pi}$ from t_{τ,Π_2} with an advantage that is non-negligible (in k).*

Proof. Suppose there exists an algorithm D that distinguishes $t_{\tau,\Pi}$ from t_{τ,Π_2} with an advantage that is non-negligible in k. Consider the following polytime algorithm M that takes as input a problem instance (τ, t_0, t_1) for TDDH where $t_0 = (X, Y, Z)$ and $t_1 = (X', Y', Z')$.

M(τ, t_0, t_1):
1. compute $(X_r, Y_r, Z_r) = f(E_{a,b}(\mathbb{F}_p), G_1, X, Y, Z)$
2. compute $(X_r', Y_r', Z_r') = f(E_{a',b'}(\mathbb{F}_p), G_1', X', Y', Z')$
3. compute $u = \texttt{SelCurv}(1^k)$ and $v = \texttt{SelCurv}(1^k)$
4. if $(u = 0)$ then set $m_A = \texttt{Encode}(T_{a,b,\beta}(\mathbb{F}_p), X_r, u)$
5. if $(u = 1)$ then set $m_A = \texttt{Encode}(T_{a,b,\beta}(\mathbb{F}_p), X_r', u)$
6. if $(u \neq v)$ then
7.   if $(v = 0)$ then choose $z \in_R \{0, 1, ..., r - 1\}$ and compute $P = zG_1$
8.   if $(v = 1)$ then choose $z \in_R \{0, 1, ..., r' - 1\}$ and compute $P = zG_1'$
9. else
10.   if $(v = 0)$ then set $P = Z_r$ else set $P = Z_r'$
11. compute $(m_k, P_\ell, c_\ell) = \texttt{ECPRBG}(T_{a,b,\beta}(\mathbb{F}_p), G_1, G_1', P, v, \ell)$
12. output $(\tau, Y_r, Y_r', m_A, m_k)$

   Suppose t_0 and t_1 are DH triples. From the correctness of algorithm f, both (X_r, Y_r, Z_r) and (X_r', Y_r', Z_r') are random DH triples. It follows that the tuple (Y_r, Y_r', m_A, m_k) is drawn from the same set and probability distribution as Π.
   Suppose t_0 and t_1 are not DH triples. Then from the correctness of f, both (X_r, Y_r, Z_r) and (X_r', Y_r', Z_r') are random 3-tuples. It follows that the tuple (Y_r, Y_r', m_A, m_k) is drawn from the same set and probability distribution as Π_2.
   It follows that $D(M(\tau, t_0, t_1))$ solves TDDH. $\diamond$

Let Π_3 be Π_2 except that GenPairA3 is used instead of GenPairA2.

GenPairA3(Y, Y'):
1. compute $u = \texttt{SelCurv}(1^k)$
2. if $(u = 0)$ then

3.   choose $w \in_R \{0, 1, ..., r - 1\}$ and set $m_A = \text{Encode}(T_{a,b,\beta}(\mathbb{F}_p), wG_1, u)$
4. else
5.   choose $w \in_R \{0, 1, ..., r' - 1\}$ and set $m_A = \text{Encode}(T_{a,b,\beta}(\mathbb{F}_p), wG_1', u)$
6. choose $m_k \in_R \{0, 1\}^\ell$ and output (m_A, m_k)

Lemma 5. *ECDL polytime reduces to the problem of distinguishing t_{τ, Π_2} from t_{τ, Π_3} with an advantage that is non-negligible in k.*

Proof. Suppose that there exists an algorithm D that distinguishes t_{τ, Π_2} from t_{τ, Π_3} with an advantage that is non-negligible in k. Consider the following poly-time algorithm M that takes as input an ℓ-bit string m_k that is either random or pseudorandomly generated using Kaliski's PRBG (an output of -1 from Kaliski's generator is converted to a 0).

$M(\tau, m_k)$:
1. choose $x \in \mathbb{Z}$ randomly such that $0 \le x \le r - 1$ and compute $Y = xG_1$
2. choose $x' \in \mathbb{Z}$ randomly such that $0 \le x \le r' - 1$ and compute $Y' = x'G_1'$
3. compute $u = \text{SelCurv}(1^k)$
4. if $(u = 0)$ then
5.   choose $w \in_R \{0, 1, ..., r - 1\}$ and set $m_A = \text{Encode}(T_{a,b,\beta}(\mathbb{F}_p), wG_1, u)$
6. else
7.   choose $w \in_R \{0, 1, ..., r' - 1\}$ and set $m_A = \text{Encode}(T_{a,b,\beta}(\mathbb{F}_p), wG_1', u)$
8. output (τ, Y, Y', m_A, m_k)

Suppose m_k is drawn from the same set and probability distribution as Kaliski's generator. Then (Y, Y', m_A, m_k) is drawn from the same set and probability distribution as Π_2. Now suppose that $m_k \in_R \{0, 1\}^\ell$. Then (Y, Y', m_A, m_k) is drawn from the same set and probability distribution as Π_3.

It follows that $D(M(\tau, m_k))$ distinguishes whether m_k is random or pseudo-random with non-negligible advantage in k. It can be shown that this implies the solution to the ECDL problem (using the results of Kaliski, see Theorem 1 in Subsection 2.3). $\diamond$

Let $\text{GenPairA4}(Y, Y')$ be an algorithm that outputs the pair (m_A, m_k) where $m_A \in_R \{0, 1\}^{k+1}$ and $m_k \in_R \{0, 1\}^\ell$. Let Π_4 be protocol Π_3 except that the algorithm GenPairA4 is used by Alice instead of GenPairA3.

Lemma 6. *t_{τ, Π_3} is statistically indistinguishable from t_{τ, Π_4}.*

Proof. The distance is $\frac{1}{2}(t_0 + t_1)$. Term t_0 is for the case that m_A is an encoded point on $T_{a,b,\beta}(\mathbb{F}_p)$. Term t_1 is for the case that m_A is not an encoded point on $T_{a,b,\beta}(\mathbb{F}_p)$. Recall that $p = 2^k - \delta$. So, $2p + 2 = 2^{k+1} - 2\delta + 2$. The terms corresponding to the selection of Y and Y' cancel out.

$$t_0 = (2p + 2)2^\ell \left| \frac{1}{2p+2} \frac{1}{2^\ell} - \frac{1}{2^{k+1}} \frac{1}{2^\ell} \right| = \left| 1 - \frac{2p+2}{2^{k+1}} \right| = 1 - \frac{2^k - \delta + 1}{2^k} = \frac{\delta}{2^k} - \frac{1}{2^k}$$

$$t_1 = (2^{k+1} - (2p + 2))2^\ell \left| 0 * \frac{1}{2^\ell} - \frac{1}{2^{k+1}} \frac{1}{2^\ell} \right| = \frac{2^{k+1} - (2p+2)}{2^{k+1}} = \frac{2\delta - 2}{2^{k+1}} = \frac{\delta - 1}{2^k} \quad \diamond$$

Observe that $t_{\tau,\Pi_4} = t_{\tau,U}$, the uniform distribution.

The success probability of protocol Π is $p_1 = (\frac{r}{2p+2})^2 + (\frac{r'}{2p+2})^2$. It can be shown using Hasse's Theorem that p_1 is overwhelmingly (in k) close to $1/2$.

Fact 1: Let D_k^1, D_k^2, and D_k^3 be probability ensembles with common security parameter k. It is well-known that if D_k^1 and D_k^2 are computationally indistinguishable and D_k^2 and D_k^3 are computationally indistinguishable, then D_k^1 and D_k^3 are computationally indistinguishable (see Lecture 7, [23]).

Combining Fact 1 with Theorem 4 and Lemmas 4, 5, and 6 gives the following theorem that shows that Property 5 of Definition 7 holds.

Theorem 6. *If ECDDH requires exponential time (in k) on both curves in $T_{a,b,\beta}(\mathbb{F}_p)$ then distinguishing $t_{\tau,\Pi}$ from $t_{\tau,U}$ is hard.*

Theorems 5 and 6 give Theorem 7.

Theorem 7. *If the fastest ECDDH algorithm for both curves in $T_{a,b,\beta}(\mathbb{F}_p)$ requires exponential time (in k) then Π is a space-efficient pseudorandom key exchange having success probability overwhelmingly (in k) close to $1/2$.*

7   Application: Kleptographic Attack Against SSL

In this section we show an asymmetric backdoor in SSL.[4] Our EC pseudorandom key exchange has other applications: It can be used to devise an asymmetric backdoor (SETUP) in RSA key generation. It can also be used to devise a public key stegosystem. These constructions are in the standard (random oracle devoid) model, but space limitations prevent us from showing them here.

In SSL the client sends a 28 byte hello nonce to the server in the client hello message. The server sends a 28 byte hello nonce to the client in the server hello message. The client then sends a 46 byte nonce to the server encrypted under the server's public key. These 28+28+46 bytes, plus additional available information is all that is needed to derive all key material, IVs, and so on for the session. So, it is enough to eavesdrop on the SSL session.

Observe that the cleartext output of the client contains a very small subliminal channel. More specifically, we identified the 224 bits (28 bytes) of the hello nonce. This is a publicly readable subliminal channel since it can be passively read by an eavesdropper on the network. The random 46 bytes that are asymmetrically encrypted are not publicly readable.

Our goals are to: (1) covertly leak SSL secrets to the designer that acts as a passive eavesdropper on the network, (2) have the ensemble corresponding to the I/O of the client that contains the backdoor be computationally indistinguishable from the ensemble corresponding to the I/O of a client that doesn't contain the backdoor under black-box queries (when the distinguisher is permitted to act as

---

[4] Freier, Karlton, and Kocher, Internet Draft "The SSL Protocol Version 3.0," Network Working Group, Nov. 18, 1996.

the SSL server and learn the 46 byte nonce and know the *entire* specification of the backdoor and recovery algorithms), and (3) maintain the security of SSL sessions against all passive eavesdroppers except the designer.

We now review the notion of an asymmetric backdoor, which is also called a secretly embedded trapdoor with universal protection (SETUP) [29,30]. The threat model involves: a designer, an eavesdropper, and an inquirer. The inquirer may act as an SSL server in order to determine if the client has a backdoor or not. Intuitively speaking, the designer is Bob and the device is Alice and they effectively conduct a space-efficient pseudorandom key exchange.

The designer devises an SSL client G_1 that appears to behave exactly like a "normal" SSL client G_0 but that has a backdoor (we call G_0 the reference client). The designer places his public keys (Y, Y') in G_1 and keeps the corresponding private keys (x, x') secret. By passively eavesdropping on the network, the designer obtains the hello nonces from the hello messages that both emanate from and that are sent to G_1.

Let $\overline{m}_A = (m_{A,1}, m_{A,2}, ..., m_{A,L})$ be a contiguous sequence of hello nonces that is output by G_1 and obtained by the designer. Let $\overline{s} = (s_1, s_2, ..., s_L)$ be session information. The session traffic s_i where $1 \le i \le L$ contains enough information to verify a key and IV guess for SSL session i. Among other things this includes the server's hello nonce. The designer passes $(\overline{m}_A, \overline{s}, x, x')$ to a recovery algorithm $\mathcal{R}_1$.

The backdoor has the property that the reverse-engineer who breaches the black-box that houses it will see that it is there. But, the backdoor is asymmetric so the reverse-engineer will not be able to use it. The reverse-engineer will learn the public keys (Y, Y') but not the needed private decryption keys (x, x'). The designer, on the other hand, learns the pre-master secret nonces using the recovery algorithm and (x, x').

Let $k = 223$ and let $\ell = 8 * 46 = 368$. The SSL client G_1 that contains the backdoor generates the client hello message m_A and pre-master secret nonce m_k using G_1. The point U is stored in non-volatile memory across calls to G_1. Initially, $U = \bot$ (denoting that U has not yet been assigned). The Boolean c and counter μ are also stored in non-volatile memory. μ is initially zero. The constant max is used to limit the number of bits from Kaliski's PRBG that the asymmetric backdoor asks for.

$G_1(Y, Y')$:
1. compute $u = \texttt{SelCurv}(1^k)$ and $v = \texttt{SelCurv}(1^k)$
2. if $(u = 0)$ then
3.   choose $w \in_R \{0, 1, ..., r - 1\}$ and set $m_A = \texttt{Encode}(T_{a,b,\beta}(\mathbb{F}_p), wG_1, u)$
4. else
5.   choose $w \in_R \{0, 1, ..., r' - 1\}$ and set $m_A = \texttt{Encode}(T_{a,b,\beta}(\mathbb{F}_p), wG'_1, u)$
6. if $(u \ne v)$ then
7.   if $((U = \bot)$ or $(\mu = max))$ then
8.   set $c = v$
9.   if $(v = 0)$ then choose $z \in_R \{0, 1, ..., r - 1\}$ and compute $P = zG_1$
10.   if $(v = 1)$ then choose $z \in_R \{0, 1, ..., r' - 1\}$ and compute $P = zG'_1$

11.   else set $P = U$ and set $\mu \leftarrow \mu + 1$
12. else
13.   if $(v = 0)$ then compute $P = wY$ else compute $P = wY'$
14.   set $\mu = 0$ and set $c = v$
15. compute $(m_k, P_\ell, c_\ell) = \texttt{ECPRBG}(T_{a,b,\beta}(\mathbb{F}_p), G_1, G_1', P, c, \ell)$
16. if $((U \neq \perp)$ or $(u = v))$ then set $(U, c) = (P_\ell, c_\ell)$
17. output (m_A, m_k)

An important observation is that in each session with probability close to $1/2$ the non-volatile memory elements (U, c, μ) will be refreshed. That is, (U, c) will be near the beginning of an entirely new PRBG sequence.

The corresponding recovery algorithm is $\mathcal{R}_1(\overline{m}_A, \overline{s}, x, x')$. It outputs the empty list or the values $(m_{k,j}, m_{k,j+1}, ..., m_{k,L})$ where $j \geq 1$ is the first exchange in which Bob (the designer) can recover the ECDH shared secret.

$\mathcal{R}_1(\overline{m}_A, \overline{s}, x, x')$:
1. set $(\mu, j) = (0, \infty)$ and set $fnd = 0$
2. for $i = 1$ to L do:
3.   compute $m_{k,i} = \texttt{RecSecret}(m_{A,i}, x, x')$
4.   compute $t = \texttt{IsCorrectPreMaster}(m_{A,i}, s_i, m_{k,i})$
5.   if $(t = 1)$
6.   if $(i < j)$ then set $j = i$
7.   compute $(U, u) = \texttt{Decode}(T_{a,b,\beta}(\mathbb{F}_p), m_{A,i})$
8.   if $(u = 0)$ then compute $P = xU$ else compute $P = x'U$
9.   set $(m_{k,i}, P_\ell, c_\ell) = \texttt{ECPRBG}(T_{a,b,\beta}(\mathbb{F}_p), G_1, G_1', P, u, \ell)$
10.   set $fnd = 1$, $P = P_\ell$, $c = c_\ell$, and set $\mu = 0$
11.   if $((t = 0)$ and $(j \neq \infty))$ then
12.   if $(\mu = max)$ then output $\emptyset$ and halt
13.   set $(m_{k,i}, P_\ell, c_\ell) = \texttt{ECPRBG}(T_{a,b,\beta}(\mathbb{F}_p), G_1, G_1', P, c, \ell)$
14.   set $P = P_\ell$, $c = c_\ell$, and set $\mu \leftarrow \mu + 1$
15. if $(fnd = 1)$ then output list $m_{k,j}, m_{k,j+1}, ..., m_{k,L}$ else output $\emptyset$

If max and L are large enough then $\emptyset$ will be output with negligible probability. This algorithm can be changed to enable better recovery of 46 byte nonces.

In practice the designer will be very successful in eavesdropping on SSL sessions. Given a list of consecutive sessions, the first DH shared secret (i.e., the first time that $u = v$ in Π and hence the first time that recovery is possible) will be in SSL session $i \geq 1$ with probability $(1 - p_1)^{i-1} p_1$. This is p_1 for $i = 1$, $(1 - p_1)p_1$ for $i = 2$, and so on. In Section 6 we showed that p_1 is overwhelmingly (in k) close to $1/2$. Furthermore, for a large enough value for max in $\mathcal{G}_1$, the designer will with overwhelming probability learn every pre-master secret nonce from then on in practice. Due to space limitations we do not include a proof of the following claims. We remark that whereas SSL relies on idealized hash functions, our construction does not.

Claim 1. *If ECDDH is exponentially hard on both curves in $T_{a,b,\beta}(\mathbb{F}_p)$ then computational indistinguishability holds for the SETUP attack on SSL.*

Claim 2. *If ECDDH is exponentially hard on both curves in $T_{a,b,\beta}(\mathbb{F}_p)$ and the SSL key exchange algorithm is secure then confidentiality holds for the SETUP attack on SSL.*

Claim 3. *If ECDDH is exponentially hard on both curves in $T_{a,b,\beta}(\mathbb{F}_p)$ and the SSL key exchange algorithm is secure then the asymmetric backdoor attack $\mathcal{G}_1$ is a SETUP version of SSL client $\mathcal{G}_0$ having recovery algorithm $\mathcal{R}_1$.*

8   Conclusion

We presented the notion of a space-efficient pseudorandom key exchange. A construction was presented in the standard model based on twists over $GF(p)$ and we applied it to build the first asymmetric backdoor in SSL in the standard model.

References

1. Adleman, L.M., Manders, K., Miller, G.: On Taking Roots in Finite Fields. In: IEEE Foundations of Computer Science—FOCS 1977, pp. 175–177. IEEE Computer Society Press, Los Alamitos (1977)
2. von Ahn, L., Hopper, N.J.: Public-Key Steganography. In: Cachin, C., Camenisch, J.L. (eds.) EUROCRYPT 2004. LNCS, vol. 3027, pp. 323–341. Springer, Heidelberg (2004)
3. Anderson, R.J.: A Practical RSA Trapdoor. Elec. Letters 29(11) (1993)
4. Anderson, R., Vaudenay, S., Preneel, B., Nyberg, K.: The Newton Channel. In: Workshop on Information Hiding, pp. 151–156 (1996)
5. Boneh, D.: The Decision Diffie-Hellman Problem. In: Third Algorithmic Number Theory Symposium—ANTS III, pp. 48–63 (1998)
6. Chevassut, O., Fouque, P., Gaudry, P., Pointcheval, D.: The Twist-AUgmented Technique for Key Exchange. In: Yung, M., Dodis, Y., Kiayias, A., Malkin, T.G. (eds.) PKC 2006. LNCS, vol. 3958, pp. 410–426. Springer, Heidelberg (2006)
7. Coppersmith, D.: Finding a small root of a bivariate integer equation; factoring with high bits known. In: Maurer, U.M. (ed.) EUROCRYPT 1996. LNCS, vol. 1070, pp. 178–189. Springer, Heidelberg (1996)
8. Crépeau, C., Slakmon, A.: Simple Backdoors for RSA Key Generation. In: The Cryptographers Track at the RSA Conference, pp. 403–416 (2003)
9. Desmedt, Y.: Abuses in Cryptography and How to Fight Them. In: Goldwasser, S. (ed.) CRYPTO 1988. LNCS, vol. 403, pp. 375–389. Springer, Heidelberg (1990)
10. Diffie, W., Hellman, M.: New Directions in Cryptography. IEEE Transactions on Information Theory IT-22(6), 644–654 (1976)
11. Damgård, I., Landrock, P., Pomerance, C.: Average Case Error Estimates for the Strong Probable Prime Test. Math. of Comput. 61(203), 177–194 (1993)
12. Dodis, Y., Gennaro, R., Håstad, J., Krawczyk, H., Rabin, T.: Randomness Extraction and Key Derivation Using the CBC, Cascade and HMAC Modes. In: Franklin, M. (ed.) CRYPTO 2004. LNCS, vol. 3152, pp. 494–510. Springer, Heidelberg (2004)
13. Gennaro, R., Krawczyk, H., Rabin, T.: Secure Hashed Diffie-Hellman over Non-DDH Groups. In: Cachin, C., Camenisch, J.L. (eds.) EUROCRYPT 2004. LNCS, vol. 3027, pp. 361–381. Springer, Heidelberg (2004)

14. Goh, E.-J., Boneh, D., Pinkas, B., Golle, P.: The Design and Implementation of Protocol-Based Hidden Key Recovery. In: Boyd, C., Mao, W. (eds.) ISC 2003. LNCS, vol. 2851, pp. 165–179. Springer, Heidelberg (2003)
15. Golebiewski, Z., Kutylowski, M., Zagorski, F.: Stealing Secrets with SSL/TLS and SSH—Kleptographic Attacks. In: Pointcheval, D., Mu, Y., Chen, K. (eds.) CANS 2006. LNCS, vol. 4301, pp. 191–202. Springer, Heidelberg (2006)
16. Hopper, N.J., Langford, J., von Ahn, L.: Provably Secure Steganography. In: Yung, M. (ed.) CRYPTO 2002. LNCS, vol. 2442, pp. 77–92. Springer, Heidelberg (2002)
17. Impagliazzo, R., Levin, L., Luby, M.: Pseudo-Random Generation from One-Way Functions. In: Symp. on the Th. of Comp.—STOC 1989, pp. 12–24 (1989)
18. Kaliski, B.S.: A Pseudo-Random Bit Generator Based on Elliptic Logarithms. In: Odlyzko, A.M. (ed.) CRYPTO 1986. LNCS, vol. 263, pp. 84–103. Springer, Heidelberg (1987)
19. Kaliski, B.S.: Elliptic Curves and Cryptography: A Pseudorandom Bit Generator and Other Tools. PhD Thesis, MIT (February 1988)
20. Kaliski, B.S.: One-Way Permutations on Elliptic Curves. Journal of Cryptology 3(3), 187–199 (1991)
21. Kaliski, B.S.: Anderson's RSA trapdoor can be broken. Elec. Letters 29(15) (1993)
22. Lenstra, A.K.: Generating RSA Moduli with a Predetermined Portion. In: Ohta, K., Pei, D. (eds.) ASIACRYPT 1998. LNCS, vol. 1514, pp. 1–10. Springer, Heidelberg (1998)
23. Luby, M.: Pseudorandomness and Cryptographic Applications. Princeton Computer Science Notes (1996)
24. Möller, B.: A Public-Key Encryption Scheme with Pseudo-Random Ciphertexts. In: Samarati, P., Ryan, P.Y A, Gollmann, D., Molva, R. (eds.) ESORICS 2004. LNCS, vol. 3193, pp. 335–351. Springer, Heidelberg (2004)
25. Rabin, M.: Probabilistic Algorithms in Finite Fields. SIAM Journal on Computing 9, 273–280 (1980)
26. Simmons, G.J.: The Prisoners' Problem and the Subliminal Channel. In: Advances in Cryptology—Crypto 1983, pp. 51–67. Plenum Press, New York (1984)
27. Simmons, G.J.: Subliminal Channels: past and present. European Tra. on Telecommunications 5, 459–473 (1994)
28. Weis, R., Lucks, S.: All your key bit are belong to us—the true story of black box cryptography. In: Proc. of SANE, pp. 27–31 (2002)
29. Young, A., Yung, M.: The Dark Side of Black-Box Cryptography, or: Should We Trust Capstone? In: Koblitz, N. (ed.) CRYPTO 1996. LNCS, vol. 1109, pp. 89–103. Springer, Heidelberg (1996)
30. Young, A., Yung, M.: Kleptography: Using Cryptography Against Cryptography. In: Fumy, W. (ed.) EUROCRYPT 1997. LNCS, vol. 1233, pp. 62–74. Springer, Heidelberg (1997)
31. Young, A., Yung, M.: A Space Efficient Backdoor in RSA and its Applications. In: Preneel, B., Tavares, S. (eds.) SAC 2005. LNCS, vol. 3897, pp. 128–143. Springer, Heidelberg (2006)
32. Young, A., Yung, M.: An Elliptic Curve Backdoor Algorithm for RSASSA. In: Information Hiding—IH 2006 (2006)

How Can Reed-Solomon Codes Improve Steganographic Schemes?

Caroline Fontaine* and Fabien Galand

CNRS/IRISA-TEMICS,
Campus de Beaulieu, 35 042 Rennes cedex, France
caroline.fontaine@irisa.fr, fabien.galand@irisa.fr

Abstract. The use of syndrome coding in steganographic schemes tends to reduce distortion during embedding. The more complete model comes from the wet papers [FGLS05] which allow to lock positions that cannot be modified. Recently, BCH codes have been investigated, and seem to be good candidates in this context [SW06]. Here, we show that Reed-Solomon codes are twice better with respect to the number of locked positions and that, in fact, they are optimal. We propose two methods for managing these codes in this context: the first one is based on a naive decoding process through Lagrange interpolation; the second one, more efficient, is based on list decoding techniques and provides an adaptive trade-off between the number of locked positions and the embedding efficiency.

1 Introduction

Steganography aims at sending a message through a cover-medium, in an *undetectable* way. *Undetectable* means that nobody, except the intended receiver of the message, should be able to tell if the medium is carrying a message or not [Sim84]. Hence, if we speak about still images as cover-media, the embedding should work with the smallest possible distortion, but also not being detectable with the quite powerful analysis tools available [BW04, Fra02]. A lot of papers have been published on this topic, and it appears that modeling the embedding and detection/extraction processes with an error correcting code point of view, usually called matrix embedding by the steganographic community, may be helpful to achieve these goals [Cra98, GK03, FGLS05, FGS05a, FGS06, FS06, SW06]. The main interest of this approach is that it decreases the number of component modifications during the embedding process. As a side effect, it was remarked in [FGLS05] that matrix embedding could be used to provide an effective answer to the adaptive selection channel: the sender can embed the messages adaptively with the cover-medium to minimize the distortion, and the receiver can extract the messages without being aware of the sender's choices. A typical steganographic application is the perturbed quantization [FGS05b]: during quantization process, e.g. JPEG compression, real values v have to be rounded between possible quantized values $x_0, ..., x_j$; when v lies close to the middle of an interval

---

* Corresponding author.

T. Furon et al. (Eds.): IH 2007, LNCS 4567, pp. 130–144, 2007.
© Springer-Verlag Berlin Heidelberg 2007

$[x_i, x_{i+1}]$, one can choose between x_i and x_{i+1} without adding too much distortion. This embeds messages under the condition that the receiver does not need to know which positions where modified.

It has been shown that if random codes may seem interesting for their asymptotic behavior, they impose to solve really hard problems: syndrome decoding and covering radius computation, which are proved to be NP-complete and Π_2-complete respectively (the Π_2 complexity class includes the NP class) [Var97, McL84]. Moreover, no efficient decoding algorithm is known, even for a small non trivial family of codes. From a practical point of view, this implies that the related steganographic schemes are too much complex to be considered as acceptable for real life applications. Hence, it is of great interest to have a deeper look at other kinds of codes, structured codes, which are more accessible and lead to efficient decoding algorithms. In this way, some previous papers studied the Hamming code [Cra98, Wes01, FGS05a], the Simplex code [FS06] and BCH codes [SW06]. Here, we focus on this latter paper, that pointed out the interest in using BCH codes. The authors distinguish two cases, as previously introduced in [FGLS05]. The first one is the more classical one: the embedder modifies any position of the cover-data (a vector which is extracted from the cover-medium, and processed by the encoding scheme), the only constraint being the maximum number of modifications. In this case, they showed that BCH codes behave well, but also pointed out that choosing the most appropriate code among the BCH family is quite hard: we do not know good complete syndrome decoding algorithm for BCH codes. In the second case, some positions are locked and cannot be used for embedding; this is due to the fact that modifying these positions lead to a degradation of the cover-medium that is noticeable. Hence, in order to remain undetectable, the sender restricts himself to keep these positions and lock them. This case is more realistic. The authors showed there is a trade-off between the number of elements that can be locked and the efficiency of the code.

Here, we propose to focus on a particular family of BCH codes: the Reed-Solomon (RS) codes. We first recall in Section 2 the framework of matrix embedding/syndrome coding. Then, we discuss the interest of using Reed-Solomon codes in this context: in Section 3, Reed-Solomon codes are presented, explicitly showing in Section 4 how they can improve realistic steganographic schemes. We show in Section 4.1 that with these codes we can go beyond the limits of BCH codes: we can lock twice the number of positions. In fact, we see that RS codes are optimal according to this criterion, since they enable to manage as many locked positions as possible. In Section 4.2, we also propose an improved algorithm based on Guruswami-Sudan list-decoding, that enables to make an adaptive trade-off between the embedding efficiency and the number of locked positions.

Before going deeper in the subject, please note that we made the choice to represent vectors horizontally . For general references to error correcting codes, we orientate the reader towards [HP03].

2 Syndrome Coding

The behavior of a steganographic algorithm can be sketched in the following way: a *cover-medium* is processed to extract a sequence of bits v, sometimes called *cover-data*; v is modified into s to embed the message m; s is sometimes called the *stego-data*; modifications on s are translated on the cover-medium to obtain the *stego-medium*. Here, we assume that the detectability of the embedding increases with the number of bits that must be changed to go from v to s (see [Wes01, KDR06] for some examples of this framework).

Syndrome coding deals with this number of changes. The key idea is to use some syndrome computation to embed the message into the cover-data. In fact, this scheme uses a linear code $\mathcal{C}$, more precisely its cosets, to hide m. A word s hides the message m if s lies in a particular coset of $\mathcal{C}$, related to m. Since cosets are uniquely identified by the so called syndromes, embedding/hiding consists exactly in searching s with syndrome m, close enough to v.

We first set up the notation and describe properly the syndrome coding scheme, and its inherent problems. Let $\mathbb{F}_q = GF(q)$ denote the finite field with q elements[1]. Let $v \in \mathbb{F}_q{}^n$ denote the cover-data and $m \in \mathbb{F}_q{}^r$ the message. We are looking for two mappings, embedding Emb and extraction Ext, such that:

$$\forall (v, m) \in \mathbb{F}_q{}^n \times \mathbb{F}_q{}^r, \ \mathrm{Ext}(\mathrm{Emb}(v, m)) = m \tag{1}$$
$$\forall (v, m) \in \mathbb{F}_q{}^n \times \mathbb{F}_q{}^r, \ d_H(v, \mathrm{Emb}(v, m)) \leq T \tag{2}$$

Eq. (1) means that we want to recover the message in all cases; Eq. (2) means that we authorize the modification of at most T coordinates in the vector v.

Let $\mathcal{C}$ be a q-ary linear code of length n, dimension k and parity check matrix H. That is, $\mathcal{C} = \{c \mid c \cdot H^t = 0\}$ is a vector subspace of $\mathbb{F}_q{}^n$ of dimension k. The *syndrome* of a vector y, with respect to the code $\mathcal{C}$, is the row vector $y \cdot H^t$ of length $n - k$; we denote it by $E(y)$. The *covering radius* of $\mathcal{C}$ is the minimum integer ρ such that $\{E(y) \mid w_H(y) \leq \rho\} = \mathbb{F}_q{}^{n-k}$. Let us denote by D the mapping that associates with a syndrome m a vector a of Hamming weight less than or equal to ρ, and which syndrome is precisely equal to m (that is, $w_H(a) \leq \rho$ and $E(a) = a \cdot H^t = m$). Remark that effective computation of D is the complete syndrome decoding problem, which is hard. It is quite easy to show that the scheme defined by

$$\mathrm{Emb}(v, m) = v + D(m - E(v))$$
$$\mathrm{Ext}(y) = E(y) = y \cdot H^t$$

enables to embed messages of length $r = n - k$ in a cover-data of length n, while modifying at most $T = \rho$ elements of the cover-data.

The parameter $(n - k)/\rho$ represents the (worst) embedding efficiency[2], that is, the number of embedded symbols per embedding changes in the worst case.

---

[1] Recall that when q is a power of two, elements of $\mathbb{F}_q$ can be regarded as blocks of bits.

[2] Remark this is with respect to symbols and not bits. If elements of $\mathbb{F}_q$ are viewed as blocks of ℓ bits, changing a symbol by an other roughly leads to $\ell/2$ flips.

In a similar way, one defines the average embedding efficiency $(n - k)/\omega$, where ω is the average weight of the output of D for uniformly distributed inputs.

A problem raised by the syndrome coding, as presented above, is that any position in the cover-data v can be changed. In some cases, it is more reasonable to keep some coordinates unchanged because they would produced too big artifacts in the stego-medium. This can be done in the following way. Let $\mathcal{I} = \{i_1, ..., i_j\}$ be the coordinates that must not be changed, let $H_{\mathcal{I}}$ be the matrix obtained from H by removing[3] the columns $i_1, ..., i_j$, and $E_{\mathcal{I}}$ and $D_{\mathcal{I}}$ the corresponding mappings. That is, $E_{\mathcal{I}}(y) = y \cdot H_{\mathcal{I}}^t$ for $y \in \mathbb{F}_q^{n-|\mathcal{I}|}$, and $D_{\mathcal{I}}(m) \in \mathbb{F}_q^{n-|\mathcal{I}|}$ is a vector of weight at most $\rho_{\mathcal{I}}$ such that its syndrome, with respect to $H_{\mathcal{I}}$, is m. Here, $\rho_{\mathcal{I}}$ is the covering radius of $\mathcal{C}_{\mathcal{I}}$, the code obtained from $\mathcal{C}$ by removing the coordinates in $\mathcal{I}$ from all the codewords. Of course, this is also the code of parity check matrix $H_{\mathcal{I}}$. Finally, let us define $D_{\mathcal{I}}^*$ as the vector of $\mathbb{F}_q^n$ such that the coordinates in $\mathcal{I}$ are zeros and the vector obtained by removing these coordinates is precisely $D_{\mathcal{I}}$. Now, we have $D_{\mathcal{I}}^*(m) \cdot H = D_{\mathcal{I}}(m) \cdot H_{\mathcal{I}}^t = m$ and, by definition, $D_{\mathcal{I}}^*(m)$ has zeros at coordinates set by $\mathcal{I}$. Naturally, the scheme defined by

$$\text{Emb}(v, m) = v + D_{\mathcal{I}}^*(m - E(v))$$
$$\text{Ext}(y) = E(y) = y \cdot H^t$$

performs syndrome coding without disturbing the positions in $\mathcal{I}$. But, it is worth noting that for some sets $\mathcal{I}$, the mapping $D_{\mathcal{I}}$ cannot be defined for all possible values of m because the equation $y \cdot H_{\mathcal{I}}^t = m$ has no solution. This always happens when $|\mathcal{I}| > k$, since $H_{\mathcal{I}}$ has dimension $(n - k) \times (n - |\mathcal{I}|)$, but can also happen for smaller sets.

Please, keep in mind that using syndrome coding leads to essentially two problems. First, the parameters n, r, ρ depend on the choice of $\mathcal{C}$, and most of the time ρ is hard to compute. Second, the mapping D is difficult to compute.

3 What Reed-Solomon Codes Are, and Why They May Be Interesting

Reed-Solomon codes over the finite field $\mathbb{F}_q$ are optimal linear codes. The *narrow-sense RS codes* have length $n = q - 1$ and can be defined as a particular sub-family of the BCH codes. But, we prefer the alternative, and larger, definition as an evaluation code, which leads to the *Generalized Reed-Solomon codes (GRS codes)*.

Roughly speaking, a GRS code of length $n \leq q$ and dimension k is a set of words corresponding to polynomials of degree less than k evaluated over a subset of $\mathbb{F}_q$ of size n. More precisely, let $\{\gamma_0, ..., \gamma_{n-1}\}$ be a subset of $\mathbb{F}_q$ and define $ev(P) = (P(\gamma_0), P(\gamma_1), \ldots, P(\gamma_{n-1}))$, for $P(X)$ a polynomial over $\mathbb{F}_q$. Then, we define $GRS(n, k)$ as

---

[3] In coding theory, this is called *shortening* the code on $\mathcal{I}$: we only keep codewords that have zero on $\mathcal{I}$, and then we remove the coordinates set by $\mathcal{I}$.

$$GRS(n,k) = \{ev(P) \mid \deg(P) < k\} \ .$$

This definition, *a priori*, depends on the choice of the γ_i and the order of evaluation, but as far as we are concerned, only the number of γ_i is important, so we consider a fixed set of γ_i and a fixed order. Remark that when $\gamma_i = \beta^i$ with β a primitive element of $\mathbb{F}_q$ and $i \in \{0, ..., q-2\}$, we obtain the *narrow-sense Reed-Solomon codes*.

GRS codes are optimal: they reach the Singleton bound, that is, the minimal distance of $GRS(n,k)$ is $d = n - k + 1$, which is the largest possible. On the other hand, the covering radius of $GRS(n,k)$ is known and equal to $\rho = n - k$.

Concerning the evaluation function, recall that if we consider $n \leq q$ elements of $\mathbb{F}_q$, then it is known that there is a unique polynomial of degree at most $n-1$ taking particular values on these n elements. This means that for every v in $\mathbb{F}_q{}^n$, one can find a polynomial V with $\deg(V) \leq n-1$, such that $ev(V) = v$; moreover, V is unique. Of course, ev is a linear mapping, $ev(\alpha \cdot P + \beta \cdot Q) = \alpha \cdot ev(P) + \beta \cdot ev(Q)$ for any polynomials P, Q and field elements α, β.

For convenience, in the sequel, we identify any polynomial of degree less than n with a vector of length n, the i-th coordinate of the vector being the coefficient of the monomial of degree i. Thus, the evaluation mapping can be represented by the matrix

$$\Gamma = \begin{pmatrix} ev(X^0) \\ ev(X^1) \\ ev(X^2) \\ \cdots \\ ev(X^{n-1}) \end{pmatrix} = \begin{pmatrix} \gamma_0^0 & \gamma_1^0 & \cdots & \gamma_{n-1}^0 \\ \gamma_0 & \gamma_1 & \cdots & \gamma_{n-1} \\ \gamma_0^2 & \gamma_1^2 & \cdots & \gamma_{n-1}^2 \\ & & \vdots & \\ \gamma_0^{n-1} & \gamma_1^{n-1} & \cdots & \gamma_{n-1}^{n-1} \end{pmatrix} \ .$$

If we denote by $\mathrm{Coeff}(V) \in \mathbb{F}_q{}^n$ the vector consisting in the coefficients of V, then $\mathrm{Coeff}(V) \cdot \Gamma = ev(V)$. On the other hand, Γ being non-singular, its inverse Γ^{-1} computes $\mathrm{Coeff}(V)$ from $ev(V)$. For our purpose, it is noteworthy that the coefficients of monomials of degree at least k can be easily computed from $ev(V)$: splitting Γ^{-1} in two parts,

$$\Gamma^{-1} = (\underbrace{A}_{k \text{ columns}} \quad \underbrace{B}_{n-k \text{ columns}}) \ ,$$

$ev(V) \cdot B$ is precisely the coefficients vector of the monomials of degree at least k in V. In fact, B is the transpose of a parity check matrix of the GRS code since a vector c is an element of the code if and only if we have $c \cdot B = 0$. So, instead of B, we write H^t, as it is usually done.

Now, let us look at the cosets of $GRS(n,k)$. A coset is a set of the type $y + GRS(n,k)$, with $y \in \mathbb{F}_q{}^n$ not in $GRS(n,k)$. As usual with linear codes, a coset is uniquely identified by the vector $y \cdot H^t$, syndrome of y. In the case of GRS code, this vector consists in the coefficients of monomials of degree at least k.

4 What Can Reed-Solomon Codes Do

Our problem is the following. We have a vector v of length n of symbols of $\mathbb{F}_q$, extracted from the cover-medium, and a message m of length r of symbols of $\mathbb{F}_q$. We want to modify v into s such that m is embedded in s, changing at most T coordinates in v.

The basic principle is to use syndrome coding with a GRS code: we use the cosets of $GRS(n,k)$ to embed the message, finding a vector s in the proper coset, close enough to v. Thus, k must be equal to $n - r$, and we suppose we have fixed $\gamma_0,...,\gamma_{n-1} \in \mathbb{F}_q$, constructed the matrix Γ whose i-th row is $ev(X^i)$, and inverted it. In particular, we denote by H^t the last $n - k$ columns of Γ^{-1} and, therefore, according to the previous section, H is a parity-check matrix. Recall that a word s embeds the message m if $s \cdot H^t = m$.

To construct s, we need a word y such that its syndrome is $m - v \cdot H^t$; thus, we can set $s = y + v$, which leads to $s \cdot H^t = y \cdot H^t + v \cdot H^t = m$. Moreover, the Hamming weight of y is precisely the number of changes we apply to go from v to s; so, we need $w(y) \leq T$.

When T is equal to the covering radius of the code corresponding to H, such a vector y always exists. But, explicit computation of such a vector y, known as the bounded syndrome decoding problem, is proved to be NP-hard for general linear codes. Even for well structured codes, we usually do not have polynomial time (in the length n) algorithm to solve the bounded syndrome decoding problem up to the covering radius. This is precisely the problem faced by [SW06].

GRS codes overcome this problem in a nice fashion. It is easy to find a vector with syndrome m: let us consider the polynomial $M(X)$ that has coefficient m_i for the monomial X^{k+i}, $i \in \{0,...,n-1-k\}$; according to the previous section, we have $ev(M) \cdot H^t = m$. Now, finding y can be done by computing a polynomial P of degree less than k such that for at least k elements $\gamma \in \{\gamma_0, ..., \gamma_{n-1}\}$ we have $P(\gamma) = M(\gamma) - V(\gamma)$. With such a P, the vector $y = ev(M - V - P)$ has at least k coordinates equal to zero, and the correct syndrome value. Hence, T can be as high as the covering radius $\rho = n - k$, and the challenge lies in the construction of P.

It is noteworthy to remark that locking the position i, that is, requiring $s_i = v_i$, is equivalent to ask for $y_i = 0$ and, thus, $P(\gamma_i) = M(\gamma_i) - V(\gamma_i)$.

4.1 A Simple Construction of P

Using Lagrange Interpolation. A very simple way to construct P is by using the Lagrange interpolating polynomials. We choose k coordinates $\mathcal{I} = \{i_1, ..., i_k\}$, and compute

$$P(X) = \sum_{i \in \mathcal{I}} (M(\gamma_i) - V(\gamma_i)) \cdot L_{\mathcal{I}}^{(i)}(X) \ ,$$

where $L_{\mathcal{I}}^{(i)}$ is the unique polynomial of degree at most $k - 1$ taking values 0 on γ_j, $j \neq i$ and 1 on γ_i, that is,

$$L_{\mathcal{I}}^{(i)}(X) = \prod_{j \in \mathcal{I} \backslash \{i\}} (\gamma_i - \gamma_j)^{-1}(X - \gamma_j) \ .$$

The polynomial P we obtain this way clearly satisfies $P(\gamma_i) = V(\gamma_i) - M(\gamma_i)$ for every $i \in \mathcal{I}$ and, thus, we can set $y = ev(M - V - P)$. As pointed out earlier, since, for $i \in \mathcal{I}$, we have $y_i = 0$, we also have $s_i = v_i + y_i = v_i$, $i.e.$ positions in $\mathcal{I}$ are locked.

The above proposed solution has a nice feature: we can choose the coordinates on which s and v are equal, and this does not require any loss in computational complexity nor embedding efficiency. This means that we can perform the syndrome decoding directly with the additional requirement of wet papers, keeping unchanged the coordinates whose modifications are detectable.

So far, what do GRS codes allow?

Optimal Management of Locked Positions. We can embed $r = n - k$ elements of $\mathbb{F}_q$, changing not more than $T = n - k$, so the embedding efficiency is equal to 1 in the worst case. But, we can lock *any* k positions to embed our information.

This is to be compared with [SW06], where BCH codes are used. The maximal number of locked positions, without failing to embed the message m, is experimentally estimated to be $k/2$. To be able to lock up to $k-1$ positions, it is necessary to allow a non-zero probability of non embedding. It is also noteworthy that the average embedding efficiency decreases fast.

In fact, embedding $r = n - k$ symbols while locking k symbols amongst n is optimal. We said in Section 2 that locking the positions in $\mathcal{I}$ leads to an equation $y \cdot H_{\mathcal{I}}^t = m$, where $H_{\mathcal{I}}$ has dimension $(n - k) \times (n - |\mathcal{I}|)$. So, when $|\mathcal{I}| > k$, there exist some values m for which there is no solution y. On the other hand, let us suppose we have a code with parity check matrix H such that for any $\mathcal{I}$ of size k, and any m, this equation has a solution, that is, $H_{\mathcal{I}}$ is invertible. This means that any $(n - k) \times (n - k)$ submatrix of H is invertible. But, it is known that this is equivalent to require the code to be MDS (see for example [HP03, Cor 1.4.14]), which is the case of GRS code. Hence, GRS codes are optimal in the sense that we can lock as many positions as possible, that is, up to k for a message length of $r = n - k$.

4.2   A More Efficient Construction of P

Using List Decoding. A natural idea to improve the results of the last section is to use decoding algorithms for GRS codes, whenever it is possible. Such algorithms compute, from a vector $ev(Q)$, polynomials P of degree at most $k-1$, such that $ev(P)$ are close to $ev(Q)$, according to the Hamming distance. Stated differently, they provide good approximations of Q. Using these algorithms reduce the average number of changes required by the embedding and, thus, improve the average efficiency.

Essentially, the output of the decoding algorithms may be: a single polynomial P, if it exists, such that the vector $ev(P)$ is at distance at most $\lfloor (n - k + 1)/2 \rfloor$

from $ev(Q)$ (remark that if such a P exists, it is unique), and nothing otherwise; or, a list of all polynomials P such that the vectors $ev(P)$ are at distance at most T from $ev(Q)$.

The second case corresponds to the so called list decoding; an efficient algorithm for GRS codes was initially provided by [Sud97], and was improved by [GS99], leading to what is known as the Guruswami-Sudan algorithm. Clearly, list decoding is the more interesting: like the first kind of decoding, it provides the solution of minimum weight if it exists; moreover, the possibility to choose between different vectors improves the undetectability targeted by the steganographic applications.

Guruswami-Sudan algorithm outlines. The reader interested in detailed exposition may refer to [GS99, McE03, HP03]. The Guruswami-Sudan algorithm uses a parameter called the interpolation multiplicity μ. For an input vector $(a_0, ..., a_{n-1})$, the algorithm computes a bivariate polynomial $R(X, Y)$ such that[4] each couple (γ_i, a_i) is a root of R with multiplicity μ. The second and last step is to compute the list of factors of R, of the form $Y - P(X)$, with $\deg(P) \leq k - 1$. For a fixed μ, the list contains all the polynomials which are at distance at most $\lambda_\mu \approx n - \sqrt{(1 + \frac{1}{\mu})(k - 1)n}$. The maximum decoding radius is, thus, $\lambda_{GS} = n - 1 - \sqrt{n \cdot (k - 1)}$. Moreover, the overall algorithm can be performed in less than $\mathcal{O}(n^2 \mu^4)$ arithmetic operations over $\mathbb{F}_q$.

Guruswami-Sudan for shortened GRS codes. The Guruswami-Sudan algorithm can be used for decoding shortened GRS codes: for a fixed set $\mathcal{I}$ of indices, we are looking for polynomials P such that $\deg(P) < k$, $P(\gamma_i) = 0$ for $i \in \mathcal{I}$ and $P(\gamma_i) = Q(\gamma_i)$ for as many $i \notin \mathcal{I}$ as possible. Such P can be written $P(X) = F(X)G(X)$ with $F(X) = \prod_{i \in \mathcal{I}}(X - \gamma_i)$. Hence, decoding the shortened code reduces to obtain G such that $\deg(G) < k - |\mathcal{I}|$ and $G(\gamma_i) = Q(\gamma_i)/F(\gamma_i)$ for as many $i \notin \mathcal{I}$ as possible. This means, we are using the GS algorithm to decode a word of $GRS(n - |\mathcal{I}|, k - |\mathcal{I}|)$.

Algorithm Description. Our general scheme becomes: try to perform list decoding on $ev(M - V)$, in order to get a P as close as possible to $ev(M - V)$; if it fails, fall back onto Lagrange interpolation – as in the previous section – to compute P.

In fact, it is still possible to keep some positions locked: Let $\mathcal{I}$ be the set of coordinates to be untouched, construct the polynomial P such that $P(\gamma_i) = M(\gamma_i) - V(\gamma_i)$; Let us consider $Y = M - V - P$ and use GS decoding to compute an approximation U of Y of degree at most $k - 1$, such that $U(\gamma_i) = 0$ for $i \in \mathcal{I}$; If GS decoding fails, add a new position to $\mathcal{I}$ and retry until it succeeds or $\mathcal{I} = k$; If no GS decoding succeeds (and, so, $\mathcal{I} = k$), define $U(X) = 0$; Finally, the stegoword is $v + ev(Y - U)$.

Figure 1 depicts the complete algorithm. The description uses two external procedures. The GSdecode procedure refers to the Guruswami-Sudan list decod-

---

[4] R must also satisfy another important constraint on the so called weighted degree.

ing: it decodes the polynomial $Y(X)$ of degree at most $k-1$, with respect to the code $GRS(n,k)$ defined by the evaluation on (γ_i), and shortened on positions set by $\mathcal{I}$. So, this procedure returns a good approximation $U(X)$ of $Y(X)$, on the evaluation set, of degree less than $k-1$, with the additional condition that $U(\gamma_i) = 0$ for $i \in \mathcal{I}$. Remark that when $\mathcal{I} = \emptyset$, we simply use the GS decoding, whereas when $\mathcal{I} \neq \emptyset$, we use the modified decoding for shortened codes. The selectposition procedure returns an integer from the set given as a parameter. This procedure is used to choose the new position to lock before retrying the list decoding.

The correctness of this algorithm follows from the fact that through the whole algorithm we have $ev(Y) \cdot H^t = m - v \cdot H^t$ and $Y(\gamma_i) = 0$ for $i \in \mathcal{I}$.

Inputs: $v = (v_0, ..., v_{n-1})$, the cover-data
         $m = (m_0, ..., m_{n-k-1})$, symbols to hide
         $\mathcal{I}$, set of coordinates to remain unchanged, $|\mathcal{I}| \leq k$
Output: $s = (s_0, ..., s_{n-1})$, the stego-data
         $(s \cdot H^t = m; s_i = v_i, i \in \mathcal{I}; d_H(s,v) \leq n-k)$

1: $V(X) \Longleftarrow v_0 X^0 + \cdots + v_{n-1} X^{n-1}$
2: $M(X) \Longleftarrow m_0 X^k + \cdots + m_{n-k-1} X^{n-1}$
3: $Y(X) \Longleftarrow M(X) - V(X)$
4: **for all** $i \in \mathcal{I}$ **do**
5:    $L_\mathcal{I}^{(i)}(X) \Longleftarrow \prod_{j \in \mathcal{I} \setminus \{i\}} (\gamma_i - \gamma_j)^{-1}(X - \gamma_j)$
6: **end for**
7: $P(X) \Longleftarrow \sum_{i \in \mathcal{I}} a_i \cdot L_\mathcal{I}^{(i)}(X)$
8: $Y(X) \Longleftarrow Y(X) - P(X)$
9: **while** $|\mathcal{I}| < k$ **and** GSdecode$(Y(X), \mathcal{I}) = \emptyset$ **do**
10:    $i \Longleftarrow$ selectposition$(\{0, ..., n-1\} \setminus \mathcal{I})$
11:    $\mathcal{I} \Longleftarrow \mathcal{I} \cup \{i\}$
12:    $L_\mathcal{I}^{(i)}(X) \Longleftarrow \prod_{j \in \mathcal{I} \setminus \{i\}} (\gamma_i - \gamma_j)^{-1}(X - \gamma_j)$
13:    $Y(X) \Longleftarrow Y(X) - Y(\gamma_i) \cdot L_\mathcal{I}^{(i)}(X)$
14: **end while**
15: **if** GSdecode$(Y(X), \mathcal{I}) \neq \emptyset$ **then**
16:    $U(X) \Longleftarrow$ GSdecode$(Y(X), \mathcal{I})$
17:    $Y(X) \Longleftarrow Y(X) - U(X)$
18: **end if**
19: $s \Longleftarrow v + ev(Y)$
20: **return** s

Fig. 1. Algorithm for embedding with locked positions using a $GRS(n,k)$ code, $(\gamma_0, ..., \gamma_{n-1})$ fixed. It embeds $r = n-k$ symbols of $\mathbb{F}_q$ with up to k locked positions and at most $n-k$ changes.

Analysis. The most important property of an embedding algorithm is the number of changes introduced during the embedding. This analysis, for our algorithm, depends on two parameters.

The first parameter is the probability $p(n, k)$ that list decoding of a word in $\mathbb{F}_q^n$ outputs a non-empty list of codewords in $\text{GRS}(n, k)$. We denote by $q(n, k)$ the probability of the complementary event, namely the return of an empty list. Thus, the probability that the first $\ell - 1$ list decodings fail and the ℓ-th succeeds is $p(n - |\mathcal{I}| - \ell, k - |\mathcal{I}| - \ell) \prod_{e=0}^{\ell-1} q(n - |\mathcal{I}| - e, k - |\mathcal{I}| - e)$.

The second parameter is the average distance $\delta(n, k)$ between the closest codewords in the (non-empty) list and the word to decode. This last parameter leads to the average number of changes required to perform the embedding:

$$\omega = \left(\sum_{\ell=0}^{k'-1} \delta'(\ell) \cdot p'(\ell) \prod_{e=0}^{\ell-1} q'(e) \right) + (n - k) \prod_{e=0}^{k'-1} q'(e) \; ,$$

where $p'(e) = p(n - |\mathcal{I}| - e, k - |\mathcal{I}| - e)$, $q'(e) = q(n - |\mathcal{I}| - e, k - |\mathcal{I}| - e)$ and $\delta'(e) = \delta(n - |\mathcal{I}| - e, k - |\mathcal{I}| - e)$.

Estimating p and δ. To (upper) estimate $p(n, k)$, we proceed as follows. Let us denote by Z the random variable equal to the size of the output list of the decoding algorithm. The Markov inequality yields $Pr(Z \geq 1) \leq \mathbb{E}(Z)$, where $\mathbb{E}(Z)$ denotes the expectation of Z. But, $Pr(Z \geq 1)$ is the probability that the list is non-empty and, thus, $Pr(Z \geq 1) = p(n, k)$. Now, $\mathbb{E}(Z)$ is the average number of elements in the output list, but this is exactly the average number of codewords in a Hamming ball of radius λ_{GS}. Unfortunately, no adequate information can be found in the literature to properly estimate it; the only paper studying a similar quantity is [McE03], but it cannot be used for our $\mathbb{E}(Z)$. So, we set

$$\mathbb{E}(Z) = \frac{q^k}{q^n} \cdot V_{\lambda_{GS}} = \frac{\displaystyle\sum_{i=0}^{\lambda_{GS}} (q-1)^i \binom{n}{i}}{q^{n-k}} \; ,$$

where $V_{\lambda_{GS}}$ is the volume of a ball of radius λ_{GS}. This would be the correct value if GRS codes were *random* codes over $\mathbb{F}_q$ of length n, with q^k codewords uniformly drawn from $\mathbb{F}_q^n$. That is, we estimate $\mathbb{E}(Z)$ as if GRS codes were random codes. Thus, we use $\overline{p} = \min(1, q^{k-n} V_{\lambda_{GS}})$ to upper estimate p.

The second parameter we need is the average number of changes required when the list is non-empty. We consider that the closest codeword is uniformly distributed over the ball of radius λ_{GS} and, therefore, we have

$$\delta(n, k) = \frac{\displaystyle\sum_{i=0}^{\lambda_{GS}} (q-1)^i \binom{n}{i} i}{V_{\lambda_{GS}}} \; .$$

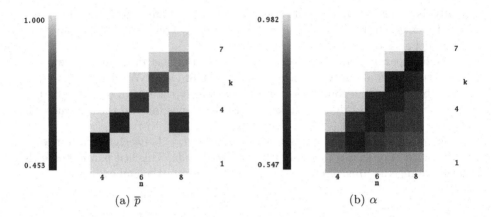

Fig. 2. Figure (a) plots the estimated probability $\overline{p}$ of list decoding success on a random input vector for $GRS(n,k)$ over $\mathbb{F}_8$. Figure (b) plots the relative average number of changes α. As usual, n is the length and k the dimension.

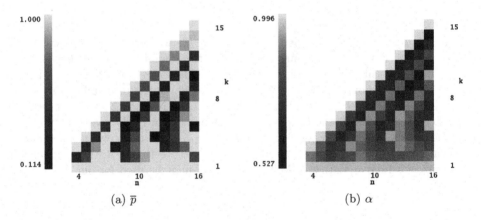

Fig. 3. Same as figure 2 for $\mathbb{F}_{16}$

A Simplified Analysis. A simple (upper) estimate of the average number of changes can be obtained by setting $\mathcal{I} = \emptyset$ and considering that if the first list decoding fails, the others will fail too. Doing so, we clearly underestimate the performance of our algorithm. This leads to the very simple quantity

$$\alpha = \frac{\delta(n,k) \cdot \overline{p}(n,k) + (n-k) \cdot (1 - \overline{p}(n,k))}{n-k}.$$

This value is plotted in Figures 2, 3, 4, 5 and 6 for small values of q (the number of elements of the field). For each figure, the left part (a) plots $\overline{p}$ and the right part (b) plots α.

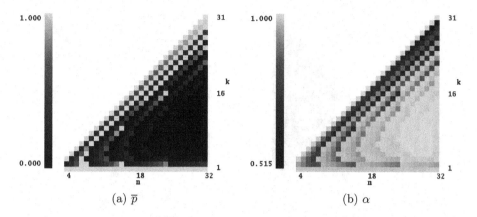

(a) $\bar{p}$ (b) α

Fig. 4. Same as figure 2 for $\mathbb{F}_{32}$

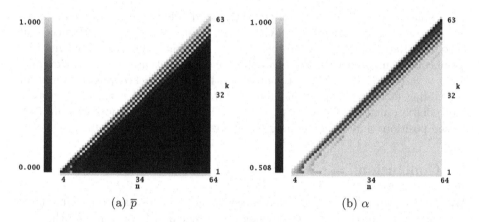

(a) $\bar{p}$ (b) α

Fig. 5. Same as figure 2 for $\mathbb{F}_{64}$

Let us first briefly depict the meaning of the colors for both figure sides. In all figures, dark colors correspond to small values, and bright colors to high values. So, on the left hand side figures, dark areas mean a decoding failure (small $\bar{p}$), and bright areas mean a successful list decoding. On the right hand side figures, dark areas correspond to a number of coordinate modifications that remains far less than $n - k$, which is the maximum value; bright pixels mean we are close to the maximum. These figures show that, when k is close to n, the code is sufficiently dense in the space to warranty a high value of $\mathbb{E}(Z)$; hence, $\bar{p}$ is close to 1 and the list decoding is successful. Other favorable cases for decoding are for small values of k, where the radius λ_{GS} is close to n, and the decoding balls cover the space quite well. On the contrary, when k is far away from its extremal values (1 and $n - 1$), the decoding balls are too small to contain enough codewords, and the decoding fails. Clearly, these figures also show that this behavior increases when q becomes higher. The previous analysis

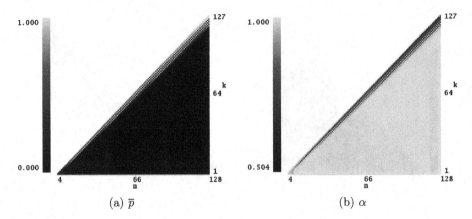

(a) $\overline{p}$

(b) α

Fig. 6. Same as figure 2 for $\mathbb{F}_{128}$

also explains what we observe on the right hand side figures, since the relative average number of changes α heavily depends on the probability of successful decoding. Remark that the improvement in the embedding efficiency may be significant, compared with the algorithm given in Section 4.1. As an example, for $q = 8$, $GRS(7,3)$ embeds 4 symbols with up to 3 locked positions and an embedding efficiency improvement up to 37.4% compared with the Lagrange interpolation algorithm. Over $\mathbb{F}_{16}$, $GRS(14,9)$ embeds 5 symbols with up to 9 locked positions and an embedding efficiency improvement up to 67.6%.

5   Conclusion

We have shown in this paper that Reed-Solomon codes are good candidates for designing realistic efficient steganographic schemes. If we compare them to the previous studied codes, like BCH codes, Reed-Solomon codes improve the management of locked positions during embedding, hence ensuring a better management of the distortion: they are able to lock twice the number of positions, that is, they are optimal in the sense that they enable to lock the maximal number of positions. We proposed two methods for managing these codes in this context: the first one is based on a naive decoding process through Lagrange interpolation; the second one, more efficient, is based on the Guruswami-Sudan list decoding and provides an adaptive trade-off between the number of locked positions and the embedding efficiency.

Acknowledgment

Dr. C. Fontaine is supported (in part) by the European Commission through the IST Programme under Contract IST-2002-507932 ECRYPT.

We are in debt to Daniel Augot for numerous comments on this work, in particular for pointing out the adaptation of the Guruswami-Sudan algorithm to shortened GRS used in the embedding algorithm.

References

[BW04]   Böhme, R., Westfeld, A.: Exploiting preserved statistics for steganalysis. In: Lester, J.C., Vicari, R.M., Paraguaçu, F. (eds.) ITS 2004. LNCS, vol. 3220, pp. 82–96. Springer, Heidelberg (2004)

[Cra98]   Crandall, R.: Some notes on steganography. Posted on steganography mailing list (1998), http://os.inf.tu-dresden.de/~westfeld/crandall.pdf

[FGLS05]   Fridrich, J., Goljan, M., Lisonek, P., Soukal, D.: Writing on wet paper. IEEE Transactions on Signal Processing 53(10), 3923–3935 (2005) (special issue "Supplement on Secure Media III")

[FGS05a]   Fridrich, J., Goljan, M., Soukal, D.: Efficient wet paper codes. In: Barni, M., Herrera-Joancomartí, J., Katzenbeisser, S., Pérez-González, F. (eds.) IH 2005. LNCS, vol. 3727, pp. 204–218. Springer, Heidelberg (2005)

[FGS05b]   Fridrich, J., Goljan, M., Soukal, D.: Perturbed quantization steganography. ACM Multimedia and Security Journal 11(2), 98–107 (2005)

[FGS06]   Fridrich, J., Goljan, M., Soukal, D.: Wet paper codes with improved embedding efficiency. IEEE Transactions on Information Security and Forensics 1(1), 102–110 (2006)

[Fra02]   Franz, E.: Steganography preserving statistical properties. In: Petitcolas, F.A.P. (ed.) IH 2002. LNCS, vol. 2578, pp. 278–294. Springer, Heidelberg (2003)

[FS06]   Fridrich, J., Soukal, D.: Matrix embedding for large payloads. IEEE Transactions on Information Security and Forensics 1(3), 390–394 (2006)

[GK03]   Galand, F., Kabatiansky, G.: Information hiding by coverings. In: Proc. ITW 2003, pp. 151–154 (2003)

[GS99]   Guruswami, V., Sudan, M.: Improved decoding of Reed-Solomon and algebraic-geometry codes. IEEE Transactions on Information Theory 45(6), 1757–1767 (1999)

[HP03]   Huffman, W.C., Pless, V.: Fundamentals of Error-Correcting Codes. Cambridge University Press, Cambridge (2003)

[KDR06]   Kim, Y., Duric, Z., Richards, D.: Modified matrix encoding technique for minimal distortion steganography. In: Proc. of the 8th International Workshop on Information Hiding. LNCS, Springer, Heidelberg (2006)

[McE03]   McEliece, R.J.: The Guruswami-Sudan decoding algorithm for Reed-Solomon codes. Technical Report 42-153, IPN Progress Report (May 2003) http://tmo.jpl.nasa.gov/progress_report/42-153/153F.pdf

[McL84]   McLoughlin, A.: The complexity of computing the covering radius of a code. IEEE Transactions on Information Theory 30(6), 800–804 (1984)

[Sim84]   Simmons, G.J.: The prisoners' problem and the subliminal channel. In: Advances in Cryptology – CRYPTO 1983, pp. 51–67. Plenum Press (1984)

[Sud97]   Sudan, M.: Decoding of Reed-Solomon codes beyond the error-correction bound. Journal of Complexity 13(1), 180–193 (1997)

[SW06]   Schönfeld, D., Winkler, A.: Embedding with syndrome coding based on BCH codes. In: Proc. of the ACM Multimedia and Security Workshop 2006, pp. 214–223. ACM Press, New York (2006)

[Var97]   Vardy, A.: The intractability of computing the minimum distance of a code. IEEE Transactions on Information Theory 43(6), 1757–1766 (1997)

[Wes01]   Westfeld, A.: F5 – a steganographic algorithm: high capacity despite better steganalysis. In: Moskowitz, I.S. (ed.) Information Hiding. LNCS, vol. 2137, pp. 289–302. Springer, Heidelberg (2001)

Reducing the Complexity of Syndrome Coding for Embedding

Dagmar Schönfeld and Antje Winkler

Technische Universität Dresden, Dresden, Germany
{Dagmar.Schoenfeld, Antje.Winkler}@tu-dresden.de

Abstract. This paper deals with strategies to dramatically reduce the complexity for embedding based on syndrome coding. In contrast to existing approaches, our goal is to keep the embedding efficiency constant, i.e., to embed less complexly without increasing the average number of embedding changes, compared to the classic Matrix Embedding scenario.

Generally, our considerations are based on structured codes, especially on BCH Codes. However, they are not limited to this class of codes.

We propose different approaches to reduce embedding complexity concentrating on both syndrome coding based on a parity check matrix and syndrome coding based on the generator polynomial.

1 Introduction

Steganography has been used since ancient times in order to communicate confidentially. In contrast to cryptography, in digital steganography the existence of the message itself is hidden by embedding a secret message in inconspicuously looking cover material, e.g., text or image files.

However, common attacks investigate statistics and try to detect statistical differences between cover and stego objects. Therefore, embedding imperceptibly does not suffice at all for secure steganographic systems. Thus, the main goals of the design of good steganographic algorithms are:

- to modify the cover data as little as possible in order to prevent detectable changes in the statistical properties, and
- to modify the cover data only in inconspicuous parts.

As numerous approaches in the past have shown, applying algorithms from coding theory to steganography can help to achieve both objectives.

One approach, first mentioned by Crandall [3] and commonly known as Matrix Embedding, was applied to reduce the number of required changes of the cover by carefully selecting the positions used for embedding. In his paper, Crandall refers to an unpublished paper [1] that discusses this topic from the point of view of a coding theorist. The relation between linear covering codes and steganography was also discussed in [9].

Another field of application of codes from coding theory is a scenario of a message being transmitted using a channel with constrained access to its symbols, e.g., by excluding conspicuous parts of the cover.

T. Furon et al. (Eds.): IH 2007, LNCS 4567, pp. 145–158, 2007.

A recent approach, based on syndrome coding using random codes, is called Wet Paper Codes [6]. This embedding scenario does not require the sender to share any knowledge about the constraints with the recipient and does not even sacrifice embedding capacity – however, this happens at the cost of an increased embedding complexity.

Apart from investigations of speeding up the embedding process of Wet Paper Codes (e.g., by using sparse random parity check matrices combined with structured Gaussian elimination [4], or by exploiting the LT process [5]), Fridrich et al. also presented an approach to minimize the number of embedding changes based on the application of Wet Paper codes to small blocks [7].

However, this topic was also investigated by [11,12] based on a class of structured codes, the BCH Codes (Bose, Chaudhuri, Hoquenghem, [2,10]). Again, both of the aforementioned objectives were considered.

Embedding based on the classic approach, by finding a coset leader using a parity check matrix $\mathbf{H}_{k \times n}$, is really complex and therefore time consuming. Thus, one aspect of [12] was the investigation of more efficient embedding strategies. Beside an improvement of the classic Matrix Embedding based on $\mathbf{H}_{k \times n}$, [12] also consider syndrome coding based on the generator polynomial $g(x)$. Particularly, the goal was to find a balanced solution between low embedding complexity and high embedding efficiency.

In this paper, we focus on embedding strategies to further reduce the embedding complexity without reducing the embedding efficiency e and without increasing the average number of embedding changes R_a respectively. Strictly speaking, our goal is to obtain $R_{a,classic}$, which can be achieved by means of the *classic* Matrix Embedding scenario. Generally, the considerations are based on structured codes, especially on BCH Codes. However, they are not limited to this class of codes.

In our investigations, we first take a closer look at the generator polynomial $g(x)$, since the authors in [12] have shown that this approach is way less complex than the classic approach based on $\mathbf{H}_{k \times n}$. The question that should be answered in this paper is, whether and how it is possible to achieve $R_{a,classic}$ by further improving this approach.

We also focus on possibilities to reduce the search domain considering syndrome coding based on $\mathbf{H}_{k \times n}$, i.e., strategies to reduce the cardinality of sequences that have to be evaluated in order to find the coset leader. Again, the question arises, whether it is possible to achieve $R_{a,classic}$ by means of these approaches.

The paper is organized as follows: In Section 2, strategies for embedding without locked elements are discussed. In this paper, the goal was to embed less complexly compared to the classic Matrix Embedding algorithm while keeping the embedding efficiency constant. Therefore, different strategies were considered: At first, an improved embedding scheme based on the generator polynomial $g(x)$ is described in Section 2.2. Secondly, Section 2.3 summarizes investigations to reduce the search domain. The adaptation of the results achieved so far for embedding regarding locked elements is described in Section 3. Finally, Section 4 summarizes the results.

2 Efficient Embedding Without Locked Elements

Within this section, the goal is to find efficient embedding strategies for an embedding scenario without considering embedding constraints first, i.e., all cover elements can be used for embedding.

The described approaches have its origin in syndrome coding based on a generator polynomial $g(x)$ as well as on a parity check matrix $\mathbf{H}_{k \times n}$. Therefore, different optimization strategies were considered, in order to reduce embedding complexity while keeping the embedding efficiency constant compared to the classic Matrix Embedding scenario. Strictly speaking, our goal is to achieve $R_{a,classic}$.

Even if the investigations are based on BCH Codes, it is possible to apply the algorithms proposed in this paper on different types of matrix construction.

2.1 Basic Considerations

Describing BCH Codes

In this paper, the investigations are based on binary BCH Codes, a class of structured codes. Generally, a (n, l, f_k) BCH Code, as any Cyclic Code, is fully defined by its generator polynomial $g(x)$[1].

The code parameter n describes the length of each codeword, and the parameter l is related to the dimension of the code. Thus, l also gives the number of information bits determining the number of codewords of the code alphabet A, i.e., $|A| = 2^l$.

The generator polynomial $g(x)$ can be seen as a function of arbitrary values of d_{min} or f_k and n, where the number of parity bits k can be identified with $k = \mathrm{degree}(g(x)) = n - l$.

The performance of a code is described by the minimum Hamming distance d_{min}, defined as the minimum distance among all possible distinct pairs of codewords in A. Only considering error correction, the maximum number of correctable errors can be calculated with $f_k = \lfloor \frac{d_{min}-1}{2} \rfloor$. Of course, a high performance f_k requires a high amount of parity bits k.

Another possibility to fully describe BCH Codes is the use of a parity check matrix $\mathbf{H}_{k \times n}$. Generally, there are several ways to derive $\mathbf{H}_{k \times n}$ by means of $g(x)$, however, the way of calculating $\mathbf{H}_{k \times n}$ has absolutely no influence on the performance of a code. For example, in this paper, the check polynomial $h(x)$ with $g(x) \cdot h(x) = x^n + 1$ is used. To derive $\mathbf{H}_{k \times n}$, the coefficients of $h(x)$ are simply shifted k times and the results are written in form of a matrix.

---

[1] A polynomial $p(x)$ is defined as $p(x) = u_k x^k + u_{k-1} x^{k-1} + \ldots + u_1 x + u_0$, in which the sequence of its coefficients can be seen as a binary vector $\mathbf{p} = (u_k u_{k-1} \ldots u_1 u_0)$ and is denoted in boldface symbols. Throughout the text, also matrices $\mathbf{M}$ are denoted in boldface symbols.

Both, the parity check matrix $\mathbf{H}_{k \times n}$ and the generator polynomial $g(x)$ can be used to generate codewords. According to the construction algorithms described in [2,10], all codewords $\mathbf{a}_i \in A$ are multiples of $g(x)$. Thus, $\mathbf{s} = \mathbf{H}_{k \times n} \cdot \mathbf{a}_i^T = \mathbf{0}$ and $\mathbf{s} = \mathrm{mod}(\mathbf{a}_i, \mathbf{g}) = \mathbf{0}$ respectively is true $\forall \mathbf{a}_i \in A$.

Classical Syndrome Coding

Generally, the goals in coding theory and in steganography are different. While in coding theory the syndrome $\mathbf{s} = \mathbf{H}_{k \times n} \cdot \mathbf{b}^T$ of length k is used for error detection and error correction, in steganographic systems it is used to embed a confidential message.

In **coding theory** it is assumed that a codeword $\mathbf{a}_i$ is transformed during transmission due to a random error pattern $\mathbf{f}$ into a sequence $\mathbf{b}$. Thus, whenever $\mathbf{s} \neq \mathbf{0}$, the goal in coding theory is to modify the received sequence $\mathbf{b}$ in a way that $\mathbf{H}_{k \times n} \cdot \mathbf{b}_{corr}^T = \mathbf{0}$.

However, using this approach in **steganographic systems**, in a first step the cover is divided into parts $\mathbf{a}$ of length n and the message into parts $\mathbf{emb}$ of length k. In a second step a sequence $\mathbf{f}$ has to be determined, to deliberately modify the cover part $\mathbf{a}$ in a way that, according to Equation (1), the resulting part $\mathbf{b}$ of the stego image fulfills $\mathbf{s} = \mathbf{emb}$.

$$\mathbf{s} = \mathbf{H}_{k \times n} \cdot (\mathbf{a} \oplus \mathbf{f})^T = \mathbf{H}_{k \times n} \cdot \mathbf{b}^T. \tag{1}$$

This approach, based on syndrome coding, is known from literature (e.g., [3]) as Matrix Embedding.

In the classic Matrix Embedding approach, based on a parity check matrix $\mathbf{H}_{k \times n}$, one tries to achieve a maximized embedding efficiency $e = \frac{k}{R_a}$, in which k is related to the number of embeddable bits per block and therefore to the number of parity bits of a code. Generally, the number of average embedding changes R_a has to be minimized. Thus, a sequence has to be chosen out of all possible 2^n sequences $\mathbf{f}$ of length n, in a way that the distance between $\mathbf{a}$ and $\mathbf{b} = \mathbf{a} \oplus \mathbf{f}$ is minimal. This sequence $\mathbf{f}$ is denoted as coset leader with the weight of $\mathbf{f}$ $w(\mathbf{f})$ being minimal.

Note that $R_{a,classic}$ based on this classic approach is the best achievable result for each specific code. Therefore, it is used as a measure to compare the different coding strategies proposed in this paper.

Whenever considering a big codeword length n, finding the optimal solution and thus finding a coset leader is an NP complete problem. Since the search domain enfolds 2^n sequences $\mathbf{f}$, exhaustive search is required. Note that it is possible to speed up the process of finding the coset leader by means of look-up tables.

Remember the look-up table in coding theory, defined as:

$$coset(\mathbf{0}) = \left\{ \mathbf{a}_i \mid \mathbf{H}_{k \times n} \cdot \mathbf{a}_i^T = \mathbf{0} \right\} = A. \tag{2}$$

In contrast, each of the 2^k possible syndromes and hence each possible sequence $\mathbf{emb}$ can be seen as a coset in steganographic systems. Each coset consists of $\frac{2^n}{2^k} = 2^l$ sequences and can be defined as:

$$coset(\mathbf{emb}) = \left\{ \mathbf{f} \mid \mathbf{H}_{k \times n} \cdot \mathbf{f}^T = \mathbf{emb} \right\} \quad \forall \mathbf{emb}. \tag{3}$$

For each syndrome **emb**, the sequence **f** with minimum distance between **a** and $\mathbf{b} = \mathbf{f}$ is called coset leader and should be chosen for embedding, whenever the goal is to minimize R_a. This will result in a reduced time complexity, since the search domain is reduced, i.e., only 2^l sequences have to be considered for exhaustive search instead of 2^n sequences. Of course, this approach based on 2^k look-up tables is limited by storing all 2^n sequences. Nevertheless, also the effort to create the 2^k look-up tables has to be considered.

Generally, there are different requirements to the embedding process. On the one hand side, the goal is to find the coset leader, i.e., to find a solution that results in a minimum number of embedding changes which will maximize the embedding efficiency. Another aspect, which has to be considered, is the embedding complexity. In this paper, we consider time complexity as well as memory complexity. A reduced embedding complexity can be achieved with a reduced embedding efficiency as shown in [12], or even with constant embedding efficiency.

In this paper, we try to find efficient embedding strategies, which will enable us to embed less complexly while keeping the embedding efficiency constant compared to the classic Matrix Embedding scenario.

2.2 Embedding Based on $g(x)$

As mentioned in Section 2.1, there are two possible ways to fully describe BCH Codes: a parity check matrix $\mathbf{H}_{k \times n}$ and a generator polynomial $g(x)$. The classic Matrix Embedding approach is based on the first one.

Within this section, we take a look at the second one, trying to answer the question, whether it is possible to embed more rapidly with no reduction in embedding efficiency compared to the classic approach, i.e., if it is possible to achieve $R_{a,classic}$.

Using the generator polynomial $g(x)$ in **coding theory**, a syndrome **s** is calculated by dividing the received sequence **b** (or the corresponding polynomial $b(x)$) by the generator polynomial $g(x)$ and analyze the remainder. Only if the sequence **b** is divisible without remainder, the received sequence is a codeword, otherwise an error is detected.

In **steganographic systems**, the remainder can be used to embed the secret message. Therefore, the cover sequence **a** is defined as $[\mathbf{a}_l \, \mathbf{a}_k]$, according to the parameters l and k.

In a first step of the *basic* embedding process, **a** is divided by **g** in order to obtain the syndrome **s** of length k as:

$$\mathbf{s} = \mathrm{mod}(\mathbf{a}, \mathbf{g}). \tag{4}$$

To achieve the positions, which have to be flipped in order to embed **emb** into **a**, this syndrome **s** has to be combined with **emb** using a XOR operation. The positions of ones are related to the positions that have to be flipped within

$\mathbf{a}_k{}^2$. The stego sequence $\mathbf{b}$ leading to the confidential message $\mathbf{emb}$ and related to $\mathbf{a}$ can be achieved according to:

$$\mathbf{b} = [\mathbf{a}_l \ (\mathbf{a}_k \oplus (\mathbf{s} \oplus \mathbf{emb}))]. \tag{5}$$

The resulting stego sequence certainly fulfills the desired property:

$$\mathbf{s} = \mathrm{mod}(\mathbf{b}, \mathbf{g}) = \mathbf{emb}. \tag{6}$$

While this simple approach enables to embed fast with only few XOR operations, we have to deal with a reduced embedding efficiency since the algorithm is not always able to find the coset leader (see Table 1).

However, the embedding efficiency can be *improved* by also considering $\mathbf{a}_l$, i.e., not only flipping bits within the k parity bits but also information bits within $\mathbf{a}_l$.

First investigations [12] considered only one additional bit within l information bits. The essential idea of this heuristic approach is to pre-flip one out of all l possible information bits, embed the confidential message and evaluate the results. Thus, the improved approach needs l pre-calculation steps:

In each step $i, (i = 1, 2, ..., l)$, one out of l information bits in $\mathbf{a}_l$ is pre-flipped. Afterward, $\mathbf{s}$ denoted as $\mathbf{s}_i$ is determined according to Equation (4). For each syndrome $\mathbf{s}_i$, the weight of $(\mathbf{s}_i \oplus \mathbf{emb})$ is determined within the evaluation step, since the goal is to find the coset leader or at least the combination with minimal Hamming weight. The total number of bits, which have to be flipped within the cover sequence $\mathbf{a}$ in order to embed the confidential message part $\mathbf{emb}$, is now

$$w_1 = \min_{i=1}^{l}(\mathrm{w}(\mathbf{s}_i \oplus \mathbf{emb}) + 1), \text{ including the pre-flipped bit.}$$

In order to determine, whether the application of the improved approach is advantageous in comparison to the basic algorithm, w_2 is calculated as well, according to Equation (4) with the basic unmodified $\mathbf{a}_l$, as $w_2 = \mathrm{w}(\mathbf{s} \oplus \mathbf{emb})$. Whenever w_1 is smaller than w_2, pre-flipping one bit is indeed advantageous in comparison to the basic method. In this case, the w_1 bits are flipped. Otherwise the basic method is applied and w_2 bits are flipped.

As a result of this heuristic approach based on pre-flipping one additional bit, the embedding efficiency can considerably be increased (see Table 1).

Continuing this thought, in the *optimal* case up to f_k pre-flipped bits are included. *Experimental investigations have shown that it is sufficient to consider up to f_k instead of l pre-flipped bits.* Again, the performance of a code matters.

By means of this approach, i.e., considering all possible flipping patterns $\binom{l}{i}$, $(i = 1, 2, ..., f_k)$, it is possible to reach $R_{a,classic}$ exactly. Thus, we are able to achieve the same embedding efficiency as by using the classic Matrix Embedding.

The results in terms of R_a are summarized in Table 1 for the three approaches described in this section. For a comparison, we also give $R_{a,classic}$.

---

[2] It is recommended to use an interleaver to pre-process the image before embedding starts in order to reduce the impact of possible attacks.

Table 1. Average number of embedding changes R_a

(n, l, f_k)	$g(x)$, basic	$g(x)$, improved	$g(x)$, optimal	$\mathbf{H}_{k \times n}$, classic
$(7, 4, 1)$	1.5	0.875	0.875	0.875
$(15, 11, 1)$	2.0	0.938	0.938	0.938
$(15, 7, 2)$	4.0	2.683	2.461	2.461
$(17, 9, 2)$	4.0	2.516	2.324	2.324
$(31, 26, 1)$	2.5	0.969	0.969	0.969
$(31, 21, 2)$	5.0	2.843	2.482	2.482
$(23, 12, 3)$	5.5	3.429	2.853	2.853

2.3   Embedding Based on $\mathbf{H}_{k \times n}$

As pointed out in the last section, using the optimal approach for syndrome coding based on the generator polynomial $g(x)$ for embedding enables us to achieve $R_{a,classic}$. However, the question whether a less time complex embedding is possible remains unanswered.

To answer this question, the results of our investigations are summarized in terms of time complexity in Table 2.

Table 2. Complexity of embedding

Approach	Number of XOR operations	Example: $(15, 7, 2)$ BCH
$\mathbf{H}_{k \times n}$, classic	$((k \cdot n) \, n + k) \, 2^n$	59244544
$\mathbf{H}_{k \times n}$, 2^k look-up tables	$n \cdot 2^l$	1920
$g(x)$, basic	$l \, (k+1) + k$	71
$g(x)$, improved	$l + (l \, (k+1) + k)(l+1)$	575
$g(x)$, optimal	$l + (l \, (k+1) + k) \sum_{i=0}^{f_k} \binom{l}{i}$	2066

As a measure of time complexity the number of XOR operations was considered, needed to embed a confidential message **emb** of length k within n cover bits. The approaches described in the last section can easily be compared to the classic approach since a division in the binary case can also be realized using XOR operations.

Table 2 confirms that embedding based on syndrome coding by means of $g(x)$ is indeed advantageous compared to the classic approach in terms of time complexity. Note that we are also able to achieve $R_{a,classic}$ using the optimal approach.

However, considering the estimated time complexity for the classic approach based on a parity check matrix $\mathbf{H}_{k \times n}$ combined with 2^k look-up tables, the results achieved so far are slightly worse.

This fact motivates us to further investigate memory complexity, i.e., to reduce the number of look-up tables on the one hand side, and the number of sequences stored in the coset on the other hand side. Thus, we investigated improved search strategies within the coset, in order to make the use of look-up tables manageable within practical systems. Of course, our goal is again to achieve $R_{a,classic}$.

Decreasing the Search Area - Working with $coset(0)$

Remember the classic approach without look-up tables, in which finding a coset leader, i.e., a coset member $\mathbf{f}$ with minimal weight, is an NP complete problem, requiring exhaustive search. In this case, the search area includes all possible sequences of length n, i.e., 2^n sequences have to be evaluated. This will, of course, be to complex for many practical systems.

Generally, it is possible to speed up the process of finding a coset leader by means of look-up tables. There are 2^k different syndromes and therefore 2^k possible sequences **emb**. Within each look-up table, all 2^l possible sequences $\mathbf{f}$ leading to each sequence **emb** are stored.

The first look-up table ($coset(0)$) belongs to the zero syndrome (and thus to **emb** $= 0$) and contains all codewords $\mathbf{a}_i \in A$ of the considered code. All remaining entries $\mathbf{f}$ in the look-up tables correspond to all possible error patterns in coding theory and are stored in the remaining $(2^k - 1)$ look-up tables. Within practical systems, this certainly causes problems with storage.

In this section, *we describe a practical algorithm using only one look-up table, strictly speaking the one containing all codewords* $\mathbf{a}_i \in A$, *i.e., one look-up table with* $coset(0) = A$.

Thereby, our goal is to achieve both a reduced time complexity and a reduced memory complexity. Therefore, all possible cosets based on $coset(0)$ are defined as:

$$coset(\mathbf{emb}) = \{\mathbf{f_m} \oplus \mathbf{a}_i \mid \mathbf{H}_{k \times n} \cdot (\mathbf{f_m} \oplus \mathbf{a}_i)^T = \mathbf{emb}\} = \mathbf{f_m} \oplus coset(0), \quad (7)$$

where the coset member $\mathbf{f_m}$ is defined as $\mathbf{f_m} = \mathbf{a} \oplus \mathbf{f}$. Based on this definition of a coset, the coset leader is defined as the sequence $\mathbf{f_m} \oplus \mathbf{a}_i$ with minimum distance to the cover sequence $\mathbf{a}$.

The following paragraph describes the adapted embedding process based on only one look-up table containing $coset(0) = A$:

The embedding process is divided into two parts. In the first part, the classic approach is used to acquire the first sequence $\mathbf{f}$ fulfilling, combined with the cover sequence $\mathbf{a}$, Equation (1) with $\mathbf{s} = \mathbf{emb}$. Thus, a coset member with $\mathbf{f_m} = \mathbf{a} \oplus \mathbf{f}$ is determined. A coset member can be identified more simply by searching for a sequence $\mathbf{f}$ independent of $\mathbf{a}$, i.e., by searching for a sequence that fulfills $\mathbf{s} = \mathbf{H}_{k \times n} \cdot \mathbf{f}^T$ with $\mathbf{s} = \mathbf{emb}$. In this case, $\mathbf{f}$ is equal to the coset member, i.e., $\mathbf{f_m} = \mathbf{f}$.

This coset member will certainly not always be the coset leader. Hence, in the second step of the embedding process, the coset leader has to be determined, i.e., the sequence with minimum distance to the cover sequence $\mathbf{a}$. This can easily be done within the coset $coset(\mathbf{emb})$ with:

$$coset(\mathbf{emb}) = \mathbf{f_m} \oplus \mathbf{a}_i \quad (i = 1, 2, ..., 2^l). \quad (8)$$

This coset indeed includes all 2^l sequences leading to **emb** if combined with the parity check matrix $\mathbf{H}_{k \times n}$:

$$\mathbf{H}_{k \times n} \cdot (\mathbf{f_m} \oplus \mathbf{a}_i)^T = \mathbf{H}_{k \times n} \cdot \mathbf{f_m}^T \oplus \mathbf{H}_{k \times n} \cdot \mathbf{a}_i^T = \mathbf{emb} \oplus \mathbf{0} = \mathbf{emb} \qquad (9)$$

is true for all $\mathbf{a}_i \in A$ (see Equation (7)). As a result, the desired stego sequence **b** can easily be identified with:

$$\mathbf{b} = \arg \min_{\mathbf{a}_i \in A} \left(\mathrm{d}(\mathbf{a}, \mathbf{f_m} \oplus \mathbf{a}_i) \right) \oplus \mathbf{f_m}. \qquad (10)$$

As a result, $R_{a,classic}$ can be achieved.

The advantage of this approach compared to the classic approach is a reduced time complexity. Instead of an exhaustive search including 2^n sequences of length n, only the first sequence $\mathbf{f_m}$ has to be acquired. This sequence can be used to determine a sequence $(\mathbf{f_m} \oplus \mathbf{a}_i)$ that has a minimum distance to the cover sequence **a** in order to replace it. The search area, included in the exhaustive search, now contains only 2^l instead of 2^n sequences.

The time needed to find the first sequence **f** leading to **emb** and thus to find a coset member $\mathbf{f_m}$ is negligible. Another advantage of the approach described above is the reduced memory complexity, since only one look-up table has to be stored, i.e., only 2^l sequences. However, when dealing with large code parameters, especially large parameters l, this storage space might be unacceptable. Therefore, approaches to further reduce $coset(\mathbf{0})$ were investigated.

Decreasing the Search Area - Working with the Reduced $coset(\mathbf{0})_{red}$
Working with $coset(\mathbf{0})$, as described in the last section, reduces the embedding complexity considerably. However, for large code parameters, especially a high number of information bits l, not only a lot of time for the exhaustive search but also a lot of storage is required for a look-up table containing all 2^l codewords. Because of this, an approach to further reduce time and memory complexity by reducing $coset(\mathbf{0})$ is discussed.

Our first investigations were motivated by the fact that the weight of the codewords of a linear code is distributed symmetrically. For example the code alphabet of the $(15, 7, 2)$ BCH Code contains $|A| = 2^l = 128$ codewords distributed by: $\mathrm{w}(A) = (1, 0, 0, 0, 0, 18, 30, 15, 15, 30, 18, 0, 0, 0, 0, 1)$. Thus, there exist, e.g., one codeword with weight 0 and 18 codewords with weight 5.

The question we would like to answer is, how far we can go with a reduction of A. Is it sufficient to store only 2^{l-1} codewords with a weight of $\mathrm{w}(\mathbf{a}_i) \leq \lfloor \frac{n}{2} \rfloor$ or maybe even less in the look-up table?

Investigations have shown that including only half of all possible codewords, i.e., reducing the searching area to 2^{l-1} sequences with

$$coset(\mathbf{0})_{red} = \left\{ \mathbf{a}_i \mid \mathrm{w}(\mathbf{a}_i) \leq \left\lfloor \frac{n}{2} \right\rfloor \wedge \mathbf{H}_{k \times n} \cdot \mathbf{a}_i^T = \mathbf{0} \right\} \qquad (11)$$

will result in only a *small deterioration* of R_a.

Some examples:

- for the $(15, 7, 2)$ BCH Code $R_a = 2.508$ can be achieved, while $R_{a,classic} = 2.461$, and
- for the $(23, 12, 3)$ BCH Code (Golay Code) $R_a = 2.864$ can be achieved, while $R_{a,classic} = 2.853$.

Nevertheless, the embedding complexity in terms of time and memory can be reduced considerably. For example using the $(15, 7, 2)$ BCH Code, only $\frac{2^{l-1}}{2^n} = \frac{2^6}{2^{15}} = 0.00195$, i.e., only 0.2% of the original search area has to be considered for embedding with only a minor loss in embedding efficiency, directly influenced by R_a.

This deterioration of R_a is caused by the reduced $coset(\mathbf{0})_{red}$. Each coset member $\mathbf{f_m}$ leads to different reduced cosets with:

$$coset(\mathbf{emb})_{red} = \mathbf{f_m} \oplus coset(\mathbf{0})_{red}. \tag{12}$$

Of course, each of this cosets is part of $coset(\mathbf{emb}) = \mathbf{f_m} \oplus coset(\mathbf{0})$. Consequently, it is not always possible to find the coset leader, i.e., the coset leader does not need to be included in the reduced coset considered here.

However, we can exploit this particularity of the reduced coset, since each of the different reduced cosets affects R_a. In order to minimize the differences between $R_{a,classic}$ and R_a, it seems reasonable to *find different sequences $\mathbf{f_m}$ and thus to evaluate different reduced cosets*.

Of course, this approach is more time consuming. Strictly speaking, *the time complexity increases by the number num of evaluated sequences $\mathbf{f_m}$ and thus by the number of different reduced cosets. However, this additional time complexity is negligible, as long as $num \cdot 2^l \ll 2^n$ and $num \ll 2^k$ respectively.*

Table 3 summarizes some of our results. Within this investigation, we reduced the alphabet and thereby the look-up table from $|A| = 2^l$ to $|A_{red}| = 2^{l-1}$. Therefore, the code sequences with the lowest weight are chosen, i.e., all sequences with $w(\mathbf{a}_i) \leq \lfloor \frac{n}{2} \rfloor$.

Table 3. Influence of the number of evaluated sequences, $num \cdot \mathbf{f_m}$

(n, l, f_k)	$R_{a,classic}$	$\lvert A_{red} \rvert$	$R_{a,1\mathbf{f_m}}$	$R_{a,5\mathbf{f_m}}$	$R_{a,10\mathbf{f_m}}$
(15,7,2)	2.461	2^6	2.508	2.461	2.461
(15,11,1)	0.938	2^{10}	0.938	0.938	0.938
(23,12,3)	2.852	2^{11}	2.864	2.853	2.853

The results confirm the assumption that evaluating different sequences $\mathbf{f_m}$ and thereby different reduced cosets $coset(\mathbf{emb})_{red}$ indeed results in an improved R_a. As can be seen, e.g., for the $(15, 7, 2)$ BCH Code, considering 5 different sequences $\mathbf{f_m}$ in the embedding process leads to $R_{a,classic}$. The time needed to evaluate additional sequences $\mathbf{f_m}$ is negligible.

However, even if it is possible to achieve enormous advantages in terms of embedding complexity compared to the classic approach, the complexity is relatively high, whenever considering codes with a high number of information bits. For these codes, reducing the code alphabet by one half does not suffice at all, since the required storage for the look-up table and the time needed for exhaustive search are still to high.

Based on this problem, the question arises, whether it is possible to further reduce the alphabet A and consequently the look-up table. *Using the approach described above, it is indeed important to use only those codewords with the lowest weight.* Investigations have shown, that variations of this criterion always results in worse results, i.e., in higher discrepancies to $R_{a,classic}$.

Table 4 summarizes the results of our investigations.

Table 4. Influence of the number of evaluated sequences, $num \cdot f_m$

(n,l,f_k)	$R_{a,classic}$	$|A_{red}|$	$R_{a,1f_m}$	$R_{a,5f_m}$	$R_{a,10f_m}$	$R_{a,15f_m}$
(31,21,2)	2.482	30443, w($\mathbf{a}_i$) $< k$	2.490	2.482	2.482	2.482
(31,21,2)	2.482	11533, w($\mathbf{a}_i$) $< (k-1)$	2.531	2.482	2.482	2.482
(31,21,2)	2.482	3628, w($\mathbf{a}_i$) $< (k-2)$	2.757	2.486	2.483	2.482

In this example, the alphabet A of the $(31, 21, 2)$ BCH Code was reduced from 2^{21} down to $\approx 2^{12}$ sequences. Nevertheless, we are able to achieve $R_{a,classic}$ considering $num = 15$ sequences $\mathbf{f_m}$, i.e., by evaluating up to 15 different reduced cosets. Whenever a negligible reduction of R_a can be accepted, considering $num = 5$ sequences $\mathbf{f_m}$ is sufficient. By means of this approach, the time complexity is low, i.e., the time needed to embed a sequence $\mathbf{emb}$ is manageable. Therefore, it can be used in practical systems.

As a result of the example illustrated above, the search area can be decreased from 2^{31} sequences to $\approx 2^{12}$, i.e., only $\frac{2^{12}}{2^{31}} = 0.000002$ of the sequences (0.0002%) have to be considered by exhaustive search in comparison to the classic approach.

Generalizing the Approach
Even if we discussed this approach for linear codes like BCH Codes, it is not limited to this class of codes. It is also possible to generalize the approach of working with $coset(\mathbf{0})$ as well as the approach working with $coset(\mathbf{0})_{red}$.

Whenever it is possible to separate $\mathbf{H}_{k \times n}$ (e.g., through permuting columns) in $\mathbf{H}_{k \times n} = [\mathbf{H}_{k \times l} \, \mathbf{H}_{k \times k}]$ under the condition that $\mathbf{H}_{k \times k}$ is non-singular, all codewords $\mathbf{a}_i \in A$ can be easily determined. In this case, all codewords are arranged systematically.

Starting with all 2^l known source sequences $\mathbf{a}_{i,l}$ of length l, $\mathbf{a}_i = [\mathbf{a}_{i,l} \, \mathbf{a}_{i,k}] \in A$ is determined by:

$$\mathbf{a}_{i,k} = \mathbf{H}_{k \times k}^{-1} \cdot \mathbf{H}_{k \times l} \cdot \mathbf{a}_{i,l}^T. \tag{13}$$

The resulting codewords $\mathbf{a}_i$, $(i = 1, 2, ..., 2^l)$ are stored in only one look-up table. Of course a reduction of this look-up table is also possible. However, to answer the question whether it is possible to always achieve $R_{a,classic}$, further investigations are required.

3   Efficient Embedding Including Locked Elements

In this section, we consider embedding including embedding constraints. Since the results for syndrome coding based on a parity check matrix $\mathbf{H}_{k \times n}$ achieved so far are much better, we focus on this scenario. After describing the basic approach, the results of the previous section are adapted to this embedding scenario. Again, we focus on embedding with reduced embedding complexity but with a constant average number of embedding changes in comparison to $R_{a,classic}$ achieved with the classic Matrix Embedding scenario.

3.1   Description of the Basic Approach

Remember, embedding based on the classic approach was done by finding a sequence $\mathbf{f}$ of minimal weight with $\mathbf{s} = \mathbf{H}_{k \times n} \cdot (\mathbf{a} \oplus \mathbf{f})^T = \mathbf{emb}$, as long as locked elements are neglected.

However, since practical steganographic applications have to deal with locked elements, it is necessary to consider these locked elements within the blocks of length n. Thus, the classic embedding algorithm has to be adapted as follows (see also [12]):

In a first pre-processing step, the matrix $\mathbf{H}_{k \times n}$ is divided for each block of length n into $\mathbf{H}_{k \times n} = [\mathbf{H}_{k \times lock} \ \mathbf{H}_{k \times unlock}]$, depending on the positions of locked elements with $n = lock + unlock$. As a result, $\mathbf{H}_{k \times lock}$ is a submatrix of $\mathbf{H}_{k \times n}$ corresponding to locked elements, and $\mathbf{H}_{k \times unlock}$ is a submatrix of $\mathbf{H}_{k \times n}$ corresponding to unlocked elements.

In order to embed, a sequence $\mathbf{f}$ of length $unlock$ has to be determined in a way that $\mathbf{s} = \mathbf{emb}$ according to:

$$\mathbf{s} = \underbrace{\mathbf{H}_{k \times lock} \cdot \mathbf{a}_{lock}^T}_{\mathbf{s}_{lock}} \oplus \underbrace{\mathbf{H}_{k \times unlock} \cdot (\mathbf{a}_{unlock} \oplus \mathbf{f})^T}_{\mathbf{s}_{unlock}}. \tag{14}$$

However, it is also possible to simplify the embedding process and thus to decrease embedding complexity, since $(\mathbf{s}_{lock} \oplus \mathbf{emb}) = \mathbf{c}$ is invariant. Instead of searching for a coset leader of length n, one can try to find a sequence $\mathbf{f}$ of length $unlock$ (a coset leader of length $unlock$) with minimum weight in a way that $\mathbf{s}_{unlock} = \mathbf{c}$. As a result, the stego sequence leads to $\mathbf{emb}$, according to Equation (1).

3.2   Description of the Improved Approach

The basic algorithm described above can also be improved in terms of embedding efficiency as described in Section 2.3. Thus, it is possible to work with only one look-up table containing all codewords $\mathbf{a}_i \in A$.

However, it is necessary to consider the fact that the positions of locked elements are distributed randomly, i.e., the number of locked elements and their positions varies from block to block. It is necessary to reduce the sequences within the look-up table by the locked positions for each block $\mathbf{a}$ of length n and thus for each pattern of locked elements. Consequently, $coset(\mathbf{0})_{unlock} = A_{unlock}$ and therefore A_{unlock} now contains sequences of length $unlock$.

The embedding process is again divided into two parts. First, a sequence $\mathbf{f}$ fulfilling (14) with $\mathbf{s} = \mathbf{emb}$ has to be found. This coset member of length $unlock$ with $\mathbf{f}_{m,unlock} = \mathbf{f}$ can be used to determine the coset leader based on $coset(\mathbf{0})_{unlock}$:

$$\mathbf{b}_{unlock} = \arg\min_{\substack{\mathbf{a}_{i,unlock} \\ \in A_{unlock}}} \left(d(\mathbf{a}_{unlock}, (\mathbf{f}_{m,unlock} \oplus \mathbf{a}_{i,unlock})) \right) \oplus \mathbf{f}_{m,unlock}. \quad (15)$$

Similarly to the embedding scenario not considering embedding constraints (Section 2.3), it is possible to reduce the alphabet A and therefore to reduce the number of sequences that have to be considered by exhaustive search. This reduction will also result in different reduced cosets for different sequences $\mathbf{f}_{m,unlock}$. Thus, it is again advantageous to evaluate different sequences $\mathbf{f}_{m,unlock}$ and consequently different reduced cosets in order to achieve $R_{a,classic}$.

This approach enables to embed faster and less complexly while achieving an average number of embedding changes similar to the basic approach. Instead of 2^{unlock} sequences of length $(unlock)$, 2^l sequences have to be considered at most. Whenever we further reduce the alphabet, we can further reduce this number.

4 Summary and Outlook

Since embedding based on the classic approach, by finding a coset leader using a parity check matrix $\mathbf{H}_{k \times n}$, is really complex and therefore time consuming, we focused on embedding strategies to reduce the embedding complexity without reducing the embedding efficiency e and without increasing the average number of embedding changes R_a respectively compared to $R_{a,classic}$, which can be achieved with the *classic* Matrix Embedding scenario.

Within first investigations, syndrome coding based on the generator polynomial $g(x)$ was considered. As the results confirm, it is indeed possible to achieve $R_{a,classic}$. Thus, it is possible to embed less time complex based on this approach.

However, the complexity of embedding can further be reduced by syndrome coding based on $\mathbf{H}_{k \times n}$ combined with look-up tables. Embedding based on look-up tables reduces time complexity dramatically compared to the classic approach based on exhaustive search. Instead of 2^n only 2^l sequences have to be considered. Nevertheless, this approach is limited by storage, since all 2^n sequences have to be stored.

Consequently, our goal was to further reduce the storage space. Therefore, we proposed an embedding strategy working within $coset(\mathbf{0})$, i.e., only 2^l sequences have to be stored. Since this can still be problematic for codes with a high number of information bits l, the cardinality of $coset(\mathbf{0})$ was further reduced.

To summarize, we are able to embed much faster due to the reduced time complexity. Additionally, the storage space can be reduced dramatically, i.e., for the $(31, 21, 2)$ BCH Code, e.g., only 0.0002% of the original search area has to be considered in our approach. However, this result does not affect R_a; it is still possible to achieve $R_{a,classic}$ by means of this approach.

Even if the considerations in this paper are based on structured codes, they are not limited to this class of codes.

Acknowledgement

Parts of this work were supported by the German Research Foundation (DFG).

References

1. Bierbrauer, J.: Crandall's problem (unpublished) (1998), http://www.ws.binghamton.edu/fridrich/covcodes.pdf
2. Bossert, M.: Channel Coding for Telecommunications. Wiley, Chichester (1999)
3. Crandall, R.: Some Notes on steganography. Posted on Steganography Mailing List (1998), http://os.inf.tu-dresden.de/~westfeld/crandall.pdf
4. Fridrich, J., Goljan, M., Lisonek, P., Soukal, D.: Writing on Wet Paper. Proc. of IEEE Transcription on Signal Processing 53, 3923–3935 (2005)
5. Fridrich, J., Goljan, M., Lisonek, P., Soukal, D.: Writing on Wet Paper. Proc. of EI SPIE San Jose 5681, 328–340 (2005)
6. Fridrich, J., Goljan, M., Soukal, D.: Perturbed Quantization Steganography with Wet Paper Codes. In: Proc. of ACM Multimedia and Security Workshop, Germany, pp. 4–15 (2004)
7. Fridrich, J., Goljan, M., Soukal, D.: Efficient Wet Paper Codes. In: Barni, M., Herrera-Joancomartí, J., Katzenbeisser, S., Pérez-González, F. (eds.) IH 2005. LNCS, vol. 3727, pp. 204–218. Springer, Heidelberg (2005)
8. Fridrich, J., Soukal, D.: Matrix Embedding for Large Payloads. Proc. of EI SPIE San Jose 6072, 727–738 (2006)
9. Galand, F., Kabatiansky, G.: Information hiding by coverings. In: Proc. of IEEE Information Theory Workshop, pp. 151–154 (2004)
10. Klimant, H., Piotraschke, R., Schönfeld, D.: Informations- und Kodierungstheorie. Teubner Verlag Wiesbaden (2006)
11. Schönfeld, D.: Einbetten mit minimaler Werkänderung (Embedding with minimal cover changes). Datenschutz und Datensicherheit DuD, Vieweg Verlag 25(11), 666–671 (2001)
12. Schönfeld, D., Winkler, A.: Embedding with Syndrome Coding Based on BCH Codes. In: Proc. of ACM Multimedia and Security Workshop, Switzerland, pp. 214–223 (2006)

Exploiting Security Holes in Lattice Data Hiding

Luis Pérez-Freire and Fernando Pérez-González*

Signal Theory and Communications Department
University of Vigo, Vigo 36310, Spain
{lpfreire, fperez}@gts.tsc.uvigo.es

Abstract. This paper presents a security analysis for data hiding methods based on nested lattice codes, extending the analysis provided by previous works. The security is quantified in an information-theoretic sense by means of the information leakage between the watermarked signals seen by the attacker and the secret key used in the embedding process. The theoretical analysis accomplished in the first part of the paper addresses important issues such as the possibility of achieving perfect secrecy and the impact of the embedding rate and channel coding in the security level. In the second part, a practical algorithm for estimating the secret key is proposed, and the information extracted is used for implementing a reversibility attack on real images.

1 Introduction

Watermarking security has emerged in the last years as a new research topic, whose basics can be found in [1],[2],[3] and the references therein. The framework for security analysis adopted in these works follows a cryptanalytic approach: all the parameters of the watermarking scheme are assumed to be public, and the security relies only on a secret key, which is assumed to remain unchanged in the contents watermarked by the same user. The main target of the security analysis is to determine whether the watermarking scheme conceals properly the secret key; if it is not the case, then we are interested in assessing the security level of the scheme, defined as the number of observations needed to achieve an estimate of the secret key up to a certain accuracy [2].

In this paper we focus on the security analysis of data hiding schemes based on nested lattice codes [4], usually known as lattice DC-DM schemes. Specifically, the work in the present paper extends the theory and algorithms developed in [5] to a more general scenario. The analysis in [5] was mainly restricted to the so-called "Known Message Attack" (KMA) scenario, where the messages embedded

* This work was partially funded by *Xunta de Galicia* under projects PGIDT04 TIC322013PR, PGIDT04 PXIC32202PM, and "Competitive Research Units" program, Ref. 150/2006; MEC project DIPSTICK, Ref. TEC2004-02551/TCM, and European Commission through the IST Programme under Contract IST-2002-507932 ECRYPT. ECRYPT disclaimer: The information in this paper is provided as is, and no guarantee or warranty is given or implied that the information is fit for any particular purpose. The user thereof uses the information at its sole risk and liability.

T. Furon et al. (Eds.): IH 2007, LNCS 4567, pp. 159–173, 2007.
© Springer-Verlag Berlin Heidelberg 2007

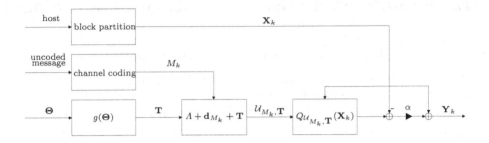

Fig. 1. Block diagram showing the lattice data hiding model

in each watermarked signal were assumed to be known by the attacker. This paper considers a general scenario (which encompasses most of the practical data hiding applications), termed "Watermarked Only Attack" (WOA), where the attacker no longer knows anything about the embedded messages. As in [5], the security level is measured by means of the mutual information (a.k.a. information leakage) between the watermarked signals and the secret key, which is related to the variance of the key estimation error. The first part of this paper measures the information leakage for lattice DC-DM schemes, paying special attention to the comparison between KMA and WOA scenarios, and considering also possible strategies that achieve good security levels. The second part shows how the information about the key provided by the observations can be extracted and used in practical scenarios, proposing a reversibility attack based on an estimate of the secret dither. The proposed estimation algorithm works with any arbitrary nested lattice code, and is applicable to high embedding rate scenarios.

The main notational conventions used in the paper are the following: Λ_f and Λ are the n-dimensional fine and coarse (shaping) lattices of the nested lattice code, respectively. The alphabet that encodes the messages to be transmitted is defined as $\mathcal{M} \triangleq \{0, 1, \ldots, p - 1\}$, with p denoting its cardinality. Random variables are denoted by capital letters, and vectors are represented by boldface letters. $H(\cdot)$ and $h(\cdot)$ denote entropy and differential entropy [6], respectively.

2 Theoretical Model

The mathematical model for lattice data hiding considered in this paper is shown in Fig. 1. First, the host signal is partitioned into non-overlapping blocks $\mathbf{X}_k$ of length n. The message to be embedded may undergo channel coding, yielding the symbols $M_k \in \mathcal{M}$ which are assumed to be equiprobable, unless otherwise stated. Each symbol M_k is embedded in one block $\mathbf{X}_k$ by means of a randomized lattice quantizer yielding a watermarked signal $\mathbf{Y}_k$ as follows:

$$\mathbf{Y}_k = \mathbf{X}_k + \alpha(Q_\Lambda(\mathbf{X}_k - \mathbf{d}_{M_k} - \mathbf{T}) - \mathbf{X}_k + \mathbf{d}_{M_k} + \mathbf{T}), \tag{1}$$

where $Q_\Lambda(\mathbf{x})$ is a nearest neighbor quantizer whose centroids are distributed according to Λ, the coarse (shaping) lattice, $\alpha \in [0, 1]$ is the distortion

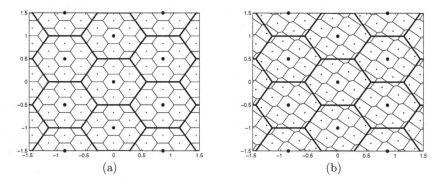

Fig. 2. Nested lattice codes of rate $R = \log(9)/2$ with hexagonal shaping lattice, obtained by means of self-similar construction (a) and Construction A with $\mathbf{g} = (1,2)^T$ (b). Voronoi regions of Λ_f and Λ are represented by thin and thick lines, respectively.

compensation parameter, $\mathbf{d}_{M_k}$ is the coset leader associated to M_k, and $\mathbf{T} = g(\boldsymbol{\Theta})$ is the secret dither signal, which remains constant in each watermarked block. The embedding distortion per dimension in a mean-squared-error sense can be computed as $D_w = \frac{1}{n}E\left[||\mathbf{X}_k - \mathbf{Y}_k||^2\right] = \alpha^2 P(\Lambda)$, where $P(\Lambda)$ denotes the second-order moment per dimension of $\mathcal{V}(\Lambda)$.

The coset leaders $\mathbf{d}_{M_k} \in \{\mathbf{d}_0, \ldots, \mathbf{d}_{p-1}\}$ that encode each symbol M_k are chosen so that $\bigcup_{k=0}^{p-1}(\mathbf{d}_k + \Lambda) = \Lambda_f$ and they coincide with the coset leaders of minimum norm of the nested lattice code. Nested lattice codes can be obtained in a number of ways; we consider in this paper self-similar lattice partitions and Construction A [7]. In self-similar lattice partitions, $\Lambda_f = p^{-\frac{1}{n}}\Lambda$, for $p^{\frac{1}{n}} \in \mathbb{N}$.[1] The lattice Λ is a sublattice of Λ_f, resulting in a "nesting ratio" $\frac{\text{vol}(\mathcal{V}(\Lambda))}{\text{vol}(\mathcal{V}(\Lambda_f))} = p$, and an embedding rate $R = \log(p)/n$. The coset leaders $\mathbf{d}_k$ can be obtained as $\Lambda_f \cap \mathcal{V}(\Lambda)$. Construction A is more flexible, and is summarized as follows:

1. Define a positive integer p. In order to construct a nested lattice code with good asymptotic properties, p must be prime.
2. Define a generating vector $\mathbf{g} \in \mathbb{Z}_p^n$ and compute the codebook $\mathcal{C} \triangleq \{\mathbf{c} \in \mathbb{Z}_p^n : \mathbf{c} = q \cdot \mathbf{g} \mod p, \ q = 0, \ldots, p-1\}$. Then, define the lattice $\Lambda' = p^{-1}\mathcal{C} + \mathbb{Z}^n$.
3. Define the generating matrix $\mathbf{G} \in \mathbb{R}^{n \times n}$ (where each row is a basis vector) of the coarse (shaping) lattice Λ. Apply the linear transformation $\Lambda_f = \Lambda'\mathbf{G}$. It follows that Λ is a sublattice of Λ_f and the nesting ratio is $\frac{\text{vol}(\mathcal{V}(\Lambda))}{\text{vol}(\mathcal{V}(\Lambda_f))} = p$, resulting in a coding rate $R = \log(p)/n$.
4. The coset leaders are given by $\Lambda_f \cap \mathcal{V}(\Lambda)$, or equivalently, $p^{-1}\mathcal{C}\mathbf{G} \mod \Lambda$.

Examples of 2-dimensional nested lattice codes are shown in Fig. 2.

With regard to the attacker's strategy, it is assumed that he manages to gather an ensemble of watermarked blocks $\{\mathbf{Y}_k, \ k = 1, \ldots, N_o\}$ (hereinafter,

---

[1] More general self-similar lattice partitions consider also rotations of Λ, but we will restrict our attention to those obtained through scaling.

observations), which may belong to different host signals, but all of them were watermarked with the same secret key $\boldsymbol{\Theta}$. He knows the parameters of the nested lattice code being used, i.e. Λ, $\{\mathbf{d}_i, \; i = 0, \ldots, p-1\}$, α, whereas he ignores the host blocks $\mathbf{X}_k$, the embedded symbols M_k, and $\mathbf{T} = g(\boldsymbol{\Theta})$. The objective of the attacker is to obtain an estimate of $\mathbf{T}$. The first step performed by him is the modulo reduction of the watermarked blocks as $\tilde{\mathbf{Y}}_k \triangleq \mathbf{Y}_k \bmod \Lambda$, where the modulo operation is defined as $\mathbf{X} \bmod \Lambda \triangleq \mathbf{X} - Q_\Lambda(\mathbf{X})$. Under the assumption (a.k.a. "flat-host assumption") that the variance of the components of $\mathbf{X}_k$ is much larger than the embedding distortion, such modulo reduction does not imply any loss of information for the attacker, as discussed in [5]. Let us define

$$f_0(\mathbf{x}) \triangleq \begin{cases} (\mathrm{vol}(\mathcal{Z}(\Lambda)))^{-1}, & \mathbf{x} \in \mathcal{Z}(\Lambda) \\ 0, & \text{otherwise,} \end{cases} \tag{2}$$

with $\mathcal{Z}(\Lambda) \triangleq (1-\alpha)\mathcal{V}(\Lambda)$, where $\mathcal{V}(\Lambda) \triangleq \{\mathbf{x} \in \mathbb{R}^n : Q_\Lambda(\mathbf{x}) = \mathbf{0}\}$ denotes the Voronoi region of Λ [8]. The probability density function of the signals seen by the attacker can be computed by taking into account that, under the flat-host assumption, $f(\tilde{\mathbf{y}}_k|m_k, \mathbf{t}) = f_0(\tilde{\mathbf{y}}_k - \mathbf{d}_{m_k} - \mathbf{t} \bmod \Lambda)$. Finally, the function $g(\cdot)$ is assumed to yield a secret dither $\mathbf{T}$ uniformly distributed in the Voronoi region $\mathcal{V}(\Lambda)$, which turns out to be the worst case for the attacker [5].

3   Theoretical Security Analysis

The amount of information that leaks from the observations is quantified by means of the mutual information $I(\tilde{\mathbf{Y}}_1, \ldots, \tilde{\mathbf{Y}}_{N_o}; \mathbf{T})$. Making use of the chain rule for entropies [6], it can be written in a more illustrative manner as

$$\begin{aligned} I(\tilde{\mathbf{Y}}_1, &\ldots, \tilde{\mathbf{Y}}_{N_o}; \mathbf{T}) \\ &= I(\tilde{\mathbf{Y}}_1, \ldots, \tilde{\mathbf{Y}}_{N_o}; \mathbf{T}, M_1, \ldots, M_{N_o}) - I(\tilde{\mathbf{Y}}_1, \ldots, \tilde{\mathbf{Y}}_{N_o}; M_1, \ldots, M_{N_o}|\mathbf{T}) \\ &= I(\tilde{\mathbf{Y}}_1, \ldots, \tilde{\mathbf{Y}}_{N_o}; \mathbf{T}|M_1, \ldots, M_{N_o}) + I(\tilde{\mathbf{Y}}_1, \ldots, \tilde{\mathbf{Y}}_{N_o}; M_1, \ldots, M_{N_o}) \\ &\quad - I(\tilde{\mathbf{Y}}_1, \ldots, \tilde{\mathbf{Y}}_{N_o}; M_1, \ldots, M_{N_o}|\mathbf{T}). \end{aligned} \tag{3}$$

The first term of (3) is the information leakage in the KMA case, that was studied in [5]. One fundamental property of the KMA scenario is that, under the assumption $\mathbf{T} \sim U(\mathcal{V}(\Lambda))$, the conditional pdf of the dither signal is [5]

$$f(\mathbf{t}|\tilde{\mathbf{y}}_1, \ldots, \tilde{\mathbf{y}}_{N_o}, \mathbf{m}) = \begin{cases} (\mathrm{vol}(\mathcal{S}_{N_o}(\mathbf{m})))^{-1}, & \mathbf{t} \in \mathcal{S}_{N_o}(\mathbf{m}) \\ 0, & \text{otherwise} \end{cases} \tag{4}$$

where $\mathbf{m} \triangleq (m_1, \ldots, m_{N_o})$,

$$\mathcal{S}_{N_o}(\mathbf{m}) \triangleq \bigcap_{j=1}^{N_o} \mathcal{D}_j(m_j), \tag{5}$$

$$\mathcal{D}_j(m_j) = (\tilde{\mathbf{y}}_j - \mathbf{d}_{m_j} - \mathcal{Z}(\Lambda)) \bmod \Lambda. \tag{6}$$

Eq. (5) denotes the "feasible region" for the secret dither, conditioned on the observations and the message sequence $\mathbf{m}$. This property will be frequently used in the remaining of this paper. The third term of (3) represents the achievable rate for a fair user, i.e., knowing the secret dither $\mathbf{T}$, whereas the second term is the rate achievable by unfair users (which is not null, in general) that do not know $\mathbf{T}$. A similar reasoning to that followed in [5, Sect. II] shows that the mutual information in (3) is concave and increasing with N_o. Notice that

$$I(\tilde{\mathbf{Y}}_1, \ldots, \tilde{\mathbf{Y}}_{N_o}; M_1, \ldots, M_{N_o}) - I(\tilde{\mathbf{Y}}_1, \ldots, \tilde{\mathbf{Y}}_{N_o}; M_1, \ldots, M_{N_o} | \mathbf{T}) < 0, \quad (7)$$

so the information leakage in the WOA case never exceeds that in the KMA case, as expected. In order to compute the asymptotic gap (when $N_o \to \infty$) between the security level of KMA and WOA scenarios, the left hand side of (7) is rewritten as $N_o \cdot H(M_1 | \tilde{\mathbf{Y}}_1, \mathbf{T}) - H(M_1, \ldots, M_{N_o} | \tilde{\mathbf{Y}}_1, \ldots, \tilde{\mathbf{Y}}_{N_o})$. Although the proof cannot be included here due to space limitations, it is possible to show that, for equiprobable message sequences,

$$\lim_{N_o \to \infty} (H(M_1, \ldots, M_{N_o} | \tilde{\mathbf{Y}}_1, \ldots, \tilde{\mathbf{Y}}_{N_o}) - N_o \cdot H(M_1 | \tilde{\mathbf{Y}}_1, \mathbf{T})) \to \log(p). \quad (8)$$

Hence, the asymptotic gap between KMA and WOA scenarios in terms of information leakage per dimension is $R = \log(p)/n$, i.e., the embedding rate. This result has important implications, since in practical scenarios we usually resort to low embedding rates that allow to recover the embedded message without the use of complex channel coding schemes. The problem is that low embedding rates may yield a security level similar to that of the KMA scenario. In spite of this, the WOA scenario still provides one major advantage over the KMA in terms of security, because in the WOA case the attacker cannot aspire to acquire perfect knowledge of the secret dither vector (even for infinite N_o) unless he has information about the a priori probabilities of the message sequences (introduced by the specific channel coding scheme being applied, for instance). This is a consequence of the following property: [2]

$$\Pr(\mathbf{m} | \tilde{\mathbf{y}}_1, \ldots, \tilde{\mathbf{y}}_{N_o})$$
$$= \Pr((\mathbf{m} + j \cdot \mathbf{1}) \mod p | \tilde{\mathbf{y}}_1, \ldots, \tilde{\mathbf{y}}_{N_o}) \cdot \frac{\Pr(\mathbf{m})}{\Pr((\mathbf{m} + j \cdot \mathbf{1}) \mod p)}, \ j \in \mathcal{M}, (9)$$

where the modulo operation is applied componentwise, and $\mathbf{1}$ denotes the n-dimensional vector with all components equal to 1. The obtention of Eq. (9) follows by combining equations (18) and (20) of the Appendix, and taking into account that the addition of a constant vector to the observations does not change the a posteriori probabilities of the embedded messages. This ambiguity makes impossible to reduce the uncertainty about $\mathbf{T}$ beyond a set of p discrete (equiprobable) points. However, such uncertainty can be further reduced by exploiting the statistical dependence between the symbols embedded in different blocks if a channel code has been applied.

---

[2] Eq. (9) holds directly for nested codes obtained through Construction A, and also for codes obtained through self-similar partitions if the coset leaders are properly arranged in $\mathcal{M}$.

3.1 Coding Strategies for Achieving Perfect Secrecy

Under certain assumptions it is possible to achieve null information leakage, a.k.a. "perfect secrecy", i.e., $I(\tilde{\mathbf{Y}}_1, \ldots, \tilde{\mathbf{Y}}_{N_o}; \mathbf{T}) = 0$. In the following lemma, two different strategies are considered.

Lemma 1. *Assuming equiprobable symbols and independence between the messages embedded in different blocks, the two following strategies achieve perfect secrecy:*

1. *Using self-similar lattice partitions with nesting ratio p and distortion compensation parameter $\alpha_k = 1 - kp^{-\frac{1}{n}}, k = 1, \ldots, p^{\frac{1}{n}} - 1$.*
2. *Making $|\mathcal{M}| \to \infty$ with the coset leaders $\mathbf{d}_k, \ k = 0, \ldots, \infty$ uniformly distributed in $\mathcal{V}(\Lambda)$.*

Outline of the proof: Due to the lack of space, a detailed proof is not included. The proof is based on the fact that, under the assumption of independence between the embedded messages, $h(\tilde{\mathbf{Y}}_1) = h(\tilde{\mathbf{Y}}_1|\mathbf{T})$ is a necessary and sufficient condition for achieving perfect secrecy. For proving the first part of the lemma, we have to prove that

$$f(\tilde{\mathbf{y}}_1|\mathbf{T} = \mathbf{t}) = \frac{1}{p}\sum_{i=0}^{p-1} f_0(\tilde{\mathbf{y}}_1 - \mathbf{t} - \mathbf{d}_i \mod \Lambda) = \frac{1}{\text{vol}(\mathcal{V}(\Lambda))} \ \forall \ \tilde{\mathbf{y}}_1 \in \mathcal{V}(\Lambda), (10)$$

where $f_0(\cdot)$ is given by (2). Intuitively, Eq. (10) turns out to be true for the considered values of α because in that case the union of p regions $\mathcal{Z}(\Lambda)$ (which are scaled versions of $\mathcal{V}(\Lambda_f)$) shifted by the corresponding coset leaders $\mathbf{d}_k, k \in \mathcal{M}$, perfectly packs in space, yielding a watermarked signal uniformly distributed in $\mathcal{V}(\Lambda)$. The proof of the second part of the lemma consists in showing that $f(\tilde{\mathbf{y}}_1|\mathbf{T} = \mathbf{t}) = (\text{vol}(\mathcal{V}(\Lambda)))^{-1} \ \forall \ \tilde{\mathbf{y}}_1 \in \mathcal{V}(\Lambda)$, which is true due to the uniform distribution of the coset leaders. $\qquad\square$

Some remarks to the results stated in Lemma 1 are in order:

1) The first strategy stated in Lemma 1 yields a finite and discrete set of values for α that permit to achieve perfect secrecy; however, the choice of these values may be in conflict with robustness requirements. Notice also that the second strategy is independent of α and the type of lattice partition.

2) Lemma 1 suggests that, for achieving good security levels, the codewords (coset leaders) must be uniformly distributed over $\mathcal{V}(\Lambda)$ in order to completely fill the space (also with help of the self-noise introduced when $\alpha < 1$). Thus, simple coding schemes (as repetition coding, see Section 3.2) do not necessarily yield good security levels, even for high embedding rates.

3) The condition of mutual independence between the symbols embedded in different observations is key to guarantee perfect secrecy. To see this, note that the conditional pdf of the dither signal can be written as

$$f(\mathbf{t}|\tilde{\mathbf{y}}_1, \ldots, \tilde{\mathbf{y}}_{N_o}) = \sum_{\mathbf{m} \in \mathcal{M}^{N_o}} f(\mathbf{t}|\mathbf{m}, \tilde{\mathbf{y}}_1, \ldots, \tilde{\mathbf{y}}_{N_o}) \cdot \Pr(\mathbf{m}|\tilde{\mathbf{y}}_1, \ldots, \tilde{\mathbf{y}}_{N_o}),$$

where $\mathcal{M}^{N_o}$ denotes the whole message space. When perfect secrecy is achieved, the probability distribution $\Pr(\mathbf{m}|\tilde{\mathbf{y}}_1,\ldots,\tilde{\mathbf{y}}_{N_o})$ makes the conditional pdf of the dither uniform over $\mathcal{V}(\Lambda)$. If the symbols m_i are not mutually independent, then the a posteriori distribution of the messages is changed, so the conditional pdf of the dither is no longer uniform. Hence, the strategies proposed in Lemma 1 in conjunction with channel coding across different blocks will provide perfect secrecy only if the attacker ignores the channel code being applied and the dependencies between symbols that it introduces.

4) The proof of the lemma resorts to the flat-host assumption to show null information leakage. In practice, small information leakages may exist due to the finite variance of the host signal, which causes the host distribution to not be strictly uniform in each quantization cell. However, this information leakage seems to be hardly exploitable in practical attacks.

3.2   Theoretical Results for Cubic Lattices with Repetition Coding

One of the most popular schemes for lattice data hiding is DC-DM with repetition coding [9], which can be seen as a particular case of Construction A using $\mathbf{g} = (1,\ldots,1)^T$ and $\Lambda = \Delta\mathbb{Z}^n$. In order to obtain the information leakage for this scheme, Eq. (3) is rewritten using the chain rule for mutual informations [6] and the results in [5, Sect. III] as (assuming equiprobable message sequences)

$$\frac{1}{n}I(\tilde{\mathbf{Y}}_1,\ldots,\tilde{\mathbf{Y}}_{N_o};\mathbf{T})$$

$$= \frac{1}{n}N_o \cdot H(M_1|\tilde{\mathbf{Y}}_1,\mathbf{T}) - \frac{1}{n}H(M_1,\ldots,M_{N_o}|\tilde{\mathbf{Y}}_1,\ldots,\tilde{\mathbf{Y}}_{N_o})$$

$$+ \sum_{i=2}^{N_o}\frac{1}{i} - \log(1-\alpha),\ N_o \geq 2. \tag{11}$$

Eq. (11) does not admit a closed-form expression, although it is possible to obtain the entropies of interest numerically. The second term of Eq. (11) is

$$E_{\tilde{\mathbf{Y}}_1,\ldots,\tilde{\mathbf{Y}}_{N_o}}\left[H(M_1,\ldots,M_{N_o}|\tilde{\mathbf{Y}}_1 = \tilde{\mathbf{y}}_1,\ldots,\tilde{\mathbf{Y}}_{N_o} = \tilde{\mathbf{y}}_{N_o})\right], \tag{12}$$

which can be computed through the a posteriori probability distribution of the message sequences, that can be obtained according to the Appendix, arriving at (assuming equiprobable message sequences again)

$$\Pr(m_1,\ldots,m_{N_o}|\tilde{\mathbf{y}}_1,\ldots,\tilde{\mathbf{y}}_{N_o}) = \frac{\mathrm{vol}(\mathcal{S}_{N_o}(m_1,\ldots,m_{N_o}))}{\sum_{\mathbf{m}\in\mathcal{M}^{N_o}}\mathrm{vol}(\mathcal{S}_{N_o}(\mathbf{m}))}, \tag{13}$$

where $\mathcal{M}^{N_o}$ denotes the whole message space for N_o observations (actually, only the message sequences with non-null probability need to be taken into account). The feasible region is always a hypercube, and as such it can be computed componentwise. Finally, the entropy (12) is obtained by averaging over the realizations

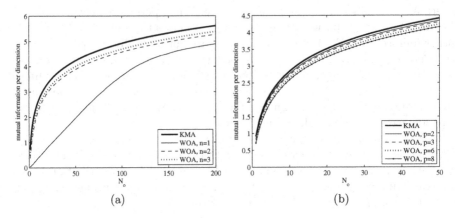

(a)   (b)

Fig. 3. Information leakage per dimension for cubic Λ using repetition coding. Impact of the repetition rate (n) for $\alpha = 0.52$ and $p = 2$ (a), and impact of the alphabet size (p) for $\alpha = 0.6$ and $n = 10$ (b).

of $\tilde{\mathbf{Y}}_1, \ldots, \tilde{\mathbf{Y}}_{N_o}$. For repetition coding, the problem of computing $H(M_1|\tilde{\mathbf{Y}}_1, \mathbf{T})$ is the dual of the computation of $h(\mathbf{T}|\tilde{\mathbf{Y}}_1, \ldots, \tilde{\mathbf{Y}}_{N_o}, M_1, \ldots, M_{N_o})$, which was addressed in [5]. For the entropy of interest, we have

$$H(M_1|\tilde{\mathbf{Y}}_1, \mathbf{T}) = H(M_1|\tilde{\mathbf{Y}}_1, \mathbf{T} = 0) = E_{\tilde{\mathbf{Y}}_1}\left[H(\mathbf{d}_{M_1}|\tilde{\mathbf{Y}}_1 = \mathbf{y}, \mathbf{T} = 0)\right]. \quad (14)$$

and $H(\mathbf{d}_{M_1}|\tilde{\mathbf{Y}}_1 = \mathbf{y}, \mathbf{T} = 0) = \log(\sum_{k=0}^{p-1} I_{\mathcal{I}}((\Delta \cdot k/p) \mod \Delta))$, where $I_{\mathcal{I}}(\cdot)$ is the indicator function:

$$I_{\mathcal{I}}(x) \triangleq \begin{cases} 1, & x \in \mathcal{I} \\ 0, & \text{otherwise,} \end{cases}$$

and $\mathcal{I} \triangleq [\max_{i=1,\ldots,n}\{\tilde{y}_i\} - (1-\alpha)\Delta/2, \ \min_{i=1,\ldots,n}\{\tilde{y}_i\} + (1-\alpha)\Delta/2]$, with y_i, $i = 1, \ldots, n$, the components of $\tilde{\mathbf{y}}_1$. The expectation (14) is obtained by averaging over the realizations of $\tilde{\mathbf{Y}}_1$.

The results are illustrated in Fig. 3 and compared to the results obtained for the KMA scenario, supporting some of the conclusions given in sections 3 and 3.1. Specifically, Fig. 3(a) shows the negative impact in the security level of increasing the dimensionality while keeping constant the embedding rate, whereas Fig. 3(b) shows the security improvement brought about by the increase of the alphabet size. Fig. 3(a) shows that the gap in the information leakage between KMA and WOA tends asymptotically to $\log(2)/n$. On the other hand, Fig. 3(b) shows that increasing p does not yield a significant improvement; in fact, it can be shown that with repetition coding is not possible to achieve perfect secrecy in any way (but for $n = 1$, which yields a self-similar partition), because the distribution of the coset leaders (in a diagonal of the n-dimensional hypercube) does not allow to fulfill the condition of perfect secrecy ($h(\tilde{\mathbf{Y}}_1) = h(\hat{\mathbf{Y}}_1|\mathbf{T})$).

4   A Practical Dither Estimator

4.1   Dither Estimator Based on Set-Membership Theory for KMA

In case the embedded symbols $\mathbf{m} = \{m_1, \ldots, m_{N_o}\}$ are known by the attacker, the algorithm proposed in [5, Sect. IV] gives an accurate estimate of the secret dither. This estimator exploits the fact that each observation defines a bounded feasible region for $\mathbf{T}$, according to Eq. (5). It works under the assumption that $\alpha > 0.5$, in order to assure convergence. The feasible region corresponding to the ith observation (Eq. (6)) is redefined as $\mathcal{D}_i(m_i) \triangleq \tilde{\mathbf{v}}_i + \mathcal{Z}(\Lambda)$, $i = 1, \ldots, N_o$, where $\tilde{\mathbf{v}}_i \triangleq (\tilde{\mathbf{y}}_i - \mathbf{d}_{m_i} - \tilde{\mathbf{y}}_1 + \mathbf{d}_{m_1})$ mod Λ. By introducing the offset $-\tilde{\mathbf{y}}_1 + \mathbf{d}_{m_1}$ in every observation, we get a convex $\mathcal{S}_k(\mathbf{m})$ for all k and $\mathbf{m}$, as discussed in [5]. Obviously, this offset must be removed from the final dither estimate.

Since the exact computation of $\mathcal{S}_{N_o}(\mathbf{m})$ is, in general, computationally prohibitive, the algorithm proposed in [5, Sect. IV] computes an outer bound of $\mathcal{S}_{N_o}(\mathbf{m})$ in order to an keep an affordable computational complexity. We will consider in this paper the "inner polytope" algorithm [5], where $\mathcal{S}_{N_o}(\mathbf{m})$ is described by means of an n-dimensional ellipsoid. This allows to describe the feasible region with a reduced and constant number of parameters, independently of its complexity.

4.2   Joint Bayesian and Set-Membership Estimation for WOA

The uncertainty about the embedded symbols m_k invalidates the straightforward application of the estimation algorithm described in Section 4.1 to the WOA scenario. A possible solution would be to consider all the possible sequences of embedded messages so as to transform the WOA problem into p^{N_o} parallel KMA problems. Obviously, this brute force approach is not practical due to the huge number of possible message sequences, which grows exponentially with the number of observations. However, the a priori search space for the correct sequence of embedded symbols can be dramatically reduced if one considers their a posteriori probability, since certain message sequences have null or negligible probability of occurrence. This is the approach that will be followed here.

From the Appendix, we know that the a posteriori probability of a certain message sequence $\mathbf{m}$ (hereinafter, a "path") reads as

$$\Pr(\mathbf{m}|\tilde{\mathbf{y}}_1, \ldots, \tilde{\mathbf{y}}_{N_o}) = \frac{\text{vol}(\mathcal{S}_{N_o}(\mathbf{m})) \cdot \Pr(\mathbf{m})}{(\text{vol}(\mathcal{Z}(\Lambda)))^{N_o} \cdot \text{vol}(\mathcal{V}(\Lambda)) \cdot f(\tilde{\mathbf{y}}_1, \ldots, \tilde{\mathbf{y}}_{N_o})}. \tag{15}$$

In the following we consider a priori equiprobable paths (either because no coding across different blocks takes place or because we do not know the actual coding scheme being applied), which represents the worst case for the attacker.[3] Under this assumption, the only term of (15) that depends on the hypothesized path is $\text{vol}(\mathcal{V}(\Lambda))$. In practical terms, the most probable paths are those with the

---

[3] If the attacker had knowledge about the coding scheme being applied, he could consider the a priori probability of each path in order to simplify the estimation.

largest feasible region, $\mathcal{S}_{N_o}(\mathbf{m})$. Hence, we can define the "score" of a path $\mathbf{m}$ as $\lambda(\mathbf{m}) \triangleq \text{vol}(\mathcal{S}_{N_o}(\mathbf{m}))$, which can be used to compare the probabilities of different paths as long as they have the same length. It follows that, given N_o observations, maximum-likelihood (ML) estimation of the most probable path is given by $\hat{\mathbf{m}} = \arg\max_{\mathbf{m}} \lambda(\mathbf{m})$, and the ML estimate (if $\mathbf{T} \sim \mathcal{U}(\Lambda)$, as assumed in this paper) of the secret dither would be given by any point in $\mathcal{S}_{N_o}(\hat{\mathbf{m}})$.

A possible implementation of the proposed estimator is by means of a tree search where each branch of the tree represents a hypothesized path with a secret dither estimate associated. The tree search can be accomplished iteratively, discarding those paths with null probability, thus producing a subexponential increase in the number of feasible paths. Nevertheless, this tree search cannot be directly applied as is, in general, due to the some computational issues: 1) despite the subexponential increase in the number of feasible paths, the computational requirements may still become unaffordable; 2) as mentioned in Section 4.1, the exact computation of the feasible regions may be unfeasible in practice, except for some simple lattices. In order to overcome these computational restrictions, the following strategies are proposed.

1) Outer bounds of the feasible regions can be computed by means of the "inner polytope" algorithm [5], as mentioned in Section 4.1, providing a huge reduction of the computational complexity. However, this approximation may impact negatively the performance of the estimation algorithm because it modifies the actual scores of the paths.

2) A fast algorithm for checking null intersections (without computing the outer bound to the feasible region) can be used for speeding up the estimation procedure. An algorithm based on the OVE algorithm [10] for set-membership estimation is suited to our purposes.

3) In order to limit the number of feasible paths in each iteration, we resort to a "beam search" strategy: let $\lambda(\mathbf{m}_0)$ be the score of the most probable path. In each iteration, those paths $\mathbf{m}_i$ for which $\lambda(\mathbf{m}_0)/\lambda(\mathbf{m}_i) > \beta$ are discarded from the tree search. The parameter $\beta > 0$ is termed "beam factor" and causes a prunning of the tree by keeping only the branches with the highest probabilities. Besides the beam search strategy, an additional prunning criterion is implemented by limiting the maximum number of allowable feasible paths.

4) The a priori path space, given by $\mathcal{M}^{N_o}$, can be divided into equivalence classes (with p elements each) defined by the relation

$$\mathbf{m}_1 \sim \mathbf{m}_2 \text{ if } \mathbf{m}_2 = (\mathbf{m}_1 + j \cdot \mathbf{1}) \bmod p, \text{ for any } j = 0, \ldots, p-1, \text{ and } \mathbf{m}_1, \mathbf{m}_2 \in \mathcal{M}^{N_o}.$$

Since the paths belonging to the same equivalence class have the same a posteriori probability (recall Eq. (9)), the search space can be reduced to one representative per equivalence class, thus reducing the cardinality of the search space by a factor p without incurring in any loss of performance.

For the sake of clarity, the steps of the proposed estimation algorithm are summarized here. The input data are the observations $\{\tilde{\mathbf{y}}_i, i = 1 \ldots, N_o\}$ and the parameters of the nested lattice code.

1. Initialization: $\mathbf{m}_0 = 0$, $\mathcal{D}_1(0) = (1 - \alpha)\mathcal{V}(\Lambda)$, and $K_1 = 1$, with K_1 denoting the number of feasible paths for the first observation (1 in our case). This

initialization takes into account the offset introduced in Section 4.1 and the division of $\mathcal{M}^{N_o}$ into equivalence classes.

2. For $i = 2, \ldots, N_o$

   (a) Let $\{\mathbf{m}_k, \ k = 1, \ldots, K_{i-1}\}$ be the set of feasible paths for the $i - 1$ first observations. Construct a set of candidate paths as $\{\mathbf{m}_{k,l} = [\mathbf{m}_k \ l], \ k = 1, \ldots, K_{i-1}, \ l = 0, \ldots, p - 1\}$.

   (b) Compute the regions $\mathcal{S}_i(\mathbf{m}_{k,l})$ using $\tilde{\mathbf{v}}_r = (\tilde{\mathbf{y}}_r - \mathbf{d}_{m_{k,l}(r)} - \tilde{\mathbf{y}}_1) \mod \Lambda$, $r = 1, \ldots, i$, where $m_{k,l}(r)$ denotes the rth element of $\mathbf{m}_{k,l}$. If the inner polytope algorithm is applied, this step yields the ellipsoids that bound the true feasible regions. Prior to this step, the algorithm that checks null intersections may be applied for saving computational resources.

   (c) Compute the score $\lambda(\mathbf{m}_{k,l})$ of each path as $\text{vol}(\mathcal{S}_i(\mathbf{m}_{k,l}))$. The paths with non-null score are added to the tree. If a prunning criterion is being applied, retain only those paths that fulfill the requirements. This step yields K_i paths $\{\mathbf{m}_0, \ldots, \mathbf{m}_{K_i-1}\}$ with non-null probability, termed "surviving paths".

3. The dither estimate is computed as the center of $\mathcal{S}_{N_o}(\mathbf{m}_0)$ (or its bounding region), where $\mathbf{m}_0$ is the path with the highest score (hence, the most likely) among the K_{N_o} surviving branches of the tree. The p paths belonging to the equivalence class $[\mathbf{m}_0]$ can be computed as $\mathbf{m}_k = (\mathbf{m}_0 + k \cdot \mathbf{1}) \mod p$, $k \in \mathcal{M}$, and the p corresponding dither estimates are given by $\hat{\mathbf{t}}_k = (\hat{\mathbf{t}}_0 + \mathbf{d}_k + \tilde{\mathbf{y}}_1)$ $\mod \Lambda$, $k \in \mathcal{M}$, where $\hat{\mathbf{t}}_0$ is the dither estimate associated to the path $\mathbf{m}_0$. Note that $\tilde{\mathbf{y}}_1$ is added for canceling the offset introduced in Step 2-b.

4.3   Experimental Results

This section presents the results of applying the estimation algorithm proposed in 4.2 over some practical schemes. The experiments have been carried out under the following assumptions: the host signals follow a Gaussian distribution with zero mean and variance $\sigma_X^2 = 10$, and the DWR is 30 dB in all cases (DWR $\triangleq$ $10 \log_{10}(\sigma_X^2 / D_w)$); the embedded messages are equiprobable (i.e., no coding is applied along different blocks), and the attacker knows the parameters of the nested lattice code being used, as stated in Section 2. In all cases, a beam factor $\beta = 10^{45/10}$ has been used, and the maximum number of feasible paths was limited to 250. The performance of the estimator is measured in terms of the mean squared error (MSE) per dimension between the dither estimate and the actual dither. In order to compute the MSE without ambiguities (due to the existence of p equiprobable paths), it is assumed that the message conveyed by the first observation corresponds to the symbol 0.

Fig. 4 shows the results obtained for a scheme using a cubic shaping lattice in 10 dimensions and repetition coding (see Section 3.2) with $\alpha = 0.6$. In this case, the simplicity of the feasible regions allows to compute them exactly. It can be seen that for $p = 4$ is still possible to attain the same accuracy as in the KMA scenario, whereas for $p = 7$ and $p = 10$ a significant degradation of the MSE is observed. This degradation is a consequence of the fact that, as p is increased, the probability of decoding the correct path decreases. In the experiments, the

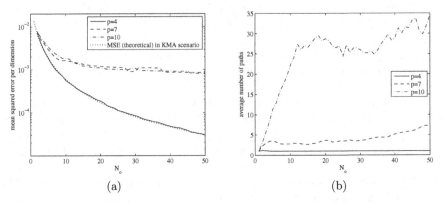

Fig. 4. MSE per dimension (a) and average number of surviving paths in the tree search (b) using cubic Λ with repetition coding ($n = 10$), $\alpha = 0.6$, and different embedding rates

probability of choosing an incorrect path has been shown to be around 0.05 and 0.1 for $p = 7$ and $p = 10$, respectively. The average number of surviving paths in the tree search is plotted in Fig. 4 for illustrating the complexity of the search procedure. In this regard, it can be seen that even in a difficult case as $p = 10$ with $\alpha = 0.6$, the tree search can still be performed with low complexity.

Fig. 5(a) shows the results obtained for a hexagonal shaping lattice and $\alpha = 0.7$, using the inner polytope algorithm in order to compute the approximate feasible regions. Notice that, although α is higher than in the former case, the maximum embedding rate considered now is substantially larger: $\frac{1}{2}\log_2(9)$ bits vs. $\frac{1}{10}\log_2(10)$ bits (the case with $p = 9$ corresponds to the lattice code shown in Fig. 2(b)). Similar comments as above apply in this case: increasing p degrades the MSE, and the spurious peaks in the plots are due to incorrect decisions about the actual path. Finally, Fig. 5(b) shows the results obtained for the E_8 shaping lattice [8], the best lattice quantizer in 8 dimensions.

An accurate dither estimate (subjected to an unknown modulo-Λ shift, as the one obtained here) allows to implement a number of harmful attacks. We are going to focus on a reversibility attack as follows: based on a dither estimate $\hat{\mathbf{t}}$ and an estimated path $\hat{\mathbf{m}}$, the host vector corresponding to the kth watermarked block can be computed as

$$\hat{\mathbf{x}}_k = \mathbf{y}_k - \frac{\alpha}{1 - \alpha}(Q_\Lambda(\mathbf{y}_k - \mathbf{d}_{\hat{m}_k} - \hat{\mathbf{t}}) - \mathbf{x}_k + \mathbf{d}_{\hat{m}_k} + \hat{\mathbf{t}}). \qquad (16)$$

It is interesting to notice that the ambiguity in the estimated message does not affect negatively the host estimation whenever the estimated path $\hat{\mathbf{m}}$ fulfills

$$\hat{\mathbf{m}} = (\mathbf{m} + k \cdot \mathbf{1}) \mod p, \quad \text{for any } k \in \mathcal{M}, \qquad (17)$$

being $\mathbf{m}$ the actual embedded path. The reason is that the dither estimate associated to any of those paths yields the same fine lattice Λ_f, and thus it is

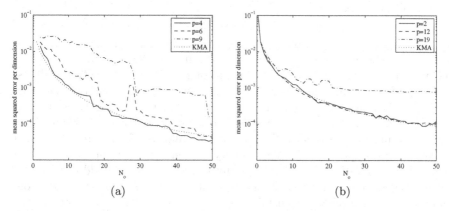

(a)   (b)

Fig. 5. MSE per dimension for $\alpha = 0.7$ and different embedding rates. Results for hexagonal $(n = 2)$ (a) and E_8 $(n = 8)$ (b) shaping lattices.

(a)   (b)

Fig. 6. Illustration of a reversibility attack based on dither estimate according to Eq. (16). Image watermarked using $\Lambda = E_8$, $\alpha = 0.7$, $p = 10$ and PSNR = 38.2 dB (a), and estimate of the original image with PSNR = 55.9 dB (b).

valid for performing a successful reversibility attack. Fig. 6 shows the result of implementing this attack on a real watermarked image. The parameters of the watermarking algorithm are the same as above, and the watermark is embedded in the low frequency coefficients of 8×8 non-overlapping DCT blocks, yielding a PSNR = 38.2 dB. The resulting host estimate, shown in Fig. 6(b), presents a PSNR of approximately 56 dB. Nevertheless, if each pixel value of this host estimate is rounded off to the closest integer, then the PSNR goes to ∞.

5 Conclusions

We have presented in this paper an investigation of the security provided by data hiding schemes based on nested lattice codes randomized by means of secret dithering. It has been shown that, although it is theoretically possible to achieve perfect secrecy, the security level of many practical scenarios (i.e., simple shaping lattices, low embedding rates) can be fairly low. In fact, the security holes of the data hiding schemes studied in this paper have been shown to be exploitable in practice with affordable complexity, allowing for instance to reverse the watermarking process with high fidelity. In general, the information leakage about the secret dither can be reduced by increasing the embedding rate, but this solution demands for more powerful error correcting codes (ECC) if one wants to guarantee reliable transmission. A possible drawback, as noted in this paper, is that the use of ECCs introduces statistical dependence between different observations that could be exploited by an attacker, specially for simple ECCs. The complexity of exploiting the information leakage provided by channel coding deserves further attention in future works.

References

1. Cayre, F., Fontaine, C., Furon, T.: Watermarking security: theory and practice. IEEE Trans. Signal Processing 53 (2005)
2. Comesaña, P., Pérez-Freire, L., Pérez-González, F.: Fundamentals of data hiding security and their application to spread-spectrum analysis. In: Barni, M., Herrera-Joancomartí, J., Katzenbeisser, S., Pérez-González, F. (eds.) IH 2005. LNCS, vol. 3727, Springer, Heidelberg (2005)
3. Pérez-Freire, L., Comesaña, P., Troncoso-Pastoriza, J.R., Pérez-González, F.: Watermarking security: a survey. Transactions on Data Hiding and Multimedia Security I 4300, 41–72 (2006)
4. Moulin, P., Koetter, R.: Data hiding codes. Proceedings of IEEE 93, 2083–2126 (2005)
5. Pérez-Freire, L., Pérez-González, F., Furon, T., Comesaña, P.: Security of lattice-based data hiding against the known message attack. IEEE Transactions on Information Forensics and Security 1, 421–439 (2006)
6. Cover, T.M., Thomas, J.A.: Elements of Information Theory. Wiley series in Telecommunications (1991)
7. Erez, U., Zamir, R.: Achieving 1/2log(1+SNR) over the Additive White Gaussian Noise channel with lattice encoding and decoding. IEEE Transactions on Information Theory 50, 2293–2314 (2004)
8. Conway, J.H., Sloane, N.J.A.: Sphere packings, lattices and groups. third edn, 3rd edn. Comprehensive Studies in Mathematics, vol. 290. Springer, New York (1999)
9. Comesaña, P., Pérez-González, F., Balado, F.: On distortion-compensated dither modulation data-hiding with repetition coding. IEEE Transactions on Signal Processing 54, 585–600 (2006)
10. Cheung, M.F., Yurkovich, S., Passino, K.M.: An optimal volume ellipsoid algorithm for parameter set estimation. IEEE Transactions on Automatic Control 38, 1292–1296 (1993)

Appendix

A Posteriori Probability of the Message Sequences

In order to compute the probability a posteriori of a message sequence $\mathbf{m} = (m_1, \ldots, m_{N_o})$ (hereinafter, a "path"), this probability is first rewritten using Bayes' rule:

$$\Pr(m_1, \ldots, m_{N_o} | \tilde{\mathbf{y}}_1, \ldots, \tilde{\mathbf{y}}_{N_o})$$

$$= \frac{f(\tilde{\mathbf{y}}_1, \ldots, \tilde{\mathbf{y}}_{N_o} | m_1, \ldots, m_{N_o}) \cdot \Pr(m_1, \ldots, m_{N_o})}{f(\tilde{\mathbf{y}}_1, \ldots, \tilde{\mathbf{y}}_{N_o})}. \tag{18}$$

The a posteriori probability of the observations can be factored as:

$$f(\tilde{\mathbf{y}}_1, \ldots, \tilde{\mathbf{y}}_{N_o} | m_1, \ldots, m_{N_o}) = \prod_{k=1}^{N_o} f(\tilde{\mathbf{y}}_k | m_1, \ldots, m_k, \tilde{\mathbf{y}}_1, \ldots, \tilde{\mathbf{y}}_{k-1})$$

$$= \prod_{k=1}^{N_o} \int_{\mathcal{V}(\Lambda)} f(\tilde{\mathbf{y}}_k | m_k, \mathbf{t}) \cdot f(\mathbf{t} | \tilde{\mathbf{y}}_1, \ldots, \tilde{\mathbf{y}}_{k-1}, m_1, \ldots, m_{k-1}) d\mathbf{t}. \tag{19}$$

In order to compute each factor of (19), we will resort to the flat-host assumption, which implies that $f(\tilde{\mathbf{y}}_k | m_k, \mathbf{t}) = f_0(\tilde{\mathbf{y}}_k - \mathbf{d}_{m_k} - \mathbf{t} \mod \Lambda)$. Thus, each factor of (19) can be seen as a circular convolution over $\mathcal{V}(\Lambda)$:

$$f(\tilde{\mathbf{y}}_1, \ldots, \tilde{\mathbf{y}}_{N_o} | m_1, \ldots, m_{N_o})$$

$$= \prod_{k=1}^{N_o} f_0(\tilde{\mathbf{y}}_k - \mathbf{d}_{m_k} \mod \Lambda) \circledast f(\mathbf{t} | \tilde{\mathbf{y}}_1, \ldots, \tilde{\mathbf{y}}_{k-1}, m_1, \ldots, m_{k-1})$$

Furthermore, under the assumption that $\mathbf{T} \sim U(\mathcal{V}(\Lambda))$, we have that the conditional pdf of the dither is given by Eq. (4). By combining (2) and (4), it can be seen that the integrand of the kth factor in (19) is given by

$$\begin{cases} (\text{vol}(\mathcal{Z}(\Lambda)) \cdot \text{vol}(\mathcal{S}_{k-1}(\mathbf{m})))^{-1}, & \mathbf{t} \in \mathcal{S}_{k-1}(\mathbf{m}) : (\tilde{\mathbf{y}}_k - \mathbf{d}_{m_k} - \mathbf{t}) \mod \Lambda \in \mathcal{Z}(\Lambda) \\ 0, & \text{otherwise.} \end{cases}$$

The condition on $\mathbf{t}$ in the equation above is equivalent to $\mathbf{t} \in \mathcal{S}_{k-1}(\mathbf{m}) : \mathbf{t} \in (\tilde{\mathbf{y}}_k - \mathbf{d}_{m_k} - \mathcal{Z}(\Lambda)) \mod \Lambda$, so each factor in (19) is proportional to the volume of $\mathcal{S}_k(\mathbf{m}) = \mathcal{S}_{k-1}(\mathbf{m}) \cap \mathcal{D}_k(m_k)$. Finally, Eq. (19) can be succinctly expressed as

$$f(\tilde{\mathbf{y}}_1, \ldots, \tilde{\mathbf{y}}_{N_o} | m_1, \ldots, m_{N_o}) = \prod_{k=1}^{N_o} \frac{\text{vol}(\mathcal{S}_k(m_1, \ldots, m_k))}{\text{vol}(\mathcal{Z}(\Lambda)) \cdot \text{vol}(\mathcal{S}_{k-1}(m_1, \ldots, m_{k-1}))}$$

$$= \frac{\text{vol}(\mathcal{S}_{N_o}(m_1, \ldots, m_{N_o}))}{(\text{vol}(\mathcal{Z}(\Lambda)))^{N_o} \cdot \text{vol}(\mathcal{V}(\Lambda))}. \tag{20}$$

Practical Security Analysis of
Dirty Paper Trellis Watermarking

Patrick Bas[1],[2] and Gwenaël Doërr[3]

[1] CIS / Helsinki University of Technology
P.O. Box 5400, FI-02015 HUT Finland
[2] Gipsa-lab CNRS INPG
961, rue de la Houille Blanche BP 46
38042 St. Martin d'Hères, France
[3] University College London
UCL Adastral Park – Ross Building 2
Martlesham IP5 3RE , United Kingdom

Abstract. This paper analyses the security of dirty paper trellis (DPT) watermarking schemes which use both informed coding and informed embedding. After recalling the principles of message embedding with DPT watermarking, the secret parameters of the scheme are highlighted. The security weaknesses of DPT watermarking are then presented: in the watermarked contents only attack (WOA) setup, the watermarked data-set exhibits clusters corresponding to the different patterns attached to the arcs of the trellis. The K-means clustering algorithm is used to estimate these patterns and a co-occurrence analysis is performed to retrieve the connectivity of the trellis. Experimental results demonstrate that it is possible to accurately estimate the trellis configuration, which enables to perform attacks much more efficient than simple additive white Gaussian noise (AWGN).

1 Introduction

Beside conventional measurements of performances such as robustness to channel transmission, receiver operating characteristics (ROC) curves or imperceptibility, *security* has recently been acknowledged to be also of fundamental importance in digital watermarking. By definition, security oriented attacks "aim at gaining knowledge about the secrets of the system (e.g. the embedding and/or the detection keys)" [1]. In practice, it implies that if the security of a scheme is compromised, different attacks such as message modification, message copy or message erasure are possible while keeping a very low distortion. Hence, watermarking schemes need to be carefully analysed to identify its *security level*, e.g. the number of contents that are needed to estimate accurately the secret key [2].

Security of watermarking schemes can be assessed either with a theoretical analysis or with a practical evaluation. Theoretical security analysis consists in calculating the information leakage occurring when observing several watermarked contents by means of information theoretic measures such as equivocation or mutual information between the secret key and the observations [2,1,3].

T. Furon et al. (Eds.): IH 2007, LNCS 4567, pp. 174–188, 2007.

These measurements prove whether or not there is some information leakage that might be exploited to estimate the secret key. However, they do not give any clue about the tools that could be used to perform this estimation.

On the other hand, practical security analysis consists in designing attacks which make possible to estimate the secret parameters used during embedding. Only a few attempts in this direction have been reported so far and they have mostly focused on basic watermarking schemes. For example, in [4,5,6], the authors propose different blind source separation methods to estimate secret patterns that are used in spread-spectrum or spread transform dither modulation schemes for both independent and identically distributed (iid) and non-iid signals. In [3], the authors adopt a set-membership approach to estimate the dither vector used during DC-DM embedding.

This paper proposes a practical security analysis of dirty paper trellis (DPT) watermarking schemes, which have been proven to achieve high performances with respect to robustness and payload [7]. Section 2 first recalls the principles of DPT watermarking. In Section 3, the different parameters that define the secret key are identified, and a worst case attack (WCA) relying on the estimation of the secret key is introduced. In Section 4, practical tools are proposed to estimate each parameter of the trellis, namely the patterns attached to the arcs and the configuration of the trellis. Section 5 reports the performances of the WCA according to both the embedding distortion and the number of observed contents. Finally, some perspectives to improve the security of DPT watermarking schemes are presented in Section 6.

2   Dirty Paper Trellis Watermarking

2.1   Notations and Parameters Definition

In this paper, the host vector is denoted $\mathbf{x}$ and the watermarked vector $\mathbf{y}$. The latter one carries a N_b bits message $\mathbf{m}$. Each bit of the message is encoded on N_v coefficients and therefore $\mathbf{x}$ and $\mathbf{y}$ are both $N_b \cdot N_v$-dimensional vectors [1]. Moreover, $\|\mathbf{v}\|$ denotes the Euclidian norm of the vector $\mathbf{v}$ and $\mathbf{v}(k)$ the kth component of $\mathbf{v}$. Finally, embedding distortions are given using the watermark to content ratio (WCR) expressed in decibels.

2.2   Trellis-Based Watermarking

The use of trellis for watermarking is a practical way to perform dirty paper coding [8]. Dirty paper coding implies the use of a codebook $\mathcal{C}$ of codewords with a mapping between codewords and messages. The key difference with conventional codes is that different codewords can map to the same message. This defines a coset $\mathcal{C}_m$ of codewords for each message $\mathbf{m}$. The watermarking process

---

[1] Note that an attacker will have the opportunity to observe N_o watermarked contents. Practical values of N_o can go from 1 (a single image for example) to several thousands (a set of videos where each frame carries a payload).

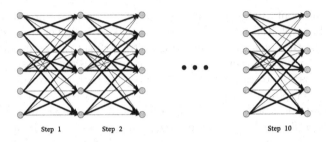

Step 1   Step 2   Step 10

Fig. 1. Example of the structure of a 10 steps trellis with 6 states and 4 arcs per states. Bold and normal arcs denote respectively 0 and 1 valued labels.

then reduces to (i) identify the codeword in the coset $\mathcal{C}_m$, related to the message to be hidden, which is the nearest from the host vector $\mathbf{x}$, and (ii) move the host vector inside the detection region of the selected codeword. According to Costa's framework, using this setup the capacity of the channel does not depend on the host $\mathbf{x}$.

DPT codes have two main assets: the generation of the codebook $\mathcal{C}$ is systematic and the search for the nearest codeword can be efficiently performed with a Viterbi decoder [9]. A DPT is defined by several parameters:

1. the number of states N_s,
2. the number of arcs per state N_a,
3. the connectivity between the states i.e. in which state an arc starts and in which state it ends,
4. the N_v-dimensional pseudo-random patterns associated to each one of the $N_a.N_s$ arcs, which can be assimilated to the carrier used in spread spectrum schemes,
5. the binary label associated to each one of the $N_a.N_s$ arcs,
6. the number of steps N_b in the trellis.

Figure 1 depicts an example of a DPT. One can notice that the configuration of the trellis is simply repeated from one step to another without any change. Moreover, the number of outgoing and incoming arcs per state is constant. These are common assumptions in trellis coding.

A DPT is thus associated with a codebook $\mathcal{C} = \{\mathbf{c_i}, i \in [1, ..., N_s \cdot N_a^{N_b}]\}$ of $N_s \cdot N_a^{N_b}$ codewords in a $N_v \cdot N_b$-dimensional space. Each codeword corresponds to a path in the trellis and encodes a N_b bits message. This message can be retrieved by concatenating the binary labels of the arcs along the corresponding path.

DPT watermarking makes makes use of both *informed coding* and *informed embedding* [7]. Informed coding consists in selecting the codeword $\mathbf{g}$ in the codebook $\mathcal{C}$ that is the closest to the host vector $\mathbf{x}$ and that encodes the desired message. The selection is done by running a Viterbi decoder with an expurgated trellis

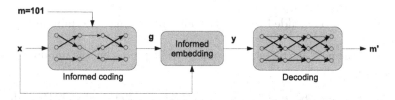

Fig. 2. Main principles of DPT watermarking. In this example $N_b = 3$, $N_s = 3$, $N_a = 2$. Three alternative codewords are available in the expurgated trellis to represent the message **m**. The codeword **g** with the highest correlation with **x** is identified using the Viterbi algorithm. Afterward, the watermarked vector **y** is computed taking into account **g**. On the receiver side, the detector uses the whole DPT to retrieve the embedded payload.

containing only arcs whose binary labels are in accordance with the message to be embedded. As a result, any path through the trellis encodes the desired message. The Viterbi decoder is then used to maximize/minimize a given function i.e. to find the *best* codeword in this subset according to some criterion. In their original article [7], the authors proposed to keep the codeword with the highest linear correlation with the host vector **x**.

At this point, informed embedding is used to reduce the distance between the host vector **x** and the selected codeword **g**. It basically computes a watermarked vector **y** that is as close as possible from **x** while being at the same time within the detection region of the desired codeword **g** with a guaranteed level of robustness to additive white Gaussian noise (AWGN). In practice, a sub-optimal iterative algorithm is used combined with a Monte-Carlo procedure to find this watermarked vector **y** [7].

On the receiver side, the embedded message is extracted by running a Vitterbi decoder with the whole DPT. The optimal path is thus identified and the corresponding message retrieved by concatenating the binary label of the arcs along this path. The whole procedure is illustrated in Figure 2.

3   DPT Secret Key and Worst Case Attack

First, some parameters of the DPT will be assumed to be public. It may not always be true in practice, but usually these parameters are fixed according to the desired robustness or payload of the algorithm. In this study for instance, the three parameters N_s, N_a and N_b will be known.

Furthermore, processed contents will be assumed not to be shuffled before embedding i.e. they are directly watermarked without prior permutation of the samples position. The problem of inverting a hypothetical shuffle relies on the security of the shuffle itself and is far beyond the scope of this paper.

To define the secret key relative to a DPT watermarking scheme, it is necessary to identify which information is required by the attacker to perform security-oriented attacks such as:

- decoding the embedded message,
- altering the embedded message while producing the minimal possible distortion,
- copying the message to another content while producing the minimal possible distortion.

To decode the embedded message, the previous section recalls that all parameters of the DPT are needed. This includes by definition the patterns attached to the arcs, the connectivity between the states, and the binary labels of the arcs. To copy a message in an optimal way, it is first necessary to decode them and then to embed them into another content. Therefore, the same parameters are required. On the other hand, to alter the embedded message, all previous parameters are needed except the binary labels. Indeed, the watermarked vector $\mathbf{y}$ only need to be moved toward another vector $\mathbf{y}_A$ so that it no longer lies in the decoding region of $\mathbf{g}$. As long as a *neighbour* codeword is selected, it is unlikely to encode the same message and it will be close enough to avoid large distortion. This threat can be seen as the worst case attack (WCA) for DPT watermarking [10].

To perform this attack, it is necessary to know the two closest codewords from the watermarked vector $\mathbf{y}$, i.e. the embedded codeword $\mathbf{g}$, and the second closest codeword from $\mathbf{y}$ ($\mathbf{b}_1$ in Figure 3 (a)). The attacker simply needs then to move the watermark content $\mathbf{y}$ somewhere inside the decoding region of this second best codeword ($\mathbf{y}_A$ in Figure 3 (a)) to make the detector fail while minimizing the distortion of the attack. In practice, this second best codeword is identified by feeding the Viterbi decoder with the watermarked vector $\mathbf{y}$ and successively forbidding a single step of the optimal path $\mathbf{g}$. This results in N_b candidates and the closest to $\mathbf{y}$ is retained as the second best codeword to be used in the WCA. This procedure is depicted in Figure 3 (b).

4   DPT Parameters Estimation

For the sake of generality, the analysis will be done according to the Watermarked content Only Attack (WOA) setup [2], where the attacker observes different contents watermarked with different messages using the same secret key. The aim of this section is to present different techniques that can be used to estimate different parameters of a DPT that constitute the secret key, namely the patterns, the connectivity and the binary labels of the arcs.

4.1   Side Effects of Informed Embedding

Let $\mathcal{U} = \{\mathbf{u}_i, i \in [1, ..., N_a \cdot N_s]\}$ be the set of patterns, also referred to as carriers, associated with the arcs of the DPT. In practice, each pattern is usually normalised, e.g. $\|\mathbf{u}_i\| = 1, \forall i$. As a result, each pattern can be seen as a point on the surface of the N_v-dimensional unit sphere. Moreover, each codeword $\mathbf{c}_i$ of the DPT is a $N_v \cdot N_b$-dimensional vector of norm $\sqrt{N_b}$ and can be considered

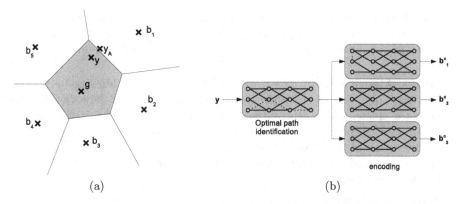

(a)   (b)

Fig. 3. Worst case attack for DPT watermarking. (a): To be optimal, the attacker needs to find the closest point to **y** outside the detection region of the embedded codeword **g** (grey area). To do so, he needs to identify the second nearest codeword from **y**, i.e. b_1 in the Figure. (b): To identify the second best codeword, the Viterbi decoder is run several times with a single step of the optimal trellis forbidden. The codeword amongst the N_b candidates which is the closest to **y** is retained.

as a point on the surface of a $N_v \cdot N_b$-dimensional sphere of radius $\sqrt{N_b}$, denoted $\mathcal{S}_c$.

Viterbi decoding aims at finding the codeword $\mathbf{c} \in \mathcal{C}$ which is the most correlated with some input vector **v**, i.e. it evaluates and maximises:

$$\text{corr}(\mathbf{c}_i, \mathbf{v}) = \frac{<\mathbf{c}_i, \mathbf{v}>}{N_b \cdot N_v} = \frac{\sum_{j=1}^{N_b \cdot N_v} \mathbf{c}_i(j)\mathbf{v}(j)}{N_b \cdot N_v}, \tag{1}$$

which is equivalent to:

$$\text{corr}(\mathbf{c}_i, \mathbf{v}) = \frac{||\mathbf{v}||.||\mathbf{c}_i|| \cos(\theta_i)}{N_b \cdot N_v}, \tag{2}$$

where θ_i denotes the angle between **v** and $\mathbf{c}_i$. Because $||\mathbf{v}||$, $||\mathbf{c}_i||$ and $N_b \cdot N_v$ are constant terms, the codeword that is selected basically maximises $\cos(\theta_i)$.

In other words, the Viterbi decoder returns the codeword which is at the smallest angular distance from the input vector. This implies that when one wants to embed a codeword **g** in a host vector **x**, it is necessary to produce a watermarked vector **y** whose angular distance with **g** is lower than with any other codeword in $\mathcal{C}$. Moreover, the higher the robustness constraint, the closer the watermarked contents to the desired codeword. Consequently, considering the distribution of normalized observations $\mathbf{y}^* = \mathbf{y}/||\mathbf{y}||$ one might observe *clusters* corresponding to the codewords in $\mathcal{C}$ on the surface of the $N_v \cdot N_b$ dimensional sphere $\mathcal{S}_c$.

4.2   Patterns Estimation Using a Clustering Method

Data clustering algorithms enable to analyse a large set of data by partitioning the set into subsets called clusters. Clusters are build such as to minimize the average distance between each data point and the nearest cluster center, also referred to as centroid. Given k the number of clusters, a clustering algorithm also returns the label of the centroid associated with each data point.

K-means Algorithm. In this work, the K-means algorithm has been used to provide a partition of the observed space. This algorithm labels each data point to the cluster whose centroid is the nearest. The centroid is defined as the center of mass of the points in the cluster, and its coordinates are given by the arithmetic mean of the coordinates of all the points in the cluster.

The implemented version of the algorithm was proposed by MacQueen [11] and is described below:

1. Choose k the number of clusters,
2. Initialise the centroids,
3. Assign each data point to the nearest centroid,
4. Update the centroid coordinates,
5. Go back to step 3 until some convergence criterion is met.

This algorithm is easy to implement, fast, and it is possible to run it on large datasets. However K-means does not yield the same result for each run, i.e. the final clusters depend on the initial random assignments. One solution to overcome this problem is to perform multiple runs with different initialisations and to keep the result which provides the lowest intra-cluster variance. To ensure that the initial clusters are evenly distributed over the data set, a random initialisation using the KZZ method [12] has been used.

Definition of the Dataset. A segment **s** is a portion of the observed watermarked vector **y** corresponding to a single step. Therefore, **s** is of size N_v and **y** is composed of N_b segments. Two alternative strategies are possible to estimate the secret parameters of the DPT:

1. Apply the K-means algorithm to estimate the centroids representing the codewords of the trellis. Then it has to find $k = N_s \cdot N_a^{N_b}$ centroids in a $N_v \cdot N_b$-dimensional space using a dataset of normalised watermarked vectors.
2. Apply the K-means algorithm to estimate the centroids representing the patterns of the trellis. Then it has to find $k = N_s \cdot N_a$ centroids in a N_v-dimensional space using a data-set of normalised watermarked segments.

Observing N_o watermarked contents is equivalent to observing $N_o \cdot N_b$ watermarked segments. As a result, the two strategies proposed earlier involve respectively $\frac{N_o}{N_s \cdot N_a^{N_b}}$ and $\frac{N_o \cdot N_b}{N_s \cdot N_a}$ observations per centroid. In other words, the second solution provides $N_b \cdot N_a^{N_b-1}$ times more observations per centroid than the first one to perform clustering. This problem is related to the *curse of dimensionality*, well known in machine learning, which states that the number of observations needed to learn topological objects such as clusters is exponential with respect to the dimension of the problem. Since the main concern here is the estimation of the patterns used in the DPT, the second solution is preferred to improve the estimation accuracy for the same number of observed contents.

Analysis of Estimation Accuracy According to Distortion. The accuracy of the estimated patterns is inherently related to the embedding distortion, and therefore with the robustness constraint. Figure 4 depicts two typical examples of 3D distributions of normalised watermarked segments for two different embedding distortions. In this case only 6 codewords are used and one bit is embedded. The yellow balls indicate the centroids estimated using the K-means algorithm and the grey balls the position of the true patterns. In this example, patterns are chosen to be either orthogonal or collinear (the set of orthogonal patterns is multiplied by -1 to obtain collinear ones). Each point of the distribution has a color depending on the center it has been associated.

In each case, the detection regions are represented by clusters which are clearly identifiable. Moreover the mapping between detection cells and embedded contents is consistent. However, for the smallest distortion (WCR=-6.6 dB), watermarked vectors are not uniformly distributed inside the embedding region. This is due to the fact that if two neighbour codewords encode the same message, their border region will have a density of codewords less important than if they encode different messages. This uneven distribution of watermarked codewords in each detection region results in a erroneous estimation of the codeword, the cluster center being "attracted" by the dense borders as illustrated on the right-hand distribution.

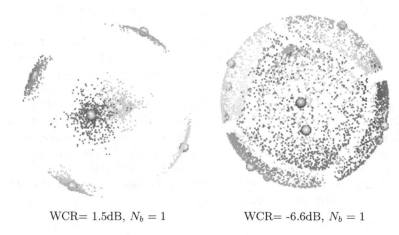

WCR= 1.5dB, $N_b = 1$ WCR= -6.6dB, $N_b = 1$

Fig. 4. Distributions of normalised watermarked contents ($N_v = 3$, $N_b = 1$, $N_s = 3$, $N_a = 2$, $N_o = 5000$). Locations of the real (gray) and estimated (yellow) patterns using the K-means algorithm. The visualization is easier using a color output.

Figure 5 shows the accuracy of the DPT patterns estimation in the case of a realistic watermarking scenario. The different parameters of the trellis are defined here by $N_v = 12$, $N_b = 10$, $N_s = 6$, $N_a = 4$, which means that the clustering algorithm has to estimate 24 patterns of 12 samples each[2]. To evaluate

---

[2] $N_v = 12$ is the number of DCT coefficients that are used in the image watermarking scheme presented in [7].

the estimation process, the average of the difference between the two largest normalised correlations between each real and estimated patterns for each pattern is computed i.e.:

$$\Delta = \frac{1}{N_s \cdot N_a} \sum_i [\max1_j(\text{corr}_N(\mathbf{cl}_i, \mathbf{u}_j)) - \max2_j(\text{corr}_N(\mathbf{cl}_i, \mathbf{u}_j))] \qquad (3)$$

where $\mathbf{cl}_i$ is the estimated centroid of the ith cluster, corr_N denotes the normalised correlation, and $\max1_j$ (resp. $\max2_j$) represents the first (resp. second) value when an array is sorted by descending order. As previously, the set of 24 patterns are orthogonal or collinear between themselves. As a result, Δ is equal to one if the estimation of each pattern is perfect and decreases with respect to the accuracy of estimations.

The difference between the two highest correlation score magnifies the contrast between accurate and non-accurate estimation of the DPT patterns when they are orthogonal or opposite. A score Δ close to 1 means that each estimated pattern is much closer to one of the original patterns than the others. On the other hand, a score Δ close to 0 means that each estimated pattern is equally distant from two original patterns. Consequently, the estimation of the original patterns is not possible. Using only $\max1()$ would have decreased the difference between accurate and non-accurate estimations because even random patterns may have an important correlation with fixed ones if N_v is low.

The evolution of the estimation accuracy with respect to different embedding distortions and different number of observations is given in Figure 5 for observations composed of either one or two segments. If the considered dataset is composed of couples of segments, the number of observations necessary to obtain the same accuracy than for one segment is roughly multiplied by 4. This confirms the "curse of dimensionality" effect mentioned earlier. Moreover, as expected, the estimation accuracy increases with the number of observed contents and the embedding distortion i.e. the robustness constraint. While more than 128000 observations are needed to obtain an accuracy of 0.9 with $WCR = -11.5dB$ and a data set of single segments, 24000 and 8000 observations are needed respectively for $WCR = -10.3dB$ and $WCR = -9.1dB$.

4.3   Note on Label Estimation

As mentioned in Section 3, the estimation of the binary label associated to each arc is not possible in the WOA framework. Note however that, for the Known Message Attack scenario (KMA) where each embedded message is known [2], the binary labels can easily be estimated by examining the bits associated to each segment. For an estimated centroid, the binary label will be determined as the most frequent bit related to the segments within the cluster.

Another way to deal with this issue is to use supervised clustering techniques such as Learning Vector Quantization [13]. This approach might be more efficient than K-Means since it considers the class of observations as a-priori information.

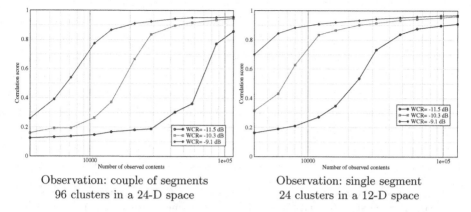

Observation: couple of segments
96 clusters in a 24-D space

Observation: single segment
24 clusters in a 12-D space

Fig. 5. Accuracy of the DPT patterns estimation ($N_v = 12$, $N_b = 10$, $N_s = 6$, $N_a = 4$). Average after 10 trials. For each trial, 10 K-means runs are performed.

4.4   Connections and State Estimation

In the DPT estimation process, the next step is to estimate the connectivity of the trellis. This can be seen as learning which patterns are emitted at step $t + 1$ knowing that a given pattern has been emitted at step t. This estimation can be done by using a co-occurrence matrix $\mathbf{C}$ which is a square matrix of size $N_s \cdot N_a$. Each element $\mathbf{C}(i, j)$ of the matrix is expressed by:

$$\mathbf{C}(i, j) = \text{occ}(\mathbf{s}_t \in \mathcal{C}{\updownarrow}_i, \mathbf{s}_{t+1} \in \mathcal{C}{\updownarrow}_j) \tag{4}$$

where $\mathcal{C}{\updownarrow}_k$ denotes the set representing the kth cluster and $\text{occ}(A, B)$ is an occurrence function that counts the number of times both A and B are true. The test $(\mathbf{s}_t \in \mathcal{C}{\updownarrow}_i)$ is performed using the classification results of the K-means algorithm used for the patterns estimation. As a result, if the pattern i has been emitted at step t, the N_a maximum values in the ith row of the co-occurrence matrix $\mathbf{C}$ indicate the index of the patterns that can be emitted at step $t + 1$. This method implicitly assumes that a different pattern is attached to each arc in the trellis. Therefore, it will fail to deal with the recent improvements proposed for DPT watermarking based on trellis coded modulation [14].

Using the established co-occurrence matrix, it is possible to check whether the estimated connectivity matches the one of the original trellis. For each line i in the matrix, the index of the N_a highest elements are retrieved. As stated before, each index points to the pattern that can be emitted at step $t + 1$ when the pattern i has been emitted at step t. This leads to $N_s \cdot N_a^2$ possible couple of patterns, that can be referred to as *connections*. The connection error rate is then defined as the ratio of connections which are actually not allowed by the original trellis. The lower the connection error rate, the more accurate the estimated connectivity. As depicted in Figure 6, the accuracy relies again on the embedding distortion and the number of observed contents. It should be noted that the number of observed contents necessary to achieve a good estimation

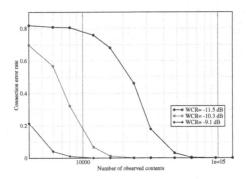

Fig. 6. Connection error rate ($N_v = 12$, $N_b = 10$, $N_s = 6$, $N_a = 4$). Observation: single segment. Average after 10 trials. For each trial, 10 K-means runs are performed.

of the connections is of the same order of magnitude than for the estimation of patterns.

At this point, using the co-occurrence matrix, it is possible to identify for each pattern, which can also be viewed as an arc, which are the incoming and outgoing states. Each state is estimated up to a permutation with respect to the original trellis. However, this permutation does not hamper the ability of the decoder to retrieve the correct succession of patterns.

All the arcs going toward a given state will give similar rows in the co-occurrence matrix $\mathbf{C}$. Indeed, the rows indicate the choice of patterns that can be emitted afterward when an arc is traversed. Same rows implies same choice i.e. for all these arcs, the same state has been reached. To deal with the potential noise in the co-occurence matrix, a K-means algorithm is run on the rows of $\mathbf{C}$ to identify N_s clusters. Each row is then labeled in accordance to the cluster it belongs to. This label indicates the outgoing state when an arc is traversed i.e. when a given pattern is emitted. For instance, in Figure 7, if the third pattern is emitted, the systems reaches state 1 and can only emit the patterns 1 and 4.

One can then build an outgoing state matrix: it is a simple matrix with entries at the estimated connection index which indicates the outgoing state when the

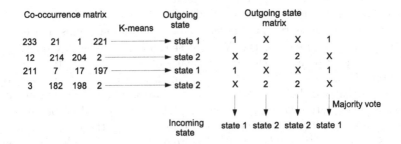

Fig. 7. Example of incoming and outgoing state estimations

pattern i is emitted at step t. An example is given in Figure 7. This matrix can be read row by row: if the pattern 3 is emitted at step t, then the system is in the third row and one can see that the state 1 is reached. Moreover, this outgoing state matrix can also be read column by column: if the pattern 3 has been emitted at step $t+1$, then the system is in the third column and the entries indicates the possible states of the system before the emission of the pattern i.e. the incoming state. A simple majority vote along each column to accommodate for potentially noisy observations gives then the most likely incoming state for each pattern. In the example depicted in Figure 7, one can see for instance that the pattern 3 is coming from state 2 and is going toward state 1.

5   Results on the Worst Case Attack

Once all the secret parameters of the DPT have been estimated, it is possible to perform the WCA described in Section 3. Results are plotted on Figure 8 for the same setup than previously: $N_v = 12$, $N_b = 10$, $N_s = 6$, $N_a = 4$ and three different embedding distortions. Two different scores are computed to assess the efficiency of the WCA: the classical bit-error rate (BER) and the message error rate (MER). The MER is the most meaningful score because it measures the ability of the WCA to move the watermarked vector $\mathbf{y}$ outside the detection region of the embedded codeword. The BER plot in Figure 8 highlights the fact that the WCA does not necessarily yield the same BER for different embedding distortions once the estimation of the trellis is accurate enough. Indeed, for different distortions, the second best codeword may be different and thus induce a different BER.

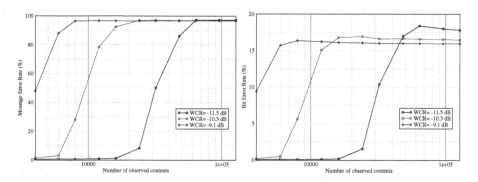

Fig. 8. Message Error Rate and Bit Error Rate after the WCA ($N_v = 12$, $N_b = 10$, $N_s = 6$, $N_a = 4$). Average after 10 trials. For each trial, 10 K-means are performed.

The security level s can be defined as the number of watermarked contents necessary to perform a successful WCA e.g. with a MER close to 100%. The values of s for different embedding distortions are reported in Table 1. This table also provides a comparison of the average watermarked signal to noise

Table 1. Comparison of the security level and the signal to noise ratio of the WCA and AWGN for equal BER. For SNR, an accurate estimation of the trellis ($N_o = 124000$) is performed.

Watermark to Content Ratio	−11.5 dB	−10.3 dB	−9.1 dB
security level s	$64\,10^3$	$24\,10^3$	$8\,10^3$
SNR for the WCA	16.9 dB	16.9 dB	16.9 dB
SNR for AWGN	4.5 dB	3.5 dB	2.4 dB

ratios (SNR) for the WCA and AWGN required to yield equivalent BER. The WCA induces a SNR that is between 12 dB and 14 dB more important than for AWGN (the comparison between MERs would have been even more dramatic).

6   Conclusion and Perspectives

This paper has investigated security issues for DPT watermarking schemes. Different properties of this class of schemes have to be highlighted:

- Using the WOA setup, it is impossible to estimate the binary labels associated with each arc of the trellis and consequently it is impossible to copy the message embedded in one content to another one without introducing unacceptable distortion. This property relies on the fact that coding is informed i.e. it is dependent of the host signal. Note that this property is not true for classical Spread Spectrum [5].
- The WOA setup enables however to perform a WCA for this scheme. Machine learning techniques can be used to identify clusters that are created in the data set during the embedding. This estimation has been performed using a K-means algorithm. Different tests suggest that an accurate estimation of the trellis is possible but depends on two parameters: the number of observations and the embedding distortion which is directly linked with the robustness of the scheme.

The assumptions made in this paper on the trellis structure may first look restrictive but encompass a large variety of practical implementations:

- The trellis structure was the same for each step. This hypothesis is important if one want to deal with synchronisation problems. Moreover, if it is not the case, because the trellis structure is the same for each content in the WOA setup, it is still possible to observe at least N_o similar segments (instead of $N_o \cdot N_b$) and to estimate the patterns for each step.
- The number of outgoing and incoming arcs per state was assumed to be constant. Nevertheless the presented connection and state estimation algorithms can also be used if the arcs change from one step to another.
- The WCR considered are was the order of -10 dB. In the case of smaller WCRs (around -20 dB) either other clustering techniques or a more important number of observations would be necessary. Nevertheless a WCR around

-10dB on a dedicated subspace, like medium frequency DCT coefficients for example, is practically realistic.
- In a more the general setup some additional techniques would be required to estimate N_s and N_a for each step, one possibility would be to use hierarchical clustering algorithms to estimate these parameters [15].

Our future works will be focused on the design of secure DPT watermarking schemes. One solution might be to perform the embedding in such a way that the distribution of codewords is similar to the distribution of secure but non-informed coding schemes such as circular watermarking [16].

Acknowledgments

Dr. Patrick Bas is supported (in part) by the European Commission through the IST Programme under Contract IST-2002-507932 ECRYPT and the National French projects ACI-SI Nebbiano, RIAM Estivale and ARA TSAR. Dr Gwenaël Doërr's research is supported in part by the Nuffield Foundation through the grant NAL/32707.

References

1. Comesaña, P., Pérez-Freire, L., Pérez-González, F.: Fundamentals of data hiding security and their application to spread-spectrum analysis. In: Barni, M., Herrera-Joancomartí, J., Katzenbeisser, S., Pérez-González, F. (eds.) IH 2005. LNCS, vol. 3727, Springer, Heidelberg (2005)
2. Cayre, F., Fontaine, C., Furon, T.: Watermarking security part I: Theory. In: Proceedings of SPIE, Security, Steganography and Watermarking of Multimedia Contents VII, San Jose, USA, vol. 5681 (2005)
3. Pérez-Freire, L., Pérez-González, F., Furon, T.: On achievable security levels for lattice data hiding in the Known Message Attack scenario. In: 8th ACM Multimedia and Security Workshop, Geneva, Switzerland, pp. 68–79 (accepted)
4. Doërr, G., Dugelay, J.L.: Security pitfalls of frame-by-frame approaches to video watermarking. IEEE Transactions on Signal Processing (formerly IEEE Transactions on Acoustics, Speech, and Signal Processing) 52 (2004)
5. Cayre, F., Fontaine, C., Furon, T.: Watermarking security part II: Practice. In: Proceedings of SPIE, Security, Steganography and Watermarking of Multimedia Contents VII, San Jose, USA, vol. 5681 (2005)
6. Bas, P., Hurri, J.: Vulnerability of dm watermarking of non-iid host signals to attacks utilising the statistics of independent components. IEE proceeding, transaction on information security 153, 127–139 (2006)
7. Miller, M.L., Doërr, G.J., Cox, I.J.: Applying informed coding and embedding to design a robust, high capacity watermark. IEEE Trans. on Image Processing 6(13), 791–807 (2004)
8. Costa, M.H.M.: Writing on dirty paper. IEEE Transactions on Information Theory 29(3), 439 (1983)
9. Viterbi, A.J.: CDMA: Principles of Spread Spectrum Communication. Addison-Wesley, Reading, pub-AW:adr (1995)

10. Koval, O., Voloshynovskiy, S., Deguillaume, F., Pérez-González, F., Pun, T.: Worst case additive attack against quantization-based data-hiding methods. In: Proceedings of SPIE, Security, Steganography and Watermarking of Multimedia Contents VII, San Jose, USA (2005)
11. MacQueen, J.: Some methods for classification and analysis of multivariate observations. In: LeCam, L.M., Neyman, J. (eds.) Proc. of the 5th Berkeley Symp. on Mathematics Statistics and Probability (1967)
12. He, J., Lan, M., Tan, C.L., Sung, S.Y., Low, H.B.: Initialization of cluster refinement algorithms: a review and comparative study. In: Proceedings of IEEE International Joint Conference on Neural Networks, pp. 25–29 (2004)
13. Kohonen, T.: Improved versions of learning vector quantization. In: IJCNN 1990, pp. 545–550 (1990)
14. Wang, C., Doërr, G., Cox, I.J.: Trellis coded modulation to improve dirty paper trellis watermarking. In: Proc. SPIE (2007)
15. Ward Jr., J.H.: Hierarchical grouping to optimize an objective function. Journal of the American Statistical Association 58, 236–244 (1963)
16. Bas, P., Cayre, F.: Achieving subspace or key security for woa using natural or circular watermarking. In: ACM Multimedia and Security Workshop, Geneva, Switzerland (2006)

Security of Invertible
Media Authentication Schemes Revisited

Daniel Dönigus, Stefan Endler, Marc Fischlin, Andreas Hülsing, Patrick Jäger,
Anja Lehmann, Sergey Podrazhansky, Sebastian Schipp, Erik Tews,
Sven Vowe, Matthias Walthart, and Frederik Weidemann

Darmstadt University of Technology, Germany
marc.fischlin@gmail.com,
www.minicrypt.de

Abstract. Dittmann, Katzenbeisser, Schallhart and Veith (SEC 2005) introduced the notion of invertible media authentication schemes, embedding authentication data in media objects via invertible watermarks. These invertible watermarks allow to recover the original media object (given a secret encryption key), as required for example in some medical applications where the distortion must be removable.

Here we revisit the approach of Dittmann et al. from a cryptographic viewpoint, clarifying some important aspects of their security definitions. Namely, we first discuss that their notion of unforgeability may not suffice in all settings, and we therefore propose a strictly stronger notion. We then show that the basic scheme suggested by Dittmann et al. achieves our notion if instantiated with the right cryptographic primitives. Our proof also repairs a flaw in the original scheme, pointed out by Hopper, Molnar and Wagner (TCC 2007).

We finally address the issue of secrecy of media authentication schemes, basically preventing unauthorized recovering of the original media object without the encryption key. We give a rigorous security statement (that is, the best security guarantee we can achieve) and prove again that the scheme by Dittmann et al. meets this security level if the right cryptographic building blocks are deployed. Together our notions of unforgeability and of secrecy therefore give very strong security guarantees for such media authentication schemes.

1   Introduction

The transition from analog to digital media facilitates many tasks but also comes along with continually improved manipulation tools, which allow various modifications of media objects. Thus, it becomes increasingly difficult to distinguish authentic from altered objects. To enable a better distinction it is therefore necessary to apply techniques that guarantee authenticity, integrity and possibly secrecy of data.

The straightforward use of digital signatures is not always a satisfying solution to provide authenticity and integrity, because an object and its signature have to be stored separately. This, however, may not be convenient in the area

T. Furon et al. (Eds.): IH 2007, LNCS 4567, pp. 189–203, 2007.

of multimedia data. To counter this problem fragile watermarks were proposed, which can be used to embed a signature directly into an object, such that any (significant) modification will destroy the watermark and thereby invalidates the signature. Unfortunately, this approach comes with the disadvantage that it always leads to irrevocable distortions in the authenticated object, which may not be acceptable in all applications, e.g., X-ray imaging objects are extremely sensitive to modifications. One solution is to use invertible watermarking schemes, which are special fragile watermarks addressing the need to re-obtain the original media object by allowing a complete removal of the embedded data.

Media Authentication Schemes. Using invertible watermarking schemes in combination with encryption and digital signatures, Dittmann, Katzenbeisser, Schallhart and Veith (DKSV) [3] introduced the notion of an invertible media authentication scheme that allows reconstruction of the original object. They also propose a framework to build such authentication schemes: To protect a media object O the $\mathcal{MAS}_{\text{DKSV}}$ scheme first applies an invertible watermarking scheme as proposed by Fridrich et al. [4], dividing O into two parts A_O, B_O by running the watermarking algorithm SEPARATE. See Figure 1. The part B_O next gets compressed and encrypted to a ciphertext X that is stored as the first part of the watermark. To achieve an appropriate compressibility level, B_O has to be chosen accordingly. The second part of the watermark contains the digital signature s of the encrypted part X and A_O, the public part of the object. Finally, the watermark (X, s) is joined with A_O to a single protected object $\overline{O}$ by using the watermarking algorithm JOIN.

Reconstruction of the original object from $\overline{O}$ is done by decrypting to recover COMPRESS(B_O) and uncompressing this value to get the part B_O. A simple join operation with A_O merges the parts together again. As for integrity and secrecy, as long as the object is not altered the signature can be verified by using the public verification key, while the reconstruction of the original object is protected by the secret reconstruction key.

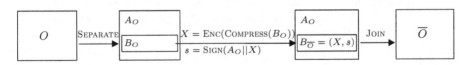

Fig. 1. Protection of media objects in the $\mathcal{MAS}_{\text{DKSV}}$ Scheme

In contrast to most known watermarking schemes where the security is only analyzed by ad-hoc methods, the media authentication scheme of Dittmann et al. comes with a formal model against malicious modification attempts, following well-known approaches for signature schemes. In [3] a media authentication scheme is called secure against forgeability if for every adversary it is infeasible to produce an object O and its protected version $\overline{O}$ for a given verification key. This should even hold if the adversary may ask for protected versions of other objects before.

Our Results (Integrity). Demanding from the adversary to output a pair $(O, \overline{O})$ seems to be overly restrictive, since the authentication system should be already considered broken if an adversary merely creates an arbitrary authenticated object $\overline{O}$ (without knowing a corresponding original object O). Consider for example a governmental organization publishing satellite data $\overline{O}$ of which parts may be classified as confidential for issues of national security (contained in the encrypted B_O part), but which should still allow public verification of authenticity. In this case, the adversary's goal could be to produce other partially protected satellite data bearing a correct signature of the governmental authority, but without any need of being able to generate a matching unprotected object. In this case, the unforgeability definition of Dittmann et al. would provide no security guarantee.

Therefore we propose a stronger definition of unforgeability, which we call strong unforgeability and which prevents attacks like the one above. To show that our definition is indeed strictly stronger than the definition of Dittmann et al., we first give a proof that strong unforgeability implies (basic) unforgeability. After that, we present an example of media authentication scheme which is secure according to the basic notion, but not according to our enhanced definition.

Before proving that the original scheme of Dittmann et al. [3] can be lifted to satisfy the notion of strong unforgeability, we need to tweak the signing process. Hopper et al. revealed in [8] that, in the original scheme, an adversary can easily find different objects that generate the same input $A_O \| X$ to the signing resp. verification process and thus straightforwardly constitute a forgery. We show that those attacks can be prevented by using an appropriate encoding for computing the signature, where A_O and X are clearly separated. Together with a strongly unforgeable signature scheme, this also provides a sufficient condition for a strongly unforgeable media authentication scheme.

Our Results (Secrecy). Another security aspect considered in our paper is secrecy of the original data contained in the protected object. In order to achieve a secure protection of the B_O part, Dittmann et al. [3] propose to use a symmetric encryption scheme. Unfortunately, they neither provide any rigorous security model, nor make any conclusions about the secrecy of their scheme.

In a companion paper, Katzenbeisser and Dittmann [9] discuss a desirable secrecy requirement, resembling semantic security of encryption schemes [5] where a ciphertext should not reveal anything about the original message. In [9] the authors conclude that a similar notion for media authentication schemes "might not be possible to satisfy" because, due to the requirement of good compressibility, the protected part B_O is typically not completely random and may statistically depend on the public part A_O. Therefore, an adversary may be able to derive some information about the encrypted part from the public part A_O. In [9] the authors thus outline an alternative (and somewhat non-standard) security definition, but remain rather informal and do not prove that the $\mathcal{MAS}_{\text{DKSV}}$ scheme achieves the desired level of secrecy.

Our starting point is to note that the fact that A_O may reveal some information about B_O does not obviate similar claims about the secrecy for the media authentication scheme. The reason, originating in the context of encryption, is that the precise idea of semantic security is that one should not be able to learn anything about a message m from a ciphertext X *than what is known about m anyway*. For instance, if m is a credit card number sent encrypted, but the card type is transmitted in clear, then the first digit is usually deducible from the type. Secrecy with respect to such side information is therefore the highest security level we can achieve and should aim for.

Adapting the notion of semantic security with side information we give a formal definition of secrecy for media authentication schemes. Our definition basically says that an authentication scheme is considered secure if whatever can be computed from a protected object $\overline{O} = (A_O, B_{\overline{O}})$ could also be derived from the public part A_O alone. We can even strengthen our notion to a more realistic scenario where the adversary is able to obtain protected and reconstructed objects of his choice. Based on the formal definition we then consider the secrecy of the media authentication scheme by Dittmann et al. and show that semantic security of the used encryption function is a sufficient condition for the authentication scheme to be semantically secure as well.

Summary. Overall, this paper here complements the work of Dittmann et al. by giving precise security models that describe the guarantees in terms of integrity and secrecy. We introduce the notion of strong unforgeability to strengthen the security against malicious modification attempts and provide the sufficient requirements for an authentication scheme to achieve this security goal. Furthermore we show that secrecy in the sense of semantic security for media authentication schemes can be defined, which is completed by proving secrecy for the construction of Dittmann et al. under reasonable assumptions about the encryption scheme.

Organization. In Section 2 we recall the definition of an invertible media authentication scheme by Dittmann et al. [3]. In Section 3 we introduce the scheme (or, to be precise, the framework) by Dittmann et al. and the underlying tools (watermarking, encryption and signatures). Section 4 deals with our refinement of integrity of media authentication schemes and relates the notions, whereas Section 5 covers the secrecy aspects of such schemes. We note that, following the terminology of [3], in this paper here we exclusively deal with *offline* media authentication. It is easy to adapt our notions and proofs to the case of *online* media authentication; we refer to the full version for details.

2   Media Authentication Schemes

An invertible media authentication scheme ($\mathcal{MAS}$), defined by Dittmann et al. [3], consists of a set of algorithms allowing to protect a media object. More precisely, an invertible $\mathcal{MAS}$ is able to produce a protected media object using the algorithm PROTECT while retaining the ability to losslessly reconstruct the original media object using algorithm RECONSTRUCT. The ability for lossless reconstruction of protected media objects is typically achieved by using invertible watermarking schemes as introduced by Honsinger et al. [7]. If a media object has been previously protected, its integrity can be unambiguously verified using algorithm VERIFY.

Usage of the above algorithms necessitates cryptographic keys for protection as well as reconstruction of media objects, which have to be kept private. However, verification of the integrity of a protected media object assumes a public verification key, thus enabling integrity checks by third parties. The generation of all necessary keys is summarized in a single algorithm GENKEY, which takes as input a security parameter and selects keys of the corresponding strength.

Definition 1. *An* invertible media authentication scheme *is a tuple of probabilistic polynomial-time algorithms*

$$\mathcal{MAS} = (\text{GENKEY}, \text{PROTECT}, \text{VERIFY}, \text{RECONSTRUCT})$$

with the following properties:

- GENKEY *takes as input a security parameter n (in unary, as 1^n) and outputs a triple of keys (K_P, K_V, K_R), where K_P is the secret protection key, K_V is the public verification key and K_R is the secret reconstruction key.*
- PROTECT *takes as input a media object O and a protection key K_P, and outputs a protected media object $\overline{O}$ or* FAIL, *if protection is not possible.*
- VERIFY *accepts as input a protected media object $\overline{O}$ and a verification key K_V, and outputs either* TRUE *or* FALSE.
- RECONSTRUCT *takes a protected media object $\overline{O}$ and a reconstruction key K_R, and outputs a media object O or* FAIL.

Furthermore, we require that verification and reconstruction for valid protected objects always succeeds, i.e., for any media object O, for all keys $(K_P, K_V, K_R) \leftarrow \text{GENKEY}(1^n)$ and any $\overline{O} \leftarrow \text{PROTECT}(O, K_P)$, we have

$$\Pr\left[\text{VERIFY}(\overline{O}, K_V) = \text{TRUE} \mid \overline{O} \neq \text{FAIL}\right] = 1,$$
$$\Pr\left[\text{RECONSTRUCT}(\overline{O}, K_R) = O \mid \overline{O} \neq \text{FAIL}\right] = 1.$$

3   The DKSV Media Authentication Scheme

In this section we first recall the basic ingredients of the media authentication scheme by Dittmann et al. [3], before presenting the actual $\mathcal{MAS}_{\text{DKSV}}$ scheme.

3.1   Tools

Recall that the basic idea of the $\mathcal{MAS}_{\text{DKSV}}$ scheme is to divide the object O into a public part A_O and a part B_O which should be protected. This splitting (and its inverse process) are performed via an invertible watermarking scheme, as described in this Section. The B_O part is then compressed, encrypted and signed. Encryption and Signatures are therefore described formally afterwards.

Watermarking. Watermarking schemes are an alternative to the concept of cryptographic signatures, designed specifically to embed authentication and integrity data within media objects, thus eliminating the need for separate storage. *Invertible* watermarking schemes are often a special case of fragile watermarks [10] and have been introduced by Honsinger et al. [7] to address the need to re-obtain the original media object. Fridrich et al. [4] later proposed a general framework for invertible watermarking schemes that uses lossless compression to allow the reversion of the embedding process. Thereby, the ability to embed data into a media object O is accomplished by two polynomial-time algorithms JOIN and SEPARATE:[1]

- SEPARATE takes a media object O as input and produces a tuple (A_O, B_O) (or the output FAIL),
- JOIN takes a pair (A'_O, B'_O) as input and returns a media object O' (or the output FAIL).

If the following equalities hold, JOIN(SEPARATE(O)) $= O$ (given SEPARATE(O) $\neq$ FAIL) for any object O, and SEPARATE(JOIN(A_O, B_O)) $= (A_O, B_O)$ (given that JOIN(A_O, B_O) $\neq$ FAIL) for all A_O, B_O, then we call the pair (JOIN, SEPARATE) an *invertible watermarking scheme.*

Note that the completeness condition above also provides some sort of collision-resistance for the SEPARATE algorithm. Namely, for any objects $O \neq O'$ with SEPARATE(O) $\neq$ FAIL, SEPARATE(O') $\neq$ FAIL we must have SEPARATE(O) $\neq$ SEPARATE(O'). Otherwise, if SEPARATE returned the same output for some $O \neq O'$, then JOIN would sometimes fail to recover the right object O or O' from these identical outputs. The analogous argument applies to JOIN. We note that we could also use a relaxed version in which "bad" objects $O \neq O'$ may exist, but then they are hard to find in reasonable time (similar to collision-resistance of hash functions). Our results remain valid under this relaxed version.

Encryption. A symmetric encryption scheme $\mathcal{E} = (\text{GENENC}, \text{ENC}, \text{DEC})$ consists of three probabilistic polynomial-time algorithms, where algorithm GENENC on input 1^n generates a key K_E, algorithm ENC on input K_E and message $m \in \{0,1\}^*$ outputs a ciphertext X, and algorithm DEC also takes K_E and a ciphertext X and returns $m \in \{0,1\}^*$ or FAIL. Furthermore, for all keys K_E produced by GENENC(1^n), all messages $m \in \{0,1\}^*$ and ciphertexts $X \leftarrow \text{ENC}(K_E, m)$, we have $m = \text{DEC}(K_E, X)$.

As for security of encryption schemes we follow the idea of semantic security, as defined by Goldwasser and Micali [5]. Informally, the idea of semantic security for encryption schemes is that any information $f_{\text{enc}}(m)$ an efficient adversary could learn about a message m from a ciphertext X could also be computed efficiently without X. All this holds of course relative to any side information

---

[1] These algorithms are often defined to be initialized with a watermarking key K_W. Here we presume for simplicity that this key is "hardwired" into the description of the algorithms, or that the key is available to all parties as a system parameter. The key K_W may also contain randomness for both algorithms (if required).

about m. This extra knowledge about m is typically formalized by having some side information hist_m about the message m.

For notational convenience we denote by $(m, \text{hist}_m) \leftarrow (\mathcal{M}, \text{hist}_{enc})(1^n)$ the joint sampling process in which the message m is picked according to distribution $\mathcal{M}(1^n)$ and, at the same time, side information hist_m is generated according to algorithm $\text{hist}_{enc}(1^n)$. Note that in this process both algorithms $\mathcal{M}$ and hist_{enc} may share state.

Definition 2. *A symmetric encryption scheme $\mathcal{E} = (\text{GENENC}, \text{ENC}, \text{DEC})$ is called* semantically secure *(with respect to side information hist_{enc}) if for every probabilistic polynomial-time algorithm $\mathcal{A}_{enc}$ there is a probabilistic polynomial-time algorithms $\mathcal{S}_{enc}$, the simulator, such that for every polynomial-time distribution $\mathcal{M}$ and any function f_{enc} the difference*

$$\Pr\left[\boldsymbol{Exp}_{\mathcal{E},\mathcal{A}_{enc}}^{sem,\mathcal{M},f_{enc},\text{hist}_{enc}}(n) = 1\right] - \Pr\left[\boldsymbol{Exp}_{\mathcal{E},\mathcal{S}_{enc}}^{sem,\mathcal{M},f_{enc},\text{hist}_{enc}}(n) = 1\right]$$

is negligible, where

Experiment $\boldsymbol{Exp}_{\mathcal{E},\mathcal{A}_{enc}}^{sem,\mathcal{M},f_{enc},\text{hist}_{enc}}(n)$	**Experiment $\boldsymbol{Exp}_{\mathcal{E},\mathcal{S}_{enc}}^{sem,\mathcal{M},f_{enc},\text{hist}_{enc}}(n)$**
$K_E \leftarrow \text{GENENC}(1^n)$	$K_E \leftarrow \text{GENENC}(1^n)$
$(m, \text{hist}_m) \leftarrow (\mathcal{M}, \text{hist}_{enc})(1^n)$	$(m, \text{hist}_m) \leftarrow (\mathcal{M}, \text{hist}_{enc})(1^n)$
$X \leftarrow \text{ENC}(K_E, m)$	
$a \leftarrow \mathcal{A}_{enc}(1^n, X, \text{hist}_m)$	$a \leftarrow \mathcal{S}_{enc}(1^n, \text{hist}_m)$
output 1 if and only if	*output 1 if and only if*
$a = f_{enc}(m, \text{hist}_m)$	$a = f_{enc}(m, \text{hist}_m)$

We note that Dittmann et al. [3] do not make any security claim about the underlying encryption scheme in their $\mathcal{MAS}$. See also the discussion in Section 5. Finally, we remark that semantic security (with respect to any side information) is a very common property of modern encryption schemes, and is usually met by all practical and theoretical solutions (cf. [6]).

Signature Schemes. A signature scheme $\mathcal{S} = (\text{GENSIGN}, \text{SIGN}, \text{SIGVERIFY})$ consists of probabilistic polynomial-time algorithms such that GENSIGN on input 1^n generates a key pair $(K_{VS}, K_{SS}) \leftarrow \text{GENSIGN}(1^n)$, algorithm SIGN for input K_{SS} and a message $m \in \{0,1\}^*$ outputs a signature $s \leftarrow \text{SIGN}(K_{SS}, m)$, and algorithm SIGVERIFY for input K_{VS}, m and s returns a decision $d \leftarrow \text{SIGVERIFY}(K_{VS}, m, s)$ which is either TRUE or FALSE. Additionally, for all security parameters n, all keys $(K_{VS}, K_{SS}) \leftarrow \text{GENSIGN}(1^n)$, all messages $m \in \{0,1\}^*$ and all signatures $s \leftarrow \text{SIGN}(K_{SS}, m)$ it holds $\text{SIGVERIFY}(K_{VS}, m, s) = $ TRUE.

Below we define a strong notion of security for signature schemes, called strong unforgeability, which supersedes the common notion of unforgeability for signatures (cf. [6]). Roughly, strong unforgeability also prevents the adversary from producing new signatures for previously signed messages (even if the adversary can see other signatures for chosen message through a signature oracle $\text{SIGN}(K_{SS}, \cdot)$):

Definition 3. *A signature scheme* $\mathcal{S} = (\text{GENSIGN}, \text{SIGN}, \text{SIGVERIFY})$ *is called strongly unforgeable if for any probabilistic polynomial-time algorithm* $\mathcal{A}_{sig}$,

$$\Pr\left[\boldsymbol{Exp}_{\mathcal{S},\mathcal{A}_{sig}}^{StUnf}(n) = 1\right]$$

is negligible, where

Experiment $\boldsymbol{Exp}_{\mathcal{S},\mathcal{A}_{sig}}^{StUnf}(n)$
  $(K_{VS}, K_{SS}) \leftarrow \text{GENSIGN}(1^n)$
  $(m^*, s^*) \leftarrow \mathcal{A}_{sig}^{\text{SIGN}(K_{SS}, \cdot)}(K_{VS})$,
    where we let m_i *denote the* i-*th query to oracle* $\text{SIGN}(K_{SS}, \cdot)$
    and s_i *the oracle's answer to this query*
  output 1 if and only if
    $\text{SIGVERIFY}(K_{VS}, m^*, s^*) = \text{TRUE} \text{ and } (m^*, s^*) \neq (m_i, s_i) \text{ for all } i.$

Note that in the regular notion of unforgeability we strengthen the requirement on (m^*, s^*) in the experiment above, and demand that $m^* \neq m_i$ for all i (such that finding another signature s^* to a given pair m_i, s_i is no longer considered a successful attack). In particular, if a scheme is strongly unforgeable, then it is also unforgeable in the basic sense. Yet, it is also easy to construct an unforgeable signature scheme which does not achieve the stronger notion, e.g., if for each signature the signing algorithm appends a redundant bit which the verification algorithm simply ignores.

Efficient strongly unforgeable schemes exist under various assumptions, e.g., [1, 2]. Existentially they can be derived from any one-way function (cf. [6]) and are thus based on the same complexity assumption as signature schemes which are unforgeable in the ordinary sense.

3.2   The $\mathcal{MAS}_{\text{DKSV}}$ Scheme

With the tools of the previous sections we can now recapture the $\mathcal{MAS}_{\text{DKSV}}$ scheme. To protect a media object O the $\mathcal{MAS}_{\text{DKSV}}$ scheme first uses the watermarking scheme to determine the parts A_O and B_O. Then the B_O part is first compressed to C_O and, together with a hash value $H(O)$ of the object, encrypted to a ciphertext X.[2] The resulting ciphertext and the public part A_O of the original media object O are signed together with the signature algorithm, $s \leftarrow \text{SIGN}(K_{SS}, (A_O, X))$. The values X and s are finally joined with A_O into a single media object $\overline{O}$.

The integrity of a protected object $\overline{O}$ can be verified by anyone by recovering A_O, X, s from the protected object and verifying the signature s for (A_O, X). This can be done without decrypting X and recovering B_O. Reconstruction

---

[2] The role of $H(O)$ concerning the security of the scheme remains somewhat unclear, i.e., Dittmann et al. [3] never specify any security requirements on H. It appears that security-wise H does not serve any purpose. We include H here only for sake of completentess; the reader may simply think of H as the function with empty output.

then can easily be achieved by first verifying $\overline{O}$ and then decrypting with K_E. After uncompressing C_O to B'_O algorithm JOIN can be applied to (A_O, B'_O). The resulting object O' is hashed to $H(O')$ which is compared to the embedded hash. If this is successful the restored object is returned as O, otherwise the reconstruction algorithm fails.

We note that, in the original scheme, Dittmann et al. use the signature algorithm to sign the concatenation $A_O\|X$ of the values A_O and X. But this introduces a weaknesses which the attack by Hopper et al. [8] exploits. Here we therefore tweak the signature process by signing (A_O, X) instead, with the usual meaning that this string (A_O, X) contains a separator between the two values. For instance, we can encode the bit length of A_O into a starting block of fixed length (say, into the first n bits for security parameter n) and then append $A_O\|X$. Other choices are possible, of course.

Construction 1 (DKSV-MAS). *Let* (JOIN, SEPARATE) *be an invertible watermarking scheme,* $\mathcal{E}$ *be a symmetric encryption scheme and* $\mathcal{S}$ *be a signature scheme. Let* (COMPRESS, UNCOMPRESS) *be a lossless compression scheme and* H *be some function (with fixed output length). Then the DKSV media authentication scheme* $\mathcal{MAS}_{DKSV}$ *is defined by the following algorithms:*

- *Algorithm* GENKEY *on input* 1^n *runs the key generation algorithms of the signature scheme and the encryption scheme,* $(K_{SS}, K_{VS}) \leftarrow$ GENSIGN(1^n) *and* $K_E \leftarrow$ GENENC(1^n)*, and outputs* $K_V = K_{VS}$*,* $K_R = (K_{VS}, K_E)$ *and* $K_P = (K_{SS}, K_E)$*.*
- *Algorithm* PROTECT *on input* K_P *and object* O *first splits the object by computing* $(A_O, B_O) \leftarrow$ SEPARATE(O)*, then compresses* $C_O \leftarrow$ COMPRESS(B_O) *and computes a ciphertext* $X \leftarrow$ ENC$(K_E, C_O\|H(O))$*. It computes a signature* $s \leftarrow$ SIGN$(K_{SS}, (A_O, X))$ *and joins the signature together with* A_O *and* X *into the protected object* $\overline{O} \leftarrow$ JOIN$(A_O, (X, s))$*. It outputs* $\overline{O}$ *(or* FAIL *if any of the deployed algorithms returns* FAIL*).*
- *Algorithm* VERIFY *on input* K_V *and a protected object* $\overline{O}$ *splits the object into* $(A_O, (X, s)) \leftarrow$ SEPARATE$(\overline{O})$ *and returns the output of the signature verification algorithm for these data,* SIGVERIFY$(K_{VS}, (A_O, X), s)$ *(which equals* FAIL *in the special case that* SEPARATE *returned* FAIL *before).*
- *Algorithm* RECONSTRUCT *takes as input* K_R *and a protected object* $\overline{O}$*, and only continues reconstruction if verification of* $\overline{O}$ *works. If so, then it recovers* $(A_O, (X, s)) \leftarrow$ SEPARATE$(\overline{O})$ *and decrypts* X *to* $C_O\|h$ *and re-computes* $B_O =$ UNCOMPRESS(C_O) *and* $O \leftarrow$ JOIN(A_O, B_O)*. If* $H(O) = h$ *then it outputs* O*; in any other case the algorithm returns* FAIL*.*

4   Integrity of Media Authentication Schemes

In this section we address integrity protection of media authentication schemes. We first review the definition of Dittmann et al. [3] about unforgeability of

$\mathcal{MAS}$[3] and then present our improved security guarantee, denoted by *strong unforgeability*. We show that strong unforgeability is strictly stronger than the notion of Dittmann et al., and finally prove that the $\mathcal{MAS}_{\text{DKSV}}$ scheme achieves the stronger notion if instantiated with the right primitives.

4.1   Definitions

The original unforgeability requirement of Dittmann et al. [3] demands that, without the protection key, it is infeasible to find an object O and its protected version $\overline{O}$, even after having seen other protected objects:

Definition 4. *Let* $\mathcal{MAS} = (\text{GenKey}, \text{Protect}, \text{Verify}, \text{Reconstruct})$ *be an invertible media authentication scheme. It is called* unforgeable *if for every probabilistic polynomial-time algorithm* $\mathcal{A}_{DKSV}$ *the value*

$$\Pr\left[\boldsymbol{Exp}^{mas\text{-}unf}_{\mathcal{MAS},\mathcal{A}_{DKSV}}(n) = 1\right]$$

is negligible, where

> **Experiment** $\boldsymbol{Exp}^{mas\text{-}unf}_{\mathcal{MAS},\mathcal{A}_{DKSV}}(n)$
> $(K_P, K_V, K_R) \leftarrow \text{GenKey}(1^n)$
> $(O, \overline{O}) \leftarrow \mathcal{A}^{\text{Protect}(\cdot, K_P)}_{DKSV}(1^n, K_V)$
>   *where* O_i *denotes the i-th query to oracle* $\text{Protect}(\cdot, K_P)$
>   *and* $\overline{O}_i$ *the oracle's answer to this query*
>   *output* 1 *if and only if*
> $\text{Verify}(\overline{O}, K_V) = \mathsf{TRUE}$ *and* $\overline{O} \in [\text{Protect}(O, K_P)]$ *and*
> $O \neq O_i$ *for all* i.

We note that Dittmann et al. [3] claim their scheme to be secure under this definition. However, as mentioned before, Hopper et al. [8] point out a gap in this proof, exploiting a weak encoding for the signing algorithm. Patching the signature and verification process as described in Construction 1 gives a version which is indeed secure according to this definition here (if the signature scheme achieves basic unforgeability). This can be easily inferred from the security proof for our stronger notion in the next section, and we therefore omit a formal proof for this simpler fact.

Our first definitional strengthening concerns the adversary's task to find a protected object $\overline{O}$ together with its original counter part O. Recall the satellite data example from the introduction, where the adversary's goal is only to produce another valid protected object without knowing a matching object in clear. Then the previous definition would provide no security guarantee in this case. In fact, as we will discuss later, there are even schemes satisfying the unforgeability

---

[3] Dittmann et al. call the property in their paper "security against existential unforgeability" but, for sake of better distinction with other security notions such as secrecy, we rename the property here to "unforgeability".

notion above but which fail to meet the stronger requirement in the example. In our refinement below we therefore reduce the requirement on the adversary's output and merely demand that the attacker outputs a new protected object $\overline{O}$.

The other strengthening refers to availability of other components of a system. Since the algorithms may operate in a highly interactive setting, we follow the conservative approach in cryptography and allow our algorithm $\mathcal{A}_{\text{strong}}$ to also communicate with a RECONSTRUCT oracle, enabling him to reconstruct objects of his choice. Note that verification can be carried out locally by the adversary with the help of the public key anyway. With these two refinements we obtain the following definition:

Definition 5. *Let* $\mathcal{MAS}$ = (GENKEY, PROTECT, VERIFY, RECONSTRUCT) *be an invertible media authentication scheme. It is called* strongly unforgeable *if for every probabilistic polynomial-time algorithm* $\mathcal{A}_{\text{strong}}$ *the value*

$$\Pr\left[\boldsymbol{Exp}^{mas\text{-}stunf}_{\mathcal{MAS},\mathcal{A}_{strong}}(n) = 1\right]$$

is negligible, where

> $\boldsymbol{Experiment\ Exp}^{mas\text{-}stunf}_{\mathcal{MAS},\mathcal{A}_{strong}}(n)$
> $(K_P, K_V, K_R) \leftarrow \text{GENKEY}(1^n)$
> $\overline{O} \leftarrow \mathcal{A}^{\text{PROTECT}(\cdot,K_P),\text{RECONSTRUCT}(\cdot,K_R)}_{strong}(1^n, K_V)$
> *where* O_i *denotes the* i-*th query to oracle* PROTECT$(\cdot, K_P)$
> *and* $\overline{O}_i$ *the oracle's answer to this query*
> *output 1 if and only if*
> VERIFY$(\overline{O}, K_V) =$ TRUE *and* $\overline{O} \neq \overline{O}_i$ *for all* i.

4.2   On the Relationship of the Notions

In this section we show that security according to our definition of strong unforgeability is strictly stronger than the one for the definition by Dittmann et al. This is done in two steps. First we will show that our definition implies the definition of Dittmann et al. After that, we provide two examples of schemes which are secure according to the basic notion but not to the enhanced definition (one example is omitted from this version here). We remark that the separating examples even hold if we augment the DKSV definition by giving $\mathcal{A}_{\text{DKSV}}$ access to a RECONSTRUCT oracle. This difference merely stems from the fact that $\mathcal{A}_{\text{DKSV}}$ has to output a pair $(O, \overline{O})$, compared to $\overline{O}$ as in our definition.

Proposition 1. *If an invertible* $\mathcal{MAS}$ *scheme is strongly unforgeable then it is also unforgeable.*

The proof is omitted for space reasons. We next give a separating example for the patched $\mathcal{MAS}_{\text{DKSV}}$ framework where we assume that the signature scheme is *not* strongly unforgeable, i.e., where one can easily transform a signature s to a message m into another valid signature $s^* \neq s$. With this instantiation choice there exists a successful attack against the strong unforgeability, but which does not constitute a break against basic unforgeability.

The adversary against the strong unforgeability calls the PROTECT oracle only once about an object O to derive a protected object $\overline{O} = \text{JOIN}(A_{\overline{O}}, (X, s))$. The attacker next runs SEPARATE$(\overline{O})$ to obtain $A_{\overline{O}} = A_O$ and (X, s). Since the signature scheme is not strongly unforgeable the attacker can now compute another valid signature $s^* \neq s$ for (A_O, X). He finally outputs $\overline{O}^* = \text{JOIN}(A_O, (X, s^*))$ as the forgery attempt.

The attack succeeds according to the strong unforgeability, because $s^* \neq s$ and thus $\overline{O}^*$ was never received from the PROTECT oracle before, and VERIFY evaluates to TRUE. In the DKSV definition of an attack, however, an attacker must output $(O, \overline{O})$. So in our case, prepending O to $\overline{O}^*$ would not constitute a successful attack as O has been sent to the PROTECT oracle before. In fact, it is easy to see from our proof in the next section that any attacker fails according to the DKSV definition if the underlying signature scheme achieves basic unforgeability.

4.3   Strong Unforgeability of the $\mathcal{MAS}_{\text{DKSV}}$-Scheme

We next prove that the $\mathcal{MAS}_{\text{DKSV}}$ scheme achieves strong unforgeability if the underlying signature scheme is strong enough. Note again that this statement necessitates the patch of the signature and verification algorithm; else the attack by Hopper er al. would still apply.

Theorem 2 (Strong Unforgeability). *If the signature scheme $\mathcal{S}$ is strongly unforgeable then the $\mathcal{MAS}_{DKSV}$ media authentication scheme in Construction 1 is strongly unforgeable.*

Proof. If there would be a successful attacker $\mathcal{A}_{\text{strong}}$ on the $\mathcal{MAS}_{\text{DKSV}}$ according to our strong definition, then by using the prerequisites we could use this attacker to construct a successful attacker $\mathcal{A}_{\text{sig}}$ against the strong unforgeability of the deployed signature scheme. In the following we will show the construction of such an attacker $\mathcal{A}_{\text{sig}}$.

The attacker $\mathcal{A}_{\text{sig}}$ on the signature scheme gets the signature public key K_{VS} as input. He chooses an encryption key K_E and passes the key $K_V = K_{VS}$ to $\mathcal{A}_{\text{strong}}$ to start a black-box simulation. In this simulation of $\mathcal{A}_{\text{strong}}$, adversary $\mathcal{A}_{\text{sig}}$ can easily answer queries of $\mathcal{A}_{\text{strong}}$ to oracle RECONSTRUCT with the help of the key $K_R = (K_E, K_{VS})$. For any query O_i of $\mathcal{A}_{\text{strong}}$ to the PROTECT oracle, $\mathcal{A}_{\text{sig}}$ calculates $(A_{O_i}, B_{O_i}) = \text{SEPARATE}(O_i)$, $C_{O_i} = \text{COMPRESS}(B_{O_i})$ and $X_i \leftarrow \text{ENC}(K_E, C_{O_i} \| H(O_i))$. If any of the algorithms returns FAIL then $\mathcal{A}_{\text{sig}}$ immediately returns FAIL to $\mathcal{A}_{\text{strong}}$, else $\mathcal{A}_{\text{sig}}$ passes $m_i = (A_{O_i}, X_i)$ to his SIGN-oracle to get a signature s_i. Thereafter he returns $\overline{O}_i = \text{JOIN}(A_{O_i}, (X_i, s_i))$ to attacker $\mathcal{A}_{\text{strong}}$. Once $\mathcal{A}_{\text{strong}}$ outputs a protected object $\overline{O}$ and stops, adversary $\mathcal{A}_{\text{sig}}$ runs SEPARATE on $\overline{O}$ to obtain A_O and (X, s). Now $\mathcal{A}_{\text{sig}}$ outputs $m^* = (A_O, X)$ and $s^* = s$.

It is obvious that $\mathcal{A}_{\text{sig}}$ perfectly mimics the PROTECT oracle as well as the RECONSTRUCT oracle in $\mathcal{A}_{\text{strong}}$'s emulation. It remains to show that $\mathcal{A}_{\text{sig}}$

succeeds in his attack whenever $\mathcal{A}_{\text{strong}}$ wins. If $\mathcal{A}_{\text{strong}}$'s output $\overline{O}$ satisfies $\text{VERIFY}(\overline{O}, K_V) = \text{TRUE}$ then in particular $\text{SIGVERIFY}(K_{VS}, m^*, s^*)$ for $\mathcal{A}_{\text{sig}}$'s output will also be TRUE and $\text{SEPARATE}(\overline{O}) = (A_O, (X, s)) \neq \text{FAIL}$. Furthermore $\overline{O} \neq \overline{O}_i$ for all i.

We have to show that the pair $(m^*, s^*) = ((A_O, X), s)$ has not appeared in $\mathcal{A}_{\text{sig}}$'s interactions with the signature oracle. This is clearly true if, in the i-th request, $\mathcal{A}_{\text{sig}}$ returned $s_i = \text{FAIL}$ before even querying the signature oracle, namely, if separation, compression or encryption failed. If, on the other hand, $\overline{O}_i = \text{FAIL}$ for the i-th interaction, because the final JOIN in the simulation of the protection query returned FAIL, but a message $m_i = (A_{O_i}, X_i)$ was still signed with s_i, then we must have $(m^*, s^*) \neq (m_i, s_i)$. Else, for equality $(m^*, s^*) = (m_i, s_i)$ we would have $\text{FAIL} = \text{JOIN}(A_{O_i}, (X_i, s_i)) = \text{JOIN}(A_O, (X, s)) = \text{JOIN}(\text{SEPARATE}(\overline{O}))$ for $\text{SEPARATE}(\overline{O}) \neq \text{FAIL}$, contradicting the completeness of the watermarking scheme. Finally, if $\overline{O}_i \neq \text{FAIL}$, then because $\overline{O} \neq \overline{O}_i$ and the SEPARATE-function is collision-resistant (see Section 3.1) we have $(A_O, (X, s)) \neq (A_{O_i}, (X_i, s_i))$.

Hence, if attacker $\mathcal{A}_{\text{strong}}$ on the media authentication scheme is successful, attacker $\mathcal{A}_{\text{Sig}}$ will also succeed with the same probability, because (m^*, s^*) was never received from the SIGN-oracle and $\text{SIGVERIFY}(K_{VS}, m^*, s^*) = \text{TRUE}$. $\square$

5   Secrecy of Media Authentication Schemes

Recall that the scheme by Dittmann et al. [3] introduces an encryption scheme in order to protect the B_O-part of an object O. However, in their paper they do not provide any claim about the secrecy under reasonable conditions about the encryption scheme, not to mention a rigorous security model. In a companion paper, though, Katzenbeisser and Dittmann [9] discuss a desirable secrecy requirement, resembling semantic security of encryption schemes (as defined in Section 3.1). Yet, their proposal advocates a somewhat elliptical mixture between semantic security and indistinguishability of encryption schemes (cf. [6]), and remains rather sketchy. It also remains unclear if, or under which conditions, the $\mathcal{MAS}_{\text{DKSV}}$ scheme meets this goal.

Recall that the idea behind semantic security of an encryption scheme was that anything an efficient adversary could learn about a message m from a ciphertext X could also be computed efficiently without X. Here we discuss that, by using appropriate notions of secrecy with side information, we can indeed define secrecy for media authentication schemes in the sense of semantic security. Our definition basically says that an $\mathcal{MAS}$ provides secrecy if whatever one can compute from a protected object $\overline{O}$ (including the public part A_O) could also be derived from A_O alone.[4] We then continue to show that semantic security of the encryption function (with respect to side information) also guarantees secrecy of the $\mathcal{MAS}_{\text{DKSV}}$ scheme.

---

[4] As usual, the adversary may have even further knowledge about (parts of) B_O (or other information about the system) and the requirement then is that the adversary cannot deduce anything beyond this additional knowledge and A_O.

5.1   Definition

The definition below follows the one for semantic security of encryption (with respect to side information) closely. Namely, we again compare the success probability of an adversary predicting some information $f_{MAS}(O)$ of an object O from the protected version $\overline{O}$ (and $hist_O$) with the prediction success of a simulator given only $hist_O$. For a secure $\mathcal{MAS}$ these probabilities should be close.

We write $\mathcal{O}$ for the distribution of the objects and $hist_{MAS}$ for the algorithm computing the side information. For notational convenience we again denote by $(O, hist_O) \leftarrow (\mathcal{O}, hist_{MAS})(1^n)$ the joint sampling process, possibly sharing state between the two algorithms.

Definition 6. *An invertible media authentication scheme $\mathcal{MAS}$ is called semantically secure with respect to side information $hist_{MAS}$ if for every probabilistic polynomial-time algorithm $\mathcal{A}_{MAS}$, there is a probabilistic polynomial-time algorithm $\mathcal{S}_{MAS}$, the simulator, such that for every polynomial-time distribution $\mathcal{O}$ of objects and for every function f_{MAS}, the difference*

$$\Pr\left[\boldsymbol{Exp}_{\mathcal{MAS},\mathcal{A}_{MAS}}^{mas\text{-}sem,\mathcal{O},f_{MAS},hist_{MAS}}(n) = 1\right] - \Pr\left[\boldsymbol{Exp}_{\mathcal{MAS},\mathcal{S}_{MAS}}^{mas\text{-}sem,\mathcal{O},f_{MAS},hist_{MAS}}(n) = 1\right]$$

is negligible, where

Exper. $\boldsymbol{Exp}_{\mathcal{MAS},\mathcal{A}_{MAS}}^{mas\text{-}sem,\mathcal{O},f_{MAS},hist_{MAS}}(n)$	**Exper.** $\boldsymbol{Exp}_{\mathcal{MAS},\mathcal{S}_{MAS}}^{mas\text{-}sem,\mathcal{O},f_{MAS},hist_{MAS}}(n)$
$(K_P, K_V, K_R) \leftarrow \textsc{GenKey}(1^n)$	$(K_P, K_V, K_R) \leftarrow \textsc{GenKey}(1^n)$
$(O, hist_O) \leftarrow (\mathcal{O}, hist_{MAS})(1^n)$	$(O, hist_O) \leftarrow (\mathcal{O}, hist_{MAS})(1^n)$
$\overline{O} \leftarrow \textsc{Protect}(K_P, O)$	
$a \leftarrow \mathcal{A}_{MAS}(K_V, \overline{O}, hist_O)$	$a \leftarrow \mathcal{S}_{MAS}(K_V, hist_O)$
output 1 if and only if	output 1 if and only if
$a = f_{MAS}(O, hist_O)$	$a = f_{MAS}(O, hist_O)$

We remark that we can even strengthen the notion above by granting $\mathcal{A}_{MAS}$ access to oracles $\textsc{Protect}(\cdot, K_P)$ and $\textsc{Reconstruct}(\cdot, K_R)$ (with the restriction that the adversary never queries the reconstruct oracle about the challenge $\overline{O}$, enabling a trivial attack otherwise). Assuming chosen-plaintext security of the underlying encryption scheme (where the adversary is also allowed to see ciphertexts of arbitrary messages via an oracle $\textsc{Enc}(K_E, \cdot)$), our result also holds under this more advanced attack model, as we will discuss in the full version. Interestingly, the proof for this extension also takes advantage of our notion of strong unforgeability.

5.2   Secrecy of the $\mathcal{MAS}_{DKSV}$-Scheme

The following theorem shows that semantic security of the encryption scheme carries over to the secrecy of the $\mathcal{MAS}_{DKSV}$ scheme:

Theorem 3. *Let $hist_{MAS}(1^n)$ be the function which takes an object O and outputs A_O where $(A_O, B_O) \leftarrow \textsc{Separate}(O)$. Let $\mathcal{E}$ be a semantically secure encryption scheme (with respect to side information $hist_{enc} = hist_{MAS}$). Then the* *invertible media authentication scheme* $\mathcal{MAS}_{DKSV}$ *in Construction 1 is semantically secure with respect to side information* $hist_{MAS}$.

The proof is by contradiction, transforming an allegedly successful adversary on the secrecy of the media authentication scheme into a successful attack against the encryption scheme. The proof appears in the full version. We also note that the result still holds if $hist_{MAS}(1^n)$, in addition to A_O, includes further information like $hist'(B_O)$ for some function $hist'$ (as long as the encryption scheme is secure for this augmented side information).

Acknowledgments

We thank the reviewers of Information Hiding 2007 for valuable comments.

Marc Fischlin and Anja Lehmann are supported by the Emmy Noether Program Fi 940/2-1 of the German Research Foundation (DFG).

References

1. Bellare, M., Rogaway, P.: The exact security of digital signatures –How to sign with RSA and Rabin. In: Maurer, U.M. (ed.) EUROCRYPT 1996. LNCS, vol. 1070, pp. 399–416. Springer, Heidelberg (1996)
2. Boneh, D., Shen, E., Waters, B.: Strongly Unforgeable Signatures Based on Computational Diffie-Hellman. In: Yung, M., Dodis, Y., Kiayias, A., Malkin, T.G. (eds.) PKC 2006. LNCS, vol. 3958, pp. 229–240. Springer, Heidelberg (2006)
3. Dittmann, J., Katzenbeisser, S., Schallhart, C., Veith, H.: Ensuring Media Integrity on Third-Party Infrastructures. In: Proceedings of SEC 2005. 20th International Conference on Information Security, pp. 493–508. Springer, Heidelberg (2005)
4. Fridrich, J., Goljan, M., Du, R.: Lossless data embedding – new paradigm in digital watermarking. EURASIP Journal of Applied Signal Processing 2, 185–196 (2002)
5. Goldwasser, S., Micali, S.: Probabilistic Encryption. Journal of Computer and System Science 28(2), 270–299 (1984)
6. Goldreich, O.: The Foundations of Cryptography, vol. 2. Cambridge University Press, Cambridge (2004)
7. Honsinger, C.W., Jones, P., Rabbani, M., Stoffel, J.C.: Lossless recovery of an original image containing embedded data. US patent application, Docket No: 77102/E/D (1999)
8. Hopper, N., Molnar, D., Wagner, D.: From Weak to Strong Watermarking. In: Vadhan, S.P. (ed.) TCC 2007. LNCS, vol. 4392, Springer, Heidelberg (2007)
9. Katzenbeisser, S., Dittmann, J.: Malicious attacks on media authentication schemes based on invertible watermarks. In: Security, Steganography, and Watermarking of Multimedia Contents. Proceedings of SPIE, vol. 5306, pp. 838–847 (2004)
10. Yeung, M., Mintzer, F.: Invisible watermarking for image verification. Journal of Electronic Imaging 7, 578–591 (1998)

A Fusion of Maximum Likelihood
and Structural Steganalysis

Andrew D. Ker

Oxford University Computing Laboratory, Parks Road, Oxford OX1 3QD, England
adk@comlab.ox.ac.uk

Abstract. This paper draws together two methodologies for the detection of bit replacement steganography: the principle of maximum likelihood, which is statistically well-founded but has lead to weak detectors in practice, and so-called structural detection, which is sensitive but lacks optimality and can suffer from complicated exposition. The key novelty is to extend structural analysis to include a hypothetical "pre-cover", from which the cover object is imagined to derive. Here, maximum likelihood detection is presented for three structural detectors. Although the algebraic derivation is long, and maximizing the likelihood function difficult in practice, conceptually the new detectors are reasonably simple. Experiments show that the new detectors are the best performers yet, very significantly so in the detection of replacement of multiple bit planes.

1 Introduction

There is no doubt that replacement of low-order bits, whether in digital images, movies, or audio, is an insecure method of embedding and there is a large body of literature on the detection of this steganographic method. Broadly, detectors fall into three categories: methods that target the *structure* of bit replacement[1], those that apply statistical techniques to derive *maximum likelihood* (ML) detectors based on features such as histogram or co-occurrence matrix, and *blind* classifier-based methods that pick ad-hoc features and train on cover and stego images.

Each class has its advantages. The structural detectors, which include (in increasing order of complexity) [1–7], are easily the most sensitive. But their exposition can become complex, and the methods themselves are often based on dubious statistical principles (for example, assuming that all observations of random variables equal the expectation). Statistical rigour is at the heart of maximum likelihood detectors [8–11] but their performance is weak. The blind classifier-based methods can detect a range of embedding methods (not limited to bit replacement) but have neither good detection power nor statistical rigour and we shall not consider this last class here.

This paper combines the theoretical rigour of ML detection with the sensitivity of structural steganalysis. Not only does this produce superior detectors, it

---

[1] An even cover sample can be incremented or unchanged, but never decremented, when the least significant bit is replaced, conversely for odd samples; similar structure occurs in replacement of other bits.

T. Furon et al. (Eds.): IH 2007, LNCS 4567, pp. 204–219, 2007.

also presents a framework which avoids some of the difficulties that plague structural steganalysis using large groups of pixels [6]. Indeed, with hindsight, this is arguably the mathematical setting within which structural steganalysis should always have been presented. We will confine our analysis to digital grayscale images with spatial-domain embedding, but the principles described here should apply in other domains too.

The contents of the paper is as follows. Section 2 is a brief survey of ML and structural steganalysis methods for detection of bit replacement. Section 3 describes ML detection of least significant bit (LSB) replacement using an extended structural analysis, deriving a likelihood function and explaining a maximization procedure (at this stage only a simple, slow, maximization is used), with experimental results following. Sections 4 and 5 repeat the same process and experiments for the detection of embedding in two lowest bit planes and then a more complex structural analysis of embedding in just the LSB plane. Finally, Sect. 6 draws conclusions. In order to include multiple detectors the later sections contain little detail; this paper aims to present the principles only, and we refer to an extended version of this paper [12] for fuller derivations, explicit likelihood functions, and wider experimental results.

2   ML Steganalysis and Structural Steganalysis

The starting point for ML steganalysis is the Neyman-Pearson Lemma, which states that the optimal discriminator between two point hypotheses is given by the likelihood ratio. Further, good performance for composite hypotheses is given by the generalized likelihood ratio (GLR) test and for parameter estimators by the method of maximum likelihood (although the optimality of these extensions is not universal). One of the earliest uses of ML in steganalysis is found in [8], which derives the effect of LSB replacement on the probability mass function (PMF) of a signal; if the PMF of the cover source is known, it is possible to create a GLR test for the presence of data hidden by LSB overwriting and a ML estimate for the size of payload.

In practice the PMF of the cover is not known: it must be estimated by either filtering the observed PMF [8] or postulating an "ideal" cover PMF ([9] uses this latter approach, in a transform domain). The detectors are weak for three reasons: estimation of the cover PMF is subject to inaccuracy; considering only the PMF discards Markovicity in the cover source; and the detectors are unable to exploit the aforementioned structure of LSB replacement. Improved detectors based on maximum likelihood principles can be found in [11], which models the source as a Markov chain, and [10] which also tries to exploit some of the structure of LSB replacement via the so-called "stair-step" effect. Nonetheless, even the improved detectors remain unable to detect even moderate payloads[2].

In contrast, the most successful class of steganalyzers for bit replacement (including LSB embedding as well as replacement of multiple bit planes) are

---

[2] We should be clear that some of the ML detectors cited are not specialised towards LSB replacement, so weak performance is expected.

those which focus on the structure of the embedding process. Their general strategy, described in [5], is as follows. First, define a feature set of stego images which depends on the size of payload p, a vector $\mathbf{S}(p)$; second, derive how $\mathbf{S}(p)$ depends on p and $\mathbf{S}(0)$ and then invert so that, given a stego image, we can hypothesise a value for p and compute what this would imply for $\mathbf{S}(0)$. Third, express a model for covers in terms of $\mathbf{S}(0)$. Then we create an estimator for the payload size p as whichever implies a value of $\mathbf{S}(0)$ closest to the model.

The structure of LSB replacement in individual samples is trivial and does not give a detector, but extending to pairs or larger groups of pixels produces extremely sensitive detectors. The earliest detector used the structure implicitly [1]; analysis of the effect of bit replacement on specific structural features was first given in [2] and extended in [4,5]. Further application, to large groups of pixels and replacement of two bit planes, can be found in [6,7]. A key novelty is the principle of *least-squares* [3], which defines the closest cover fit to be when the features' sum-square deviation (from an ideal) is minimized.

Although very effective, the structural detectors have drawbacks. The analysis of the effect of bit replacement on groups of three or more pixels can be handled in an elegant manner [5], but specification of the cover model for such groups can become desperately complicated, as demonstrated in [6]. And the statistical methodology is poor: it is not truly the case that stego features $\mathbf{S}(p)$ depend deterministically on p and $\mathbf{S}(0)$ (it also depends on the payload content, usually assumed random) and it is necessary to take expectations. Neither is the cover model exact. Moreover a least-squares cover fit, while plausible, cannot be shown optimal (indeed we shall later be able to see that it is not).

3   Maximum Likelihood and the "Couples" Structure

We now present a fusion of the sensitive features used by the structural detectors with the principles of maximum likelihood. In this section we consider the features used by the detectors known as *Sample Pairs* (SPA) [2,3] or *Couples* [5] (other possibilities will be examined in later sections).

We assume a single-channel cover image[3] which consists of N pixels with intensities $s_1, s_2, \ldots, s_N$ in the range $0 \ldots 2M+1$ (typically $M = 127$). A *sample pair* is a pair of pixels (j, k) for some $j \neq k$. Let $\mathcal{P}$ be the set of all pairs that represent adjacent pixels and define some subsets of $\mathcal{P}$, called the *trace subsets*:

$$\mathcal{D}_m = \{(j, k) \in \mathcal{P} \mid s_k = s_j + m\}$$
$$\mathcal{E}_m = \{(j, k) \in \mathcal{P} \mid s_k = s_j + m, \text{ with } s_j \text{ even}\}$$
$$\mathcal{O}_m = \{(j, k) \in \mathcal{P} \mid s_k = s_j + m, \text{ with } s_j \text{ odd}\}$$

for $-2M + 1 \leq m \leq 2M + 1$. Analysis of the movement of sample pairs among these subsets, when payload is embedded by LSB replacement, is the key to structural steganalysis. The cover model in [2,3] is $|\mathcal{E}_m| = |\mathcal{O}_m|$, although only odd indices can be used for steganalysis.

---

[3] Colour images are usually separated into colour channels, whose signals are either treated separately or concatenated.

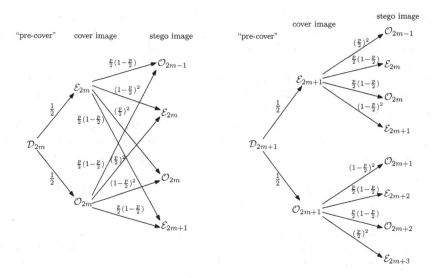

Fig. 1. The evolution of the *Couples* trace subsets, from "pre-cover" to stego-image, when proportion $\frac{p}{2}$ least significant bits are flipped

3.1 Derivation of Likelihood Function

We present here a new analysis of trace subsets. To model trace subsets in cover images, we use the technique of [13], which proposed a model as part of the analysis of errors in least-squares steganalysis. Imagine that, for each m, the set $\mathcal{D}_m$ is first determined (in what we will call a "pre-cover") and then partitioned binomially to make the cover image, with each sample pair in $\mathcal{D}_m$ placed independently and equiprobably into $\mathcal{E}_m$ or $\mathcal{O}_m$. Of course this bears no relationship to the physical processes which create, for example, an image in the CCD of a digital camera – there is no "pre-cover" except in our imagination – but it is a natural explanation of the cover property $|\mathcal{E}_m| = |\mathcal{O}_m|$ and it is demonstrated, in [13], very accurate in most circumstances[4].

Second, we model how LSB replacement converts trace subsets in the cover to trace subsets in a stego image, depending on the size of payload. We suppose that the LSB of each sample is flipped, independently, with probability $\frac{p}{2}$ – this corresponds to embedding a payload (uncorrelated with the cover) of length pN by randomized LSB replacement, or perhaps the embedding of a longer payload when LSB flipping is used as part of a source coding scheme [14] (of course the estimator will be truly for twice the number of flipped pixels, regardless of the connection this has with payload size; it could be nothing else). Under this

---

[4] In [13] the limitations of this model are explored; it is not very accurate for m near zero and there is observed a negative correlation between the sizes of $\mathcal{E}_1$ and $\mathcal{E}_{-1}$; in fact it is possible to explain these features in terms of over-saturated images, but that is not within the scope of this paper. We content ourselves with using the model as is, in the knowledge that it is not perfect.

embedding operation each quartet of trace subsets $\mathcal{O}_{2m-1}$, $\mathcal{E}_{2m}$, $\mathcal{O}_{2m}$, $\mathcal{E}_{2m+1}$ undergoes permutation, with probabilities determined by p. We will not repeat that analysis, since it can be found in much of the other steganography literature including [2, 3, 5].

The overall evolution of sample pairs, from "pre-cover", through cover, to stego image, with the probability of each transition, is shown in Fig. 1. Note that transitions originating from $\mathcal{D}_m$ are of different structure depending on whether m is even or odd, because $\mathcal{E}_{2m}$ and $\mathcal{O}_{2m}$ can be interchanged by embedding whereas $\mathcal{E}_{2m+1}$ and $\mathcal{O}_{2m+1}$ cannot. Figure 1 is the foundation from which we will derive a likelihood for an observed stego image, given the sizes of the $\mathcal{D}_m$ in the pre-cover and p.

Consider for example the trace subset $\mathcal{E}_{2m+1}$ in the stego image. A sample pair has arrived there by one of four possible paths:

(i) Beginning in $\mathcal{D}_{2m}$ in the pre-cover, it was placed into $\mathcal{E}_{2m}$ in the cover and moved to $\mathcal{E}_{2m+1}$ under embedding; the probability of a pair beginning in $\mathcal{D}_{2m}$ making these transitions is $\frac{1}{2}\frac{p}{2}(1 - \frac{p}{2})$.

(ii) Beginning in $\mathcal{D}_{2m}$, it was placed into $\mathcal{O}_{2m}$ and moved to $\mathcal{E}_{2m+1}$ under embedding; again the probability of a pair in $\mathcal{D}_{2m}$ making such transitions is $\frac{1}{2}\frac{p}{2}(1 - \frac{p}{2})$.

(iii) Beginning in $\mathcal{D}_{2m+1}$, it was placed into $\mathcal{E}_{2m+1}$ and did not move under embedding; the probability of a pair in $\mathcal{D}_{2m+1}$ doing so is $\frac{1}{2}(1 - \frac{p}{2})^2$.

(iv) Beginning in $\mathcal{D}_{2m-1}$, it was placed into $\mathcal{O}_{2m-1}$ and moved to $\mathcal{E}_{2m+1}$ under embedding; the probability of a pair in $\mathcal{D}_{2m+1}$ doing so is $\frac{1}{2}(\frac{p}{2})^2$.

Similar calculations can be carried out for all trace subsets $\mathcal{E}_m$ and $\mathcal{O}_m$: each can have arisen from one of three of the $\mathcal{D}_m$ in the pre-cover. We display these probabilities in Tab. 1, with the columns corresponding to the source $\mathcal{D}_m$ and the rows to the $\mathcal{E}_m$ and $\mathcal{O}_m$ in the stego image. Therefore the full table, for 8 bit images, has 511 columns (trace subsets $\mathcal{D}_m$ exist for $-255 \leq m \leq 255$) and 1020 rows ($\mathcal{O}_{-255}, \mathcal{E}_{-254}, \mathcal{O}_{-254}, ..., \mathcal{E}_{254}, \mathcal{O}_{254}, \mathcal{E}_{255}$) and only a portion is displayed, from which the rest can be constructed. We have made the convenient abbreviation $\pi_i = \frac{1}{2}(\frac{p}{2})^i(1 - \frac{p}{2})^{2-i}$ for $i = 0, 1, 2$. Observe that fifth displayed row corresponds to our analysis, above, of trace subsets finishing in $\mathcal{E}_{2m+1}$.

Now suppose that an image is observed, with unknown payload. Let us form a vector of the observed sizes of trace subsets in the stego image, interleaving as $\boldsymbol{A}' = (O'_{-255}, E'_{-254}, O'_{-254}, ..., E'_{255})^T$, to correspond with the row labels of the complete table excerpted in Tab. 1. We write $\boldsymbol{p}_m$ for the column of Tab. 1 headed by the pre-cover trace subset $\mathcal{D}_m$ and suppose that the size of this subset was d_m. Because each sample pair beginning in the pre-cover must end up in some trace subset of the stego image, and under the assumption of random uncorrelated payload all destinations are independent, we have that the number of pairs in each trace subset originating from $\mathcal{D}_m$ takes a multinomial distribution. Summing up over all subsets $\mathcal{D}_m$ in the pre-cover, we thus deduce that $\boldsymbol{A}' = \sum_m \boldsymbol{A}'_m$, where each $\boldsymbol{A}'_m$ has a multinomial distribution with size parameter d_m and probability vector $\boldsymbol{p}_m$.

Table 1. Table showing the probability that, given a random payload of pN, each sample pair from a trace subset $\mathcal{D}_m$ in the pre-cover is observed in each trace subset $\mathcal{E}_m$ or $\mathcal{O}_m$ in a stego image

	$\mathcal{D}_{2m-1}$	$\mathcal{D}_{2m}$	$\mathcal{D}_{2m+1}$	$\mathcal{D}_{2m+2}$
$\mathcal{E}_{2m-1}$	π_0	0	0	0
$\mathcal{O}_{2m-1}$	π_0	$2\pi_1$	π_2	0
$\mathcal{E}_{2m}$	π_1	$\pi_0 + \pi_2$	π_1	0
$\mathcal{O}_{2m}$	π_1	$\pi_0 + \pi_2$	π_1	0
$\mathcal{E}_{2m+1}$	π_2	$2\pi_1$	π_0	0
$\mathcal{O}_{2m+1}$	0	0	π_0	$2\pi_1$
$\mathcal{E}_{2m+2}$	0	0	π_1	$\pi_0 + \pi_2$
$\mathcal{O}_{2m+2}$	0	0	π_1	$\pi_0 + \pi_2$
$\mathcal{E}_{2m+3}$	0	0	π_2	$2\pi_1$
$\mathcal{O}_{2m+3}$	0	0	0	0

In order to find the likelihood for this sum of distributions we make the standard multivariate Gaussian approximation to the multinomial distribution (generally accurate as long as the size of the original trace subset is not very small):

$$A \overset{.}{\sim} N(\boldsymbol{\mu}, \boldsymbol{\Sigma})$$

where $\boldsymbol{\mu} = \sum_m d_m \boldsymbol{p}_m$, $\boldsymbol{\Sigma} = \sum_m d_m (\boldsymbol{\Delta}_{\boldsymbol{p}_m} - \boldsymbol{p}_m \boldsymbol{p}_m^T)$, and $\boldsymbol{\Delta}_{\boldsymbol{v}}$ represents a diagonal matrix with $\boldsymbol{v}$ on the diagonal. This allows us to compute the (log-)likelihood that a given image with trace subsets $\boldsymbol{a}$ arose from a pre-cover with specific trace subset sizes $\boldsymbol{d}$ and a particular proportionate payload p:

$$l(\boldsymbol{a}; p, \boldsymbol{d}) = -\frac{L}{2}\log(2\pi) - \frac{1}{2}\log|\boldsymbol{\Sigma}| - \frac{1}{2}(\boldsymbol{a} - \boldsymbol{\mu})^T \boldsymbol{\Sigma}^{-1}(\boldsymbol{a} - \boldsymbol{\mu})$$

where L is the length of the vector of observations $\boldsymbol{a}$.

Although we omit the intermediate calculations, it is worthwhile to see the full form of the mean vector $\boldsymbol{\mu} = (\ldots, \mathrm{E}[O'_{2m-1}], \mathrm{E}[E'_{2m}], \mathrm{E}[O'_{2m}], \mathrm{E}[E'_{2m+1}], \ldots)^T$ and covariance matrix $\boldsymbol{\Sigma}$ whose entries are $\mathrm{Cov}[E'_m, O'_m]$. Extracting $\boldsymbol{p}_m$ from Tab. 1 and using $\boldsymbol{\mu} = \sum_m d_m \boldsymbol{p}_m$, we derive

$$\mathrm{E}[O'_{2m-1}] = \pi_0 d_{2m-1} + 2\pi_1 d_{2m} + \pi_2 d_{2m+1}$$
$$\mathrm{E}[E'_{2m}] = \pi_1(d_{2m-1} + d_{2m+1}) + (\pi_0 + \pi_2)d_{2m}$$
$$\mathrm{E}[O'_{2m}] = \pi_1(d_{2m-1} + d_{2m+1}) + (\pi_0 + \pi_2)d_{2m}$$
$$\mathrm{E}[E'_{2m+1}] = \pi_2 d_{2m-1} + 2\pi_1 d_{2m} + \pi_0 d_{2m+1}$$

for each m. From $\boldsymbol{\Sigma} = \sum_m d_m (\boldsymbol{\Delta}_{\boldsymbol{p}_m} - \boldsymbol{p}_m \boldsymbol{p}_m^T)$ we can compute all covariances; they are displayed in the following table. We make a further abbreviation, $\sigma = \pi_0 + \pi_2$, and elide the covariances of O'_{2m} (which are almost identical to those of E'_{2m}) in order to fit the table onto the page.

	O'_{2m-1}	E'_{2m}	O'_{2m}	E'_{2m+1}
O'_{2m-3}	$-\pi_0\pi_2 d_{2m-1}$	$-\pi_1\pi_2 d_{2m-1}$	←	$-\pi_2^2 d_{2m-1}$
E'_{2m-2}	$-\pi_0\pi_1 d_{2m-1}$	$-\pi_1^2 d_{2m-1}$	←	$-\pi_1\pi_2 d_{2m-1}$
O'_{2m-2}	$-\pi_0\pi_1 d_{2m-1}$	$-\pi_1^2 d_{2m-1}$	←	$-\pi_1\pi_2 d_{2m-1}$
E'_{2m-1}	$-\pi_0^2 d_{2m-1}$	$-\pi_0\pi_1 d_{2m-1}$	←	$-\pi_0\pi_2 d_{2m-1}$
O'_{2m-1}	$\pi_0(1-\pi_0)d_{2m-1}$ $+2\pi_1(1-2\pi_1)d_{2m}$ $+\pi_2(1-\pi_2)d_{2m+1}$	$-\pi_0\pi_1 d_{2m-1}$ $-2\pi_1\sigma d_{2m}$ $-\pi_1\pi_2 d_{2m+1}$	←	$-\pi_0\pi_2 d_{2m-1}$ $-4\pi_1^2 d_{2m}$ $-\pi_0\pi_2 d_{2m+1}$
E'_{2m}	$-\pi_0\pi_1 d_{2m-1}$ $-2\pi_1\sigma d_{2m}$ $-\pi_1\pi_2 d_{2m+1}$	$\pi_1(1-\pi_1)d_{2m-1}$ $+\sigma(1-\sigma)d_{2m}$ $+\pi_1(1-\pi_1)d_{2m+1}$	╱	$-\pi_1\pi_2 d_{2m-1}$ $-2\pi_1\sigma d_{2m}$ $-\pi_0\pi_1 d_{2m+1}$
O'_{2m}	$-\pi_0\pi_1 d_{2m-1}$ $-2\pi_1\sigma d_{2m}$ $-\pi_1\pi_2 d_{2m+1}$	$-\pi_1^2 d_{2m-1}$ $-\sigma^2 d_{2m}$ $-\pi_1^2 d_{2m+1}$	╲	$-\pi_1\pi_2 d_{2m-1}$ $-2\pi_1\sigma d_{2m}$ $-\pi_0\pi_1 d_{2m+1}$
E'_{2m+1}	$-\pi_0\pi_2 d_{2m-1}$ $-4\pi_1^2 d_{2m}$ $-\pi_0\pi_2 d_{2m+1}$	$-\pi_1\pi_2 d_{2m-1}$ $-2\pi_1\sigma d_{2m}$ $-\pi_0\pi_1 d_{2m+1}$	←	$\pi_2(1-\pi_2)d_{2m-1}$ $+2\pi_1(1-2\pi_1)d_{2m}$ $+\pi_0(1-\pi_0)d_{2m+1}$
O'_{2m+1}	$-\pi_0\pi_2 d_{2m+1}$	$-\pi_0\pi_1 d_{2m+1}$	←	$-\pi_0^2 d_{2m+1}$
E'_{2m+2}	$-\pi_1\pi_2 d_{2m+1}$	$-\pi_1^2 d_{2m+1}$	←	$-\pi_0\pi_1 d_{2m+1}$
O'_{2m+2}	$-\pi_1\pi_2 d_{2m+1}$	$-\pi_1^2 d_{2m+1}$	←	$-\pi_0\pi_1 d_{2m+1}$
E'_{2m+3}	$-\pi_2^2 d_{2m+1}$	$-\pi_1\pi_2 d_{2m+1}$	←	$-\pi_0\pi_2 d_{2m+1}$

These hold for all m, and other covariances are zero. Although fairly appalling to look at, the matrix can quickly be computed from p and d.

It is worthwhile to contrast the principle of structural ML estimation with the standard structural estimators. Consider, for example, [2]: the cover model used there (with a minor variation) is that $|\mathcal{E}_{2m+1}| = |\mathcal{O}_{2m+1}|$ for each m. In Fig. 1 we can see that this is true *in expectation*, but a more sophisticated model can quantify deviations from exact equality. Similarly, the standard structural analysis of embedding is the same as the transitions from cover to stego object in Fig. 1, but it assumes that the observed stego image trace subset sizes are exactly their expectation, not allowing for random variation. The ML method allows us, in effect, to take account of the fact that such approximations are more accurate when the numbers involved are larger. Finally, the principle of least-squares estimation [3, 7] is optimal if the random variables whose least squares are minimized are Gaussian and independent. Under our model they are Gaussian, but considering the covariance matrix Σ, one can show that the relevant quantities are not independent, and hence least-squares steganalysis is, at best, an approximation to optimality.

3.2   Implementing a ML Estimator

In principle, the rest is simple: given an image we observe the trace subsets a and find the value of p (along with, as nuisance parameters, all the d) which maximizes the log-likelihood. In practice there are some difficulties.

First, how to find the maximum? There is no apparent closed form for it so we must proceed numerically. The function is differentiable, but computing the derivative (particularly with respect to p) seems extremely difficult and we have not yet completed the calculation. This prevents us from using standard iterative/scoring methods to locate the maximum. So that we can test the accuracy of a structural ML detector, without being unduly distracted by implementation issues, we have settled on a temporary, computationally expensive, solution: the maximization method of Nelder and Mead [15] which walks a simplex through the surface to be optimized and does not require derivatives. Of course, such a method converges only slowly to a maximum. We must also find a point from which to start the optimization: we used one of the standard methods for estimating LSB replacement payload [2] as an initial value of p, and created initial values for $\boldsymbol{d}$ by inverting the second half of the transition diagram in Fig. 1 (such an inversion is already part of the standard method for structural steganalysis of LSB replacement).

Unfortunately, maximization of the full likelihood function is computationally unfeasible: it is a 512-dimensional problem, which is simply too complex to optimize in any reasonable amount of time. But we can cheaply reduce the dimensionality by discarding the parameters d_m for $|m|$ large: very few adjacent pairs of pixels have a large difference, and discarding a minority of pairs does not reduce the evidential base too much. We found that considering only $\mathcal{D}_{-11}$ to $\mathcal{D}_{11}$ still gave excellent performance (in our test set of cover images, 75.1% of sample pairs are found in this range) and reduces the dimensionality of the maximization to 24.

We can further ameliorate the computational cost by evaluating the log-likelihood efficiently: because the matrix in Tab. 1 has many zeros (recall that each trace subset in the stego image can come from only one of three subsets in the pre-cover) the covariance matrix $\boldsymbol{\Sigma}$ is zero except near to the diagonal and there exist efficient methods to compute $|\boldsymbol{\Sigma}|$ and $(\boldsymbol{a} - \boldsymbol{\mu})^T \boldsymbol{\Sigma}^{-1} (\boldsymbol{a} - \boldsymbol{\mu})$ exploiting the *Cholesky decomposition* of $\boldsymbol{\Sigma}$.

A final improvement is to observe that $\mathcal{E}_{2m}$ and $\mathcal{O}_{2m}$ are always treated equally in Tab. 1, $\boldsymbol{\mu}$, and $\boldsymbol{\Sigma}$. This means that it is safe to combine such subsets, observing and computing likelihood of only the sum $E'_{2m} + O'_{2m}$, but still separating E'_{2m+1} and O'_{2m+1}. This leaves the dimensionality of the maximization unchanged, but reduces the size of the quadratic form which must be computed for each evaluation of the likelihood, from $L = 44$ to $L = 33$.

Nonetheless the ML estimator is still quite slow due to the inefficient maximization method. Using a moderately-optimized implementation in C, and a computer with a 64-bit processor running at 2Ghz, we timed the standard *SPA* estimator [2], a least-squares variant *Couples/LSM* [3], and our new *Couples/ML* estimator, on various image sizes. The results are displayed in Tab. 2; observe that the size of the images is almost irrelevant to the ML estimator which spends almost all of its time maximizing the likelihood function, whereas the standard methods spend most of their time simply counting the trace subsets and hence their time complexity is roughly linear in the image size.

Table 2. Images processed per second, for three detectors and three image sizes

Detector	Image size		
	0.5Mpixel	1.0Mpixel	1.5Mpixel
SPA	36.1	21.0	15.11
Couples/LSM	36.7	21.5	15.26
Couples/ML	0.401	0.392	0.387

There still remains a difficulty with implementing the estimator. As p tends to zero, the covariance matrix Σ becomes singular. Thus the likelihood function can grow without bound as p approaches zero, if the d are chosen in a certain way, and the likelihood optimizer can find its way to an incorrect "solution". This is a standard problem and can be seen as either overfitting – some of the observed trace subsets can match their expectations with arbitrarily good accuracy, at the expense of others – or a breakdown in the multivariate Gaussian approximation to the multinomial when the probabilities involved are small. The common solution is to place a prior distribution on the difficult parameter (here p) and convert the ML estimator to a maximum a posteriori (MAP) estimator. If the prior is Gaussian this amounts to placing a quadratic penalty on the log-likelihood function.

We already needed to find another estimate $\hat{p}$ from which to begin the optimization, and found that using a Gaussian prior with mean $\hat{p}$ and variance $\hat{p}^2/100$ (knowing that we want to keep the estimator away from $p = 0$ without fixing it too closely to the less-accurate prior estimate) was an effective solution.

3.3   Experimental Results

We now benchmark the MAP estimator *Couples/ML* against the best of the other structural detectors based on pairs of pixels: *SPA* [2], *Couples/LSM* (in the form described in [7]) and a new weighted least-squares version *Couples/WLSM* [16]. We report only results which use a set of 3000 never-compressed grayscale covers, which have been downsampled to approximately 0.3Mpixels from scanned high-resolution originals. LSB replacement steganography was simulated with embedding rates $0, 0.05, \ldots 1$, and accuracy of the resulting estimates compared.

Making a comparison of estimator accuracy is not quite straightforward because the shape of error distribution is not necessarily the same for all estimators. Therefore it can be misleading to compare, for example, only mean-square error (such a measure will heavily penalize estimators with a few large outliers) or only interquartile range (which is completely insensitive to outliers). Furthermore, there is both estimator bias (least-squares estimators consistently underestimate large payloads) and spread to consider.

We will display a number of measures in order to give a balanced assessment: mean-square error encompasses both bias and spread, sample mean estimates

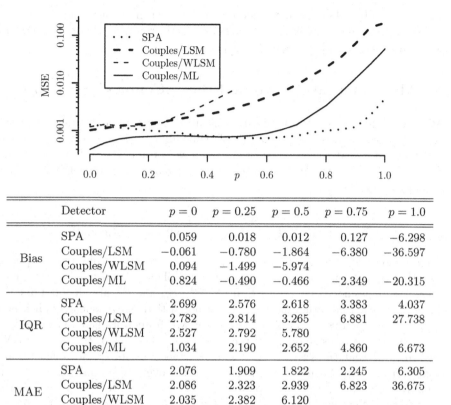

	Detector	$p = 0$	$p = 0.25$	$p = 0.5$	$p = 0.75$	$p = 1.0$
Bias	SPA	0.059	0.018	0.012	0.127	−6.298
	Couples/LSM	−0.061	−0.780	−1.864	−6.380	−36.597
	Couples/WLSM	0.094	−1.499	−5.974		
	Couples/ML	0.824	−0.490	−0.466	−2.349	−20.315
IQR	SPA	2.699	2.576	2.618	3.383	4.037
	Couples/LSM	2.782	2.814	3.265	6.881	27.738
	Couples/WLSM	2.527	2.792	5.780		
	Couples/ML	1.034	2.190	2.652	4.860	6.673
MAE	SPA	2.076	1.909	1.822	2.245	6.305
	Couples/LSM	2.086	2.323	2.939	6.823	36.675
	Couples/WLSM	2.035	2.382	6.120		
	Couples/ML	0.826	1.725	1.843	3.525	21.039

Fig. 2. Above, chart displaying how the estimator mean-square error (MSE; log axis) of the structural detectors depends on the proportionate payload p. Below, table displaying other measures of estimator accuracy: sample bias, interquartile range (IQR), mean absolute error (MAE), all displayed $\times 10^2$, for five payload sizes.

bias, interquartile range is a measure of spread without regard to outliers, and mean absolute error is a combination measure which is robust but not insensitive to outliers. The first of these is charted, and the others tabulated, in Fig. 2.

Observe that the *Couples/ML* estimator is uniformly superior to both *Couples/LSM* and *Couples/WLSM* (the latter is not benchmarked for proportionate payloads greater than 50% because its "optimal" weighting depends on the true payload being small). It is also superior to the standard *SPA* method for payloads $p < 0.5$, and particularly for very small payloads. Of course, in some applications the increased computational costs of the maximization will outweigh the accuracy advantages. The slight positive bias at zero payloads, for the ML method, is because negative estimates can never happen.

It is curious that one of the very first payload estimators, which claims no optimality, should appear the best performer for large payloads. In fact this can be explained by reference to a weakness in the cover model used here, which the standard SPA method coincidentally does exactly the right thing to avoid, but such an explanation is beyond the scope of this work.

4   Maximum Likelihood and the "2Couples" Structure

We now outline the extension of ML structural analysis to embedding in the two lowest bit planes; this was called "2LSB" embedding in [7], where a least-squares structural steganalyzer was presented. Again we consider pairs of pixels evolving from a "pre-cover" through a cover to a stego-image. The trace subsets, which we re-use from [7], are

$$\mathcal{D}_m = \{(j, k) \in \mathcal{P} \mid s_k = s_j + m\}$$
$$\mathcal{B}_m^i = \{(j, k) \in \mathcal{P} \mid s_k = s_j + m, \text{ with } s_j \equiv i \ (\text{mod } 4)\}$$

for $i = 0, 1, 2, 3$. They serve the same purpose as in the Couples case, exposing exactly the structure of replacement of two bit planes. Traditional least-squares steganalysis assumes that the sizes of $\mathcal{B}_m^0$, $\mathcal{B}_m^1$, $\mathcal{B}_m^2$ and $\mathcal{B}_m^3$ are all equal in cover images, for each m, although in [7] it was noted that not all such equalities are useful for steganalysis – a difficulty that the ML framework is able to avoid.

As before, we must model differences between the sizes of $\mathcal{B}_m^i$ in covers. We will imagine that the "pre-cover" has fixed trace subsets $\mathcal{D}_m$ for each m, and that every pair in $\mathcal{D}_m$ moves to one of $\mathcal{B}_m^i$ in the cover object, independently and equiprobably. Again, this corresponds with traditional structural steganalysis in expectation. Next, embedding a payload of length $2pN$ (or randomizing the two least bits of each pixel with probability p) causes the 16 trace subsets $\mathcal{B}_{4m}^0$, $\mathcal{B}_{4m+1}^0$, $\mathcal{B}_{4m+2}^0$, $\mathcal{B}_{4m+3}^0$ $\mathcal{B}_{4m-1}^1$, $\mathcal{B}_{4m}^1$, $\mathcal{B}_{4m+1}^1$, $\mathcal{B}_{4m+2}^1$ $\mathcal{B}_{4m-2}^2$, $\mathcal{B}_{4m-1}^2$, $\mathcal{B}_{4m}^2$, $\mathcal{B}_{4m+1}^2$ $\mathcal{B}_{4m-3}^3$, $\mathcal{B}_{4m-2}^3$, $\mathcal{B}_{4m-1}^3$, $\mathcal{B}_{4m}^3$ to be permuted with certain probabilities, which are described in [7] and will not be repeated here.

The added complexity means that we cannot fit in a diagram analogous to Fig. 1: a pair in $\mathcal{D}_m$ in the pre-cover can move to any one of 32 trace subsets in the stego image. We will skip directly to the analogue of Tab. 1, which we display in Tab. 3 using the abbreviation $\pi_i = \frac{1}{4}(\frac{p}{4})^i(1 - \frac{3p}{4})^{2-i}$.

It would be horrendous to display the mean and covariance matrices here, which are much more complex than those in Sect. 3, and we omit all calculations. But the principle of ML estimation can now proceed as in the previous section: concatenate the observed trace subset sizes into a vector $\boldsymbol{a}$, and maximize the log-likelihood function

$$l(\boldsymbol{a}; p, \boldsymbol{d}) = -\frac{L}{2} \log(2\pi) - \frac{1}{2} \log |\boldsymbol{\Sigma}| - \frac{1}{2}(\boldsymbol{a} - \boldsymbol{\mu})^T \boldsymbol{\Sigma}^{-1}(\boldsymbol{a} - \boldsymbol{\mu})$$

where $\boldsymbol{\mu} = \sum_m d_m \boldsymbol{p}_m$, $\boldsymbol{\Sigma} = \sum_m d_m(\boldsymbol{\Delta}_{\boldsymbol{p}_m} - \boldsymbol{p}_m \boldsymbol{p}_m^T)$, and $\boldsymbol{p}_m$ are the columns of Tab. 3. We must convert to a MAP estimator to avoid overfitting (the same prior is appropriate) and again we find it necessary to reduce the dimensionality of the optimization by considering only $\mathcal{D}_{-11}$ to $\mathcal{D}_{11}$, for a 24 dimensional surface.

Table 3. Table showing the probability that, given a random payload of $2pN$ embedded by 2LSB replacement, each sample pair from a trace subset $\mathcal{D}_m$ in the pre-cover is observed in each trace subset $\mathcal{B}^i_m$ in a stego image

	$\mathcal{D}_{4m-3}$	$\mathcal{D}_{4m-2}$	$\mathcal{D}_{4m-1}$	$\mathcal{D}_{4m}$	$\mathcal{D}_{4m+1}$	$\mathcal{D}_{4m+2}$	$\mathcal{D}_{4m+3}$
$\mathcal{B}^3_{4m-3}$	π_0	$2\pi_1$	$2\pi_1+\pi_2$	$2\pi_1+2\pi_2$	$3\pi_2$	$2\pi_2$	π_2
$\mathcal{B}^3_{4m-2}$	π_1	$\pi_0+\pi_2$	$2\pi_1+\pi_2$	$2\pi_1+2\pi_2$	$\pi_1+2\pi_2$	$2\pi_2$	π_2
$\mathcal{B}^3_{4m-1}$	π_1	$\pi_1+\pi_2$	$\pi_0+2\pi_2$	$2\pi_1+2\pi_2$	$\pi_1+2\pi_2$	$\pi_1+\pi_2$	π_2
$\mathcal{B}^3_{4m}$	π_1	$\pi_1+\pi_2$	$\pi_1+2\pi_2$	$\pi_0+3\pi_2$	$\pi_1+2\pi_2$	$\pi_1+\pi_2$	π_1
$\mathcal{B}^2_{4m-2}$	π_1	$\pi_0+\pi_2$	$2\pi_1+\pi_2$	$2\pi_1+2\pi_2$	$\pi_1+2\pi_2$	$2\pi_2$	π_2
$\mathcal{B}^2_{4m-1}$	π_2	$2\pi_1$	$\pi_0+2\pi_2$	$2\pi_1+2\pi_2$	$2\pi_1+\pi_2$	$2\pi_2$	π_2
$\mathcal{B}^2_{4m}$	π_2	$\pi_1+\pi_2$	$2\pi_1+\pi_2$	$\pi_0+3\pi_2$	$2\pi_1+\pi_2$	$\pi_1+\pi_2$	π_2
$\mathcal{B}^2_{4m+1}$	π_2	$\pi_1+\pi_2$	$\pi_1+2\pi_2$	$2\pi_1+2\pi_2$	$\pi_0+2\pi_2$	$\pi_1+\pi_2$	π_1
$\mathcal{B}^1_{4m-1}$	π_1	$\pi_1+\pi_2$	$\pi_0+2\pi_2$	$2\pi_1+2\pi_2$	$\pi_1+2\pi_2$	$\pi_1+\pi_2$	π_2
$\mathcal{B}^1_{4m}$	π_2	$\pi_1+\pi_2$	$2\pi_1+\pi_2$	$\pi_0+3\pi_2$	$2\pi_1+\pi_2$	$\pi_1+\pi_2$	π_2
$\mathcal{B}^1_{4m+1}$	π_2	$2\pi_2$	$2\pi_1+\pi_2$	$2\pi_1+2\pi_2$	$\pi_0+2\pi_2$	$2\pi_1$	π_2
$\mathcal{B}^1_{4m+2}$	π_2	$2\pi_2$	$\pi_1+2\pi_2$	$2\pi_1+2\pi_2$	$2\pi_1+\pi_2$	$\pi_0+\pi_2$	π_1
$\mathcal{B}^0_{4m}$	π_1	$\pi_1+\pi_2$	$\pi_1+2\pi_2$	$\pi_0+3\pi_2$	$\pi_1+2\pi_2$	$\pi_1+\pi_2$	π_1
$\mathcal{B}^0_{4m+1}$	π_2	$\pi_1+\pi_2$	$\pi_1+2\pi_2$	$2\pi_1+2\pi_2$	$\pi_0+2\pi_2$	$\pi_1+\pi_2$	π_1
$\mathcal{B}^0_{4m+2}$	π_2	$2\pi_2$	$\pi_1+2\pi_2$	$2\pi_1+2\pi_2$	$2\pi_1+\pi_2$	$\pi_0+\pi_2$	π_1
$\mathcal{B}^0_{4m+3}$	π_2	$2\pi_2$	$3\pi_2$	$2\pi_1+2\pi_2$	$2\pi_1+\pi_2$	$2\pi_1$	π_0

But there are twice as many trace subsets to count and there is less symmetry than before, so each evaluation of the likelihood involves a quadratic form of dimension 80; accordingly the estimator is even slower than that of the previous section (about ten times slower, in our poorly-optimized implementation).

We benchmark this MAP estimator for 2LSB replacement, which we call *2Couples/ML*, against the least-squares version *2Couples/LSM* [7]. We also include another detector of multiple bit plane replacement, which is a modification of the method known as *WS* and found in [17] (we will call it *2LSB WS*). Results for the corresponding experiments to those in Sect. 3 are displayed in Fig. 3.

Observe that the new estimator is many times more accurate than the others, except for very large payloads. It remains more accurate than the LSM detector for all embedding rates, but above proportionate payloads of about 80% the WS-based detector is the only one not to suffer from weak performance (this seems to be a general feature of WS detectors, and their area of strength). Clearly the method of maximum likelihood has made a vast improvement to the reliability of payload estimation, particularly in the difficult case of small payloads.

5   Maximum Likelihood and the "Triples" Structure

Finally, we sketch how the ML technique can be applied to a more intricate structural analysis of (single plane) LSB replacement, based on triplets of pixels.

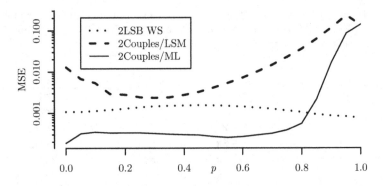

	Detector	$p = 0$	$p = 0.25$	$p = 0.5$	$p = 0.75$	$p = 1.0$
	2LSB WS	0.148	1.612	2.033	1.535	0.093
Bias	2Couples/LSM	0.806	−0.990	−2.765	−10.243	−20.521
	2Couples/ML	0.600	−0.239	−0.094	−0.374	4.806
	2LSB WS	3.466	3.912	4.129	3.658	2.991
IQR	2Couples/LSM	1.905	1.954	2.849	9.270	41.608
	2Couples/ML	0.774	1.488	1.599	2.192	41.863
	2LSB WS	2.341	2.828	3.050	2.647	2.028
MAE	2Couples/LSM	2.624	1.921	3.154	10.371	20.521
	2Couples/ML	0.601	1.134	1.116	1.456	28.516

Fig. 3. Above, chart displaying how the MSE (log axis) of the *2Couples/LSM* structural estimator [7], *2LSB WS* [17], and the proposed *2Couples/ML* estimator, depends on the proportionate payload p. Below, table displaying other measures of estimator accuracy: sample bias, IQR, and MAE, all displayed $\times 10^2$, for five payload sizes.

Let $\mathcal{T}$ be the set of horizontal groups of three adjacent pixels with notation analogous to Sects. 3 and 4, and define trace subsets as follows:

$$\mathcal{D}_{m,n} = \{(j, k, l) \in \mathcal{T} \mid s_k = s_j + m, s_l = s_k + n\}$$
$$\mathcal{E}_{m,n} = \{(j, k, l) \in \mathcal{T} \mid s_k = s_j + m, s_l = s_k + n, \text{ with } s_j \text{ even}\}$$
$$\mathcal{O}_{m,n} = \{(j, k, l) \in \mathcal{T} \mid s_k = s_j + m, s_l = s_k + n, \text{ with } s_j \text{ odd}\}$$

These capture the third-order effects of replacing LSBs; in covers we expect that $\mathcal{E}_{m,n}$ and $\mathcal{O}_{m,n}$ will be of approximately equal size, and the corresponding least-squares structural payload estimators [5] are generally (although not uniformly) more accurate than those based on Couples structure.

For an ML detector we again imagine that $\mathcal{E}_{m,n}$ and $\mathcal{O}_{m,n}$ derive binomially from $\mathcal{D}_{m,n}$. This time it is the eight trace subsets $\mathcal{O}_{2m-1,2n}$, $\mathcal{O}_{2m-1,2n+1}$, $\mathcal{E}_{2m,2n}$, $\mathcal{E}_{2m,2n+1}$, $\mathcal{O}_{2m,2n-1}$, $\mathcal{O}_{2m,2n}$, $\mathcal{E}_{2m+1,2n-1}$, $\mathcal{E}_{2m+1,2n}$ which are permuted by LSB operations – see [5] for the transition probabilities – and the analogy to Tab. 1 is displayed in part in Tab. 4. All instances of the displayed transitions make up

Table 4. Extract from table showing probabilities of transition from pre-cover trace subsets to stego object trace subset, when the Triples structure is analyzed

	$\mathcal{D}_{2m-1,}$ $2n$	$\mathcal{D}_{2m-1}$ $2n+1$	$\mathcal{D}_{2m}$ $2n-1$	$\mathcal{D}_{2m}$ $2n$	$\mathcal{D}_{2n}$ $2n+1$	$\mathcal{D}_{2m+1}$ $2n-1$	$\mathcal{D}_{2m+1}$ $2n$
$\mathcal{O}_{2m-1,2n}$	π_0	π_1	π_1	$\pi_1 + \pi_2$	π_2	π_2	π_3
$\mathcal{O}_{2m-1,2n+1}$	π_1	π_0	π_2	$\pi_1 + \pi_2$	π_1	π_3	π_2
$\mathcal{E}_{2m,2n}$	π_1	π_2	π_2	$\pi_0 + \pi_3$	π_1	π_1	π_2
$\mathcal{E}_{2m,2n+1}$	π_2	π_1	π_3	$\pi_1 + \pi_2$	π_0	π_2	π_1
$\mathcal{O}_{2m,2n-1}$	π_1	π_2	π_0	$\pi_1 + \pi_2$	π_3	π_1	π_2
$\mathcal{O}_{2m,2n}$	π_2	π_1	π_1	$\pi_0 + \pi_3$	π_2	π_2	π_1
$\mathcal{E}_{2m+1,2n-1}$	π_2	π_3	π_1	$\pi_1 + \pi_2$	π_2	π_0	π_1
$\mathcal{E}_{2m+1,2n}$	π_3	π_2	π_2	$\pi_1 + \pi_2$	π_1	π_1	π_0

the complete table and the abbreviation is $\pi_i = \frac{1}{2}(\frac{p}{2})^i(1 - \frac{p}{2})^{3-i}$. Then a MAP estimator can be derived in the same way as for Couples and 2Couples structure.

The optimization problem for this likelihood is much harder than those occurring in Sects. 3 and 4, because the number of nuisance parameters (the sizes of $\mathcal{D}_{m,n}$ in the pre-cover) is squared by the finer categorization of pixel differences. We must radically reduce the number of subsets under consideration in order to achieve a tractable optimization. For now we consider only $|m| \leq 3$ and $|n| \leq 3$, but only 36.1% of sample triplets in our test covers are found in this range so we are ignoring quite a large proportion of the evidence. Even so, this leads to 48 dimensional optimization problem, and each likelihood evaluation involves a quadratic form of length 72, so this *Triples/ML* estimator is much slower to evaluate than *Couples/ML* of Sect. 3 (over a minute per image).

Because of its complexity we have not yet conducted as full benchmarks as for *Couples/ML* and *2Couples/ML*. Some reduced experiments are reported in Fig. 4. In order to make a fair comparison with least-squares Triples [5] (denoted *Triples/LSM*) we weakened the standard estimator by similarly limiting it to trace subsets with maximum absolute index of 3. The experimental results indicate that the *Triples/ML* estimator is more accurate only for small payloads, with the critical payload being somewhere between 25% and 50%. It is not clear that the performance gain is worth the hugely inflated computational costs.

6 Conclusions and Directions for Further Research

Bringing together the statistical foundations of the maximum likelihood method with the sensitivity of structural steganalysis has been fruitful in terms of new and more accurate payload estimators for bit replacement steganography. At the moment there is a large computational cost associated with maximizing the likelihood function, but it is likely to be significantly reduced when the function is differentiated. There is no fundamental bar to this: the problem is only one

	Detector	$p = 0$	$p = 0.1$	$p = 0.25$	$p = 0.5$
Bias	Triples/LSM⁻	−0.128	−0.478	−0.857	−0.326
	Triples/ML	0.785	−0.695	−0.828	−1.031
IQR	Triples/LSM⁻	3.127	3.262	3.495	1.914
	Triples/ML	0.957	1.998	2.537	2.631
MAE	Triples/LSM⁻	2.362	2.584	2.899	1.522
	Triples/ML	0.785	1.750	1.990	2.027
MSE	Triples/LSM⁻	0.153	0.182	0.237	0.076
	Triples/ML	0.042	0.074	0.099	0.095

Fig. 4. Comparison of estimator accuracy for weakened *Triples/LSM* (denoted *Triples/LSM⁻*) and *Triples/ML* methods, with four payload sizes

of algebraic complexity. Another possibility for reducing the complexity is to formulate a parametric model for the pixel difference parameters d. However, no such model will be perfect and inaccuracies modelling d could damage the accuracy of the ML estimator.

Regardless of computational cost, there is a certain elegance to the combined method, particularly in that it avoids the potentially extremely complex question of which equalities between trace subsets should be included in the cover model. We believe that the ML foundation provides the "ultimate" structural steganalyzers and that, once the efficiency is improved and one hole in the cover model patched, these detectors will be the last and best bit replacement detectors.

The next application of a likelihood calculation might be the development of a likelihood ratio test for the presence of hidden data (it may also be possible to develop tests for which type of bit replacement – LSB, 2LSB, etc – have been used). In some preliminary experiments we did implement such a detector but its performance was disappointing – as a classifier for the presence or absence of hidden data it was better to use simply the payload estimate. Very likely this is because of the necessity of imposing a prior distribution, to avoid overfitting, so that the usual generalized likelihood ratio statistic is not available.

We should note, though, that there is no guarantee of complete optimality with maximum likelihood estimators, let alone the MAP estimator we have to use in practice: their unbiased and minimum variance properties only apply asymptotically. Indeed for a single image we have only one observation of the trace subset sizes which make up the multinomial likelihood, although it can be seen as many observations: the type of each sample pair or triplet. Finally, the trace subsets used here have been demonstrated highly sensitive but this does not completely preclude the possibility that better feature sets exist.

Even so, the experimental results included in this paper demonstrate that the fusion of ML methods with structural analysis has practical value as well as a well-principled derivation.

Acknowledgements

The author is a Royal Society University Research Fellow.

References

1. Fridrich, J., Goljan, M., Du, R.: Detecting LSB steganography in color and grayscale images. IEEE Multimedia 8, 22–28 (2001)
2. Dumitrescu, S., Wu, X., Wang, Z.: Detection of LSB steganography via sample pair analysis. IEEE Transactions on Signal Processing 51, 1995–2007 (2003)
3. Lu, P., Luo, X., Tang, Q., Shen, L.: An improved sample pairs method for detection of LSB embedding. In: Fridrich, J. (ed.) IH 2004. LNCS, vol. 3200, pp. 116–127. Springer, Heidelberg (2004)
4. Dumitrescu, S., Wu, X.: A new framework of LSB steganalysis of digital media. IEEE Transactions on Signal Processing 53, 3936–3947 (2005)
5. Ker, A.: A general framework for the structural steganalysis of LSB replacement. In: Barni, M., Herrera-Joancomartí, J., Katzenbeisser, S., Pérez-González, F. (eds.) IH 2005. LNCS, vol. 3727, pp. 296–311. Springer, Heidelberg (2005)
6. Ker, A.: Fourth-order structural steganalysis and analysis of cover assumptions. In: Security, Steganography and Watermarking of Multimedia Contents VIII. Proc. SPIE, vol. 6072, pp. 25–38 (2006)
7. Ker, A.: Steganalysis of embedding in two least significant bits. IEEE Transactions on Information Forensics and Security 2, 46–54 (2007)
8. Dabeer, O., Sullivan, K., Madhow, U., Chandrasekaran, S., Manjunath, B.: Detection of hiding in the least significant bit. IEEE Transactions on Signal Processing 52, 3046–3058 (2004)
9. Hogan, M., Hurley, N., Silvestre, G., Balado, F., Whelan, K.: ML detection of steganography. In: Security, Steganography and Watermarking of Multimedia Contents VII. Proc. SPIE, vol. 5681, pp. 16–27 (2005)
10. Draper, S., Ishwar, P., Molnar, D., Prabhakaran, V., Ramchandran, K., Schonberg, D., Wagner, D.: An analysis of empirical PMF based tests for least significant bit image steganography. In: Barni, M., Herrera-Joancomartí, J., Katzenbeisser, S., Pérez-González, F. (eds.) IH 2005. LNCS, vol. 3727, pp. 327–341. Springer, Heidelberg (2005)
11. Sullivan, K., Madhow, U., Chandrasekaran, S., Manjunath, B.: Steganalysis for Markov cover data with applications to images. IEEE Transactions on Information Forensics and Security 1, 275–287 (2006)
12. Ker, A.: A fusion of maximum likelihood and structural steganalysis, extended technical report in preparation (2007)
13. Ker, A.: Derivation of error distribution in least-squares steganalysis. IEEE Transactions on Information Forensics and Security 2, 140–148 (2007)
14. Fridrich, J., Soukal, D.: Matrix embedding for large payloads. In: Security, Steganography and Watermarking of Multimedia Contents VIII. Proc. SPIE, vol. 6072 (2006)
15. Nelder, J., Mead, R.: A simplex algorithm for function minimization. Computer Journal 7, 308–313 (1965)
16. Ker, A.: Optimally weighted least-squares steganalysis. In: Security, Steganography and Watermarking of Multimedia Contents IX. Proc. SPIE, vol. 6505 (2007)
17. Yu, X., Tan, T., Wang, Y.: Extended optimization method of LSB steganalysis. In: Proc. IEEE International Conference on Image Processing, vol. 2, pp. 1102–1105 (2005)

Traffic Analysis Attacks on a Continuously-Observable Steganographic File System

Carmela Troncoso, Claudia Diaz, Orr Dunkelman, and Bart Preneel

K.U.Leuven, ESAT/COSIC,
Kasteelpark Arenberg 10, B-3001 Leuven-Heverlee, Belgium
firstname.lastname@esat.kuleuven.be

Abstract. A continuously-observable steganographic file system allows to remotely store user files on a raw storage device; the security goal is to offer plausible deniability even when the raw storage device is continuously monitored by an attacker. Zhou, Pang and Tan have proposed such a system in [7] with a claim of provable security against traffic analysis. In this paper, we disprove their claims by presenting traffic analysis attacks on the file update algorithm of Zhou *et al*. Our attacks are highly effective in detecting file updates and revealing the existence and location of files. For multi-block files, we show that two updates are sufficient to discover the file. One-block files accessed a sufficient number of times can also be revealed. Our results suggest that simple randomization techniques are not sufficient to protect steganographic file systems from traffic analysis attacks.

1 Introduction

The goal of a steganographic file system is to protect the user from compulsion attacks, where the user is forced to hand over file decryption keys under the threat of legal sanctions or physical intimidation. In order to achieve this goal, the steganographic file system must conceal the files it stores, so that the user can plausibly deny their very existence.

Several proposals in the literature provide plausible deniability to the user against attackers that take one or more snapshots of the raw storage. To the best of our knowledge, the proposal by Zhou *et al*. [7] is the only one that claims to resist attackers who can continuously monitor accesses to the storage. It relies on dummy updates and relocations of data that are supposed to conceal accesses to the hidden files.

Zhou *et al*. [7] present two separate mechanisms for reading and updating files; we present traffic analysis attacks which are effective against the file update mechanism. Our attacks succeed in revealing the existence and location of hidden files, depriving the user of plausible deniability. We describe the theory behind the attacks, and the impact of the system's parameters on their effectiveness. We have also simulated the attacks, and obtained empirical results that confirm our theoretical analysis.

T. Furon et al. (Eds.): IH 2007, LNCS 4567, pp. 220–236, 2007.

The rest of this paper is organized as follows: in Sect. 2, we summarize previous work on steganographic file systems. Section 3 describes the update algorithm of [7]. Section 4 explains theoretically how to attack the system. The empirical results of our implementation are presented in Sect. 5. We present our conclusions in Sect. 6, where we also suggest lines for future research. Finally, Appendix A shows the attack algorithms that have been used in our implementation.

2   Related Work

The concept of a steganographic file system was first proposed by Anderson, Needham and Shamir in [1] together with two implementations. The first approach consists of hiding the information in cover files such that it can be retrieved by XOR-ing a subset of them. In the second approach, the file system is filled with random data and the real files are hidden by writing the encrypted blocks in pseudo-random locations derived from the name of the file and a password.

Kuhn and McDonald proposed StegFS in [5]. They use a block allocation table (BAT) to have control over the file system contents. In this table, each entry is encrypted with the same key as the block it corresponds to. The file system is organized in levels in such a way that opening a level (decrypting all the entries in the BAT) opens also all the lower levels.

There is another proposal called StegFS by Zhou, Pang and Tan in [6]. This scheme tracks for each block of the file system whether it is free or it has been allocated. Each hidden file has a header placed in a pseudo-random free location derived from its name and a secret key. This header suffices to locate all the blocks of the file, as it contains links to their locations.

All of the previous systems are intended to run on a single machine on top of a standard file system. There are, in addition, two approaches for distributed steganographic file systems, Mnemosyne and Mojitos. The former has been proposed by Hand and Roscoe in [4]. In order to hide a file, they write it to a location chosen pseudo-randomly by hashing the file name, the block number and a secret key. The latter was proposed by Giefer and Letchner in [2], and it combines ideas from Mnemosyne and StegFS (by Kuhn and McDonald [5]).

3   Hiding Data Accesses in StegFS

The steganographic file systems presented in the previous section are secure towards an attacker who is able to get snapshots of the state of the file system (sufficiently spaced in time so it cannot be considered to be continuous surveillance). They are vulnerable, however, towards attackers who can continuously monitor the system.

Continuous attackers are able to continuously scan the contents of the file system and detect block updates. They can also observe the I/O operations on the storage, and perform traffic analysis on the accessed (read and written) block locations. Zhou, Pang and Tan proposed in [7] mechanisms to hide the data accesses in their StegFS [6] against this attack model. In the system model (Fig. 1) of [7], users send the file requests to a trusted agent over a secure channel. The agent translates these requests into I/O operations on the storage, and returns the results to the user. Whenever there is no user activity, the agent performs dummy I/O operations. The terminology used to distinguish the block types and update operations (also called "accesses") is:

- **Data blocks** are all the storage blocks that contain the user's data. We refer as **file blocks** to the data blocks of a particular file that is being updated by the user.
- **Dummy blocks** are empty (free) blocks that contain random data.
- When the user requests a **file update**, this triggers **data updates** on all the blocks that belong to the file.
- The system performs **dummy updates** (i.e., change the appearance of the block without changing its actual content) on both dummy and data blocks, in order to hide the data updates.

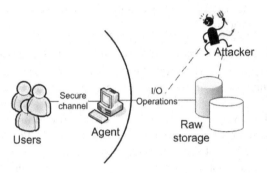

Fig. 1. System model in [7]

The authors of [7] give the following definition of security for hiding data accesses in a steganographic file system:

"Let X denote the sequence of accesses the agent performs on the raw storage. Its probability distribution is P_X. Y denotes the set of access requests users submit to the agent, and when there is no request, $Y = \emptyset$. $P_{X|Y}$ is the conditional probability distribution of X given a particular Y. (Thus, $P_{X|\emptyset}$ is the probability distribution of dummy accesses.) A system is secure if and only if, whatever Y is, $P_{X|Y}$ and $P_{X|\emptyset}$ are so similar that it is computationally infeasible for an attacker to distinguish between them from a sufficiently large set of samples. A system is perfectly secure if and only if $P_{X|Y}$ and $P_{X|\emptyset}$ are exactly the same."

The mechanism proposed in [7] to hide data updates works as follows. Whenever there is no user activity, the user agent issues dummy updates on blocks selected uniformly at random in the storage volume. For a dummy update, the agent reads the selected block, decrypts it, changes the initialization vector (IV) which serves as initial value for the CBC mode, encrypts the block and writes it back in the same location of the file system.

When the user agent receives a request to update a file, it updates all its blocks. The update algorithm relocates file blocks each time they are updated, so that subsequent operations on the file do not result in accesses to the same storage locations. In order to update file block B1, the agent first chooses a block B2 uniformly at random from the storage space. If the selected block B2 is the same as the requested one (B1), the data update is performed in the same way as a dummy update. If B2 is a dummy block, the agent swaps it with the file block B1 and updates their contents. Finally, if B2 is a data block, the agent performs a dummy update on it and re-starts the selection process. Alg. 1 shows the update algorithm provided in [7].

Algorithm 1. Update algorithm of [7]

```
 1: if there is a request to update block B1 then
 2:     Re: randomly pick a block B2 from the storage space
 3:     if B2=B1 then
 4:         read in B1, decrypt it
 5:         update B1 IV's and data field
 6:         encrypt B1, write it back
 7:     else if B2 is a dummy block then
 8:         read in B1,
 9:         substitute B2 for B1
10:         update B2 IV's and data field
11:         encrypt B2, write it back
12:     else
13:         read in B2,
14:         decrypt it, update B2's IV
15:         encrypt B2, write it back
16:         go to Re:
17: else {dummy update}
18:     randomly pick up a block B3 from the storage space;
19:     read in B3,
20:     decrypt it, update B3's IV,
21:     encrypt B3, write it back;
```

The authors of [7] claim that the update algorithm is perfectly secure on the basis of the following proof:

> "For a data update, each block in the storage space has the same probability of being selected to hold the new data. Hence the data updates produce random block I/Os, and follow exactly the same pattern as the dummy updates. Therefore, whether there is any data update or not, the updates on the raw storage follow the same probability distribution as

that of dummy updates. According to the previous definition of security, the scheme is perfectly secure. Without knowing the agent's encryption key, attackers can get no information on the hidden data no matter how long they monitor the raw storage."

In this paper we show that, although all blocks have the same probability of being selected to hold the updated data, I/Os produced by file updates follow different patterns than dummy updates. Thus, the probability distributions of updates in the raw storage are different depending on whether there is user activity or not. Consequently, file updates can be distinguished by an adversary performing traffic analysis on the system.

For a data update, we note that there are two possible interpretations of the algorithm:

1. If we only look at the pseudo-code, when B2 is a dummy block, the updated content of B1 is stored in B2, but the original block location, B1, keeps its old value.
2. If we take in account the text of the paper, when B2 is a dummy block, B1 and B2 are *swapped*; i.e., the agent reads B1 and overwrites it with random data. Then, it reads B2 and overwrites it with the updated content of B1.

Implementing the update algorithm as in the first interpretation implies that the updated content of the file block B1 is transferred to B2, while B1 remains intact. This approach has an obvious problem: the information contained in B1 remains there until it is overwritten (when the block is chosen as B2 in a future data update), meaning that deleted file contents and old versions could still be recovered from the storage.

Moreover, from a traffic analysis perspective, dummy and data updates produce easily distinguishable access patterns: in dummy updates, the same block location is read and written; while in data updates, the read and written block locations are different. We present an example in Fig. 2, where a file located in blocks 1, 2 and 3 is updated and transferred to positions 34, 345 and 127. We can easily see where the file blocks were and where they have been transferred, eliminating the user's plausible deniability on the existence and location of the "hidden" file. Note that a series of data updates made very close to each other indicate that, with very high probability those blocks are part of the same file. Therefore, the dummy updates performed in between file block updates (blocks 479, 290 and 47 in the example) must have been on data blocks. This reveals the existence and location of additional data blocks, besides the ones that have been updated by the user.

In the next section, we show that the security proof given by Zhou, Pang and Tan is wrong even for what seems to be a more clever implementation. Assuming that users do not update their files simultaneously, a continuous attacker can distinguish between data and dummy updates and learn, as a result, the existence and location of hidden files.

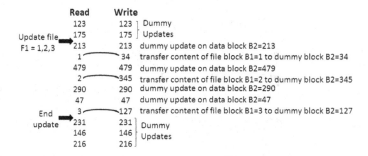

Fig. 2. Update of a three-block file (locations 1,2,3) according to the first interpretation of the update algorithm of [7]

4   Traffic Analysis Attacks on StegFS

We recall the notation presented in the pseudo-code of Algorithm 3 of Sect. 3:

- B1 is the file block to be updated.
- B2 is the candidate block (selected uniformly at random) to hold the updated information of B1. B2 may be a data block or a dummy block. If B2 is a data block, a dummy update is performed on it, and a new B2 is selected. This process is repeated until B2 is a dummy block. Then, B1 is overwritten with random data and the updated content of B1 is stored in B2.
- B3 is the block selected uniformly at random for a dummy update while there are no user requests.

We have developed two attack strategies. The first one applies to multi-block files, and is based on exploiting file block correlations, as explained in Sect. 4.1. The second strategy, explained in Sect. 4.2, applies to one-block files, and is based on the assumption that a file block is updated with higher frequency than a dummy block.

4.1   Attack on Multi-block Files

Identifying file update patterns. Each of the data updates follows a pattern with: first, as many dummy updates on data blocks as data data blocks B2 are chosen in the updating algorithm; second, an update on the file block (B1); and finally, an update on the dummy block B2 to which the data is transferred. In Fig. 3 we can see the same example as in the previous section, where a file located in blocks 1, 2 and 3 is updated and moved to blocks 34, 345 and 127.

The updates on blocks belonging to the same file are separated by a number of dummy updates on data blocks B2. As there are more empty blocks in the storage, it is easier to randomly pick a free block, and therefore file blocks B1 are accessed closer in time to each other (together with their updated locations B2).

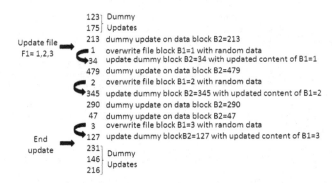

Fig. 3. Update of a three-block file (locations 1,2,3) according to the second interpretation of the update algorithm of [7]

Let R be the occupation rate of the file system. The maximum number of block updates (including data and dummy updates) a file update is expected to need is given by a negative binomial distribution, where the size b of the file is the number of successes and $1 - R$ the success probability. With probability greater than $1 - \epsilon$, a file of b blocks will be updated in at most $A = b + k$ blocks, where k can be derived from the probability mass function of the negative binomial: $\binom{k+b-1}{k} \cdot R^k \cdot (1 - R)^r < \epsilon$. For example, for an occupation rate $R = 0.5$, a complete update on a file of $b = 4$ blocks will be contained in a maximum of $A = 29$ updates with probability greater than $1 - \epsilon = 1 - 10^{-5}$.

As shown in Fig. 4, we can find similar patterns each time the file is updated (i.e., a set of locations updated closely together at two different points in time). By identifying these patterns, we can tell when a file has been updated and where exactly the file blocks are in the storage space. Once we find the most recent pattern, we know that the file will be in the location updated just after the repeated locations that have created the pattern. In the example shown in Fig. 4, the file will be in the positions 12, 60 and 125 of the storage space.

Probability of false positives. We must not forget that these patterns could have been produced by dummy updates (the attacker would think he has found a file update, but actually the access pattern has been randomly generated). We call the probability of this event as *probability of false positive*, and denote it P_{f+}. We now explain how P_{f+} can be computed.

Lemma 1. *Let B be the number of blocks in the storage, let b be the file size and A the expected length of the windows we analyze (i.e., we expect a file of b blocks to be updated in A updates). Let P_A be the probability that in A random accesses all the b blocks of the file are accessed. Then*

$$P_A \leq \left[\frac{e}{\frac{B}{A}} \right]^{\frac{B-A}{A} \cdot \frac{bA}{B}} \approx \left(\frac{eA}{B} \right)^b .$$

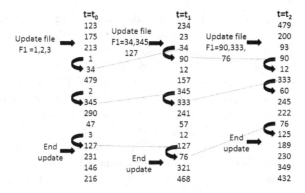

Fig. 4. Three updates on a three-block file according to the second interpretation of the algorithm of [7]

Proof. Let I_i $(i = 1, \ldots, b)$ be an indicator variable whether block i of the file has been accessed. It is easy to see that $\Pr[I_i] = 1 - (1 - \frac{1}{B})^A \leq \frac{A}{B}$. We note that the set of events $\{I_i\}$ is not independent, but as these events are negatively correlated and as we are interested in an upper bound, by assuming that they are independent we obtain a bound which is not tight.

Denote $X = \sum_{i=1}^{b} I_i$, then there all the blocks of the file are accessed if $X = b$. If we treat the events as independent, we can apply the Chernoff inequality which states that $\Pr[X > (\delta + 1)\mu] \leq (\frac{e}{\delta+1})^{\delta\mu}$, where $\mu = E[X]$. As $E[X] = \sum_{i=1}^{b} E[I_i] = \sum_{i=1}^{b} \Pr[I_i] \leq \frac{bA}{B}$, we obtain that

$$P_A = \Pr[X = b] = Pr[X > \underbrace{(\delta + 1)\frac{bA}{B}}_{b}] \leq \left[\frac{e}{\frac{B}{A}}\right]^{\frac{B-A}{A} \cdot \frac{bA}{B}} \approx \left(\frac{eA}{B}\right)^b .$$

Lemma 2. *Let T be the number of dummy accesses, and let $C = T/A$ be the number of subsets of A consecutive accesses each. Under the assumption that these subsets are independent of each other.[1] The probability P_{f+} of having a false positive in at least one of the C subsets is: $P_{f+} \leq 1 - (1 - P_A)^C$.*

Proof. The probability that a false positive happens for one of the subsets is P_A. Thus, the probability that a false positive have not occurred for a given A accesses is $1 - P_A$. All C subsets do not produce any false positive with probability $(1 - P_A)^C$, and the result follows from that immediately.

The probability P_{f+} of having a false positive decreases both with the size b of the file and the number B of blocks in the storage. P_{f+} increases with the number T of dummy updates taken into account, and the occupation rate R.

---

[1] This is an approximation supported by our experimental results. The adaptive algorithm used in our implementation (see Appendix A) deals with accesses straddling two subsets of length A.

We denote $P_{f+}(i)$ as the probability of false positive, given $i + 1$. Figure 5(a) shows the probability, $P_{f+}(1)$, of false positive (logarithmic scale) for two file updates. We can see that, as the file size increases (from five blocks on), the probability of false positive becomes negligible even when there are only two updates on the file. $P_{f+}(i)$ also decreases with i (see Fig. 5(b)), as it becomes less likely that more repetitions of patterns happen just by coincidence. Note that we have considered in the figures up to two million accesses, meaning that on average each block in the storage is read 200 times. We can see that even with these large numbers of accesses, real operations are detected with low false positive rate. This is because our detection algorithm takes into account the correlations between accessed locations, and not the amount of times they have been selected.

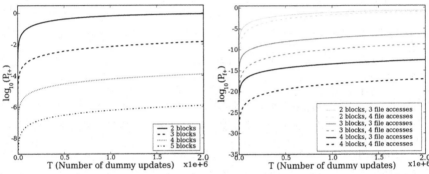

(a) Probability of false positive with two updates per file (logarithmic scale)

(b) Probability of false positive with more than two updates per file (logarithmic scale)

Fig. 5. Probability of false positive for multi-block files ($B = 10000$; $R = 0.5$; $\epsilon = 5 \cdot 10^{-4}$)

4.2 Attack on One-Block Files

Now, we assume that the user updates one-block files with a higher frequency than dummy updates occur on random blocks. Instead of searching for a file update pattern, we analyze the distance between two accesses to the same block (note that each time the file is updated it is transferred to a different location). In the example of Fig. 6 we show three updates on file F1. The distance between the first and second updates (file in block 479) is three, and the distance between the second and third updates (file in block 231) is seven.

Let B be the total number of blocks in the file system. When there are only dummy updates, the probability $P_D(i)$ of having a distance i in between two updates of the same block, follows a geometric distribution:

$$P_D(i) = \left(1 - \frac{1}{B}\right)^{i-1} \cdot \left(\frac{1}{B}\right) . \tag{1}$$

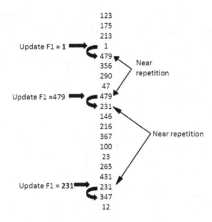

Fig. 6. Example of 3 updates on a one-block file

This equation provides a lower bound on the distance between dummy updates on the same block. The distance between random block updates increases as the user requests data updates more frequently, because the user requests particular data blocks, therefore reducing the frequency with which random blocks are selected.

Let f $(0 < f < 1)$ be the access frequency to a one-block file. The probability $P_F(i)$ of having a distance i between two updates of the file is given by:

$$P_F(i) = (1 - f)^{i-1} \cdot f \ . \tag{2}$$

As long as the file update frequency f is significantly higher than $1/B$, distance analysis can be used to distinguish user updates on one-block files from dummy updates on random blocks.

Although the distance between accesses is, on average, much smaller for the file blocks than for the dummy blocks, it is also possible that two dummy updates on a block happen to be close to each other. If we look just for two accesses (as we do in the multi-block case), we have a high probability of false positive. Therefore, we need to find more than one *near* access in order to statistically prove that a block really contains a file. *Near* means that two data updates could be separated this distance with non-negligible probability.

Let D_C, such that $P_F(D_C) < \epsilon_C$ (see (2)), denote the maximum distance we consider *near*. The probability of false positive (i.e., consider random updates as produced by user requests) for one near access is given by $P_{f+}(1) = \sum_{i=0}^{D_C} P_D(i)$ (see (1)). As the number h of hops (consecutive near accesses) increases, the probability of a false positive decreases: $P_{f+}(h) = P_{f+}(1)^h$. On the other hand, the probability of a false negative (i.e., considering that a file update has been a dummy update) in one near access happens when a file update occurs further than expected: $P_{f-}(1) = \sum_{i=D_C}^{\infty} P_F(i)$. If we consider h near accesses as bound to consider a chain caused by user actions, we will miss a file if any of the h hops happens further than expected: $P_{f-}(h) = \sum_{i=1}^{h} \binom{h}{i} P_{f-}(1)$. We show in

Fig. 7(a) the probability of having a false positive with respect to the number
of hops, for different access frequencies and values of ϵ_C.

In Fig. 7(b), we show the number of hops needed to ensure that a series of
near updates belongs to a file, as a function of the access frequency. We note that
a small number of hops is sufficient, even for relatively low access frequencies (in
the figure we show a maximum frequency of 10^{-3}).

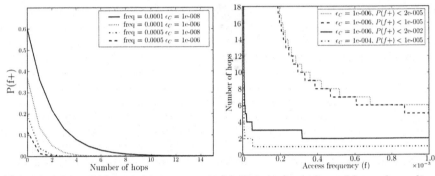

(a) Probability of false positives vs number of hops

(b) Required number of hops depending on access frequency

Fig. 7. Analysis of the number of hops ($B = 100\,000$)

5   Results

In order to test the effectiveness of the attacks, we have implemented a simulation of the update algorithms and the attacks in Python.[2] In this section, we
summarize the empirical results.

5.1   Implementation of the Attack on Multi-block Files

We have tested the attack using favorable parameters for the user, with few files,
a very low update frequency and only two updates per file. The parameters of
the simulation can be seen in Table 1. As the attack becomes more efficient for
larger files, we present results for two sets of files. The first set of files have sizes
between 2 and 3 blocks, and the second considers files of sizes between 4 and 10.

Even though we are in a bad case as attackers, the attack has a high success
probability. We summarize the results in Table 2. In both tests we found more
than 99% of the files hidden in the system, although the guessed file size differs
from the real one in some cases (2% for files of 2-3 blocks, and 1% for files of 4
blocks or bigger). Found files may appear slightly larger than they are because
sometimes we assign "extra blocks" to the file (when there is a dummy update
that fits the pattern next to the end or the beginning of the real file blocks). With

---

[2] The code is available upon request to the authors.

Table 1. Parameters of attack on multi-block files

Size of files (blocks)	Number of files per size	File update frequency	Size of storage space
2-3	10	3%	10000
4-10	10	3%	10000

probability ϵ, the separation between file block updates is larger than expected. This results in either some block of the file being lost (when the block with extra separation is the one accessed at the beginning or the end of the file update); or in a file being found split and considered as two smaller files (when the extra separation happens in the middle of a file). While searching for 2 and 3 block files, we find some false positives, as this occurs with non-negligible probability for very small file sizes (see Fig. 5(a)).

Table 2. Results of the attack on multi-block files

Size of files	Files found	Wrong size	False positives
2-3	> 99%	< 2%	< 2%
4-10	> 99%	< 1%	0%

5.2 Implementation of the Attack on One-Block Files

We have considered a file system with $B = 100\,000$ blocks, where 10 one-block files are accessed 12 times each. We have tested the efficiency of the attack for several access frequencies. In the implementation of the attack, we consider we have found a file when we find a chain of 10 or more near accesses. We have set the probability of false negatives by fixing $\epsilon_C = 10^{-12}$.

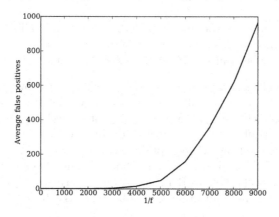

Fig. 8. False positives vs. $1/f$ ($B = 100\,000$; $\epsilon_C = 10^{-12}$)

As expected, the performance of the attack heavily depends on the access frequency f to one-block files. We show this dependence in Fig. 8, where we represent the number of false positives as a function of the access frequency. For frequencies greater than $4 \cdot 10^{-4}$ (in Fig. 8 this corresponds to $1/f = 2500$), we can find all one-block files without obtaining any false positives. As the access frequency decreases, the performance of the attack degrades, and more false positives appear. We note that the number of false positives depends on the access frequency, but not on the number of files in the system.

6   Conclusions and Future Work

In this paper we have analyzed the update algorithm proposed by Zhou, Pang and Tan in [7], and found that it is vulnerable to traffic analysis attacks. We have described the theory behind the attacks, explained how the system's parameters influence their performance, and presented empirical results on their effectiveness.

Our results show that the security claims in [7] are unsubstantiated. Their algorithms do not produce the same patterns for file and dummy updates, therefore, the probability distribution of updated locations in the storage is different whether there is user activity in the system or not. Our attacks exploit these changes and successfully distinguish file and dummy updates, finding the locations of hidden files. Multi-block files are very easy to find (two updates are sufficient to reveal their existence and location), while several file updates are needed in order to find one-block files. Our (non-optimized) implementation successfully finds most of the files hidden in the storage, and more efficient implementations could further increase the accuracy of the attacks.

The two key weaknesses in the update algorithm proposed in [7] are:

- Blocks are rarely relocated, and when they are, their new location appears next to the old one in the history of accessed locations. This greatly reduces the uncertainty on the possible locations to which block contents may have been moved.
- While the "dummy updates" select block locations uniformly at random, multi-block file updates generate correlations between accessed locations that could not have been plausibly generated at random.

The traffic analysis strategies presented in this paper show that introducing "a bit of randomness" is not sufficient to effectively conceal user accesses to files in a steganographic file system. More sophisticated mechanisms are required in order to design a traffic analysis resistant steganographic file system; developing such mechanisms is left as an open problem.

The authors of [7] also propose a method to conceal read accesses to files, based on a multi-level oblivious RAM [3]. A line of future research could analyze whether or not this mechanism resists traffic analysis attacks.

Acknowledgments

We would like to thank the anonymous "Reviewer 1", whose comments have substantially improved the quality of this paper. This work was supported by the IWT SBO ADAPID project (Advanced Applications for e-ID cards in Flanders), GOA Ambiorics and IUAP p6/26 BCRYPT. Carmela Troncoso is funded by a grant of the Foundation Barrie De la Maza from Spain.

References

1. Anderson, R.J., Needham, R.M., Shamir, A.: The steganographic file system. In: Aucsmith, D. (ed.) IH 1998. LNCS, vol. 1525, pp. 73–82. Springer, Heidelberg (1998)
2. Giefer, C., Letchner, J.: Mojitos: A distributed steganographic file system. Technical report, University of Washington (2004)
3. Goldreich, O., Ostrovsky, R.: Software protection and simulation on oblivious RAMs. J. ACM 43(3), 431–473 (1996)
4. Hand, S., Roscoe, T.: Mnemosyne: Peer-to-peer steganographic storage. In: Druschel, P., Kaashoek, M.F., Rowstron, A. (eds.) IPTPS 2002. LNCS, vol. 2429, pp. 130–140. Springer, Heidelberg (2002)
5. McDonald, A.D., Kuhn, M.G.: StegFS: A steganographic file system for linux. In: Pfitzmann, A. (ed.) IH 1999. LNCS, vol. 1768, pp. 462–477. Springer, Heidelberg (2000)
6. Pang, H., Tan, K.-L., Zhou, X.: StegFS: A steganographic file system. In: Proceedings of the 19th International Conference on Data Engineering, pp. 657–667. IEEE Computer Society Press, Los Alamitos (2003)
7. Zhou, X., Pang, H., Tan, K.-L.: Hiding data accesses in steganographic file system. In: Proceedings of the 20th International Conference on Data Engineering, pp. 572–583. IEEE Computer Society Press, Los Alamitos (2004)

A   Algorithms for Detecting Patterns

We show first the algorithm used to uncover multi-block files, and afterwards the one to reveal one-block files. We note that these algorithms are not optimized. An attacker could run them several times, and use the information gained in the first runs to refine the results in later ones.

A.1   Multi-block Files

Worst Case Scenario. We checked the effectiveness of the algorithm in a worst case scenario. We made two simulations with a file system of $B = 10000$ blocks, with files with sizes of $2 - 3$ blocks and $4 - 10$ blocks, respectively, and only 10 files of each size. The file access frequency has been set to 3%, so that accesses to files are on average far away from each other. Finally, we considered only 2 updates per file.

The algorithm (Alg. 2). The algorithm used to find multi-block files works as follows. For b-block files we first calculate the expected number A of blocks its update is expected to occupy. Denote by $G_F(A)$ the most recent chunk of A consecutive accesses. We compare $G_F(A)$ (as shown in Fig. 9(a)) with the previous chunk of A accesses $G_M(A)$. If there is more than one element in the intersection (i.e., locations that have been accessed in both chunks), we increase the size of the chunks and compare them again, in order to detect file updates that do not fit exactly inside the chunks. Finally, if the intersection contains b (or more) elements, we conclude these are due to a file update. If not, we take a new $G_M(A)$ and compare it again with the $G_F(A)$. Once $G_F(A)$ has been compared with all prior $G_M(A)$'s, we choose a new $G_F(A)$ and restart the process.

Fig 9(a) shows an example of this algorithm, where a 3-block file (1, 2 and 3) is detected in positions 34, 345 and 127. In Step 1, we define a first chunk $G_F(A)$, and a first chunk $G_M(A)$, we can easily see that the intersection of the fixed chunk with the rest of the accesses is void. Then, in Step 2, new $G_F(A)$ and $G_M(A)$ are chosen. We can see that, after a couple of comparisons (Step 3), $G_F(A) \bigcap G_M(A) > 1$. Then, in Step 4, we increase their sizes to check if the intersection grows. From this result we can derive that a 3-block file is located in positions 34, 345 and 127.

A.2   One-Block Files

Worst case scenario. For one-block files, the simulation was made with a file system of $B = 100000$ blocks, only 10 one-block files accessed 12 times each, and frequencies higher than 10^{-4}. We consider we have found a file when at least $h = 10$ near accesses are chained.

The algorithm (Alg. 4). In order to find one-block files, we start with the most recent access and search near repetitions of it, if there are not, we move to the next position and so on. Once we find a first near access, we build a tree of near accesses (given that there can be more than one near access to a position) and, if one of its branches has more than h elements, we conclude that we have found a one-block file.

We illustrate in Fig 9(b) how a one-block file is found. Assuming that 123 has been the latest access to the storage and that we are looking for chains of $h = 5$ hops, the first candidate we find is 479, which has two possible *newCandidates*, 231 and 431. Following the algorithm, we arrive at the tree showed in the figure, and can conclude that there is a file in location 1, that comes from position 222 after having passed by locations 278, 347, 231 and 479.

Algorithm 2. Algorithm to search multi-block files patterns

1: $FixPointer$ = last access to the system
2: **while** there are accesses to make a new fixed chunk **do**
3:    we choose $G_F(A)$, a chunk of A accesses from $FixPointer$ to $FixPointer - A$
4:    $MovPointer = FixPointer - A + 1$
5:    **while** there are accesses to compare with $G_F(A)$ **do**
6:       we choose $G_M(A)$, a chunk of A accesses from $MovPointer$ to $MovPointer - A$

7:       $MovPointer = MovPointer - A - 1$
8:       **if** $Int = G_F(A) \bigcap G_M(A) > 1$ **then**
9:          **repeat**
10:             $IntOld = Int$
11:             we increase the size of the chunk in x blocks $A = A + x$
12:             $Int = G_F(A) \bigcap G_M(A)$
13:          **until** $size(IntOld) = size(Int)$
14:          **if** $size(Int) >= b$ **then**
15:             there is a file in the locations belonging to the intersection
16:          **else**
17:             false alarm, continue searching
18:       $MovPointer+ = A$
19:    $FixPointer+ = A$

Algorithm 3. searchCandidates($Location$, $Tree$) (near accesses to a given location)

1: $candidates$ = list of "near" repeated accesses to $Location$
2: **if** $size(candidates) >= 1$ **then**
3:    **for** $candidate$ in $candidates$ **do**
4:       $newCandidate$ = location accessed immediately before $candidate$
5:       append $newCandidate$ to $Tree$
6:       $Tree = searchCandidates(newCandidate, Tree)$
RETURN: Tree

Algorithm 4. Search one-block pattern Algorithm

1: $Location$ = last access to the system
2: $tree = NULL$
3: **while** there are accesses in the list **do**
4:    $treeCandidates = searchCandidates(Location, tree)$
5:    **if** there is a branch with more than h elements **then**
6:       the block right before the root of the tree has a file
7:    **else**
8:       $tree = NULL$

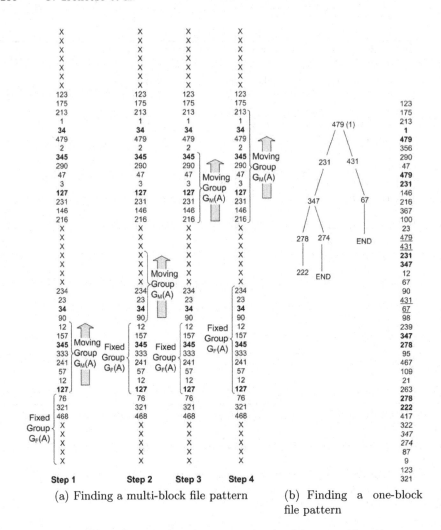

(a) Finding a multi-block file pattern

(b) Finding a one-block file pattern

Fig. 9. Algorithms used to detect patterns in the accessed locations

Soft Feature-Based Watermark Decoding with Insertion/Deletion Correction

Mathias Schlauweg, Dima Pröfrock, and Erika Müller

Institute of Communications Engineering,
Faculty of Computer Science and Electrical Engineering,
University of Rostock,
Rostock 18119, Germany
{mathias.schlauweg, dima.proefrock, erika.mueller}@uni-rostock.de

Abstract. Hard decisions constitute the major problem in digital watermarking applications, especially when content adaptive embedding methods are used. Soft-decision decoding, on the other hand, has proved to be performance gaining, often realized during forward error correction. But despite this insight, no adaptive watermarking approach integrates the adaptation process into soft decoding, up to now. Further, insertion/deletion errors can occur in a content dependent watermarking system due to hard decisions if data is embedded only in some selected regions of the host signal. This kind of error usually desynchronizes the decoder and disables the correct watermark extraction. In this paper, we work out three fundamental properties of content dependent quantization-based watermarking. We show how the coupling between these properties and common soft-decision forward error correction decoding can be used to build up an overall soft processing watermarking. No pre-distortion has to be used, and hence, the image quality is not degraded. Even adaptation techniques can be used where it is computational infeasible to project a pre-distortion back onto the host image. Afterwards, we describe how to modify a common Viterbi decoder to enable the correction of insertion/deletion errors combined with our new soft decoding approach and hence improve the overall performance.

Keywords: Digital watermarking, image segmentation, adaptive decoding, soft-decision forward error correction, re-synchronization.

1 Introduction

After several years of watermarking research, more and more sophisticated methods have been developed to embed additional data into multimedia content. All these methods have in common that they strive after a good compromise between invisibility and robustness of the embedding. In image watermarking, invisibility means that degradations of the perceptual quality of the host image must be avoided. Hence, newer content adaptive watermarking methods take advantage of the property that the HVS (human visual system) is less sensitive to changes

T. Furon et al. (Eds.): IH 2007, LNCS 4567, pp. 237–251, 2007.

in textured regions than in smooth regions of an image [1]. Data can be embedded with higher robustness against watermark attacks in stronger textured regions without being visible, commonly known as *perceptual shaping* [2].

Basically, there are two kinds of adaptive watermarking outlined in literature. The first embeds data into all regions. Less as well as more perceptually significant areas are used, whereas the embedding strength is adapted to the image content, as in [1], [2]. The second approach is based on the idea only embedding in regions where the perceivable distortion is low and leaving perceptually sensitive areas undisturbed [3], [4], [6]. In both cases, the image has to be separated into regions with different HVS properties, and during the extraction process, the same separation has to be determined from the host signal. Discrepancies yield errors, even if no attack has been applied [5]. While the former approach has to deal with common substitution errors (binary: $0{\rightarrow}1$ or $1{\rightarrow}0$), the later would result in catastrophic de-synchronization. That means a deletion error occurs when an embedded symbol is not detected by the receiver and an insertion error occurs when the receiver detects a symbol that was not transmitted.

The most often applied technique to circumvent discrepancies between both separation feature maps is to form a gap around the separation threshold. In other words, the used feature is pre-distorted to leave a margin. As a consequence the image quality is degraded. Furthermore, there are separation approaches where it is computational infeasible or even impossible to project the pre-distortion back onto the host image. For example, the separation feature could have been calculated using *higher order statistics* from extensive data. In this case, errors are ignored or tried to be corrected by FEC (forward error correction), usually with moderate success, because common forward error correction schemes are designed to correct substitutions. They cannot detect or correct insertions/deletions. In such systems, synchronization loss will result in a sequence or burst of errors until synchronization is re-established.

In this paper, we propose to integrate commonly used hard region separation into an overall soft processing framework, as in Fig. 1 c). Three interesting key properties deviated from content dependent quantization-based watermarking

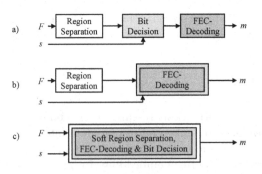

Fig. 1. Overall hard processing a), hard region separation with soft bit decoding b), overall soft processing c). F = separation feature, s = host signal, m = watermark.

are presented in section 2. These properties can be used to combine HVS-based region separation and watermark decoding with impressive improvements in error correction capability. Afterwards in section 3, we give an overview of recent insertion/deletion/substitution error correction approaches and present a new solution to the problem of bit re-synchronization in adaptive watermarking. Experimental results for the combination of both new techniques are shown in section 4 and conclusions will be given in section 5.

2   Soft-Decoded Adaptive Watermarking

As mentioned earlier, if there are discrepancies of the region separation during adaptively embedding and extracting the watermark m, as in Fig. 2 b) and c), then wrong parameters are used and errors can occur. If both less as well as more perceptually significant areas are used, for example, with different embedding strengths, "only" single bit errors occur. In the case of bit sensitive, signature-based applications such as image authentication [1] these bit errors are problematic but can be corrected using common forward error correction. But if data are only embedded in regions where the perceivable distortion is low, long bursts of errors occur until re-synchronization. For example, the nine mask differences in Fig. 2 c) would result in three insertions and six deletions anywhere in the extracted watermark stream if the decoder assumes that data is only embedded in the white blocks.

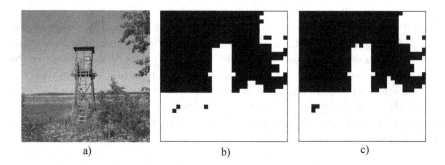

a)   b)   c)

Fig. 2. Original image a). Hard embedding mask b), hard extraction mask after JPEG compression with quality factor QF = 50 c) using the DWT-based segmentation ($\tau=2$).

Thus, the first goal must be to find a segmentation scheme that yields less decision errors. Furthermore, we require the segmentation feature map F to consist of real values, $F \in \mathbb{R}$. These soft values, the soft mask, will be used during our new soft-decision decoding for weighting the input signal s. In section 2.1 and 2.2, we propose two separation approaches that fulfill these requirements. Afterwards in 2.3, three interesting properties of content adaptive quantization-based watermarking are presented. We show how these properties can be combined and integrated into a soft-decision decoding in section 2.4.

2.1 DWT-Based Soft Mask Generation

In [1], we applied texture segmentation in the DWT (discrete wavelet transform) domain for an image authentication scheme. Large DWT-coefficients indicate image positions with strong texture, whereas small ones stand for homogenous regions. As in Fig. 3 except for the LL^4-subband, all coefficients of the fourth decomposition level are compared to a threshold. Afterwards, the known morphologic operations *closing* and *erosion* are used to eliminate small gaps and to refine the separation. The binary masks are combined logically and used during embedding as well as extraction to select between two different watermarking strengths Δ_1 and Δ_2.

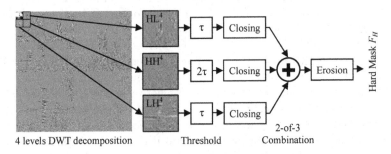

Fig. 3. Hard mask generation for adaptive embedding as described in [1]

But the described DWT segmentation approach was originally designed for a hard region separation and hard FEC-decoding. Now, in this paper we modify it to a soft version, whereas the texture threshold τ is subtracted rather than being used for binarization. As shown in Fig. 4, the resulting three matrices are summed and multiplied element-wise by the signed hard mask values F_H, which are calculated as described above. Compared to the original image the homogenous sky yields negative values, whereas for stronger textured regions the feature F_S is positive.

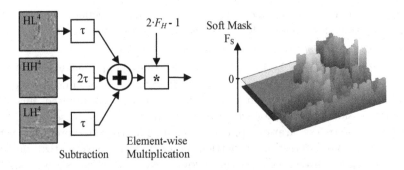

Fig. 4. Soft mask generation based on DWT coefficient amplitude

2.2   Gradient-Based Soft Mask Generation

For the proposed DWT segmentation approach it would be easy to pre-distort the feature to leave a margin to lower the number of segmentation errors at the decoder. But for another approach that turns out to be even more robust to signal processing a feature pre-distortion is computational more complex. In this second, gradient-based segmentation we propose to detect horizontal, vertical and diagonal edges using the *Sobel* operator. That means the image is filtered using the Sobel filter matrices from Fig. 5 at first. Afterwards, a Gaussian low pass filtering is applied and the four feature maps are compared to a threshold and summed as in the DWT-based approach. Again, morphologic operations are used for the binary hard mask to refine the segmentation, whereupon the filtered edge masks are multiplied element-wise by the hard mask similar to Fig. 4.

$$
\begin{matrix}
1 & 2 & 3 & 2 & 1 \\
0 & 0 & 0 & 0 & 0 \\
0 & 0 & 0 & 0 & 0 \\
0 & 0 & 0 & 0 & 0 \\
-1 & -2 & -3 & -2 & -1
\end{matrix}
\qquad
\begin{matrix}
1 & 0 & 0 & 0 & -1 \\
2 & 0 & 0 & 0 & -2 \\
3 & 0 & 0 & 0 & -3 \\
2 & 0 & 0 & 0 & -2 \\
1 & 0 & 0 & 0 & -1
\end{matrix}
\qquad
\begin{matrix}
3 & 2 & 1 & 0 & 0 \\
2 & 0 & 0 & 0 & 0 \\
1 & 0 & 0 & 0 & -1 \\
0 & 0 & 0 & 0 & -2 \\
0 & 0 & -1 & -2 & -3
\end{matrix}
\qquad
\begin{matrix}
0 & 0 & 1 & 2 & 3 \\
0 & 0 & 0 & 0 & 2 \\
-1 & 0 & 0 & 0 & 1 \\
-2 & 0 & 0 & 0 & 0 \\
-3 & -2 & -1 & 0 & 0
\end{matrix}
$$

a)   b)   c)   d)

Fig. 5. Sobel filter matrices for horizontal a), vertical b), diagonal c-d) edge detection

The following figure indicates the robustness of both described segmentation methods determined from several tests on natural images. By the term robustness here the probability of occurrence of a feature threshold transition is meant, which would yield additional errors to be corrected by the FEC-decoder.

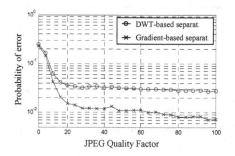

	DWT-based separation	Gradient-based separation
gaussian filtering (mask size 3x3)	1.342 %	1.252 %
gaussian filtering (mask size 5x5)	3.723 %	3.611 %
unsharp masking (mask size 5x5)	1.928 %	1.373 %

Fig. 6. Probability of occurrence of a feature threshold transition during region segmentation at the receiver site due to non-malicious signal processing

2.3   Three Key Properties Towards Soft Decoding

For watermark embedding we use QIM (*quantization index modulation*) in the DWT domain as it is described in [1]. But for the extraction site, we found three new interesting properties to be used for soft-decoding during nearest-neighbor quantization. Thereby, Λ_1 and Λ_2 denote the two quantization lattices that each consist of sub-lattices marked with × and ○ accordingly. Although here we describe the embedding for the DWT domain, other domains, e.g., DCT (discrete cosine transform) or pixel domain could be used as well.

Firstly, we assume that data is embedded in both less as well as more textured regions. Later on, in section 3, we consider the case that data is embedded only in strong textured regions but not in homogenous parts of the image. We show that this so-called selective watermarking is a special case of adaptive watermarking where the embedding strength Δ_1 is zero at the encoder.

Property I - Lattice Point Coverage. In Fig. 7, the "natural" covers of Λ_1 and Λ_2 are shown for the case of lattice crossings due to false feature separation. The shaded areas indicate "natural positive crossings". For example, suppose Λ_1 has been used during watermark embedding and the host signal was quantized to the highlighted point ○. If afterwards the mask changes slightly as in Fig. 2 c), then Λ_2 would be used during extraction. In this case the nearest-neighbor quantization would yield the correct bit decision as long as the sample keeps inside the shaded area, even if the separation feature has passed over the decision threshold. But if the point × right beside it has been used, it would be falsely decided to a point ○ in lattice Λ_2. In this case, a bit substitution error would occur.

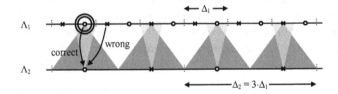

Fig. 7. Covers of two different QIM lattices ($\Delta_2 = 3 \cdot \Delta_1$)

However, the possibility is highest that no error occurs during a transition $\Lambda_1 \leftrightarrow \Lambda_2$ in the case of an exactly three times larger quantization interval Δ_2. Thereby, in at least 50 percent of all cases there is no problem if a transition occurs if the distortion to the quantized signal is less than $\Delta_1/2$.

Property II - Distortion Probability Function. In [11], Vila-Forcén et al. studied additive attacks against quantization-based watermarking. For attacks such as lossy compression, noise adding or filtering the distortion to the quantized signal can be expected to be Gaussian distributed. Since the variance of this distribution is the same for both lattices Λ_1 and Λ_2, following distortion probability density functions $pdf(s_i)$ can be expected (see Fig. 8). Due to the nearest-neighbor quantization $s_i = \{-1 \leq s_i \leq +1 : s_i \in \mathbb{R}\}, \forall i \in \{1,2\}$ for one periodic quantization bin, if we consider $s_1 = s/\Delta_1$ and $s_2 = s/\Delta_2$.

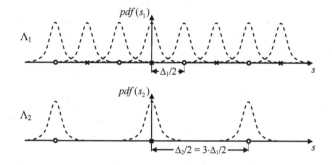

Fig. 8. Probability density functions of the disturbed signal $(\Delta_2/\Delta_1 = 3)$

Both probability density functions are drawn one upon the other in Fig. 8 to visualize that there are spaces at the second lattice where it is unlikely that a signal sample is located. In other words, if the feature is close to the decision threshold and the signal sample is somewhere in the space where $pdf(s_2)$ is small, it is more likely that the sample was originally embedded using lattice Λ_1.

Property III - Certainty of Decision. We define C as certainty of how close the input feature F is to the selected feature threshold τ. That means if the feature is close to the decision threshold, it is uncertain which QIM lattice has to be used. In this case the certainty is zero. If the feature is far from the threshold and it is oblivious which lattice was chosen during embedding, the certainty is high. Using this certainty we propose two weighting functions, f_1 and f_2, for the input signals in Λ_1 and Λ_2.

$$C = F - \tau \tag{1}$$

$$f_1(C) = \frac{1}{2} - \frac{\arctan(C)}{\pi} \tag{2}$$

$$f_2(C, s_2, O) = 1 - f_1(C \cdot (|s_2| + O)) \tag{3}$$

C_x	$f_1(C)$	$f_2(C, s_2, O)$
0	0,5	0,5
$-\infty$	1	0
$+\infty$	0	1

The weighting function f_2 for lattice Λ_2 depends on the absolute value of input signal s_2 to implement Property II. The value O should be set to the ratio Δ_1/Δ_2, e.g., $O = 1/3$. For one periodical quantization bin the weighting functions are visualized in Fig. 9. Considering the input signal both functions are drawn opposed to each other.

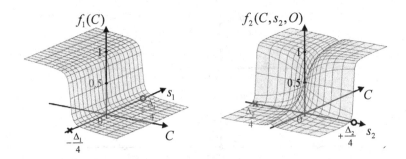

Fig. 9. Soft feature input signal weighting functions

Since data embedded using the weaker embedding strength Δ_1 is less robust to attacks or common signal processing than data embedded using Δ_2 afterwards we stretch the signal s_w by the factor Δ_2/Δ_1 at all mask positions where the separation feature is larger than the threshold τ.

$$s_w = \frac{s_1 \cdot f_1(C) + s_2 \cdot f_2(C, s_2, O)}{2} \tag{4}$$

$$s_w^* = \begin{cases} s_w & C < 0 \\ \Delta_2/\Delta_1 \cdot s_w & C \geq 0 \end{cases} \tag{5}$$

2.4   Soft-Decision Decoding of the Weighted Signal

After the weighing process, the FEC-decoder receives a stream containing information about the reliability of each received symbol. For example, the common *Viterbi decoder* with soft-decision input used to decode *convolutional codes* can be employed to determine the embedded message m. By observing a sequence of symbols this decoder determines multiple paths of message states in a kind of *state machine*. Each of these states is valuated by a path metric, representing the reliability of each bit-decision. Afterwards, in a trace back process the maximum likelihood path survives. The weighting approach directly influences this metric.

The improvement of the described input signal weighting approach concerning substitution error correction performance will be presented in section 4. Prior to this in the following section, we discuss the case that data is embedded exclusively in stronger textured regions, whereas perceptually sensitive areas are left undisturbed. This embedding can yield insertions as well as deletions at unpredictable locations within the watermarking sequence at the decoder.

3   Insertion/Deletion Error Correction

The term watermark de-synchronization is used twice in literature. The term sometimes often refers to the whole embedded message in consequence of geometric attacks such as shifting, rotation, or scaling. But it may also refer to a non-linear drift within the message sequence. This second kind of de-synchronization caused by bit insertions and deletions is the major problem in content adaptive watermarking. Known approaches such as ESD (exhaustive search detection) or TMD (template matching detection), recently analyzed by Barni [7], usually applied to re-synchronize the whole message are computational infeasible in the case of IDS (insertions/deletions/substitutions).

Most error correction schemes are designed to correct substitution errors. It is assumed that the decoder knows the block boundaries in the case of *block codes* or the message length in the case of *convolutional codes*. They can neither detect nor correct insertions/deletions. In such systems, synchronization loss will result in a sequence or burst of errors until synchronization is re-established.

Basically, there are two categories of re-establishing synchronization. While the first detects synchronization loss and discards incorrect code words to regain synchronization, the second is able to correct insertions/deletions and hence to recover the transmitted data. In [5] and [10], the authors give an overview of recent approaches to channel re-synchronization. One technique is, for example, to use an inner code to infer the positions of insertion/deletion errors and an outer code to correct errors in a *concatenated coding* scheme, as in [4], [5]. Thereby, carrier signals (marker) are provided for the outer burst-error-correcting decoder. If these markers are not in their expected positions, the outer decoder can infer the insertion/deletion positions. In this case, exhaustive search detection can be used for the inner code partition with reduced computational effort. Another technique, published by Solanki *et al.*, treats the host signal locations where no data is embedded as erasures [6]. Similar to the idea of *punctured channel coding*, the encoder simply drops the code symbols at these locations. Afterwards, the decoder inserts don't-care states for the assumed locations knowing only the selection criterion but not the explicit locations. Insertions now become errors, and deletions become additional don't-care states that can be corrected by the decoder. Both these solutions require extra coding effort at the sender. In contrast, a third technique that works only at the receiver is the use of extended *dynamic programming* during FEC-decoding. Here, existing codes and standard encoding methods are used. Only the decoder is slightly modified, as in [8] - [10].

3.1   Interconnected Viterbi Decoders

The first extended dynamic programming approach for the purpose of IDS-error correction in a watermarking system with selective embedding was proposed by Mansour and Tewfik [8]. Their technique recovers the correct message if extra bits (*false alarms*) are added to the body of the message at random locations. They modify the Viterbi algorithm used to decode the embedded watermark that was previously encoded with convolutional codes. The decoder is designed to handle substitution as well as insertion errors, but no deletions. To get only substitutions and insertions the threshold τ for selecting embedding positions at the decoder is chosen to be less than the threshold at the embedding site. The new threshold is $\tau - T$. Hence, the probability of occurrence of deletion errors is lower than for insertion errors (see Fig. 10). But in this case all embedding positions with a feature value in the distance $d \leq T$ to the threshold unavoidably turn out to be insertions. As a consequence the FEC-decoder has to deal with an extra error rate that degrades the overall correction capability.

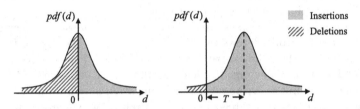

Fig. 10. Probability density functions of the occurrence of threshold transitions (zero-crossings) and hence insertion/deletion errors at the decoder (left). If the threshold at the decoder is chosen to be less than the threshold at the embedding, most deletions turn out to be insertions (right).

Recently, another approach was described by Swart *et al.* [10]. Multiple parallel Viterbi decoders are used to correct IDS-errors. Each decoder receives a stream containing information about the reliability of each received symbol. By observing a sequence of symbols the common decoder determines several paths of message states in a kind of state machine. Each of these states is valuated by a metric, representing the reliability of each bit-decision. Afterwards, in a trace back process the maximum likelihood path survives. Synchronization errors result in all metrics to have high rate of change for the decoders that are out of sync. Since each of the parallel-interconnected Viterbi decoders is one bit out of sync with the others (see Fig. 11), by monitoring the rate of change for the accumulated error metrics, one is able to ascertain which of the Viterbi decoders is in synchronization. Based on the idea in [9], where several standalone decoders were used, Swart *et al.* integrated the framework into one larger Viterbi decoder and called it super trellis decoder.

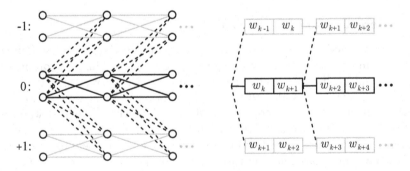

Fig. 11. Representation of the super trellis [10] (left). Another illustration of the super trellis to better visualize the indices of the input samples, for an 1/2-rate code (right). The sub decoder lagging by one bit is denoted by -1, the sub decoder leading by one bit is denoted by +1.

We implemented the proposed algorithm and made some modifications on the super trellis decoder. These modifications allow us to directly input the previously described soft-weighted samples s_w to the decoder stage.

A further input to the decoder must be the feature decision certainty C to infer the subset of s_w that is assumed to be the embedded watermark w_k at the host signal positions p_k prior re-synchronization. That means if N is the number of all possible candidates of embedding locations and K is the number of, e.g., coefficients for data embedding selected using the local perceptual criterion C, $w_k := s_w(p_k)$, whereas $p_k = \{p_k \in \mathbb{N} : 0 \le C(p_k), 1 \le k \le K\}$.

Modifications:

1. Deletions can only have been occured at those positions where $p_k < p_{k+1} - 1$. This reduces the computational effort as well as the number of *false positives*.
2. Swarts decoder simply repeats the previous sample, e.g., w_{k+1} in Fig. 11, if a deletion is assumed for a symbol in the range $p_k...p_{k+1}$. But since the decoder has knowledge about all samples, we propose to integrate the sample delivered by the watermark extractor that is assumed to be deleted. In the example in Fig. 12, such a deleted sample is labeled D. If $p_k < p_{k+1} - n$, where $2 \le n$, or in other words if there are more than one deletion candidate, we suggest from all n samples $D(p_k + 1)...D(p_k + n)$ to chose the one with the lowest absolute value $|C|$.
3. Considering Fig. 11, the old super trellis decoder is not able to deduce the actual insertion/deletion position within a pair of symbols, e.g., the tupel $[w_k, w_{k+1}]$ in the case of a 1/2-rate code. As can be seen in Fig. 12, our trellis extension checks for all possible combinations of insertion/deletion positions and hence, finds as well as corrects the actual error location.
4. Additionally, we apply a weighting to the first pair of samples within the window for the decoders out of sync using the certainty of the sample positions assumed to be inserted or deleted, respectively.

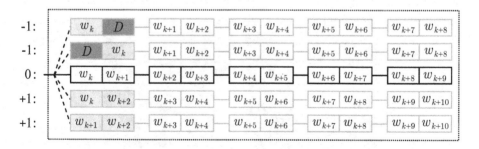

Fig. 12. Modified super trellis for a 1/2-rate code, where 2 input samples form a pair of symbols. Here, the decoder considers the input within a window of length 5.

4   Experimental Results

The probability of mask transitions using the described soft region segmentation is very low, as shown in Fig. 6. Thus, we had to perform a huge number of simulations to assess the improvement in bit error correction during watermark retrieval. To get an impression of how the image from Fig. 2 a) is changed due to the embedding process, in Fig. 13 and Fig. 14 the watermarked image is displayed. In the first image, less as well as more perceptually significant regions are used for data embedding. Here, only bit substitution errors have to be expected if the segmentation mask changes during watermark extraction. On the other hand, in Fig. 14, the host image is only watermarked in regions where the separation feature is larger than the threshold. That means for this approach also insertion/deletion errors have to be expected. As already mentioned, we call the second approach selective embedding and claim that selective embedding is a special form of adaptive embedding, where Δ_1 is zero.

a)   b)

Fig. 13. Adaptively watermarked image a). 1024 bits are embedded in less as well as more perceptually significant regions, $\Delta_2 = 3 \cdot \Delta_1$, where $\Delta_1 = 2$, PSNR = 45.91 dB. Difference to original b).

a)   b)

Fig. 14. Selectively watermarked image a). 541 bits are only embedded ($\Delta_2 = 6$) in regions where the separation feature is larger than the threshold, PSNR = 46.32 dB. Difference to original b).

All results shown in this paper have been calculated for the same parameters for a set of 32 natural photos. We show the results of our new solution for JPEG compression. Other watermark attacks such as filtering or noise-adding have similar effect on the probability of mask transitions and hence, functionality of our approach. In this paper, malicious attacks such as *cropping* or *geometric attacks* are not considered since the original intention was to propose an extension for the image authentication watermarking system in [1].

4.1   Adaptive Watermarking

Fig. 15 shows that our soft-mask/soft-FEC solution outperforms common adaptive watermarking using hard region separation combined with either soft or hard forward error correction. The soft-masking approach helps to lower the bit error rate approximately by a factor 5 for commonly used JPEG compression (QF $\geq$ 10) without any extra coding effort or quality degradations during watermark embedding.

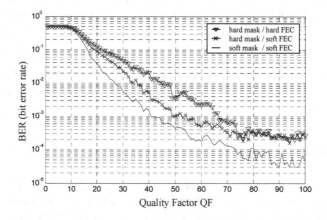

Fig. 15. Empirical bit error rate for lossy JPEG compression for different values of quality factor after forward error correction for the adaptive watermarking approach

4.2   Selective Watermarking

If in Equ. 3 (section 2.3) the step size Δ_1 is zero and no data is embedded in the perceptually sensitive regions, it follows that O, and s_1 are zero too. Although this special form, the weighting function $f_2(C, s_2)$ and hence the segmentation feature have still influence. That means if the feature is far from the threshold, the probability of occurrence of an insertion/deletion error is low. On the other hand, if the feature is close to the threshold the new super trellis decoder can benefit from this knowledge since the weighting process raises the error metric for all interconnected decoders that are out of sync.

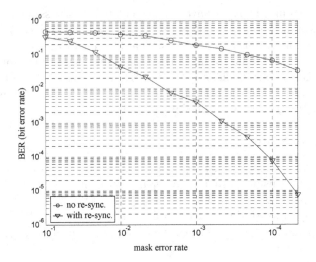

Fig. 16. Empirical mask error rate against the bit error rate after forward error correction with and without re-synchronization for the selective watermarking approach

In Fig. 16, the propability of occurence of mask transitions, which we denote as mask error rate, is shown against the bit error rate (BER). The bit error rate also includes burst errors that result from de-synchronization due to insertions/deletions.

5   Conclusions

In this paper, an integration of perceptual watermarking adaptation into the soft-decision decoding of common forward error correction was proposed. In prior watermarking approaches this adaptation process was always excluded from soft-decoding. We proved that a soft-integration yields impressive improvements in bit error correction during watermark retrieval. No pre-distortion has to be used to avoid adaptation errors during watermark extraction. Hence, the host image quality is not degraded. Furthermore, even adaptation techniques can be used where it is computational infeasible to project a pre-distortion back onto the host image. We showed that the performance can be further gained by combining our soft-decoding approach with a recently proposed channel coding technique capable of correcting insertion/deletion errors at the decoder site. We introduced some modifications for this insertion/deletion correction algorithm to improve the overall performance. Our proposed technique can be integrated very easily into numerous watermarking applications without loss of security, performance or functionality.

References

1. Schlauweg, M., Pröfrock, D., Müller E.: JPEG2000-Based Secure Image Authentication. In: Proc. of ACM Multimedia and Security Workshop, Geneva, Switzerland, pp. 62–67 (2006)
2. Wolfgang, R.B., Podilchuk, C.I., Delp, E.J.: Perceptual Watermarks for Images and Video. Proc. of IEEE - Special Issue on Identification and Protection of Multimedia 87(7), 1108–1126 (1999)
3. Hernández, J.R., Delaigle, J.-F., Macq, B.: Improving Data Hiding by Using Convolutional Codes and Soft-Decision Decoding. In: Proc. of SPIE Security and Watermarking of Multimedia Contents, San José, USA, pp. 24–47 (2000)
4. Sharma, G., Coumou, D.J.: Watermark Synchronization: Perspectives and a New Paradigm. In: Proc. of Conference on Information Sciences and Systems, Princeton, USA, pp. 1182–1187 (2006)
5. Davey, M.C., MacKay, D.J.C.: Reliable Communication over Channels with Insertions, Deletions and Substitutions. IEEE Transactions on Information Theory 47(2), 687–698 (2001)
6. Solanki, K., Jacobsen, N., Madhow, U., Manjunath, B.S., Chandrasekaran, S.: Robust Image-Adaptive Data Hiding Using Erasure and Error Correction. IEEE Transactions on Image Processing 13(12), 1627–1639 (2004)
7. Barni, M.: Shedding Light on Some Possible Remedies Against Watermark De-Synchronization: A Case Study. In Proc. of SPIE Security, Steganography, and Watermarking of Multimedia Contents VII, San José, USA, pp.106–113 (2005)
8. Mansour, M.F., Tewfik, A.H.: Efficient Decoding of Watermarking Schemes in the Presence of False Alarms. In Proc. of IEEE Workshop on Multimedia and Signal Processing, Cannes, France, pp. 523–528 (2001)
9. Dos Santos, M.P.F., Clarke, W.A., Ferreira, H.C., Swart, T.G.: Correction of Insertions/Deletions using Standard Convolutional Codes and the Viterbi Decoding Algorithm. In: Proc. of IEEE Information Theory Workshop, Paris, France, pp. 187–190 (2003)
10. Swart, T.G., Ferreira, H.C., dos Santos, M.P.F.: Using Parallel-Interconnected Viterbi Decoders to Correct Insertion/Deletion Errors. In: Proc. of IEEE AFRICON Conference in Africa, Gaborone, Botswana, pp. 341–344 (2004)
11. Vila-Forcén, J.E., Voloshynovskiy, S., Koval, O., Pun, T., Pérez-González, F.: Worst Case Additive Attack against Quantization-Based Data-Hiding Methods. In: Proc. of SPIE Security, Steganography, and Watermark of Multimedia Contents VII, San José, USA, pp. 136–146 (2005)

Noise Robust Speech Watermarking with Bit Synchronisation for the Aeronautical Radio

Konrad Hofbauer[1,2] and Horst Hering[2]

[1] Graz University of Technology, Austria
Signal Processing and Speech Communication Laboratory
konrad.hofbauer@TUGraz.at
[2] Eurocontrol Experimental Centre, France
horst.hering@eurocontrol.int

Abstract. Analogue amplitude modulation radios are used for air/ ground voice communication between aircraft pilots and controllers. The identification of the aircraft, so far always transmitted verbally, could be embedded as a watermark in the speech signal and thereby prevent safety-critical misunderstandings. The first part of this paper presents an overview on this watermarking application. The second part proposes a speech watermarking algorithm that embeds data in the linear prediction residual of unvoiced narrowband speech at a rate of up to 2 kbit/s. A bit synchroniser is developed which enables the transmission over analogue channels and which reaches the optimal limit within one to two percentage points in terms of raw bit error rate. Simulations show the robustness of the method for the AWGN channel.

1 Introduction

Tactical air traffic control (ATC) guidance over continental areas currently relies on voice communication between pilots and controllers. Analogue amplitude modulation (AM) radios are and have been used worldwide for this purpose for more than fifty years, and the standards have not been modified in any significant way since. The aeronautical transceivers operate in the very high frequency (VHF) band (118-137 MHz) with double-sideband amplitude modulation (DSB-AM). They are known for their poor signal quality and sensitivity to disturbances along the propagation path such as noise, fading and Doppler effect. This technology is expected to remain in use for the provision of air traffic management (ATM) for many years to come, even if the use of data communications will progressively increase in the medium and long terms [1].

To reduce the complexity of air traffic to a level that can be handled by air traffic controllers, the traffic is organised in volumes of airspace, called sectors. In a particular ATC sector, all pilots and the controller use a single radio channel, which is called the party line. In order for the controller to have a clear picture of the traffic and to be able to give appropriate instructions, the controller must know exactly which pilot he is in contact with at a given point in time. Pilots therefore give their call sign at the start of every voice message.

T. Furon et al. (Eds.): IH 2007, LNCS 4567, pp. 252–266, 2007.

The identification step is inherently threatened by, among others, poor quality of the audio signal and human error (where the call sign is misunderstood or the wrong call sign is given by accident). The dangers of failed or mistaken identification are obvious: incidents caused by instructions being given to the wrong aircraft. The risk of miscommunication rises where aircraft with similar call signs are present within the same ATC sector. Reducing the risk and thereby increasing the level of safety in ATC had motivated research in this area.

The Aircraft Identification Tag (AIT) concept has been developed in order to reduce call sign ambiguity, to secure identification and to thereby enhance general safety and security in commercial aviation [2]. AIT relies on digital speech watermarking technology to embed identifiers, such as the call sign, into the voice signal before the signal is transmitted to the ground. The embedded tag is a sort-of digital signature of the aircraft. The tag is hidden in the air-ground voice message as watermark. It is meant to be extracted on the ground and for example transformed into a visual signal on the radar screen (Fig. 1). The goal of AIT is to visually animate the aircraft the pilot is communicating with at the time, and in so doing, increase the chances of successful identification.

The following section describes hypothetical operational concepts of AIT. Section 3 proposes a novel speech watermarking method with a special focus on synchronisation. Simulation results which demonstrate the synchronisation performance and the noise robustness of the method are shown in Section 4.

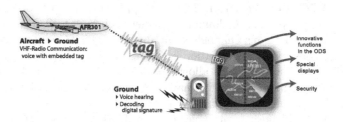

Fig. 1. Identification of transmitting aircraft through embedded watermark

2   Operational Concepts

The operational requirements within the AIT concept specify the necessary performance figures of the watermarking system. Real-time availability of the identification in less than one second implies a certain data rate for the digital transmission. A robust transmission of the message and a verification of the validity of the received data is indispensable. From the user's point of view, the system should not degrade the perceptual quality of the voice transmission. Additionally, it should be autonomous and transparent to the user and not require changes to the well-established procedures in air traffic control and on-board the aircraft.

2.1   AIT Applications

In view of a possible transfer to the industry and a wide-scale implementation, an "AIT Initial Feasibility Study" was performed to provide directions for a full feasibility analysis [3]. This study named three candidate AIT applications.

Identification of Transmitting Aircraft. Highlighting the transmitting aircraft on the controllers' human machine interface is the basic-most scenario. For this AIT application the aircraft has to embed its digital signature as a watermark in every transmitted voice message, with the signature being transmitted in less than one second. The embedded data consists of an up to 36 bit long flight or aircraft identifier, such as flight number, aircraft registration number, etc., and does not change within a flight.

In order to be useful for the controller, the embedded tag must be available on the ground within about one second after the start of a voice message. After correlating the AIT signature with available flight plan and radar data, the representing aircraft symbol on the radar screen can be transformed into a visual stimulus until the end of the aircraft voice message. The visual stimulus such as the flashing of the symbol or the animation of the corresponding speed vector as a sinusoid focuses the controller's attention on the speaking aircraft track and thereby supports the understanding of the message.

Uplink of ATC Identification. This AIT application consists of the transmission of a non-encrypted ATC domain identifier such as the ATC centre ID, over the voice communications channels from the ground ATC systems to the aircraft. The purpose of this application is to provide a basic authentication of the transmitting ATC station. This allows the pilots to verify that they communicate with the designated sector and have not mistakenly selected a wrong sector frequency. This application is simple and is relatively easy to implement. It is a first step towards more secure voice communication as it identifies 'phantom' controllers who use simple equipment.

Secure Authentication. The third AIT application provides pilots and controllers with a real-time confirmation that the received voice message is indeed transmitted by a trusted source. In order to allow proper authentication of the transmitting station or aircraft, the system transmits secured digital signatures in both air-ground and ground-air directions. The digital signatures are exchanged via AIT. The use of secured digital signatures relies on cryptography and therefore on the deployment of cryptographic keys. Key infrastructure and key management for a worldwide aeronautical system is outside the scope of this paper and AIT.

Also within the European Commission FP6 project SAFEE (Security of Aircraft in the Future European Environment [4]) it is aimed to embed a secured authentication in the voice communication using a watermark with an estimated required payload data size of 100 to 150 bits.

2.2 Operational Use and Deployment

The AIT equipment reports the voice message as having positive authentication, negative authentication, or missing authentication.

Positive authentication means that secured digital signatures are embedded in the voice message, that they are correct, and there is no threat. A negative authentication means that secured digital signatures are embedded but that they are incorrect, and that there is a recognised potential threat. This threat could for example result from an attacker playing a recorded voice message including AIT data that does not fit cryptographic keys and time stamps actually in use. A missing authentication may mean that the voice message was too short (less than one second), that the AIT data contains errors that could not be corrected (e.g. due to very poor radio quality), or that there was no AIT data embedded in the voice message (due to equipment failure or lack of equipment).

The system could be put in place gradually over time with subject to deadlines or by select sectors of airspace (ex. the airspace covered by the European Civil Aviation Conference). The different AIT applications could form separate packages and be implemented one after the other. Notably, only a complete and mandatory employment of AIT would deliver the full safety and security benefits.

3 Watermarking Speech

A watermarking algorithm for this particular AIT application faces quite different challenges compared to many other watermarking domains.

The first obvious difference is the host signal domain. A comparably small fraction of watermarking research focuses in particular on speech and its properties. A few QIM-based speech watermarking algorithms have been proposed, which quantise or modulate the line spectrum pair parameters [5], the linear prediction residual [6] or the frequency of partials of a sinusoidal speech representation [7].

The second big difference compared to the classical copyright protection application is that due to the real-time broadcast environment only an ephemeral protection for the moment of the transmission is required, and that an attacker should be unable to produce fake authenticated speech.

Third, again due to the real-time broadcast environment, those types of attacks that would maliciously try to render the watermark unreadable do not apply. Besides attacks such as transformations and collisions, especially the fact that no speech coding is involved removes a big constraint. Embedding can occur in perceptually *irrelevant* speech parameters, which would normally be likely to be removed by a speech coder.

However, the watermark has to be robust against transmission over a radio channel which is time-varying, analogue, narrow-band and noisy. Further on the duration of the watermark must be rather short, as a quick availability of the data is required.

An early AIT prototype which was based on spread-spectrum watermark techniques demonstrated the *feasibility* of the AIT concept [2]. It does not quite fulfil the operational requirements though, which is the motivation for the development of a better performing speech watermarking algorithm, especially when considering the large payload data size that secured authentication requires.

We previously presented a speech watermarking algorithm which exploits the aforementioned differences [8]. However, the system was not tested against the noisy analogue transmission channel. First, perfect synchronisation between the transmitter and receiver was assumed. But, as the watermarking channel is an analogue channel, the digital watermark embedder and decoder are in general *not* synchronised and a synchronisation error is always present. Second, a noise-less transmission channel was assumed. This also does not hold for the desired application since the aeronautical voice radio is in general a noisy transmission channel. The algorithm proposed in this paper is an extension on this work and presents a system which is capable of symbol synchronisation and watermark detection in the presence of channel noise.

3.1   Speech Signal Properties

In general, for a modern watermarking system it is crucial to consider the way the host signal is perceived [9]. Perceptual models are used for this very purpose. It is likewise important to consider the way the host signal is produced, which can provide significant insight into its properties. The following paragraphs outline some speech signal parameters which the proposed watermarking system is based on.

Speech Production and Linear Prediction. Linear prediction coding is a powerful and widely used technique for speech processing and coding [10]. Linear prediction (LP) models predict future values of a signal $s(n)$ from a linear combination of the past P signal values $s(n-k)$,

$$\hat{s}(n) = \sum_{k=1}^{P} a_k s(n-k).$$

The prediction coefficients a_k are chosen so that the prediction error (prediction residual)

$$e(n) = s(n) - \hat{s}(n) \tag{1}$$

is minimum in a mean squared error sense. The P-dimensional vector $\mathbf{a}$ of predictor coefficients a_k is given by

$$\mathbf{a} = \mathbf{R}_{ss}^{-1}\mathbf{r}_{ss} \tag{2}$$

where $\mathbf{R}_{ss}$ is the autocorrelation matrix and $\mathbf{r}_{ss}$ is the autocorrelation vector of the past P input samples. Given the excitation signal $e(n)$ and the predictor coefficients $\mathbf{a}$ as input, the LP synthesis model output is

$$s(n) = e(n) + \sum_{k=1}^{P} a_k s(n-k). \tag{3}$$

Inversely, given a recorded signal $s(n)$, the LP analysis model computes the residual $e(n)$ using (2) and (1).

The LP model is an all-pole filter model and particularly well suited for speech signals as the poles can model the resonances of the vocal tract. This is applied in the so-called source-filter model of speech production depicted in Fig. 2. In speech signals mostly two types of excitation signals e can be found. In so-called *voiced* speech sounds, such as the vowels, the vocal chords open and close periodically with a certain *pitch* and the excitation signal resembles to a pulse train with a time variant gain g. In *unvoiced* speech sounds, such as the fricatives, the vocal chords are permanently open and create turbulences in the air flow and therefore a white-noise-like excitation signal e, again with a time-variant gain. Speech in regular English language consists of approximately two thirds of voiced and one third of unvoiced segments [11].

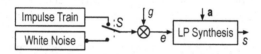

Fig. 2. Source filter model of speech production

Unvoiced Speech Perception and Noise Excitation In *unvoiced* speech it is possible to replace the excitation signal e by a white noise signal of equal power. Previous studies showed that this does not introduce perceptual distortion as long as the time-variant gain g is maintained [11]. This effect is made use of in low-rate speech coding algorithms: In unvoiced segments it is sufficient to code and transmit the LP synthesis model parameters and the running gain—the residual e is substituted on the decoder side by using white noise. This property can also be exploited for embedding a watermark [8]. Our algorithm is also based on this very same principle.

3.2 Watermarking in Unvoiced Speech

Watermark Embedding. A block diagram of the watermarking scheme is shown in Fig. 3. The digital discrete-time speech signal with a sampling frequency $f_s = 8\,\mathrm{kHz}$ is split up into voiced and unvoiced segments based on whether a pitch can be found in the signal or not. We use the PRAAT implementation of an autocorrelation-based pitch tracking algorithm [12]. Based on a local cross-correlation value maximisation the individual pitch cycles and the glottal closure instants (the physical counterpart to the aforementioned pulse train) are identified. All regions with pitch marks are considered as voiced regions, whereas all other regions, including pauses, are considered as unvoiced.

In parallel, the linear prediction residual e of the speech signal s is computed. An LP analysis of the order $P = 10$ is performed every 30 samples using (1)

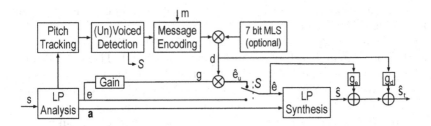

Fig. 3. Watermark embedding in unvoiced segments of speech

and a signal block (window length) of 160 samples. The predictor coefficients **a** are interpolated using their line spectral frequency (LSF) representation so that finally an updated set of coefficients is used every $L = 15$ samples. A running gain g is extracted from the residual e by computing the root mean square value within a time window of length L around each sample using a moving average filter on the squared residual $e(n)^2$.

In the unvoiced segments the residual itself is discarded and only its gain g_u is used further on. An entirely new residual is created for the unvoiced segments, which consists of a data signal that carries the watermark information m. The watermark encoding block shown in Fig. 3 outputs a binary-valued signal $d_i \in \{-1, 1\}$: In unvoiced speech segments, d is a sequence of packets of small parts of the watermark message m, in binary encoding. Each packet is prepended by a defined identification sequence which marks the beginning of a packet. In voiced speech segments, d is a uniformly distributed random binary signal. As an optional step in order to increase robustness, the original rate of d of 2000 bit/s is reduced by a factor of seven and each block of seven then identical samples is multiplied with a maximum length sequence (MLS) of equal length. Thus each sample (and bit) of d is spread in time. In both cases, the binary signal d is multiplied by the running gain g in order to form the new residual $\hat{e}_u = gd$ for the unvoiced segments. The unmodified voiced residual e_v and the artificial watermark residual $\hat{e}_u$ are re-joined into a continuous watermarked residual $\hat{e}$ by switching among the two according to the same voiced-unvoiced decision. The speech is resynthesised by LP synthesis according to (3) using the watermarked residual $\hat{e}$ and the predictor coefficients **a** that were obtained in the LP analysis.

Two optional measures that impair perceptual quality but, as we will show in Section 4, greatly enhance noise robustness are possible: One is the emphasis of the noise-like and high-frequency components of the signal by adding the residual $\hat{e}$ itself to the synthesised speech $\hat{s}$ with a constant gain g_e.[1] This could under some circumstances even increase the speech intelligibility. The second option is to create a watermark floor by adding the data signal d with a constant gain g_d to the synthesised speech signal, which is perceived as background noise.[2]

---

[1] In the simulations the residual is usually not added at all, but if stated so at a level of -20 dB relative to $\hat{s}$.

[2] The watermark floor is applied only where explicitly stated, at a level of -20 dB.

The transmitted watermarked speech signal $\hat{s}_t$ can therefore be expressed by $\hat{s}_t = \hat{s} + g_e \hat{e} + g_d d$ with g_e and g_d being zero by default.

Watermark Detection. We first assume a digital channel with everything being perfectly synchronised.[3] The basic detection scheme is outlined in Fig. 4. From the received watermark speech signal s' the LP residual e' is computed using LP analysis with the same parameters as in Section 3.2. The estimate d' of the original data signal is given by the sign of the residual, so $d' = \text{sgn}(e')$. If data spreading was used in the embedding, the residual e' is first cross-correlated with the previously applied spreading sequence and then the sign of the correlator output is used as an estimate d'. Using the predefined identification sequence, the embedded data packets, which only occur in unvoiced segments, are located. The data is extracted from these packets, decoded, and results in the message estimate m'.

Fig. 4. Watermark detection in the residual domain

3.3 Synchronisation

Synchronisation between the watermark embedder and the watermark detector is a multi-layered problem, certainly so for an analogue radio channel. We address the different aspects of sychronisation from the longest to the shortest time interval.

Synchronisation of the Voiced-Unvoiced Segmentation. The previously proposed method contained a voiced-unvoiced detection in the embedder as well as in the detector and requires that the segmentations run perfectly in sync [8]. This is difficult to achieve in practise, as there is a mismatch even with a clean channel due to artifacts introduced by the watermark embedding. One possibility to overcome this issue could be to use an error coding scheme that is capable of handling not only substitution but also insertion and deletion errors [13].

However, with the packet-based method proposed in Section 3.2 the voiced-unvoiced segmentation in the detector can be completely omitted, since the algorithm simply finds no valid data packets in the voiced regions. The details concerning the packet-based coding of the data as well as its pitfalls and improvements such as packet detection, packet loss recovery, etc. are outside the scope of this paper. Likewise Section 4 focuses on the raw bit error rate (BER) within the unvoiced segments.

Synchronisation of the LP Analysis Frames. One might intuitively assume that the block boundaries for the linear prediction analysis in the embedder and detector have to be identical. However, using LP parameters as given above and

---

[3] We will deal with synchronisation extensively in Section 3.3.

real speech signals, the predictor coefficients do not change rapidly in between the relatively short update intervals. As a consequence, a synchronisation offset in LP block boundaries is not an issue. Figure 5(a) shows the bit error rate of the proposed watermarking system using a noiseless discrete-time channel. The LP block boundaries in the detector are offset by an integer number of samples compared to the embedder. It can be observed that the bit error rate is not affected.

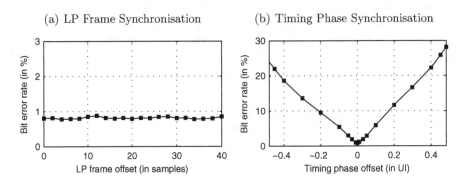

Fig. 5. Robustness of baseline system with respect to synchronisation errors

Data Frame Synchronisation. Frame synchronisation is achieved by the periodical embedding of a synchronisation sequence in the digital data stream. The sequence can be detected using, among others, the simple correlation rule, maximum-likelihood estimation or soft-decoding supported methods [14]. This is a well-explored topic in the context of digital communications and is not further treated herein.

Bit Synchronisation and Timing Recovery. If the watermarked signal is transmitted over a discrete-time channel, then with the above three measures synchronisation is established. If the channel is however an analogue channel as in the application described in Section 2, the issue of bit or symbol synchronisation arises. The digital clocks in the embedder and detector are in general time-variant, have a slightly different frequency, and have a different timing phase (which is the choice of sampling instant within the symbol interval). It is therefore necessary that the detector clock synchronises itself to the incoming data sequence. Figure 5(b) shows the resulting bit error rate when there is phase shift of a fractional sample in the sampling instants of the watermark embedder and detector. We measure this timing phase error in 'unit intervals' (UI), which is the fraction of a sampling interval $T = \frac{1}{f_s}$.

Although bit synchronisation is a well explored topic, it is still a major challenge in every modern digital communication system due to the strong impact on the detection performance. Prominent methods for non-data aided bit synchronisation are among others the transmission of a clock signal, early-late gate synchronisers, minimum mean-square-error methods, maximum likelihood methods and spectral line methods [15,16].

Spectral Line Bit Synchronisation We present in the following a watermark synchronisation scheme based on the classical spectral line method, due to its simple structure and low complexity.[4] Figure 6 shows the block diagram of the proposed synchroniser. The mathematical derivation of the general spectral line method is given in literature [16] and not repeated herein.

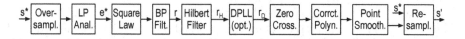

Fig. 6. Synchronisation system based on spectral line method

The received watermarked analogue signal s^* is oversampled by a factor k compared to the original sampling rate f_s.[5] The linear prediction residual e^* of the oversampled speech signal s^* is again computed using LP analysis of the same order $P = 10$ as in the embedder and with intervals of equal length in time. This results in a window length of $k * 160$ samples and an update interval of $k * 15$ samples after interpolation.

We exploit the fact that the (oversampled) residual shows some periodicity with the embedding period $T = \frac{1}{f_s}$ due to the data embedding at these instances. We extract the periodic component r at f_s from the squared residual $(e^*)^2$ with an FIR bandpass filter with a bandwidth of b=480 Hz centred at f_s. The output r of the bandpass filter is a sinusoid with period T, and is phase-shifted by $\frac{\pi}{2}$ with an FIR Hilbert filter resulting in the signal r_H. The Hilbert filter can be designed with a large transition region given that r is a bandpass signal.

The zero-crossings of r_H are determined using linear interpolation between the sample values adjacent to the zero-crossings. The positions of the zero-crossings in the positive direction are a first estimate of the positions of the ideal sampling points of the analogue signal s^*. It was found that the LP framework used in the simulations introduces a small but systematic fractional delay which depends on the oversampling factor k and results in a timing offset. We found that this timing offset can be corrected using a third order polynomial $t_\Delta = a_0 + a_1 k^{-1} + a_2 k^{-2} + a_3 k^{-3}$. The coefficients a_i have been experimentally determined to be $a_0 = 0$, $a_1 = 1.5$, $a_2 = -7$ and $a_3 = 16$.

Since the estimated sampling points contain gaps and spurious points, all points whose distance to a neighbour is smaller than 0.75 UI (unit interval) are removed in a first filtering step. In a second step all gaps larger than 1.5 UI are

---

[4] Whether the proposed structure could be implemented even in analogue circuitry could be subject of further study.

[5] In the later simulations a factor $k = 32$ is used. Values down to $k = 8$ are possible at the cost of accuracy.

filled with new estimation points which are based on the position of previous points and the observed mean distance between two points. The analogue signal is now re-sampled at these estimated positions. The output is a discrete-time signal with rate f_s, which is synchronised to the watermark embedder and which serves as input to the watermark detector.

Digital Phase-Locked Loop. The bit synchronisation can be further improved by the use of a digital phase-locked loop (DPLL), as indicated in Fig. 6. The DPLL still provides a stable output in the case of the synchronisation signal r_H being temporarily corrupt or unavailable. In addition, the use of a DPLL renders the previous point filtering and gap filling steps obsolete.

There is a vast literature on the design and performance of both analogue and digital phase-locked loops [17]. Our loop is based on a regular second order all digital phase-locked loop [18]. Inspired by dual-loop gear-shifting DPLLs [19] we use a dual-loop structure to achieve fast locking of the loop. We also dynamically adapt the bandwidth of the second loop in order to increase its robustness against spurious input signals. The exact structure and operation of the implemented loop is presented in an addendum note [20].

4   Simulation Results

The results of simulations of the proposed speech watermarking system using a short sequence of noisy air traffic control radio speech with a sampling rate of $f_s = 8\,\text{kHz}$ are presented hereafter. Out of 45800 samples of the speech signal 12527 samples have been marked unvoiced by the algorithm and used for data embedding, resulting in a raw data rate of 2188 bit/s without spreading or 312 bit/s with spreading. It is important to note that this rate is a variable rate which is dependent on the speech signal. In TIMIT, which is a large English language speech corpus, 36% of the speech is labelled as unvoiced [11].

4.1   Noise Robustness

We first show the robustness of the watermarking system with respect to additive white Gaussian noise (AWGN) on the radio channel assuming perfect synchronisation. Figure 7 shows the raw bit error rate for various signal-to-noise ratios (SNR) of the channel. One bit is embedded per unvoiced sample and the results are given for the cases with and without a watermark floor of $g_d = -20\,\text{dB}$ and for the cases with and without a residual emphasis of $g_e = -20\,\text{dB}$. Both watermark floor and residual emphasis increase the watermark energy in the signal at the expense of perceptual quality.

4.2   Synchronisation Performance

We already showed in Fig. 5 the adverse effect of a timing phase error on the bit error rate. This timing phase error results from the unsynchronised resampling of the signal. We use a piecewise cubic Hermite interpolating polynomial

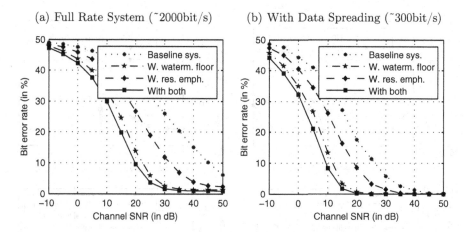

Fig. 7. Raw bit error rate at different AWGN channel SNR with perfect synchronisation

(PCHIP) to simulate the reconstruction of the continous-time signal and resample the resulting piecewise polynomial structure at equidistant sampling points at intervals of $\frac{1}{f_s}$ or $\frac{1}{kf_s}$ respectively.

In the reconstruction each sample of the embedder output $\hat{s}_t$ serves as a data point in the interpolation. The nodes of these data points would ideally reside on an evenly spaced grid with intervals of $\frac{1}{f_s}$. In order to simulate an unsynchronised system we move these nodes of the data points to different positions according to three parameters:

Timing phase offset: All nodes are shifted by a fraction of the regular grid interval $\frac{1}{f_s}$ (unit interval, UI).

Sampling frequency offset: The distance between all nodes is changed from one unit interval to a slightly different value.

Jitter: The position of each single node is shifted randomly following a Gaussian distribution with variance σ_J^2.

The proposed synchronisation system is capable of estimating the original position of the nodes, which is where the continous-time signal has to be re-sampled for optimal performance. The phase estimation error is the distance between the original and the estimated node position in unit intervals. Its root-mean-square value across the entire signal is shown in Fig. 8 for the above three types of synchronisation errors. The figure also shows the bit error rate for different sampling frequency offsets. The bit error rate as a function of the uncorrected timing phase offset was already shown in Fig. 5(b).

4.3   Overall Performance

Figure 9 shows the raw bit error rate of the overall system including watermark floor, residual emphasis and synchroniser at different channel SNR. Compared

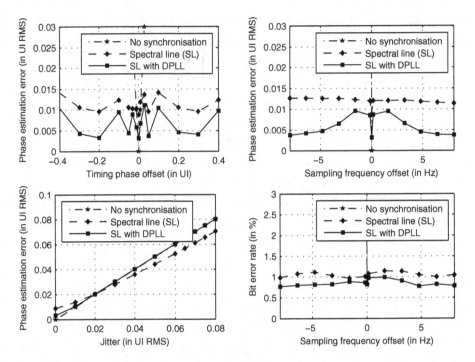

Fig. 8. Synchronisation system performance: Phase estimation error and bit error rate for various types of node offsets

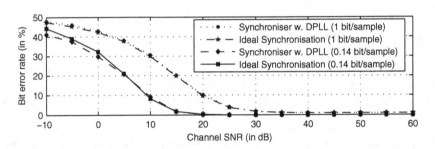

Fig. 9. Overall system performance with watermark floor and residual emphasis, with ideal (assumed) synchronisation and with the proposed synchroniser

to the case where ideal synchronisation is assumed, the raw BER increases by less than two percentage points accross all SNR.

The perceptual quality of the watermarked speech has not yet been formally evaluated. The short sample used in the simulations is available online for demonstration [21]. The difference between the original signal and both the baseline system and the system with the residual emphasis is audible but does not seem disturbing, especially for noisy signals. The watermark floor is clearly audible and its level would in practise be adjusted to the expected channel noise level. The watermark floor is then at least partially masked by the channel noise.

5 Conclusion

We presented a speech watermarking algorithm that makes use of the specific properties of speech signals and also exploits perceptual properties of the human auditory system. We showed the robustness of the system against AWGN attacks and also presented a synchronisation scheme for the analogue channel that performs within a range of one to two percentage points of raw bit error rate compared to the theoretical optimum at simulated ideal synchronisation. By limiting ourselves to a certain type of application we are able to allow complete non-robustness to certain types of attacks but can therefore achieve exceptionally high bit rates in comparison to the available channel bandwidth. Further refinement and testing is required to make the method robust against radio channel influences that are beyond AWGN and desynchronisation.

Our method is motivated by, but not limited to the described ATC application. It might also become useful for other legacy system enhancements that require backward-compatibility such as bandwidth extension for wire-line telephone systems, or for broadcast monitoring, archiving, or copyright monitoring for commercial text-to-speech systems. We also hope that the presentation of the potential aeronautical application will inspire further researchers to come up with even better methods for watermarking radio speech.

References

1. van Roosbroek, D.: EATMP communications strategy. Technical Description, vol. 2 (ed. 6.0), Eurocontrol (2006)
2. Hering, H., Hagmüller, M., Kubin, G.: Safety and security increase for air traffic management through unnoticeable watermark aircraft identification tag transmitted with the VHF voice communication. In: Proceedings of the 22nd Digital Avionics Systems Conference (DASC 2003), Indianapolis, USA (2003)
3. Celiktin, M., Petre, E.: AIT initial feasibility study. Technical report, EUROCONTROL European Air Traffic Management Programme (EATMP) (2006)
4. SAFEE: Security of aircraft in the future european environment (2007), http://www.safee.reading.ac.uk/
5. Hatada, M., Sakai, T., Komatsu, N., Yamazaki, Y.: Digital watermarking based on process of speech production. In: Proceedings of SPIE - Multimedia Systems and Applications V (2002)
6. Geiser, B., Jax, P., Vary, P.: Artificial bandwidth extension of speech supported by watermark-transmitted side information. In: Proceedings of the 9th European Conference on Speech Communication and Technology EUROSPEECH (2005)
7. Girin, L., Marchand, S.: Watermarking of speech signals using the sinusoidal model and frequency modulation of the partials. In: Proceedings of the IEEE International Conference on Acoustics, Speech, and Signal Processing (ICASSP) (2004)

8. Hofbauer, K., Kubin, G.: High-rate data embedding in unvoiced speech. In: Proceedings of the International Conference on Spoken Language Processing (INTERSPEECH), Pittsburgh, PY, USA, 2006 (2006)
9. Cox, I.J., Miller, M.L., Bloom, J.A.: Digital Watermarking. Morgan Kaufmann, San Francisco (2001)
10. Vary, P., Martin, R.: Digital Speech Transmission. John Wiley and Sons, Chichester (2006)
11. Kubin, G., Atal, B.S., Kleijn, W.B.: Performance of noise excitation for unvoiced speech. In: Proceedings of the IEEE Workshop on Speech Coding for Telecommunications (1993)
12. Boersma, P., Weenink, D.: PRAAT: doing phonetics by computer. [progr.] (2006)
13. Coumou, D.J., Sharma, G.: Watermark synchronization for feature-based embedding: Application to speech. In: Multimedia and Expo, 2006 IEEE International Conference on, Toronto, ON, Canada, pp. 849–852 (2006)
14. Cassaro, T.M., Georghiades, C.N.: Frame synchronization for coded systems over AWGN channels. IEEE Transactions on Communications 52 (2004)
15. Franks, L.E.: Carrier and bit synchronization in data communication–a tutorial review. IEEE Transactions on Communications 28 (1980)
16. Proakis, J.G., Salehi, M.: Comm. Systems Engineering. Prentice-Hall, Englewood Cliffs (2001)
17. Gardner, F.M.: Phaselock Techniques, 3rd edn. John Wiley and Sons Ltd, Chichester (2005)
18. Shayan, Y.R., Le-Ngoc, T.: All digital phase-locked loop: concepts, design and applications. IEE Proceedings F Radar and Signal Processing 136, 53–56 (1989)
19. Kim, B.: Dual-loop DPLL gear-shifting algorithm for fast synchronization. Circuits and Systems II: Analog and Digital Signal Processing, IEEE Transactions on 44, 577–586 (1997)
20. Hofbauer, K., Hering, H.: An addendum to Noise robust speech watermarking with bit synchronisation for the aeronautical radio (2007),
http://www.spsc.tugraz.at/people/hofbauer/papers/
Hofbauer_IH07_Addendum.pdf
21. Hofbauer, K.: Audio demonstration files of Noise robust speech watermarking with bit synchronisation for the aeronautical radio (2007),
http://www.spsc.tugraz.at/people/hofbauer/ih07/

A Geometrical Robust Image Data Hiding Scheme Using FCA-Based Resynchronization⋆

Peizhong Lu and Dan Wang

Fudan University, Shanghai 200433, P.R. China
pzlu@fudan.edu.cn

Abstract. This paper proposes a data hiding scheme composed of a synchronization technique by using content of the image and a DCT payload embedding method. The position of the center of gravity of each Delaunay triangle is embedded inside the red channel of the corresponding triangle. This information called synchronization information is afterward decoded robustly by fast correlation attacks used commonly in cryptanalysis. The synchronization information is used to recover the affine transform that has been done on the image. The best merit of correlation attack is its powerful error-correcting ability which can be used not only to get rid of false position information caused by a few missed or imagined features, but also to obtain enough error-free synchronization information in spite of the feature points undergoing geometry transformations. A DCT-based algorithm is used to embed secret messages in the blue channel of the image. The paper also explicitly analyses the channel noise model so as to provide a basis on which some important parameters used in fast correlation attacks are designed. Simulation results show that our data-hiding scheme is highly robust to geometrical distortions including RST and most of affine transformations, and common signal processing such as JPEG compression.

Keywords: data hiding, geometrical attacks, fast correlation attacks, affine transformations.

1 Introduction

Geometrical attack is considered as a destructive processing to most of image data hiding systems. A minor geometrical distortion often causes the hidden data undetectable due to the loss of insertion position in the attacked images. Usually, data hiding scheme for steganography requires larger embedding payload than watermark, which makes the problem more intractable. So far there exist some geometrical invariant watermark schemes [1,2,3,4,10,11,12]. But it is still an open problem to find a data hiding method with high robustness to geometrical attacks.

Watermarking algorithms combating geometrical attacks can be roughly classified into four categories based on the original image [12], invariant transform ,

---

⋆ This work was supported by the National Natural Science Foundation of China (60673082,90204013), and Special Funds of Authors of Excellent Doctoral Dissertation in China(200084).

T. Furon et al. (Eds.): IH 2007, LNCS 4567, pp. 267–278, 2007.

templates insertion [11], and the image-self content [1,2]. Among all these algorithms, the method based on the image-self content has received much more attention than others because the content of the image has permanent features remained in the attacked image. P. Bas et al. [1] utilize such features to propose a successful content-based watermarking scheme. But it is a one-bit watermark scheme, which is obviously not suitable for a data-hiding scheme for communications.

Inspired by Bas's scheme [1], a data-hiding scheme with high-embedded capacity is presented in the paper [2]. It can resist some geometrical distortions. However it has its shortcoming since the robustness to the common signal processing such as JPEG compression is very weak.

In this paper, we propose a data hiding scheme that uses content of the image to achieve synchronization and a DCT embedding scheme to embed the payload. In the scheme, we first use a new detector based on the scale-space theory to obtain feature points with inherent geometrical robustness. Then we utilize Delaunay tessellation (DT) to partition the image into different triangles. The center coordinate vector of each Delaunay triangle, considered as synchronization information (SI), is extended to a linear recurring sequence by a linear feedback shift register (LFSR). The sequence is embedded inside the red channel of the corresponding triangle. A DCT-based algorithm is used to embed communication messages in the blue channel of the image. During the extraction procedure, the synchronization information is firstly extracted according to the fast correlation attack (FCA) technique. This synchronization information is used subsequently to reconstruct the disturbed image. After this step, the data embedded in the blue channel of the image can be extracted from the resynchronized image. The general diagram of our scheme is shown in the Fig. 1, in which (a) is the insertion procedure and (b) is the extraction procedure.

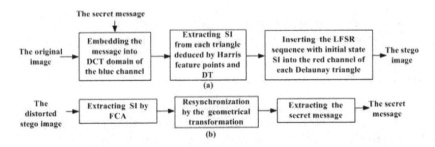

Fig. 1. The general diagram of the coding and decoding scheme

Simulation results show that the powerful error-correcting ability of the fast correlation attack brings a remarkable geometrical robustness to our scheme.

The rest of this paper is organized as follows. In section 2, the extraction of feature points based on the scale-space theory is described briefly. In Section 3, the fast correlation attack technique is introduced in detail. In Sections 4 the details of our scheme that includes insertion and extraction are proposed. In

Sections 5 experimental results are presented. Finally we conclude this paper in Section 6.

2   Feature Point Extraction Based on Scale-Space Theory

The feature point extraction has been one of the most important issues in pattern recognition and computer visualization. Among various feature point detectors, the Harris detector [5] shows the best performance in terms of restoration. The Harris points are geometrically stable under various image processing attacks including rotation, noise addition and illumination change. However, it is unstable under scaling with a large ratio since the size of the window used in extracting Harris points is fixed. So, in this paper, we improve the Harris corner detector based on scale space theory [6] to find the feature points with more robustness against scaling and other attacks.

The scale-space representation that is a set of images at different levels of resolutions can be described as follows.

$$I\left(x,y,\sigma\right) = G\left(x,y,\sigma\right) * I\left(x,y\right)$$

where $G\left(x,y,\sigma\right)$ is the Gaussian kernel with standard deviation σ and mean zero, and $*$ represents the linear convolution operator.

The function in scale-space Harris corner detector in scale σ at point (x,y) is given as follows:

$$C(x,y,\sigma) = \sigma^2 G(x,y,\sigma) * \begin{pmatrix} I_x^2(x,y,t) & I_x I_y(x,y,t) \\ I_x I_y(x,y,t) & I_y^2(x,y,t) \end{pmatrix}$$

where $I_x = \partial/\partial_x I\left(x,y,\sigma\right)$, and t is a multiple of $\sigma/2$.

Then the scale-space Harris points measure $R(x,y)$ is given in terms of $C(x,y,\sigma)$ as follows:

$$R(x,y) = \det\left(C(x,y,\sigma)\right) - 0.04\left(\text{trace}\left(C(x,y,\sigma)\right)\right)^2. \tag{1}$$

Harris points are extracted as the local maxima at each level of the scale space as follows:

$$S = \{(x,y)\,|R(x,y) > \eta, \forall(u,v) \in V_{x,y}, R(x,y) \geq R(u,v)\},$$

where η is a threshold, and $V_{x,y}$ is a small neighbor at (x,y).

Moreover, the scale-space Harris corner detector is improved by this paper in the following aspects:

a) In order to upgrade the robustness of the detector, we do twice feature point extractions. Firstly, the scale-space Harris corner detector is performed on the image to deduce a set of feature points. Secondly, the scale-space Harris corner detector is performed on the scaled and rotated image to deduce another set of feature points. Then we choose the feature points with inherent geometrical robustness in both sets for our next triangulation.

b) In our experiments, we use a mask $[-2, -1, 0, 1, 2]$ to do convolution product to get gradient magnitude, which has more accuracy than the mask used by P. Bas in [1].

c) We exploit a blur operation before detection to increase the robustness of the detector.

3   FCA-Based Coding

Fast correlation attack (FCA) is one of the most important methods in cryptanalysis, which is suitable to attack a large class of keystream generators based on linear feedback shift register (LFSR) [7][8].

Let $u = (u_1, u_2, ..., u_N)$ be an unknown keystream sequence of an LFSR with a known generator polynomial $g(x)$, $z = (z_1, z_2, ..., z_N)$ be the corresponding noisy sequence received from a binary symmetric channel (BSC) with error transition probability p, such that the two sequences have a correlation of $\Pr\{z_i = u_i\} = 1 - p$, where N is the length of the output sequence of the LFSR and $p \leq 0.5$. The so-called FCA technique is usually used to solve the following problem: for a given noisy output sequence z, how to recover the initial state $(u_1, u_2, ..., u_L)$ of the LFSR, where L is the degree of the polynomial $g(x)$.

In our scheme, each SI, the position of the center of gravity of each Delaunay triangle, is considered as the initial state of LFSR. The further generated sequence u of the LFSR is embedded inside the Delaunay triangle. During the extraction, the corresponding noisy sequence z will be extracted firstly from the distorted image. Thus the sequences of u and z have a correlation of $\Pr\{z_i = u_i\} = 1 - p$, where p should be estimated. Then, FCA is used to recover the initial state of u, namely the desired SI, from z accurately. The resynchronization can be established after we obtain enough correct SIs. The procedure of the decoding based on FCA in our scheme is introduced in detail as follows.

3.1   Parameter Design for FCA

According to Shannon's theory, a necessary condition to realize unique decoding is that the length N must be no less than $N_0 = L/C(p)$, where p is the transition probability and $C(p)$ is the channel capacity of the BSC, namely

$$C(p) = 1 + p \log_2 p + (1 - p) \log_2(1 - p). \tag{2}$$

According to the simulation results in [7], if the length N of the sequence z is not less than N_0, the correctly probability for reconstructing the initial state of u from z is larger than 0.5. If $N \geq 2N_0$, the probability of the correct decoding approximates to 1.

To determine the suitable length N, we firstly evaluate the error transition probability p of the channel used to embed synchronization information in the image. So we do statistical experiments on the channel's bit error rate (BER) for images Lena, Peppers, and Fruits. A sequence S with $M = 1024$ bits is embedded in the synchronization channel of the original images. Then another sequence S' is extracted in the geometrical distorted images. After comparing the sequences S and S', we obtain the BER of the channel in Table 1. From the results in Table 1, we claim that the average BER of the synchronization channel, namely the transition probability p, is less than 0.33.

Table 1. The BER of the synchronization channel (M: mean, V: variation)

		Rotation	Scale	Shearing	Affine
Lena	M	0.312	0.302	0.296	0.304
	V	0.044	0.037	0.040	0.030
Peppers	M	0.294	0.280	0.325	0.328
	V	0.029	0.035	0.037	0.040
Fruits	M	0.304	0.327	0.282	0.280
	V	0.049	0.042	0.039	0.038

In our scheme, we set $L = 15$, $N = 482$. Since transition probability of the synchronization channel satisfies $p \leq 0.33$, the Shannon bound is $N_0 = 15/C(p) \leq 176.31$. Thus $N \geq 2.73 N_0$ which is large enough to guarantee that the SI can be estimated successfully by FCA with the correctly decoding probability approximating to 1.

3.2 Pre-computing

Let G be a $N \times 15$ matrix such that each LFSR sequence u generated by $g(x)$ satisfies that

$$G \cdot (u_1, u_2, ..., u_{15})^t = (u_1, u_2, ..., u_N)^t, \tag{3}$$

where t denotes the transpose of matrix.

For a given received sequence z, the problem of FCA is to find the best initial vector $(x_1, x_2, ..., x_{15})$ such that the number of the correct equations in

$$G \cdot (x_1, x_2, ..., x_{15})^t = (z_1, z_2, ..., z_N)^t \tag{4}$$

is maximum.

We compute the sums of every two rows of the above equations to find all the equations such that the unknown variables $x_9, x_{10}, ..., x_{15}$ are eliminated. The number of such equations is approximately $(482 \times 481)/(2 \times 2^8) \approx 453$.

We consider the left coefficients of these equations as the binary representation of the integer, and rearrange equations into the following equations:

$$i \cdot (x_1, x_2, ..., x_8)^t = z_{i_{j,1}} \oplus z_{i_{j,2}}, i = 0, 1, ..., 255, j = 0, ..., t_i, \tag{5}$$

where i is considered as an 8-dimensional binary vector, and t_i is the number of equations with the left side $i \cdot (x_1, x_2, ..., x_8)^t$. Hence $t_0 + t_1 + \cdots + t_{255} \approx 453$, $0 \leq i_{j,1} < i_{j,2} \leq 482$.

3.3   Fast Walsh Transformation

How to efficiently find the best initial vector such that the number of the correct equations in (5) reaches maximum is a key step in FCA. We accomplish it by Walsh transformation.

Let us define f_d as a function from F_2^{15} to the real number field R such that if $t_i > 0$, then

$$f_d(i) = \sum_{1 \leq j \leq t_i} (-1)^{z_{ij,1}+d \oplus z_{ij,2}+d},$$

else $f_d(i) = 0$, where $d=0$ or 7. The Walsh transformation F_d of f_d is defined by

$$F_d(x) = \sum_{i \in F_2^{15}} f_d(i)(-1)^{i \cdot x^t}, x \in F_2^{15}.$$

By searching maximums of

$$F_0(u') = \max\left\{F_0(x) \,|\, x \in F_2^{15}\right\}$$

and

$$F_0(u'') = \max\left\{F_0(x) \,|\, x \in F_2^{15}, x \neq u'\right\},$$

we can determine whether $F_0(u') - F_0(u'') < T$, and T is the threshold. If so, we throw away the initial state as SI since there are too many errors occur at the embedded sequence. If not, we can obtain the first 8 bits initial vector $(u_1, u_2, ..., u_8)$. The remaining 8 bits of $(u_8, u_9, ..., u_{15})$ can be obtained by calculating $F_7(x)$. If the overlapped bit u_8 is the same, the preceding 15 bits of u are obtained, namely, the initial state of LFSR is obtained. In this case, we obtain the synchronization information.

4   The Proposed Data Hiding Scheme

Geometrical distortions in image, such as RST, can be modeled by a 6-parameters affine transformation A:

$$A(x_0, y_0) = \begin{pmatrix} x_t \\ y_t \end{pmatrix} = \begin{pmatrix} a & b \\ c & d \end{pmatrix} \begin{pmatrix} x_0 \\ y_0 \end{pmatrix} + \begin{pmatrix} e \\ f \end{pmatrix}$$

where (x_0, y_0) and (x_t, y_t) denote the coordinates of the original point and the transformed point respectively. The main aim of our scheme is to obtain the affine transformation A from the attacked image accurately so that the resynchronization can be realized by performing the inverted transformation A^{-1} to the distorted image.

We embed synchronization information for resynchronization and secret message for communications in the original image. The procedure of the overall insertion is depicted in Fig. 2. Since the human visual system (HVS) is insensitive to the change of the blue color in a color image, we choose the blue channel of the image as the covert communication channel for a large amount of secret message and another color channel as the synchronization channel. In our paper, the red channel is used to insert SI.

The data hiding method [13] based on DCT and convolutional codes (CC) is utilized here to accomplish the secret message insertion. In order to improve the security of the scheme, we use interleaving and spread spectrum technique (SS) to provide a random distribution of data bits. There is a HVS analyzer which calculates the just noticeable distortion (JND) mask of each color channel. The JNDs are used to control the watermark strength in different color channels respectively.

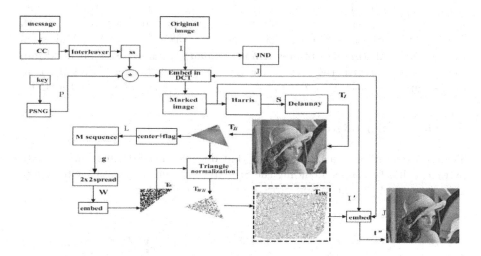

Fig. 2. Data Insertion Process

The SI insertion is described in following steps.

Step A. Feature points extraction and Delaunay tessellation

The SI is inserted into the red channel of the original image. So, the first step is to extract the feature points by the scale-space Harris detector from the red channel of the original image. Then we utilize Delaunay tessellation [9] according to the feature point set to partition the image into different triangles. Thus we obtain the Delaunay triangle set $T_I = \{T_{Ii} | i = 1, 2, \ldots, N_T\}$, where N_T is the number of Delaunay triangles.

Step B. Generation of the Synchronization Information

If v_1, v_2, v_3 are three vertices of a Delaunay triangle T_{Ii}, and $v = \frac{v_1 + v_2 + v_3}{3}$ is the center of gravity of the triangle. It can be represented by a binary bit sequence with length 20, supposing that the maximum dimension of the image is 1024×1024. For example, if the center coordinates pair (X, Y) of a triangle is (92,107), the binary bit sequence is (0001011100, 0001101011).

The fixed flag bits (11000) are added to the head of the binary bit sequence of coordinates X and Y respectively in order to increase the exactness of extraction. Then two 15-bits sequences are respectively extended into the linear recurring sequences $(a_1, a_2, \cdots, a_N)$ and $(b_1, b_2, \cdots, b_N)$ through the LFSR. The joint sequence $(u_1, u_2, ..., u_{2N}) = (a_1, a_2, ..., a_N, b_1, b_2, ..., b_N)$ will be embedded into the triangle T_{Ii} in the next step.

Step C. Triangle normalization and SI embedding

The triangle-normalized procedure [2] will transform each Delaunay triangle into a standard triangle which is a 96×96 isosceles right triangle with almost $96 \times 97/2$ pixels. Every bit of sequence u is expanded into a 2×2 block. All the blocks are then arranged in the shape of a standard triangle T_w by the scanning from center to edge. The standard triangle T_w is transformed into the Delaunay triangle T_{WIi} via the invert triangle normalization. In order to avoid the overlapping in the edge of the triangle, we choose $4656 - 800 = 3856$ bits from center to edge to embed synchronization information. Therefore the length of the embedding sequence u is $2N$, where $N = (3856/4)/2 = 482$. Multiplied by the JNDs, all the SIs obtained from Delauany triangles are embedded into the image I' in which the secret message has been embedded. Thus the final marked image I'' such that $I'' = I' + J \cdot T_{IW}$ is obtained, where J is the JND.

5   Data Extraction

The data extraction is a blind process that does not need original image. Data extraction has two steps including the SI extraction and the message extraction. The diagram of the extraction procedure is depicted in Fig.3.

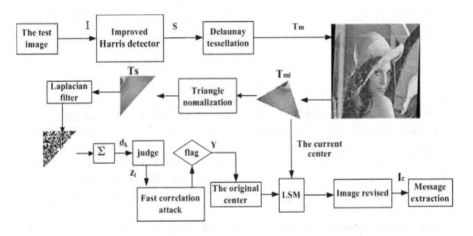

Fig. 3. Resynchronization and Decoding Process

The SI extraction is described in the following steps.

Step A. Feature points extraction and Delaunay tessellation

In the first step, the feature points and Delaunay tessellation are performed on the stego image. Let $T_m = \{T_{mi} | 0 \leq i < N_T\}$ be the triangle set, where N_T is the number of Delaunay triangles.

Step B. Triangle normalization and contaminated sequence extraction

The Delaunay triangle T_{mi} is mapped into a 96×96 standard triangle T_{si} by triangle normalization. The normalized triangle T_{si} is filtered using the 3×3 Laplacian filter that removes main energy of the original image. The filtered triangle T'_{si} is scanned from center to edge by the unit of 2×2 block, and the average value of every 2×2 block forms the sequence $\{d_i\}$. We use the hard decision to get the final output sequence z: $z_i = (1 + sign(d_i))/2, 1 \le i \le 2N$.

Step C. FCA-based decoding and the synchronization information extraction

Let $z^{(X)} = (z_1, z_2, ..., z_N)$, $z^{(Y)} = (z_{N+1}, z_{N+2}, ..., z_{2N})$. After using the FCA on $z^{(X)}$ and $z^{(Y)}$ according to the algorithm in Section 3, we obtain the initial state of the LFSR $x = (x_{14}, x_{13}, ..., x_0)$ and $y = (y_{14}, y_{13}, ..., y_0)$. If the flags at the head of x and y is checked right, we obtain a SI which is the center (X^e, Y^e) $= (x_9, x_8, \cdots, x_0, y_9, y_8, \cdots, y_0)$ of the corresponding triangle.

Step D. Affine transformation estimated by least square method

Now we obtain the set ϕ consisting of all the extracted centers (X_k^e, Y_k^e) and all the centers of the current Delaunay triangles (X_k^c, Y_k^c), namely

$$\phi = \{((X_k^e, Y_k^e), (X_k^c, Y_k^c)) | 0 \le k < N_e\},$$

where N_e denotes the number of extracted synchronization information (**NESI**). We can estimate the desired affine transformation A by means of the least square method (LSM) according to the set ϕ.

Step E. Geometrical revision and decoding for the hidden message

At last the attacked image can be calibrated by the inverted affine transformation A^{-1}. The hidden secret message can be extracted from the revised image by using the de-interleaving and Viterbi soft decoding algorithm [13].

6   Experimental Results

In order to demonstrate the effectiveness of the proposed approach, we do experiments on many images. Especially, we give the results on the popular color images including *Lena, Peppers, Girls, Milkdrop,* and *Fruit.* The size of all images is 512×512. In our scheme, let $g(x) = x^{15} + x^{14} + x^{11} + x + 1$ be the generator polynomial of the LFSR. The peak signal to noise ratio (PSNR) between the original image and the final stego image are 46.68dB, 43.72dB, 39.78dB, 43.12dB, 42.31dB respectively. Our proposed method satisfies the requirement of invisibility.

6.1   Capacity Analysis

There is no interference between the insertion of SI and the secret message because they are embedded in the different color channels. The FCA guarantees the extraction of SI exactly, which results in increasing of the embedding capacity considerably. Table 2 shows the embedded capacity of the secret message in *Lena* under the condition that BER of the received secret message is less than 0.069 for the different schemes. We can conclude that our method is a high-capacity data-hiding scheme.

Table 2. The embedded capacity of different schemes (bits)

	Bas's[1]	Pereira's[11]	Kang's[4]	Ours
Capacity	1	72	264	5120

6.2 NESI Analysis

We compare the number of extracted synchronization information (NESI) between Bas scheme [1] and our scheme in Table 3. The results show that our scheme can extract enough synchronization information from the distorted images.

Table 3. NESI

	Rotation 0.5		Scale 1.5	
	Bas's	Our	Bas's	Our
Lena	31	47	26	26
Peppers	26	44	40	46
Girls	57	54	48	48
Milk	30	43	28	39
Fruit	45	47	25	49

6.3 Robustness

We use StirMark 4.0[10] to do geometrical attacks that include: (1) scaling, (2) aspect ratio change, (3) rotation, (4) shearing, (5) general geometric affine transformation, (6) JPEG, (7) cropping, where parameters of attacks except cropping are all same as Dong's method [3], and the cropping proportion are 0.05,0.15,0.25 respectively; Table 4 shows average BER of the extracted secret message from five marked images after different attacks.

Moreover, we do mixed attacks that include geometrical attacks and common signal processing as follows: JPEG compression with quality factor 85 to the stego image after cropping and rotation. The cropping proportion is 0.05. The

Table 4. Robustness results (the data is BER)

	(1)	(2)	(3)	(4)	(5)	(6)	(7)
Dong[3]	0.002	0.001	0	0	0.001	0	0.516
Ours	0	0	0	0	0.002	0.012	0.001

Table 5. The robustness to mixed attacks(the data is BER)

	(1)	(2)	(3)	(4)	(5)
Mixed 1	0	0	0	0.068	0.048
Mixed 2	0	0	0.001	0.066	0.015

scaling proportion is 1.1, and the rotation angles are:(1) 0.25; (2) 0.5;(3) 0.75;(4) 1;(5) 2. Table 5 shows the average BER value of the extracted message from five marked images by the mixed attacks.

From above experimental results, we can conclude that our scheme is highly robust to both geometrical attacks and common signal processing. The performances of our scheme obviously exceeds to that of Dong's method [3] in almost all aspects except in the case of lower JPEG's quality factor. However, our scheme is immune to the cropping, but Dong's method does not have this ability because it badly depends on the whole image when they calculate the moment of image.

7   Conclusions

In this paper, we propose a new data-hiding scheme with high capacity and strong robustness for color image. Our scheme has three advantages to combat geometrical attacks. Firstly, since we exploit the improved Harris detecting approach based on scale-space theory, most of Harris feature points extracted by our method are inherent immune to geometrical attacks, which enhances the robustness to geometrical transformations, especially to scaling. Secondly, although some feature points may be missed or changed after geometrical attacks, the resynchronization can also be established if only 3 center coordinates of Delaunay triangle are evaluated accurately. Finally and the most importantly, the FCA technique guarantees to extract enough SI efficiently and exactly even the BER of the channel is very large. We do not design our own FCA in this paper. We only choose the particular FCA proposed by Chose [8]. Recently, there are a plentiful researches on FCA in cryptography which made the solutions more and more efficient. All the new advanced FCAs with the state of the art will be more suitable for our information hiding scheme.

References

1. Bas, P., Chassery, J.M., Macq, B.: Geometrically invariant watermarking using feature points. IEEE Trans. on Image Processing 11(9), 1014–1028 (2002)
2. Xue, G., Lu, P.: A counter-geometric distortions data hiding scheme using double channels in color images. In: Cox, I., Kalker, T., Lee, H.-K. (eds.) IWDW 2004. LNCS, vol. 3304, pp. 33–44. Springer, Heidelberg (2005)
3. Dong, P., Brankov, J.G.: Digital watermarking robust to geometric distortions. IEEE Trans. on Image Processing 14(12), 2140–2150 (2005)

4. Kang, X., Huang, J., Shi, Y.Q., et al.: A DWT-DFT composite watermarking scheme robust to both affine transform and JPEG compression. IEEE Trans. Circuits Syst. Video Technol. 13(8), 776–785 (2003)
5. Harris, C., Stephen, M.: A combined corner and edge detector. In: Proc. of the 4th Alvey Vision Conf., pp.147–151 (1988)
6. Lowe, D.G.: Distinctive image features from scale-invariant keypoints. Int. J. Compute Vision 60, 99–110 (2004)
7. Siegenthaler, T.: Decrypting a class of stream ciphers using ciphertext only. IEEE Trans. on Comput. 34, 81–85 (1985)
8. Chose, P., Joux, A., Mitton, M.: Fast correlation attacks: an algorithmic point of view. In: Knudsen, L.R. (ed.) EUROCRYPT 2002. LNCS, vol. 2332, pp. 76–88. Springer, Heidelberg (2002)
9. Mitchell, D.P., Netravali, A.N.: Reconstruction filters in computer graphics, Computer Graphics. Proceedings of SIGGRAPH 22(4), 221–228 (1988)
10. Lin, C.Y., Wu, M., Bloom, J.A., et al.: Rotation, scale, and translation resilient watermarking for images. IEEE Trans. on image Processing 10(5), 767–782 (2001)
11. Pereira, S., Pun, T.: Robust template matching for affine resistant image watermarks. IEEE Trans. Image Process. 9(6), 1123–1129 (2000)
12. Dong, P., Brankov, J., Galatsanos, N., Yang, Y.: Geometric robust watermarking based on a new mesh model correction approach. In: Proc. IEEE Int. Conf. Image Processing, pp. 493–496 (June 2002)
13. Hernández, J.R., Amado, M., Perez, F.: DCT-Domain watermarking techniques for still images: Detector performance analysis and a new structure. IEEE Trans. on Image Processing 9(1), 55–68 (2000)
14. Petitcolas, F.: Stirmark4.0, [Online] (2006), http://www.cl.cam.ac.uk/users/fapp2/watermarking/stirmark/

Optimization of Tardos's Fingerprinting Codes in a Viewpoint of Memory Amount*

Koji Nuida[1], Manabu Hagiwara[1], Hajime Watanabe[1], and Hideki Imai[1,2]

[1] Research Center for Information Security (RCIS), National Institute of Advanced
Industrial Science and Technology (AIST)
Akihabara-Daibiru room 1102, 1-18-13 Sotokanda, Chiyoda-ku, Tokyo 101-0021,
Japan
http://www.rcis.aist.go.jp/index-en.html
{k.nuida, hagiwara.hagiwara, h-watanabe, h-imai}@aist.go.jp
[2] Chuo University
1-13-27 Kasuga, Bunkyo-ku, Tokyo 112-8551, Japan

Abstract. It is known that Tardos's collusion-secure probabilistic fingerprinting code (Tardos code) has length of theoretically minimal order. However, Tardos code uses certain continuous probability distribution, which causes that huge amount of extra memory is required in a practical use. An essential solution is to replace the continuous distributions with finite discrete ones, preserving the security. In this paper, we determine the optimal finite distribution for the purpose of reducing memory amount; the required extra memory is reduced to less than 1/32 of the original in some practical setting. Moreover, the code length is also reduced (to, asymptotically, about 20.6% of Tardos code), and some further practical problems such as approximation errors are also considered.

Keywords: fingerprinting code, Tardos code, optimization, watermarking, digital rights management.

1 Introduction

As the amount of secret or commercial digital objects (e.g. movies, musics, customers' data) grows rapidly, nowadays several serious information leakage and spreads of illegal copies have been reported as well. Many of them were in fact caused by users who obtained the object in a right manner. Such illegal copying itself is very hard to be prevented; an alternative and more realistic solution is to embed secret identification information of each user into the digital object by watermarking technique, making the guilty users ("pirates") traceable from the copied object. For this purpose, the embedded information should be secure against "collusion-attacks", that is detection or modification by a group of pirates. A *c-secure fingerprinting code* is such identification information which is designed as being secure against up to c pirates.

---

* This study has been sponsored by the Ministry of Economy, Trade and Industry, Japan (METI) under contract, New-generation Information Security R&D Program, and by JSPS Grants-in-Aid for Scientific Research.

T. Furon et al. (Eds.): IH 2007, LNCS 4567, pp. 279–293, 2007.

It is known that Tardos's c-secure probabilistic fingerprinting code [8] has length of theoretically minimal order with respect to c. However, in Tardos code, biases of bit values of codewords for each position are decided by outputs of certain *continuous* probability distribution, which we call a *bias distribution* in this paper, and those outputs will be reused for pirates tracing. This means that some approximation of bias distributions is necessary in implementation of Tardos codes; however, effects of such approximation on the security performance has not been clarified so far. Moreover, since (even approximated) values of such continuous distributions have high accuracy, the contents server must store distinct output values for every position as well as the codebook itself, therefore huge amount of extra memory is required in a practical use of this code.

A simple but essential solution for these problems is to replace the bias distributions with *finite discrete* ones. For example, if a bias distribution has 4 possibilities of outputs, then only 2 bits of memory (expressing "which of the 4 values") are required to record one output. This solution was first explored by Hagiwara, Hanaoka and Imai in [3] (*HHI scheme*); they established a formula of sufficient code length achieving desired security performance, in terms of data for given (finite) bias distribution. They also proposed a condition "c-indistinguishability" for suitable bias distribution, and gave three examples of such distributions which reduced the code lengths to about 60% of Tardos codes.

However, for the purpose of reducing memory amount, it has not been discussed whether their choice of bias distribution is optimal or not. Moreover, although their code requires us to compute some "score" of each user for tracing the pirates, and the scores cannot be explicitly representable on computers in general, effects of approximation of scores have not been considered. The central aim of this paper is to solve these problems.

This paper is organized as follows. After some preliminary (Sect. 2) on the model of fingerprinting codes and some preceding works, first we show (Sect. 3) a strong evidence that the c-indistinguishability property of bias distributions contributes essentially to reduce the resulting code lengths. Thus we restrict our attention to bias distributions with this property. Then we determine both the c-indistinguishable (c-ind, in short) bias distributions (Sect. 4) and the optimal distributions among them (Sect. 5). We refer to the optimal distributions as *Gauss-Legendre* (*GL*) *distributions*, since these are closely related to Gauss-Legendre quadrature (a classical approximation method for integral). The c-ind GL distribution has only $\lceil c/2 \rceil$ possibilities of outputs, where $\lceil x \rceil$ denotes as usual the smallest integer n with $x \leq n$, so only $\lceil \log_2 \lceil c/2 \rceil \rceil$ bits of memory are required to store one output. Table 1 gives a comparison of required memory amount to store outputs of bias distributions (for Tardos codes, the outputs are approximated by single-precision binary floating-point numbers); this shows that our proposal can reduce the memory amount dramatically.

Secondly, we improve the formula of code lengths given in [3] in order to reduce code lengths further and to consider effects of approximation in computation of users' scores (Sect. 6). The combination of our new formula and GL distributions provides much shorter code lengths than Tardos codes. Figure 1 shows the ratio

Table 1. Comparison of required extra memory amount

In case 1, No. of pirates = 2, No. of users = 200, error probability = 10^{-11}.
In case 2, No. of pirates = 4, No. of users = 400, error probability = 10^{-11}.

		bits / position	code length	total bits
Case 1	Tardos [8]	32	12,400	396,800
	Ours	0	**6,278**	0
	%	0	**50.6**	0
Case 2	Tardos [8]	32	51,200	1,638,400
	Ours	1	**19,750**	**19,750**
	%	**3.1**	**38.6**	**1.2**

of lengths given by our formula and the original one [3] applied to the same GL distributions, relative to Tardos codes. In particular, although details are omitted here due to limited pages, we are indeed able to prove that the ratio of our length converges to about 20.6% as $c \to \infty$. Some more numerical examples are given in Sect. 6.1.

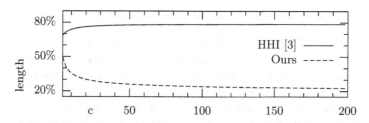

Fig. 1. Ratio of code lengths relative to Tardos codes

At the end of this paper, we give remarks on some recent works on Tardos codes (Sect. 7), and collect the proofs of our theorems as an appendix.

2 Preliminary

2.1 Our Model for Fingerprinting Codes

In our model, a contents server embeds a codeword $c_i = (c_{i,1}, c_{i,2}, \ldots, c_{i,n})$, where n is the code length and $c_{i,j} \in \{0, 1\}$, into a digital object distributed to i-th user u_i by certain watermarking technique. When an illegal copy of the object is found, which contains a codeword $y = (y_1, \ldots, y_n)$ (called *forged codeword*), the contents server perform some *tracing algorithm* with y and all the c_is as input for detecting the *pirates* (users who created the illegal copy). Note that some bits in y are possible to be undecodable, which are denoted by a symbol '?'.

If there are ℓ pirates, they try to detect the fingerprint from differences of the contents they have, and to modify the detected parts of fingerprint in their illegal copy by some strategy. As well as most of the preceding works on fingerprinting codes (e.g. [1,3,8]), here we assume the followings about the pirates' strategy:

Marking Assumption: If all the bits $c_{i_1,j}, c_{i_2,j}, \dots$ in codewords of the pirates $u_{i_1}, u_{i_2}, \dots$ at the same position j coincide, then $y_j = c_{i_1,j}$.

Pirates' Knowledge: Pirates have no knowledge about innocent (non-pirate) users' codewords, so y is independent of those codewords.

To discuss on the error probability of tracing algorithms, here we clarify the meaning of the following terms:

false-negative: the tracing algorithm outputs *no pirates*;
false-positive: the tracing algorithm outputs *at least one innocent user*;
tracing error: false-negative or false-positive (or possibly both) occurs.

A fingerprinting code (equipped with a tracing algorithm) is called *c-secure* (*with ε-error*) if the probability of tracing error is bounded above by a negligibly small value ε whenever the number of pirates does not exceed c (i.e. $\ell \le c$).

2.2   Tardos Code and Its Generalization

The construction and tracing algorithms of c-secure Tardos codes [8] and its generalization given in [3] are summarized as follows. First, the contents server chooses the random values $p^{(j)}$, $0 < p^{(j)} < 1$, independently for every $1 \le j \le n$ according to a given probability distribution $\mathcal{P}$ (which we refer to as the *bias distribution*). Note that we only consider the bias distributions *symmetric* with respect to $1/2$; i.e. outputting p and $1-p$ with the same probability. The obtained sequence $P = (p^{(1)}, p^{(2)}, \dots, p^{(n)})$ should be stored and be kept secret (pirates are allowed to guess the values $p^{(j)}$ from the distribution $\mathcal{P}$ and their codewords, but not to know about the actual choices of $p^{(j)}$). Then, secondly, the server decides each codeword c_i in the following probabilistic manner: $Prob(c_{i,j} = 1) = p^{(j)}$ and $Prob(c_{i,j} = 0) = 1 - p^{(j)}$ for j-th position. All the bits $c_{i,j}$ should be chosen independently.

In the tracing algorithm, the server computes a score S_i of each user u_i by $S_i = \sum_{j=1}^n S_i^{(j)}$, where $S_i^{(j)} = \sqrt{(1 - p^{(j)})/p^{(j)}}$ if $(y_j, c_{i,j}) = (1,1)$, $S_i^{(j)} = -\sqrt{p^{(j)}/(1 - p^{(j)})}$ if $(y_j, c_{i,j}) = (1,0)$, and $S_i^{(j)} = 0$ if $y_j \in \{0, ?\}$. The output of the algorithm is the (possibly empty) set of *all* users u_i with $S_i \ge Z$, where Z is a suitably chosen threshold parameter.

2.3   Problems

As mentioned in Introduction, Tardos code uses *continuous* bias distribution $\mathcal{P}$, which causes that explicit implementation on computers seems to be impossible. Moreover, when we would like to approximate $\mathcal{P}$ by e.g. floating-point numbers, we face following two problems; the original security proof does not consider effects of such approximation; and huge amount of extra memory is required to store the approximated values of $\mathcal{P}$.

To solve these problems, HHI scheme in [3] used *finite* bias distributions, and gave a formula of corresponding code length and threshold parameter making the code c-secure. They also proposed a condition "c-indistinguishability" for bias distributions so that the resulting code length will be shorter.

However, it has been open whether their choice of bias distributions is optimal or not for the purpose of reducing extra memory amount. Moreover, although the users' scores become irrational numbers in many practical cases and so approximation is necessary, effects of such approximation on the error probability has not been discussed. We solve these problems in the following sections.

3   A Characterization of c-Indistinguishability

Before solving these problems, first we study the c-indistinguishability property (or c-*ind* in short) for bias distributions proposed in [3]. (See the Appendix for definition, since it requires some more notations.) This condition was first introduced for reducing code lengths determined by the formula in [3]. In contrast, here we give a strong evidence that this condition essentially contributes to decrease error probability of the resulting code, thus for reducing code lengths.

We start with an arbitrary finite bias distribution $\mathcal{P}$. Let $u_1, u_2, \ldots, u_\ell$ ($\ell \leq c$) be the pirates and $c_1, c_2, \ldots, c_\ell$ their codewords. Their aim is that none of them will be outputted by the tracing algorithm, therefore they try to create the forged codeword y by a strategy so that all of their scores will be as small as possible. Thus they would hope that at least the sum S of their scores will be small. Now by Marking Assumption (see Sect. 2.1) and the definition of the tracing algorithm (see Sect. 2.2), we have $S = S' + S''$, where S' denotes the sum of scores corresponding to positions j in which either all bits $c_{1,j}, \ldots, c_{\ell,j}$ are equal or pirates choose $y_j \in \{0, ?\}$, which is independent of the pirates' strategy, and S'' denotes the sum of scores corresponding to the remaining positions.

Now for each position j of the latter type, we denote (for $I \subset \{1, 2, \ldots, \ell\}$) the event that $c_{i,j} = 1$ if $i \in I$ and $c_{i,j} = 0$ if $i \notin I$ by $\mathcal{B}_I$, and the event that $\mathcal{B}_I$ occurs and $y_j = 1$ by $\mathcal{B}'_I$. Then the contribution of j-th position for S'' under the event $\mathcal{B}'_I$ is $x\sqrt{(1 - p^{(j)})/p^{(j)}} - (\ell - x)\sqrt{p^{(j)}/(1 - p^{(j)})}$, where $x = |I|$. Thus its expected value over the choices of $p^{(j)}$ conditioned on $\mathcal{B}'_I$ is

$$\sum_p Prob(p^{(j)} = p \mid \mathcal{B}'_I) \left(x\sqrt{\frac{1-p}{p}} - (\ell - x)\sqrt{\frac{p}{1-p}} \right) \tag{1}$$

where the sum is taken over all possible outputs of the bias distribution $\mathcal{P}$. Regarding this value, we will prove the following result in Appendix.

Proposition 1. *The expected value Eq.(1) is always 0 if and only if $\mathcal{P}$ is c-indistinguishable.*

Hence no strategy better for pirates than the others in average exists if $\mathcal{P}$ is c-ind; this fact is an essential importance of c-indistinguishability. By this observation, we may restrict our attention to c-ind distributions.

4   Determining c-Indistinguishable Distributions

In this section, we determine all the c-ind bias distributions $\mathcal{P}$ for an arbitrary c. More explicitly, we prove that the c-ind bias distributions are in one-to-one correspondence with the following mathematical objects:

Definition 1. *A pair $\mathcal{Q} = (X, w)$ of a finite subset X of the interval $(-1, 1)$ and a positive function $w > 0$ on X is called a* quadrature system *(QS in short) of degree d if $\int_{-1}^{1} F(t)dt = \sum_{\xi \in X} w(\xi)F(\xi)$ for any real polynomial $F(t)$ of degree up to d. We refer to the size $|X|$ of X as* order *of $\mathcal{Q}$, and we say that $\mathcal{Q}$ is* symmetric *if $-X = \{-\xi \mid \xi \in X\} = X$ and $w(-\xi) = w(\xi)$ for all $\xi \in X$.*

Example 1. Let $X = \{0, \pm\sqrt{15}/5\}$, $w(0) = 8/9$ and $w(\pm\sqrt{15}/5) = 5/9$. Then it can be verified that $\int_{-1}^{1} F(t)dt = (5/9)F(-\sqrt{15}/5) + (8/9)F(0) + (5/9)F(\sqrt{15}/5)$ for any polynomial $F(t)$ of degree at most 5. Thus (X, w) is a (symmetric) QS of order 3 and degree 5.   □

Our aforementioned result (proved in Appendix) is expressed as follows.

Theorem 1. *The c-ind bias distributions are in one-to-one correspondence with the symmetric QS of degree $c - 1$. Namely, for a symmetric QS $\mathcal{Q} = (X, w)$ of degree $c - 1$, define a probability distribution $\mathcal{P}(\mathcal{Q})$ by*

$$\mathcal{P}(\mathcal{Q}) = \left\{ \left(\frac{1+\xi}{2}, \frac{w(\xi)}{C\sqrt{1-\xi^2}} \right) \mid \xi \in X \right\} \quad \text{where } C = \sum_{\xi \in X} \frac{w(\xi)}{\sqrt{1-\xi^2}} \quad (2)$$

(the above expression means that $\mathcal{P}(\mathcal{Q})$ outputs the value $(1+\xi)/2$ with probability $w(\xi)/(C\sqrt{1-\xi^2})$). On the other hand, for a c-ind distribution $\mathcal{P} = \{(p_i, q_i) \mid 1 \le i \le m\}$, define $\mathcal{Q}(\mathcal{P}) = (\{\xi_1, \ldots, \xi_m\}, w)$ by $\xi_i = 2p_i - 1$ and

$$w(\xi_i) = \frac{\sqrt{p_i(1-p_i)}q_i}{C'} \quad \text{for } 1 \le i \le m \text{ where } C' = \frac{1}{2}\sum_{i=1}^{m} \sqrt{p_i(1-p_i)}q_i \ . \quad (3)$$

Then $\mathcal{P}(\mathcal{Q})$ is c-ind, $\mathcal{Q}(\mathcal{P})$ is a symmetric QS of degree $c - 1$, and we have $\mathcal{Q}(\mathcal{P}(\mathcal{Q})) = \mathcal{Q}$ and $\mathcal{P}(\mathcal{Q}(\mathcal{P})) = \mathcal{P}$.

Thus the c-ind distributions are determined in terms of symmetric QS. Note that any symmetric QS of even degree $2d$ is also a QS of degree $2d + 1$ by definition, so this theorem infers that c-ind distributions are also $(c + 1)$-ind if c is odd. Thus we may concentrate our attention on the case that c is even.

5   The Optimal Bias Distribution

Among the c-ind bias distributions, in this section we determine the optimal distributions for the purpose of reducing extra memory. As mentioned in Introduction, the optimal c-ind distributions are exactly the ones with minimal number of possible outputs. By Theorem 1, such distributions correspond to the symmetric QSs of degree $c - 1$ with minimal order. Moreover, the following classical result tells us the complete characterization of such QSs.

Theorem 2 (See [2,7] etc.). *For $m \geq 1$, let $L_m(t) = (\frac{d}{dt})^m(t^2-1)^m/(2^m \cdot m!)$ be the m-th Legendre polynomial. Let X be the set of zeroes of $L_m(t)$ (i.e. the values ξ with $L_m(\xi) = 0$), and for $\xi \in X$, put $w(\xi) = 2/((1-\xi^2)L'_m(\xi)^2)$. Then $\mathcal{Q}_m = (X, w)$ is a symmetric QS of order m and degree $2m-1$.*

Moreover, no QS of degree $2m-1$ other than the above QS has order less than or equal to m. Hence the above QS is the unique QS of minimal order.

(For example, the QS in Example 1 is $\mathcal{Q}_3$.) We refer to the QS $\mathcal{Q}_m$ given in this theorem as *Gauss-Legendre QS*, since this is deeply related to Gauss-Legendre quadrature formula, a classical approximation method of integral (see e.g. [7]). Thus the optimal distributions (*GL distributions*) are completely determined by Theorems 1 and 2.

Owing to these results, we can also describe the GL distributions explicitly as follows (its proof will be given in Appendix). See Table 2 for examples.

Theorem 3. *Let $\tilde{L}_m(t) = (\frac{d}{du})^m(u^2-1)^m|_{u=2t-1}$, a polynomial in t of degree m. Then the unique optimal $(2m)$-ind distribution is equal to*

$$\mathcal{P} = \mathcal{P}_{2m} = \left\{ \left(p, \frac{C}{(p(1-p))^{3/2}\tilde{L}'_m(p)^2} \right) \;\middle|\; \tilde{L}_m(p) = 0 \right\}, \tag{4}$$

where C is the normalized constant (this expression means that $\mathcal{P}$ outputs each value p such that $\tilde{L}_m(p) = 0$, with probability $C/((p(1-p))^{3/2}\tilde{L}'_m(p)^2)$). This distribution has m possible outputs.

Table 2. The optimal c-ind distributions $\mathcal{P}_c$

Here we omit the output values less than $1/2$ by symmetry.

c	$\tilde{L}(t)$	value	probability
2	$2(2t-1)$	$1/2$	1
4	$8(6t^2 - 6t + 1)$	$1/2 + \sqrt{3}/6$	$1/2$
6	$48(2t-1)$	$1/2$	$(20\sqrt{10} - 32)/93$
	$\cdot(10t^2 - 10t + 1)$	$1/2 + \sqrt{15}/10$	$(125 - 20\sqrt{10})/186$
8	$384(70t^4 - 140t^3$	$1/2 + \sqrt{525 - 70\sqrt{30}}/70$	$1/4 + (41\sqrt{30} - 49\sqrt{21})/12$
	$+ 90t^2 - 20t + 1)$	$1/2 + \sqrt{525 + 70\sqrt{30}}/70$	$1/4 - (41\sqrt{30} - 49\sqrt{21})/12$

6   Formula of Code Lengths

We have determined the optimal c-ind bias distributions above. In this section, we improve the formula of code lengths and thresholds in [3] to reduces code lengths further and to consider effects of approximation of scores. Since (as suggested by Table 2) we would be required to approximate the optimal distributions in a practical case, we start with an arbitrary finite bias distribution $\mathcal{P}$.

We prepare several notations. Let $p_0, p_1, \ldots, p_k$ (with $p_0 < p_1 < \cdots < p_k$) be the possible outputs of $\mathcal{P}$ and $q_i = Prob(\mathcal{P}$ outputs $p_i)$, so $p_{k-i} = 1 - p_i$ and $q_{k-i} = q_i$ by our assumption on $\mathcal{P}$ (see Sect. 2.2). Let $\delta \geq 0$ be a bound of approximation error of users' scores, and U_i a value such that $|U_i - \sqrt{(1-p_i)/p_i}| \leq \delta$, for $0 \leq i \leq k$. Put $r(t) = (e^t - 1 - t)/t^2$ for $t > 0$, $f_{\ell,x}(p) = p^x(1-p)^{\ell-x}\left(x\sqrt{(1-p)/p} - (\ell - x)\sqrt{p/(1-p)}\right)$. Moreover, let $R_{\ell,x} = \max\{0, E_p[f_{\ell,x}(p)]\}$ for $0 \leq x \leq \ell$, where E_p denotes the expected value over outputs p of $\mathcal{P}$, and $\mathcal{R}_{\ell,p} = E_p[-f_{\ell,0}(p)] - \sum_{x=1}^{\ell-1}\binom{\ell}{x}R_{\ell,x}$ for $1 \leq \ell \leq c$. (Some numerical example will be given later.)

Based on these values, choose a positive value $\mathcal{R}$ such that $\mathcal{R} \leq \mathcal{R}_{\ell,p}$ for all $1 \leq \ell \leq c$, two approximated values ψ_1 and ψ_2 of $\sqrt{(1-p_0)/p_0}$ such that $0 < \psi_1 \leq \sqrt{(1-p_0)/p_0} \leq \psi_2$, and two positive values x_i' $(i = 1, 2)$ so that $0 < x_i'r(x_i') \leq \eta_i\mathcal{R}\psi_i/c$; where $\eta_1 = 1/2$ and $\eta_2 = \sqrt{c}/2$. (The resulting code length will be reduced as $\mathcal{R}$ increases, approximated values ψ_1 and ψ_2 become sharper, and x_1' and x_2' increase.) Moreover, take A_i $(i = 1, 2)$ such that

$$A_i \geq \frac{c}{(1 - \eta_1 - \eta_2/c)\mathcal{R} - 2\delta c} \cdot \frac{\psi_2}{x_i'} \log \frac{1}{\varepsilon_i} , \tag{5}$$

where ε_1 and ε_2 are security parameters and the base of log is e. (The code length will be shorter as A_1 and A_2 become smaller.)

Now we determine the code length n and threshold Z for our code by

$$n = A_1 + A_2 \text{ and } Z = \left(\left(1 - \frac{\eta_2}{c}\right)\frac{\mathcal{R}}{c} - \delta\right)A_1 + \left(\frac{\eta_1\mathcal{R}}{c} + \delta\right)A_2 . \tag{6}$$

Note that, even if the value $R_{\ell,x}$ or $\mathcal{R}_{\ell,p}$ (determined by $\mathcal{P}$) is not explicitly representable on computers, all values $\mathcal{R}$, ψ_i and x_i' can be chosen as explicitly representable, and A_i (therefore the code length) can be chosen as integers.

Moreover, in the tracing algorithm, the server computes the "approximated score" $\widehat{S}_i$ of i-th user by $\widehat{S}_i = \sum_{j=1}^n \widehat{S}_i^{(j)}$, where

$$\widehat{S}_i^{(j)} = \begin{cases} U_m & \text{if } y_j = 1, \ c_{i,j} = 1 \text{ and } p^{(j)} = p_m , \\ -U_{k-m} & \text{if } y_j = 1, \ c_{i,j} = 0 \text{ and } p^{(j)} = p_m , \\ 0 & \text{if } y_j \in \{0, ?\} . \end{cases} \tag{7}$$

(Note that this $\widehat{S}_i$ is an approximated value of the true score S_i with approximation error $|\widehat{S}_i - S_i| \leq n\delta$.) Then this algorithm is slightly modified as outputting the i-th user as a candidate of pirates if and only if $\widehat{S}_i \geq Z$.

Theorem 4. *In the above setting, the probability of false-positive is less than $1 - (1 - \varepsilon_1)^{N-1} \leq (N-1)\varepsilon_1$ if there are N users in total. On the other hand, the probability of false-negative is less than ε_2. Hence the tracing error probability is bounded by ε if we put $\varepsilon_1 = \varepsilon_2 = \varepsilon/N$.*

The proof of this theorem will be given in Appendix. Note that the original formula in [3] can be recovered by putting $\delta = 0$, $\eta_1 = 1/4$ and $\eta_2 = c/2$. Figure

1 above shows the ratio of code lengths given by our formula Eq.(6) and the original formula, both applied to the same GL distributions, relative to lengths of Tardos codes. In fact, we can prove that the ratio of our length converges to about 20.6% as $c \to \infty$ (detail is omitted here due to limited pages and will appear in the full version of this paper).

6.1 Numerical Example

We use the bias distributions given in the left-hand side of Table 3, with $c \in \{2, 4, 6, 8\}$. We choose approximated bitwise scores U_i as in the right-hand side of Table 3, with $\delta = 0$ if $c = 2$ and $\delta = 10^{-5}$ if $c \in \{4, 6, 8\}$. Then we can compute the auxiliary values $\mathcal{R}$, ψ_1, ψ_2, x_1', x_2', A_1 and A_2 as in Table 4, where $\varepsilon_1 = \varepsilon_2 = \varepsilon/N$, $N = 100c$ and $\varepsilon = 10^{-11}$ (recall that $\eta_1 = 1/2$ and $\eta_2 = \sqrt{c}/2$).

Now if $c = 2$, then the code length n and threshold Z are given by

$$ n = A_1 + A_2 \text{ and } Z = \left(\frac{1}{4} - \frac{1}{8\sqrt{2}} \right) A_1 + \frac{1}{8} A_2 . \tag{8} $$

On the other hand, if $c \in \{4, 6, 8\}$, then we have

$$ n = A_1 + A_2 \text{ and } Z = \left(\left(1 - \frac{1}{2\sqrt{c}} \right) \frac{\mathcal{R}}{c} - 10^{-5} \right) A_1 + \left(\frac{\mathcal{R}}{2c} + 10^{-5} \right) A_2 . \tag{9} $$

The resulting values of n and Z are shown in Table 4, where the row '%' gives the percentage of our code length relative to Tardos code. This shows that our contribution indeed reduces the code lengths.

Table 3. Bias distributions $\mathcal{P}$ and approximated scores in the example

c	p	q	c	p	q
2	0.50000	1.00000	8	0.06943	0.24833
4	0.21132	0.50000		0.33001	0.25167
	0.78868	0.50000		0.66999	0.25167
6	0.11270	0.33201		0.93057	0.24833
	0.50000	0.33598			
	0.88730	0.33201			

c	U_0	U_1	U_2	U_3
2	1			
4	1.93187	0.51763		
6	2.80590	1	0.35639	
8	3.66101	1.42485	0.70182	0.27314

7   Remarks on Relations with Recent Works

In [6], Škorić et al. investigated code lengths of c-secure probabilistic fingerprinting codes in certain wide class, including Tardos codes. They concluded that the lengths of c-secure codes in their scope cannot be shorter than $4\pi^2 c^2 \lceil \log(N/\varepsilon) \rceil$. Moreover, by using Gaussian approximation for distributions of users' scores, they suggested a possibility of the lengths to attain smaller values $2\pi^2 c^2 \log(N/\varepsilon)$ (about $2\pi^2\% \approx 19.7\%$ of Tardos codes) asymptotically due to the sharpest estimate of error probability. Since our code lengths are asymptotically about 20.6%

Table 4. Auxiliary values, lengths and thresholds for the example

	c	2	4	6	8
	N	200	400	600	800
Tardos	n	12400	51200	115200	211200
	$\mathcal{R}$	0.5	0.408	0.377	0.362
	ψ_1	1	1.931	2.805	3.661
	ψ_2	1	1.932	2.806	3.662
	x_1'	0.231	0.184	0.166	0.155
	x_2'	0.315	0.347	0.377	0.406
	A_1	3622	12907	28878	51783
	A_2	2656	6843	12716	19769
Ours	n	**6278**	**19750**	**41594**	**71552**
	%	**50.6**	**38.6**	**36.1**	**33.9**
	Z	$917.3\cdots$	1336.31786	$1843.45024\cdots$	$2375.91448\cdots$

of Tardos codes (as mentioned in Sect. 6), our codes are breaking the former limit and almost realizing the latter one.

On the other hand, Isogai et al. [4,5] reduced code lengths of Tardos codes by improving the estimate of the error probability. Table 5 shows comparison of code lengths and of asymptotic lengths when $c \to \infty$ in some case. Although their code lengths are shorter than ours, their codes use continuous bias distributions and so several problems discussed in this paper, e.g. huge memory amount and implementation of bias distributions, have been left unsolved. Their result suggests that there remains a room of our code lengths to be reduced further.

Table 5. Comparison of code lengths for $N = 10^9$ and $\varepsilon = 10^{-6}$

c	4	8	16	32	64	$\to \infty$
Tardos [8]	5.60×10^4	2.24×10^5	8.96×10^5	3.58×10^6	1.43×10^7	100%
IM06 [4]	1.40×10^4	5.98×10^4	2.33×10^5	8.93×10^5	3.40×10^6	22.0%
IM07 [5]	—	—	—	—	—	19.7%
Ours	2.18×10^4	7.72×10^4	2.78×10^5	1.01×10^6	3.75×10^6	20.6%

8   Conclusion

We discussed on problems of Tardos's fingerprinting codes [8], such as huge required memory amount in a practical use. We investigated the probability distributions used in construction of a generalization [3] of Tardos codes, and determined the distributions optimal for the purpose of reducing required memory amount. Our contribution indeed reduces the memory amount dramatically. We also reduced the code lengths significantly by improving the formula of code lengths given in [3], and considered the effects of certain approximation, needed in a practical use, on security performance of our codes.

Acknowledgments. The authors would like to express gratitude to Kazuto Ogawa and Satoshi Fujitsu at Japan Broadcasting Corporation (NHK), and to Takashi Kitagawa and Rui Zhang at AIST, for several significant comments.

References

1. Boneh, D., Shaw, J.: Collusion-secure Fingerprinting for Digital Data. IEEE Trans. Inform. Th. 44, 1897–1905 (1998)
2. Engels, H.: Numerical Quadrature and Cubature. Academic Press, London (1980)
3. Hagiwara, M., Hanaoka, G., Imai, H.: A Short Random Fingerprinting Code against a Small Number of Pirates. In: Fossorier, M.P.C., Imai, H., Lin, S., Poli, A. (eds.) AAECC 2006. LNCS, vol. 3857, pp. 193–202. Springer, Heidelberg (2006)
4. Isogai, T., Muratani, H.: Reevaluation of Tardos's Code. IEICE Technical Report, ISEC2006-96, pp. 7–12 (2006)
5. Isogai, T., Muratani, H.: An Evaluation of Tardos's Asymptotic Code Length. In: Proc. of the 2007 Symposium on Cryptography and Information Security (SCIS 2007). The Institute of Electronics, Information and Communication Engineers (2007)
6. Škorić, B., Vladimirova, T.U., Celik, M., Talstra, J.C.: Tardos Fingerprinting is Better than We Thought. e-print arXiv:cs.CR/0607131 (2006)
7. Szegö, G.: Orthogonal Polynomials. American Mathematical Society (1939)
8. Tardos, G.: Optimal Probabilistic Fingerprint Codes. J. ACM. Preliminary version appeared. In: Proc. of ACM Symposium on Theory of Computing 2003, Association for Computing Machinery, pp. 116–125 (to appear)

Appendix: Proofs of Theorems

c-Indistinguishable Distributions

Definition 2 ([3, Sect. 5]). *We call a (finite, symmetric) probability distribution $\mathcal{P}$ c-indistinguishable if $\sum_{x=1}^{\ell-1} \binom{\ell}{x} R_{\ell,x} = 0$ for any $2 \leq \ell \leq c$ (see Sect. 6 for notations).*

First we prepare some auxiliary results. The following lemma can be immediately verified, since each value $R_{\ell,x}$ is non-negative by definition.

Lemma 1. *A bias distribution $\mathcal{P}$ is c-ind if and only if $R_{\ell,x} = 0$ for any $2 \leq \ell \leq c$ and $1 \leq x \leq \ell - 1$; or equivalently, if and only if $E_p[f_{\ell,x}(p)] \leq 0$ for any $2 \leq \ell \leq c$ and $1 \leq x \leq \ell - 1$.*

In the following argument, we put for simplicity

$$g_{\ell,x}(p) = f_{\ell,x}(p)/\sqrt{p(1-p)} = xp^{x-1}(1-p)^{\ell-x} - (\ell-x)p^x(1-p)^{\ell-x-1} . \quad (10)$$

Now observe that $g_{\ell,\ell-x}(p) = -g_{\ell,x}(1-p)$ and so $f_{\ell,\ell-x}(p) = -f_{\ell,x}(1-p)$, therefore (since we assumed that any bias distribution $\mathcal{P}$ is symmetric with respect to $1/2$) we have

$$E_p[f_{\ell,\ell-x}(p)] = -E_p[f_{\ell,x}(1-p)] = -E_p[f_{\ell,x}(p)] . \quad (11)$$

This infers the following properties of c-ind distributions.

Proposition 2. *Let $2 \leq \ell \leq c$.*

1. A bias distribution $\mathcal{P}$ is c-ind if and only if, for any $1 \leq x \leq \ell - 1$

$$E_p \left[f_{\ell,x}(p) \right] = 0 \ . \tag{12}$$

2. If ℓ is even, then Eq.(12) always holds for $x = \ell/2$. Thus any bias distribution $\mathcal{P}$ is 2-ind (cf. [3, Proposition 1]).
3. Eq.(12) holds for $x = x_0$ if and only if Eq.(12) holds for $x = \ell - x_0$.

Proof. For the first claim, by Eq.(11), $E_p \left[f_{\ell,\ell-x}(p) \right] \geq 0$ for all $1 \leq x \leq \ell - 1$ whenever $E_p \left[f_{\ell,x}(p) \right] \leq 0$ for all $1 \leq x \leq \ell - 1$. Thus the claim follows from Lemma 1. The other claims are also straightforward by Eq.(11). $\square$

Proof of Proposition 1. Since the value $p^{(j)}$ is secret for the pirates, the conditional probability $Prob(y_j = 1 \mid \mathcal{B}_I \wedge (p^{(j)} = p))$ that $y_j = 1$ under the events $\mathcal{B}_I$ and $p^{(j)} = p$ is constant on $p^{(j)}$, denoted by $Prob(y_j = 1 \mid \mathcal{B}_I)$. On the other hand, we have $Prob(\mathcal{B}_I \mid p^{(j)} = p) = p^x (1 - p)^{\ell - x}$ by code construction. Thus, by putting $C = Prob(y_j = 1 \mid \mathcal{B}_I)/Prob(\mathcal{B}_I')$, we have

$$Prob(p^{(j)} = p \mid \mathcal{B}_I') = C \cdot Prob((p^{(j)} = p) \wedge \mathcal{B}_I) = C \cdot Prob(p^{(j)} = p) p^x (1-p)^{\ell - x} \ , \tag{13}$$

so Eq.(1) is equal to

$$C \sum_p Prob(p^{(j)} = p) p^x (1 - p)^{\ell - x} \left(x \sqrt{\frac{1-p}{p}} - (\ell - x) \sqrt{\frac{p}{1-p}} \right) \tag{14}$$

$$= C \cdot E_p \left[f_{\ell,x}(p) \right] \ .$$

Thus by Proposition 2, this value is always 0 if and only if $\mathcal{P}$ is c-ind. $\square$

Proof of Theorem 1. First, we show that $\mathcal{P} = \mathcal{P}(\mathcal{Q})$ is a c-ind distribution for any symmetric QS $\mathcal{Q}$ of degree $c-1$. By definition, $\mathcal{P}$ is indeed a finite probability distribution; i.e. the probabilities are all positive and their sum is 1. The outputs of $\mathcal{P}$ are in the interval $(0, 1)$ since X is a subset of the interval $(-1, 1)$, while $\mathcal{P}$ is symmetric with respect to $1/2$ since $\mathcal{Q}$ is symmetric. So the remaining task is (by Proposition 2) to show that $E_p \left[f_{\ell,x}(p) \right] = E_p \left[\sqrt{p(1-p)} g_{\ell,x}(p) \right] = 0$ for all $2 \leq \ell \leq c$ and $1 \leq x \leq \ell - 1$. Since $g_{\ell,x}$ is a polynomial of degree $\ell - x \leq c - 1$, we have

$$E_p \left[\sqrt{p(1-p)} g_{\ell,x}(p) \right] = \frac{1}{2C} \sum_{\xi \in X} w(\xi) g_{\ell,x} \left(\frac{1+\xi}{2} \right) \tag{15}$$

$$= \frac{1}{2C} \int_{-1}^{1} g_{\ell,x} \left(\frac{1+t}{2} \right) dt = \frac{1}{C} \int_0^1 g_{\ell,x}(z) \, dz = 0$$

(note that $g_{\ell,x}(z) = \frac{d}{dz}(z^x (1 - z)^{\ell - x})$). Thus the first claim is verified.

Secondly, we show that $\mathcal{Q} = \mathcal{Q}(\mathcal{P})$ is a symmetric QS of degree $c - 1$ for any c-ind distribution $\mathcal{P}$. The set X is included in $(-1, 1)$ since $0 < p_i < 1$ for all i, while $\mathcal{Q}$ is symmetric since $\mathcal{P}$ is symmetric. So the remaining task is to show that $\int_{-1}^{1} F(t)dt = \sum_{\xi \in X} w(\xi)F(\xi)$ for any polynomial $F(t)$ of degree up to $c - 1$. Now note that any such $F(t)$ can be expressed as a linear combination of the polynomials $g_{\ell,1}(\frac{1+t}{2})$ (with $2 \leq \ell \leq c$) and constant polynomial 1, while $\sum_i w(\xi_i) = 2 = \int_{-1}^{1} 1 \, dt$ by definition. Thus it suffices to show the above claim only for $F(t) = g_{\ell,1}(\frac{1+t}{2})$. Now we have

$$C' \int_{-1}^{1} g_{\ell,1}\left(\frac{1+t}{2}\right) dt = 2C' \int_{0}^{1} g_{\ell,1}(z)dz = 0$$

$$= E_p\left[\sqrt{p(1-p)}g_{\ell,1}(p)\right] = C' \sum_{i=1}^{m} w(\xi_i)g_{\ell,1}\left(\frac{1+\xi_i}{2}\right) \tag{16}$$

since $\mathcal{P}$ is c-ind (see Proposition 2), so our claim follows. Thus the second claim is also proved.

Finally, since $\sum_{\xi \in X} w(\xi) = 2$ and $\sum_i q_i = 1$, a straightforward computation can verify that $\mathcal{Q}(\mathcal{P}(\mathcal{Q})) = \mathcal{Q}$ and $\mathcal{P}(\mathcal{Q}(\mathcal{P})) = \mathcal{P}$. Hence the proof is concluded.
□

Proof of Theorem 3. Put $\widehat{L}_m(t) = L_m(2t - 1)$, so $\widehat{L}_m$ is proportional to $\widetilde{L}_m$. First, note that $\widehat{L}_m(\frac{1+\xi}{2}) = 0$ if and only if $L_m(\xi) = 0$, so the set of outputs of $\mathcal{P}_c = \mathcal{P}(\mathcal{Q}_m)$ is (by definition) the set of zeroes of $\widehat{L}_m$, which is also the set of zeroes of $\widetilde{L}_m$.

Secondly, note that $1 - \xi^2 = 4p(1 - p)$ if $p = (1 + \xi)/2$, and

$$\frac{d}{dt}L_m(t)|_{t=2p-1} = \frac{d}{dt}\widehat{L}_m\left(\frac{1+t}{2}\right)\Big|_{t=2p-1}$$

$$= \frac{1}{2}\left(\frac{d}{du}\widehat{L}_m(u)\Big|_{u=(1+t)/2}\right)\Big|_{t=2p-1} = \frac{1}{2}\frac{d}{du}\widehat{L}_m(u)\Big|_{u=p} = C''\widetilde{L}'_m(p) \tag{17}$$

where C'' is some constant. Then the probability that $\mathcal{P}_c$ takes the value $p = (1 + \xi)/2$ with $\xi \in X$ is

$$\frac{w(\xi)}{C\sqrt{1-\xi^2}} = \frac{2}{C(1-\xi^2)^{3/2}L'_m(\xi)^2} = \frac{1}{4CC''^2(p(1-p))^{3/2}\widetilde{L}'_m(p)^2} \cdot \tag{18}$$

Thus the claim follows, since the factor $1/(4CC''^2)$ is common for all p.
□

Proof of Theorem 4

First, we recall the results in [3] on false-positive and false-negative error probabilities. Since our code is basically the same as theirs (with length and threshold modified), these results can be used for estimating behavior of users' scores. In the following, let $x_1, x_2 > 0$, $\alpha = \sqrt{p_0/(1-p_0)}x_1$ and $\beta = \sqrt{p_0/(1-p_0)}x_2/c$.

Lemma 2 (Markov's Inequality). *Let Y be a finite positive random variable and $t > 0$. Then $Prob(Y > t) < E[Y]/t$ and $Prob(Y \geq t) \leq E[Y]/t$ where $E[Y]$ denotes the expected value of Y.*

Theorem 5 ([3, Lemma 1]). *Let u_i be an innocent user. For any fixed $P = (p^{(1)}, \ldots, p^{(n)})$ and any fixed $y = (y_1, \ldots, y_n)$, we have*

$$Prob_{c_i}(S_i \geq Z) < e^{r(x_1)\alpha^2 n - \alpha Z} \, , \tag{19}$$

where the probability is taken over all codewords c_i chosen according to P.

Remark 1. 1. The proof of [3, Lemma 1] is still valid even if y is an *arbitrary* codeword with $y_j \in \{0, 1, ?\}$, which need not satisfy the *Marking Assumption*; only the required property is that y is independent of the codeword of u_i.
2. Although [3, Lemma 1] bounds the probability $Prob(S_i > Z)$ only, the same proof infers the above stronger bound (since the inequality $1 + r_1\alpha^2 \leq e^{r_1\alpha^2}$ with $\alpha > 0$ and $r_1 > 0$ used in the proof actually holds strictly). Moreover, the bound also holds even if Z is not the threshold but an *arbitrary* positive parameter, and the assumption $\alpha\sqrt{(1-p)/p} < x_1$ in [3, Lemma 1] can be replaced by a weaker one $\alpha\sqrt{(1-p)/p} \leq x_1$.

Theorem 6 ([3, Lemma 2]). *Let $u_1, \ldots, u_\ell$ be the pirates with $\ell \leq c$. For any fixed pirates' strategy, we have*

$$E_{(P,c_1,\ldots,c_\ell,y)}\left[e^{-\beta \sum_i S_i}\right] \leq e^{\beta(c\beta r(x_2) - \mathcal{R}_{\ell,P})n} \, , \tag{20}$$

so by Lemma 2, we have

$$Prob_{(P,c_1,\ldots,c_\ell,y)}(S_i < Z \text{ for all } i) \leq Prob_{(P,c_1,\ldots,c_\ell,y)}\left(\sum_{i=1}^{\ell} S_i < \ell Z\right)$$

$$\leq Prob_{(P,c_1,\ldots,c_\ell,y)}\left(e^{-\beta \sum_i S_i} > e^{-\beta \ell Z}\right) \tag{21}$$

$$< E_{(P,c_1,\ldots,c_\ell,y)}\left[e^{-\beta \sum_i S_i}\right]/e^{-\beta \ell Z}$$

$$\leq e^{\beta(c\beta r(x_2) - \mathcal{R}_{\ell,P})n + \beta \ell Z} \, ,$$

where the probabilities and expected values are taken over all P, all $c_1, \ldots, c_\ell$ and all y chosen according to $\mathcal{P}$, P and the pirates' strategy, respectively.

Remark 2. The proof of [3, Lemma 2] indeed allows pirates' strategies to be probabilistic though it was not clear (cf. Remark 1 in [8, Sect. 1.2]). Moreover, although [3] only considers the restricted case that y containing no '?', the argument in [8, Lemma 5.3] can generalize the proof to our general situation.

Now we start to derive our formula Eq.(6) by using the above properties. First, recall that in our tracing algorithm considering approximation errors (given in Sect. 6), a user is outputted if and only if $\widehat{S} \geq Z$ where $\widehat{S}$ is the approximated score; while $\widehat{S} \geq Z$ yields $S \geq Z - n\delta$ and $\widehat{S} < Z$ yields $S < Z + n\delta$. Thus to achieve $Prob(u_{i_0}$ is outputted$) < \varepsilon_1$, where u_{i_0} is an arbitrary innocent user, and $Prob$(no pirate is outputted) $< \varepsilon_2$, it suffices to satisfy that

$$Prob(S \geq Z - n\delta) < \varepsilon_1 \text{ and } Prob(S_i < Z + n\delta \text{ for all } i) < \varepsilon_2 , \qquad (22)$$

where S is an innocent user's true score and $S_1, \ldots, S_\ell$ are ℓ pirates' true scores with $\ell \leq c$. By the same arguments as Theorems 5 and 6 (see also Remark 1), the following conditions yield Eq.(22):

$$\begin{aligned} r(x_1)\alpha^2 n - \alpha(Z - n\delta) &\leq \log \varepsilon_1 , \\ \beta(c\beta r(x_2) - \mathcal{R}_{\ell,\mathcal{P}})n + \beta\ell(Z + n\delta) &\leq \log \varepsilon_2 \text{ for } \ell \leq c . \end{aligned} \qquad (23)$$

Moreover, since n, Z and β are all positive, the following conditions

$$r(x_1)\alpha^2 n - \alpha(Z - n\delta) = \log \varepsilon_1 \text{ and } \beta(c\beta r(x_2) - \mathcal{R})n + \beta c(Z + n\delta) = \log \varepsilon_2 \quad (24)$$

also yield Eq.(22). Now we determine x_1 and x_2 by $x_i r(x_i) = \sqrt{(1 - p_0)/p_0} \, \eta_i \mathcal{R}/c$ for $i = 1, 2$. These x_i are uniquely determined since $tr(t)$ for $t > 0$ is a strictly increasing continuous function with image $(0, \infty)$. Solving Eq.(24) with our choices $\alpha = \sqrt{p_0/(1 - p_0)}x_1$ and $\beta = \sqrt{p_0/(1 - p_0)}x_2/c$ of parameters, we have

$$n = \frac{c\sqrt{(1 - p_0)/p_0}}{(1 - \eta_1 - \eta_2/c)\mathcal{R} - 2\delta c} \left(\frac{1}{x_1} \log \frac{1}{\varepsilon_1} + \frac{1}{x_2} \log \frac{1}{\varepsilon_2} \right) ,$$

$$Z = \frac{\sqrt{(1 - p_0)/p_0}}{(1 - \eta_1 - \eta_2/c)\mathcal{R} - 2\delta c} \left(\frac{(1 - \eta_2/c)\mathcal{R} - \delta c}{x_1} \log \frac{1}{\varepsilon_1} + \frac{\eta_1 \mathcal{R} + \delta c}{x_2} \log \frac{1}{\varepsilon_2} \right)$$
$$\qquad (25)$$

which is a generalization of the formula in [3] (the original is recovered by putting $\eta_1 = 1/4$, $\eta_2 = c/2$ and $\delta = 0$).

Now if we take the values ψ_i, x_i' and A_i ($i = 1, 2$) as in Sect. 6, and modify code length $\widehat{n}$ and threshold $\widehat{Z}$ as

$$\widehat{n} = A_1 + A_2 \text{ and } \widehat{Z} = \left(\left(1 - \frac{\eta_2}{c}\right) \frac{\mathcal{R}}{c} - \delta \right) A_1 + \left(\frac{\eta_1 \mathcal{R}}{c} + \delta \right) A_2 , \qquad (26)$$

then by comparing Eq.(25) and Eq.(26), we can observe that Eq.(22) holds with ε_i replaced by e^{-k_i} where

$$k_i = \frac{(1 - \eta_1 - \eta_2/c)\mathcal{R} - 2\delta c}{c} \sqrt{\frac{p_0}{1 - p_0}} x_i A_i \text{ for } i = 1, 2 . \qquad (27)$$

Moreover, since $\psi_2 \geq \sqrt{(1 - p_0)/p_0}$ and $x_i' \leq x_i$ ($i = 1, 2$) by definition, we have $e^{-k_i} \leq \varepsilon_i$ by the choice of A_i. This means that the code length $\widehat{n}$ and threshold $\widehat{Z}$, which are precisely those used in Theorem 4 (see Eq.(6)), provide the desired security performance. Hence Theorem 4 is proved. $\square$

Combining Tardos Fingerprinting Codes and Fingercasting

Stefan Katzenbeisser[1], Boris Škorić[1], Mehmet U. Celik[1],
and Ahmad-Reza Sadeghi[2]

[1] Philips Research Europe, Information and System Security Group,
Eindhoven, The Netherlands
{stefan.katzenbeisser,boris.skoric,mehmet.celik}@philips.com
[2] Horst Görtz Institute for IT Security, Ruhr-Universität Bochum,
Bochum, Germany
sadeghi@crypto.rub.de

Abstract. Forensic tracking faces new challenges when employed in mass-scale electronic content distribution. In order to avoid a high load at the server, the watermark embedding process should be shifted from the secure server to the client side, where (1) the security of the watermark secrets must be ensured, and (2) collusion-resistance against a reasonably sized coalition of malicious users needs to be guaranteed. The combination of secure content broadcasting, secure embedding and collusion tolerance aspects has been recently addressed and termed as Fingercasting. However, the proposed solution does not apply a special collusion-resistant code, but derives a limited resistance against collusion attacks from the underlying spread spectrum watermark. In this paper, we make the first step towards tackling this problem: we propose a construction that provides collusion-resistance against a large coalition in a secure watermark embedding setting. In particular, we propose to incorporate a variant of the collusion resistant random code of Tardos, currently the code with best asymptotic behavior, into a Fingercasting framework. Through statistical analysis we show that the combination is feasible for a small subset of possible Fingercasting system parameters.

1 Introduction

In the past few years we have experienced a shift from classic content distribution channels, such as CDs or DVDs, towards electronic content distribution (ECD). Although these new distribution models offer new possibilities for content providers, the risk of unauthorized mass re-distribution complicates the introduction of large-scale ECD systems. Forensic watermarking can be used besides (or instead of) encryption in a classic Digital Rights Management architecture as a deterrence against unauthorized distribution. In a forensic tracking system, each authorized copy of the distributed content is watermarked with a unique transaction mark, linking that copy either to a particular user or to a specific device. When an unauthorized copy is found, the embedded watermark

T. Furon et al. (Eds.): IH 2007, LNCS 4567, pp. 294–310, 2007.

(carrying the transaction mark) uniquely identifies the source of the copy, and allows the distributor to trace the user who has re-distributed the content.

Traditionally, forensic watermarks are directly embedded into the content by a trusted distribution server before content is delivered to a customer. However, this approach has two obvious drawbacks. First, the distribution mechanism does not scale well. As individualized content has to be delivered to each customer, forensic watermarking puts a high computational load on the distribution server and prevents the use of network caching that would reduce the transmission overhead. Second, server-based embedding scenarios are unsuitable for de-centralized distribution networks (such as peer-to-peer systems) or architectures that allow super-distribution of content. In mass-scale distribution systems, these drawbacks become major issues that limit deployment of forensic tracking watermarks.

Client-side embedding, where the watermark embedding process is shifted from the distribution server to the clients, solves the scalability issue. However, as the client device resides in a potentially hostile environment, the major obstacle for client-side embedding is the security risk. The watermark embedder needs the watermarking secrets (keys), which when exposed allow the attackers to effectively remove watermarks. Thus, watermark embedding at the client must be done in a way which does not compromise the security of the keys; in addition, neither the watermark nor the unmarked original content should be available to the client. Security of the client-side embedding can be provided by *secure watermark embedding* schemes [8,9,2,1,4]. (See Section 2 for an overview of methods proposed in the literature.)

Another area of concern in forensic tracking is the "collusion attack". In a collusion attack, a coalition of authorized users (colluders), who posses personalized copies of the same content, pool their copies together and examine the differences. Using the difference information, they try to create a content copy that is not traceable to any member of the coalition. If the coalition is sufficiently large, they evade detection with very high probability.

In server-based forensic tracking architectures the problem is usually solved by the use of collusion-resistant codes as an additional layer on top of the watermarking scheme [3,13]: the watermarks given to individual users are encoded in such a way that, assuming an upper bound on the number of colluders, enough tracing information is present in the attacked copy to accuse at least one member of the coalition.

Although several different approaches have been proposed for secure embedding, their collusion resistance has received little attention so far. Restrictions imposed on the watermark construction by the secure embedding mechanism have prevented the application of collusion-secure codes in a straightforward manner.

In this paper, we propose the first construction that combines a lookup-table based secure embedding mechanism with a collusion-secure code. In particular, we choose Fingercasting [1] as a secure embedding method due to its low complexity and low transmission overhead. Fingercasting employs a lookup-table based encryption approach, where each content symbol is encrypted by pseudo-randomly adding S entries of a random encryption table; S is a system parameter that can be used to find a trade-off between the security of the encryption algorithm and the transparency of the embedded watermark. For the security of the encryption, larger values of S (such as $S \geq 2$) are desirable, whereas for the watermark transparency low values of S (such as $S \leq 5$) are preferable. As the collusion-secure code, we use a 'symmetric' variant of Tardos' randomized fingerprinting code [13], recently proposed by some of the authors in [14], which achieves the optimal asymptotic code length, while supporting large coalition sizes and low false accusation and false rejection probabilities.

In our approach, we embed a fingerprint in the lookup tables used by Fingercasting, which translates into a fingerprint embedded in the decrypted content. (Due to the random encryption and watermark embedding method of Fingercasting, fingerprinting codes cannot be applied directly to the content.) Through tedious statistical analysis, we show that the proposed construction yields a practical collusion-resistant secure embedding scheme only for the specific parameter choices of $S = 1$ or $S = 2$ in the Fingercasting scheme.

The rest of the paper is organized as follows. Section 2 surveys related work, and Section 3 gives a brief overview of both Fingercasting and Tardos codes. Our construction is outlined in Section 4; furthermore, we perform a statistical analysis of the scheme in Section 5 which shows that it indeed provides a collusion resistant secure embedding scheme for $S = 1$ and $S = 2$, but fails for larger S. Finally, in Section 6 we discuss future research challenges.

2 Related Work

Several approaches for secure watermark embedding have been proposed in the literature. In broadcast environments, Crowcroft et al. [5] and Parviainen et al. [10] proposed a client-side watermark insertion technique based on stream switching. In their method, they divide the content stream into small chunks and broadcast two versions of the stream, watermarked with different watermarks. Each chunk is encrypted by a different key. Clients are given a personalized set of decryption keys that allows them to selectively decrypt chunks of the two broadcast streams such that each client obtains the full stream. The way the full decrypted stream is composed out of the two broadcast versions encodes the watermark. However, this scheme has a limited collusion resistance. Emmanuel et al. [6] proposed a client-side embedding method in which a pseudo-random mask is blended over each video frame; each client is given a different mask, which, when subtracted from the masked broadcast video, leaves an additive watermark in the content. The scheme has security problems, as a constant mask is used for all frames of a video, which can be estimated by averaging attacks. Kundur and Karthik [8] were the first to use techniques from partial encryption in order to fingerprint digital images. Their method is based on encrypting the signs of DCT coefficients in an image; during decryption some signs are left unchanged, which leaves a detectable fingerprint in the image. As the sign bits of DCT coefficients are perceptually significant, the partially encrypted version of the content is heavily distorted. However, as some DCT coefficients are left scrambled during decryption, the watermark can be visible; visibility of the watermark must be traded for optimal detection. Lemma et al. [9] overcome these problems and propose a practical partial encryption-based secure embedding solution for audio-visual content. However, both schemes still have limited robustness against collusion attacks.

Anderson et al. [2] designed a special stream cipher, called Chameleon, which allows one, by appropriate design of keys, to decrypt Chameleon-encrypted content in slightly different ways and thus leave a key-dependent trace in the decrypted data stream. Recently Adelsbach et al. [1] showed how to generalize the Chameleon cipher in order to be able to embed spread spectrum watermarks in audio-visual content. Their construction, called *Fingercasting*, does not apply a special collusion-resistant code, but draws a limited resistance against collusion attacks from the underlying spread spectrum watermark. As Fingercasting forms the basis of the method proposed in this paper, we review it in detail in the next section.

The construction of collusion-resistant codes has been an active research topic since the late 1990s, see e.g. [7,3,11,13]. The constructions depend strongly on assumptions that restrict the type of manipulations an attacker is allowed to perform; often, one assumes the *marking assumption*, stating that the colluders can only change those parts of the content where they have obtained different versions. In this paper, we make use of the fingerprinting code by Tardos [13], which is a fully randomized binary code and exhibits the currently best known asymptotic behavior (see Section 3.2 for a brief overview).

3 Preliminaries

3.1 Fingercasting

Fingercasting, as described in [1], combines broadcast encryption, a lookup-table based encryption scheme and a watermark embedder in order to distribute uniquely marked copies of a content to multiple users. In the following, we discuss the joint encryption/embedding operations performed by Fingercasting; for a complete overview of the scheme we refer to [1].

Fingercasting employs a secret master lookup table (encryption key) $\mathbf{E}$ of length L and a set of client lookup tables $\mathbf{D}_1, \ldots, \mathbf{D}_n$. Client k gets a unique table $\mathbf{D}_k$, which forms a long-term decryption key, and is a "distorted version" of the master lookup table: each table $\mathbf{D}_k$ is constructed as $\mathbf{D}_k = \mathbf{E} - \mathbf{W}_k$, where $\mathbf{W}_k$ will be referred to as watermark table. Before distribution, content is encrypted using the master lookup table $\mathbf{E}$; a client uses his personalized lookup table $\mathbf{D}_k$ to decrypt. Decrypting a piece of content with $\mathbf{D}_k$ rather than with $\mathbf{E}$ leaves a detectable spread-spectrum watermark in the decrypted content.

Fingercasting can be parameterized by a constant S, which represents the number of entries from the encryption lookup-table $\mathbf{E}$ added to each content element during encryption. The choice of S strikes a balance between the security of the encryption process (for which S should be large enough, e.g., $S \geq 2$) and the transparency of the watermark (for which S should be chosen small, e.g., $S \leq 5$).

A piece of content will be denoted as a vector $\mathbf{c} = (c_1, \ldots, c_M)$ of length M; depending on the watermark embedding domain, the values c_i may e.g. represent baseband samples or DCT coefficients. To encrypt a piece of plaintext content $\mathbf{c}$, the distributor uses a pseudorandom generator to derive $S \cdot M$ indices $t_{i\alpha}$ pointing to entries in the lookup table, where $1 \leq i \leq M$, $1 \leq \alpha \leq S$ and $1 \leq t_{i\alpha} \leq L$, and encrypts $\mathbf{c}$ according to

$$z_i = c_i + \sum_{\alpha=1}^{S} \mathbf{E}[t_{i\alpha}] \bmod p, \tag{1}$$

where p is a sufficiently large prime, and $\mathbf{E}[x]$ denotes the content of the lookup table $\mathbf{E}$ at index x. All ciphertexts z_i are collected to form the encrypted content $\mathbf{z} = (z_1, \ldots, z_M)$. A client can decrypt $\mathbf{z}$ by reversing the encryption operation with his own lookup table $\mathbf{D}_k$ to obtain the watermarked content $\mathbf{y}_k$,

$$y_i^{(k)} = z_i - \sum_{\alpha=1}^{S} \mathbf{D}_k[t_{i\alpha}] \bmod p = c_i + \sum_{\alpha=1}^{S} \mathbf{W}_k[t_{i\alpha}]. \tag{2}$$

Here, we assume that the prime p is selected in such a way that no overflow occurs when the watermark is added.

In the following we will denote the watermark embedded in the content in the above manner by $\mathbf{w}_k = (w_1^{(k)}, \ldots, w_M^{(k)})$. Note that each $w_i^{(k)}$ is formed by summing S entries of the watermark table $\mathbf{W}_k$ of user k:

$$w_i^{(k)} = \sum_{\alpha=1}^{S} \mathbf{W}_k[t_{i\alpha}]. \tag{3}$$

Thus, even if the entries in $\mathbf{W}_k$ are binary, the embedded watermark will in general be non-binary.

3.2   The Tardos Fingerprinting Code

In the Tardos fingerprinting method, each user receives a unique fingerprint, which is represented as a binary codeword of length M. The code length M determines the collusion resistance, expressed as the maximum coalition size c the system can resist, for given false positive and false negative probabilities of the code. We refer to [13,12] for details and estimates of M. Let N be the total number of users to be accommodated in the distribution system. All codewords can be arranged as a $N \times M$ matrix $\mathbf{X}$, where the k-th row corresponds to the fingerprint given to the k-th user.

The distributor stochastically generates the matrix $\mathbf{X}$ in the following way. In a first step, he chooses M independent and identically distributed random variables $\{p_1^{(i)}\}_{i=1}^M$ from the real interval $p_1^{(i)} \in [t, 1-t]$, where t is a small parameter satisfying $ct \ll 1$. In this paper we set $t = 0$, see [14] for a justification. We define $p_0^{(i)} = 1 - p_1^{(i)}$. Each $p_1^{(i)}$ is sampled according to a density function f, which is symmetric around $p_1^{(i)} = 1/2$ and heavily biased towards values of $p_1^{(i)}$ close to t and $1 - t$:

$$f(p) = \frac{1}{2 \arcsin(1 - 2t)} \frac{1}{\sqrt{p(1-p)}}. \tag{4}$$

In a second step, the distributor fills the columns of the matrix $\mathbf{X}$ by independently drawing random bits $\mathbf{X}_{ki} \in \{0, 1\}$ with $\mathbb{P}[\mathbf{X}_{ki} = 1] = p_1^{(i)}$. Consequently, we have $\mathbb{P}[\mathbf{X}_{ki} = 0] = p_0^{(i)}$. When content is released to customer k, it is watermarked with the k-th row of $\mathbf{X}$.

The colluders, pooling together their personalized content copies, use a (possibly randomized) strategy to obtain an attacked content copy $\mathbf{y}$, which they make publicly available. Having spotted a copy with embedded mark $\mathbf{w}$, the distributor wants to determine at least one person from the coalition who created the copy. To achieve this, he computes for each user $1 \leq k \leq N$ an accusation sum S_k as

$$S_k = \sum_{i=1}^M w_i\, U(\mathbf{X}_{ki}, p_1^{(i)}), \quad \text{with} \quad U(\mathbf{X}_{ki}, p_1^{(i)}) = \begin{cases} g_1(p_1^{(i)}) \text{ if } \mathbf{X}_{ki} = 1 \\ g_0(p_1^{(i)}) \text{ if } \mathbf{X}_{ki} = 0, \end{cases} \tag{5}$$

where g_1 and g_0 are the 'accusation weight functions'

$$g_1(p) = \sqrt{\frac{1-p}{p}} \quad \text{and} \quad g_0(p) = -\sqrt{\frac{p}{1-p}}. \tag{6}$$

The accusation sum S_k is computed by summing over all symbols of $\mathbf{w}$. All '0' symbols are ignored. For each '1' symbol, the accusation sum S_k is either increased or decreased, depending on how much suspicion arises from that symbol: if user k has a one in the same position, then the suspicion is increased by a positive amount $g_1(p_1^{(i)})$, where the suspicion decreases with higher probability $p_1^{(i)}$. If user k has a zero in the position, the overall suspicion is corrected by the negative amount $g_0(p_1^{(i)})$, which gets more pronounced for large values of $p_1^{(i)}$. Finally, the distributor decides a user k to be guilty (i.e., part of the coalition that produced the attacked copy in question), if S_k is greater than a certain threshold. The exact value of the threshold depends on the desired false positive and false negative probabilities.

In this work, we use a 'symmetric' version of Tardos' code, as proposed in [14], which achieves a shorter code length by judging the guilt of users according to a modified accusation sum

$$S_k' = \sum_{i=1}^M \delta(w_i, \mathbf{X}_{ki}) g_1(p_{w_i}^{(i)}) + [1 - \delta(w_i, \mathbf{X}_{ki})] g_0(p_{w_i}^{(i)}),$$

where $\delta(\cdot, \cdot)$ denotes the Kronecker delta. Thus, to judge the guilt of user k, the accusation algorithm compares the elements of the extracted fingerprint with the elements of the fingerprint given to user k. If the symbols agree, the accusation is increased, otherwise decreased. For a thorough analysis we refer to [14].

4   Collusion-Resistant Fingercasting

In this section, we propose a construction that combines a Tardos fingerprinting code with Fingercasting in order to yield a collusion-resistant secure embedding scheme. In particular, we show in Section 5 that the construction works for the choice of Fingercasting parameters $S = 1$ and $S = 2$.

4.1   Attack Model and Marking Assumption

In order to derive results regarding the collusion security, we follow the widely adopted approach of introducing a *marking assumption*, which is suitable for the Fingercasting scheme. The fingerprinting code assigns each user a codeword, which is embedded into the distributed content by the use of a watermarking algorithm; we assume that each symbol of the fingerprint gets embedded in a dedicated part of the content. Due to the personalized nature of the fingerprint, some parts ('positions') of the content are different in the copies the colluders pool together, while others are identical. The latter positions are called *undetectable*. Traditionally, the marking assumption is stated as follows: a group of colluders is unable to change the fingerprint symbols embedded in undetectable positions.

In the context of secure lookup-table based embedding, this traditional marking assumption is not sufficient. During the decryption process, the attackers have not only access to c copies of the content, but also to a set of c decryption tables $\mathbf{D}_1, \ldots, \mathbf{D}_c$, which they can compare to notice differences between the watermark table $\mathbf{W}_1, \ldots, \mathbf{W}_c$ internally used by the distributor. (For simplicity of notation and without loss of generality, we enumerate the colluders by $k = 1, \ldots, c$). Thus, we distinguish between detectable table and detectable content positions. We call an index $1 \leq l \leq L$ a *detectable table position*, if there exist two tables $\mathbf{W}_k$ and $\mathbf{W}_{k'}$ with $1 \leq k, k' \leq c$ and $\mathbf{W}_k[l] \neq \mathbf{W}_{k'}[l]$. Conversely, a position $1 \leq i \leq M$ in the content is called a *detectable content position*, if a detectable index was used to encrypt that position, i.e., there exists an index $l \in \{t_{i,1}, \ldots, t_{i,S}\}$ which is a detectable table position. Otherwise, a content portion is called undetectable.

In the rest of the paper, we assume a modified version of the marking assumption, more suitable for Fingercasting: The colluders cannot change a fingerprint symbol embedded in an undetectable content position. Note that this assumption is *weaker* than the traditional marking assumption: even a content position that is identical in all the personalized copies of the attackers may be *detectable*, in case detectable table positions were used in the watermark embedding process and the individualized watermark symbols cancel due to the summation of S lookup-table entries.

Besides this weaker marking assumption, we work with an attack model known as *restricted digit model*. In this model, it is assumed that the colluders only 'mix-and-match' detectable entries in their decryption lookup-tables, i.e., decrypt the content using a lookup-table that is a combination of entries of the attacker's tables. Note that we allow the attackers to independently perform this mixing operation every time they access one entry from a decryption table.

4.2 Construction

In the following, we construct a Fingercasting scheme that incorporates a Tardos code. Intuitively, we use a Tardos codeword to construct the individualized watermark table $\mathbf{W}_k$ of length L; as mentioned in Section 3.1, this causes a non-binary watermark $\mathbf{w}_k$ (of length $M \geq L$) to be embedded into the content, where each element of $\mathbf{w}_k$ is a sum of S terms from $\mathbf{W}_k$. For tracing purposes, we 'condense' the watermark $\mathbf{w}_k$ back into a table $\mathbf{Z}$ of length L, which serves as an estimate of the table $\mathbf{W}_k$ from which $\mathbf{w}$ was created. Finally, we judge the guilt of a user k by the similarity between $\mathbf{Z}$ and $\mathbf{W}_k$.

Fingerprint creation. The distributor constructs a Tardos matrix $\mathbf{X}$ of dimensions $N \times L$, as described in Section 3.2. The length L of the codewords is a system parameter that will be determined later (L is also the length of the encryption and decryption lookup-tables). Finally, the distributor sets up a Fingercasting scheme by picking a sufficiently large prime p and a master encryption table $\mathbf{E}$ of length L where for all $1 \leq l \leq L$, $\mathbf{E}[l] \leftarrow_R \mathbb{Z}_p$.

Client key generation. For client k, the distributor selects the k-th row of the matrix $\mathbf{X}$ and derives a watermark table $\mathbf{W}_k$ from it; more precisely, he sets

$$\mathbf{W}_k[l] = \begin{cases} -1 & \text{if } \mathbf{X}_{k,l} = 0 \\ 1 & \text{if } \mathbf{X}_{k,l} = 1 \end{cases}$$

and computes the k-th client decryption key as $\mathbf{D}_k = \mathbf{E} - \mathbf{W}_k$.

Content encryption and decryption. As in Fingercasting, the distributor encrypts the content $\mathbf{c}$ using the master table $\mathbf{E}$ and sends it to the client, who uses his own table $\mathbf{D}_k$ to decrypt according to Equation (2). Note that this decryption process essentially embeds a non-binary watermark $\mathbf{w}_k$ into the content, as each value of the embedded watermark is a sum of S binary values from the watermark table $\mathbf{W}_k$, see Equation (3).

Tracing. The distributor finds an unauthorized content copy. He first performs watermark extraction on each content segment in order to recover an estimate of the (non-binary) embedded watermark $\mathbf{w}$. Note that, in case no collusion attacks have been performed, each element of $\mathbf{w}$ is a sum of S different entries of one single watermark table $\mathbf{W}_k$.

From $\mathbf{w}$ he computes a lookup table $\mathbf{Z}$ of length L in the following manner. Initially, he sets $\mathbf{Z}[l] = 0$ for all $1 \leq l \leq L$. He then iterates over all content

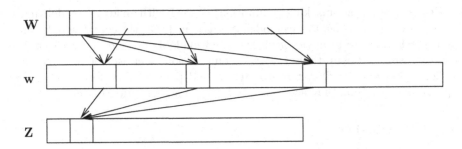

Fig. 1. Construction of the table $\mathbf{Z}$ (illustrated for $S = 2$ and one table entry). Note that there are T_l contributions of $\mathbf{W}[l]$ to $\mathbf{Z}[l]$ and that there are also other entries from $\mathbf{W}$ that contribute to $\mathbf{Z}[l]$.

positions $1 \leq i \leq M$, reconstructs the indices $\{t_{i,1}, \ldots, t_{i,S}\}$ and increases each value $\mathbf{Z}[t_{i\alpha}]$, for all $1 \leq \alpha \leq S$, by w_i. Thus, he obtains a table $\mathbf{Z}$ as

$$\mathbf{Z}[l] = \sum_{i=1}^{M} \mathbf{w}_i \sum_{\alpha=1}^{S} \delta(l, t_{i\alpha}).$$

This process is depicted in Figure 1. Finally, he computes for each user k an accusation sum

$$A_k = \sum_{l=1}^{L} [1 - \delta(\mathbf{Z}[l], 0)] \left[\delta(\operatorname{sgn} \mathbf{Z}[l], \mathbf{W}_k[l]) \, g_1(p_{\operatorname{sgn} \mathbf{Z}[l]}^{(l)}) + \right.$$
$$\left. (1 - \delta(\operatorname{sgn} \mathbf{Z}[l], \mathbf{W}_k[l])) \, g_0(p_{\operatorname{sgn} \mathbf{Z}[l]}^{(l)}) \right], \tag{7}$$

where $\operatorname{sgn} x$ denotes the sign of x. Here, in abuse of notation, we identify $p_{-1}^{(l)}$ with the probability $p_0^{(l)}$ as defined in Section 3.2.

A user k gets accused if $A_k > Z$, for some threshold Z, which will be determined later; see Equation 9.

4.3 Motivation of the Accusation Sum

The choice of the accusation sum A_k is motivated by the following two arguments.

1. Given the embedded fingerprint sequence $\mathbf{w}$, we attempt to recover an estimate of the watermarking table that was used to create it. Let us first assume that no attack occurred, i.e., each entry of $\mathbf{w}$ is the sum of S entries of a table $\mathbf{W}_k$. We obtain such an estimate by constructing a table $\mathbf{Z}$ and using the signs of the entries in $\mathbf{Z}$. Each individual entry of $\mathbf{Z}[l]$ accumulates all values in $\mathbf{w}$ that were computed as a sum involving $\mathbf{W}_k[l]$ as summand. The purpose of this step is essentially to reduce the non-binary embedded watermark $\mathbf{w}$ to the binary lookup-table from which it was created.

Note that the length of $\mathbf{Z}$ is smaller than the content ($L < M$); thus, some entry $\mathbf{W}_k[l]$ will be used multiple times in decrypting the content. We denote with T_l a random variable that counts the number of times one such entry $\mathbf{W}_k[l]$ is used during decryption. Note that each T_l follows a Binomial distribution,

$$\mathbb{P}[\mathbf{W}_k[l] \text{ is used } T_l \text{ times}] = \binom{M}{T_l}(S/L)^{T_l}(1 - S/L)^{M-T_l}.$$

Each value $\mathbf{Z}[l]$ is then a sum of T_l entries $\mathbf{W}_k[l]$ and $(S - 1)T_l$ other entries of $\mathbf{W}_k$, which are uniformly randomly chosen (according to the index generation function in Fingercasting). Due to the random choice of indices and the randomized construction of $\mathbf{W}_k$, the contribution of these other terms will average out. Consequently, the sign of $\mathbf{Z}[l]$ is dominated by the T_l summands $\mathbf{W}_k[l]$. Thus, the sign of $\mathbf{Z}[l]$ should give a good estimate of the value $\mathbf{W}_k[l]$. Note that S has a strong influence on the values in $\mathbf{Z}$: whereas for each $\mathbf{Z}[l]$ the contribution of the 'good' terms $\mathbf{W}_k[l]$ increases linearly with S, the number of the other random summands (that may potentially influence the signs of $\mathbf{Z}$) increases quadratically in S. This can be seen by noting that T_l is on average of the order SM/L.

2. The reconstructed estimate $\mathbf{Z}$ is compared with the watermark table $\mathbf{W}_k$ of a user k to judge his 'guilt'. All zero entries in the table $\mathbf{Z}$ are ignored, which is enforced by the factor $[1 - \delta(\mathbf{Z}[l], 0)]$ in Equation (7). While the basic Fingercasting scheme [1,4] uses correlation for the comparison of $\mathbf{W}_k$ and $\mathbf{w}$, we use a variant of Tardos' accusation sum: If the symbol $\mathbf{W}_k[l]$ agrees with the sign of $\mathbf{Z}[l]$, then user k is accused by a positive amount $g_1(p_{\text{sgn }\mathbf{Z}[l]}^{(l)})$. If the symbols differ, then he is accused by a negative amount $g_0(p_{\text{sgn }\mathbf{Z}[l]}^{(l)})$.

Note, however, that this informal reasoning assumes that no collusion attack occurs, i.e., the attackers do not deliberately influence the sign of the reconstructed table $\mathbf{Z}$. In the following section we show that the proposed construction still allows tractability in the restricted digit model if the Fingercasting parameter S is set to 1 or 2. It turns out that in this case, the attackers have no statistically significant influence on the signs of the values in $\mathbf{Z}$.

5   Analysis of the Construction

In this section we show that the construction works for $S = 1$ and $S = 2$. The intuitive reason for this lies in the construction of the table $\mathbf{Z}$: as noted in Section 4.3, each entry $\mathbf{Z}[l]$ accumulates a sum of T_l terms $\mathbf{W}[l]$; if $\mathbf{W}[l]$ is an undetectable table position, the colluders—according to the marking assumption—cannot influence these terms. However, they can try to adjust the remaining $(S - 1)T_l$ terms (in case they belong to detectable table positions) contributing to $\mathbf{Z}[l]$ in order to flip its sign.

For the case of $S = 1$ there are no such terms, thus the colluders have no influence on the value $\mathbf{Z}[l]$ at undetectable table positions. In the case of $S = 2$, the number of table positions under control and outside control of the colluders is almost equal (as for $S = 2$ we have $T_l = (S - 1)T_l$), which implies that they only have a small chance of influencing the signs in $\mathbf{Z}$. Note that typically not all of the other $(S-1)T_l$ terms can be changed by the colluders, as some of them may still come from undetectable table positions.

However, for $S \geq 3$ the construction fails, as the number of terms potentially under control of the colluders, $(S - 1)T_l$, exceeds the number of 'good' terms T_l.

5.1   Bound on the Lookup-Table Length L

We analyze the construction of Section 4.2 in a similar way as the Tardos scheme was analyzed in [12], using a statistical approach. In particular, we will make use of a result from [12], showing that the required code length in a Tardos-like scheme mainly depends on the statistical properties of a quantity called 'collective accusation sum'.

The collective accusation sum of a coalition C of c users is defined as the sum of the individual accusations of each user in C:

$$A_C = \sum_{k \in C} A_k. \tag{8}$$

The statistics of A_C and the accusation sums A_k for innocent users k determine to a great extent the performance of the fingerprinting code. We denote by $\tilde{\mu}_j$ and $\tilde{\sigma}_j$ the mean and variance of the accusation sum A_j of an innocent user $j \notin C$, scaled by L, whereas $\tilde{\mu}$ and $\tilde{\sigma}$ denote the mean and variance of the collective accusation sum, again scaled by L:

$$\tilde{\mu}_j = \mathbb{E}[A_j]/L \qquad \tilde{\sigma}_j^2 = (\mathbb{E}[A_j^2] - \mathbb{E}^2[A_j])/L$$
$$\tilde{\mu} = \mathbb{E}[A_C]/L \qquad \tilde{\sigma}^2 = (\mathbb{E}[A_C^2] - \mathbb{E}^2[A_j])/L.$$

Here, the expectation value is taken over all stochastic degrees of freedom in the system (both at the side of the distributor and the colluders); $\mathbb{E}$ is formally defined in Section 5.2. By construction (in particular the specific choice of g_0 and g_1, the idempotency of Kronecker deltas and the relation $\mathbb{E}[\delta(\operatorname{sgn} \mathbf{Z}[l], \mathbf{W}_k[l])] = p_{\operatorname{sgn} \mathbf{Z}[l]}^{(l)})$ we immediately obtain $\tilde{\mu}_j = 0$ and $\tilde{\sigma}_j = 1$, whereas the computation of $\tilde{\mu}$ turns out to be less straightforward (see Section 5.2).

A similar reasoning as the one applied in [12] for the original Tardos scheme shows that, under the assumption that both A_j and A_C follow a Gaussian distribution (which is justified due to the Central Limit Theorem), a threshold Z of

$$Z \geq \sqrt{2}L\tilde{\sigma}_j \operatorname{Erfc}^{\operatorname{inv}}(2\varepsilon_1) \tag{9}$$

and a code length of

$$L \geq 2c^2 \left(\frac{\tilde{\sigma}_j}{\tilde{\mu}} \operatorname{Erfc}^{\operatorname{inv}}(2\varepsilon_1)\right)^2 \left(1 + \frac{\tilde{\sigma}}{c\tilde{\sigma}_j} \frac{\operatorname{Erfc}^{\operatorname{inv}}(2\varepsilon_2)}{\operatorname{Erfc}^{\operatorname{inv}}(2\varepsilon_1)}\right)^2 \tag{10}$$

suffices to achieve a collusion resistance against any coalition of at most c colluders, while having a false positive (accusation) probability of ε_1 and a false negative probability of ε_2. In the regime $\varepsilon_1 \ll \varepsilon_2$, which is relevant for practical content distribution systems, ε_2 has only a small influence on the code length, as $\text{Erfc}^{\text{inv}}(2\varepsilon_2) < \text{Erfc}^{\text{inv}}(2\varepsilon_1)$. Ignoring the ε_2-term in (10), using $\tilde{\sigma}_j = 1$ and the Taylor expansion of the error function leads to the following estimate of the required code length

$$L \approx \frac{2}{\tilde{\mu}^2} c^2 \ln(\frac{1}{\varepsilon_1}). \tag{11}$$

Thus, the parameter $\tilde{\mu}$ determines the length of the Fingercasting lookup table L required to resist a coalition of c users in our construction. A scheme with good traceability will have a short value L (and thus a moderately large value of $\tilde{\mu}$), whereas a scheme that offers only moderate or bad traceability will have a $\tilde{\mu}$ close to zero, thus requiring a huge code length, which is infeasible in practice. The rest of this section is devoted to obtaining an estimate of $\tilde{\mu}$ in our construction.

5.2   Computing $\tilde{\mu}$

Recall that $\tilde{\mu}$ was defined as the scaled average of the collective accusation sum A_C of a coalition of c users, i.e., $\tilde{\mu} = \mathbb{E}[A_C]/L$, where the average is computed over all stochastic processes in the construction. A careful examination of the construction shows that there are four different stochastic processes involved:

- The distributor generating the numbers $p_1^{(1)}, \ldots, p_1^{(L)}$. Computing the expected value with respect to the distribution of $p_1^{(l)}$, whose density is given in (4), will be denoted by $\mathbb{E}_{\mathbf{p}}$. (Note that $\mathbb{E}_{\mathbf{p}}$ corresponds to an L-dimensional integral).
- The distributor filling the Tardos matrix $\mathbf{X}$ according to the probabilities $p_1^{(l)}$. Without loss of generality, we assume that the coalition's attack strategy for the l-th position in $\mathbf{Z}$ only depends on the number of symbols $\{+1, -1\}$ that are present in the colluder's watermark tables $\mathbf{W}_1, \ldots, \mathbf{W}_c$ at the position l. We denote with b_l the number of $+1$ symbols seen by the coalition at position l. Note that $b_l \in \{0, \ldots, c\}$. We write $\mathbf{b} = (b_1, \ldots, b_L)$. Averaging over the Tardos matrix $\mathbf{X}$ thus reduces to averaging over all integers $(b_1, \ldots, b_L)$. As noted in [13], these symbol counters follow a multinomial distribution. The average with respect to $\mathbf{b}$ will be denoted by $\mathbb{E}_{\mathbf{b}}$.
- The distributor generating indices $t_{i\alpha}$ according to the Fingercasting index generator. We assume the index generator to be a random oracle, thus all indices are chosen independently and uniformly. Averaging with respect to this distribution will be denoted by $\mathbb{E}_t$.
- The colluders' stochastic attack strategy (influencing the sign of $\mathbf{Z}[l]$), given the vector $\mathbf{b}$. We define $P_{\mathbf{b}}^{(l)}(\alpha) := \mathbb{P}[\text{sgn}\,\mathbf{Z}[l] = \alpha \mid \mathbf{b}]$. Averaging over this distribution will be denoted by $\mathbb{E}_w$. Furthermore, we define $P_{\mathbf{b},b_l=x}^{(l)}(\alpha) = \mathbb{P}[\text{sgn}\,\mathbf{Z}[l] = \alpha \mid \mathbf{b} \text{ with } b_l = x]$.

Applying the above averages, we obtain $\tilde{\mu}$ as $\tilde{\mu} = \mathbb{E}_p[\mathbb{E}_t[\mathbb{E}_\mathbf{b}[\mathbb{E}_w[A_C]]]]$. After straightforward but tedious manipulations (see Appendix), we get

$$\tilde{\mu} = \frac{2}{\pi}\mathbb{E}_{\mathbf{p}\backslash p^{(l)}}\left[\mathbb{E}_t[\mathbb{E}_{\mathbf{b}\backslash b_l}[\,P^{(l)}_{\mathbf{b},b_l=c}(+1) - P^{(l)}_{\mathbf{b},b_l=c}(-1)\,]]\right], \qquad (12)$$

where l denotes any *undetectable table position* with $b_l = c$. Here, $\mathbb{E}_{\mathbf{p}\backslash p^{(l)}}$ and $\mathbb{E}_{\mathbf{b}\backslash b_l}$ denote averaging over all probabilities and $\mathbf{b}$ values, except those at the l-th position. Note that the above expression depends only on undetectable table positions; the two probabilities $P^{(l)}_{\mathbf{b},b_l=c}(-1)$ and $P^{(l)}_{\mathbf{b},b_l=c}(+1)$ intuitively capture the ability of the colluders to alter the sign in the reconstructed table $\mathbf{Z}[l]$ for an undetectable table position l by using all the other detectable positions in $\mathbf{W}_1, \ldots, \mathbf{W}_c$ that they have at their disposal.

Thus, for determining the value of $\tilde{\mu}$ it suffices to consider the special case of an undetectable table position l with $\mathbf{W}[l] = +1$, and to determine the probability that the colluders can force the sign of $\mathbf{Z}[l]$ to be positive or negative. The fact that the average is taken over all remaining degrees of freedom $(\mathbb{E}_{\mathbf{p}\backslash p^{(l)}}, \mathbb{E}_t, \mathbb{E}_{\mathbf{b}\backslash b^{(l)}})$ allows us to reduce the analysis to a 'typical set' argument.

5.3   The Case $S = 1$

For the special case $S = 1$ it is easy to compute $\tilde{\mu}$ from Equation (12). Recall from Section 4.3 that for $S = 1$, in an undetectable table position l, $\mathbf{Z}[l]$ only depends on the value of $\mathbf{W}[l]$, which is not controllable by the colluders due to our table-level marking assumption.

Since the table position l in question is undetectable and the l-th entries in the colluders' watermark tables $\mathbf{W}_1, \ldots, \mathbf{W}_c$ are all filled with $+1$ (recall that $b_l = c$), the colluders can only produce a positive value $\mathbf{Z}[l]$. Consequently, we have $P^{(l)}_{\mathbf{b},b_l=c}(+1) = 1$ and $P^{(l)}_{\mathbf{b},b_l=c}(-1) = 0$. Thus, $\tilde{\mu} = 2/\pi$. Plugging this value into Equation (11) yields a code size of $L \approx \frac{\pi^2}{2}c^2 \ln(1/\varepsilon_1)$. This shows that the construction of Section 4.2 allows a good traceability of colluders; the scheme has the same performance as Tardos' fingerprinting code of length L.

The drawback of choosing $S = 1$ lies in the limited security of the encryption step in Equation (1): The distribution of the blinding factors added for encryption (sum of S entries of the encryption lookup table $\mathbf{E}$) does not have a sufficiently small statistical distance to a uniform distribution. This problem can be avoided by choosing a longer lookup table than necessary for tracing. However, this comes at the expense of reduced overall efficiency.

5.4   The Cases $S = 2$ and $S \geq 3$

An exact analysis of the cases $S \geq 2$ is nontrivial due to the averages in Equation (12). We therefore proceed by giving estimates for the probabilities $P^{(l)}_{\mathbf{b},b_l=c}(+1)$ and $P^{(l)}_{\mathbf{b},b_l=c}(-1)$ and subsequently of $\tilde{\mu}$. As an exact computation of Equation (12) seems intractable, we use a 'typical set' argument; we replace the three averaging steps by evaluating the probabilities $P^{(l)}_{\mathbf{b},b_l=c}(+1)$ and $P^{(l)}_{\mathbf{b},b_l=c}(-1)$ for a 'typical' configuration of parameters.

In order to enforce a bad traceability, the colluders' goal is to make $\tilde{\mu}$ as small as possible. This can be achieved by a strategy that results in $P^{(l)}_{\mathbf{b},b_l=c}(+1) \approx P^{(l)}_{\mathbf{b},b_l=c}(-1)$. Recall from the discussion at the beginning of Section 5 that the entry $\mathbf{Z}[l_0]$ consists of T_{l_0} copies of $\mathbf{W}[l_0]$ and $(S-1)T_{l_0}$ other summands $\mathbf{W}[l]$ for various $l \neq l_0$. When l_0 is an undetectable $+1$ position, the attackers cannot change $\mathbf{W}[l_0] = +1$. The contribution of these positions to $\mathbf{Z}[l_0]$ will be $+T_{l_0}$. Of the remaining $(S-1)T_{l_0}$ summands, the majority will, for large coalition sizes, come from detectable positions. Whenever a detectable table position is used in the decryption, due to the restricted digit model, the colluders can make a decision on the sign of the watermark symbol to use. We denote the number of such decisions by θ. The colluders must use these decisions to overcome the $+T_{l_0}$ 'bias'. They will succeed with probability

$$P^{(l)}_{\mathbf{b},b_l=c}(-1) = \frac{1}{2}\mathbb{P}[\theta > T_{l_0}].$$

The factor $1/2$ originates from the fact that the colluders only see an undetectable position l_0, but do not know the sign of the watermark symbol used. Thus, they can only guess whether they have a positive or negative bias to overcome. The probability $\mathbb{P}[\theta > T_{l_0}]$ can be expressed as

$$\mathbb{P}[\theta > T_{l_0}] = \sum_{\theta=T_{l_0}+1}^{(S-1)T_{l_0}} \binom{(S-1)T_{l_0}}{\theta}(1-\delta)^\theta \delta^{(S-1)T_{l_0}-\theta}, \qquad (13)$$

where δ denotes the probability that a certain table entry $\mathbf{W}[l]$ is undetectable. Note that $\delta = 2\int f(p)p^c\,dp \propto 1/\sqrt{c}$; we will assume that the coalition is so large that $\delta < 0.5$.

For $S = 2$ we have $\mathbb{P}[\theta > T_{l_0}] = 0$, since the summation interval is nonexistent. Next, we estimate the probability $P^{(l)}_{\mathbf{b},b_l=c}(+1)$, which we can express as

$$P^{(l)}_{\mathbf{b},b_l=c}(+1) = 1 - P^{(l)}_{\mathbf{b},b_l=c}(-1) - P^{(l)}_{\mathbf{b},b_l=c}(0).$$

Note that $P^{(l)}_{\mathbf{b},b_l=c}(0) = 1/2\,\mathbb{P}[\theta = T_{l_0}]$. From the binomial form (13) we get $\mathbb{P}[\theta = T_{l_0}] = (1-\delta)^{T_{l_0}}$. Thus, in contrast to the $S = 1$ case, the expectation term in Equation (12) for $\tilde{\mu}$ is not exactly equal to 1, but slightly smaller,

$$\tilde{\mu} \approx \frac{2}{\pi}[1 - \tfrac{1}{2}(1-\delta)^{T_l}],$$

which forces the distributor to use a slightly larger code length. T_l is on average equal to SM/L. Hence, $S = 2$ provides a good tradeoff between the security of the encryption and the traceability of colluders.

For $S = 3$, however, the sum in (13) is close to unity. This is seen as follows. The peak of the binomial distribution lies at $\theta = 2(1-\delta)T_{l_0} > T_{l_0}$, while the summation interval starts at $\theta = T_{l_0}$. Thus, the summation covers most of the probability mass of the distribution, especially if $\delta \ll 0.5$ and if the ratio M/L is large. For higher values of S, the summation (13) covers even more of the probability mass. Hence, for $S \geq 3$ the attackers can choose a strategy that makes $P^{(l)}_{\mathbf{b}, b_l = c}(+1) \approx P^{(l)}_{\mathbf{b}, b_l = c}(-1)$ and the attack succeeds with very high probability. The reason for the failure for higher S values lies in the degrees of freedom the attackers have to influence the signs of the entries in $\mathbf{Z}$. Thus, for $S \geq 3$ the accusation method needs to be changed; the most promising solution is to accuse based on $\mathbf{w}$ instead of $\mathbf{Z}$. We leave this for future research.

6 Conclusions and Future Work

In this paper, we presented the first secure watermark embedding scheme that combines a lookup-table based stream cipher with an efficient fingerprinting code, recently proposed by Tardos. This enables efficient fingerprinting of distributed content, as the joint decryption and fingerprinting step is performed securely at the client side. We determined the required tracing algorithms and discussed the main design parameters and their trade-off. Our analysis shows that the construction works for the choice of parameters $S = 1$ or $S = 2$ in Fingercasting. Whereas $S = 1$ is unfavorable in terms of security, the choice $S = 2$ yields a practical solution. Future work includes improvement of the tracing algorithm in order to handle the case $S \geq 3$ and designing Chameleon-based stream ciphers that allow for a better trade-off between security of the encryption and the length of the fingerprint code.

Acknowledgements. The work described in this paper has been supported by the European Commission through the IST Programme under contract IST-2006-034238 SPEED. The information in this document reflects only the author's views, is provided as is and no guarantee or warranty is given that the information is fit for any particular purpose. The user thereof uses the information at its sole risk and liability.

References

1. Adelsbach, A., Huber, U., Sadeghi, A.-R.: Fingercasting—joint fingerprinting and decryption of broadcast messages. In: Batten, L.M., Safavi-Naini, R. (eds.) ACISP 2006. LNCS, vol. 4058, pp. 136–147. Springer, Heidelberg (2006)
2. Anderson, R.J., Manifavas, C.: Chameleon—a new kind of stream cipher. In: FSE 1997. Proceedings of the 4th International Workshop on Fast Software Encryption, London, UK, pp. 107–113. Springer, Heidelberg (1997)
3. Boneh, D., Shaw, J.: Collusion-secure fingerprinting for digital data. IEEE Transactions on Information Theory 44(5), 1897–1905 (1998)
4. Celik, M., Lemma, A., Katzenbeisser, S., Veen, M.v.d.: Secure embedding of spread-spectrum watermarks using look-up tables. In: ICASSP 2007. International Conference on Acoustics, Speech and Signal Processing, IEEE Computer Society Press, Los Alamitos (2007)

5. Crowcroft, J., Perkins, C., Brown, I.: A method and apparatus for generating multiple watermarked copies of an information signal. WO Patent 00/56059 (2000)
6. Emmanuel, S., Kankanhalli, M.S.: Copyright protection for MPEG-2 compressed broadcast video. In: IEEE International Conference on Multimedia and Expo (ICME 2001), pp. 206–209 (2001)
7. Hollmann, H.D.L., van Lint, J.H., Linnartz, J.-P., Tolhuizen, L.M.G.M.: On codes with the identifiable parent property. Journal of Combinatorial Theory 82, 472–479 (1998)
8. Kundur, D.: Video fingerprinting and encryption principles for digital rights management. Proceedings of the IEEE 92(6), 918–932 (2004)
9. Lemma, A., Katzenbeisser, S., Celik, M., van der Veen, M.: Secure watermark embedding through partial encryption. In: Shi, Y.Q., Jeon, B. (eds.) IWDW 2006. LNCS, vol. 4283, pp. 433–445. Springer, Heidelberg (2006)
10. Parviainen, R., Parnes, P.: Large scale distributed watermarking of multicast media through encryption. In: Proceedings of the International Federation for Information Processing, Communications and Multimedia Security Joint working conference IFIP TC6 and TC11, pp. 149–158 (2001)
11. Peikert, C., Shelat, A., Smith, A.: Lower bounds for collusion-secure fingerprinting. In: Proceedings of the 14th Annual ACM-SIAM Symposium on Discrete Algorithms (SODA), pp. 472–478 (2003)
12. Škorić, B., Vladimirova, T.U., Celik, M., Talstra, J.C.: Tardos fingerprinting is better than we thought. Technical report, arXiv repository, cs.CR/0607131 (2006), http://www.arxiv.org/abs/cs.CR/0607131
13. Tardos, G.: Optimal probabilistic fingerprint codes. In: Proceedings of the 35th Annual ACM Symposium on Theory of Computing (STOC), pp. 116–125 (2003)
14. Škorić, B., Katzenbeisser, S., Celik, M.U.: Symmetric tardos fingerprinting codes for arbitrary alphabet sizes. Cryptology ePrint Archive, Report 2007/041 (2007), http://eprint.iacr.org/2007/041

A   Appendix: Derivation of Equation (12)

Recall that $\tilde{\mu} = \mathbb{E}_p[\mathbb{E}_t[\mathbb{E}_b[\mathbb{E}_w[A_C]]]]$, where A_C denotes the collective accusation sum of a coalition C of c users as defined in Equation (8). We denote with $b_\alpha^{(l)}$ the number of α symbols in the l-th entry of the tables $\mathbf{W}_1, \ldots, \mathbf{W}_c$ of the colluders. A_C can be written as

$$
A_C = \sum_{l=1}^{L}[1 - \delta(\mathbf{Z}[l], 0)] \sum_{k \in C} \Big[\delta(\mathrm{sgn}\,\mathbf{Z}[l], \mathbf{W}_k[l])\, g_1(p_{\mathrm{sgn}\,\mathbf{Z}[l]}^{(l)}) +
$$
$$
(1 - \delta(\mathrm{sgn}\,\mathbf{Z}[l], \mathbf{W}_k[l]))\, g_0(p_{\mathrm{sgn}\,\mathbf{Z}[l]}^{(l)}) \Big]
$$
$$
= \sum_{l=1}^{L}[1 - \delta(\mathbf{Z}[l], 0)]\, [b_{\mathrm{sgn}\,\mathbf{Z}[l]}^{(l)} g_1(p_{\mathrm{sgn}\,\mathbf{Z}[l]}^{(l)}) + (c - b_{\mathrm{sgn}\,\mathbf{Z}[l]}^{(l)}) g_0(p_{\mathrm{sgn}\,\mathbf{Z}[l]}^{(l)})].
$$

Taking the expectation $\mathbb{E}_w$ of A_C yields, using the definition of $P_\mathbf{b}^{(l)}(\alpha)$,

$$
\mathbb{E}_w[A_C] = \sum_{\alpha \in \{1, -1\}} \sum_{l=1}^{L} P_\mathbf{b}^{(l)}(\alpha)\, [b_\alpha^{(l)} g_1(p_\alpha^{(l)}) + (c - b_\alpha^{(l)}) g_0(p_\alpha^{(l)})].
$$

Taking the expected value $\mathbb{E}_t$, writing the two terms of the sum over α explicitly and noting that $b_{-1}^{(l)} = c - b_1^{(l)}$ yields:

$$\mathbb{E}_t[\mathbb{E}_w[A_C]] = \sum_{l=1}^{L} \mathbb{E}_t[P_{\mathbf{b}}^{(l)}(1)]\ [b_1^{(l)}g_1(p_1^{(l)}) + [c - b_1^{(l)}]g_0(p_1^{(l)})] +$$

$$\mathbb{E}_t[P_{\mathbf{b}}^{(l)}(-1)]\ [b_{-1}^{(l)}g_1(p_{-1}^{(l)}) + [c - b_{-1}^{(l)}]g_0(p_{-1}^{(l)})]$$

$$= \sum_{l=1}^{L} \mathbb{E}_t[P_{\mathbf{b}}^{(l)}(1) - P_{\mathbf{b}}^{(l)}(-1)]\frac{b_1^{(l)} - cp_1^{(l)}}{\sqrt{p_1^{(l)}(1 - p_1^{(l)})}}.$$

To simplify the notation, we write b_l as abbreviation for $b_1^{(l)}$; similarly, we write p_l for $p_1^{(l)}$. Next, we jointly take the averages $\mathbb{E}_{\mathbf{b}}$ and $\mathbb{E}_p$. We do this by first taking the average $\mathbb{E}_{\mathbf{b}\backslash b_l}$ over all values $\mathbf{b}$, except the l-th position, then over b_l (which follows a Binomial distribution) and finally over the probabilities $p_1, \ldots, p_L$ chosen during fingerprint creation. Applying these three averages we obtain

$$\tilde{\mu} = \frac{1}{L}\mathbb{E}_p\left[\sum_{l=1}^{L}\sum_{b_l=1}^{c}\binom{c}{b_l}\mathbb{E}_t[\mathbb{E}_{\mathbf{b}\backslash b_l}[P_{\mathbf{b}}^{(l)}(1) - P_{\mathbf{b}}^{(l)}(-1)]]\frac{b_l - cp_l}{\sqrt{p_l(1 - p_l)}}p_l^{b_l}(1 - p_l)^{c - b_l}\right].$$

By the independence of columns, we can first take the average over p_l and subsequently over all other values, yielding

$$\tilde{\mu} = \frac{1}{L}\mathbb{E}_{\mathbf{p}\backslash p^{(l)}}\left[\sum_{l=1}^{L}\sum_{b_l=1}^{c}\binom{c}{b_l}\mathbb{E}_t[\mathbb{E}_{\mathbf{b}\backslash b_l}[P_{\mathbf{b}}^{(l)}(1) - P_{\mathbf{b}}^{(l)}(-1)]]\right.$$

$$\left.\mathbb{E}_{p_l}\left[\frac{b_l - cp_l}{\sqrt{p_l(1 - p_l)}}p_l^{b_l}(1 - p_l)^{c - b_l}\right]\right]. \tag{14}$$

The innermost expectation value can, using the density function f defined in Equation (4), be computed explicitly, as

$$\mathbb{E}_{p_l}\left[\frac{b_l - cp_l}{\sqrt{p_l(1 - p_l)}}p_l^{b_l}(1 - p_l)^{c - b_l}\right] = \frac{1}{\pi}p_l^{b_l}(1 - p_l)^{c - b_l}\Big|_0^1 = -\frac{1}{\pi}\delta(b_l, 0) + \frac{1}{\pi}\delta(b_l, c).$$

Thus, in the sum over b_l in Equation (14), all summands except $b_l = 0$ and $b_l = c$ vanish and $\tilde{\mu}$ can be written as

$$\tilde{\mu} = \frac{1}{\pi}\mathbb{E}_{\mathbf{p}\backslash p^{(l)}}\left[-\mathbb{E}_t[\mathbb{E}_{\mathbf{b}\backslash b_l}[P_{\mathbf{b}, b_l=0}^{(l)}(1) - P_{\mathbf{b}, b_l=0}^{(l)}(-1)]] +\right.$$

$$\left.\mathbb{E}_t[\mathbb{E}_{\mathbf{b}\backslash b_l}[P_{\mathbf{b}, b_l=c}^{(l)}(1) - P_{\mathbf{b}, b_l=c}^{(l)}(-1)]]\right],$$

where l denotes any index of an undetectable table position. By symmetry, Equation (12) follows.

Exposing Digital Forgeries Through Specular Highlights on the Eye

Micah K. Johnson and Hany Farid

Department of Computer Science
Dartmouth College
Hanover, NH 03755
{kimo,farid}@cs.dartmouth.edu
www.cs.dartmouth.edu/~{kimo,farid}

Abstract. When creating a digital composite of two people, it is difficult to exactly match the lighting conditions under which each individual was originally photographed. In many situations, the light source in a scene gives rise to a specular highlight on the eyes. We show how the direction to a light source can be estimated from this highlight. Inconsistencies in lighting across an image are then used to reveal traces of digital tampering.

Keywords: Digital Tampering, Digital Forensics.

1 Introduction

The photograph in Fig. 1 of the host and judges for the popular television show *American Idol* was scheduled for publication when it caught the attention of a photo-editor. Coming on the heels of several scandals that rocked major news organizations, the photo-editor was concerned that the image had been doctored. There was good reason to worry – the image was a composite of several photographs. Shown in Fig. 1 are magnifications of the host's and judge's eyes. The inconsistencies in the shape and position of the specular highlight on the eyes suggest that the people were originally photographed under different lighting conditions. In this work, we show how the location of a specular highlight can be used to determine the direction to the light source. Inconsistencies in the estimates from different eyes, as well as differences in the shape and color of the highlights, can be used to reveal traces of digital tampering.

In related work, the authors of [5] showed how to estimate the light source direction in 2-D. While this approach has the benefit of being applicable to arbitrary objects, it has the drawback that it can only determine the direction to the light source within one degree of ambiguity. In contrast, we estimate the full 3-D light source direction by leveraging a 3-D model of the human eye. Although not specifically developed for a forensic setting, the authors of [7] described a technique for computing an environment map from eyes that embodies the illumination in the scene. While the environment map provides a rich source of information about the lighting, it has the drawback of requiring a relatively high-resolution image of the eye.

T. Furon et al. (Eds.): IH 2007, LNCS 4567, pp. 311–325, 2007.
© Springer-Verlag Berlin Heidelberg 2007

Fig. 1. This photograph of the *American Idol* host and judges is a digital composite of multiple photographs. The inconsistencies in the shape and position of the specular highlight on the eyes suggest that these people were originally photographed under different lighting conditions. Photo courtesy of Fox News and the Associated Press.

We describe how to estimate the 3-D direction to a light source from specular highlights on the eyes. We show the efficacy of this approach on synthetic and real images and visually plausible forgeries.

2 Methods

The position of a specular highlight is determined by the relative positions of the light source, the reflective surface and the viewer (or camera). In Fig. 2, for example, is a diagram showing the creation of a specular highlight on an eye. In this diagram, the three vectors L, N and R correspond to the direction to the light, the surface normal at the point at which the highlight is formed, and the direction in which the highlight will be seen. For a perfect reflector, the highlight is seen only when the view direction $V = R$. For an imperfect reflector, a specular highlight can be seen for viewing directions V near R, with the strongest highlight seen when $V = R$.

We will first derive an algebraic relationship between the vectors L, N, and V. We then show how the 3-D vectors N and V can be estimated from a single image, from which the direction to the light source L is determined.

The law of reflection states that a light ray reflects off of a surface at an angle of reflection θ_r equal to the angle of incidence θ_i, where these angles are measured with respect to the surface normal N, Fig. 2. Assuming unit-length

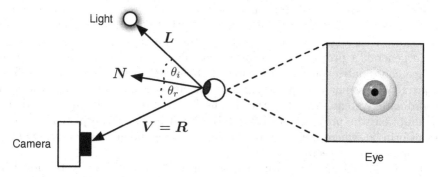

Fig. 2. The formation of a specular highlight on an eye (small white dot on the iris). The position of the highlight is determined by the surface normal N and the relative directions to the light source L and viewer V.

vectors, the direction of the reflected ray R can be described in terms of the light direction L and the surface normal N:

$$R = L + 2(\cos(\theta_i)N - L)$$
$$= 2\cos(\theta_i)N - L. \qquad (1)$$

By assuming a perfect reflector ($V = R$), the above constraint yields:

$$L = 2\cos(\theta_i)N - V$$
$$= 2\left(V^T N\right)N - V. \qquad (2)$$

The light direction L can therefore be estimated from the surface normal N and view direction V at a specular highlight. In the following sections, we describe how to estimate these two 3-D vectors from a single image.

Note that the light direction is specified with respect to the eye, and not the camera. In practice, all of these vectors will be placed in a common coordinate system, allowing us to compare light directions across the image.

2.1   Camera Calibration

In order to estimate the surface normal N and view direction V in a common coordinate system, we first need to estimate the projective transform that describes the transformation from world to image coordinates. With only a single image, this calibration is generally an under-constrained problem. In our case, however, the known geometry of the eye can be exploited to estimate this required transform. Throughout, upper-case symbols will denote world coordinates and lower-case will denote camera/image coordinates.

The limbus, the boundary between the sclera (white part of the eye) and the iris (colored part of the eye), can be well modeled as a circle [7]. The image of the limbus, however, will be an ellipse except when the eye is directly facing the camera. Intuitively, the distortion of the ellipse away from a circle will be related to the pose and position of the eye relative to the camera. We therefore seek the transform that aligns the image of the limbus to a circle.

In general, a projective transform that maps 3-D world coordinates to 2-D image coordinates can be represented, in homogeneous coordinates, as a 3×4 matrix. We assume that points on a limbus are coplanar, and define the world coordinate system such that the limbus lies in the $Z = 0$ plane. With this assumption, the projective transformation reduces to a 3×3 planar projective transform [2], where the world points X and image points x are represented by 2-D homogeneous vectors.

Points on the limbus in our world coordinate system satisfy the following implicit equation of a circle:

$$f(\boldsymbol{X};\boldsymbol{\alpha}) = (X_1 - C_1)^2 + (X_2 - C_2)^2 - r^2 = 0, \qquad (3)$$

where $\boldsymbol{\alpha} = (\,C_1 \quad C_2 \quad r\,)^T$ denotes the circle center and radius.

Consider a collection of points, $\boldsymbol{X_i}$, $i = 1, \ldots, m$, each of which satisfy Equation (3). Under an ideal pinhole camera model, the world point $\boldsymbol{X_i}$ maps to the image point $\boldsymbol{x_i}$ as follows:

$$\boldsymbol{x_i} = H\boldsymbol{X_i}, \qquad (4)$$

where H is a 3×3 projective transform matrix.

The estimation of H can be formulated in an orthogonal distance fitting framework. Let $E(\cdot)$ be an error function on the parameter vector $\boldsymbol{\alpha}$ and the unknown projective transform H:

$$E(\boldsymbol{\alpha}, H) = \sum_{i=1}^{m} \min_{\hat{\boldsymbol{X}}} \left\| \boldsymbol{x_i} - H\hat{\boldsymbol{X}} \right\|^2, \qquad (5)$$

where $\hat{\boldsymbol{X}}$ is on the circle parametrized by $\boldsymbol{\alpha}$. The error embodies the sum of the squared errors between the data, $\boldsymbol{x_i}$, and the closest point on the model, $\hat{\boldsymbol{X}}$. This error function is minimized using non-linear least squares via the Levenberg-Marquardt iteration [9] (see Appendix A for details).

Once estimated, the projective transform H can be decomposed in terms of intrinsic and extrinsic camera parameters [2]. The intrinsic parameters consist of the camera focal length, camera center, skew and aspect ratio. For simplicity, we will assume that the camera center is the image center, that the skew is 0 and the aspect ratio is 1, leaving only the focal length f. The extrinsic parameters consist of a rotation matrix R and translation vector t that define the transformation between the world and camera coordinate systems. Since the world points lie on a single plane, the projective transform can be decomposed in terms of the intrinsic and extrinsic parameters as:

$$H = \lambda K (\,\boldsymbol{r_1} \quad \boldsymbol{r_2} \quad t\,), \qquad (6)$$

where the 3×3 intrinsic matrix K is:

$$K = \begin{pmatrix} f & 0 & 0 \\ 0 & f & 0 \\ 0 & 0 & 1 \end{pmatrix}, \tag{7}$$

λ is a scale factor, the column vectors r_1 and r_2 are the first two columns of the rotation matrix R, and t is the translation vector.

With a known focal length f, and hence a known matrix K, the world to camera coordinate transform $\hat{H}$ can be estimated directly:

$$\frac{1}{\lambda} K^{-1} H = \begin{pmatrix} r_1 & r_2 & t \end{pmatrix}$$

$$\hat{H} = \begin{pmatrix} r_1 & r_2 & t \end{pmatrix}, \tag{8}$$

where the scale factor λ is chosen so that r_1 and r_2 are unit vectors. The complete rotation matrix is given by:

$$R = \begin{pmatrix} r_1 & r_2 & r_1 \times r_2 \end{pmatrix}, \tag{9}$$

where $\times$ denotes cross product.

If the focal length is unknown, it can be directly estimated as described in Appendix B.

2.2   View Direction

Recall that the minimization of Equation (5) yields both the transform H and the circle parameters α for the limbus. The unit vector from the center of the limbus to the origin of the camera coordinate system is the view direction, v. Let $X_c = \begin{pmatrix} C_1 & C_2 & 1 \end{pmatrix}$ denote the estimated center of a limbus in world coordinates. In the camera coordinate system, this point is given by:

$$x_c = \hat{H} X_c. \tag{10}$$

The view direction, as a unit vector, in the camera coordinate system is then given by:

$$v = -\frac{x_c}{\|x_c\|}, \tag{11}$$

where the negative sign reverses the vector so that it points from the eye to the camera.

2.3   Surface Normal

The 3-D surface normal N at a specular highlight is estimated from a 3-D model of the human eye [6]. The model consists of a pair of spheres as illustrated in Fig. 3(a). The larger sphere, with radius $r_1 = 11.5$ mm, represents the sclera and the smaller sphere, with radius $r_2 = 7.8$ mm, represents the cornea. The

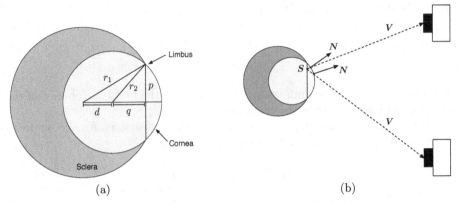

Fig. 3. (a) A side view of a 3-D model of the human eye. The larger sphere represents the sclera and the smaller sphere represents the cornea. The limbus is defined by the intersection of the two spheres. (b) The surface normal at a point S in the plane of the limbus depends on the view direction V.

centers of the spheres are displaced by a distance $d = 4.7$ mm. The limbus, a circle with radius $p = 5.8$ mm, is defined by the intersection of the two spheres. The distance between the center of the smaller sphere and the plane containing the limbus is $q = 5.25$ mm. These measurements vary slightly among adults, and the radii of the spheres are approximately 0.1 mm smaller for female eyes [3,6].

Consider a specular highlight in world coordinates at location $S = (\begin{array}{cc} S_x & S_y \end{array})$, measured with respect to the center of the limbus. The surface normal at S depends on the view direction V. In Fig. 3(b) is a schematic showing this relationship for two different positions of the camera. The surface normal N is determined by intersecting the ray leaving S, along the direction V, with the edge of the sphere. This intersection can be computed by solving a quadratic system for k, the distance between S and the edge of the sphere,

$$(S_x + kV_x)^2 + (S_y + kV_y)^2 + (q + kV_z)^2 = r_2^2$$
$$k^2 + 2(S_xV_x + S_yV_y + qV_z)k + (S_x^2 + S_y^2 + q^2 - r_2^2) = 0, \qquad (12)$$

where q and r_2 are specified by the 3-D model of the eye. The view direction $V = (\begin{array}{ccc} V_x & V_y & V_z \end{array})$ in the world coordinate system is given by:

$$V = R^{-1}v, \qquad (13)$$

where v is the view direction in camera coordinates, Section 2.2, and R is the estimated rotation between the world and camera coordinate systems, Section 2.1. The surface normal N in the world coordinate system is then given by:

$$N = \begin{pmatrix} S_x + kV_x \\ S_y + kV_y \\ q + kV_z \end{pmatrix}, \qquad (14)$$

and in camera coordinates: $n = RN$.

2.4   Light Direction

Consider a specular highlight $\boldsymbol{x_s}$ specified in image coordinates and the estimated projective transform H from world to image coordinates. The inverse transform H^{-1} maps the coordinates of the specular highlight into world coordinates:

$$\boldsymbol{X_s} = H^{-1}\boldsymbol{x_s} \tag{15}$$

The center $\boldsymbol{C}$ and radius r of the limbus in the world coordinate system determine the coordinates of the specular highlight, $\boldsymbol{S}$, with respect to the model:

$$\boldsymbol{S} = \frac{p}{r}\left(\boldsymbol{X_s} - \boldsymbol{C}\right), \tag{16}$$

where p is specified by the 3-D model of the eye. The position of the specular highlight $\boldsymbol{S}$ is then used to determine the surface normal $\boldsymbol{N}$, as described in the previous section. Combined with the estimate of the view direction $\boldsymbol{V}$, Section 2.2, the light source direction $\boldsymbol{L}$ can be estimated from Equation (2). In order to compare light source estimates in the image, the light source estimate is converted to camera coordinates: $\boldsymbol{l} = R\boldsymbol{L}$

3   Results

We tested our technique for estimating the 3-D light source direction on both synthetically generated and real images. In all of these results the direction to the light source was estimated from specular highlights in both eyes. This required a slight modification to the minimization in Equation (5) which is described in Appendix A. The view direction, surface normal and light direction were then estimated separately for each eye.

3.1   Synthetic Images

Synthetic images of eyes were rendered using the `pbrt` environment [8]. The shape of the eyes conformed to the 3-D model described in Section 2.3 and the eyes were placed in one of 12 different locations. For each location, the eyes were rotated by a unique amount relative to the camera. The eyes were illuminated with two light sources: a fixed light directly in line with the camera, and a second light placed in one of four different positions. The twelve locations and four light directions gave rise to 48 images, Fig. 4. Each image was rendered at a resolution of 1200 × 1600 pixels, with the cornea occupying less than 0.1% of the entire image. Shown in Fig. 4 are several examples of the rendered eyes, along with a schematic of the imaging geometry.

The limbus and position of the specular highlight(s) were automatically extracted from the rendered image. For each highlight, the projective transform H, the view direction $\boldsymbol{v}$ and surface normal $\boldsymbol{n}$ were estimated, from which the direction to the light source $\boldsymbol{l}$ was determined. The angular error between the estimated $\boldsymbol{l}$ and actual $\boldsymbol{l_0}$ light directions is computed as:

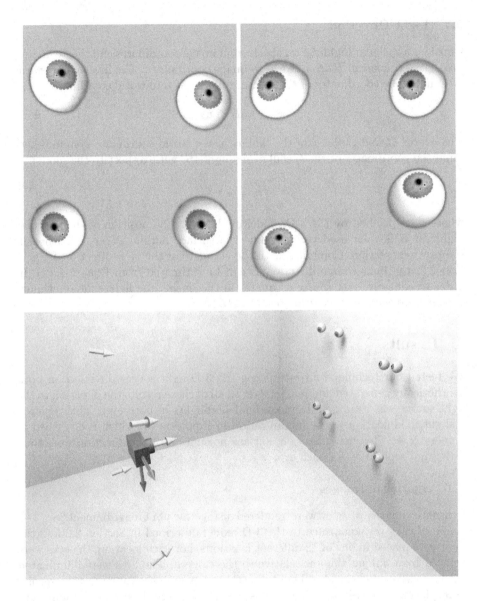

Fig. 4. Synthetically generated eyes. Each of the upper panels corresponds to different positions and orientations of the eyes and locations of the light sources. The ellipse fit to each limbus is shown in dashed green, and the red dots denote the positions of the specular highlights. Shown below is a schematic of the imaging geometry: the position of the lights, camera and a subset of the eye positions.

$$\phi = \cos^{-1}\left(l^T l_0\right). \tag{17}$$

where the vectors are normalized to be unit length.

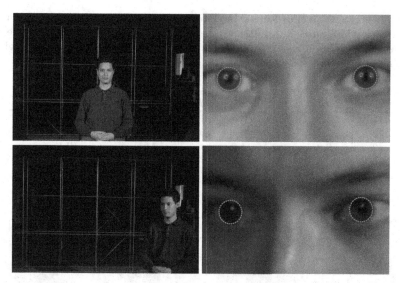

Fig. 5. A subject at different locations and orientations relative to the camera and two light sources. Shown to the right are magnified views of the eyes. The ellipse fit to each limbus is shown in dashed green and the red dots denote the positions of the specular highlights. See also Table 1.

With a known focal length, the average angular error in estimating the light source direction was 2.8° with a standard deviation of 1.3° and a maximum error of 6.8°. With an unknown focal length, the average error was 2.8° with a standard deviation of 1.3° and a maximum error of 6.3°.

3.2   Real Images

To further test the efficacy of our technique, we photographed a subject under controlled lighting. A camera and two lights were arranged along a wall, and the subject was positioned 250 cm in front of the camera and at the same elevation. The first light L_1 was positioned 130 cm to the left of and 60 cm above the camera. The second light L_2 was positioned 260 cm to the right and 80 cm above the camera. The subject was placed in five different locations and orientations relative to the camera and lights, Fig. 5. A six mega-pixel Nikon D100 camera with a 35 mm lens was set to capture in the highest quality JPEG format.

For each image, an ellipse was manually fit to the limbus of each eye. In these images, the limbus did not form a sharp boundary – the boundary spanned roughly 3 pixels. As such, we fit the ellipses to the better defined inner outline [4], Fig. 5. The radius of each limbus was approximately 9 pixels, and the cornea occupied 0.004% of the entire image.

Each specular highlight was localized by specifying a bounding rectangular area around each highlight and computing the centroid of the selection. The weighting function for the centroid computation was chosen to be the squared (normalized) pixel intensity.

Table 1. Angular errors (degrees) in estimating the light direction for the images shown in Fig. 5. On the left are the errors for a known focal length, and on the right are the errors for an unknown focal length. A '–' indicates that the specular highlight for that light was not visible on the cornea.

image	left eye L_1	L_2	right eye L_1	L_2	left eye L_1	L_2	right eye L_1	L_2
1	5.8	7.6	3.8	1.6	5.8	7.7	3.9	1.7
2	–	8.7	–	0.8	–	10.4	–	18.1
3	9.3	–	11.0	–	17.6	–	10.1	–
4	12.5	16.4	7.5	7.3	10.4	13.6	7.4	5.6
5	14.0	–	13.8	–	17.4	–	16.5	–

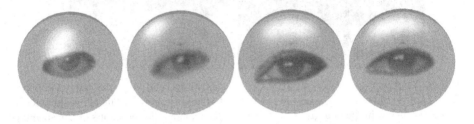

Fig. 6. The estimated light source direction for each person in Fig. 1 is depicted as Gaussian blobs on a hemisphere, each centered about the estimated 3-D direction. Superimposed on each hemisphere is an image of one of the eyes from which the estimates were made. Note that the inconsistencies in the light source direction suggest that the photograph is a composite of at least three photographs.

The location to the light source(s) was estimated for each pair of eyes assuming a known and unknown focal length. The angular errors, Equation (17), for each image are given in Table 1. Note that in some cases an estimate for one of the light sources was not possible when the highlight was not visible on the cornea. With a known focal length, the average angular error was 8.6°, and with an unknown focal length, the average angular error was 10.5°.

There are several reasons for the increase in error over the synthetic images. First, the average size of the cornea in our real images is much smaller than the size of the cornea in the synthetic images, 256 pixels^2 versus over 1000 pixels^2. Second, the limbus in an adult human eye is slightly elliptical, being 1 mm wider than it is tall [3], while our model assumes a circular limbus.

Shown in Fig. 1 is a photograph of the host and judges of the television show *American Idol*, and shown in Fig. 6 are the results of estimating the direction to the light source for each person. These estimates are rendered as Gaussian blobs ($\sigma = 15°$) on a hemisphere. The final estimate is depicted as a sum of Gaussians, one for each specular highlight. Note that the estimates in the two right-most plots are visually consistent with one another, but are significantly different from the two left-most estimates.

Fig. 7. A composite where rock star Gene Simmons' face has been inserted into a family portrait

Shown in Fig. 7 is a composite where the father's face has been replaced with a different face. Two specular highlights are visible on each of the children's eyes. The light direction was estimated from each specularity and for each eye. Across the children's eyes, the average pair-wise difference in orientation for the first specularity was 8.5° with a maximum difference of 11.6°. The average difference for the second specularity was 9.4° with a maximum difference of 13.9°. By comparison, the average difference in orientation between the father's specularities to those of the children was 40.3°. We did not estimate the light direction for the woman because we have found that glasses distort the shape and location of the specularity on the eye.

4   Discussion

When creating a composite of two or more people it is often difficult to match the lighting conditions under which each person was originally photographed. Specular highlights that appear on the eye are a powerful cue as to the shape, color and location of the light source(s). Inconsistencies in these properties of the light can be used as evidence of tampering. We have described how to measure the 3-D direction to a light source from the position of the highlight on the eye. While we have not specifically focused on it, the shape and color of a highlight are relatively easy to quantify and measure and should also prove helpful in exposing digital forgeries.

Since specular highlights tend to be relatively small on the eye, it is possible to manipulate them to conceal traces of tampering. To do so, the shape, color and location of the highlight would have to be constructed so as to be globally consistent with the lighting in other parts of the image. Inconsistencies in this lighting may be detectable using the technique described in [5]. Also working in our favor is that even small artifacts on the eyes are visually salient. Nevertheless, as with all forensic tools, it is still possible to circumvent this technique.

We expect this technique, in conjunction with a growing body of forensic tools, to be effective in exposing digital forgeries.

Acknowledgments

We are grateful to Fabio Pellacini for many helpful conversations and suggestions. This work was supported by a Guggenheim Fellowship, a gift from Adobe Systems, Inc., a gift from Microsoft, Inc., a grant from the United States Air Force (FA8750-06-C-0011), and under a grant (2005-DD-BX-1091) awarded by the Bureau of Justice Assistance (points of view or opinions in this document are those of the author and do not represent the official position or policies of the United States Department of Justice).

References

1. Ahn, S.J.: Least Squares Orthogonal Distance Fitting of Curves and Surfaces in Space. LNCS, vol. 3151. Springer, Heidelberg (2004)
2. Hartley, R., Zisserman, A.: Multiple View Geometry in Computer Vision. Cambridge University Press, Cambridge (2004)
3. Hogan, M.J., Alvarado, J.A., Weddell, J.E.: Histology of the Human Eye. W.B Saunders Company (1971)
4. Iskander, D.R.: A parametric approach to measuring limbus corneae from digital images. IEEE Transactions on Biomedical Engineering 53(6), 1134–1140 (2006)
5. Johnson, M.K., Farid, H.: Exposing digital forgeries by detecting inconsistencies in lighting. In: ACM Multimedia and Security Workshop, New York, NY (2005)
6. Lefohn, A., Caruso, R., Reinhard, E., Budge, B., Shirley, P.: An ocularist's approach to human iris synthesis. IEEE Computer Graphics and Applications 23(6), 70–75 (2003)
7. Nishino, K., Nayar, S.K.: Eyes for relighting. ACM Transactions on Graphics 23(3), 704–711 (2004)
8. Pharr, M., Humphreys, G.: Physically Based Rendering: From Theory to Implementation. Morgan Kaufmann, San Francisco (2004)
9. Ruszczyński, A.: Nonlinear Optimization. Princeton University Press, Princeton (2006)

Appendix A

In this appendix we describe the minimization of the error function:

$$E(\alpha, H) = \sum_{i=1}^{m} \min_{\hat{X}} \left\| x_i - H\hat{X} \right\|^2, \tag{18}$$

which yields the perspective transform H and circle parameters α. For notational convenience, we express this error function as $E(u)$ where $u = (\alpha \quad h)$, and where the vector h contains the nine elements of the 3×3 matrix H.

This error function is minimized in nested iterations as described in [1]. The inner iteration computes the closest point $\hat{X}$ on the model for each image point x_i, where the model is specified by the current state of u. The outer iteration then updates the parameter vector u according to the results of the inner model fitting. This process is repeated and terminates when the norm of the update to u is below a specified threshold.

Closest point: For a given point x_i in image coordinates, we seek the closest point $\hat{X}$ on the model. The point $\hat{X}$ that satisfies this condition must, of course, be on the model, $f(\hat{X}; \alpha) = 0$. Recall that $f(\cdot)$ is the equation of a circle, Equation (3). In order to contend with the scale ambiguity inherent to homogeneous coordinates, this model takes on a slightly different form:

$$f(X; \alpha) = (X_1/X_3 - C_1)^2 + (X_2/X_3 - C_2)^2 - r^2 \tag{19}$$

For $\hat{X}$ to be the closest point, it must satisfy two additional criteria. First, the vector between the image point x_i and the model point $H\hat{X}$ (expressed in image coordinates) must be parallel to the gradient of the model in image coordinates, $H^{-T}\nabla f$, yielding the following constraint:

$$z^T((x_i - H\hat{X}) \times H^{-T}\nabla f) = 0, \tag{20}$$

where $z^T = (0 \quad 0 \quad 1)$ restricts this constraint to the image plane. Second, the model point $H\hat{X}$ must lie in the image plane (recall that the homogeneous points x_i lie in the plane $z = 1$):

$$z^T(x_i - H\hat{X}) = 0. \tag{21}$$

These three constraints form a system of non-linear equations that can be solved using the Gauss-Newton method, where the vector-valued function to be minimized is:

$$g(u, x_i, X) = \begin{pmatrix} f(X, \alpha) \\ z^T((x_i - HX) \times H^{-T}\nabla f) \\ z^T(x_i - HX) \end{pmatrix}. \tag{22}$$

In practice, the image point x_i is expressed in terms of world coordinates $x_i = HX_i$. This error function is given by:

$$g(u, X_i, X) = \begin{pmatrix} f(X, \alpha) \\ z^T(H(X_i - X) \times H^{-T}\nabla f) \\ z^T H(X_i - X) \end{pmatrix}. \tag{23}$$

This inner iteration is initialized with H equal to the identity matrix, and $\boldsymbol{\alpha}$, the circle parameters, equal to a bounding circle fit to the image data.

Parameter update: Once the inner iteration completes and the closest points $\hat{\boldsymbol{X}}$ have been computed for each image point $\boldsymbol{x}_i$, the parameter vector $\boldsymbol{u}$ can be updated. The outer iteration uses a Levenberg-Marquardt minimization, which requires the derivative of $\boldsymbol{x}_i - H\boldsymbol{X}$ with respect to $\boldsymbol{u}$, evaluated at the closest point $\hat{\boldsymbol{X}}$:

$$\frac{\partial}{\partial u}(\boldsymbol{x}_i - H\boldsymbol{X})\Big|_{\boldsymbol{X}=\hat{\boldsymbol{X}}} = -\left(\frac{\partial H}{\partial u}\right)[\boldsymbol{X}]\Big|_{\boldsymbol{X}=\hat{\boldsymbol{X}}} - H\frac{\partial \boldsymbol{X}}{\partial u}\Big|_{\boldsymbol{X}=\hat{\boldsymbol{X}}}, \qquad (24)$$

where $[\boldsymbol{X}]$ is a block-diagonal matrix with $\boldsymbol{X}$ on the diagonal. The derivative $\partial H/\partial u$ is computed by simply differentiating the matrix H with respect to each of its components h_i. The derivative $\partial X/\partial u$ is computed by implicitly differentiating $\boldsymbol{g}(\cdot)$ with respect to $\boldsymbol{u}$:

$$\frac{\partial \boldsymbol{g}}{\partial u} + \frac{\partial \boldsymbol{g}}{\partial \boldsymbol{X}}\frac{\partial \boldsymbol{X}}{\partial u} + \frac{\partial \boldsymbol{g}}{\partial \boldsymbol{X}_i}\frac{\partial \boldsymbol{X}_i}{\partial u} = 0, \qquad (25)$$

and solving for $\partial X/\partial u$:

$$\frac{\partial \boldsymbol{X}}{\partial u} = -\left(\frac{\partial \boldsymbol{g}}{\partial \boldsymbol{X}}\right)^{-1}\left(\frac{\partial \boldsymbol{g}}{\partial u} + \frac{\partial \boldsymbol{g}}{\partial \boldsymbol{X}_i}\frac{\partial \boldsymbol{X}_i}{\partial u}\right). \qquad (26)$$

The individual derivatives in this expression are determined by straight-forward differentiation of each function with respect to its unknowns. The derivatives for all m image points, $\boldsymbol{x}_1$ to $\boldsymbol{x}_m$, are then stacked into a $3m \times 12$ Jacobian matrix, where 12 corresponds to the total number of unknowns (9 elements of H and 3 circle parameters $\boldsymbol{\alpha}$). This Jacobian matrix is used by the Levenberg-Marquardt minimization to compute the update to the parameter vector $\boldsymbol{u}$.

Constraints: The minimization described above can be extended to handle two circles by creating a block-diagonal Jacobian matrix from the Jacobian matrices of the individual eyes. In addition, constraint equations can be added to the error function $E(\boldsymbol{u})$, Equation (18), to ensure that the transform H for both eyes is the same and that the radii of the circles are equal to 5.8 mm. The error function for both eyes with constraints is then given by:

$$\begin{aligned}
\hat{E}(\boldsymbol{u}_1, \boldsymbol{u}_2) = &\; E(\boldsymbol{u}_1) + E(\boldsymbol{u}_2) \\
&+ w\left(\|\boldsymbol{h}_1 - \boldsymbol{h}_2\|^2 + (\det(H_1) - 1)^2 + (\det(H_2) - 1)^2\right. \\
&\left.+ (r_1 - 5.8)^2 + (r_2 - 5.8)^2\right),
\end{aligned} \qquad (27)$$

where w is a scalar weighting factor. The Jacobian of this system is:

$$J(\boldsymbol{u}_1, \boldsymbol{u}_2) = \begin{pmatrix} J_1(\boldsymbol{u}_1) & \\ & J_2(\boldsymbol{u}_2) \\ \hat{J}_1(\boldsymbol{u}_1) & \hat{J}_2(\boldsymbol{u}_2) \end{pmatrix}, \qquad (28)$$

where J_1 and J_2 are the Jacobian matrices from the individual eyes, and $\hat{J}_1$ and $\hat{J}_2$ are the Jacobians of the constraint equations with respect to u_1 and u_2. The transforms H_1 and H_2 are initially set to the identity matrix, and the circle parameters were chosen to enclose the limbus of each eye.

Appendix B

In this appendix we describe how to decompose the projective transform H in Equation (6) in the case when the focal length f is unknown.

The transform H has eight unknowns: the focal length f, the scale factor λ, the three rotation angles θ_x, θ_y and θ_z for the rotation matrix R, and the three coordinates of the translation vector t. By multiplying the matrices on the right-hand side of Equation (6), H can be expressed in terms of these unknowns:

$$H = \lambda \begin{pmatrix} fc_yc_z & fc_ys_z & ft_x \\ f(s_xs_yc_z - c_xs_z) & f(s_xs_ys_z + c_xc_z) & ft_y \\ c_xs_yc_z + s_xs_z & c_xs_ys_z - s_xc_z & t_z \end{pmatrix}, \tag{29}$$

where $c_x = \cos(\theta_x)$, $s_x = \sin(\theta_x)$, etc, and where the rotation matrix follows the "x-y-z" convention.

Consider the upper-left 2×2 sub-matrix of H rewritten in terms of the four unknowns θ_x, θ_y, θ_z, and $\hat{f} = \lambda f$. These unknowns are estimated by minimizing the following error function using non-linear least-squares:

$$E(\theta_x, \theta_y, \theta_z, \hat{f}) = (\hat{f}c_yc_z - h_1)^2 + (\hat{f}c_ys_z - h_2)^2 + (\hat{f}(s_xs_yc_z - c_xs_z) - h_4)^2 \\ + (\hat{f}(s_xs_ys_z + c_xc_z) - h_5)^2, \tag{30}$$

where h_i corresponds to the ith entry of H. A Gauss-Newton iterative approach is employed to minimize $E(\cdot)$. In practice, we have found that $\theta_z = \tan^{-1}(h_2/h_1)$, $f = 1$ and random values for θ_x and θ_y provide good starting conditions for this minimization. These estimated parameters then yield two possible estimates of the focal length:

$$f_1 = \frac{\hat{f}(c_xs_yc_z + s_xs_z)}{h_7} \quad \text{and} \quad f_2 = \frac{\hat{f}(c_xs_ys_z - s_xc_z)}{h_8}. \tag{31}$$

These two estimates are combined using the following weighted average:

$$f = \frac{h_7^2 f_1 + h_8^2 f_2}{h_7^2 + h_8^2}. \tag{32}$$

Note that the focal length f is undefined for $h_7 = h_8 = 0$. In addition, this estimation is vulnerable to numeric instabilities for values of h_7 and h_8 near zero. As such, the weighting was chosen to favor larger values of h_7 and h_8.

Tamper Hiding: Defeating Image Forensics

Matthias Kirchner and Rainer Böhme

Technische Universität Dresden
Institute for System Architecture
01062 Dresden, Germany
matthias.kirchner@acm.org, rainer.boehme@tu-dresden.de

Abstract. This paper introduces novel hiding techniques to counter the detection of image manipulations through forensic analyses. The presented techniques allow to resize and rotate (parts of) bitmap images without leaving a periodic pattern in the local linear predictor coefficients, which has been exploited by prior art to detect traces of manipulation. A quantitative evaluation on a batch of test images proves the proposed method's efficacy, while controlling for key parameters and for the retained image quality compared to conventional linear interpolation.

1 Introduction

Within just one decade, digital signal processing has become the dominant technology for creating, processing and storing the world's pictorial memory. While this new technology clearly has many advantages, critics have expressed concern that it has never been so easy to manipulate images, often in such a perfection that the forgery is visually indistinguishable from authentic photographs. Hence, digitalisation reduces the trustworthiness of pictures in particularly those situations where society is used to base important decisions on them: in the courtroom (photographs as pieces of evidence), in science (published photographs as empirical proofs), and at the ballot box (press photographs).

As a result, research on digital image forensics and tamper detection has gained ground. These techniques can be broadly divided into two branches. One direction tracks particularities of the image acquisition process and reports conspicuous deviations as indications for possible manipulation. Typical representatives of this category include [1,2,3,4,5]. The other approach tries to identify traces from specific image processing functions [6,7,8,9]. Although forensic toolboxes are already quite good at unveiling naive manipulations, they still solve the problem only at its surface. The key question remains open: How reliable are these forensic techniques against a farsighted counterfeiter who is aware of their existence?

To the best of our knowledge, this paper is the first to focus on hiding techniques that help the counterfeiter to defeat forensic tools. We believe that research on "attacks" against forensic techniques is important to evaluate and ultimately improve detectors, as is steganography for steganalysis and vice versa.

Continuing the analogy with steganalysis, one can distinguish *targeted* and *universal* attacks. A targeted attack is a method that avoids traces detectable

T. Furon et al. (Eds.): IH 2007, LNCS 4567, pp. 326–341, 2007.

with one particular forensic technique, which the developer of the attack usually knows. Conversely, universal attacks try to maintain or correct (i.e. make plausible) as many statistical properties of the image to conceal manipulations even when presented to unknown forensic tools. In this sense, a low quality JPEG compression of doctored images can be interpreted as universal attack. While compression often is both plausible and effective—the dominant artefacts from quantisation in the frequency domain are likely to override subtle statistical traces of manipulation—it goes along with a loss in image quality. This highlights the fact that the design space for some attacks against forensic techniques is subject to a trade-off between security (i.e. undetectability) and quality (transparency). This is another parallel to steganography and watermarking.

Tamper hiding techniques can also be classified by their position in the process chain. We call a method *integrated* if it replaces or interacts with the image manipulation operation (e.g. an undetectable copy-move tool as plug-in to image processing software) as opposed to *post-processing*, which refers to algorithms that try to cover all traces after a manipulation with conventional methods.

In this paper we present targeted attacks against a specific technique to detect traces of resampling in uncompressed images proposed by Popescu and Farid [7]. Section 2 recalls the details of this detection method before our countermeasures are discussed in Section 3, together with experimental results. To generalise from single examples and provide a more valid assessment of the proposed methods' performance, a quantitative evaluation on a larger set of test images has been conducted. Its setup and results are given in Section 4. Finally, Section 5 addresses implications for future research on both forensics and counter-forensics.

2   Detecting Traces of Resampling

Most attempts of image forgery rely on scaling and rotation operations, which involve a resampling process. As a result, scholars in image forensics have developed methods to detect traces of resampling in bitmap images. This section reviews the state-of-the-art method proposed by Popescu and Farid [7].

Interpolation algorithms are key to smooth and visually appealing image transformation, however a virtually unavoidable side effect of interpolation is that it introduces linear dependencies between groups of adjacent pixels [10]. The idea of Popescu and Farid's detection method is in identifying these artefacts. They presume that the intensity of each pixel $y_{i,j}$ can be approximated as the weighted sum of pixels in its close neighbourhood (window of size $N \times N$, with $N = 2K + 1$ and K integer) and an independent residual ϵ.

$$y_{i,j} = f(\boldsymbol{\alpha}, \boldsymbol{y}) + \epsilon_{i,j} = \sum_{(k,l)\in\{-K,...,K\}^2} \alpha_{k,l} \cdot y_{i+k,j+l} + \epsilon_{i,j} \qquad (1)$$

They further demonstrate that after interpolation, the degree of dependence from its neighbours differs between pixels. These differences turn out to appear systematically and in a periodic pattern.

The pattern is referred to as p-map and can be obtained from a given image as follows: Using a simplified model, pixels y, $y_{i,j} \in [0, 255]$, are assigned to one of two classes $\mathcal{M}_1$ and $\mathcal{M}_2$. Set $\mathcal{M}_1$ contains those pixels with high linear dependence whereas set $\mathcal{M}_2$ comprises all pixels without it. The *expectation maximisation* (EM) algorithm [11], an iterative two-stage procedure, allows to estimate simultaneously both, the set a specific pixel most likely belongs to, and the unknown weights $\boldsymbol{\alpha}$. First, the E-step uses the Bayes theorem to calculate the probability for each pixel belonging to set $\mathcal{M}_1$.

$$p_{i,j} = \mathrm{Prob}(y_{i,j} \in \mathcal{M}_1 | y_{i,j}) = \frac{\mathrm{Prob}(y_{i,j} | y_{i,j} \in \mathcal{M}_1) \cdot \mathrm{Prob}(y_{i,j} \in \mathcal{M}_1)}{\sum_{k=1}^{2} \mathrm{Prob}(y_{i,j} | y_{i,j} \in \mathcal{M}_k) \cdot \mathrm{Prob}(y_{i,j} \in \mathcal{M}_k)} \tag{2}$$

Evaluating this expression requires

1. a conditional distribution assumption for $\boldsymbol{y}$: $y \sim \mathcal{N}(f(\boldsymbol{\alpha}, \boldsymbol{y}), \sigma_{\mathcal{M}_1})$ for $y_{i,j} \in \mathcal{M}_1$ and $y \sim \mathcal{U}(0, 255)$ for $y_{i,j} \in \mathcal{M}_2$,
2. knowledge of weights $\boldsymbol{\alpha}$ (initialised with $1/(N^2 - 1)$ in the first round),
3. knowledge of $\sigma_{\mathcal{M}_1}$ (initialised with the signal's empirical standard deviation),
4. another assumption saying $\mathrm{Prob}(y_{i,j} \in \mathcal{M}_1) = \mathrm{Prob}(y_{i,j} \in \mathcal{M}_2)$.

In the M-step, vector $\boldsymbol{\alpha}$ is updated using a weighted least squares estimator:

$$\boldsymbol{\alpha} = (\boldsymbol{Y}'\boldsymbol{W}\boldsymbol{Y})^{-1}\boldsymbol{Y}'\boldsymbol{W} \cdot \boldsymbol{y} \tag{3}$$

Matrix $\boldsymbol{Y}$ has dimension $|\boldsymbol{y}| \times (N^2 - 1)$ and contains the non-center elements of all windows as stacked row vectors. Matrix $\boldsymbol{W}$ holds the corresponding conditional probabilities $p_{i,j}$ of (2) as weights on its diagonal, hence $\boldsymbol{p} = \mathrm{diag}(\boldsymbol{W})$. Given new estimates for $\boldsymbol{p}$ and $\boldsymbol{\alpha}$, $\sigma_{\mathcal{M}_1}$ can be computed as weighted standard deviation from the residuals $\boldsymbol{\epsilon}$. E-step and M-step are iterated until convergence.

Previous resampling operations leave periodical pattern in the so-obtained p-maps. This pattern becomes most evident after a transformation into the frequency domain, using a Discrete Fourier Transformation (DFT), where it causes distinct peaks that are typical for the specific resampling parameters. To enhance the visibility of the characteristic peaks, Popescu and Farid propose to apply a contrast function C [7]. The contrast function is composed of a radial weighting window, which attenuates very low frequencies, and a gamma correction step. The absolute values of the resulting complex plane can be visualised and presented to a human forensic investigator.

Figure 1 illustrates the detection process by comparing an original greyscale image to a processed version that has been scaled up[1] with linear interpolation to 105 % of the original (left column). The resulting p-maps are displayed in the centre. As expected, the rather chaotic p-map of the original image shows a very

---

[1] We show upscaling because it is particularly likely to leave detectable traces in the redundancy of newly inserted pixels. So it forms a critical test for our methods.

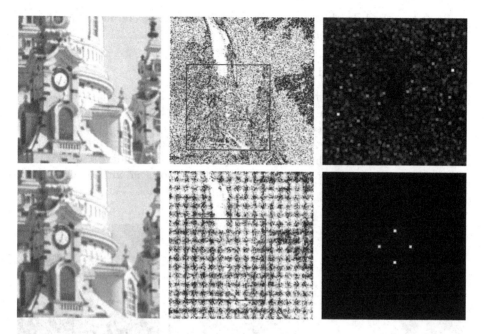

Fig. 1. Results of resampling detection for original image (top row) and 5 % upsampling (bottom row). Complete p-maps are displayed in the centre column; frames mark the parts depicted on the left. Periodic resampling artefacts lead to characteristic peaks in the corresponding spectrum (rightmost pictures).

clear periodic structure after transformation, which also explains the different appearance of the spectrum (right column). To enhance the quality in print, each spectrum graph in this paper is normalized to span the full intensity range. We further apply a maximum filter to improve the visibility of the peaks.

In general, this detection method is known as an effective and powerful tool. Robustness against several image manipulation operations (except lossy compression) has already been proven in the original publication and could be confirmed by us, also with respect to non-linear interpolation methods, such as B-splines.

3   Countermeasures Against Resampling Detection

In the hand of forensic investigators, this powerful detection method might raise the temptation to use its results as proof of evidence in legal, social and scientific contexts. However, one must bear in mind that forensic methods merely provide indications and are by orders of magnitude less dependable than other techniques, such as decent cryptographic authentication schemes. In contrast to cryptography, multimedia forensics remains an inexact science without rigourous security proofs. To draw attention to this problem, we will present three methods to perform image transformations that are almost undetectable by the above described method. In this sense, these techniques can be considered as attacks against the detection algorithm.

3.1 Attacks Based on Non-linear Filters

The detection method is based on the assumption of systematic linear dependencies between pixels in close neighbourhood (see Eq. (1)). Hence, all kinds of non-linear filters, applied as post-processing step, are candidates for possible attacks. The *median filter*, a frequently used primitive in image processing [12], replaces each pixel with the median of all pixels in a surrounding window of defined shape and size. This acts as a low-pass filter, however with floating cutoff frequency.

Fig. 2. Results after upsampling by 5 % and post-processing with a 5 × 5 median filter: characteristic peaks in the spectrum vanish, however the image appears excessively blurred

Figure 2 shows the results of the detection algorithm applied on a transformed image that has been post-processed with a 5 × 5 square median filter. This attack is successful as the characteristic peaks in the spectrum have disappeared. Note that the amplitudes corresponding to the brightest spots in the rightmost graph are by magnitudes smaller than the peaks in Fig. 1. However, a simple median filter negatively affects the quality of the post-processed image, which is reflected in noticeable blurring. Therefore, despite effective, naive non-linear filters are suboptimal for mounting relevant attacks in practice.

3.2 Attacks Based on Geometric Distortion

Inspired by the effectiveness of geometric attacks against watermarking schemes [13], we have explored geometric distortion as building blocks for attacks against tamper detection. We expect it to be effective in our application as well because the detection method exploits the periodic structure in mapping discrete lattice position from source to destination image, where the relative position of source and target pixels is repeated over the entire plane. This systematic similarity allows to separate it statistically from residual image content. To break

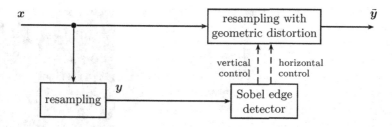

Fig. 3. Block diagram of geometric distortion with edge modulation

the similarity, each individual pixel's target position is computed from the transformation relation with a random disturbance vector e superimposed.

$$\begin{bmatrix} i \\ j \end{bmatrix} = A \cdot \begin{bmatrix} i_x \\ j_x \end{bmatrix} + \begin{bmatrix} e_{1,i,j} \\ e_{2,i,j} \end{bmatrix} \quad \text{where} \quad e \sim \mathcal{N}(0, \sigma) \quad \text{i. i. d.} \tag{4}$$

A is the transformation matrix and indices i_x, j_x refer to source positions as opposed to i, j which index the resampled image. Parameter σ controls the degree of distortion. However, naive geometric distortion may cause visible artefacts, such as jitter, which is perceived most visually disturbing at straight lines and edges. To evade such quality loss, we modulate the strength of distortion adaptively from the local image content. The modulation is controlled by two edge detectors, one for horizontal and one for vertical disturbance, as follows:

$$\begin{bmatrix} i \\ j \end{bmatrix} = A \cdot \begin{bmatrix} i_x \\ j_x \end{bmatrix} + \begin{bmatrix} e_{1,i,j} \cdot (1 - 1/255 \cdot \text{sobelH}(y, i_y, j_y)) \\ e_{2,i,j} \cdot (1 - 1/255 \cdot \text{sobelV}(y, i_y, j_y)) \end{bmatrix} . \tag{5}$$

Functions sobelH and sobelV return the value of a linear Sobel filter for horizontal and vertical edge detection, respectively [12]. This construction applies fewer distortion to areas with sharp edges, where the visible impact would be most harmful otherwise. The Sobel filter coefficients are defined as

$$H = \begin{bmatrix} 1 & 2 & 1 \\ 0 & 0 & 0 \\ -1 & -2 & -1 \end{bmatrix} \quad \text{and} \quad V = \begin{bmatrix} -1 & 0 & 1 \\ -2 & 0 & 2 \\ -1 & 0 & 1 \end{bmatrix} .$$

Our implementation ensures that the range is truncated to the interval $[0, 255]$. Note that the filter is applied to a transformed image without any distortion y. As a consequence, this attack requires the image to be transformed twice, as depicted in the block diagram of Fig. 3.

The results demonstrate that geometric distortion is capable to eliminate the characteristic traces from the p-map spectrum (Fig. 4). In line with our expectations, the edge modulation mitigates the loss in image quality considerably.

3.3 A Dual Path Approach to Undetectable Resampling

While geometric distortion with edge modulation generates already good results, we found from a comprehensive evaluation of many different transformation pa-

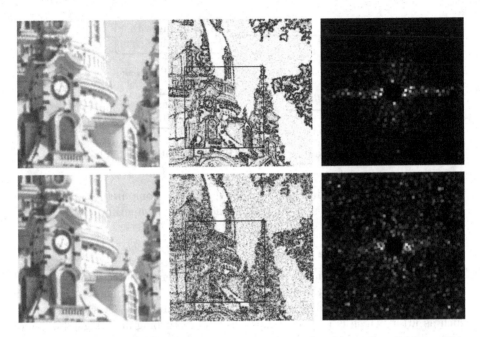

Fig. 4. Results after upsampling by 5 % with geometric distortion of strength $\sigma = 0.4$. Comparison between naive distortion (top) and edge modulation using horizontal and vertical Sobel filters (bottom).

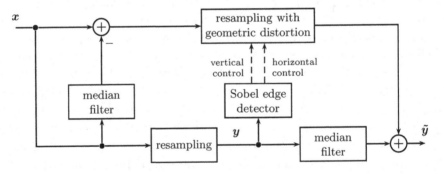

Fig. 5. Block diagram of dual path approach: combination of median filter for low frequency image component and geometric distortion with edge modulation for the high frequency component

rameters that the undetectability can be improved further by applying different operations to the high and low frequency components of the image signal. Such approaches have already been applied successfully in noise reduction [14] and watermarking attacks [15]. Figure 5 illustrates the proposed process. The two frequency components are separated with a median filter. First, the low frequency component of the output image is obtained by applying a median filter

Fig. 6. Dual path method: 5 % upsampling, 7 × 7 median filter for low frequency component combined with geometric distortion ($\sigma = 0.3$) and edge modulation

directly to the resampled source image (see Sect. 3.1). Second, a high frequency component is extracted from the source image x by subtracting the result of a median filter (other low-pass filters are conceivable as well). This component is resampled with geometric distortion and edge modulation (see Sect. 3.2), where the edge information is obtained from the resampled image y prior to the median filter. The final image $\tilde{y}$ is computed by summing up both components. This attack has two parameters, the size of the median filter and the standard deviation of the geometric distortion σ.

Figure 6 finally reports the results of the dual path approach. It becomes evident that the obtained p-map is most similar to the p-map of the original (see Fig. 1 above). Further, no suspicious peaks appear in its spectrum. The image quality is preserved and shows no visible artefacts.

4   Quantitative Evaluation

For a quantitative evaluation of our attacks against resampling detection, we built a database of 168 never-compressed 8 bit greyscale images, each of dimension 426×426 pixels. All images were derived from a smaller set of 14 photographs taken with a Nikon Coolpix 4300 digital camera at full resolution (2272 × 1704). Therefore we first cut every photograph into twelve 852 × 852 parts with maximum 50 % overlap. Then each part was downsampled by factor two to avoid possible interference from periodic patterns that might stem from a *colour filter array* (CFA) interpolation inside the camera [2].

As described in Sect. 2, the resampling detector relies on finding periodic dependencies between pixels in a close neighbourhood. To identify forgeries automatically, Popescu and Farid propose to measure the similarity between the p-map of a given image and a set of synthetically generated periodic patterns [7]. The synthetic map $s^{(A)}$ for transformation A is generated by computing the distance between each point in the resampled lattice and the closest point in the original lattice,

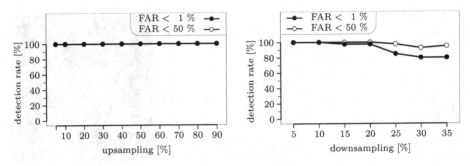

Fig. 7. Results of resampling detection after upsampling (left) and downsampling (right) by varying amounts. Each data point corresponds to the resampling of 40 images.

$$s_{i,j}^{(A)} = \left\| A \cdot \begin{bmatrix} i \\ j \end{bmatrix} - \left\lfloor A \cdot \begin{bmatrix} i \\ j \end{bmatrix} + \begin{bmatrix} 1/2 \\ 1/2 \end{bmatrix} \right\rfloor \right\| . \qquad (6)$$

In the absence of prior information about the actual transformations parameters A, an automatic detector conducts an exhaustive search in a set $\mathcal{A}$ of candidate transformation matrices A_q. In all our experiments, $\mathcal{A}$ contains 256 synthetic maps for upsampling in the range of 1 % to 100 % as well as 128 synthetic maps for downsampling in the range of 1 % to 50 % using equidistant steps of 0.4 percentage points. The maximum pairwise similarity between an empirical p-map and all elements of $\mathcal{A}$ is taken as a decision criterion d.

$$d = \max_{A \in \mathcal{A}} \sum_{i,j} \left| C(\mathrm{DFT}(p)) \right| \cdot \left| \mathrm{DFT}\left(s^{(A)} \right) \right| \qquad (7)$$

Function C is the contrast function (see above) and DFT applies a 2D discrete Fourier transformation. If d exceeds a specific threshold d_T then the corresponding image is flagged as resampled. We have determined d_T empirically for a defined *false acceptance rate* (FAR) by applying the detector to all 168 original images in the database. Our performance measures are detection rates, i.e. the fraction of correctly detected manipulations, for FAR < 1 % and FAR < 50 %, respectively.

Figure 7 reports the **baseline detection results** for upsampling and downsampling using plain linear interpolation. Each data point is computed as average from 40 resampled images.[2] We find perfect detection for upsampling and very high detection accuracy for downsampling. This confirms the general effectiveness of the detection method in the range of tested transformation parameters. Thus, Figure 7 may serve as reference for the evaluation of our attacks with respect to their capability to hide such image transformations.

---

[2] The detector parameters were set to $N = 2$ and $\|\alpha_n - \alpha_{n-1}\| < 0.001$ as convergence criterion for the EM algorithm. The modest amount of images is due to the computational complexity of about 50 seconds computation time for one single p-map using a C implementation on a 1.5 Ghz G4 processor.

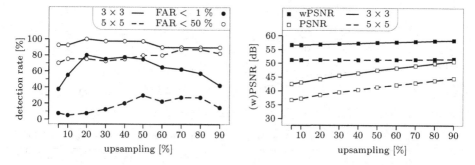

Fig. 8. Evaluation of median filter at different window sizes. Detection rates (left) and average image quality (right). Larger window sizes reduce both detection rates and image quality.

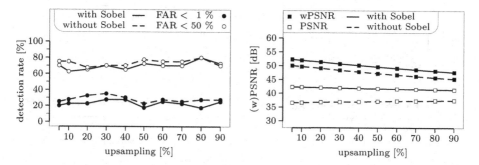

Fig. 9. Evaluation of geometric distortion ($\sigma = 0.4$) with and without edge modulation. Detection rates (left) and image quality (right). Edge modulation yields substantially better quality and slightly superior detection results.

Any attempt to conceal resampling operations should not only be judged by the achieved level of undetectability but also by the amount of image degradation. For our quantitative evaluation we resort to common image quality metrics Q to assess the visual impact of our proposed attacks.

$$Q = 20 \, \log \frac{255}{\|(\boldsymbol{y} - \tilde{\boldsymbol{y}}) \cdot \boldsymbol{v}\|} \tag{8}$$

We report the metrics PSNR, where $\boldsymbol{v} = \mathbf{1}$, as well as a variant adjusted for human visual perception wPSNR ('w' for *weighted*). It has been argued that the latter metric is a more valid indicator for the evaluation of watermarking attacks [16]. Weights $\boldsymbol{v}$ are computed from a *noise visibility function* (NVF), which emphasises image regions with high local variance and attenuates flat regions and soft gradients. Among the two NVFs proposed in [17] we have chosen the one based on a stationary Generalised Gaussian image model. Both metrics are measured in dB. Higher values indicate superior image quality.

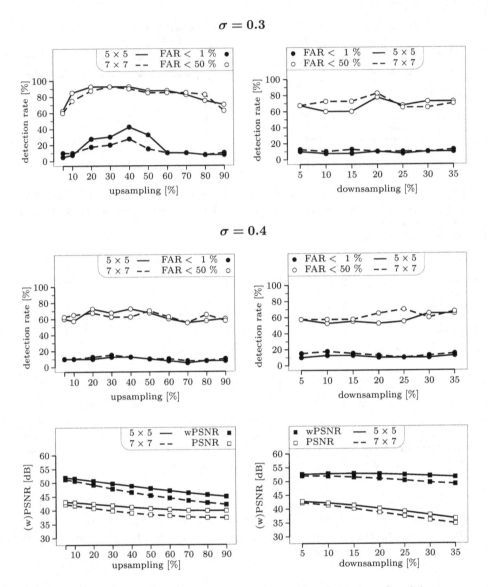

Fig. 10. Evaluation of dual path approach for upsampling (left column) and downsampling (right column). Detection rates for $\sigma = 0.3$ (top row) and $\sigma = 0.4$ (centre row); average image quality for $\sigma = 0.4$ (bottom row). Breakdown by window size of the median filter (5×5 vs 7×7) and false acceptance rates (FAR: 1 % vs 50 %). Stronger distortion in the high frequency component decreases detectability. Smaller windows sizes in the low frequency component retain better image quality.

Figure 8 reports detection rates (left) and average image quality (right) for upsampled images, post-processed with **median filters** of sizes 3×3 and 5×5, respectively. As larger window sizes introduce a higher degree of non-linearity, the 5×5 median filter yields noticeable less detectable results than the smaller 3×3 filter. However, this comes at a cost of substantial losses in visual image quality, which can be expressed both in terms of PSNR and wPSNR.

Note that the success of this attack depends on the upsampling ratio in a non-linear manner. The results for downsampling are omitted for the sake of brevity.

Since, at practical window sizes, median-filtered images suffer from extensive blurring, we have further investigated the effect of **geometric distortion** in the resampling process. Figure 9 shows the results for upsampling by varying amounts with distortion of strength $\sigma = 0.4$. As can be seen from the graphs, using edge modulation is a reasonable extension to the general approach. While detection rates remain stable on a relatively low level for all tested transformation parameters both with and without edge modulation, the latter yields a considerable improvement in image quality between 2–6 dB on average.

Finally, Figure 10 presents the results for the **dual path approach**. Since we consider this method as benchmark for future research, graphs for both upsampling (left column) and downsampling (right column) are displayed. The top four charts show detection rates for distortion strengths $\sigma = 0.3$ and $\sigma = 0.4$, respectively. Average image quality for $\sigma = 0.4$ is reported in the bottom row. The frequency components have been separated with 5×5 and 7×7 median filters. While a higher degree of geometric distortion generally reduces detection rates, we found that the choice of σ is more important for upsampling than for downsampling. Note that both 5×5 and 7×7 median filter lead to similar detection rates, however the former might be preferred with regard to image quality metrics. A direct comparison of the dual path approach with geometric distortion as described in Sect. 3.2 (Fig. 9) reveals a clear advantage of the dual path approach. For $\sigma = 0.4$, the latter achieves considerably better undetectability whereas image quality metrics indicate only marginal losses.

The very low detection rates of the dual path approach for $\sigma = 0.4$ demonstrate how successfully resampling operations can be concealed with the proposed method. At a practically relevant false acceptance rate $< 1\,\%$, only about $10\,\%$ of all image transformations were correctly identified as resampled (5×5 median filter, $\sigma = 0.4$). To allow for a better comparability with future research, detailed numeric results including summary statistics for the decision criterion d are given in Table 2 in the appendix. We further found that the few successful detections were concentrated within just a couple of original images, which suggests that image-specific factors may determine the efficacy of our attack.

Note that we have also tested the robustness of our results for detectors with smaller ($N = 1$) and larger ($N = 3$) neighbourhoods. As the corresponding dual path detection rates do not differ substantially from the reported figures, we conclude that our results are fairly robust and refrain from reporting them separately.

5   Concluding Remarks

This paper has taken a critical view on the reliability of forensic techniques as tools to generate evidence of authenticity for digital images. In particular, we have presented and evaluated three approaches to defeat a specific method of resampling detection, which has been developed to unveil scaling and rotation operations of digital images or parts thereof. These attacks have turned out to be the most effective ones in a broader research effort, which also led to a number of dead ends. Table 1 in the appendix briefly documents our less successful attempts as guidelines for future research in the area. Among the successful methods, the dual path approach, which applies geometric distortion with edge modulation to the high frequency component of an image signal and a median filter to the (low frequency) residual, achieved the best performance and should be regarded as benchmark for other specific tamper hiding techniques. At the same time, we would like to point out that the resampling detector of Popescu and Farid [7], against which our work in this paper is targeted, is certainly not a weak or unreliable tool when applied to plain interpolation. On the contrary, we have selected this particular detector with the aim to build an example attack against a powerful and challenging method. And we believe that many other published techniques would be vulnerable to targeted attacks of comparable sophistication.

Apart from the detailed results presented in the previous section, there are at least two more general conclusions worth mentioning. First, attacks which are integrated in the manipulation operation appear to be more effective than others that work at a post-processing step. This is plausible, since information about the concrete transformation parameters is not available at the post-processing stage and therefore much stronger interference with the image structure is necessary to cover up statistical artefacts of all possible transformations in general. Second, a closer look at all quantitative results suggests that it is easier to conceal downscaling than upscaling. This is plausible as well, since downscaling causes information loss, whereas it is more difficult to impute new pixels with idiosyncratic information. This implies that larger window sizes (for the median filter approach) and stronger geometric distortion are necessary for upscaling to achieve similar levels of (un)detectability as for downscaling.

As to the limitations, we consider this work as a first and modest attempt in an interesting sub-field. It is obvious that our results hold only for the specific detection method and we cannot rule out that image manipulations conducted with our proposed methods are detectable with a) other existing forensic techniques or b) new targeted detection methods that are build with the intention to discover our attacks. While this might trigger an new cat-and-mouse race between forensic and counter-forensic techniques, we believe that such creative competition is fruitful and contributes to a more holistic picture on the possibilities and limitations of image forensics, an area where much prior research has been done against the backdrop of a fairly naive 'adversary model'—a term borrowed from cryptography, where dealing with strong adversaries has a longer tradition [18]. On a more abstract level, one may ask the question whether it is possible at all to construct provable secure techniques under gentle assumptions. We conjecture that an ultimate response is far distant and it is probably linked to related questions, such as the search for provable secure high capacity steganography (with realistic cover assumptions), and to the development of better stochastic image models. In the meantime, more specific research questions are abundant.

Acknowledgements

The first author gratefully acknowledges receipt of a student travel grant awarded by Fondation Michel Métivier, France.

References

1. Ng, T.-T., Chang, S.-F.: A Model for Image Splicing. In: Proc. of ICIP 2004, vol. 2, pp. 1169–1172 (2004)
2. Popescu, A., Farid, H.: Exposing Digital Forgeries in Color Filter Array Interpolated Images. IEEE Trans. on Signal Processing 53, 3948–3959 (2005)
3. Lukáš, J., Fridrich, J., Goljan, M.: Detecting Digital Image Forgeries Using Sensor Pattern Noise. In: Delp, E.J., Wong, P.W. (eds.) Proc. of SPIE: Security and Watermarking of Multimedia Content VII, vol. 6072, pp. 60720Y-1–60720Y-11 (2006)
4. Johnson, M., Farid, H.: Exposing Digital Forgeries through Chromatic Aberration. In: Proc. of ACM MM-Sec., pp. 48–55 (2006)
5. Swaminathan, A., Wu, M., Liu, K.: Image Tampering Identification Using Blind Deconvolution. In: Proc. of ICIP 2006, pp. 2311–2314 (2006)
6. Fridrich, J., Soukal, D., Lukáš, J.: Detection of Copy-Move Forgery in Digital Images. In: Proc. of the Digital Forensic Research Workshop (2003)
7. Popescu, A.C., Farid, H.: Exposing Digital Forgeries by Detecting Traces of Resampling. IEEE Trans. on Signal Processing 53, 758–767 (2005)
8. Johnson, M.K., Farid, H.: Exposing Digital Forgeries by Detecting Inconsistencies in Lighting. In: Proc. of ACM MM-Sec., pp. 1–10 (2005)
9. Farid, H.: Exposing Digital Forgeries in Scientific Images. In: Proc. of ACM MM-Sec. pp. 29–36 (2006)
10. Thévenaz, P., Blu, T., Unser, M.: Interpolation Revisited. IEEE Trans. on Medical Imaging 19, 739–758 (2000)
11. Dempster, A.P., Laird, N.M., Rubin, D.: Maximum Likelihood from Incomplete Data via the EM Algorithm. Journal of the Royal Statistical Society, Series B 39, 1–38 (1977)
12. Pitas, I.: Digital Image Processing Algorithms and Applications. John Wiley & Sons, Inc., Chichester (2000)
13. Petitcolas, F., Anderson, R., Kuhn, M.: Attacks on Copyright Marking Systems. In: Aucsmith, D. (ed.) IH 1998. LNCS, vol. 1525, pp. 219–239. Springer, Heidelberg (1998)
14. Bernstein, R.: Adaptive Nonlinear Filters for Simultaneous Removal of Different Kinds of Noise in Images. IEEE Trans. on Circuits and Systems 34, 1275–1291 (1987)
15. Langelaar, G.C., Biemond, J., Lagendijk, R.L.: Removing Spatial Spread Spectrum Watermarks by Non-Linear Filtering. In: Proc. of EUSIPCO 1998, pp. 2281–2284 (1998)

16. Voloshynovskiy, S., Pereira, S., Herrigel, A., Baumgaertner, N., Pun, T.: Generalized Watermarking Attack Based on Watermark Estimation and Perceptual Remodulation. In: Wong, P.W., Delp, E.J. (eds.) Proc. of SPIE: Security and Watermarking of Multimedia Content II, vol. 3971, pp. 358–370 (2000)
17. Voloshynovskiy, S., Herrigel, A., Baumgaertner, N., Pun, T.: A stochastic Approach to Content Adaptive Digital Image Watermarking. In: Pfitzmann, A. (ed.) IH 1999. LNCS, vol. 1768, pp. 212–236. Springer, Heidelberg (2000)
18. Kerckhoffs, A.: La cryptographie militaire. Journal des sciences militaires IX, 5–38, 161–191 (1883)

Appendix

Table 1. Summary of alternative attack methods investigated in the literature and in the course of this research

Method	Type[a]	Success[b]	Image quality[c]
Existing literature [7]			
Additive noise	P	−	−
Gamma correction	P	−	−
JPEG compression	P	+	+
JPEG2000 compression	P	○	+
Our research			
Mean filter	P	−	−
Binomial filter	P	−	−
Multistage median filter	P	−	○
Incremental resampling 1	P	−	−
Incremental resampling 2	I	+	−
Locally correlated geometric distortion	I	−	+
Dual path with extremum filter (HF)	P	−	○

[a] I integrated, P post-processing
[b] + manipulation undetectable, − manipulation detectable, ○ parameter dependent
[c] + good quality (only plausible artefacts), − visible distortion, ○ parameter dependent

Table 2. Detailed results for dual path approach ($\sigma = 0.4$, window size 5×5)

	d		detection rate [%]		average image quality [a]	
	median	IQR [b]	FAR $< 1\%$	FAR $< 50\%$	wPSNR [dB]	PSNR [dB]
Originals (168 images)						
	20.32	37.20	–	–	–	–
Upsampling (40 images each)						
5 %	29.74	91.97	10.0	60.0	51.89 (1.65)	43.03 (4.71)
10 %	32.60	101.54	10.0	57.5	51.51 (1.76)	42.86 (4.77)
20 %	39.88	82.96	10.0	72.5	50.60 (1.93)	42.24 (4.94)
30 %	32.04	58.53	12.5	67.5	49.61 (2.10)	41.68 (5.03)
40 %	32.80	40.14	12.5	72.5	48.73 (2.23)	41.07 (5.14)
50 %	29.35	84.09	10.0	67.5	47.82 (2.39)	40.60 (5.26)
60 %	28.26	65.28	7.5	60.0	47.00 (2.65)	40.22 (5.50)
70 %	27.20	62.12	5.0	55.0	46.21 (2.82)	39.88 (5.51)
80 %	27.10	56.06	7.5	57.5	45.50 (3.00)	39.80 (5.51)
90 %	29.06	46.01	7.5	60.0	44.88 (3.40)	39.79 (5.77)
average detection rate [a]			**9.3** (2.4)	**63.0** (6.4)		
Downsampling (40 images each)						
5 %	23.80	106.98	10.0	57.5	52.54 (1.62)	42.72 (4.69)
10 %	23.89	100.14	12.5	52.5	52.72 (1.66)	42.13 (4.79)
15 %	24.44	84.18	12.5	55.0	52.78 (1.63)	41.29 (4.85)
20 %	25.57	78.95	10.0	52.5	52.67 (1.74)	40.19 (4.94)
25 %	39.67	84.89	10.0	55.0	52.37 (1.87)	39.06 (4.98)
30 %	39.85	96.21	10.0	65.0	51.97 (2.06)	37.79 (5.04)
35 %	48.54	85.13	12.5	65.0	51.57 (2.07)	36.46 (5.03)
average detection rate [a]			**11.1** (1.3)	**57.5** (5.4)		

[a] standard deviation in brackets [b] inter-quartile range (measure of dispersion)

Imaging Sensor Noise as Digital X-Ray for Revealing Forgeries

Mo Chen, Jessica Fridrich, Jan Lukáš, and Miroslav Goljan

Dept. of Electrical and Computer Engineering, SUNY Binghamton,
Binghamton, NY 13902-6000, USA
{mchen0,fridrich,jan.lukas,mgoljan}@binghamton.edu

Abstract. In this paper, we describe a new forensic tool for revealing digitally altered images by detecting the presence of photo-response non-uniformity noise (PRNU) in small regions. This method assumes that either the camera that took the image is available to the analyst or at least some other non-tampered images taken by the camera are available. Forgery detection using the PRNU involves two steps – estimation of the PRNU from non-tampered images and its detection in individual image regions. From a simplified model of the sensor output, we design optimal PRNU estimators and detectors. Binary hypothesis testing is used to determine which regions are forged. The method is tested on forged images coming from a variety of digital cameras and with different JPEG quality factors. The approximate probability of falsely identifying a forged region in a non-forged image is estimated by running the algorithm on a large number of non-forged images.

1 Introduction

The practice of forging photographs is probably as old as the art of photography itself. Digital photography and powerful image editing software make it very easy today to create believable forgeries of digital pictures even for a non-specialist. Verifying the content of digital images or identifying forged regions can be very crucial when digital pictures or video are presented as evidence in the court of law, for example, in child pornography and movie piracy cases (http://www.mpaa.org/piracy.asp) and even in cases involving scientific fraud [1,2].

Recently, several different methods for detecting digital forgeries were proposed [3–11]. For each of these methods, there are circumstances when they will fail to detect a forgery. For example, the copy-move detection method [9,10] is limited to one particular case of forgeries, when a certain part of the image was copied and pasted somewhere else in the same image (e.g., to cover an object). Methods based on detecting traces of resampling [6] or color filter array (CFA) interpolation artifacts [7] may produce less reliable results for processed images stored in the JPEG format. The method based on detection of inconsistencies in lighting [8] assumes nearly Lambertian surfaces for both the forged and original areas and might not work accurately when the object does not have a compatible surface, when pictures of both the

T. Furon et al. (Eds.): IH 2007, LNCS 4567, pp. 342–358, 2007.
© Springer-Verlag Berlin Heidelberg 2007

original and forged objects were taken under approximately similar lighting conditions, or during a cloudy day when no directional light source was present.

Detection of digital forgeries is a complex problem with no universally applicable solution. What is needed is a set of different tools that can be all applied to the image at hand. The decision about the content authenticity is then reached by interpreting the results obtained from different approaches. This accumulative evidence may provide a convincing enough argument that each individual method cannot.

In this paper, we describe another digital forensic tool by extending previous work on detection of forgeries [12] and employ the methodology recently proposed for camera identification [13]. The method localizes tampered image regions using the sensor pattern noise that each camera involuntarily inserts into each image as an authentication watermark. This approach is applicable whenever we are in a situation when the forged image is claimed to have been taken by a camera that we have in possession or, at least, we have other non-forged images taken by the camera. Because the pattern noise appears to be a unique stochastic fingerprint of digital imaging sensors [13], forged regions could be identified by verifying the consistency of their noise residual with the corresponding part of the pattern noise.

In the next section, we describe the sensor output model from which we derive in Section 3 and 4 an estimator and detector of the photo-response non-uniformity (PRNU). The pdf of the test statistics is obtained through a correlation predictor discussed in Section 5. The complete algorithm for forgery detection based on Neyman-Pearson hypothesis testing is detailed in Section 6. Experimental results are included in Section 7, while the last section contains a summary and discussion of limitations.

We use boldface font for vectors or matrices with $\mathbf{X}[i]$ denoting the i-th component of $\mathbf{X}$. Unless mentioned otherwise, all operations among vectors or matrices, such as product, ratio, or raising to a power, are *element-wise*. The norm of $\mathbf{X}$ is denoted as $\|\mathbf{X}\| = \sqrt{\mathbf{X} \odot \mathbf{X}}$ with $\mathbf{X} \odot \mathbf{Y} = \sum_{i=1}^{n} \mathbf{X}[i]\mathbf{Y}[i]$ being the dot product of two vectors. Denoting the sample means with a bar, the normalized correlation is

$$corr(\mathbf{X}, \mathbf{Y}) = \frac{(\mathbf{X} - \bar{\mathbf{X}}) \odot (\mathbf{Y} - \bar{\mathbf{Y}})}{\| \mathbf{X} - \bar{\mathbf{X}} \| \cdot \| \mathbf{Y} - \bar{\mathbf{Y}} \|}.$$

2 Sensor Output Model

Each digital camera contains a sensor that digitizes the image created by the optics by converting photons hitting each pixel to electrical signal. The signal then goes through a complex chain of processing that includes signal quantization, white balance, demosaicking, if the sensor is equipped with a CFA, color correction, gamma correction, filtering, and, optionally, JPEG compression. The processing details may vary greatly between cameras and are not always easily available.

In this section, we present a simplified model of in-camera processing [14] that includes the steps that are most relevant to our approach to forgery detection. We denote by $\mathbf{I}[i]$ the signal in one color channel at pixel i, $i = 1, \ldots, n$, generated by the sensor before demosaicking is applied and by $\mathbf{Y}[i]$ the incident light intensity at pixel *i*. Here, we assume that the pixels are indexed, for example, in a row-wise manner and $n = n_1 n_2$, where $n_1 \times n_2$ are image dimensions. Dropping the pixel indices for better readability, we use the following model of the sensor output

$$\mathbf{I} = g^\gamma \cdot \left[(1 + \mathbf{K})\mathbf{Y} + \mathbf{\Theta}_n \right]^\gamma + \mathbf{\Theta}_q, \tag{1}$$

where g is the color channel gain, γ is the gamma correction factor (typically, $\gamma \approx 1/2.2$), $\mathbf{K}$ is a zero-mean multiplicative factor responsible for PRNU (the sensor fingerprint [13]), $\mathbf{\Theta}_q$ is the quantization noise and $\mathbf{\Theta}_n$ is a combination of various noise sources, such as dark current, shot noise, read-out noise, etc. [15,16]. The gain factor g adjusts the pixel intensity level according to the sensitivity of the pixel in the red, green, and blue spectral bands to obtain the correct white balance. We remind that all operations in (1) are element-wise.

We linearize (1) by factoring out the dominant term $\mathbf{Y}$ and leaving the first two terms in the Taylor expansion of $(1 + x)^\gamma = 1 + \gamma x + O(x^2)$

$$\mathbf{I} = \mathbf{I}^{(0)} + \gamma \mathbf{I}^{(0)} \mathbf{K} + \mathbf{\Theta}, \tag{2}$$

where we denoted $\mathbf{I}^{(0)} = (g\mathbf{Y})^\gamma$ the sensor output in the absence of noise; $\mathbf{\Theta}$ is a complex of independent random noise components.

3 PRNU Estimation

In this section, we describe the first step in our approach to forgery detection, which is the estimation of the PRNU $\mathbf{K}$ from a set of N images taken by the camera.

We first perform host signal rejection to improve the SNR between the signal of interest and observed data. The influence of the noiseless image $\mathbf{I}^{(0)}$ is suppressed by subtracting from both sides of (2) an estimate $\hat{\mathbf{I}}^{(0)} = F(\mathbf{I})$ of $\mathbf{I}^{(0)}$ obtained using a denoising filter[1] F

$$\mathbf{W} = \mathbf{I} - \hat{\mathbf{I}}^{(0)} = \gamma \mathbf{I} \mathbf{K} + \mathbf{I}^{(0)} - \hat{\mathbf{I}}^{(0)} + \gamma(\mathbf{I}^{(0)} - \mathbf{I})\mathbf{K} + \mathbf{\Theta} = \gamma \mathbf{I} \mathbf{K} + \mathbf{\Xi}. \tag{3}$$

The noise term $\mathbf{\Xi}$ contains $\mathbf{\Theta}$ and additional distortion introduced by the denoising filter.

Let $\mathbf{I}_1, \ldots, \mathbf{I}_N$ be N non-tampered images obtained by the camera. Assuming that the images are relatively smooth and non-saturated, the model (3) is approximately accurate. From (3), we have for each $k \in \{1, \ldots, N\}$

$$\frac{\mathbf{W}_k}{\gamma \mathbf{I}_k} = \mathbf{K} + \frac{\mathbf{\Xi}_k}{\gamma \mathbf{I}_k}, \quad \mathbf{W}_k = \mathbf{I}_k - \hat{\mathbf{I}}_k^{(0)}, \quad \hat{\mathbf{I}}_k^{(0)} = F(\mathbf{I}_k). \tag{4}$$

Under the assumption that for each pixel i the sequence $\mathbf{\Xi}_1[i], \ldots, \mathbf{\Xi}_N[i]$ is WGN (white Gaussian noise), the maximum likelihood estimate of $\mathbf{K}$ is (for detailed derivation and further discussion, see [13])

---

[1] We use a wavelet based denoising filter [17] that removes from images additive Gaussian noise with variance σ_F^2 (e.g., $\sigma_F^2 = 3$ for images with 256 levels of gray).

$$\hat{\mathbf{K}} = \frac{1}{\gamma} \frac{\sum\limits_{k=1}^{N} \mathbf{W}_k \mathbf{I}_k}{\sum\limits_{k=1}^{N} (\mathbf{I}_k)^2}, \tag{5}$$

which we calculate up to the multiplicative constant γ.

4 Detection of PRNU in Blocks

Having estimated the PRNU $\mathbf{K}$, we identify tampered regions in an image by detecting the absence of PRNU in small blocks. Our basic assumption is that regions that have been tampered will not contain the PRNU from the camera. This is certainly true if the region has been copied from another image from a different camera. It is also true if the region is coming from an image obtained using the same camera as long as its spatial alignment in the image is different than in the forged image. We note that local "tampering" consisting of local image enhancement, such as contrast/brightness adjustment, sharpening, softening, or recoloring does not remove the PRNU and thus will not be detected by this forgery detection method.

If the forged image was modified using some known geometrical transformation, such as resizing or cropping, the PRNU must be pre-processed in the same manner before applying our forgery detection algorithm. If the geometrical operation is not known, the forgery detection algorithm might still apply after the geometrical transformation is identified. For this purpose, we might use the PRNU itself as a registration pattern or apply other forensic techniques, such as detection of resampling [6].

The forgery detection algorithm follows a similar structure as the method reported in [12]. In this paper, however, we use a more sophisticated algorithm that produces more reliable results. The presence of PRNU in block $\mathcal{B}$ is detected using binary hypothesis testing

$$H_0: \ \mathbf{W}[i] = \Xi[i]$$

$$H_1: \ \mathbf{W}[i] = \tau \mathbf{I}[i]\hat{\mathbf{K}}[i] + \Xi[i], \quad i \in \mathcal{B} \tag{6}$$

where $\mathcal{B}$ is the index set characterizing the block. In (6), we assume that *within the tested block* Ξ is WGN with unknown mean and variance and τ is an unknown attenuation factor due to further processing that the image of interest might have been subjected to, such as kernel filtering, enhancement, or lossy compression.

The optimal detector for (6) is the normalized correlation (see, for example, [18]).

$$\rho = corr\left(\mathbf{I}\hat{\mathbf{K}}, \mathbf{W}\right). \tag{7}$$

where all signals in (7) are constrained to the block $\mathcal{B}$.

We can easily obtain the distribution of the test statistics ρ under hypothesis H_0 simply by correlating the known signal $\mathbf{I}[i]\hat{\mathbf{K}}[i]$, $i \in \mathcal{B}$, with noise residuals from other cameras. The distribution of ρ under H_1 is much harder to obtain. In spatially uniform and relatively smooth blocks, the statistical model in (6) is relatively accurate. However, in highly textured blocks, Ξ is not stationary or independent and the attenuation factor is not constant either because in such blocks the denoising filter is less successful in separating the image content and the noise (see (3)). To estimate the distribution of ρ under H_1 for a specific block, we construct a *predictor* of the test statistics as a function of selected factors that have a major influence on it. This predictor is obtained from blocks coming from a few non-tampered images from the same camera. In essence, the predictor tells us what the value of ρ and its distribution should be if the block was not tampered. We describe the predictor in the next section.

5 Correlation Predictor

In this section, we construct a predictor of the correlation ρ under H_1 on small blocks. From experiments, we determined that the most influential factors are image intensity, texture, and signal flattening.

The predictor is a mapping from some feature vector to a real number in the interval $[0,1]$—the predicted value of ρ. In order for the algorithm to have good localization properties, the block size should not be too large. However, it can not be too small either otherwise the correlation would have large variance. As a compromise, for typical sizes of digital camera images with 1 million pixels or more, square blocks with $b \times b$ pixels, $b = 128$, gave us quite good performance.

The correlation is higher in areas of high intensity because the PRNU signal $\mathbf{I}\hat{\mathbf{K}}$ is multiplicative. However, due to the finite dynamic range, it is not present in saturated regions ($\mathbf{I}[i] = 255$ for 8-bit per channel images) and is attenuated for $I_{crit} \leq \mathbf{I}[i] \leq 255$, where the critical value of intensity I_{crit} is typically in the range 240–250. Thus, we define the *intensity feature* $f_\mathbf{I}$ as the average attenuated image intensity

$$f_\mathbf{I} = \frac{1}{|\mathcal{B}|} \sum_{i \in \mathcal{B}} att(\mathbf{I}[i]), \tag{8}$$

where $att(x)$ is the attenuation function

$$att(\mathbf{I}[i]) = \begin{cases} e^{-(\mathbf{I}[i]-I_{crit})^2/\beta}, & \mathbf{I}[i] > I_{crit}, \\ \mathbf{I}[i]/I_{crit}, & \mathbf{I}[i] \leq I_{crit}, \end{cases} \tag{9}$$

and β is a constant. For example, for our tested Canon G2 camera, we experimentally determined $I_{crit} = 250$, $\beta = 6$.

We calculate the *texture feature* $f_\mathbf{T}$ from the high-frequency component of the image. Since the denoising filter performs wavelet transform, we conveniently use this intermediate data and generate a high-pass filtered image $\mathbf{F}$ as the inverse wavelet transform of the two outmost high-frequency wavelet subbands. The texture feature is then computed as

$$f_{\mathbf{T}} = \frac{1}{|\mathcal{B}|}\sum_{i\in\mathcal{B}}\frac{1}{1+\mathrm{var}_5(\mathbf{F}[i])} , \tag{10}$$

where $\mathrm{var}_5(\mathbf{F}[i])$ is the variance of $\mathbf{F}$ in the 5×5 neighborhood of the ith pixel. The reciprocal normalizes $f_{\mathbf{T}}$ to the interval [0, 1].

Image processing that is of low-pass filtering nature, such as JPEG compression, further attenuates the PRNU and thus decreases the correlation. In a relatively flat and high intensity unsaturated region, the predictor would thus incorrectly predict a high correlation. These "flattened" areas will typically have a low value of the local variance. Thus, we added the *flattening feature* $f_{\mathbf{S}}$ defined as the ratio of pixels in the block with average local variance above a certain threshold

$$f_{\mathbf{S}} = \frac{1}{|\mathcal{B}|}\Big|\{i\in\mathcal{B}\,|\,\mathrm{var}_5(\mathbf{I}[i]) > c\mathbf{I}[i]+d\}\Big|, \tag{11}$$

where c and d are appropriately chosen constants that depend on the sample variance of $\hat{\mathbf{K}}$ (e.g., $c = 0.03$, and $d = 0.1$ for Canon G2).

The correlation also strongly depends on the collective influence of texture and intensity. Sometimes, highly textured regions are also high-intensity regions. Thus, we included the following *texture-intensity feature*

$$f_{\mathbf{TI}} = \frac{1}{|\mathcal{B}|}\sum_{i\in\mathcal{B}}\frac{att(\mathbf{I}[i])}{1+\mathrm{var}_5(\mathbf{F}[i])} . \tag{12}$$

To capture the relationship between the features and the correlation, we chose a simple polynomial multivariate least square fitting because it is fast and gave us results comparable to more sophisticated tools, such as neural networks. We denote by ρ the column vector of K normalized correlations (7) calculated for K image blocks and $\mathbf{f}_{\mathbf{I}}$, $\mathbf{f}_{\mathbf{T}}$, $\mathbf{f}_{\mathbf{S}}$, and $\mathbf{f}_{\mathbf{TI}}$ the corresponding K-dimensional feature vectors. We model ρ as a linear combination of the 4 features and their 10 second-order terms

$$\rho[k] = \theta_0 + \theta_1\mathbf{f}_{\mathbf{I}}[k] + \theta_2\mathbf{f}_{\mathbf{T}}[k] + \theta_3\mathbf{f}_{\mathbf{S}}[k] + \theta_4\mathbf{f}_{\mathbf{TI}}[k] + \theta_4\mathbf{f}_{\mathbf{I}}[k]\mathbf{f}_{\mathbf{I}}[k] + \theta_5\mathbf{f}_{\mathbf{I}}[k]\mathbf{f}_{\mathbf{T}}[k] + ..., \tag{13}$$

where $\theta = (\theta_0, \theta_1,..., \theta_{14})$ is the vector of 15 coefficients determined using the least square estimator $\theta = \left(\mathbf{H}^T\mathbf{H}\right)^{-1}\mathbf{H}^T\rho$ and $\mathbf{H}$ is a $K{\times}15$ matrix of features with a vector of ones in its first column. The estimated correlation is

$$\hat{\rho} = [1, f_{\mathbf{I}}, f_{\mathbf{T}}, f_{\mathbf{S}}, f_{\mathbf{TI}}, f_{\mathbf{I}}f_{\mathbf{I}}, f_{\mathbf{I}}f_{\mathbf{T}},...]\theta . \tag{14}$$

In order to train the predictor, it is not necessary to use many images because one can extract a large number of overlapping blocks from a single image. In practice, good predictors can be obtained from as few as 8 images with diverse content. If the image under investigation is a JPEG image, it pays off to train the predictor on JPEG images of approximately the same quality factor as it leads to more accurate forgery detection.

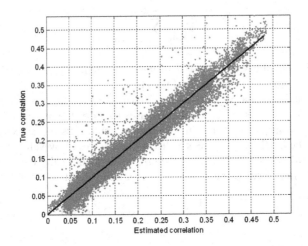

Fig. 1. Scatter plot ρ vs. $\hat{\rho}$ for K=30,000 128×128 blocks from 20 images from Canon G2

6 Forgery Detection Algorithm

The algorithm starts by sliding a 128×128 block across the image and calculating the value of the test statistics $\rho_{\mathcal{B}}$ for each block $\mathcal{B}$. The pdf $p(x|H_0)$ of $\rho_{\mathcal{B}}$ under H_0 is estimated by correlating the PRNU with noise residuals from other cameras and is modeled as generalized Gaussian (GG). For each block, the pdf $p(x|H_1)$ is obtained from the predictor and is modeled again as GG. We basically fit the GG model with pdf $(\alpha/2\sigma\Gamma(1/\alpha))e^{-(|x-\mu|/\sigma)^{\alpha}}$ through the data displayed in Fig. 1 with $\hat{\rho} \in (\rho_{\mathcal{B}} - \varepsilon, \rho_{\mathcal{B}} + \varepsilon)$ for some small $\varepsilon > 0$.

For each block $\mathcal{B}$, we first perform the Neyman-Pearson (NP) hypothesis testing by fixing the false alarm rate α. We decide that $\mathcal{B}$ has been tampered if $\rho_{\mathcal{B}} < Th$ and attribute this decision to the central pixel i of $\mathcal{B}$. The threshold Th is determined from the condition $\alpha = \int_{Th} p(x|H_0)dx$. As a result, we obtain a $(n_1-127)\times(n_2-127)$ binary array $\mathbf{T}[i] = \rho_{\mathcal{B}}[i] < Th$ indicating the tampered pixels i with $\mathbf{T}[i] = 1$.

While calculating $\mathbf{T}$, we evaluate the p-values for each block (its central pixel i)

$$p[i] = \int_{-\infty}^{Th} p(x|H_1)dx \qquad (15)$$

which tell us how much we should trust our decision. We next remove from $\mathbf{T}$ tampered pixels i for which $p[i] > \beta$ and only label as tampered those pixels for which the p-value is smaller than β. The purpose of this step is to control falsely identified pixels as tampered. The resulting binary map identifying forged regions is what we call Digital X-ray. The forged objects show up as regions lacking the PRNU in the same manner as bones show up in X-rays as they shield the radiation. The PRNU serves the same role as the X-rays.

The block dimensions impose a lower bound on the size of tampered regions that our algorithm can identify. Thus, we remove all simply connected regions from **T** that contain fewer than $b/2 \times b/2$ (64×64) pixels. Finally, we dilate the resulting binary map **T** with a square 20×20 kernel. The purpose of this final step is to compensate for the fact that we attribute the decision about the whole block only to its central pixel and thus potentially miss portions of the tampered boundary region.

7   Results

In this section, we subject our forgery detection algorithm to practical tests on forged images from 3 cameras: Canon G2 with a 4.1 megapixel (MP) CCD, Olympus C765 with a 4.1 MP CCD, and Olympus C3030 with a 3.3 MP CCD. We manipulated two images from each camera and stored them as TIFF and JPEG with quality factors 90 and 75. The forgeries varied from a simple copy-move within one image to object adding or removing. The PRNU was calculated from 30 blue sky images or uniformly lit test images obtained using a light box. If regular images were used, about 50 images would be required to have the PRNU of the same quality. The predictors were trained on more than 30,000 blocks from 20 regular images.

First, we calculated the test statistics for the unmatched cases by correlating 15,000 128×128 blocks from the PRNU with blocks from 100 images obtained using other cameras. A GG model was then fit through the data. The threshold Th was set to twice the standard deviation of the observed data. Since the GG fit was close to Gaussian for all tested cameras, this choice of threshold is equivalent to setting the false alarm rate α to approximately 3%. The threshold β for $p[i]$ was set to $\beta = 0.01$.

The performance of the proposed forgery detection technique is shown in Figs. 2–7, each of which includes the original image, the forged image, the NP decision result, and the forgery detection result (the X-ray) with tampered regions highlighted in the forged image.

As an implementation detail, we note that the sliding-window calculation of image features for the predictors can be computed efficiently using convolution implemented using FFT. For example, a full forgery X-ray of a 4 MP image takes between 4–5 minutes on a Pentium 3.4 GHz computer using Matlab.

To estimate the probability of false alarms for our method (detecting a tampered region in a non-forged image), we applied our algorithm to more than 400 non-forged images from the same three cameras in the JPEG format with quality 90. All false alarms have occurred in regions containing saturated background with dark regions, often combined with a complex texture, such as saturated sky shining through a mesh of black tree branches (two examples are shown in Fig. 8). Such regions naturally lack the PRNU and thus cannot be authenticated using our algorithm. Although not incorporated in this paper, these singularities could be removed by post-processing or expanding the predictor by adding a suitable feature.

We next subjected the forgery detection algorithm to a large scale test in order to better evaluate its real performance. We prepared 345 forged images, all from Canon G2, into which we pasted rectangular regions from images taken using other cameras. The shape and the linear size of the pasted regions was selected randomly and no

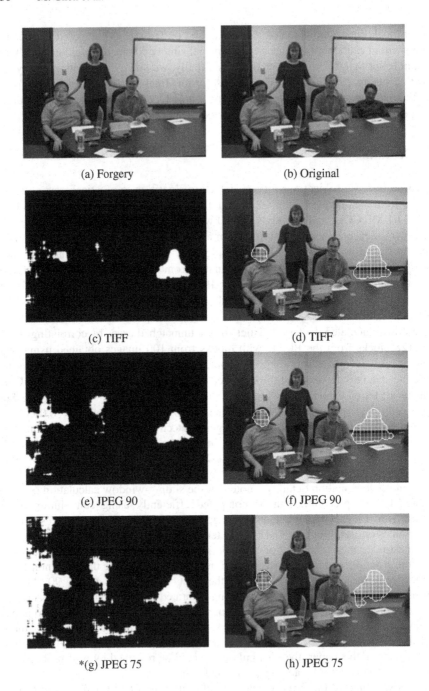

(a) Forgery

(b) Original

(c) TIFF

(d) TIFF

(e) JPEG 90

(f) JPEG 90

*(g) JPEG 75

(h) JPEG 75

Fig. 2. Forgery detection performance for a forged image from Canon G2 with $\alpha = 0.023$ and $\beta = 0.01$: (a) forged image; (b) original image; (c), (e), (g) is the NP decision for TIFF, JPEG 90, and JPEG 75, while (d), (f), (h) display the final forgery detection result

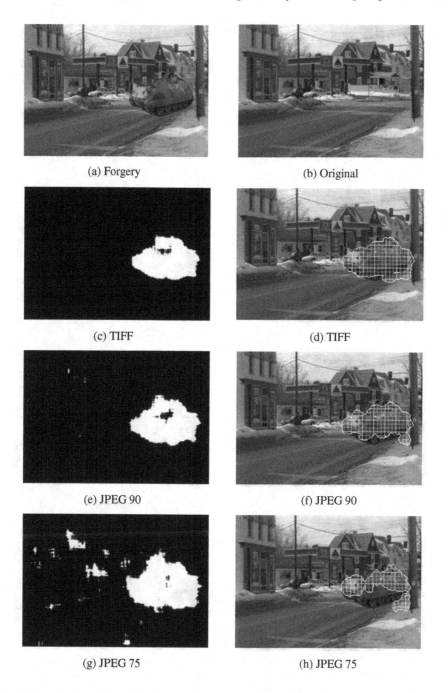

(a) Forgery

(b) Original

(c) TIFF

(d) TIFF

(e) JPEG 90

(f) JPEG 90

(g) JPEG 75

(h) JPEG 75

Fig. 3. Forgery detection performance for a forged image from Canon G2 with $\alpha = 0.023$ and $\beta = 0.01$. (a) forged image; (b) original image; (c), (e), (g) is the NP decision for TIFF, JPEG 90, and JPEG 75, while (d), (f), (h) display the final forgery detection result.

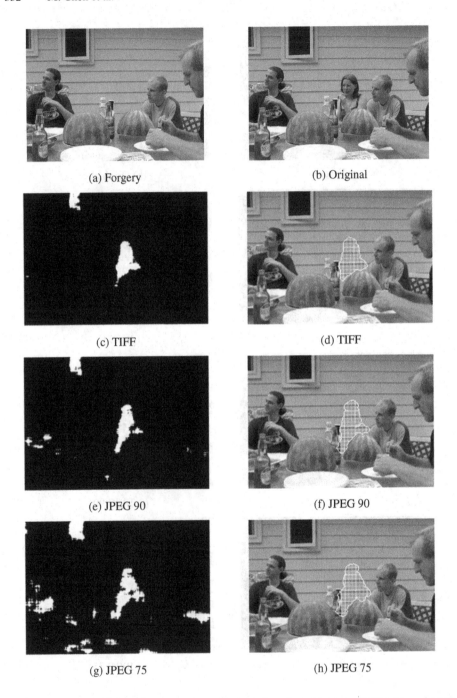

Fig. 4. Forgery detection performance for a forged image from Olympus C765 with $\alpha = 0.023$ and $\beta = 0.01$. (a) forged image; (b) original image; (c), (e), (g) is the NP decision for TIFF, JPEG 90, and JPEG 75, while (d), (f), (h) display the final forgery detection result.

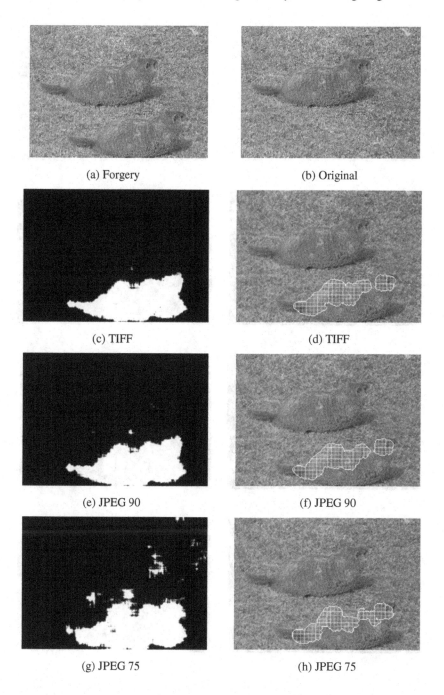

(a) Forgery

(b) Original

(c) TIFF

(d) TIFF

(e) JPEG 90

(f) JPEG 90

(g) JPEG 75

(h) JPEG 75

Fig. 5. Forgery detection performance for a forged image from Olympus C765 with $\alpha = 0.023$ and $\beta = 0.01$. (a) forged image; (b) original image; (c), (e), (g) is the NP decision for TIFF, JPEG 90, and JPEG 75, while (d), (f), (h) display the final forgery detection result.

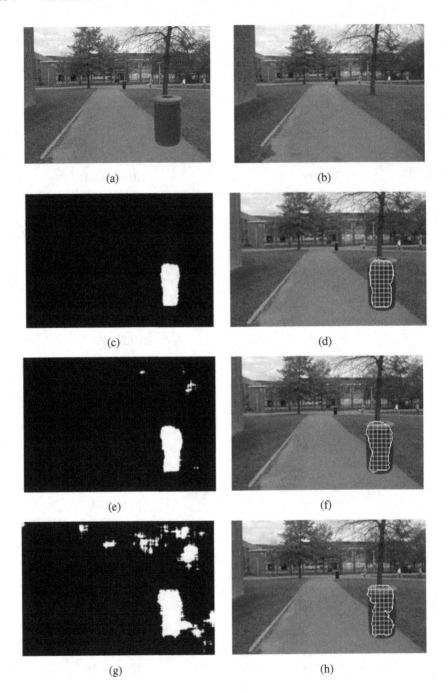

Fig. 6. Forgery detection performance for a forged image from Olympus C3030 with $\alpha = 0.023$ and $\beta = 0.01$. (a) forged image; (b) original image; (c), (e), (g) is the NP decision for TIFF, JPEG 90, and JPEG 75, while (d), (f), (h) display the final forgery detection result.

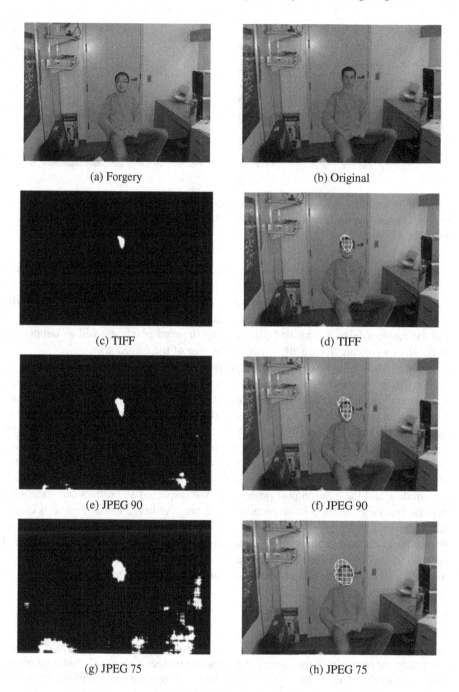

(a) Forgery

(b) Original

(c) TIFF

(d) TIFF

(e) JPEG 90

(f) JPEG 90

(g) JPEG 75

(h) JPEG 75

Fig. 7. Forgery detection performance for a forged image from Olympus C3030 with $\alpha = 0.023$ and $\beta = 0.01$. (a) forged image; (b) original image; (c), (e), (g) is the NP decision for TIFF, JPEG 90, and JPEG 75, while (d), (f), (h) display the final forgery detection result.

(a)   (b)

Fig. 8. Representative examples of image patterns giving rise to false alarms. (a) and (b) are two non-forged images from Canon G2. The highlighted regions were falsely identified as tampered.

effort was made to make the forged regions look "naturally." The smallest and the largest sides of the rectangles were 228 and 512 pixels, respectively. All forgeries were saved with two JPEG quality factors – 90 and 75 and then inspected using the Digital X-ray algorithm while registering the ratio of correctly detected forged pixels and the ratio of falsely identified pixels (non-tampered pixels marked as tampered). Both ratios were calculated with respect to the size of the forged area.

Figure 9 shows the histograms of these two ratios expressed as percentage for all 345 tested images. For the JPEG quality factor 90, at least 2/3 of the forged region was correctly identified in 85% of forgeries. On the other hand, only 23% of forgeries contained more than 20% of falsely identified pixels (again with respect to the size of the forged region). For the JPEG quality factor 75, in 73% cases the X-ray correctly detected at least 2/3 of the forged area, while 21% of forgeries contained more than 20% of falsely identified pixels. The falsely identified areas were generally located around the boundary of the real forged area due to the 128×128 block size of the sliding window and the dilation post processing. We inspected all outliers and concluded that the few cases when a large portion of the tampered region was missed occurred when the pasted region contained a large dark region. The conservative values of thresholds in our algorithm are the reason why the region was not labeled as tampered because in such regions the PRNU is naturally suppressed. The few large false positives were all of the type already mentioned above and shown in Fig. 8.

8 Summary

In this paper, we described a new method for revealing digitally manipulated images. Assuming we have either the camera that took the image or some other non-tampered images from the camera, we first estimate the photo-response non-uniformity, which serves as an authentication watermark. By detecting it in individual image blocks, one can localize the tampered region in the image. We use Neyman-Pearson hypothesis testing to identify the forged areas. The pdf of the test statistics is obtained from tests on images from other cameras (non-matched case) and using a correlation predictor (for the matched case). The proposed method can reliably identify forged areas larger than 64×64 pixels in JPEG images (tested with quality factor 75) while providing no falsely identified regions if regions that naturally lack the PRNU are excluded.

Among the potential future directions, we mention the possibility to construct a single predictor of the test statistics that would work for all cameras and calibrate it on a single non-forged image for a specific camera. This would further decrease the need for non-forged images taken with the same camera.

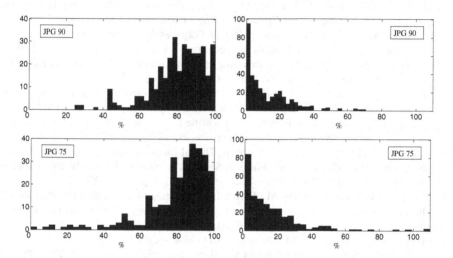

Fig. 9. Percentage of correctly identified tampered pixels (left) and falsely identified pixels (right) for 345 forged images from Canon G2 compressed using the JPEG with quality factor 90 (top) and 75 (bottom)

Acknowledgements

The work on this paper was supported by the AFOSR grant number FA9550-06-1-0046. The U.S. Government is authorized to reproduce and distribute reprints for Governmental purposes notwithstanding any copyright notation there on. The views and conclusions contained herein are those of the authors and should not be interpreted as necessarily representing the official policies, either expressed or implied, of Air Force Research Laboratory, or the U.S. Government.

References

1. Kennedy, D.: Editorial retraction. Science 211(5759), 335 (2006)
2. Pearson, H.: Image manipulation: CSI: Cell biology. Nature 434, 952–953 (2005)
3. Ng, T.-T., Chang, S.-F., Sun, Q.: Blind Detection of Photomontage Using Higher Order Statistics. In: IEEE International Symposium on Circuits and Systems, Vancouver, Canada, vol. 5, pp. v688–v691 (2004)

4. Avcibas, I., Bayram, S., Memon, N., Ramkumar, M., Sankur, B.: A Classifier Design for Detecting Image Manipulations. In: IEEE Int. Conf. Image Proc., vol. 4, pp. 2645–2648 (2004)
5. Lin, Z., Wang, R., Tang, X., Shum, H.-Y.: Detecting Doctored Images Using Camera Response Normality and Consistency. In: IEEE Computer Society Conference on Computer Vision and Pattern Recognition, vol. 1, pp. 1087–1092 (2005)
6. Popescu, A.C., Farid, H.: Exposing Digital Forgeries by Detecting Traces of Resampling. IEEE Transactions on Signal Processing 53(2), 758–767 (2005)
7. Popescu, A.C., Farid, H.: Exposing Digital Forgeries in Color Filter Array Interpolated Images. IEEE Transactions on Signal Processing 53(10), 3948–3959 (2005)
8. Johnson, M.K., Farid, H.: Exposing Digital Forgeries by Detecting Inconsistencies in Lighting. In: Proc. ACM Multimedia and Security Workshop, New York, pp. 1–9 (2005)
9. Fridrich, J., Soukal, D., Lukáš, J.: Detection of Copy-Move Forgery in Digital Images. In: Proc. Digital Forensic Research Workshop, Cleveland (August 2003)
10. Popescu, A.C., Farid, H.: Exposing Digital Forgeries by Detecting Duplicated Image Regions. Technical Report, TR2004-515. Dartmouth College, Computer Science (2004)
11. Farid, H.: Exposing Digital Forgeries in Scientific Images. In: Proc. ACM Multimedia & Security Workshop, Geneva, Switzerland, pp. 29–36 (2006)
12. Lukáš, J., Fridrich, J., Goljan, M.: Detecting Digital Image Forgeries Using Sensor Pattern Noise. In: Proc. SPIE, Electronic Imaging, Security, Steganography, and Watermarking of Multimedia Contents VIII, San Jose, California, vol. 6072, pp. 0Y1–0Y11 (2006)
13. Chen, M., Fridrich, J., Goljan, M.: Digital Imaging Sensor Identification (Further Study). In: Proc. SPIE, Electronic Imaging, Security, Steganography, and Watermarking of Multimedia Contents IX, San Jose, California, vol. 6505, pp. 0P–0Q (2007)
14. Healey, G., Kondepudy, R.: Radiometric CCD Camera Calibration and Noise Estimation. IEEE Transactions on Pattern Analysis and Machine Intelligence 16(3), 267–276 (1994)
15. Janesick, J.R.: Scientific Charge-Coupled Devices. SPIE PRESS Monograph, vol. PM83, SPIE–The International Society for Optical Engineering (2001)
16. Holst, G.C.: CCD Arrays, Cameras, and Displays, 2nd edn. JCD Publishing & SPIE Press, USA (1998)
17. Mihcak, M.K., Kozintsev, I., Ramchandran, K.: Spatially Adaptive Statistical Modeling of Wavelet Image Coefficients and its Application to Denoising. In: Proc. IEEE Int. Conf. Acoustics, Speech, and Signal Processing, Phoenix, Arizona, vol. 6, pp. 3253–3256 (1999)
18. Kay, S.M.: Fundamentals of Statistical Signal Processing, vol. II. Detection theory, Prentice Hall, Englewood Cliffs (1998)

Pros and Cons of Mel-cepstrum Based Audio Steganalysis Using SVM Classification

Christian Kraetzer and Jana Dittmann

Research Group Multimedia and Security
Department of Computer Science,
Otto-von-Guericke-University of Magdeburg, Germany

Abstract. While image steganalysis has become a well researched domain in the last years, audio steganalysis still lacks a large scale attentiveness. This is astonishing since digital audio signals are, due to their stream-like composition and the high data rate, appropriate covers for steganographic methods.

In this work one of the first case studies in audio steganalysis with a large number of information hiding algorithms is conducted. The applied trained detector approach, using a SVM (support vector machine) based classification on feature sets generated by fusion of time domain and Mel-cepstral domain features, is evaluated for its quality as a universal steganalysis tool as well as a application specific steganalysis tool for VoIP steganography (considering selected signal modifications with and without steganographic processing of audio data). The results from these evaluations are used to derive important directions for further research for universal and application specific audio steganalysis.

1 Introduction and State of the Art

When comparing steganalytical techniques a well used classification is to group them into specific and universal steganalysis techniques [1]. In the image domain a large number of examples for both classes can be found as well as research building "composite" steganalysis techniques by fusing existing techniques as described by Kharrazi et. al in [1]. In the research presented in [1] a fusion of steganalytical approaches on different levels (pre-classification and post-classification (in measurement or abstract level)) in image steganalysis is considered. This has been done by addressing the question "How to combine different (special and universal) steganalysers to gain an improved classification reliability?".

While such mature research exists in the domain of image steganalysis, the domain of audio steganalysis is much less considered in literature. This fact is quite remarkable for two reasons. The first one is the existence of advanced audio steganography schemes. The second one is the very nature of audio material as a high capacity data stream which allows for scientifically challenging statistical analysis. Especially inter-window analysis (considering the evolvement of the signal over time), which is only possible on this continuous media, distinguish audio signals from the image domain.

T. Furon et al. (Eds.): IH 2007, LNCS 4567, pp. 359–377, 2007.

The research presented in this work is based on the audio steganography approach introduced in [2]. The audio steganalysis tool (AAST; AMSL Audio Steganalysis Toolset) introduced there in the context of VoIP steganography and steganalysis is enhanced and used here to perform a set of tests to further evaluate its performance in intra-window based universal audio steganalysis.

The current version of the AAST uses a SVM classification on pre-trained models for classifying audio signals into un-marked signals and signals marked by known information hiding algorithms in its intra-window analysis. The latter approach is used here and was enhanced to allow for measurements regarding the quality of a model in terms of detection rate, errors of Type I and II and discriminatory power. In these evaluations the performance of the AAST as universal steganalysis tool as well as its specific performance on selected algorithms and the application scenario of VoIP steganography is rated.

As its scientific contribution to the research field of steganalysis, in this work first the usefulness of the presented approach in universal steganalysis is evaluated. Second, important knowledge is gained and presented in the field of VoIP specific steganalysis, which shows for the first time the importance of such profile or application scenario based evaluations, by directly comparing them to results gained under the assumption of universal analysis.

The chosen application scenario of VoIP steganography and steganalysis allows for very restrictive assumptions about the type and quality of considered audio material. To name a few of these assumptions we consider the behaviour of the source (unchanging recording conditions in an end-to-end speech communication with one human speaker on each channel) or the quality of the transmission (a streaming protocol with static data rates and QoS enhancing mechanisms). To model the two approaches considered (universal steganalysis and VoIP steganalysis) two different test sets are specified and used in the evaluations. It is shown in this work that evaluations which adapt to this assumptions (and thereby our VoIP scenario) will lead to far higher detection rates in the informed classificator approach used. The chosen application scenario also implies the existence of non-steganographic signal modifications like signal amplifications, resampling or packet drops. These possible influences to the VoIP signal and their impact to the classification accuracy will also be considered within this work.

From the evaluations performed a new set of questions for further work is derived. These questions regard the following aspects: the scalability of the used trained classification approach, the distribution of the classification errors and the impact of this knowledge on the applicability and improvement of the models for classification, the inter operability of the computed models, the possibility of grouping models for the identification of the embedding domain as well as the construction of a meta-classifier on the decision level of the introduced classification approach.

This work has the following structure: In section 2 the AAST (AMSL Audio Steganalysis Toolset) is described briefly, paying special attention to the model generation and classification phases of its intra-window analysis. Section 3 describes the test set-up, test procedure and the test objectives. This is followed by section 4, the presentation of the test results for the evaluations as an universal steganalysis approach (with an additional focus on the classification on unmarked material and the resulting false negative errors) as well as for the applicability as a specific VoIP steganalysis tool (in the latter case also the impact of non-steganographic signal modifications is evaluated). Section 5 ends the work by drawing conclusions from the tests and deriving ideas for further research in this field.

2   The AAST (AMSL Audio Steganalysis Toolset)

In [2] the basic composition of the AAST (AMSL Audio Steganalysis Toolset) is described in detail. This toolset, which is in development since 2005 and provides different steganalytical analysis methods, consists of four modules:

1. pre-processing of the audio/speech data
2. feature extraction from the signal
3. post-processing of the resulting feature vectors (for intra- or inter-window analysis)
4. analysis (classification for steganalysis)

The toolset was modified in this work for evaluation by methods for computing the Type I and II errors in the intra-window SVM (support vector machine) based classification. This was necessary because the addressed scenario of a universal audio steganalysis tool requires an evaluation of the error behaviour for the models tested. A Type I error (also known false positive) is the error of rejecting a null hypothesis (in our case the assumption that a vector is computed from a marked signal) when it is actually true. In other words, this is the error of classifying a vector as belonging to an unmarked file when it belongs to a marked signal. A Type II error (also known as a false negative) is the error of not rejecting a null hypothesis when the alternative hypothesis is the true state of nature. In our case this is the equivalent of classifying a vector as belonging to a marked file when it actually belongs to a unmarked signal.

The general principles of an AAST based steganalysis are discussed in detail in [2], here special attention shall be paid to the model generation and the model quality evaluation. A model M_{A_i} from the set of models $\mathbb{M}$ used in the analysis step of AAST is considered to be a function of the:

- pre-processing steps on the audio/speech data, influencing the parameters: The information hiding algorithm ($A_i \in A$) to be applied, the set of audio signals used for evaluation ($TestFiles$), the number of windows ($numwin$) computed per file and other parameters pa for AAST (like window size and offset for the windows of the intra-window statistical analysis ($winsize$ and $offset$), silence detection, etc.)
- feature extraction from the signal; parameters: The feature sets ($FS \subseteq \mathbb{FS}$) composed from the fs ($fs \in \mathbb{FS}$) for evaluation with their $fusion function$ (here an unweighted fusion is used)

– post-processing of the resulting feature vector sets vs for intra-window analysis; parameters: The post-processing functions (ppf) applied to the vector sets (e.g. normalisation) and the SVM used for training (and consecutive classification) with its parameters (svm_{para})

In the following sections the model generation the classification procedure is described in detail.

2.1   Training Phase (Model Generation)

The formalised model generation process is constructed as follows:

$$TestFiles^M = \text{embedding}_{A_i}(TestFiles, parameters\_of\_A_i, message) \tag{1}$$

$$vs = \text{feature computation}(TestFiles, FS, numwin, winsize, pa) \tag{2}$$

$$vs^M = \text{feature computation}(TestFiles^M, FS, numwin^M, winsize, pa) \tag{3}$$

$$vs_P = \text{ppf}(vs, classification = cover, nf) \tag{4}$$

$$vs_P^M = \text{ppf}(vs^M, classification = stego, nf) \tag{5}$$

$$vs_t = \text{join}(vs_P, vs_P^M) \tag{6}$$

$$M_{A_i} = \text{svm\_train}(vs_t, svm_{para}) \tag{7}$$

As a first step in the model generation the marked version ($TestFiles^M$) of the set of (if necessary pre-processed) test signals $TestFiles$ is generated for the $A_i \in A$ by using the embedding function $embedding_{A_i}$ of A_i. Equation (1) indicates the dependency on the algorithm parameters (including the key used for embedding and user definable parameters (e.g. embedding strength)) of this step as well as the message chosen. In a second step a vector set vs of $numwin$ (number of windows) vectors is computed for $TestFiles$ (one vector for each window in this intra-window based analysis). Equation (2) describes this process. The output vs is a function of the test signals ($TestFiles$), the feature set FS chosen for evaluation from the feature space $\mathbb{FS}$, the number of windows computed with their size and a set of application specific parameters like offset, overlap of the windows, etc. The same computation of a vector set vs^M is $TestFiles^M$ (see equation (3)). For the evaluations with AAST the sizes (in number of vectors computed per file) of vs and vs^M were chosen so far to be equal ($numwin = numwin^M$). For the generation of a valid model all other parameters ($FS, winsize, pa$) have to be the same in the computations of vs and vs^M.

After vs and vs^M are generated they are identified by the post-processing function ppf with the appropriate classification ($classification = cover$ in the case of vs and $classification = stego$ in the case of vs^M) and normalised with a common normalisation factor nf. In AAST the normalisation is done by using the corresponding function of the *libsvm* SVM package. The results of this process are vs_P and vs_P^M (see equations (4) and (5)). As a last step prior to the training phase the vector sets vs_P and vs_P^M are joined by concatenation to compose the training set vs_t (equation (6)).

The training is done by using the training function of the *libsvm* SVM package with the parameter set svm_{para} on vs_t (equation (7)).

2.2 Classification Phase

By using a model $M \in \mathbb{M}$ generated by a training phase as described above in the analysis phase of AAST on an vector set vs_c (with characteristics of vs_c = characteristics of vs_t, i.e. the same values for *winsize, pa, FS, svm_{para}* and the same post-processing function *ppf* applied), a classification accuracy p_D is computed as described in equation (8).

$$p_D = \text{svm\_classify}(M_{A_i}, vs_c) \tag{8}$$

3 Test Scenario

Two test goals are to be defined for this work: The first goal is to evaluate the performance of the AAST as a universal steganalysis tool. The second goal is to further evaluate the quality of AAST when being used as a specific steganalyser. For both test goals the performance (in terms of classification accuracy) of FM-FCC (filtered Mel-frequency cepstral coefficients, see [2]) based models is compared to the performance of strictly time domain based models. In the following the defined sets, set-ups, procedures and objectives for the tests necessary for the evaluation of these goals are described.

3.1 Test Sets and Test Set-Up

Test files used: Based on the intended application scenario the same set of 389 audio files (classified by context into 4 classes with 25 subclasses like female and male speech, jazz, blues, etc.; characteristics: average duration 28.55 seconds, sampling rate 44.1 kHz, stereo, 16 bit quantisation in uncompressed PCM coded WAV-files) is used here as described in [3] and [2] in order to provide comparability of the results with regard to the detection performance. This set of test signals is denoted in the following with $TestFiles = 389 files$.

One additional test on the impact of the size of M on the classification accuracy was made using the same long audio file as in [2]. The characteristics of this file, which was used in [2] to simulate a VoIP communication channel, are: duration 27 min 24 sec, sampling rate 44.1 kHz, stereo, 16 bit quantisation in an uncompressed PCM coded WAV-file. It contains only speech signals of one speaker. This set of test files is denoted in the following with $TestFiles = longfile$.

Algorithms, fused feature sets and parameter sets used: The parameters required for the training phase (as it is described in section 2.1) of the tests in this work are derived and enhanced from the settings in [2]. For all tests, except the ones based on the *longfile* test set[1], the following sets of parameters are applied:

---

[1] Here the parameter setting from [2] is used.

- $A_i, parameters\_of\_A_i, message$: For this work A_i, $A_i \in A$ denotes a specific information hiding algorithm with a fixed parameter set. The same algorithm with a different parameter set (e.g. lower embedding strength) would be identified as A_j with $j \neq i$. The set of A is considered in this work to consist of the subsets A_S (audio steganography algorithms) and A_W (audio watermarking algorithms) with $A = A_S \cup A_W$.

    The following A (with their corresponding $parameters\_of\_A_i$) are used for testing:

Table 1. Algorithms A_i used in the evaluation

	Name	Description	Parameters
A_{S_1}	LSB (version Heutling051208)	see [8] and [3]	see [2]
A_{S_2}	Publimark (version 0.1.2)	see the Publimark web site [5] and [7]	none (default)
A_{S_3}	WaSpStego	see [2]	see [2]
A_{S_4}	Steghide (version 0.4.3)	see the Steghide web site [4] and [6]	default
A_{S_5}	Steghide (version 0.5.1)	see A_{S4} above	default
A_{W_1}	Spread Spectrum[2]	see [6]	see [2]
A_{W_2}	2A2W (AMSL Audio Water Wavelet)	see [6]	see [2]
A_{W_3}	Least Significant Bit	see [6]	$ECC = on$
A_{W_4}	VAWW (Viper Audio Water Wavelet)	see [6]	see [2]

The *message* chosen is an ASCII coded version of Goethe's "Faust" taken from [9]. The embedding is done for every file in $TestFiles$ in a way that the complete file is marked in the generation of $TestFiles^M$ described in equation (1). For each A_i the maximum embedding strength is set, which assumably will lead to the strongest impact on the statistical transparency achievable with the evaluated A_i. The result of using the maximum embedding strength for each A_i are different payloads (e.g. one Bit per sample (44100 Bits per second) for A_{S_1} or 172 Bits per second for A_{S_3}).

- FS: from the feature fusion sets $FS \subseteq \mathbb{FS}$ defined in [2] the two sets showing the highest performance (in terms of classification accuracy) were chosen for the tests. These FS (SF_{std} and $SF_{std \cup FMFCC}$) are composed as follows: $SF_{std} = \{sf_{ev}, sf_{cv}, sf_{entropy}, sf_{LSB_{rat}}, sf_{LSB_{flip}}, sf_{mean}, sf_{median}\}$ and $SF_{std \cup FMFCC} = SF_{std} \cup \{sf_{melf_1}, ..., sf_{melf_C}\}$. The seven single features used in the composition of SF_{std} are: sf_{ev} empirical variance, sf_{cv} covariance, $sf_{entropy}$ entropy, $sf_{LSB_{rat}}$ LSB ratio, $sf_{LSB_{flip}}$ LSB flipping rate, sf_{mean} mean of samples in time domain, sf_{median} median of samples in time domain. Additionally to these seven single features in $SF_{std \cup FMFCC}$ the 29 filtered Mel-cepstral coefficients (FMFCCs) $sf_{melf_1}, ..., sf_{melf_C}$ ($C = 29$ for CD quality audio material) introduced in [2] are used.

- $winsize, numwin, numwin^M, pa$: The following parameters were chosen for all tests performed on the set of $TestFiles = 389 files$, $winsize = 1024$, $numwin = numwin^M = 256$ and $pa = \{$offset=0, overlap of the windows=0, silence detection = off$\}$. For the tests on the set of $TestFiles = longfile$ the two sets of parameters for $numwin$ and $numwin^M$ chosen are equal to the ones used in [2] ($numwin = numwin^M = 400$ and $numwin = numwin^M = 2200$).

The parameters $winsize$ and pa in the case of $TestFiles = longfiles$ were the same as in the case of $TestFiles = 389files$.

- svm_{para}: For the classification in the intra-window evaluations the $libsvm$ SVM (support vector machine) package by Chih-Chung Chang and Chih-Jen Lin [10] was used. Due to reasons of computational complexity it was decided not to change the SVM parameters (the $default$ settings are: the SVM type is a C-SVC, the kernel chosen is RBF (radial basis function) with the parameters γ (default: $\gamma = 1/k$ where k is the number of attributes in the input data) and the cost parameter C (per default set to 1)) for the duration of the tests. This set of SVM parameters as well as the SVM chosen ($libsvm$) is denoted in the following by $svm_{para} = default$.

Generation of the training and testing sets used:

For the evaluations done for this work vs_t and vs_c are generated from the same sets of audio files $TestFiles$ and $TestFiles^M$ by splitting for each file the set of $s_{tr} + s_{te}$ computed feature vectors vs_P (each vector representing the characteristics of one window of the file) into the two disjoint subsets vs_t and vs_c. This split is done by using the user defined ratio of $s_{tr}{:}s_{te}$ to assign s_{tr} vectors to the training set and s_{te} vectors to testing. More specifically the first s_{tr} feature vectors $vs_{P_1}...vs_{P_{s_{tr}}}$ of vs_P are assigned to vs_{Ptrain} and the last s_{te} feature vectors of vs_P $vs_{P_{s_{tr}+1}}...vs_{P_{s_{tr}+s_{te}}}$ to vs_{Ptest}. This procedure is shown in figure 1 for the example of $s_{tr}{:}s_{te} = 256{:}64$.

The same splitting is done with the feature vectors contained in vs_P^M. With this we get vs_{Ptrain}^M and vs_{Ptest}^M in the same ratio $s_{tr}{:}s_{te}$. Then vs_{Ptrain} and vs_{Ptrain}^M are joined to form the training set vs_t and vs_{Ptest} and vs_{Ptest}^M are joined to constitute the test set vs_c. This procedure is shown in figure 2.

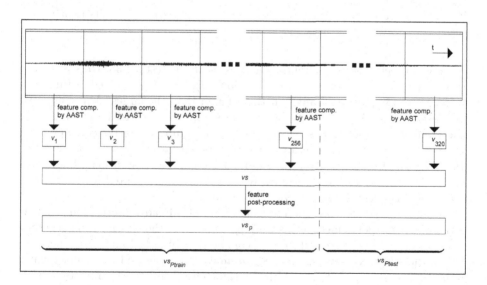

Fig. 1. Generation of vs_{Ptrain} and vs_{Ptest} for one exemplary audio file

Figure 2 shows the complete process of training and testing set generation from a given audio test set $Testfiles$.

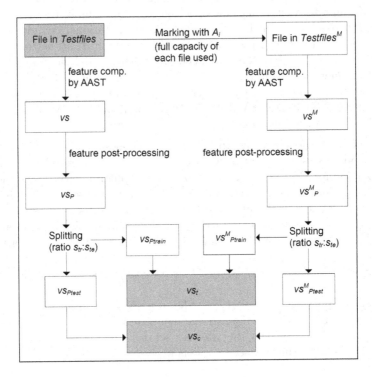

Fig. 2. Generation of the two vector sets for training (vs_t) and classification/testing (vs_c)

Consecutively the vs_t computed for each A_i on the test set $389\,files$ is used to train a model M_{A_i} as described in equation (7). The M_{A_i} derived in this work by SVM training are generally four times larger than the largest M_{A_i} computed on $TestFiles = 389\,files$ in [2] (where the $s_{tr}{:}s_{te}$ ratios of 16:4 and 64:16 were considered on this set of $TestFiles$). The results computed for the corresponding models derived in the tests performed are compared with the results for the ratios 16:4 and 64:16 as being given in [2]. By this comparison additional knowledge on the impact of the model size (in terms of vectors computed for each file in $TestFiles$) is derived and presented in section 4.

In addition to cross evaluation tests and the tests already described in [2] a new series of tests is performed in this work by computing the classification accuracy $p_{D_{A_i}}$ of each of the generated M_{A_i} on completely unmarked material. Therefore an additional vector set vs_c labelled *unmarked* is generated by independently computing vs_P from $389\,files$ with the same characteristics (parameters used) as in the computations described above. This vs_P is consecutively not split, since no model training is intended on this vector set. Instead, it is completely used in the vs_c *unmarked*. This set is then employed in the tests to evaluate the occurrence of Type I errors for a classification using all $M_{A_i} \in \mathbb{M}$.

3.2 Test Procedure

In this work the test procedure described in [2] for the intra-window analysis using AAST is followed closely to guarantee comparability of the results. Additionally in the classification module of the AAST the error occurrence of Type I and II errors is computed for selected tests as described in section 2. The complete list of parameter sets for the tests is given is section 3.1, where special attention was paid to the exact description of the generation of training and testing vector sets. The classification module of AAST is used on different models and testing vector sets as it is necessary to address the test objectives identified below.

3.3 Test Objectives

From the two major test goals of this work (evaluation of the performance of the AAST as universal and special steganalysis tool) the following test objectives are derived:

- **Algorithm cross-evaluation tests:** when the AAST is used as a universal steganalysis tool, contrary to being a specific one, the performance would largely depend on finding classifiers which show good results for a large number of algorithms. With the introduced SVM classification approach this is synonymous with finding models M in the model space $\mathbb{M}$ which have a high classification accuracy on sets of audio material (partially) marked by different information hiding algorithms. To evaluate this test objective a cross evaluation of M_{A_i} generated for all algorithms A_i against vector sets vs_c each (partially) marked by A_i are performed, measuring the classification accuracy in each case. The s_{tr} for the tests performed for this objective is set to $s_{tr} = 256$, $s_{te} = 64$.
- **Tests on the *unmarked* vector set:** The occurrence of false positives in the classification of completely unmarked material in the context of this work is considered an important indicator for a possible practical application of the AAST as a specific steganalysis tool. The occurrence (in percent) of such Type II errors is measured in the classifications of all M_{A_i} against vs_c (partially) marked by the corresponding A_i. The size of the vs_c for these tests is set to $s_{tr} = 256$, $s_{te} = 64$.
- **Scaling of the classification accuracy with an increased model size:** For this test objective M_{A_i} with different model sizes are generated for each A_i. The impact of the model size on the classification accuracy in this specific steganalysis scenario is measured (without considering the *unmarked* test set).
- **Expansion of the *longfile* tests from [2]:** In [2] this second set of test signals was used to simulate the application scenario of VoIP steganography.

The results from [2] for the only algorithm evaluated there for the application scenario of VoIP steganography indicated a possible detection accuracy of 100% under very specific conditions. In this work those tests will be extended to all $A_i \in A$ in order to confirm or dispute the findings from [2].

Additionally a test on the performance of the applied classification under signal modifications common to VoIP communications is performed and compared to an unmarked case. As examples for such common modifications the signal amplification (global amplification, normalisation or amplification of the signal in a limited frequency band), the resampling of the audio signal and the removal of frames (equivalent to the dropping of VoIP-frames) are considered.

4   Test Results

In this section the results for all tests performed are shown (following the order of the test objectives as it is given above).

4.1   Algorithm Cross-Evaluation Tests

In the tests performed for the evaluation of this test objective the M_{A_i} generated (with $s_{tr}=256$ and $FS = \{SF_{std}, SF_{std \cup FMFCC}\}$) for all A_i are used to classify vector sets vs_c generated for all A_i as described in section 3.1. The vs_c for these tests is set to $s_{te} = 64$.

The basic assumption for these tests is that the highest classification accuracy for all M_{A_i} would be found in the case when the vector set generated by using A_i is classified by the model for the same algorithm (e.g. vs_c from A_{S_1} classified by M_{S_1}; those cases are printed in tables 2 and 3 in bold face). When a model for an algorithm, being different from the one used to generate the actual vs_c, is used in the classification, the classification accuracy (in percent) should be significantly lower (if the models for both algorithms considered have completely disjunctive sets of discriminating features, the value for the classification accuracy would be 50% $\pm$ ϵ with ϵ=2%, see [2]).

Table 2. Results (classification accuracy in percent) for the cross-algorithm evaluation using the feature set SF_{std} ($s_{tr}:s_{te} = 256:64$)

	M_{S_1}	M_{S_2}	M_{S_3}	M_{S_4}	M_{S_5}	M_{W_1}	M_{W_2}	M_{W_3}	M_{W_4}
vs_c from A_{S_1}	**61.83**	56.66	51.90	50.49	50.82	49.96	52.03	59.50	53.01
vs_c from A_{S_2}	54.51	**58.07**	47.56	47.34	47.34	50.19	47.25	49.93	52.70
vs_c from A_{S_3}	57.14	46.08	**62.15**	60.71	61.31	50.62	61.27	59.36	56.88
vs_c from A_{S_4}	55.68	45.01	59.38	**60.00**	59.48	49.95	59.20	58.16	53.53
vs_c from A_{S_5}	55.68	44.67	60.10	59.07	**60.37**	51.11	60.11	57.60	54.16
vs_c from A_{W_1}	49.09	56.33	82.30	46.32	47.32	**90.17**	65.38	60.33	74.72
vs_c from A_{W_2}	58.84	45.25	61.31	60.52	62.16	50.38	**61.58**	60.00	56.56
vs_c from A_{W_3}	56.77	54.33	53.94	55.94	52.44	50.59	56.31	**59.54**	52.78
vs_c from A_{W_4}	50.53	52.50	51.18	50.55	50.55	50.87	51.11	50.97	**55.71**

In the results for the feature set SF_{std} (table 2) in the columns for M_{S_3}, M_{S_4}, M_{S_5}, M_{A_2}, M_{A_3} and M_{A_4} the classification accuracy of the model on at least one vector set marked by a different algorithm was higher than on the one marked by the actual watermarking algorithm (i.e. a higher value in the same column than the one on the principal diagonal line). As an example M_{S_1} is considered significant (classification accuracy $\geq 52\%$) for all A_S as well as A_{W_2} and A_{W_3} (results in the range [54.51%...61.87%]). In general every model except M_{W_1} shows significant results on more than one result.

Nevertheless, if the results are reviewed from the perspective of the vs_c, only one case is identified where a model origination from a different algorithm than the one used in the generation of the vs_c can be found (in the row for A_{W_2} one higher accuracy (in percent) is achieved by an algorithm being different to the one used in the set generation). Therefore the basic assumption stated above is true in nearly all cases evaluated.

To summarise the two findings from this test it can be stated that, while more than one of the generated M_{A_i} might be used to classify a given (partially) marked vector set with a accuracy higher than 52%, the best results for all but one of the 81 tests presented in table 2 have been achieved by using the appropriate model M_{A_i} for A_i.

Table 3. Results (classification accuracy in percent) for the cross-algorithm evaluation using the feature set $SF_{std \cup FMFCC}$ (s_{tr}:s_{te} = 256:64)

	M_{S_1}	M_{S_2}	M_{S_3}	M_{S_4}	M_{S_5}	M_{W_1}	M_{W_2}	M_{W_3}	M_{W_4}
vs_c from A_{S_1}	**62.19**	51.89	60.95	56.87	57.46	52.81	61.74	56.08	52.98
vs_c from A_{S_2}	52.61	**62.21**	61.99	59.45	57.50	66.73	57.73	60.39	51.66
vs_c from A_{S_3}	54.01	55.85	**72.94**	58.93	59.11	44.67	64.67	58.41	57.08
vs_c from A_{S_4}	54.21	56.52	63.13	**62.19**	61.27	49.22	61.44	61.11	50.78
vs_c from A_{S_5}	53.60	53.23	62.61	60.55	**62.05**	50.91	63.27	59.99	51.45
vs_c from A_{W_1}	50.14	50.14	50.20	50.02	51.26	**99.10**	50.25	49.99	50.33
vs_c from A_{W_2}	53.49	53.16	65.53	57.63	58.38	42.88	**74.86**	56.49	54.86
vs_c from A_{W_3}	55.48	59.23	63.08	60.82	60.61	50.63	60.99	**62.62**	51.39
vs_c from A_{W_4}	52.91	53.02	65.74	53.90	54.61	43.70	62.57	53.89	**63.92**

The results for the feature set $SF_{std \cup FMFCC}$ (table 3) show a slightly different behaviour compared to their counterparts in table 2. Here in every column the value on the principal axis is the highest value (i.e. the model shows the best results for the test set (partially) marked by the same algorithm). In these tests five vector sets could be identified where the best classification accuracy was achieved by a different algorithm than the one used in the generation of the vs_c. As an example the best classification accuracy with 66.73% on vs_c from A_{S_2} was returned by M_{W_1}.

When comparing the results for both fused feature sets considered here the results show generally two things: first, a very low discrimination power on most vs_c has to be observed. The case closest to ideal is seen for $SF_{std \cup FMFCC}$ in the case of the classifications on vs_c from A_{W_1}. Here the accuracy for the corresponding model is above 99% and the results for every other algorithm are below

52%. The second noticeable result is that seven models (one based on SF_{std} and six based on $SF_{std \cup FMFCC}$) return significant ($\geq 52\%$) classification results for the vs_c generated from eight (or in one case even all nine) of the nine A_i in the evaluation. In [2] the relevance tests for all single features sf in the feature space $\mathbb{SF}$ did show that several features are relevant for more than one (or even for all) A_i. Some of these features are incorporated in the models $SF_{std \cup FMFCC}$ and SF_{std} used here and might be the reason for the low discriminatory power observed. If comparing the performance of the SF_{std} and $SF_{std \cup FMFCC}$ based features the latter show in general a better performance (in terms of classification accuracy).

4.2   Tests on the *unmarked* Vector Set

An evaluation of the quality of a model has to take into account the performance in the case of classifying (completely) unmarked material. Table 4 shows the classification accuracy (in percent) of all models on the vector set *unmarked*. These tests are considered extreme tests in the context of this work since they are using a test set which violates the null hypothesis for the tests performed (i.e. the set is completely unmarked and not partially marked as in the other tests).

Table 4. Results for p_{A_i} (classification accuracy in percent) for the selected FS and all M_{A_i} on $vs_c = unmarked$ (($s_{tr}{:}s_{te} = 256{:}64$)

	M_{S_1}	M_{S_2}	M_{S_3}	M_{S_4}	M_{S_5}	M_{W_1}	M_{W_2}	M_{W_3}	M_{W_4}
SF_{std}	55.03	64.60	81.56	89.57	89.57	81.80	90.10	63.14	66.00
$SF_{std \cup FMFCC}$	54.23	63.61	75.29	79.38	89.41	98.96	77.54	66.77	61.56

From the classification accuracy (the number of vectors correctly classified as unmarked) given in table 4 the Type II (false negatives) errors for the classification using the M_{A_i} are computed as $100\% - p_{A_i}$ of the results presented in table 4. The results for these errors are shown in table 5.

Table 5. Results for the Type II errors (false negatives; $100\% - p_{A_i}$) in percent for the selected FS and all M_{A_i} on $vs_c = unmarked$

	M_{S_1}	M_{S_2}	M_{S_3}	M_{S_4}	M_{S_5}	M_{W_1}	M_{W_2}	M_{W_3}	M_{W_4}
SF_{std}	44.97	35.40	18.44	10.43	10.43	18.20	9.90	36.86	34.00
$SF_{std \cup FMFCC}$	45.77	36.39	24.71	20.62	10.60	1.04	22.46	33.24	38.44

The results in table 5 show a very inhomogeneous behaviour of the different models. While in the case of M_{S_1} the results are only slightly below 50% (which would be similar to guessing the result) the best result with an occurrence of false negatives of only 1.04% (in the case of M_{W_1} and $SF_{std \cup FMFCC}$, the combination which also shows the best results in section 4.1) is considered nearly perfect.

These 1.04% false negatives are equal to $389 * 64 * 1.043/100 = 260$ falsely as "marked" classified vectors. In seven of the nine cases it is noticed that the results for $SF = SF_{std}$ are better than the results for $SF_{std \cup FMFCC}$. From the high rate of Type II errors in the tests on this *unmarked* vector set, a lower number of Type I errors on partially or completely marked test sets can be assumed. Results for partially marked vector sets are given in section 4.3. To perform the computation of Type I errors on completely marked sets will be a task for further research.

4.3   Scaling of the Classification Accuracy by Increasing the Model Size Tests

In [2] the changes in the classification accuracy of a model was tested on $389 files$ for two scaling steps (s_{tr}=16 and s_{tr}=64 windows per file). Here the results for a further scaling step (s_{tr}=256) are computed to reliably identify the correlation between model size and classification accuracy. Tables 6 and 7 summarise the results from [2] and compare them with the corresponding results from the new computations. In each column of tables 6 and 7 the highest classification accuracy (in percent) is marked in bold face for better readability.

Table 6. Classification accuracy (in percent) for different model sizes and the feature set SF_{std} for all A_i considered for the classification against the appropriate M_{A_i}

	M_{S_1}	M_{S_2}	M_{S_3}	M_{S_4}	M_{S_5}	M_{W_1}	M_{W_2}	M_{W_3}	M_{W_4}
$s_{tr}:s_{te}$=16:4	55.30	57.14	59.61	**60.93**	59.09	85.89	**62.32**	59.09	52.02
$s_{tr}:s_{te}$=64:16	57.10	54.55	61.01	60.42	**61.20**	88.85	61.85	59.31	54.90
$s_{tr}:s_{te}$=256:64	**61.84**	**58.07**	**62.15**	60.00	60.37	**90.17**	61.58	**59.54**	**55.71**

Table 7. Classification accuracy (in percent) for different model sizes and the feature set $SF_{std \cup FMFCC}$ for all A_i for the classification against the appropriate M_{A_i}

	M_{S_1}	M_{S_2}	M_{S_3}	M_{S_4}	M_{S_5}	M_{W_1}	M_{W_2}	M_{W_3}	M_{W_4}
$s_{tr}:s_{te}$=16:4	51.58	60.46	63.63	59.74	59.82	93.45	70.39	59.16	55.75
$s_{tr}:s_{te}$=64:16	56.45	59.97	67.22	60.65	60.87	97.52	71.63	60.56	59.50
$s_{tr}:s_{te}$=256:64	**62.19**	**62.21**	**72.94**	**62.19**	**62.05**	**99.10**	**74.86**	**60.99**	**63.92**

When comparing both tables 6 and 7 it is obvious that the results for the $SF_{std \cup FMFCC}$ are not only showing a more homogeneous behaviour (for increasing model sizes a general increase of the classification accuracy is noticeable as well), also the general performance (in terms of the maximum classification accuracy reached) is higher for all algorithms compared to SF_{std}.

The error distribution, split into Type I and II errors, for the test of classifying each A_i with its corresponding model and $s_{tr}:s_{te}$=256:64 (last rows in tables 6 and 7) is given in tables 8 and 9. A Type I error (false positive) in our case is the error of classifying a vector as belonging to an unmarked file when in reality it belongs to a marked signal. A Type II error (false negative) in our case this is the equivalent of classifying a vector as belonging to a marked file when in fact it belongs to a unmarked signal.

Table 8. Type I and II errors (in percent of all vector classifications) at $s_{tr}{:}s_{te}$ =256:64 and feature set SF_{std} for all A considered

	A_{S_1}	A_{S_2}	A_{S_3}	A_{S_4}	A_{S_5}	A_{W_1}	A_{W_2}	A_{W_3}	A_{W_4}
Type I error (false positive)	15.68	19.59	28.63	34.78	37.94	0.73	33.58	22.03	27.29
Type II error (false negative)	22.49	18.20	9.22	5.22	2.60	9.10	4.90	18.43	17.00

Table 9. Type I and II errors (in percent of all vector classifications) at $s_{tr}{:}s_{te}$ =256:64 and feature set $SF_{std \cup FMFCC}$ for all A considered

	A_{S_1}	A_{S_2}	A_{S_3}	A_{S_4}	A_{S_5}	A_{W_1}	A_{W_2}	A_{W_3}	A_{W_4}
Type I error (false positive)	14.93	18.21	14.70	27.50	33.64	0.38	14.04	20.77	16.86
Type II error (false negative)	22.89	16.89	12.36	10.31	5.35	0.52	11.25	16.62	19.22

The different classes of results can be seen in tables 8 and 9: first, the case where both errors are not dependent on the choice of the fused feature set (see algorithms A_{S_1}, A_{S_2} and A_{W_3}), second, the case where choosing $SF_{std \cup FMFCC}$ in stead of SF_{std} decreased the Type I errors by a large amount, but at the same time increased the Type II errors slightly (see algorithms A_{S_3}, A_{S_4}, A_{S_5}, A_{W_2} and A_{W_4}), and third, the case where the number of Type II errors was nearly eliminated by choosing $SF_{std \cup FMFCC}$ (A_{W_1}).

4.4   Results for $TestFiles = longfile$

In [2] this test set was used to simulate the application scenario of VoIP steganography under the basic assumption that a VoIP communication can be generally modelled as a two channel speech communication with one invariant speaker per channel. One of these channels was simulated by using $longfile$. The tests in [2] used only A_{S_1} which is the steganography algorithm used in the VoIP steganography prototype described in [8] and [3]. Since the results of those tests (which computed models of a larger size than possible with $389 files$) did show very interesting results for the classification accuracy achieved, they are expanded in this work to the complete set of algorithms A. All parameters are chosen as in [2] to guarantee a comparability of results. Unfortunately the algorithms A_{S_4}, A_{S_5}, A_{W_1} and A_{W_3} were not capable of marking the long file composing the test set $longfile$. In the case of A_{W_1} the embedding process was terminated with a "segmentation fault", in the case of A_{W_3} and A_{S_5} the embedding function terminated with the message "aborted" without generating the marked output file. For A_{S_4} the embedding process was aborted manually after running 40 hours without termination or showing any form of progress. The behaviour of those four algorithms (which is considered to be a result of the large file size) is marked in tables 10 and 11 with "n.a." (result not available).

Table 10. $p_{D_{A_i}}$ for SF_{std} and $SF_{std \cup FMFCC}$ for all A_i and $TestFiles = longfile$ ($s_{tr}:s_{te} = 400:2200$)

	M_{S_1}	M_{S_2}	M_{S_3}	M_{S_4}	M_{S_5}	M_{W_1}	M_{W_2}	M_{W_3}	M_{W_4}
SF_{std}	72.89	61.98	55.45	n.a.	n.a.	100	n.a.	n.a.	59.75
$SF_{std \cup FMFCC}$	96.93	96.11	95.73	n.a.	n.a.	100	n.a.	n.a.	97.21

Table 11. $p_{D_{A_i}}$ for SF_{std} and $SF_{std \cup FMFCC}$ for all A_i and $TestFiles = longfile$ ($s_{tr}:s_{te} = 2200:400$)

	M_{S_1}	M_{S_2}	M_{S_3}	M_{S_4}	M_{S_5}	M_{W_1}	M_{W_2}	M_{W_3}	M_{W_4}
SF_{std}	77.88	72.25	68.50	n.a.	n.a.	100	n.a.	n.a.	64.75
$SF_{std \cup FMFCC}$	100	100	100	n.a.	n.a.	100	n.a.	n.a.	100

Both tables show very good or even perfect results for the large models used here for classification. A classification accuracy of $p_{D_{S_1}} = 100\%$ indicates that, by applying the corresponding model to a intra-window based classification of a vector field generated by AAST using the feature set $SF_{std \cup FMFCC}$ on audio material of the same type as $longfile$ or $longfile^M$ (i.e. (partially marked) speech) and with the same parameterisations as described, the result would be a perfect classification into marked and un-marked material. Additionally it means that the Type I and II errors for these tests are at 0%. Like in most of the preceding tests the results for $SF_{std \cup FMFCC}$ again outperform the results obtained by a classification using SF_{std}.

In table 12 the results from a small scale cross-algorithm evaluation on A_{S_1} and A_{S_2} using the feature sets $SF_{std \cup FMFCC}$ and SF_{std} and a $s_{tr}:s_{te}$ ratio of 2200:400 are shown. These results confirm the problems with the discriminatory power already noticed in the cross-algorithm evaluation results shown in tables 2 and 3. The results for the cross-classification of vs_c from A_{S_1} with M_{S_2} and vs_c from A_{S_2} with M_{S_1} are far above 95% in the case of $SF_{std \cup FMFCC}$ and above 60% for SF_{std}. To summarise the findings from tables 2, 3 and 12 it has to be stated that models for one algorithm sometimes return significant ($\geq 52\%$) classification results for the vs_c generated from other algorithms. In the case of the results for $SF_{std \cup FMFCC}$ in table 12 the classification results in cross-classification even reach values larger than 99%. Further research should be invested into this result in order to determine how a AAST based universal steganalysis approach will benefit from selected models which show a good performance on several algorithms.

Table 12. Classification accuracy (in percent) for the cross-algorithm evaluation on A_{S_1} and A_{S_2} using the feature sets $SF_{std \cup FMFCC}$ and SF_{std} ($s_{tr}:s_{te} = 2200:400$)

	$M_{S_1}, SF_{std \cup FMFCC}$	$M_{S_2}, SF_{std \cup FMFCC}$	M_{S_1}, SF_{std}	M_{S_2}, SF_{std}
vs_c from A_{S_1}	100	97.38	77.88	79.13
vs_c from A_{S_2}	99.75	100	62	72.25

Another test performed under the basic assumption of evaluating a VoIP communication focuses on the non-steganographic processing of data. This test is similar to the tests performed in section 4.2 but here the quality of the classifier used is evaluated using five audio modifications common to VoIP communications. Test material is generated from $TestFiles = longfile$ by using five attacks from the SMBA audio watermark benchmarking suite [11]. The attacks chosen ($Amplify$, $BassBoost$, $CutSamples$, $Normalizer1$ and $Resample$) present possible signal modifications which can occur in a VoIP application. All five attacks are used with their default parameters (for a detailed description of the attacks, their implementation and parameterisation see [11]).

Table 13 summarises the results of a classification of $TestFiles = attacks(longfile)$ using the same M_{A_i} as in table 11 for all algorithms where these models could be computed. The test hypothesis for the tests is that the evaluated audio material is not marked by an algorithm taken from A (i.e. unmarked material).

Table 13. $p_{D_{A_i}}$ for $SF_{std \cup FMFCC}$ for all A_i and $TestFiles = attacks(longfile)$ ($s_{tr}:s_{te}$ = 2200:400) and on unmarked longfiles; under the hypothesis $TestFiles = cover$

	M_{S_1}	M_{S_2}	M_{S_3}	M_{S_4}	M_{S_5}	M_{W_1}	M_{W_2}	M_{W_3}	M_{W_4}
Amplify	99.5	98.25	100	n.a.	n.a.	100	n.a.	n.a.	98.25
BassBoost	97	99.25	100	n.a.	n.a.	100	n.a.	n.a.	96.25
CutSamples	82	0.25	83	n.a.	n.a.	100	n.a.	n.a.	0
Normalizer1	100	100	100	n.a.	n.a.	98.75	n.a.	n.a.	90.75
Resample	0	0	100	n.a.	n.a.	88.75	n.a.	n.a.	0
None	100	100	100	n.a.	n.a.	100	n.a.	n.a.	100

The results in table 13 imply that the classification applied is, in all tests performed, very robust (correctly classified samples > 90%) against the $Amplify$, $BassBoost$ and $Normalizer1$ attacks. A strong inhomogeneity in the results can be seen for the $CutSamples$ and $Resample$ attacks where the rate of correctly classified samples is either very good (82 to 100%) or catastrophic (0 to 0.25%). When looking at the algorithms it can be noted that the models generated for A_{S_3} and A_{W_1} (M_{S_3} and M_{W_1}) allow for a very accurate classification (correctly classified samples > 83%) of the attacked material. The other three evaluated A_i show worse results. On the unmarked longfiles table 13 (the row for the attack $None$) shows for each of the five algorithms a 100% classification accuracy.

5   Conclusion and Summary

Regarding the first goal of evaluating the performance of the AAST as a universal steganalysis tool the results presented in section 4 show that the selected classification approach of using SVM classification is not suitable if the application scenario does not limit the selection of the information hiding algorithm to be detected. Especially the results of the algorithm cross-evaluation in section 4.1

show that the discriminatory power of most of the models used in the testing was too low to accurately distinguish between the algorithms evaluated. On the other hand the high classification accuracy of some of the models on more than one algorithm might make these models a good wide range indicator for hidden channels when applied to audio material. Nevertheless, the results prove that a different classification (i.e. multi-class classifier based) approach has to be chosen for AAST to be useful in scenarios where the number of possible steganographic methods is not limited to one.

For the second test goal of this paper (the evaluation of the quality of AAST when it is used as a specific steganalyser) section 4 shows generally very good results for all algorithms considered for larger models (here generated by training on 256 feature vectors per file in the set of audio signals). These results are supported by the ones computed on the second set of test signals (*longfile*) where the large models generated on this set allowed for 100% classification accuracy on all five algorithms which were able to mark this test set.

When considering the sets of fused features used to generate the models M it has to be stated that the models including FMFCCs outperform the strictly time domain based models in every test except for the false positive alert generation on "unmarked" vector sets.

For further research the computation of Type I errors on completely marked sets (as it is done in section 4.2 for Type II errors on completely unmarked material) might give another indicator for AAST current classification approach in universal steganalysis. Furthermore the problems with the low discriminative power shown in this work might be addressed by narrowing down the number of features fused in the feature sets used for classification by removing non-relevant features for each algorithm. Also choosing different parameters for the SVM classification might improve the classification accuracy and enable the construction of receiver operation curves (ROC) in the evaluations.

More tests under the assumption of the VoIP scenario (i.e. on speech material similar to the *longfile* material) could give a indication on how to optimise (in terms of minimising the number of features and feature vectors to be computed for a reliable classification) the classification process in the consideration of the VoIP scenario. The scalability of the used trained classification approach has to be evaluated by adding new information hiding algorithms to the test set.

The impact of knowledge gained on the distribution of classification errors of each model on the content and tests on the interoperability of the computed models might lead to a reliable grouping of models for the identification of the embedding domain, a step which would dramatically improve the performance of the introduced approach with regards to universal steganalysis. Furthermore the possibility of constructing a meta-classifier on the decision level of the introduced classification approach and the impact to the classification accuracy should be evaluated. For example if no a priory knowledge exists on the algorithm used to mark a file then a classification against all M_i might be done as a naive implementation of such a meta-classifier, using for example the tables 3 or 5 as lookup tables. A different approach could be to use the arithmetic mean of the model based classifications as a decision level fusion function. If a priori knowledge on the quality of selected classifiers exists, then this knowledge could also be incorporated into a decision level fusion, e.g. in form of a weighting function.

Acknowledgements

The work about FMFCC features as well as the implementation of parts of the AAST described in this paper has been supported in part by the European Commission through the IST Programme under Contract IST-2002-507932 ECRYPT. The information in this document is provided as is, and no guarantee or warranty is given or implied that the information is fit for any particular purpose. The user thereof uses the information at its sole risk and liability.

We wish to thank Andreas Lang for providing the SMBA benchmarking suite for the tests described in section 4.4, Claus Vielhauer for his idea of transferring the Mel-cepstral based signal analysis from biometric speaker verification to the domain of steganalysis and Stefan Kiltz for his help in revising the paper.

References

1. Kharrazi, M., Sencar, H.T., Memon, N.: Improving Steganalysis by Fusion Techniques: A Case Study with Image Steganography. In: Shi, Y.Q. (ed.) Transactions on Data Hiding and Multimedia Security I. LNCS, vol. 4300, Springer, Heidelberg (2006)
2. Kraetzer, C., Dittmann, J.: Mel-Cepstrum Based Steganalysis for VoIP-Steganography, To appear in Security, Steganography, and Watermarking of Multimedia Contents IX. In: Delp III, E.J., Wong, P.W. (eds.) Proceedings of the 19th Annual Symposium of the Electronic Imaging Science and Technology, SPIE and IS&T, San Jose, California, USA (January 28th-February 2nd 2007)
3. Kraetzer, C., Dittmann, J., Vogel, T., Hillert, R.: Design and Evaluation of Steganography for Voice-over-IP. In: Proceedings of the 2006 IEEE International Symposium on Circuits and Systems, Kos, Greece (May 21-24th, 2006)
4. Hetzl, S.: Steghide, http://steghide.sourceforge.net
5. Le Guelvouit, G.: Publimark, http://perso.wanadoo.fr/gleguelv/soft/publimark
6. Kraetzer, C., Dittmann, J., Lang, A.: Transparency Benchmarking on Audio Watermarks and Steganography. In: SPIE conference, at the Security, Steganography, and Watermarking of Multimedia Contents VIII, IS&T/SPIE Symposium on Electronic Imaging, San Jose, USA, January 15-19th (2006)
7. Lang, A., Dittmann, J.: Profiles for Evaluation and their Usage in Audio WET. In: Wong, P.W., Delp, E.J. (eds.) Proceedings of the IS&T/SPIE's 18th Annual Symposium, Electronic Imaging 2006: Security and Watermarking of Multimedia Content VIII, San Jose, California, USA, vol. 6072 (January 2006)
8. Vogel, T., Dittmann, J., Hillert, R., Kraetzer, C.: Design und Evaluierung von Steganographie für Voice-over-IP, Sicherheit 2006 GI FB Sicherheit, GI Proceedings, Magdeburg, Germany (February 2006)

9. Gutenberg, P.: Project Gutenberg Literary Archive Foundation,
   `www.gutenberg.org`
10. Chang, C.-C., Lin, C.-J.: LIBSVM: a Library for Support Vector Machines (2001),
    available at: `http://www.csie.ntu.edu.tw/~cjlin/libsvm`
11. Dittmann, J., Kraetzer, C. (eds.): ECRYPT Deliverable D.WVL.10 - Audio Bench-
    marking Tools and Steganalysis; Rev. 1.1 (2006)

Generalised Category Attack—Improving Histogram-Based Attack on JPEG LSB Embedding

Kwangsoo Lee[1], Andreas Westfeld[2], and Sangjin Lee[1]

[1] Center for Information Security Technologies (CIST),
Korea University, Seoul, Korea
kslee@cist.korea.ac.kr, sangjin@korea.ac.kr
[2] Technische Universität Dresden,
Institute for System Architecture,
01062 Dresden, Germany
westfeld@inf.tu-dresden.de

Abstract. We present a generalised and improved version of the category attack on LSB steganography in JPEG images with straddled embedding path. It detects more reliably low embedding rates and is also less disturbed by double compressed images. The proposed methods are evaluated on several thousand images. The results are compared to both recent blind and specific attacks for JPEG embedding. The proposed attack permits a more reliable detection, although it is based on first order statistics only. Its simple structure makes it very fast.

1 Introduction

LSB embedding is probably the most widespread and most frequently analysed steganographic method. It is instinctively considered weak. Hence many alternatives have been proposed in the last years. The JPEG file format is popular for digital photos not only in e-mail attachments. One of the first steganographic methods for JPEG files is Jsteg [1], which overwrites the LSB of DCT coefficients. The chi-square attack [2] demonstrated the weakness of Jsteg. Outguess [3] is an alternative that preserves the first order statistics and thus prevents the chi-square attack. It reserves a number of DCT coefficients to compensate for the changes. After embedding, the exact histogram is recovered by additional specific changes. This renders the chi-square attack ineffective, since it considers the histogram only. The chi-square attack is also prevented by F5 [4], which does not flip LSBs at all, but decreases the absolute value of coefficients by one, if necessary. F5 also increases the embedding efficiency, i. e., the message bits per change ratio. Another interesting approach is model-based steganography [5]. It uses an arithmetic decoder to adapt the stream of message bits to expected frequencies derived, e. g., from a Cauchy model of DCT coefficients. All the successors of Jsteg are immune against the chi-square attack. However, higher order statistical attacks, especially the complex blind attacks with a large feature space like

T. Furon et al. (Eds.): IH 2007, LNCS 4567, pp. 378–391, 2007.

the 324 Markov features by Shi et al. [6] and the 274 merged Markov and DCT features by Pevný and Fridrich [7] can also detect the presence of embedded messages for the advanced steganographic JPEG methods.

Our motivation to consider again LSB embedding is twofold: With very low embedding rates and straddling the changes over the whole medium, LSB embedding is still hard to detect. This is not surprising at all. There are elaborate attacks for the spatial domain (Pairs analysis, RS, SPA [8,9,10]) and improved versions (scanning pixels along a space filling curve [11], adaptive hypotheses for natural images [12]). These are not easily applied to the DCT domain. It is unsatisfactory that the aforementioned complex blind attacks perform better than current specific attacks (Yu et al. [13], Zhang and Ping [14]). Recent measurements have shown that our previous approach [15] is not significantly better than the blind attack with 274 mixed features for images from one particular source. Jsteg length information can also be used to increase the detection power of targeted Jsteg attacks as shown by Westfeld [16], however, this improvement can easily be prevented by encryption. In practice, the images come from many different sources, are scaled and recompressed. This drops the performance of the blind attacks considerably. For our experiments, we use 900 images from CBIR [17], which is a very heterogeneous set of images and, since this set too small to train a classifier with more than 100 features, another set with 3000 never compressed TIFF images from NRCS [18]. We try to construct a similarly heterogeneous set from this second source, scale to different sizes and compress with different qualities. The aforementioned specific attacks do without a long training phase, without calibrated statistics, and without a large training set: They quickly return their result when directly applied to the suspect JPEG medium. In this paper we propose several improved versions of this attack, which seem to be less sensitive to double compression.

The paper construction is as follows: In the next section, we describe basic notations and definitions, and discuss AC JPEG distribution shapes. In Section 3, we propose a general version of the category attack proposed by Lee et al. [15]. In Section 4, the experimental results are presented for Jsteg and Jphide. Finally, we conclude this paper.

2   Preliminaries

2.1   Notations and Definitions

Let $h(x)$ denote the histogram of DCT coefficients in the cover image and let N be the total number of DCT coefficients. For the ease of description, we will use probabilistic terms. Let X be the random variable of DCT coefficients in a cover image, and $f(x)$ be the probability distribution of X, i.e., $f(x) = P_X(x)$. The relation between the two distributions is

$$f(x) = \frac{1}{N}h(x) \ . \tag{1}$$

Let X' be the random variable of DCT coefficients in a stego image in which a random message is embedded in the cover image with Jsteg. And let $f'(x)$ be the probability distribution of X' i. e., $f(x) = P_{X'}(x)$.

Let $U = \sum_{x \neq 0} h(x)$ denote the number of nonzero DCT coefficients (all AC and DC) and L the number of message bits to be embedded in the JPEG image. We will measure the capacity on a common basis: bits per nonzero coefficients or

$$\text{bpc} = \frac{L}{U} , \qquad (2)$$

with $0 \leq \text{bpc} \leq 1$. The bpc is for all JPEG embedding algorithms the same while their particular capacities differ. For example, Jsteg is an application of the LSB embedding to JPEG format. It is identical with the LSB embedding except that the coefficient values 0 and 1 are not used for embedding. Consequently, for Jsteg, $U_1 = \sum_{x \notin \{0,1\}} h(x)$ and its relative capacity usage $\ell = \frac{L}{U_1}$.

We assume that the message bits are random. In other words, the message bits are assumed to be independent of the cover image and are uniformly distributed. Because the embedding path is pseudorandomly chosen, the probability of flipping the LSB of a coefficient $x \notin \{0,1\}$ is $\ell/2$. Hence, one can establish a basic relation between the cover and the stego distributions as follows: for $x \neq 0$,

$$f'(2x) = f(2x) - \frac{\ell}{2} \left(f(2x) - f(2x+1) \right) , \qquad (3)$$

$$f'(2x+1) = f(2x+1) + \frac{\ell}{2} \left(f(2x) - f(2x+1) \right) . \qquad (4)$$

2.2   Consideration of AC JPEG Coefficient Distribution

The distribution of AC coefficients in JPEG images is often regarded to follow either the Laplacian distribution [19] or the generalised Cauchy distribution [5]. The Laplacian distribution

$$h(x) = \frac{\lambda}{2} e^{-\lambda |x|} \qquad (5)$$

and the generalised Cauchy distribution

$$h(x) = \frac{p-1}{2s} \left(\left| \frac{x}{s} \right| + 1 \right)^{-p} . \qquad (6)$$

have common properties: the symmetry about 0 and the unimodality.

The distributions AC coefficients of DCT transformed blocks are generally well approximated for images that are compressed for the first time. It is reasonable to believe that the quantisation does not affect the symmetry, however, we have found a considerable number of images with multimodal distribution, probably due to the effect of double compression. For example, Fig. 1 displays the quantisation table and the AC coefficient histogram of Y channel data of a JPEG image obtained from CBIR [17]. Clearly, the distribution is not unimodal.

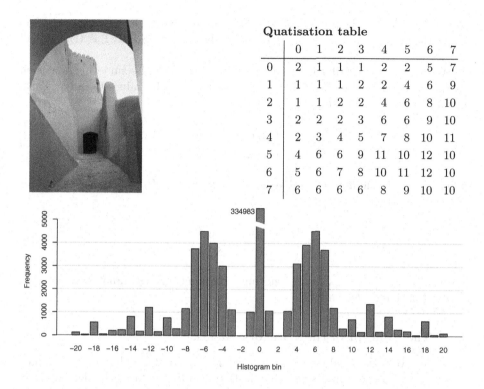

Quatisation table

	0	1	2	3	4	5	6	7
0	2	1	1	1	2	2	5	7
1	1	1	1	2	2	4	6	9
2	1	1	2	2	4	6	8	10
3	2	2	2	3	6	6	9	10
4	2	3	4	5	7	8	10	11
5	4	6	6	9	11	10	12	10
6	5	6	7	8	10	11	12	10
7	6	6	6	6	8	9	10	10

Fig. 1. A JPEG image from CBIR [17] and its quantisation table for Y channel and the histogram of AC coefficients showing the case of the multimodal; the frequency of the value 0 was reduced for display

In CBIR, one can observe many JPEG images having multimodal "comb" distributions, which require special handling in steganalysis [20].

From this observation, the steganographic technique depends on the model parameters regarding the above distributions [5]. For example, the steganalytic technique by Yu et al. uses these model parameters [13]. One remedy for the steganalyst is to filter out the images of the unexpected case in the test domain. A more advanced one is to develop non-parametric solutions for the detection like the method of Zhang and Ping (ZP) [14] and the category attack by Lee et al. [15].

3 Generalised Category Attack

3.1 Histogram Modification for Detection

For the sake of simple description of the attack, we delete some bars in the histogram. We need two separate histogram modifications, one for Jsteg and another one for Jphide. After the modification, the histogram considers only values that are usable for LSB embedding.

Let $f(x)$ denote the probability distribution of the samples in a digital image. Then the relations of $f(x)$ and $f'(x)$ described in the Sect. 2.1 is true for all $x \in Z$.

We change the distribution in a way that keeps both, its smoothness as well as the effect of LSB embedding. Jsteg does not use the values 0 and 1. For a given histogram $h(x)$, we put

$$f(x) = \begin{cases} h(x)/U_1 & , \text{ for } x > 1 , \\ h(x-2)/U_1 & , \text{ for } x \leq 1 , \end{cases} \tag{7}$$

where U_1 is the number of usable coefficients, that is, $U_1 = \sum_{x \notin \{0,1\}} h(x)$. For the Jphide attack, we put

$$f(x) = \begin{cases} h(x)/U_2 & , \text{ for } x > 1 , \\ h(x-3)/U_2 & , \text{ for } x \leq 1 , \end{cases} \tag{8}$$

where $U_2 = \sum_{x \notin \{-1,0,1\}} h(x)$ ignoring occasional changes and the negligible cases of usable coefficients.

3.2 The Concept of the Category Attack

Consider two pairs of values: $(2m, 2m+1)$ and $(2m-1, 2m)$. The former is named the *induced* category in a sense that LSB embedding induces the decrement of the frequency difference,

$$|f'(2m) - f'(2m+1)| = (1-\ell)|f(2m) - f(2m+1)| , \tag{9}$$

which is derived from (3) and (4). This fact was earlier used in the chi-square attack [2,21], a categorical data analysis for the detection of steganography.

The latter is named the *shifted* category in a sense that the values are shifted by 1. Induced and shifted categories have been termed direct and shifted pairs in the literature before [8]. However, apart from the correspondence of these terms, the category attack has little resemblance with the Pairs analysis that exploits higher order statistics creating two binary vectors and evaluating their number homogeneous and inhomogeneous pairs. The main idea of the category attack is to use the shifted category in which the frequency differences have a different pattern with LSB embedding compared to that in the induced category: Because the values can be changed within an induced category containing it, the effect of LSB embedding on the frequency difference is covered by at least two induced categories, $(2m - 2, 2m - 1)$ and $(2m, 2m + 1)$, which are overlapped by the shifted category $(2m - 1, 2m)$. In other words, the effect is dependent on the state of the distribution $f(x)$ on the four consecutive sample values $\{2m - 2, 2m - 1, 2m, 2m + 1\}$.

The assumed sample distribution is varying, and thus, we expect that $f(x)$ is monotonically increasing or decreasing on many intervals with a significant portion. For the JPEG domain, this is clear regardless of what the modality of the distribution is. Consider a monotone decreasing interval. The equalisation of both frequencies in the induced category implies that $f(2m - 1)$ will increase and $f(2m)$ will decrease after LSB embedding. This means that the frequency difference in the shifted category $(2m-1, 2m)$ grows when the embedded message size is increasing. This is also true for the monotone increasing case. This makes a difference to the pattern in the induced category.

In Fig. 2, the left side shows the difference between both changes of the frequency difference in the induced and the shifted categories. The curves represent the monotone decreasing function $f(x)$. Two adjacent circles with the same colour represent the values in an induced category. For each circle, the arrow indicates the changing pattern of the frequency of the sample value by LSB embedding. The top-left and the bottom-left figure show both patterns in the induced and the shifted categories respectively. The two arrows in one category point in opposite directions. The category attack evaluates these differences in a relative way using some measurements.

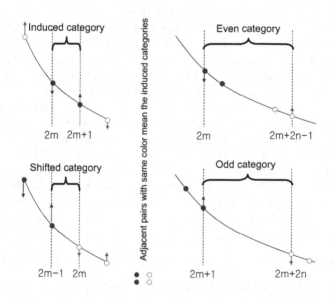

Fig. 2. The concept of general categories

3.3   General Categories

In this section, we will generalise the concept of the category attack. A category means a pair of values, say (a, b), such that $a, b \in Z$ and $a < b$. It is more convenient to represent the category by the small value a and the distance $d = b - a$. Let Ω_d be the collection of categories in which values differ by d, i.e., $\Omega_d = \{(a, a+d) : a \in Z\}$. For a distance d, the categories in Ω_d can be classified into LSB types of their small values. Let $\Omega_{0,d}$ be the sub-collection of Ω_d whose members are of the form $(2m, 2m + d)$, $m \in Z$, i.e., categories having even values as their small values. Similarly, let $\Omega_{1,d}$ be the sub-collection of Ω_d whose members are of the form $(2m + 1, 2m + d + 1)$, $m \in Z$, i.e., categories having odd values as their small values. Then the collection Ω_d is the disjoint union of the sub-collections, $\Omega_{0,d}$ and $\Omega_{1,d}$.

When the distance d is an odd value, $\Omega_{0,d}$ and $\Omega_{1,d}$ have some distinctive characteristics under LSB embedding. In this case, say $d = 2n-1$ for some $n \in N$, the category collections can be rewritten as $\Omega_{0,2n-1} = \{(2m, 2m + 2n - 1) : m \in Z\}$ and $\Omega_{1,2n-1} = \{(2m + 1, 2m + 2n) : m \in Z\}$. We will refer to $\Omega_{0,2n-1}$ as the collection of even categories with a distance $2n - 1$ (briefly the even categories) and to $\Omega_{1,2n-1}$ the collection of odd categories with a distance $2n-1$ (briefly the odd categories) respectively. The induced categories and the shifted categories referred to in the previous section are the special case of the even and the odd categories with the distance 1, respectively.

Let us look again at Fig. 2. The right side displays the different changing patterns (arrows) of the frequency differences in the even and the odd categories by LSB embedding. For the even category $(2m, 2m + 2n - 1)$ with a distance greater than 1, the two induced categories overlapped by the even category are $(2m, 2m+1)$ and $(2m+2n-2, 2m+2n-1)$. Consider the monotone decreasing interval with $f(x)$ again. As shown in the top-right figure, the frequency $f(2m)$ will decrease and the frequency $f(2m+2n-1)$ will increase after LSB embedding. Their difference $f(2m) - f(2m + 2n - 1)$ will decrease. On the other hand, for the odd category $(2m+1, 2m+2n)$ with a distance greater than 1, both induced categories overlapped by the even category are $(2m, 2m+1)$ and $(2m+2n, 2m+2n+1)$. Considering a monotone decreasing interval of $f(x)$ again (cf. bottom-right in the figure), the frequency $f(2m + 1)$ will increase and the frequency $f(2m+2n)$ will decrease after LSB embedding. Their frequency difference $f(2m+1) - f(2m + 2n)$ will increase. The frequency difference in the even and the odd categories will grow with the LSB embedding rate. And this is also true for a monotone increasing interval. Therefore, the even and the odd categories can be viewed as the generalised concept of the induced and the shifted categories.

3.4   Measurements of the Frequency Differences in Categories

For each type of categories with a distance $2n - 1$, an easy calculation of the frequency difference as overall statistics is the sum of absolute values of the frequency differences in the categories:

$$S_1(0, n) = \sum_{x \in Z} |f(2x) - f(2x + 2n - 1)| , \tag{10}$$

$$S_1(1, n) = \sum_{x \in Z} |f(2x + 1) - f(2x + 2n)| . \tag{11}$$

These have linear patterns of the embedding rate ℓ in their change. Another measure is of the form of the squared sum of frequency differences:

$$S_2(0, n) = \sum_{x \in Z} (f(2x) - f(2x + 2n - 1))^2 , \tag{12}$$

$$S_2(1, n) = \sum_{x \in Z} (f(2x + 1) - f(2x + 2n))^2 . \tag{13}$$

In general, the p-th powered sum of the absolute values of the frequency differences can be considered. However, our experiments have shown no improved detection power compared with the above measures. The following χ^2-like measure was used in the original version of the category attack:

$$\chi^2(0, n) = \sum_{x \in Z} \frac{(f(2x) - f(2x + 2n - 1))^2}{f(2x) + f(2x + 2n - 1)}, \tag{14}$$

$$\chi^2(1, n) = \sum_{x \in Z} \frac{(f(2x + 1) - f(2x + 2n))^2}{f(2x + 1) + f(2x + 2n)}. \tag{15}$$

After LSB embedding, we would expect that

$$S_i'(0, n) < S_i(0, n) \quad \text{but} \quad S_i'(1, n) > S_i(1, n), \tag{16}$$

$$\chi^{2'}(0, n) < \chi^2(0, n) \quad \text{but} \quad \chi^{2'}(1, n) > \chi^2(1, n), \tag{17}$$

where $i \in \{1, 2\}$. Furthermore, we expect each measurement to be more sensitive to higher embedding rates ℓ; for example, the change of $S_1(0, n)$ and $S_1(1, n)$ is linearly decreased and increased on ℓ respectively, if $f(x)$ is increasing in all intervals.

For a fixed distance $2n - 1$, we compare both measurements in the even and the odd categories in a relative way. Put

$$R_{S_i}(n) = \frac{S_i(1, n) - S_i(0, n)}{S_i(1, n) + S_i(0, n)}, \tag{18}$$

$$R_{\chi^2}(n) = \frac{\chi^2(1, n) - \chi^2(0, n)}{\chi^2(1, n) + \chi^2(0, n)}, \tag{19}$$

We assume that cover images have a stable pattern of the relativities, $R_{S_i}(n)$ and $R_{\chi^2}(n)$. If the relativity is above a threshold, then we suppose a stego image.

Let us consider the distance $2n - 1$. We have also evaluated the following combined relativities:

$$CR_{S_i}(n) = \frac{\sum_{k=1}^{n} S_i(1, k) - \sum_{k=1}^{n} S_i(0, k)}{\sum_{k=1}^{n} S_i(1, k) + \sum_{k=1}^{n} S_i(0, k)}, \tag{20}$$

$$CR_{\chi^2}(n) = \frac{\sum_{k=1}^{n} \chi^2(1, k) - \sum_{k=1}^{n} \chi^2(0, k)}{\sum_{k=1}^{n} \chi^2(1, k) + \sum_{k=1}^{n} \chi^2(0, k)}. \tag{21}$$

When n is growing, it is reasonable that the relativity becomes more stable for cover images. However, at the same time the relativity becomes less sensitive to LSB embedding as our experiments have shown. There seems to exist some trade-off between the stability and the sensitivity.

3.5   Discussion of the Applications to Jsteg and Jphide

Assume that JPEG images have the symmetry around 0. (7) yields

$$f(1 + x) = h(1 + x)/U_1 = h(-1 - x)/U_1 = f(1 - x) \tag{22}$$

This means that the symmetry is also true for the modified distribution with Jsteg but the center is changed to 1. Let $y = 2 - 2x - 2n$, then $|f(2x) - f(2x + 2n - 1)| = |f(2y + 1) - f(2y + 2n)|$, and thus,

$$S_i(0, n) = S_i(1, n) \ . \tag{23}$$

Similarly, one can deduce

$$\chi^2(0, n) = \chi^2(1, n) \ . \tag{24}$$

We have

$$R_{S_i}(n) = 0 \ \text{ and } \ CR_{S_i}(n) = 0 \ . \tag{25}$$

$$R_{\chi^2}(n) = 0 \ \text{ and } \ CR_{\chi^2}(n) = 0 \tag{26}$$

As an improvement of the category attack for Jsteg, instead of $h(-1)$, we suggest to use $h(1)$ for the calculation in the odd categories. So we introduce a new histogram modification $f_{ICA}(x)$ that is equivalent to those defined in Eqns. (7) and (8) except for $f_{ICA}(1) = h(1)/U_1$. Due to the symmetry $h(x) = h(-x)$ this will not change the cover statistics. However, because $h(1)$ is not changed while $h(-1)$ decreases after embedding, the measurement of frequency difference in the odd categories will be greater than its original version after LSB embedding. This will boost the sensitivity to Jsteg. We will call this improved category attack (ICA).

If the cover distribution has no symmetry around a sample value, the relativity can be hardly predictable. The initial quantities of the relative differences will fluctuate much more and consequently deviate from the mean. This is the reason of why the category attack is worse for Jphide than Jsteg. Using the combined version of the generalised category attack (GCA), this will be more improved. However, there is no better way of guessing the parameter n than by experiments.

4   Experimental Results

The results are based on two image sources. About 900 JPEG images were downloaded from the CBIR [17]. These 900 images are from mixed sources, different size, colour and greyscale, and possibly double compressed. These images were classified by all versions of the specific attacks.

For the blind attacks we faced the same problem that an investigating officer has if he only has a small set of images to test but no sufficiently large training set. A set of 900 images is too small to be separated into subsets for training and test with about 300 features. So another 3000 large colour TIFF images (2100×1500)

Table 1. Selected reliabilities and false positive rates of the proposed GCA and ICA methods in comparison to existing specific and blind attacks

Attack	$2n-1$	bpc=0.01		bpc=0.02		bpc=0.04	
		ρ	$\text{FPR}_{0.5}$	ρ	$\text{FPR}_{0.5}$	ρ	$\text{FPR}_{0.5}$
Jsteg					(900 CBIR images)		
$\text{GCA}_{AC}\ \text{CR}_{\chi^2}$	1	0.334	0.239	0.599	0.094	0.877	0.012
$\text{GCA}_{AC}\ \text{CR}_{\chi^2}$	3	0.366	0.240	0.643	0.078	0.911	0.010
$\text{GCA}_{AC}\ \text{CR}_{\chi^2}$	5	0.341	0.237	0.612	0.098	0.897	0.020
$\text{GCA}_{AC}\ \text{CR}_{\chi^2}$	7	0.313	0.280	0.573	0.130	0.876	0.027
$\text{GCA}_{AC}\ \text{CR}_{\chi^2}$	9	0.288	0.305	0.535	0.152	0.846	0.033
$\text{ICA}_{AC}\ \text{CR}_{\chi^2}$	1	0.353	0.265	0.632	0.127	0.898	0.028
$\text{ICA}_{AC}\ \text{CR}_{\chi^2}$	3	0.277	0.319	0.513	0.191	0.805	0.067
$\text{ICA}_{AC}\ \text{CR}_{\chi^2}$	5	0.250	0.323	0.471	0.220	0.759	0.084
$\text{ICA}_{AC}\ \text{CR}_{\chi^2}$	7	0.239	0.331	0.452	0.228	0.738	0.099
$\text{ICA}_{AC}\ \text{CR}_{\chi^2}$	9	0.230	0.332	0.437	0.234	0.720	0.109
CA ($\text{GCA}_{DC}\ \text{CR}_{\chi^2}$	1)	0.322	0.251	0.583	0.098	0.866	0.012
ZP β.....................		0.193	0.343	0.366	0.252	0.632	0.140
$\text{ZP}_{AC}\ \beta$.................		0.198	0.349	0.376	0.249	0.645	0.138
Yu α....................		0.056	0.487	0.110	0.477	0.209	0.441
Yu α w/o zero bin.......		0.059	0.467	0.118	0.444	0.228	0.394
23 DCT (NRCS).........		0.062	0.455	0.129	0.411	0.247	0.301
324 Markov (NRCS).....		0.075	0.456	0.151	0.407	0.271	0.339
274 Merged (NRCS).....		0.234	0.315	0.432	0.165	0.687	0.016
Jphide					(900 CBIR images)		
$\text{GCA}_{AC}\ \text{CR}_{S_2}$	1	0.154	0.361	0.296	0.250	0.526	0.119
$\text{GCA}_{AC}\ \text{CR}_{S_2}$	3	0.163	0.404	0.313	0.286	0.564	0.112
$\text{GCA}_{AC}\ \text{CR}_{S_2}$	5	0.178	0.388	0.344	0.272	0.623	0.095
$\text{GCA}_{AC}\ \text{CR}_{S_2}$	7	0.166	0.408	0.318	0.301	0.577	0.108
$\text{GCA}_{AC}\ \text{CR}_{S_2}$	9	0.163	0.406	0.313	0.330	0.570	0.118
$\text{ICA}_{AC}\ \text{CR}_{\chi^2}$	1	0.172	0.343	0.322	0.222	0.556	0.115
$\text{ICA}_{AC}\ \text{CR}_{\chi^2}$	3	0.176	0.430	0.327	0.325	0.571	0.128
$\text{ICA}_{AC}\ \text{CR}_{\chi^2}$	5	0.172	0.443	0.316	0.363	0.545	0.185
$\text{ICA}_{AC}\ \text{CR}_{\chi^2}$	7	0.163	0.448	0.303	0.378	0.525	0.201
$\text{ICA}_{AC}\ \text{CR}_{\chi^2}$	9	0.156	0.430	0.294	0.370	0.516	0.212
CA ($\text{GCA}_{DC}\ \text{CR}_{\chi^2}$	1)	0.151	0.383	0.293	0.267	0.536	0.157
23 DCT (NRCS).........		0.005	0.493	0.015	0.488	0.034	0.478
324 Markov (NRCS).....		0.136	0.420	0.258	0.354	0.386	0.272
274 Merged (NRCS).....		0.159	0.378	0.305	0.283	0.524	0.182

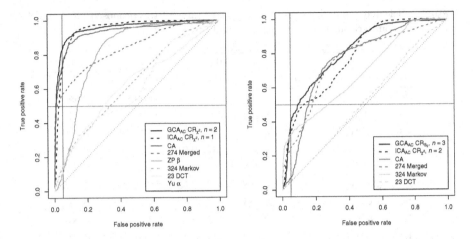

Fig. 3. ROC curves based on 900 CBIR images [17] for selected attacks to 0.04 bpc Jsteg (left) and 0.04 bpc Jphide (right). The three blind classifiers have been trained on a reasonable subset of 100,000 images derived from NRCS images [18].

were downloaded from the NRCS Photo Gallery [18], to construct a training set. We downscaled the images using pnmscale (smaller side 600, 400, 200, 80, and 40 pixels), and converted to greyscale JPEG using pnmtojpeg (qualities 99, 95, 90, 80, 70, 60, 50). Sufficiently large subsets of these about 100,000 images[1] were used to train the blind classifiers. We implemented the blind attacks by Fridrich with 23 DCT features [22], by Shi et al. with 324 Markov features [6], and by Pevný and Fridrich with 274 merged extended DCT and reduced Markov features [7], the specific attacks on randomised Jsteg by Yu et al. (the model-based approach) [13], the attack by Zhang and Ping [14], and by Lee et al. [15], together with their attack on Jphide. We focussed on low embedding rates (0.01, 0.02, and 0.04 bits per nonzero coefficient [bpc]).

Table 1 shows selected results for the attacks on Jsteg and Jphide. Figure 3 presents the ROC curves for the proposed attacks (GCA and ICA) with their best selection of n together with previous attacks. The ROC curve of some attacks (e. g., the attack by Yu et al. based on their α value) is very sensitive to the heterogeneous composition of the image set. These curves show cavities that disappear if the same attack is applied to a homogeneous set with equally sized images from one source. The detection power is evaluated using two measures: one is the reliability ρ of the ROC curve, which is twice the area under the curve minus one, and $FPR_{0.5}$, the false positive rate (FPR) at true positive rate (TPR) 0.5. We applied the three blind attacks (23 DCT, 324 Markov, and 274 merged features), the attack by Lee et al. (CA) and the two proposed attacks GCA and ICA to both, Jsteg and Jphide. Our canonical name for the CA is GCA_{DC} CR_{χ^2} with $n = 1$. There are some more specific attacks that can only detect Jsteg:

---

[1] The size of the training set was chosen according to the number of features, not smaller than 10 images per feature and class.

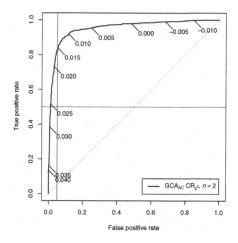

Fig. 4. ROC curve with threshold annotation

the attack by Zhang and Ping (ZP) and the attack by Yu et al. (Yu). We also modified the latter two for a marginal improvement: In "ZP_{AC}" we discarded DC coefficients, since they have a different marginal distribution and "pollute" the statistics. In "Yu w/o zero bin" we excluded the zero bin from the Cauchy model approximation, since this bin shrinks when nonzero bins are growing. For the GCA and ICA we present the cases for $n = 1 \ldots 5$ for the best available measures. In general the best measure was CR_{χ^2}, except for the GCA when applied to Jphide, where we used CR_{S_2}. The overall best result was achieved for Jsteg with the GCA ($n = 2$). Next in rank follow the ICA ($n = 1$), but not significantly worse ($p = 0.07$ for bpc= 0.04), CA, and the 274 merged Markov and DCT features. These four attacks fulfil Ker's criterion ($FPR_{0.5} \leq 0.05$) [23] for an embedding rate of 0.04 bpc. In general, the results for Jphide detection are worse for the same embedded message length. Compared to Jsteg, Jphide seems to be the better choice for steganography.

Note that there is no particular threshold that belongs to the ROC curve. Every point on the ROC curve has its own threshold that determines a false and true positive rate. To construct a classifier, we can give such a rate, and determine the threshold, which is compared to the detector output. Figure 4 shows the ROC curve for the proposed attack with the highest reliability at 0.4 bpc.

5   Conclusion

In this paper, we improved the Category Attack (CA) by Lee et al. to LSB steganography in JPEG images. By using the AC JPEG histogram, the attack was shown to be improved. Also, using the general concept of categories (GCA) and measure extensions (ICA), the attack performed with better detection reliability. It is also based only on the first order statistics, but seems to be more robust against the effect of double compression. We will study this in more detail in our ongoing work.

Acknowledgements

The work on this paper was partially supported by grant No. M10640010005-06N4001-00500 from the national R&D Program of MOST and KOSEF (first author) and by the Air Force Office of Scientific Research, Air Force Material Command, USAF, under the research grant number FA8655-06-1-3046 (second author). The U. S. Government is authorised to reproduce and distribute reprints for Governmental purposes notwithstanding any copyright notation there on. Travel to the Information Hiding Workshop was supported in part by the European Commission through the IST Programme under contract IST-2002-507932 ECRYPT.

References

1. Upham, D.: Jsteg (1993), Online available at `http://munitions.vipul.net/software/steganography/jpeg-jsteg-v4.diff.gz`
2. Westfeld, A., Pfitzmann, A.: Attacks on steganographic systems. In: Pfitzmann, A. (ed.) IH 1999. LNCS, vol. 1768, pp. 61–76. Springer, Heidelberg (2000)
3. Provos, N.: Outguess (2001), Online available at `http://www.outguess.org`
4. Westfeld, A.: F5—a steganographic algorithm: High capacity despite better steganalysis. In: Moskowitz, I.S. (ed.) Information Hiding. LNCS, vol. 2137, pp. 289–302. Springer, Heidelberg (2001)
5. Sallee, P.: Model-based steganography. In: Kalker, T., Ro, Y.M., Cox, I.J. (eds.) IWDW 2003. LNCS, vol. 2939, pp. 154–167. Springer, Heidelberg (2004)
6. Shi, Y.Q., Chen, C., Chen, W.: A Markov process based approach to effective attacking JPEG steganography. In: Camenisch, J., Collberg, C., Johnson, N.F., Sallee, P. (eds.) Information Hiding (8th International Workshop), Berlin Heidelberg. LNCS, vol. 4437, Springer, Heidelberg (2007)
7. Pevný, T., Fridrich, J.: Merging Markov and DCT features for multi-class JPEG steganalysis. In: Delp III, E.J., Wong, P.W. (eds.) Security, Steganography and Watermarking of Multimedia Contents IX (Proc. of SPIE), San Jose, CA (2007)
8. Fridrich, J., Goljan, M., Soukal, D.: Higher-order statistical steganalysis of palette images. In: Delp III, E.J., Wong, P.W. (eds.) Security, Steganography and Watermarking of Multimedia Contents V (Proc. of SPIE), San Jose, CA, pp. 178–190 (2003)
9. Fridrich, J., Goljan, M., Du, R.: Detecting LSB steganography in color and grayscale images. IEEE Multimedia 8(4), 22–28 (2001)
10. Dumitrescu, S., Wu, X., Wang, Z.: Detection of LSB steganography via sample pair analysis. In: Petitcolas, F.A.P. (ed.) IH 2002. LNCS, vol. 2578, pp. 355–372. Springer, Heidelberg (2003)
11. Westfeld, A.: Space filling curves in steganalysis. In: Delp III, E.J., Wong, P.W. (eds.) Security, Steganography and Watermarking of Multimedia Contents VII (Proc. of SPIE), San Jose, CA, pp. 28–37 (2005)

12. Lu, P., Luo, X., Tang, Q., Shen, L.: An improved sample pairs method for detection of LSB embedding. In: Fridrich, J. (ed.) IH 2004. LNCS, vol. 3200, pp. 116–127. Springer, Heidelberg (2004)
13. Yu, X., Wang, Y., Tan, T.: On estimation of secret message length in Jsteg-like steganography. In: Proceedings of the 17th International Conference on Pattern Recognition (ICPR 2004), pp. 673–676 (2004)
14. Zhang, T., Ping, X.: A fast and effective steganalytic technique against Jsteg-like algorithms. In: SAC 2003. Proceedings of the 2003 ACM Symposium on Applied Computing, Melbourne, Florida, USA, March 9–12, 2003, pp. 307–311. ACM Press, New York (2003)
15. Lee, K., Westfeld, A., Lee, S.: Category Attack for LSB steganalysis of JPEG images. In: Shi, Y.Q., Jeon, B. (eds.) IWDW 2006. LNCS, vol. 4283, pp. 35–48. Springer, Heidelberg (2006)
16. Westfeld, A.: Steganalysis in the presence of weak cryptography and encoding. In: Shi, Y.Q., Jeon, B. (eds.) IWDW 2006. LNCS, vol. 4283, pp. 19–34. Springer, Heidelberg (2006)
17. University of Washington: CBIR image database (2004), http://www.cs.washington.edu/research/imagedatabase/groundtruth
18. NRCS: Photo gallery of the USDA Natural Resources Conservation Service (2006), http://photogallery.nrcs.usda.gov/
19. Smoot, S.R., Rowe, L.A.: Study of DCT coefficient distributions. In: Proceedings of the SPIE Symposium on Electronic Imaging, San Jose, CA, vol. 2657, pp. 403–411 (1996)
20. Fridrich, J., Goljan, M., Hogea, D.: Steganalysis of JPEG images: Breaking the F5 algorithm. In: Petitcolas, F.A.P. (ed.) IH 2002. LNCS, vol. 2578, pp. 310–323. Springer, Heidelberg (2003)
21. Provos, N., Honeyman, P.: Detecting steganographic content on the Internet (2001), http://www.citi.umich.edu/techreports/reports/citi-tr-01-11.pdf
22. Fridrich, J.: Feature-based steganalysis for JPEG images and its implications for future design of steganographic schemes. In: Fridrich, J. (ed.) IH 2004. LNCS, vol. 3200, pp. 67–81. Springer, Heidelberg (2004)
23. Ker, A.D.: Improved detection of LSB steganography in grayscale images. In: Fridrich, J. (ed.) IH 2004. LNCS, vol. 3200, pp. 97–115. Springer, Heidelberg (2004)

Author Index

Lecture Notes in Computer Science

Sublibrary 4: Security and Cryptology

Vol. 4329: R. Barua, T. Lange (Eds.), Progress in Cryptology - INDOCRYPT 2006. X, 454 pages. 2006.

Vol. 4318: H. Lipmaa, M. Yung, D. Lin (Eds.), Information Security and Cryptology. XI, 305 pages. 2006.

Vol. 4307: P. Ning, S. Qing, N. Li (Eds.), Information and Communications Security. XIV, 558 pages. 2006.

Vol. 4301: D. Pointcheval, Y. Mu, K. Chen (Eds.), Cryptology and Network Security. XIII, 381 pages. 2006.

Vol. 4300: Y.Q. Shi (Ed.), Transactions on Data Hiding and Multimedia Security I. IX, 139 pages. 2006.

Vol. 4298: J.K. Lee, O. Yi, M. Yung (Eds.), Information Security Applications. XIV, 406 pages. 2007.

Vol. 4296: M.S. Rhee, B. Lee (Eds.), Information Security and Cryptology – ICISC 2006. XIII, 358 pages. 2006.

Vol. 4284: X. Lai, K. Chen (Eds.), Advances in Cryptology – ASIACRYPT 2006. XIV, 468 pages. 2006.

Vol. 4283: Y.Q. Shi, B. Jeon (Eds.), Digital Watermarking. XII, 474 pages. 2006.

Vol. 4266: H. Yoshiura, K. Sakurai, K. Rannenberg, Y. Murayama, S.-i. Kawamura (Eds.), Advances in Information and Computer Security. XIII, 438 pages. 2006.

Vol. 4258: G. Danezis, P. Golle (Eds.), Privacy Enhancing Technologies. VIII, 431 pages. 2006.

Vol. 4249: L. Goubin, M. Matsui (Eds.), Cryptographic Hardware and Embedded Systems - CHES 2006. XII, 462 pages. 2006.

Vol. 4237: H. Leitold, E.P. Markatos (Eds.), Communications and Multimedia Security. XII, 253 pages. 2006.

Vol. 4236: L. Breveglieri, I. Koren, D. Naccache, J.-P. Seifert (Eds.), Fault Diagnosis and Tolerance in Cryptography. XIII, 253 pages. 2006.

Vol. 4219: D. Zamboni, C. Krügel (Eds.), Recent Advances in Intrusion Detection. XII, 331 pages. 2006.

Vol. 4189: D. Gollmann, J. Meier, A. Sabelfeld (Eds.), Computer Security – ESORICS 2006. XI, 548 pages. 2006.

Vol. 4176: S.K. Katsikas, J. López, M. Backes, S. Gritzalis, B. Preneel (Eds.), Information Security. XIV, 548 pages. 2006.

Vol. 4117: C. Dwork (Ed.), Advances in Cryptology - CRYPTO 2006. XIII, 621 pages. 2006.

Vol. 4116: R. De Prisco, M. Yung (Eds.), Security and Cryptography for Networks. XI, 366 pages. 2006.

Vol. 4107: G. Di Crescenzo, A. Rubin (Eds.), Financial Cryptography and Data Security. XI, 327 pages. 2006.

Vol. 4083: S. Fischer-Hübner, S. Furnell, C. Lambrinoudakis (Eds.), Trust and Privacy in Digital Business. XIII, 243 pages. 2006.

Vol. 4064: R. Büschkes, P. Laskov (Eds.), Detection of Intrusions and Malware & Vulnerability Assessment. X, 195 pages. 2006.

Vol. 4058: L.M. Batten, R. Safavi-Naini (Eds.), Information Security and Privacy. XII, 446 pages. 2006.

Vol. 4047: M.J.B. Robshaw (Ed.), Fast Software Encryption. XI, 434 pages. 2006.

Vol. 4043: A.S. Atzeni, A. Lioy (Eds.), Public Key Infrastructure. XI, 261 pages. 2006.

Vol. 4004: S. Vaudenay (Ed.), Advances in Cryptology - EUROCRYPT 2006. XIV, 613 pages. 2006.

Vol. 3995: G. Müller (Ed.), Emerging Trends in Information and Communication Security. XX, 524 pages. 2006.

Vol. 3989: J. Zhou, M. Yung, F. Bao (Eds.), Applied Cryptography and Network Security. XIV, 488 pages. 2006.

Vol. 3969: Ø. Ytrehus (Ed.), Coding and Cryptography. XI, 443 pages. 2006.

Vol. 3958: M. Yung, Y. Dodis, A. Kiayias, T.G. Malkin (Eds.), Public Key Cryptography - PKC 2006. XIV, 543 pages. 2006.

Vol. 3957: B. Christianson, B. Crispo, J.A. Malcolm, M. Roe (Eds.), Security Protocols. IX, 325 pages. 2006.

Vol. 3956: G. Barthe, B. Grégoire, M. Huisman, J.-L. Lanet (Eds.), Construction and Analysis of Safe, Secure, and Interoperable Smart Devices. IX, 175 pages. 2006.

Vol. 3935: D.H. Won, S. Kim (Eds.), Information Security and Cryptology - ICISC 2005. XIV, 458 pages. 2006.

Vol. 3934: J.A. Clark, R.F. Paige, F.A.C. Polack, P.J. Brooke (Eds.), Security in Pervasive Computing. X, 243 pages. 2006.

Vol. 3928: J. Domingo-Ferrer, J. Posegga, D. Schreckling (Eds.), Smart Card Research and Advanced Applications. XI, 359 pages. 2006.

Vol. 3919: R. Safavi-Naini, M. Yung (Eds.), Digital Rights Management. XI, 357 pages. 2006.

Vol. 3903: K. Chen, R. Deng, X. Lai, J. Zhou (Eds.), Information Security Practice and Experience. XIV, 392 pages. 2006.

Vol. 3897: B. Preneel, S. Tavares (Eds.), Selected Areas in Cryptography. XI, 371 pages. 2006.

Vol. 3876: S. Halevi, T. Rabin (Eds.), Theory of Cryptography. XI, 617 pages. 2006.

Vol. 3866: T. Dimitrakos, F. Martinelli, P.Y.A. Ryan, S. Schneider (Eds.), Formal Aspects in Security and Trust. X, 259 pages. 2006.

Vol. 3860: D. Pointcheval (Ed.), Topics in Cryptology – CT-RSA 2006. XI, 365 pages. 2006.

Vol. 3858: A. Valdes, D. Zamboni (Eds.), Recent Advances in Intrusion Detection. X, 351 pages. 2006.

Vol. 3856: G. Danezis, D. Martin (Eds.), Privacy Enhancing Technologies. VIII, 273 pages. 2006.

Vol. 3786: J.-S. Song, T. Kwon, M. Yung (Eds.), Information Security Applications. XI, 378 pages. 2006.

Vol. 3108: H. Wang, J. Pieprzyk, V. Varadharajan (Eds.), Information Security and Privacy. XII, 494 pages. 2004.

Vol. 2951: M. Naor (Ed.), Theory of Cryptography. XI, 523 pages. 2004.

Vol. 2742: R.N. Wright (Ed.), Financial Cryptography. VIII, 321 pages. 2003.